SECOND EDITION

Crisis Intervention Strategies

SECOND EDITION

Crisis Intervention Strategies

Burl E. Gilliland
Richard K. James
Memphis State University

Brooks/Cole Publishing Company
Pacific Grove, California

I⊤**P** ™
The trademark ITP is used under license.

We dedicate this book to all the readers and users of this work, with the fervent hope that the strategies and perspectives contained herein may be helpful in alleviating the emotional stress, pain, and trauma that unfortunately pervade so many lives.

Most particularly, we dedicate the book to that group of readers, our students, who try out and develop their wings as volunteer interventionists in crisis centers and agencies where their learning makes a real difference in the lives of people who need them.

A CLAIREMONT BOOK

Brooks/Cole Publishing Company
A Division of Wadsworth, Inc.

Printed in the United States of America
10 9 8 7 6 5 4

Library of Congress Cataloging in Publication Data
Gilliland, Burl E.
    Crisis intervention strategies / Burl E. Gilliland, Richard K.
James. — 2nd ed.
        p.   cm.
    Includes bibliographical references and index.
    ISBN 0-534-19494-X
    1. Crisis intervention (Psychiatry)   I. James, Richard K., [date]
. II. Title.
RC480.6.G55   1992
616.89′025—dc20   92-10291
                                                          CIP

Sponsoring Editor: Claire Verduin
Editorial Assistant: Gay C. Bond
Production Editor: Linda Loba
Manuscript Editor: Lorraine Anderson
Permissions Editor: Carline Haga
Interior Design: Sharon L. Kinghan
Cover Design: Susan Haberkorn
Art Coordinator: Susan Haberkorn
Typesetting: Shepard Poorman Communications
Printing and Binding: R. R. Donnelley & Sons, Crawfordsville

Preface

PURPOSE OF THE BOOK

The primary purpose of this book is to present applied therapeutic counseling in general, and crisis intervention in particular, in a way that effectively describes actual strategies. In our experience, most clients who enter counseling or psychotherapy do so because of some sort of crisis in their lives. Although "preventive" counseling is the ideal, personal crisis generally provides the impetus that impels real clients into contact with a helping person. We have endeavored to provide a perspective that *puts you into the crisis situation as it is occurring,* enabling you to experience what the crisis worker is experiencing.

RATIONALE

The Primacy of Crisis Intervention

We believe that practically all counseling is initiated as crisis intervention. As much as we would prefer otherwise, people tend either to avoid presenting their problems to a helper until those problems have grown to crisis proportions, or to allow themselves to become ensconced in situational dilemmas that wind up in unforeseen crises. Our ideal objective, as human services workers, is to establish primary prevention programs so effective that crisis intervention will seldom be needed. However, it appears that people will not be as quick to adopt preventive measures for their psychological health as for their physical health. Therefore, we believe that crisis intervention strategies can be applied in practically all counseling, not just in crisis situations. From that perspective, we consider this book to be applicable to the total scope of counseling.

The Case for an Applied Viewpoint

The material and techniques we promote in this book come from two sources: first, our own experiences in teaching and counseling in crisis situations; second, interviews with people who are currently in the trenches, successfully performing counseling and crisis intervention. We have obtained opinions from many different individuals in the helping professions, whose daily and nightly work is dealing directly with human dilemmas, and related their views to the best of current theory and practice from the professional literature. Through many hours of dialogue, these experts have provided the most contemporary strategies and techniques in use in their particular fields. They have also reviewed our rendition of each crisis category and have provided much helpful commentary and critique on the ecology and etiology, tactics and procedures, terminology, and developmental stages of the specific crises with which they work. Therefore, what you read in the case-handling strategies comes from the horse's mouth.

Where controversies exist in regard to treatment modalities, we have attempted to present as many perspectives as possible. If you encounter problems with the tactics and techniques presented, the fault is undoubtedly in our rendition and not in the modalities themselves, which work well for the people who described them to us.

We have endeavored to incorporate, synthesize, and integrate the case-handling strategies of these resource people in a comprehensive, fluid, and dynamic way that will provide crisis workers with a basic set of tenets about effective crisis intervention. The book is not about long-term therapy or theory. Neither is it a volume dealing with crisis from only one theoretical perspective, such as a psychoanalytic approach or a behavioral system. The book incorporates a wide diversity of therapeutic modalities and reflects our eclectic approach.

Specific crises demand specific interventions that span the whole continuum of therapeutic strategies. The strategies presented in this book should not be construed as the only ones available for a particular crisis. They are presented as "best bets" based on what current research and practice indicate to be appropriate and applicable. Yet these strategies may not be appropriate for all practitioners with all clients in all situations. Good crisis intervention, as well as good therapy of any other kind, is a serious professional activity that calls for creativity and the ability to adapt to changing conditions of the therapeutic moment. To that extent, crisis intervention at times is more art than science and is not always prescriptive. Therefore, we would caution you that there are no clear-cut prescriptions or simple cause-and-effect answers in this book.

The Case for an Experiential Viewpoint

The fact that no single theory or strategy applies to every crisis situation is particularly problematic to those who are looking for simple, concrete answers to resolve the client problems they will face. If you are just beginning your career in the human services, we hope that while reading and trying out activities in this book you will suspend your judgment for a while and be open to the experience.

Basic relationship skills. The listening and responding skills described in Chapter 2 are critical to everything else the worker does in crisis intervention. Yet on cursory inspection these techniques and concepts may seem at best simplistic and at worst inane. They do not appear to fix anything because they are not "fixing" skills. What they do is give the crisis worker a firm basis of operation to explore clearly the dilemmas the client is facing. Basic listening and responding skills are the prerequisites for all other therapeutic modalities. Our experience has shown us over and over that students and trainees who scoff at and dismiss these basic relationship skills are the ones who invariably have the most trouble meeting the experiential requirements of our courses and workshop training sessions. We feel very strongly about this particular point and thus ask you to read Chapter 2 with an open mind.

Role play. If this volume is used as a structured learning experience, the case studies and the exercises at the end of each chapter are a valuable resource for experiential learning. It is essential that you observe effective crisis intervention models at work and then follow up by actually practicing and enacting the procedures you have observed. Intensive and extensive role play is an excellent skill builder.

A critical component of training is not just talking about problems but practicing the skills of handling them as well. Talking about a problem is fine, but attempting to handle a live situation enables the trainee to get involved in the business of calming, managing, controlling, and motivating clients. Role play is one of the best ways of practicing what is preached, and it prepares human services workers for developing creative ways to deal with the variety of contingencies they may face. Role play gives human services workers the chance to find out what works and does not work for them in the safety of a training situation and affords their fellow students and trainees an opportunity to give them valuable feedback.

A major problem in role play is the embarrassment of standing up in a class or workshop and risking making a fool of oneself. We want to assure you that in our classes and training sessions we do not expect perfection. If our students and trainees were perfect at crisis intervention, they would not be taking instruction in the first place! Therefore, put your inhibitions on the shelf for a while and become engaged in the role plays as if the situations were real, live, and happening right now. Further, be willing and able to accept critical comments from your peers, supervisors, or instructors. Your ego may be bruised a bit in the process, but that is far better than waiting until you are confronted with an out-of-control client before you think about what you are going to do.

Give the exercises provided in each chapter your best effort, process them with fellow students or trainees, and see what fits best with your own feelings, thoughts, and behaviors. Many times our students and trainees attempt to imitate us. Although it is gratifying to see students or trainees attempting to be "Burl" or "Dick," it is generally an exercise in futility for them. What they need to do is view us critically as we model the procedures and then incorporate their own style and personhood into the procedures. We would urge you to do the same.

ORGANIZATION OF THE BOOK

Part One: Crisis Intervention Theory and Application

Part One of the book introduces the basic concepts of crisis intervention. It is comprised of Chapters 1, 2, and 3.

Chapter 1, Approaching Crisis Intervention. Chapter 1 contains the basic rationale and the theoretical and conceptual information needed for understanding applied crisis intervention. New to this edition, the multicultural context of crisis and crisis intervention is examined as a key part of strategies and tactics.

Chapter 2, Basic Crisis Intervention Skills. Chapter 2 is a conceptual as well as skill-building model of crisis intervention that applies to all crisis categories. It contains background information and describes relationship skills, strategies, and practical guidelines for initial intervention in all crises.

Chapter 3, Crisis Case Handling. Chapter 3 is a new chapter that emphasizes how case handling in crisis intervention is different from long-term therapy. Specific strategies to use with phone, walk-in, and long-term clients in crisis are provided and the reader is introduced to a triage model for rapidly assessing the severity of the crisis in a multidimensional way.

Part Two: Handling Specific Crises: Going into the Trenches

Part Two (Chapters 4 through 9) addresses a variety of important types of crises. For each chapter in Part Two the background and dynamics of the particular crisis type are detailed to provide a basic grasp of the driving forces behind the dilemma. While some theory is presented to highlight the therapeutic modalities used, comprehensive theoretical systems are beyond the scope of this book. For sources of that information, turn to the reference section at the end of each chapter.

In Part Two we have provided scripts from real interventions, highlighted by explanations of why the crisis workers did what they did. Throughout this section the emphasis is on live tryout, experiencing, and processing of the cases and issues.

Chapter 4, Suicide. Chapter 4 focuses on strategies that crisis workers need in working with suicidal people. Suicidal ideation permeates many other problems that assail people the human services worker is likely to confront and is a consideration for all providers of crisis intervention services.

Chapter 5, Posttraumatic Stress Disorder. Although Chapter 5 concentrates heavily on PTSD among war veterans, the background, principles, and strategies explained here are relevant to PTSD clients whose traumas derive from any human-generated source.

Chapter 6, Sexual Assault. Chapter 6 addresses another societal crisis that practically every human services worker will eventually encounter— clients who have either experienced or been affected by sexual abuse. Sexually abused clientele are a special population because of the negative moral and social connotations associated with the dehumanizing acts perpetrated on them. New to this edition are crisis intervention techniques for use with a recently emerging treatment population, adult survivors of child sexual/ physical abuse.

Chapter 7, Woman Battering. Chapter 7 deals with the crisis that many women face: being treated violently by their partners. Battering also refers to being psychologically abused. This chapter provides strategies to help women who are attempting to work their way out of such pernicious relationships. The chapter also deals with emerging treatment techniques for the batterers themselves.

Chapter 8, Chemical Dependency: The Crisis of Addiction. Chapter 8 deals with one of the most timely and pressing issues of our day, addiction to substances. Since addiction is such a pervasive scourge in society, no human services worker in the public arena can escape dealing with its effects. Workers need to know about addiction and possess competence in helping people with crises of addiction or codependency. Adult children from alcoholic families represent another client group the human services worker must be prepared to help. New to this edition are descriptions of and intervention techniques to use with allied chemical dependency crises of children, codependency, and adult children of alcoholics.

Chapter 9: Personal Loss: Bereavement and Grief. Chapter 9 presents a type of crisis that every person will sooner or later face: personal loss. Even though the phenomenon of loss has been with us as long as the human species has existed, many people in our culture are poorly prepared and ill-equipped to deal with it. This chapter provides models and strategies for coping with unresolved grief. It uses ultimate loss, death, to examine a variety of problems associated with termination of relationships, both for the client and the crisis worker.

Part Three: Crisis in the Human Services Workplace

Part Three (Chapters 10, 11, and 12) concentrates on the problems of crisis workers and their employing institutions.

Chapter 10, Violent Behavior in Institutions. Chapter 10 tackles the little-publicized, and badly neglected, type of crisis that workers in many institutions face daily: violent behavior within the walls of the institution. Regardless of the organizational settings where they are employed, workers will find in this chapter useful concepts and practical strategies that they can put to immediate use with agitated and potentially assaultive clients.

Chapter 11, Hostage Crises. Chapter 11 presents another hot topic in our modern world. The taking of hostages has become well publicized through terrorism and other acts of violence. However, many hostage takings occur within the confines of human services work settings. This chapter provides basic negotiation strategies that may enable a human services worker to contain and survive a hostage situation.

Chapter 12, Human Services Workers in Crisis: Burnout. Chapter 12 is about us: all human services workers who are in the helping professions. No worker is immune to stress, burnout, and the crises that go with human services work. Chapter 12 should prove to be invaluable for any worker anywhere whose work environment is frenetic or whose personality tends to generate compulsive behavior, perfectionism, or other stressors that may lead to burnout.

Part Four: New Directions

Part Four focuses on recent developments and the future of the field of crisis intervention.

Chapter 13, Off the Couch and into the Streets. Chapter 13 is a new chapter that traces the evolution of crisis intervention into what is rapidly becoming a clinical specialty. It presents the reader with examples of innovative models of proactive and preventive crisis intervention strategies and tactics.

In summary, we have not been as concerned with intellectualizing, philosophizing, or using theoretical interpretations as with simply focusing on practical matters of how to respond in crisis situations.

ACKNOWLEDGMENTS

In writing a book that covers so many diverse areas of the human condition, it would be extremely presumptuous of us to rely solely on our own expertise and theories of truth, beauty, and goodness to propose crisis intervention techniques. While we tend at times to have a high opinion of ourselves as therapists, we are not so vain or foolish as to believe we have all the answers to all the problems one may encounter in this book. We decided the only realistic and honest way to present the most current, reliable, and practical techniques available would be to go straight to the human services workers who deal with the problems you will encounter in this book. The people are not "big names" in the therapy business. In fact, they consider themselves to be normal human services workers who meet their clientele day in and day out. What makes them "world class" in the human services business is that on a day-in and day-out basis, they do their job very, very well. They are an encyclopedia of practical knowledge in dealing with the gut-wrenching problems addressed in this text.

All of these people graciously agreed to be interviewed at length by us.

Taped transcriptions were made of each interview session. Techniques and cases presented by the human services workers were then incorporated and blended into each chapter. Upon completion of each chapter's rough draft, the manuscripts were sent to the respective workers for their critical review. We hope the final product reflects clearly what these people so skillfully do in crisis intervention.

In alphabetical order we would like to thank the following human services professionals: Steve Allen, Counseling Department, Newman School District, Newman, Illinois; Bill Brewi, Veterans Hospital, Little Rock, Arkansas; Sharon Butts, Marriage and Family Practice, Urbana, Illinois; Dr. Rich Cevasco, New Jersey State Juvenile Corrections Department; Lt. Sam Cochran, Crisis Intervention Team Program, Memphis Police Department; Dr. Pam Cogdal, Center for Student Development, Memphis State University.

Walter Crews, Commander, East Precinct, Memphis Police Department; Angie Dagastino, Aid to AIDS Center, Memphis, Tennessee; Dotsie Graham and Ollie Mannino, Charter Lakeside Hospital, Memphis, Tennessee; Dr. Jesse Jones, Federal Correctional Institution, Memphis, Tennessee; Carol McCown, Southeast Mental Health Center, Memphis, Tennessee; Dr. Rick Myer, Northern Illinois University.

Dr. Marilyn Miller Patterson, Chair, Department of Gerontology, California State University, California, Pennsylvania; Ron Pope, Midtown Mental Health Center, Memphis, Tennessee; Bruce Reed, Frayser-Millington Mental Health Center, Memphis, Tennessee; Ray Richardson, ACE Care Unit, St. Francis Hospital, Memphis, Tennessee.

Dr. Mike Rohr, LeBonheur Children's Medical Center, Memphis, Tennessee; B. J. Stone and Ed Wallin, Vietnam Veterans Center, Memphis, Tennessee; Dr. Milton Trapold, Department of Psychology, Memphis State University; Anne Tuttle, Executive Director, The Crisis Center, Memphis, Tennessee; Dr. Barry Vinick, Psychologist, Memphis, Tennessee.

Dr. Carolyn Willette, Psychologist, Rediscovery Unit, Jackson Regional Hospital, Jackson, Tennessee; Betty Winter and Kathy Scales, Family Trouble Center of the Memphis Police Department and Doctoral Students, Memphis State University.

We would like to thank the students in our Crisis Intervention and Theories of Counseling courses at Memphis State University, who served as willing guinea pigs as we field tested the exercises in this book.

A special note of thanks goes to the men in the Wednesday night rap group at the Memphis Vietnam Veterans Center for their willingness to include us in their group and to share openly some of the trauma they are still experiencing.

We thank also the reviewers of our manuscript for their helpful comments: Dr. Steven Atchley, Delaware Technical Community College; Dr. Sherry Cormier, West Virginia University; Dr. Dwight Fultz, Bemidji State; Dr. Patrick McGrath, National-Louis University; and Dr. Fred Stultz, Cal Poly San Luis Obispo.

We wish to express the utmost appreciation and gratitude for the editorial expertise, assistance, support, and encouragement provided by Brooks/Cole during the entire writing and production process. Our admiration and thanks are particularly accorded to Claire Verduin, publisher; Gay Bond, editorial associate; Linda Loba, production editor; and Lorraine Anderson, manuscript editor. We believe they are the best of the best in the book publishing business.

Finally, we would like to thank our spouses, Martha and Susan, for again refraining from taking us to divorce court while we were having this love affair for two editions and six years.

Burl Gilliland and Dick James

Contents

PART ONE

CRISIS INTERVENTION THEORY AND APPLICATION   1

CHAPTER 1

Approaching Crisis Intervention   3

Definitions of Crisis   3

Characteristics of Crisis   4

Transcrisis States   5

Characteristics of Effective Crisis Workers   7

Multicultural Perspectives in Crisis Intervention   12

Theories of Crisis and Crisis Intervention   16

Crisis Intervention Models   19

Eclectic Crisis Intervention Theory   22

Summary   23

References   24

CHAPTER 2

Basic Crisis Intervention Skills   27

Introduction   27

The Six-Step Model of Crisis Intervention   27

    Step 1: Defining the Problem   28

    Step 2: Ensuring Client Safety   28

    Step 3: Providing Support   29

    Step 4: Examining Alternatives   29

    Step 5: Making Plans   31

    Step 6: Obtaining Commitment   31

Client States of Being and Coping   32

Assessing in Crisis Intervention   33
Listening in Crisis Intervention   38
Acting in Crisis Intervention   50
Counseling Difficult Clients   59
Summary   62
References   63
Classroom Exercises   63

CHAPTER 3

Crisis Case Handling   74

Crisis Case Handling Versus Long-Term Case
  Handling   74
The Triage Assessment System   79
Neurological Assessment   85
Case Handling on Telephone Crisis Lines   86
Case Handling at Walk-in Crisis Facilities   101
Transcrisis Handling in Long-Term Therapy   107
Confidentiality in Case Handling   116
Summary   120
References   121
Classroom Exercises   124

PART TWO

HANDLING SPECIFIC CRISES: GOING INTO THE TRENCHES   127

CHAPTER 4

Suicide   129

Background   129
Dynamics of Suicide   130
Counseling Suicidal Clients   136
Intervention Strategies   147
Prevention   154
When Prevention Fails   156
Summary   156
References   158
Classroom Exercises   161

CHAPTER 5

Posttraumatic Stress Disorder   163

Background   163
Dynamics of PTSD   165
Intervention Strategies   183
The Veterans Center Model of Treatment   190
Summary   211
References   212
Classroom Exercises   222

CHAPTER 6

Sexual Assault   225

Background   225
Dynamics of Rape   229
Dynamics of Sexual Abuse of Children   232
Dynamics of Survivors of Childhood Sexual
  Abuse   235
Intervention Strategies   238
Summary   253
References   255
Classroom Exercises   260

CHAPTER 7

Woman Battering   261

Background   261
Dynamics of Woman Battering   265
Intervention Strategies   275
Center and Shelter   289
Courtship Violence   296
Treating Batterers   297
If You Are in an Abusive Relationship   311
Summary   312
References   314
Classroom Exercises   319

CHAPTER 8

Chemical Dependency: The Crisis of Addiction   322

Background   322
Dynamics of Addiction   333
Intervention Strategies   348
Intervention with the ACOA   388
Summary   394
References   395
Classroom Exercises   403

CHAPTER 9

Personal Loss: Bereavement and Grief   406

Background   406
Dynamics of Bereavement   407
Intervention Strategies   418
Some Representative Referral Services   444
Summary   447
References   447
Classroom Exercises   451

PART THREE

CRISIS IN THE HUMAN SERVICES WORKPLACE   453

CHAPTER 10

Violent Behavior in Institutions   455

Background   455
Dynamics of Violence in Human Services
  Settings   458
Intervention Strategies   462
The Violent Geriatric Client   482
Follow-up with Staff Victims   492
Summary   493
References   494
Classroom Exercises   500

CHAPTER 11

Hostage Crises   503

Background   503
Dynamics of Hostage Taking   504
Intervention Strategies   515
If You Are Held Hostage   529
Summary   532
References   533
Classroom Exercises   534

CHAPTER 12

Human Services Workers in Crisis: Burnout   537

Background   537
Dynamics of Burnout   539
Intervention Strategies   551
Summary   572
References   572
Classroom Exercises   576

PART FOUR

NEW DIRECTIONS   581

CHAPTER 13

Off the Couch and into the Streets   583

The Evolution of the Crisis Intervention
  Subspecialty   583
Proactive and Preventive Models of Crisis
  Intervention   588
Emergent Trends in Crisis Intervention   590
Community Development of Proactive-Preventive
  Crisis Intervention Services   607
Summary   610
References   611

Index   615

CRISIS INTERVENTION THEORY AND APPLICATION

Part One introduces you to the fundamental concepts, theories, strategies, and skills needed to understand and conduct effective crisis intervention. Chapter 1 introduces the conceptual and multicultural dimensions of crisis work. Chapter 2 serves as a key to the application of relationship skills and counseling strategies to the whole scope of crisis intervention. Chapter 3 informs you of two major components of crisis intervention: systematic crisis assessment and effective case management. Crisis workers will find that the principles, skills, and strategies represented here also apply broadly to *all* human problems, crisis or otherwise.

CHAPTER 1

Approaching Crisis Intervention

DEFINITIONS OF CRISIS

There are many definitions of *crisis*. Five are presented here for your thought and study. We believe that they collectively represent and define *crisis*, as well as prepare you to consider the theoretical constructs that follow in this chapter. These definitions should also set the stage for the remainder of the book.

    1. People are in a state of crisis when they face an obstacle to important life goals—an obstacle that is, for a time, insurmountable by the use of customary methods of problem solving. A period of disorganization ensues, a period of upset, during which many abortive attempts at solution are made (Caplan, 1961, p. 18).

    2. Crisis results from impediments to life goals that people believe they cannot overcome through customary choices and behaviors (Caplan, 1964, p. 40).

    3. Crises are crises because the individual knows no response to deal with a situation (Carkhuff & Berenson, 1977, p. 165).

    4. Crises are personal difficulties or situations that immobilize people and prevent them from consciously controlling their lives (Belkin, 1984, p. 424).

    5. Crisis is a state of disorganization in which people face frustration of important life goals or profound disruption of their life cycles and methods of coping with stressors. The term *crisis* refers usually to a person's feelings of fear, shock, and distress *about* the disruption, not the disruption itself (Brammer, 1985, p. 94).

    To summarize these definitions, *crisis is a perception of an event or situation as an intolerable difficulty that exceeds the resources and coping mechanisms of the person.* Unless the person obtains relief, the crisis has the potential to cause severe affective, cognitive, and behavioral malfunctioning.

CHARACTERISTICS OF CRISIS

The following discussion of characteristics of crisis represents an expanded definition of what *crisis* means.

Presence of Both Danger and Opportunity

Crisis is a danger because it can overwhelm the individual to the extent that it may result in serious pathology, including homicide and suicide. It is also an opportunity because the nature of the pain it induces impels the person to seek help (Aguilera & Messick, 1982, p. 1). If the individual takes advantage of the opportunity, the intervention can help plant the seeds of self-growth and self-realization (Brammer, 1985, p. 95).

Individuals can react in any one of three ways to crisis. Under ideal circumstances, many individuals can cope effectively with crisis by themselves and develop strength from the experience. They change and grow in a positive manner and come out of the crisis both stronger and more compassionate. Other people appear to survive the crisis, but effectively block the hurtful affect from awareness, only to have it haunt them in innumerable ways throughout the rest of their lives. There are also those who break down psychologically at the onset of the crisis and clearly demonstrate that they are incapable of going any further with their lives unless provided with immediate and intensive assistance.

Complicated Symptomology

Crisis is *not* simple; it is complex and difficult to understand, and it defies cause-and-effect description (Brammer, 1985, p. 91; Kliman, 1978, p. xxi). The symptoms that overlay precipitating crisis events become tangled webs that crisscross all environments of an individual. When an event reaches a fulminating point, there may be so many compounding problems that the worker has to intervene directly in a variety of areas. Further, the environment of individuals in crisis figures prominently in the ease or difficulty with which the crisis can be handled. Families, employing organizations, and the state of the economy are among the salient factors that may have direct effects on problem resolution and a return to stability.

Seeds of Growth and Change

In the disequilibrium that accompanies crisis, anxiety is always present, and the discomfort of anxiety provides an impetus for change (Janosik, 1984, p. 39). Many times the dilemma is that anxiety must reach the boiling point before an individual is ready to admit that the problem has gone beyond control. One need look no further than the substance abuser for affirmation of this point. By waiting so long, the substance abuser may be so entrenched that a therapeutic jackhammer has to be applied to break the addiction down into manageable pieces. Even so, a threshold point for change is reached, albeit in last-ditch desperation, where the abuser finally surrenders to the fact that something must be done.

The Absence of Panaceas or Quick Fixes

People in crisis are generally amenable to help through a variety of forms of intervention, some of which can be described as *brief therapy* (Cormier & Hackney, 1987, p. 240). For problems of long duration, quick fixes are rarely available. Many of the problems of clients who are suffering from severe crises stem from the fact that they sought quick fixes in the first place, usually through a pill. Whereas the "fix" may dampen the dreadful responses, it does nothing for the instigating stimulus, and therefore the crisis deepens.

Necessity of Choice

Life is a process of interrelated crises and challenges that we confront or not, deciding to live or not (Carkhuff & Berenson, 1977, p. 173). When we *choose to act* we are making a choice that is clearly pro-life! When we *choose not to act,* we are signing a death warrant for ourselves. In the realm of crisis, *not to choose is a choice,* and this choice usually turns out to be negative and destructive. *Choosing to do something* at least contains the seeds of growth and allows a person the chance to set goals and formulate a plan to begin to overcome the dilemma.

Universality and Idiosyncrasy

Disequilibrium or disorganization accompanies every crisis, whether universal or idiosyncratic (Janosik, 1984, p. 13). Crisis is universal because no one is immune to breakdown, given the right constellation of circumstances. It is idiosyncratic because what one person may successfully overcome, another may not, even though the circumstances are virtually the same. Maintaining a belief that one is immune to psychic assaults, that one can handle any crisis in a stable, poised, and in-command fashion is foolhardy. Thousands of "tough" Vietnam veterans suffering from Posttraumatic Stress Disorder (PTSD) who have turnstiled through VA hospitals and veterans' centers are convincing proof that when a crisis boils over, disorganization, disequilibrium, disorientation, and fragmentation of an individual's coping mechanisms will occur no matter how conditioned against psychological trauma the person may be.

TRANSCRISIS STATES

Crises are time limited, usually persisting a maximum of six to eight weeks, at the end of which the subjective discomfort diminishes (Janosik, 1984,

p. 9). However, what occurs during the immediate aftermath of the crisis event determines whether or not the crisis will become a disease reservoir that will be transformed into a chronic and long-term state. Although the original crisis event may be submerged below awareness and the individual may believe the problem has been resolved, appearance of new stressors may bring the individual to the crisis state again. This emotional roller coaster may occur frequently and for extended periods of time, ranging from months to years. An adult who was sexually abused as a child is an excellent example of a person who is in a *transcrisis state*. The adult may have attained what appears to be good mental health. However, this appearance is gained at the cost of warding off and repressing the original trauma from conscious memory. Later, during the stress of divorce, for instance, the repressed material from the original event may resurface in symptomatic ways that seem to have nothing in common with the original traumatic event or the current stressful problem. Another example would be the client with a history of sexual abuse entering treatment for an acute substance abuse problem. While the substance abuse problem becomes a high priority for treatment, it is also a symptom of the psychological roller coaster ride that started with the childhood sexual abuse. The divorce may be reconciled or the substance abuse treated, but the original crisis has not been expunged. It has merely subsided and a temporary state of equilibrium has been achieved, but the original trauma will usually reemerge and instigate a new crisis the moment new stressors are introduced. Dynamically, this pattern is defensive repression. Therapeutically, this transcrisis state calls for crisis intervention techniques.

Transcrisis points.   A frequent part of transcrisis states are *transcrisis points* occurring within the therapeutic intervention. These points are generally marked by the client coming to grips with new developmental stages or other dimensions of the problem.

Transcrisis points do not occur in regular, predictable, linear progression. For example, an abused spouse may go through transcrisis point after transcrisis point talking to a helper over the telephone before making a decision to leave the battering relationship, often calling helping persons a dozen times in the course of a few days. The abused spouse may then make a decision to leave the battering relationship and go to a spouse abuse shelter only to find that the necessity of making a geographical move or finding a job may instigate a crisis that is almost as potent as the battering. Many times, human services workers who practice long-term therapy are shocked, confused, and overwhelmed by the sudden disequilibrium their clients experience. Handling these transcrisis points may be the psychological equivalent of trying to gather quicksilver from the floor. Behaviorally, such clients may vacillate from a placid to an agitated state so fast that the worker puts out one brushfire only to be confronted by yet another. It is at these transcrisis points that standard therapeutic strategies and techniques are suspended and the human services worker must operate in a crisis intervention mode.

Once the individual has made a clear-cut choice to seek help, transcrisis points continue to occur in therapy and may be seen as benchmarks that are critical to progressive stages of positive therapeutic growth. These points are characterized by approach-avoidance behavior in seeking help, taking risks, and initiating action steps toward forward movement. Encountering these transcrisis points, a person will experience the same kind of disorganization, disequilibrium, and fragmentation that surrounded the original crisis event.

Leaping one hurdle does not necessarily mean that the entire crisis is successfully overcome. Quite the contrary is true. Spouse-abuse victims may extricate themselves from a battering relationship, only to become so terrified at having to make their own way in the world that they return to the batterer. Substance abusers may become detoxified in a difficult battle with their drug of choice, only to be undone by an inability to come to terms with another member of the family. Survivors of a catastrophe may expunge the event from memory and then be faced with repairing gaping wounds in personal relationships that have been torn apart by their long-term pathological behavior. Persons having spinal cord injuries may be successfully rehabilitated physically but retreat into substance addiction or become depressed and/or suicidal as they attempt to begin a new lifestyle from a wheelchair. Crisis workers may be faced with a series of these transcrisis points as they help clients work through their problems.

Therefore, it is not only the initial crisis with which the worker must contend but also each transcrisis point, as it occurs, if clients are not to slip back into the pathology that assailed them in the first place. Transcrisis points should not be confused with the jumps and starts that go with the working through of typical adjustment problems. Although these points may be forecast with some degree of reliability by workers who are expert in the particular field, their onset is sudden, dramatic, and extremely potent. In that regard, these psychological aftershocks can be just as damaging as the initial tremor and may require extraordinary effort on the part of the human services worker to assist the client in regaining control. It is with these transcrisis states and points that this book is also concerned; cases have been portrayed that consider both of these components.

CHARACTERISTICS OF EFFECTIVE CRISIS WORKERS

Effective crisis workers need to have not only comprehensive life experiences, but also professional and personal skills commensurate with the intensity of crisis intervention. Many crisis workers begin in the field as volunteers or support persons. They may or may not have been victims of crisis in the particular category with which they work. If these people remain in the field for any length of time they usually find that their initial zeal and commitment need to be enhanced by professional training. Many volunteers professionalize themselves by returning to school just to take a course "because they don't know enough" and end up seeking a degree in the human services field.

Our own classes and workshop sessions comprise people as diverse as homemakers, business executives, and retirees enrolled in counseling courses and specialized training because of a desire to learn in a systematic manner the therapeutic skills necessary to do their volunteer work. It is not uncommon for us also to find people who are successful in a vocation completely unrelated to human services work but who decide, by virtue of the intrinsic rewards they receive from their volunteer or support work, to make a career shift into the helping professions. A classic example is recovering alcoholics who turn the twelfth step of Alcoholics Anonymous, helping others, into a profession, seeking a graduate degree to go with their personal experience of substance abuse.

Life Experiences

The worker handles a crisis or not as he or she is a whole person or not (Carkhuff & Berenson, 1977, pp. 162–163). A whole person has a rich and varied background of life experiences. These life experiences serve as a resource for emotional maturity that, combined with training, enables workers to be stable, consistent, and well integrated not only within the crisis situation but also in their daily lives.

However, life experiences alone are not sufficient to qualify one to be a crisis worker and may be debilitating if they continue to influence the worker in negative ways. This issue is central to crisis intervention because many of the people who work as volunteers, support personnel, and professionals are products of their own crisis environments. They have chosen to work with people experiencing the same kind of crisis they themselves have suffered, and they use their experiential background as a resource in working with others. For example, there are recovering addicts who work in alcohol and drug units, battered women who work in spouse-abuse centers, and PTSD victims who counsel in Vietnam veterans' centers. These professionals have had firsthand experience with the trauma that their clients have experienced. Does this background give them an edge over the other workers who have not suffered the malady?

The answer is a qualified yes: qualified in that the person who carries emotional baggage into the helping relationship may be even less effective than the person who has had few if any life experiences. We see examples of emotional carryover into the intervention process in the proselytizing alcoholic who vilifies others in order to assuage his own insecurities and fears about "falling off the wagon" and in the child-abuse worker, herself a former victim of sexual abuse, who castigates mothers for their failure to confront abusing fathers. Such human services workers may have tremendous difficulties because they commingle many of their own problems with those of their clients. These workers alternate among feeling states characterized by sympathy, anger, disappointment, and cynicism, which are detrimental both to themselves and to their clients.

We do not believe that crisis workers must have "lived in the crisis" to be able to understand and deal with it effectively. We do believe that interventionists who have successfully overcome some of life's problems and have put those problems into perspective will have assets of maturity, optimism, tenacity, and tough-mindedness that will help them marshal their psychological resources to aid their clients.

We are not proposing that people lacking a variety of life experiences should actively pursue trauma as a means of becoming seasoned enough to be effective interventionists. We would also caution that on-the-job training in this business is a very arduous way to win one's spurs, particularly for a worker who has spent a sheltered, constricted life and decides through misguided idealism to become a Florence Nightingale and fix the problems of the world. This rose-colored view does little for clients in general and may do much harm to workers as their good intentions pave the road to burnout. We hasten to add that chronological age has very little to do with having or not having self-enhancing life experiences and a broader, more resilient viewpoint. We know people ranging in age from 21 to 65 who are emotional adolescents. They are threatened by face-to-face encounters with the real world and may be characterized by rigidity, insularity, and insecurity.

The ideal crisis worker we envision is one who has experienced life, has learned and grown from those experiences, and supports those experiences in his or her work by thorough training, knowledge, and supervision. This individual constantly seeks to integrate all these aspects into his or her therapeutic intervention in particular and into living in general.

Professional Skills

Professionally, we seek to inculcate in our students the following helping skills:

attentiveness
accurate listening and responding
congruence between thinking, feeling, and acting therapeutically
reassuring and supporting skills
rudimentary ability to analyze, synthesize, and diagnose
basic assessment and referral skills
ability to explore alternatives and solve problems
specific techniques such as behavioral contracting, relaxation training, and
    assertion skills

This is not an all-inclusive list, but it should provide a flavor of the outcome we expect of people who go through our crisis intervention course at Memphis State University.

Although these skills would be the hallmark of those who perform any human services work, the difference in crisis intervention is that these skills must be used when problem onset is sudden and dramatic, emotions are highly volatile, and background information may be sketchy at best. Although we can model and process the therapeutic skills necessary to intervene in these circumstances, inculcating the personal skills necessary to do effective crisis intervention work is another matter.

Poise

The nature of crisis intervention is that the worker is often confronted with shocking and threatening material from clients who are completely out of control. Probably the most significant help the interventionist can provide at this juncture is to remain calm, poised, and in control (Belkin, 1984, p. 427). Creating a stable and rational atmosphere provides a model for the client that is conducive to restoring equilibrium to the situation. Practicing relaxation techniques is one way of keeping calm in such highly charged situations, but more important is the worker's faith that the client can be pulled through the crisis. In our teaching we can model patience and understanding with troubled clients. What we cannot model is faith and belief in the client's ability to overcome the situation. This trait is one that must abide deep within the interventionist; we know of no easy way to teach it.

Creativity and Flexibility

Creativity and flexibility are major assets to those confronted with perplexing and seemingly unsolvable problems (Aguilera & Messick, 1982, p. 24). It is one thing to teach a person a repertoire of skills. It is quite another thing to teach the use of those skills in ways that are adaptable to clients' needs. Clearly, most traditional schooling has to do with learning material in rote ways. Most training programs known to us pay scant attention to creative therapeutic functioning. In our own courses and training workshops, students and trainees have difficulty when confronted with conducting role plays with peers because they have no formula for getting the "right" answer. Although practice in tough role-play situations builds confidence, how creative individuals are in difficult situations depends to a large measure on how well they have nurtured their own creativity over the course of their lives by taking risks and practicing divergent thinking.

Energy

Functioning in the unknown areas that are characteristic of crisis intervention requires energy, organization, direction, and systematic action (Carkhuff & Berenson, 1977, p. 194). Professional training can provide organizational guidelines and principles for systematic acting. What it cannot do is provide the energy requisite to perform this work. The chapter on burnout in this book (Chapter 12) speaks to many of the maladies that workers suffer and suggests ways to bolster morale, but being energized is still largely incumbent on the worker. Feeling good enough about oneself to tackle perplexing problems day after day calls for not only an initial desire to do the work but also the ability to take care of one's physical and psychological needs so that energy levels remain high.

Quick Mental Reflexes

Crisis work is different from typical therapeutic intervention in that time is a critical factor. Crisis intervention requires more activity and directiveness than ordinary therapeutic endeavors usually do. Time to reflect and mull over problems is a rare commodity in crisis intervention. The worker must have fast mental reflexes to deal with the constantly emerging and changing issues that occur in the crisis. We know of no video tape or spa that provides fitness activities in these areas. The worker who cannot think fast and accurately is going to find the business very frustrating indeed.

Other Characteristics

The following chapters will reveal that tenacity, the ability to delay gratification, courage, optimism, a reality orientation, calmness under duress, objectivity, a strong self-concept, and abiding faith that human beings are strong, resilient, and capable of overcoming seemingly insurmountable odds are all attributes of world-class crisis interventionists. Poll yourself on these traits. All of them are of utmost importance to you and your clients.

We also want you to understand that admission into the inner circle of the profession is not solely reserved for a few supermen and superwomen. Most interventionists we know, including ourselves, are at times perplexed, frustrated, angry, afraid, threatened, incompetent, foolish, vain, troubled, and otherwise unequal to the task. We allow ourselves and our students and trainees at least one mistake a day and go on from there. We would like you to remember that cognitive billboard and place it squarely in the forefront of your mind.

Crises and the Personhood of Crisis Workers

The pattern of helping, as of life, consists of a series of interrelated crises. We benefit or not as we act constructively or not. Each crisis encapsulates a process leading to the potential for constructive change, not only for the client but also for the helper (Carkhuff & Berenson, 1977, pp. 162–163).

The crisis helping relationship is reciprocal and is greater than the sum of its parts. The helper changes as a result of every contact with a client. Successful resolution of the crisis results in two products: (1) helping the client overcome the crisis and (2) effecting positive change in the helper as a result of the encounter.

Positive change is not merely summed up in so many cases successfully handled or so many techniques effectively employed. Successful intervention is enhancing, not only professionally but also personally, to the extent that what has impact upon us in the therapeutic moment transfers to the rest of our environment. Successfully helping a client negotiate a crisis enables us to incorporate the experience into our own life and become more holistic, enabling, and competent in all our endeavors. The power and benefit are not merely arithmetically additive but geometrical in their potential impact. Seen from this standpoint, successful intervention with another human being is one of the most intrinsically rewarding endeavors a professional helper can undertake.

If you are now feeling pessimistic about going into the field of crisis intervention or even reading this book, do not give up yet. Standing up to the intense heat of the crisis situation to help people through seemingly unsolvable problems is some of the most gratifying and positively reinforcing work we know. The intense personal rewards that accrue to crisis workers lead us to believe that this work would be high on Glasser's (1976) list of positively addicting behaviors.

If you are not starting out in the field, but are a seasoned veteran of the human services wars, the utility of this book should become readily apparent. We know of no human services workers who have not encountered or will not encounter crisis situations at some time in their career. This book has a variety of resources that should be helpful in those situations and add to the effectiveness of your short-term work.

For those who may decide that human services work (and particularly crisis intervention) is not their calling, this book also has applicability. Consider, for a moment, yourself as a client. Everyone is at times subject to the whims of a randomly cruel universe, and the kinds of crises that are dealt with in this book are apt to be visited upon all of us. Understanding how to navigate through these constellations of problems is a valuable resource. How well we live depends on our ability to handle the problems that confront us when we least expect them. As you read through the material you may find yourself "living into" some of these problems and asking yourself, "I wonder how I'd fare if I were a client?" We believe that this too is a worthwhile perspective if one can look beyond the dilemmas to the coping techniques and bank them for future reference and use.

MULTICULTURAL PERSPECTIVES IN CRISIS INTERVENTION

We are living in a pluralistic world. In the United States, whether we realize it or not, we are living in a pluralistic culture. Derald Wing Sue (1992) reminds us that failure to understand the world view of clients may lead human services workers to make erroneous interpretations, judgments, and conclusions that result in doing serious harm to clients, especially the culturally different (p. 12). This reality alone makes it mandatory for individuals concerned with the personal and professional development of crisis workers to ensure that the recruitment and training of those workers take into account a multicultural perspective. Pedersen (1987) reminds us that Western cultural biases in our conventional thinking pertain less to geography than to social, economic, political, and ethnocentric values. A vast majority of the world's population lives by a non-Western perspective. Despite the fact that the world is culturally pluralistic, many of our books, professional teachings, research findings, and implicit theories and assumptions in the field of counseling are specific to North American and European culture. Such theories and assumptions are usually so ingrained in our thinking that they are taken for granted and seldom challenged even by our most broad-minded leaders and professionals.

Unexamined, and sometimes unrealized, cultural assumptions can have a deleterious effect upon the functioning of counselors and crisis workers. It is of the utmost importance that the recruitment, screening, orientation, training, evaluation, and retention of workers deal with the realities of a multicultural clientele. A multicultural perspective in the thought processes, emotional attitudes, and behaviors of crisis workers can go a long way toward eliminating the negative effects of institutionalized racism, ethnocentrism, ageism, religionism, able-bodiedism, sexism, and other forms of cultural and personal bias that clients may encounter in some crisis agencies (Pedersen, 1987, p. 18). Ivey (1987) emphasizes that counseling and therapy should begin with awareness of cultural and group differences on the part of counselors prior to considering individual variations on those themes. He states that "only by placing multicultural counseling at the core of counseling curricula can we as counselors truly serve and be with those whom we would help" (p. 169).

Culturally Biased Assumptions

Pedersen (1987) discusses ten frequent culturally biased assumptions that crisis agency directors might consider in their preservice and in-service training programs. These assumptions are listed here for identification purposes.

1. The assumption that people all share a common measure of "normal" behavior (the presumption that problems, emotional responses, behaviors, and perceptions of crises are more or less universal across social, cultural, economic, or political backgrounds) (p. 17).

2. The assumption that individuals are the basic building blocks of all societies (the presumption that crisis intervention and counseling are directed primarily toward the individual rather than units of individuals or groups such as the family, organizations, political groups, or society) (p. 18).

3. The assumption that the definition of problems can be limited by academic discipline boundaries (the presumption that the identity of the

crisis worker or counselor is separate from the identity of the theologian, medical doctor, sociologist, anthropologist, attorney, or representative from some other discipline) (p. 19).

4. The assumption that Western culture depends on abstract words (the presumption of crisis workers and counselors in the United States that others will understand these abstractions in the same way as workers intend them) (pp. 19–20).

5. The assumption that independence is valuable and dependencies are undesirable (the presumption of Western individualism that people should not be dependent on others or allow others to be dependent on them) (p. 20).

6. The assumption that formal counseling is more important than natural support systems surrounding a client (the presumption that clients prefer the support offered by counselors over the support of family, peers, and other support groups) (pp. 20–21).

7. The assumption that everyone depends on linear thinking (the presumption by counselors and crisis workers that each cause has an effect, and each effect is tied to a cause—to explain how the world works—and that everything can be measured and described in terms of good or bad, appropriate or inappropriate, and/or other common dichotomies) (pp. 21–22).

8. The assumption that counselors need to change individuals to fit the system (the presumption that the system does not need to change to fit the individual) (p. 22).

9. The assumption that the client's past (history) has little relevance to contemporary events (the presumption that crises are mostly related to here-and-now situations and that crisis workers and counselors should pay little attention to the client's background connections) (pp. 22–23).

10. The assumption that counselors and crisis workers already know all of their assumptions (the presumption that, if counselors and crisis workers were prone toward reacting in closed, biased, and culturally encapsulated ways that promote domination by an elitist group, they would be aware of it) (p. 23).

All ten assumptions are, of course, flawed and untenable in a pluralistic world. Cormier and Hackney (1987) warn that human services workers who do not understand their own cultural biases and the cultural differences and values of others may misinterpret the behaviors and attitudes of clients from other cultures. Such workers may incorrectly label some client behavior as resistant and noncooperative. They may expect to see certain client behaviors (such as self-disclosure) that are contrary to the basic values of some cultural groups. The culturally insensitive counselor or crisis worker may also stereotype, label, or use unimodal or ineffective counseling approaches in an attempt to help clients from other cultures (pp. 256–258).

Culturally Effective Helping

Sue (1992) states that multicultural helping is enhanced when the human services worker "uses methods and strategies and defines goals consistent with the life experiences and culture [sic] values of the client" (p. 13). Belkin (1984) points out that cross-cultural counseling does not have to be negative; that it may provide effective resolution of client problems as well as serve as a unique learning experience for both client and helper; and that the main "barrier to effective cross-cultural counseling is the traditional counseling role itself, which is not applicable to many cross-cultural interactions" (p. 527). Belkin further states that the principal cross-cultural impediments are (1) language differences, (2) class-bound values, and (3) culture-bound values (p. 534). Belkin also identifies both *barriers* to and *benefits* of intracultural counseling. The *barriers* cited are (1) unjustified assumption of shared feelings, (2) client transference, and (3) counselor countertransference. The *benefits* given are (1) shared experience, which may enhance rapport, (2) client willingness to self-disclose some materials, and (3) common mode of communication, which may enhance the counseling process (p. 542). Belkin concludes that perhaps the most positive discovery and/or belief of the effective cross-cultural counselor is that humans everywhere are more alike than they are different (p. 543).

Cormier and Hackney (1987) cite several strategies that culturally effective helpers use. For instance, such helpers (1) examine and understand the world from the *client's* viewpoint, (2) search for alternative roles that may be more appealing and adaptive to clients from different backgrounds, and (3) help clients from other cultures to make contact with and elicit help from indigenous support systems (p. 259).

Cormier and Hackney (1987) also specify that to be culturally effective, helpers should *not* (1) impose their values and expectations on clients from different backgrounds, (2) stereotype or label clients, client behaviors, or cultures, and (3) try to force unimodal counseling approaches upon clients (pp. 258–259). Sue (1992) cites an example of such unimodal expectations: traditional helpers may tend to emphasize the need for clients to verbalize their emotions. He points out that some clients (such as traditional Japanese) may have been taught as children not to speak until addressed; that many cultures highly value restraint in expressing strong feelings; that patterns of communication, contrary to ours in the United States, may "tend to be vertical, flowing from those of higher prestige and status to those of lower prestige and status" (p. 12). The unenlightened worker seeking to help such a client may perceive that person to be inarticulate, unintelligent, lacking in spontaneity, or repressed (p. 13).

If agency directors and trainers of crisis workers are to prepare crisis workers to meet the needs of all people who come to crisis agencies for assistance, they must include, in their orientation and training curricula, the examination of culturally learned assumptions, presumptions, values, biases, and stereotypes about people and their behaviors. As Sue (1992) reminds us, "without this awareness and understanding, we may inadvertently assume that everyone shares our world view. When this happens, we may become guilty of cultural oppression, imposing values on the culturally different client" (p. 10).

THEORIES OF CRISIS AND CRISIS INTERVENTION

There is no single theory or school of thought that encompasses every view of human crisis or all the models or systems of crisis intervention. We will give a brief overview of theories relevant both to crisis (as a phenomenon) and to crisis intervention (as an intentional helping response). Janosik (1984) conceptualizes crisis theory on three different levels: basic crisis theory, expanded crisis theory, and applied crisis theory.

Basic Crisis Theory

The research, writings, and teachings of Lindemann (1944, 1956) gave professionals and paraprofessionals a new understanding of crisis. Lindemann helped caregivers to promote crisis intervention for many sufferers of loss who had no specific pathological diagnosis but who were exhibiting symptoms that appeared to be pathological. Lindemann's basic crisis theory and work made a substantive contribution to our understanding of behavior in clients whose grief crises were precipitated by loss. He helped professionals and paraprofessionals to recognize that behavioral responses to crises associated with grief are normal, temporary, and amenable to alleviation through short-term intervention techniques. These "normal" grief behaviors include (1) preoccupation with the lost one, (2) identification with the lost one, (3) expressions of guilt and hostility, (4) some disorganization in daily routine, and (5) some evidence of somatic complaints (Janosik, 1984, p. 11). Lindemann negated the prevailing perception that clients manifesting crisis responses should necessarily be treated as abnormal or pathological.

Whereas Lindemann focused mainly on immediate resolution of grief after loss, Caplan (1964) expanded Lindemann's constructs to the total field of traumatic events. Caplan viewed crisis as a state resulting from impediments to life goals that cannot be overcome through customary behaviors. These impediments can arise from both developmental and situational events. Both Lindemann and Caplan dealt with crisis intervention following psychological trauma using an equilibrium/disequilibrium paradigm. The stages in Lindemann's paradigm are (1) disturbed equilibrium, (2) brief therapy or grief work, (3) client's working through the problem or grief, and (4) restoration of equilibrium (Janosik, 1984, pp. 10–12). Caplan linked Lindemann's concepts and stages to all developmental and situational events and extended crisis intervention to eliminating the cognitive, emotional, and behavioral distortions that precipitated the psychological trauma in the first place.

The work of both Lindemann and Caplan gave impetus to the use of crisis intervention strategies in counseling and brief therapy with people manifesting universal human reactions to traumatic events. Basic crisis theory, following their lead, focuses on helping people in crisis recognize and correct temporary cognitive, emotional, and behavioral distortions brought on by traumatic events.

All people experience psychological trauma at some time during their lives. Neither stress nor the emergency conditions of the trauma in themselves constitute crisis. It is only when the traumatic event is subjectively perceived as a threat to need fulfillment, safety, or meaningful existence that an individual enters a state of crisis (Caplan 1964). A crisis is accompanied by temporary disequilibrium and contains potential for human growth. The resolution of crisis may lead to positive and constructive outcomes such as self-enhancing coping ability and a decrease in negative, self-defeating, dysfunctional behavior (Janosik, 1984, pp. 3–21).

Expanded Crisis Theory

Expanded crisis theory was developed because basic theory, which depended on a psychoanalytic approach alone, did not adequately address the social, environmental, and situational factors that make an event a crisis. As crisis theory and intervention have expanded, it has become clear that an approach that identifies predisposing factors as the main or only causal agent falls short of the mark. A prime example of this restrictive view was the erroneous diagnosis by practitioners who first encountered PTSD victims that pathology preceding the crisis event was the real cause of the trauma. As crisis theory and intervention have grown it has become apparent that given the right combination of developmental, sociological, psychological, environmental, and situational determinants, anyone can fall victim to transient pathological symptoms. Therefore, expanded crisis theory draws not only from psychoanalytic but also from general systems, adaptational, and interpersonal theory (Janosik, 1984). The following are synopses of the major theoretical components of an expanded view.

Psychoanalytic theory.   Psychoanalytic theory (Fine, 1973), applied to expanded crisis theory, is based on the view that the disequilibrium that accompanies a person's crisis can be understood through gaining access to the individual's unconscious thoughts and past emotional experiences. Psychoanalytic theory presupposes that some early childhood fixation is the primary explanation of why an event becomes a crisis. This theory may be used to help clients develop insight into the dynamics and causes of their behavior as the crisis situation acts upon them.

Systems theory.   Systems theory (Haley, 1973, 1976) is based not so much on what happens within an individual in crisis as on the interrelationships and interdependence among people and between people and events. The fundamental concept of systems theory is analogous "to ecological systems in which all elements are interrelated, and in which change at any level of those interrelated parts will lead to alteration of the total system" (Cormier & Hackney, 1987, p. 217). Belkin (1984) adds that this theory "refers to an emotional system, a system of communications, and a system of need fulfillment and request" in which all members within an intergenerational relationship bring something to bear on the others and each derives something from the others (pp. 350–351).

Systems theory represents a turning away from traditional approaches, which focus only on what is going on within the client, and adopts an interpersonal-systems way of thinking. There is great value in looking at crises in their total social and environmental settings—not simply as one individual being affected in a linear progression of cause-and-effect events.

Adaptational theory.   Adaptational theory, in our use of the term, depicts a person's crisis as being sustained through maladaptive behaviors, negative thoughts, and destructive defense mechanisms. Adaptational crisis theory is based on the premise that the person's crisis will recede when these maladaptive coping behaviors are changed to adaptive behaviors.

Breaking the chain of maladjusted functioning means changing to adaptive behavior, promoting positive thoughts, and constructing defense mechanisms that will help the person overcome the immobility created by the crisis and move to a positive mode of functioning. As maladaptive behaviors are learned, so may adaptive behaviors be learned. Aided by the interventionist, the client may be taught to replace old, debilitating behaviors with new, self-enhancing ones. Such new behaviors may be applied directly to the context of the crisis and ultimately result in either success or reinforcement for the client in overcoming it (Cormier & Cormier, 1985, p. 148).

Interpersonal theory.   Interpersonal theory (Rogers, 1977) is built on many of the dimensions that Cormier and Hackney (1987) describe as enhancing personal self-esteem (openness, trust, sharing, safety, unconditional positive regard, accurate empathy, and genuineness) (pp. 35–64). The essence of interpersonal theory is that people cannot sustain a personal state of crisis for very long if they believe in themselves and others and have confidence that they can become self-actualized and overcome the crisis.

When people confer their locus of self-evaluation on others, they become dependent on others for validation of their being. Therefore, as long as a person maintains an external locus of control the crisis will persist. The outcome goal, in interpersonal theory, is returning the power of self-evaluation to the person. Doing so enables the person once again to control his or her own destiny and regain the ability to take whatever action is needed to cope with the crisis situation.

Applied Crisis Theory

The application of crisis theory requires a flexible approach. Each person and each crisis situation is different. Thus, crisis workers must view each person and the events precipitating the crisis as unique. Brammer (1985, pp. 94–95) characterizes applied crisis theory as encompassing three domains: (1) normal *developmental* crises, (2) *situational* crises, and (3) *existential* crises.

Developmental crises.   Developmental crises are events in the normal flow of human growth and evolvement whereby a dramatic change or shift occurs that produces abnormal responses. For example, developmental crises may occur in response to the birth of a child, graduation from college, midlife career change, or retirement. Developmental crises are considered normal; however, all persons and all developmental crises are unique and must be assessed and handled in unique ways.

Situational crises.   A situational crisis emerges with the occurrence of uncommon and extraordinary events that an individual has no way of forecasting or controlling. Situational crises may follow such events as automobile accidents, kidnappings, rapes, corporate buyouts and loss of jobs, and sudden illness and death. The key to differentiating a situational crisis from other crises is that a situational crisis is random, sudden, shocking, intense, and catastrophic.

Existential crises.   "Existential crisis" refers to the inner conflicts and anxieties that accompany important human issues of purpose, responsibility, independence, freedom, and commitment. An existential crisis might accompany the realization, at age 40, that one will never make a significant and distinct impact upon a particular profession or organization; remorse, at age 50, that one chose never to marry or leave one's parents' home, never really made a separate life, and now has lost forever the possibility of being a fully happy and worthwhile person; or a pervasive and persistent feeling, at age 60, that one's life is meaningless—that there is a void that can never be fulfilled in a meaningful way.

CRISIS INTERVENTION MODELS

Three basic crisis intervention models discussed by both Leitner (1974) and Belkin (1984) are the *equilibrium* model, the *cognitive* model, and the *psychosocial transition* model. These three models provide the groundwork for many different crisis intervention strategies and methodologies. All crisis intervention models are based on theory. Nowhere is this fact better exemplified than in the work of Strickler and Bonnefil (1974, p. 38), who link crisis theory with a psychosocial approach to psychotherapy through the following points:

1. Treatment goals are structured to enhance the client's competency in coping with difficulties by using problem-solving skills.
2. The treatment targets specific and pertinent problem areas that involve the client's interpersonal conflicts and role dysfunctioning.

3. The client's attention is kept on the specific problem area through active focusing techniques.
4. The treatment is geared primarily to the level of the client's conscious and near-conscious emotional conflicts. These conflicts are handled by searching out their situational references and by keeping a focus within them.
5. Precipitating events are recognized as very important to the dynamics of the problem situation.
6. The modification of the client's character traits or personality patterns is not a fundamental objective of the treatment.
7. The phenomenon of client transference to the interventionist is normally not considered important to the therapeutic process unless such transference presents an impediment to treatment.
8. Treatment is based on background information derived from a knowledge of personality, ego functioning, and sociocultural functioning.

These important principles provide the bridge between crisis theory and intervention. They clearly demonstrate that the principles of crisis psychology provide the foundation for clinical practice (Belkin, 1984, p. 427). They also set the stage for a brief examination of the equilibrium, cognitive, and psychosocial transition models of crisis intervention.

The Equilibrium Model

The equilibrium model is really an equilibrium/disequilibrium model. People in crisis are in a state of psychological or emotional disequilibrium in which their usual coping mechanisms and problem-solving methods fail to meet their needs. The goal of the equilibrium model is to help people reattain a state of precrisis equilibrium (Caplan, 1961).

The equilibrium model would seem most appropriate for early intervention, when the person is out of control, disoriented, and unable to make appropriate choices. Until the person has regained some coping abilities, the main focus is on stabilizing the individual. Up to the time the person has reacquired some definite measure of stability, little else can or should be done. For example, it does little good to dig into the underlying factors that cause suicidal ideation until the person can be stabilized to the point of agreeing that life is worth living for at least another week. This is probably the purest model of crisis intervention and is most likely to be used at the onset of the crisis (Caplan, 1961; Leitner, 1974; Lindemann, 1944).

The Cognitive Model

The cognitive model of crisis intervention is based on the premise that crises are rooted in *faulty thinking* about the events or situations that surround the crisis—not in the events themselves or the facts about the events or situations (Ellis, 1962). The goal of this model is to help people become aware of and to change their views and beliefs about the crisis events or situations. The basic tenet of the cognitive model is that people can gain control of crises in their lives by changing their thinking, especially through recognizing and disputing the irrational and self-defeating parts of their cognitions, and by retaining and focusing on the rational and self-enhancing elements of their thinking.

The messages that people in crisis send themselves become very negative and twisted in context of the reality of the situation. Dilemmas that are constant and grinding wear people out, pushing their internal state of perception more and more toward negative self-talk about the situation until their cognitive sets are such that no amount of preachment can convince them that anything positive will ever come from the situation. Their behavior soon follows this negative self-talk and begets a self-fulfilling prophecy that the situation is hopeless. At this juncture, crisis intervention becomes a job of rewiring the individual's thoughts to more positive feedback loops by practicing and rehearsing new self-statements about the situation until the old, negative, debilitating ones are expunged. The cognitive model seems most appropriate after the client has been stabilized and returned to an approximate state of precrisis equilibrium. Basic components of this approach are found in the rational-emotive work of Ellis (1982), the cognitive-behavioral approach of Meichenbaum (1977), and the cognitive system of Beck (1976) and Beck, Rush, Shaw, and Emery (1987).

The Psychosocial Transition Model

The psychosocial transition model assumes that people are products of their hereditary endowments plus the learning they have absorbed from their particular social environments. Since people are continually changing, developing, and growing, and their social environments and social influence (Dorn, 1986) are continuously evolving, crises may be related to internal or external (psychological, social, or environmental) difficulties. The goal of crisis intervention is to collaborate with clients in their assessment of both internal and external difficulties contributing to the crises and to help them choose workable alternatives to their current behaviors, attitudes, and use of environmental resources. The incorporation of adequate internal coping mechanisms, social supports, and environmental resources may be needed to assist the clients in attainment of autonomous (noncrisis) control over their lives.

The psychosocial model does not perceive crisis as simply an internal state of affairs that resides totally within the individual. It reaches outside the individual and asks what systems need to be changed. Peers, family, occupation, religion, and community are but a few of the external dimensions that promote or hinder psychological adaptiveness. With certain kinds of crisis problems, few lasting gains will be made unless the social systems that affect the individual are also changed or the individual comes to terms with and understands the dynamics of those systems and how they affect adaptation to the crisis. Like the cognitive model, the psychosocial transition model seems to be most appropriate after the client has been stabilized. Theorists who have contributed to the psychosocial transition model include Adler (Ansbacher & Ansbacher, 1956), Erikson (1963), and Minuchin (1974).

ECLECTIC CRISIS INTERVENTION THEORY

Eclectic crisis intervention involves the intentional and systematic selection and integration of valid concepts and strategies from all available approaches to helping clients. As such, eclecticism has few major concepts but is a hybrid of all other available approaches. As opposed to concepts, it operates from a task orientation. Its major tasks (Gilliland, James, & Bowman, 1989, pp. 297–298; Thorne, 1973, p. 451) are (1) to identify valid elements in all systems and to integrate them into an internally consistent whole that does justice to the behavioral data to be explained; (2) to consider all pertinent theories, methods, and standards for evaluating and manipulating clinical data according to the most advanced knowledge of time and place; and (3) to identify with no specific theory, keep an open mind, and continuously experiment with those formulations and strategies that produce successful results.

Throughout this volume, the reader will find an eclectic theory integrated into interventions presented. Distinctive threads of the equilibrium/disequilibrium model, the cognitive model, and the psychosocial transition model will be woven into the fabric of crisis intervention strategies for each type of crisis explored. The eclectic theory fuses two pervasive themes: (1) all people and all crises are unique and distinctive, and (2) all people and all crises are similar. We do not see these themes as mutually exclusive.

All people and all crises are similar in that there are global elements to specific crisis types. The dynamics of bereavement are generic and provide us with general guidelines for intervention. However, treating individual cases of bereavement is anything but generic. How a family perceives the impact of the death of a member depends on a number of factors: the deceased member's place in the family, what each member of the family does in response to the death, and how the changed family system now operates. Treatment of surviving family members who have lost a child after rearing five others, as opposed to those who have lost their only child, born late in the parents' life, who had become the focus of existence for the couple, may call for far different interventional strategies even if bereavement is the generic issue.

An eclectic approach does not mean taking a therapeutic shotgun and aimlessly blasting away at the crisis. Using an eclectic approach means not being bound by and locked into any one theoretical approach in a dogmatic fashion. Rather, it means being well versed in a number of approaches and theories and being able to assess the client's needs so that appropriate techniques can be planned and fitted to them. Many human services workers avow an eclectic approach but in actuality use the word as a rationalization for not being able to do anything very well. Being a true eclectic means doing lots of hard work, reading, studying, experiencing, and being supervised and critiqued by other professionals. It also means taking risks and having a willingness to abandon an approach that on first inspection might seem reasonable and proper but, once entered, is fruitless for the particular situation.

Eclecticism performed well is equal parts of skill and intuition. Paying attention to one's feeling as much as to one's cognition about the situation is critical. Many times changing to a more effective intervention is based on nothing more scientific than a feeling that something is amiss. Although having a feeling is little justification in the scientific sense for doing something, it can nevertheless be a sound basis for action. We know of no formula for deciding when to move from a nondirective to a highly directive stance with a client in crisis, nor is there an equation that tells us that mental imagery may be more effective than confrontation as an interventional technique. Unabashedly, we believe that in an eclectic approach the performing art of crisis intervention clearly reaches its zenith.

SUMMARY

In this chapter we discussed five definitions of crisis. We consider all of these definitions of crisis to be valid and useful and we have incorporated elements of all of them into the book. Our composite definition of crisis, derived from all five sources, is *a perception of an event or situation as an intolerable difficulty that exceeds the resources and coping mechanisms of the person.* This general definition is useful throughout the book, but the worth of the definition is enhanced by considering several important principles and characteristics of crisis:

1. Crisis embodies both danger and opportunity for the person experiencing the crisis.
2. Crisis is usually time limited but may develop into a series of recurring transcrisis points.
3. Crisis is oftentimes complex and difficult to resolve.
4. The life experiences of workers may greatly enhance their effectiveness in crisis intervention.
5. Crisis contains the seeds of growth and impetus for change.
6. Panaceas or quick fixes are not applicable to crisis situations.
7. Crisis confronts people with choices.
8. Emotional disequilibrium and disorganization accompany crisis.
9. The resolution of crisis and the personhood of crisis workers interrelate.

Workers will find these principles and characteristics of crisis to be of enormous value in their role as helpers.

We have identified and discussed a number of characteristics of effective crisis workers. Effective workers demonstrate competency in their professional skills. They maintain poise while confronting the difficult issues of clients from different cultures. They are both creative and flexible in their dealing with client problems. They possess a great deal of energy and know how to organize and direct their energy toward systematic action. They can think and react quickly. Finally, effective crisis workers are positive in their outlook, work, philosophy, and approach to helping clients.

Three theoretical thrusts were discussed in the chapter: basic, expanded, and applied. *Basic crisis theory,* founded in the works of Lindemann (1944; 1956) and Caplan (1964), helps us to view crisis as situational or developmental rather than pathological in nature. *Expanded crisis theory* adds to and enhances basic theory by incorporating and adapting components from general systems, psychoanalytic, adaptational, and interpersonal theory. *Applied crisis theory* integrates the concepts of developmental, situational, and existential crises into a holistic theoretical structure containing both basic and expanded crisis theory concepts. Applied crisis theory provides the conceptual framework for us to put both basic and expanded theory into practice.

Three fundamental crisis intervention models were identified and discussed: equilibrium, cognitive, and psychosocial transition. The *equilibrium model,* probably the most widely known model of the three, defines equilibrium as an emotional state in which the person is stable, in control, or psychologically mobile. It also defines disequilibrium as an emotional state that accompanies instability, loss of control, and psychological immobility. The *cognitive model* views the crisis state as resulting from faulty thinking and belief about life's dilemmas and traumas. The *psychosocial transition model* assumes that people are products of both hereditary endowment and environmental learning and that crisis may be caused by psychological, social, or environmental factors. The psychosocial transition model therefore instructs us to look for intervention strategies in all three realms: psychological, social, and environmental.

An eclectic theoretical position, which we believe incorporates and integrates all valid concepts of crisis intervention, was presented and discussed. The strength of eclectic crisis intervention theory is that it encourages workers to select, integrate, and apply useful concepts and strategies from all available approaches to helping clients.

REFERENCES

Aguilera, D. C., & Messick, J. M. (1982). *Crisis intervention: Theory and methodology* (4th ed.). St. Louis: C. V. Mosby.

Ansbacher, H. L., & Ansbacher, R. R. (1956). *The individual psychology of Alfred Adler.* New York: Greenberg.

Beck, A. T. (1976). *Cognitive therapy and the emotional disorders.* New York: International Universities Press.

Beck, A. T., Rush, A. J., Shaw, B. F., & Emery, G. (1987). *Cognitive therapy of depression.* New York: Guilford Press.

Belkin, G. S. (1984). *Introduction to counseling* (2nd ed.). Dubuque, IA: William C. Brown.

Brammer, L. M. (1985). *The helping relationship: Process and skills* (3rd ed.). Englewood Cliffs, NJ: Prentice-Hall.

Caplan, G. (1961). *An approach to community mental health.* New York: Grune & Stratton.

Caplan, G. (1964). *Principles of preventive psychiatry.* New York: Basic Books.

Carkhuff, R. R., & Berenson, B. G. (1977). *Beyond counseling and therapy* (2nd ed.). New York: Holt, Rinehart & Winston.

Cormier, L. S. & Hackney, H. (1987). *The professional counselor: A process guide to helping.* Englewood Cliffs, NJ: Prentice-Hall.

Cormier, W. H., & Cormier, L. S. (1985). *Interviewing strategies for helpers: Fundamental skills and cognitive behavioral interventions* (2nd ed.). Pacific Grove, CA: Brooks/Cole.

Dorn, F. J. (Ed.). (1986). *The social influence process in counseling and psychotherapy.* Springfield, IL: Charles C Thomas.

Ellis, A. E. (1962). *Reason and emotion in psychotherapy.* New York: Lyle Stuart.

Ellis, A. E. (1982). Major systems. *Personnel and Guidance Journal, 61,* 6–7.

Erikson, E. (1963). *Childhood and society* (2nd ed.). New York: Norton.

Fine, R. (1973). Psychoanalysis. In R. J. Corsini (Ed.), *Current psychotherapies* (pp. 1–33). Itasca, IL: F. E. Peacock.

Gilliland, B. E., James, R. K., & Bowman, J. T. (1989). *Theories and strategies in counseling and psychotherapy* (2nd ed.). Englewood Cliffs, NJ: Prentice-Hall.

Glasser, W. (1976). *Positive addiction.* New York: Harper & Row.

Haley, J. (1973). *Uncommon therapy.* New York: Norton.

Haley, J. (1976). *Problem-solving therapy.* New York: McGraw-Hill.

Ivey, A. E. (1987). Cultural intentionality: The core of effective helping. *Counselor Education and Supervision, 26,* 168–172.

Janosik, E. H. (1984). *Crisis counseling: A contemporary approach.* Monterey, CA: Wadsworth Health Sciences Division.

Kliman, A. S. (1978). *Crisis: Psychological first aid for recovery and growth.* New York: Holt, Rinehart & Winston.

Leitner, L. A. (1974). Crisis counseling may save a life. *Journal of Rehabilitation, 40,* 19–20.

Lindemann, E. (1944). Symptomatology and management of acute grief. *American Journal of Psychiatry, 101,* 141–148.

Lindemann, E. (1956). The meaning of crisis in individual and family. *Teachers College Record, 57,* 310.

Meichenbaum, D. H. (1977). *Cognitive-behavior modification: An integrative approach.* New York: Plenum.

Minuchin, S. (1974). *Families and family therapy.* Cambridge, MA: Harvard University Press.

Pedersen, P. (1987). Ten frequent assumptions of cultural bias in counseling. *Journal of Multicultural Counseling and Development, 15,* 16–24.

Rogers, C. R. (1977). *Carl Rogers on personal power: Inner strength and its revolutionary impact.* New York: Delacorte.

Strickler, M., & Bonnefil, M. (1974). Crisis intervention and social casework: Similarities and differences in problem solving. *Clinical Social Work Journal, 2,* 36–44.

Sue, D. W. (1992, Winter). The challenge of multiculturalism: The road less traveled. *American Counselor, 1,* 6–14.

Thorne, F. C. (1973). Eclectic psychotherapy. In R. Corsini (Ed.), *Current psychotherapies* (pp. 445–486). Itasca, IL: F. E. Peacock.

CHAPTER 2

Basic Crisis Intervention Skills

INTRODUCTION

The purpose of this chapter is to provide a general overview of crisis intervention from a practitioner's standpoint. To that end we present and fully describe an applied crisis intervention model. We augment the model by discussing fundamental skills and intervention concepts. We illustrate many of the skills and concepts with dialogues between client and worker. Finally, we share some thoughts on using referrals, give some suggestions regarding counseling difficult clients, and provide a laboratory exercise.

This chapter is a prerequisite for succeeding chapters, and we urge you to consider this foundation material carefully. Read, think, and react. Examine the examples of the techniques carefully. Discuss our responses and formulate your own. Practice the laboratory exercises. To obtain the necessary skills to become a successful crisis worker, you will need to learn some new practices in the ways you deal with people in volatile situations. What we propose in this chapter will not make you perfect, but it will give you, with practice, some proven methods and abilities as a starting point. We have never, repeat never, seen a consistently successful crisis interventionist who did not practice what we are about to preach to you. If you can learn the techniques in this chapter, you should find them adaptable to any crisis situation.

We do not repeat the fundamental skills and steps of crisis intervention in every chapter or apply them in a step-by-step explicit manner to every crisis category in the book. Nevertheless, these basic principles should be applied in the process of helping every client in every category of crisis.

THE SIX-STEP MODEL OF CRISIS INTERVENTION

Even though human crises are never simple, we have found that it is desirable for the crisis worker to have a relatively straightforward and efficient model of intervention. The six steps described here and summarized in Figure 2-1 (Gilliland, 1982) can be used as such a model. Volunteers and professional human services workers such as nurses, ministers, police officers, psychologists, social workers, and counselors may be called upon at any time to deal with a unique crisis surprising in content and heavy in emotional tone. We have found that many crisis workers, especially telephone counselors and other workers in centers dealing with acute crises, appreciate a set of guidelines that are uncomplicated and practical. The six steps of our model have been used by both professional counselors and lay workers in helping clients with many different kinds of crises.

This action-oriented, situationally based method of crisis intervention is our preferred method for systematically applying several worker-initiated skills. The process of applying these skills is fluid rather than mechanistic. The entire six-step process is carried out under an umbrella of *assessment* by the crisis worker. The first three steps of (1) defining the problem, (2) ensuring client safety, and (3) providing support are more *listening* activities than they are acting. The final three steps of (4) examining alternatives, (5) making plans, and (6) obtaining commitment to positive action are largely *action* behaviors on the part of the worker, even though listening is always present along with assessment.

The six-step model is the hub around which the crisis intervention strategies in this book revolve. The effective crisis worker is flexible and resilient in the use of the six steps. In the actual intervention process, Steps 4, 5, and 6, for instance, appear to flow together in a natural, smooth, and systematic whole. The steps are designed to operate as an integrated problem-solving process.

Step 1: Defining the Problem

The first step in crisis intervention is to define and understand the problem from the client's point of view. Unless the worker perceives the crisis situation as the client perceives it, all the intervention strategies and procedures the helper might use may miss the mark and be of no value to the client. Throughout the crisis intervention process, workers direct their listening and acting skills according to the dictates of the definition. As an aid to defining crisis problems, we recommend that intervention sessions begin with crisis workers practicing what we call the *core listening skills:* empathy, genuineness, and acceptance or positive regard (Cormier & Cormier, 1991, pp. 21–39). These skills and the exercises described later in this chapter should greatly enhance your competency in this first step of crisis intervention.

Step 2: Ensuring Client Safety

It is imperative that crisis workers continually keep client safety at the forefront of all crisis intervention procedures. We define client safety simply as minimizing the physical and psychological danger to self and others. Although we position client safety in the second step, we apply this step in a fluid way, meaning that safety is a primary consideration throughout crisis intervention. The dimension of safety receives equal consideration in the worker's assessing, listening, and acting strategies. In this book and pervading our teaching and practice of crisis intervention, client safety is present, whether we overtly state it or not. We encourage students and crisis workers to make the safety step a natural part of their thinking and behaving.

Step 3: Providing Support

The third step in crisis intervention emphasizes communicating to the client that the worker is a person who cares about the client. Workers cannot assume that a client experiences feeling valued, prized, or cared for. The support step provides an opportunity for the worker to assure the client that "here is one person who really cares about you."

In Step 3, the person providing the support is the worker. This means that workers must be able to accept, in an unconditional and positive way, all their clients, whether the clients can reciprocate or not. The worker who can truly provide support for clients in crisis is able to accept and value the person no one else is willing to accept and to prize the client no one else prizes.

Step 4: Examining Alternatives

Step 4 in crisis intervention addresses an area that both clients and workers often neglect—exploring a wide array of appropriate choices available to the client. Many times clients, in their immobile state, do not adequately examine their best options. Some clients in crisis actually believe there are no options.

In the fourth step, effective workers help clients to recognize that many alternatives are available and that some choices are better than others. It may help for workers to realize that there are different ways to think about alternatives: (1) *situational supports,* which may represent excellent sources of help, are people known to the client in the present or past who might care about what happens to the client; (2) *coping mechanisms* are those actions, behaviors, or environmental resources the client might use to help get through the present crisis; and (3) *positive and constructive thinking patterns* on the part of the client are ways of thinking that might substantially alter the client's view of the problem and lessen the client's level of stress and anxiety. Crisis workers who can objectively examine a number of alternatives from these three perspectives can be of great assistance to clients who are feeling hopelessly stuck and lacking in choices.

The effective crisis worker may think about an infinite number of alternatives pertaining to the client's crisis but discuss only a few of them with the client. Clients experiencing crisis do not need a lot of choices; they need appropriate choices that are realistic to their situation.

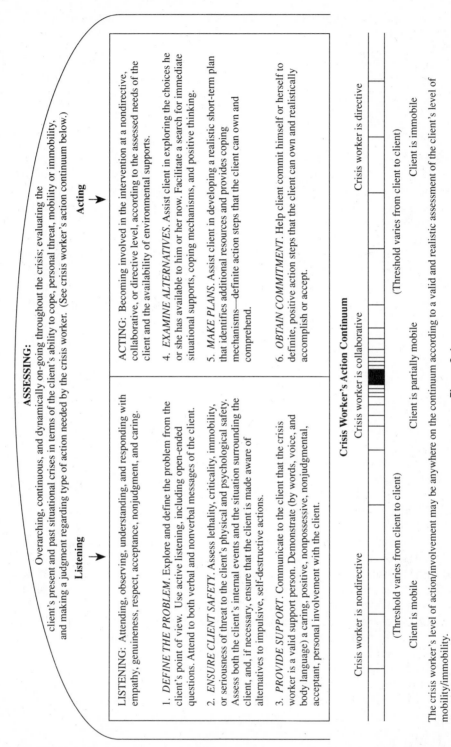

ASSESSING:

Overarching, continuous, and dynamically on-going throughout the crisis; evaluating the client's present and past situational crises in terms of the client's ability to cope, personal threat, mobility or immobility, and making a judgment regarding type of action needed by the crisis worker. (See crisis worker's action continuum below.)

Listening →

LISTENING: Attending, observing, understanding, and responding with empathy, genuineness, respect, acceptance, nonjudgment, and caring.

1. *DEFINE THE PROBLEM.* Explore and define the problem from the client's point of view. Use active listening, including open-ended questions. Attend to both verbal and nonverbal messages of the client.

2. *ENSURE CLIENT SAFETY.* Assess lethality, criticality, immobility, or seriousness of threat to the client's physical and psychological safety. Assess both the client's internal events and the situation surrounding the client, and, if necessary, ensure that the client is made aware of alternatives to impulsive, self-destructive actions.

3. *PROVIDE SUPPORT.* Communicate to the client that the crisis worker is a valid support person. Demonstrate (by words, voice, and body language) a caring, positive, nonpossessive, nonjudgmental, acceptant, personal involvement with the client.

Acting →

ACTING: Becoming involved in the intervention at a nondirective, collaborative, or directive level, according to the assessed needs of the client and the availability of environmental supports.

4. *EXAMINE ALTERNATIVES.* Assist client in exploring the choices he or she has available to him or her now. Facilitate a search for immediate situational supports, coping mechanisms, and positive thinking.

5. *MAKE PLANS.* Assist client in developing a realistic short-term plan that identifies additional resources and provides coping mechanisms—definite action steps that the client can own and comprehend.

6. *OBTAIN COMMITMENT.* Help client commit himself or herself to definite, positive action steps that the client can own and realistically accomplish or accept.

Crisis Worker's Action Continuum

Crisis worker is nondirective   Crisis worker is collaborative   Crisis worker is directive

(Threshold varies from client to client)   (Threshold varies from client to client)

Client is mobile   Client is partially mobile   Client is immobile

The crisis worker's level of action/involvement may be anywhere on the continuum according to a valid and realistic assessment of the client's level of mobility/immobility.

Figure 2-1

Step 5: Making Plans

The fifth step in crisis intervention, making plans, flows logically and directly from Step 4. Much of the material throughout this book focuses either directly or indirectly on the crisis worker's involvement with clients in planning action steps that have a good chance of restoring the emotional equilibrium of the clients. A plan should (1) identify additional persons, groups, and other referral resources that can be contacted for immediate support, and (2) provide coping mechanisms—something concrete and positive for the client to do now, definite action steps that the client can own and comprehend. The latter may include a variety of constructive psychomotor activities, such as running, playing a musical instrument, or reading. The plan should focus on systematic problem solving for the client and be realistic in terms of the client's coping ability. It may include collaboration between the client and crisis worker—for example, facilitation of relaxation techniques or emotive imagery.

It is important that planning be done in collaboration with clients so that clients feel a sense of ownership of the plan. We have seen too many instances where helpers decided for clients what they should do. The critical element in developing a plan is that clients do not feel robbed of their power, independence, and self-respect. Some clients may not object when a helper decides for them what they should do. At the moment, such clients may be so engrossed in their crisis that it really does not matter to them. They may even believe that a plan imposed on them is what they should have. It is often easy to manipulate emotionally distraught clients to accept a plan benevolently imposed upon them. The central issues in planning are *control* and *autonomy* of clients. The reasons for clients to carry out plans are to restore their sense of control and to ensure that they do not become dependent on support persons such as the worker.

Step 6: Obtaining Commitment

The sixth step, obtaining commitment, flows directly from Step 5, and the issues of control and autonomy apply equally to the process of obtaining an appropriate commitment. If the planning step is effectively done, the commitment step is apt to be easy. Many times the commitment step is brief and simple, consisting of asking the client to verbally summarize the plan: "Now that we have gone over what you plan to do next time you start to get angry with her, summarize for me what actions you will take to ensure that you do not lose your temper and what you will do to make sure you keep it from escalating into another crisis." During this step, the crisis worker demonstrates responsibility in carrying out his or her part of the plan if a collaboration has been agreed upon.

During the sixth step the crisis worker does not forget about all the other helping steps and skills such as assessing, ensuring safety, and providing support. The worker is careful to obtain an honest, direct, and appropriate commitment from the client before terminating the crisis intervention session. Later, when the worker checks up on the client's progress, the checking is done in an empathic and supportive stance. The core listening skills are as important to the commitment step as they are to the problem definition or any other step.

CLIENT STATES OF BEING AND COPING

Our six-step model of crisis intervention emphasizes actively, assertively, intentionally, and continuously assessing, listening, and acting to systematically help the client regain as much of the precrisis equilibrium, mobility, and autonomy as possible. Two of those terms, *equilibrium* and *mobility,* and their antonyms, *disequilibrium* and *immobility,* are commonly used by crisis workers to identify client states of being and coping. Since we will be using these terms as common parlance, we would like to define them first by their dictionary meaning and then give a common analogy so their meaning becomes thoroughly understood.

Equilibrium. A state of mental or emotional stability, balance, or poise in the organism.

Disequilibrium. Lack or destruction of emotional stability, balance, or poise in the organism.

Mobility. A state of physical being whereby the person can autonomously change or cope in response to different moods, feelings, emotions, needs, conditions, influences; being flexible or adaptable to the physical and social world.

Immobility. A state of physical being whereby the person is not immediately capable of autonomously changing or coping in response to different moods, feelings, emotions, needs, conditions, influences; unable to adapt to the immediate physical and social world.

A healthy person is in a state of approximate equilibrium, like a motorist driving, with some starts and stops, down the road of life—in both the short and the long haul. The person may hit some potholes but does not break any psychological axles. Aside from needing an occasional tune-up, the person remains more or less equal to the task of making the drive. In contrast, the person in crisis, whether it be acute or chronic, is experiencing serious difficulty in steering and successfully navigating life's highway. The individual is at least temporarily out of control, unable to command personal resources or those of others in order to stay on safe psychological pavement.

A healthy person is capable of negotiating hills, curves, ice, fog, stray animals, and most other obstacles that impede progress. No matter what roadblocks may appear, such a person adapts to changing conditions, applying brakes, putting on fog lights, and estimating passing time. This person may have fender-benders from time to time but avoids head-on collisions.

The person in a dysfunctional state of equilibrium and mobility has failed to pass inspection. Careening down hills and around dangerous curves, knowing the brakes have failed, the person is frozen with panic and despair and has little hope of handling the perilous situation. The result is that the person has become a victim of the situation, has forgotten all about emergency brakes, downshifting, or even easing the car into guard railings. He or she flies headlong into catastrophe and watches transfixed as it happens.

Our analogy of equilibrium and mobility applies to most crisis situations. Thus, it becomes every crisis worker's job to figuratively get the client back into the driver's seat of the psychological vehicle. As we shall demonstrate, sometimes this means leaving the driving to us, sometimes sitting alongside and pointing out the rules of the road, and sometimes just pretty much going along for the ride!

ASSESSING IN CRISIS INTERVENTION

Overarching the six-step model is assessment. Assessment is a pervasive, intentional, and continuous activity of the crisis worker. Assessment is critically important because it enables the worker to (1) determine the severity of the crisis, (2) determine the client's current emotional status—the client's level of emotional mobility or immobility, (3) determine the alternatives, coping mechanisms, support systems, and other resources available to the client, and (4) determine the client's level of lethality (danger to self and others).

Assessing Severity of Crisis

It is important for the crisis worker to evaluate the crisis severity as quickly as possible during the initial contact with the client. Crisis workers generally do not have time to perform complete diagnostic workups or obtain indepth client histories. Therefore, we propose a rapid assessment procedure, such as the triage assessment system described in detail in Chapter 3, as a quick and efficient way of obtaining information relevant to the specific crisis situation. The triage system enables the worker to gauge the severity of the client's current functioning across affective, cognitive, and behavioral domains. The degree of severity of the crisis may affect the client's mobility, which in turn gives the worker a basis for judging how directive to be. The length of time the client has been in the present crisis will determine how much time the worker has to safely defuse the crisis. Crisis is time limited; that is, most acute crises persist only a matter of days before some change—for better or worse—occurs. The severity of the crisis is assessed from the client's subjective viewpoint and from the worker's objective viewpoint. Objective assessment is based on an appraisal of the client's functioning in three areas: cognitive (thinking patterns), affective (feeling or emotional tone), and psychomotor (behavior).

Cognitive state. The worker's assessment of the client's thinking patterns may provide answers to several important questions: How realistic and consistent is the client's thinking about the crisis? To what extent, if any, does the client appear to be rationalizing, exaggerating, or believing part-truths, to exacerbate the crisis? How long has the client been engaged in crisis thinking? How open does the client appear to be to changing beliefs about the crisis situation? The answers to these and other questions about the client's thought patterns may provide some directions for crisis intervention. The worker may use such cognitive assessment to determine how to help the client refute irrational or confused thinking and develop more positive and productive thought patterns about the crisis and about workable alternatives.

Affective state. The crisis worker who is sensitive to the client's emotional tone can mentally record affective reactions to assess the seriousness of the crisis as well as discern ways to help the client. Abnormal or impaired affect is often the first sign that the client is in a state of disequilibrium. The client may be overemotional and out of control or severely withdrawn and detached. Often the worker can assist the client to regain control and mobility by helping that person express feelings in appropriate and realistic ways. Some questions the worker may address are: Do the client's affective responses indicate that the client is denying the situation or attempting to avoid involvement in it? Is the emotional response normal or congruent with the situational crisis? Do people typically show this kind of affect in situations such as this? Certainly, to ignore an unusual or unhealthy display of affect would be a mistake on the part of the worker.

Psychomotor activity. The crisis worker focuses much attention upon *doing, acting out, taking active steps, behaving,* or any number of other psychomotor activities. In crisis intervention we believe that the quickest (and often the best) way to get the client to become mobile is to facilitate positive actions that the client can take at once. Persons who successfully cope with crisis and later evaluate their experiences report that the most helpful alternative during a crisis is to engage in some concrete and immediate activity. However, it is important for the worker to remember that it may be very difficult for immobilized people to take independent and autonomous action even though that is what they need to do most. These are appropriate questions that the worker might ask the client in order to get the client to take constructive action. "In cases like this in the past, what actions did you take that helped you get back in control? What would you have to do now to get back on top of the situation? Name one or two persons who, if you contacted them right now, would be supportive to you in the crisis." The fundamental problem in immobility is loss of control. Once the client becomes involved in doing something concrete, which is a step in a positive direction, an element of control is restored, a degree of mobility is provided, and the climate for forward movement is established.

The crisis worker uses these action steps in helping a client move toward equilibrium.

Assessing the Client's Current Emotional Status

Two major factors in assessing the client's emotional stability are the *duration* of the crisis and the *degree* of emotional stamina or coping at the disposal of the client at the moment. The duration factor has to do with the time frame of the crisis. Is it a one-time crisis? Is it recurring? Has it been plaguing the client for a long period of time? A one-time, relatively short-duration crisis is what we call *acute* or *situational.* We would label a long-term pattern of recurring crisis as *chronic, long-term,* or *transcrisis.* (The latter recurring crisis is described in detail in Chapter 1.) The degree factor refers to the client's current reservoir of emotional coping stamina. Whereas during normal periods of the client's life the coping reservoir is relatively full, during crisis periods the client's reservoir is relatively empty. Assessment of the degree factor, then, involves the crisis worker's determination of how much emotional coping strength is left in the client's reservoir. Has the client run out of gas or can the client make it over a small hill?

Client's current acute or chronic state.   In assessing the crisis client's emotional functioning, it is important that the crisis worker determine whether the client is a normal individual who is in a *one-time* situational crisis or a person with a *chronic,* crisis-oriented life history. The one-time crisis is assessed and treated quite differently from the chronic crisis. The one-time crisis client usually requires direct intervention to facilitate getting over the one event or situation that precipitated the crisis. Having reached a state of precrisis equilibrium, the client can usually draw on normal coping mechanisms and support persons and manage independently. The chronic crisis client usually requires a greater length of time in counseling. That individual typically needs the help of a crisis worker in examining adequate coping mechanisms, finding support persons, rediscovering strategies that worked during previous crisis periods, generating new coping strategies, and gaining affirmation and encouragement from the worker and others as sources of strength by which to move beyond the present crisis. The chronic case frequently requires referral for long-term professional help.

Client's reservoir of emotional strength.   The client who is totally devoid of emotional strength needs more direct response from the crisis worker than the client who obviously retains a good deal of emotional strength. The worker must be very sensitive to the client's emotional functioning in order to formulate an objective judgment. A feeling of hopelessness or helplessness is a clue to a low reservoir of emotional strength. In some cases, the assessment can be enhanced by asking open-ended questions for the specific purpose of measuring that reservoir. Typically, if the reservoir is low the client will have a distorted view of the past and present and will not be able to envision a future. Questions like these can reveal the *degree* of emotional stamina remaining: "Picture yourself after the current crisis has been solved. Tell me what you're seeing yourself doing and how you're feeling. How would you wish to be feeling? How were you feeling about this before the crisis got so bad? Where do you see yourself headed with this problem?" The answers may be of great value to the worker in establishing the degree of emotional control retained by the client. In general, the lower the reservoir of emotional strength, the less the client can get hold of the future. The client with an empty reservoir might respond by a blank stare or by saying something like "There are no choices" or "No, I can't see anything. The future is blank. I can see no future." The worker's assessment of the client's current degree of emotional strength will have definite implications for the strategies and level of action to be employed by the worker during the remainder of the counseling.

Strategies for assessing emotional status.   The crisis worker who assesses the client's total emotional status may look at a wide array of factors that affect both the duration (chronic versus acute) and the degree (reservoir of strength) of emotional stability. Some of the factors to be considered are the client's age, educational level, family situation, marital status, vocational maturity and job stability, financial stability and obligations, drug and/or alcohol use, legal history (arrests, convictions, probations), social background, level of intelligence, lifestyle, religious orientation, ability to sustain close personal relationships, tolerance for ambiguity, physical health, medical history, and past history of dealing with crises. A candid look at factors like these helps the crisis worker decide whether the client will require quick referral (for medical treatment or examination), brief counseling, long-term therapy, or referral to a specific agency.

Every client's profile of emotional stability can be expected to be different. No one factor alone can ordinarily be used to conclude that the client's reservoir of emotional coping ability is empty. However, some patterns often can be pieced together to form a general picture. A person in middle age who has experienced many disappointments related to undereducation would be viewed differently from a young person who has experienced a first career disappointment. A person who has been through several bitter divorces would be expected to respond differently from a person who has recently begun to sense the first strains of marital discord. A person who was raised as an only child in a protected environment would be expected to respond differently from one who grew up in the milieu of a large family with lots of freedom. A person who has experienced many serious medical problems and hospital stays would feel differently from a person who is having a first encounter with a medical problem.

Carefully phrased open-ended questions are a valuable assessment tool for judging the client's emotional background and status and for involving the client in the ongoing assessment in a way that is facilitative for the client. For example, the worker might ask: "How is your current treatment different from the treatments you've received in the past?" "How has your increased level of drinking affected your feelings toward your wife and children?" "What could you do to make yourself feel better?" Open-ended questions can be worded in an infinite number of ways. (See the section on open-ended questions on pages 39 and 69.)

What we have been talking about is the facilitative assessment of the individual. By "facilitative assessment" we mean that data gleaned about the client are used as a part of the ongoing helping process, not simply filed away or kept in the worker's head. The key to facilitative assessment is to focus on the client's inner emotional world—not the worker's analysis of that world.

Assessing Alternatives, Coping Mechanisms, Support Systems, and Other Resources

Throughout the helping process the crisis worker keeps in mind and builds a repertory of options, evaluating their appropriateness for the client. In assessing alternatives available to the client, the worker must first consider the client's viewpoint, mobility, and capability of taking advantage of the alternatives. The worker's own objective view of available alternatives is an additional dimension. Alternatives include a repository of appropriate referral resources available to the client. Even though the client may be looking for only one or two concrete action steps or options, the worker brainstorms, in collaboration with the client, to develop a list of possibilities that can be evaluated. Most of them will be discarded before the client can own and commit to a definite course of action. The word *own* has a special connotation in planning and committing to a course of action. "Owning" means that options are not imposed on the client by the worker. The important thing for clients is that they feel a deep and genuine commitment to their choices and that they do not depend upon or merely agree to choices they believe workers have discovered for them.

The worker ponders questions such as, What actions or choices does the client have now that would restore the person to a precrisis state of autonomy? What realistic actions can the client take? What institutional, social, vocational, or personal strengths or supports are available? Who would care about and be open to assisting the client? What are the financial, social, vocational, and personal impediments to client progress?

Assessing for Suicide Potential

Not every crisis involves the client's contemplating suicide. However, in dealing with crisis clients, workers must always explore the possibility of suicide, because suicidal behavior takes many forms and wears many masks. What may appear to the crisis worker as the main problem may camouflage the real issue: the intent of the client to take his or her life. Contrary to popular belief, most suicidal clients give definite clues and believe they are calling out for help. However, even the client's closest friends may ignore those clues and do nothing about them. For that reason, we believe that every crisis problem should be assessed as to its potential for suicide. The most important aspect of suicidal evaluation is the crisis worker/evaluator's realization that suicide is an ever-present possibility in all types of clients. A more detailed coverage of assessing for suicide potential can be found in Chapter 4.

Summary of Assessment

One of the major differences between crisis intervention and other human services endeavors such as counseling, social work, and psychotherapy is that the crisis worker generally does not have time to either gather or analyze all the background and other assessment data that might normally be available under less stressful conditions. A key component of a highly functioning crisis worker is the ability to take the data available and make some meaningful sense out of it. This may be somewhat unsettling to those students who are accustomed to having complete social and psychological workups available to them before they proceed with intervention. However, the ability to make a quick evaluation of the degree of client disequilibrium and immobility—and to be flexible enough to change one's evaluation as changing conditions warrant—is a priority skill that students should seek to cultivate.

From onset to resolution of crisis, assessment is a central, continuous process. It is essential that the crisis worker not assume that because the crisis appears on the surface to have been resolved, assessment is no longer needed. The balance sheet of assessing the client's crisis in terms of severity, current emotional status, alternatives, situational supports, coping mechanisms, resources, and level of lethality is never complete until the client has achieved his or her precrisis level of mobility, equilibrium, and autonomy. Only then are the psychological debts of the client reconciled.

The resumption of precrisis equilibrium does not imply that the client needs no developmental or long-term therapy or medical treatment. It does mean that the worker's job is done, and the acute phase of the crisis is over.

LISTENING IN CRISIS INTERVENTION

Crisis intervention is a pragmatic system of counseling, helping, and assisting individuals that abbreviates the therapeutic schedule and condenses strategies. Crisis intervention is not a long, drawn-out procedure that deals with either restorative or developmental issues. This compression of time and strategies often requires the crisis worker to be more proactive and assertive than the long-term counselor or therapist. It is a procedure that may be used by both professionals and laypersons with some training. We believe that accurate and well-honed listening skills are a necessary and, indeed, sometimes sufficient skill that all helping persons must have, whether lay or professional, performing short- or long-term counseling, and this is absolutely true for crisis workers.

For that reason, listening skills are a major component of our six-step intervention model. Our preferred conceptual model for effective listening comes from person-centered counseling (Egan, 1982, 1990; Rogers, 1977). We will present brief descriptions of selected techniques that are applicable to any kind of helping relationship, crisis or otherwise.

Open-ended Questions

Often workers are frustrated by a client's lack of response and enthusiasm. Workers may make statements such as "All my clients ever do is grunt or shake their heads indicating yes or no." We can do something about getting fuller, more meaningful responses if we ask questions that are not dead ends.

There are two types of questions: *open-ended* and *closed*. Closed questions usually begin with verbs like *do, did, does, can, will,* and *doesn't.* Closed questions elicit one-word, abrupt responses. Examples: "Do you like this story?" "Yup." "Did you have fun on vacation?" "Nope."

Open-ended questions encourage clients to respond with full statements and at deeper levels of meaning. Remember that open-ended questions are used to elicit from clients something about their feelings, thoughts, and behaviors. Here are some guidelines for forming open-ended questions.

1. Request description: "Please tell me . . . ," "Tell me about . . . ," "Show me . . . ," "In what way does . . . ?"
2. Focus on plans: "What will you do . . . ?" "How will you make it happen?" "How will that help you to . . . ?"
3. Own your own desires: "I'd like you to add more to what you've said . . . ," "I want you to describe what that means to you," "Tell me specifically what you'd like to have happen in the relationship."

Owning Feelings

Owning means communicating possession: "That's mine." Often in conversation we avoid specific issues by "disowning" statements with phrases like these: "They say . . . ," "I heard the other day that you . . . ," "It's not right for you to . . . ," and "Don't you think you ought to . . . ?" Whether it is intentional or not, such verbal manipulation functions to avoid ownership of responsibility for what's being said or to avoid awareness of one's own position on thoughts and feelings concerning an issue.

When working with a client it is very important to *own* your feelings and behaviors, because many clients are using you as a model. So if you imply "We think this way" (meaning I and the world, the universe, all other people) or "God thinks this way," then the client doesn't have much chance to question such an awesome cast of thinkers.

Also, many of us chronically disown many human qualities. As workers, we are never confused, jealous, shallow, bored, or proud! Small wonder that some clients learn to distrust such all-knowing, well-integrated individuals. Let's just take, for example, my feeling of confusion. If I am pretending to understand when I'm really confused, I have split my energy right down the middle, and the client who is listening to me is doubly confused.

A deeper aspect of checking my own behavior and eliciting responses from clients is to own confusions. This means that I am aware of being confused by a client's response or behavior and that I do not pretend that I understand. Being willing to own my confusion or frustration and to attempt to eliminate it is a trust-reinforcing event for the client for two reasons: (1) both client and worker can reduce the need to pretend or fake understanding one another and begin to see more clearly where communication wires are getting crossed, and (2) the client can begin to become actively involved with the worker in an attempt to work together.

Further, to be genuine is to say what *I* feel at times. When a client has done well and I'm happy and feel good about it, I say it! Likewise, when clients start trying to control, browbeat, or otherwise put me on the hot seat, it does little good to try to hide my anger, disappointment, or hurt feelings. If I am congruent I need to let the client know how I feel.

Climate of Human Growth

According to Rogers (1977), the most effective helper is one who can provide three necessary and sufficient conditions for client growth. These conditions he named *empathy, genuineness,* and *acceptance* (pp. 9–12). To create a climate of empathy means that the crisis worker accurately senses the inner feelings and meanings the client is experiencing and directly communicates to the client that the worker understands how it feels to be the client. The condition of genuineness (also called *realness, transparence,* or *congruence*) means that the worker is being completely open in the relationship; that nothing is being hidden; that there are no facades; that there are no professional fronts. If the worker is clearly open and willing to be fully himself or herself in the relationship, the client is encouraged to reciprocate. The term *acceptance* (also referred to as *caring* or *prizing*) means that the crisis worker feels an unconditional positive regard for the client. It is an attitude of accepting and caring for the client without the client's necessarily reciprocating. The condition of acceptance is provided for no other reason than that the client is a human being in need. If these conditions of empathy, genuineness, and acceptance can be provided for the client, then the probability that the client will experience positive emotional movement is increased.

Communicating Empathy

In describing the use of empathy to help clients, we will focus on four important techniques: (1) attending, (2) verbally communicating empathic understanding, (3) nonverbally communicating empathic understanding, and (4) silence as a way of communicating empathic understanding (Cormier & Cormier, 1991; Gilliland, James, & Bowman, 1989).

Attending.   The first step in listening has little to do with words and a lot to do with looking, acting, and being attentive. In most initial counseling and therapy sessions the client enters with some anxiety related to the therapy itself in addition to the stress brought on by the crisis. In crisis situations, such anxiety is increased exponentially. Shame, guilt, rage, and sorrow are but a few of the feelings that may be manifested. Such feelings may be blatant and rampant or subtle and disguised. Whatever shape or form such feelings take, the inattentive crisis worker can miss the message the client is attempting to convey. Worse, an inattentive attitude implies lack of interest on the part of the worker and does little to establish a trusting relationship.

The effective crisis worker focuses fully on the client both in facial expression and in body posture. By nodding, keeping eye contact, smiling, showing appropriate seriousness of expression, leaning forward, keeping an open stance, and sitting or standing close to the client without invading the client's space, the crisis worker conveys a sense of involvement, concern, commitment, and trust.

Vocal tone, diction, pitch, modulation, and smoothness of delivery also tell clients a great deal about the attentiveness of crisis workers. Crisis workers, by attending closely to clients' verbal and nonverbal responses, can quickly tell whether they are establishing an empathic relationship or exacerbating the clients' feelings of distrust, fear, and uncertainty about becoming involved in the relationship.

Attentiveness, then, is both an attitude and a skill. It is an attitude in that the worker focuses fully on the client right here and now. In such moments the crisis worker's own concerns are put on hold. It is a skill in that conveying attending takes practice. It is just as inappropriate for the crisis worker to look too concerned and be too close in proximity as it is to lean back with arms folded and legs crossed, giving a cold stare. An example of an appropriate blend of both verbal and nonverbal skill in attending to a client may help to clarify what we mean. Rita is a client who is having serious marital problems. (Rita's case history is recounted in the Classroom Exercises at the end of this chapter; we suggest that you read it for background.)

Rita: [*Enters room, sits down in far corner, warily looks about the room, crosses her legs and fidgets with her purse, and avoids direct eye contact, manifesting the appearance of a distraught woman who is barely holding together.*]

CW: [*Rises behind desk. Observing the behavior and physical appearance of the client, moves to a chair a comfortable distance and a slight angle from Rita's, sits down, leans forward in an open stance, and with an appearance of concern and inquisitiveness looks directly at Rita.*] I'd like to be of help. Where would you like to start?

The crisis worker sees the apprehension in the client and immediately becomes proactive. The crisis worker moves close to the client but does not sit directly in front of her in what could be construed as a confronting stance. The worker inclines forward to focus attention—eyes, ears, brain, and whole body—into the client's world. The whole posture of the crisis worker is congruent with the verbal message of offering immediate acceptance and willingness to help. In summary, effective attending is unobtrusive, natural, and without pretense. It is a necessary condition for effective listening.

Verbally communicating empathic understanding.   When we can accurately hear and understand the core emotional feelings that are inside the client and accurately and caringly communicate that understanding to the client, we are demonstrating effective listening. The deeper our level of listening (understanding), the more helpful we will be to our clients. For instance, reflecting a client's message at the interchangeable level is helpful.

Rita: I'm thinking about just walking in and telling Jake I want a divorce—regardless of what Sam is ready to do. I don't think I can go on much longer. My ulcer is beginning to act up, I'm an emotional wreck, and everyone is expecting more of me than I can give.

CW: You're feeling a sense of urgency because it's adversely affecting your physical and emotional being.

A deeper level of listening and communicating empathic understanding to Rita might be expressed thus:

CW: Rita, your sense of urgency is getting to the point where you're about ready to take a big risk with both Jake and Sam. I sense that your physical and emotional stresses have about reached their limits and you're realizing that no one else is going to act to give you relief—that you are the one who is going to have to decide and act.

The second response is more helpful because it confirms to Rita a deeper understanding than the first response. Both responses are helpful because they are accurate and neither add to nor detract from the client's verbal, nonverbal, or emotional messages. Whereas the first response is considered minimally helpful, the second response is more facilitative because it lets the client know the worker heard a deeper personal meaning (risk) and a personal ownership of possible action. A word of caution to the worker, however: beware of reading into the client's statements more than the client is saying, and take care to keep your response as brief as possible.

Effective communication of empathic understanding to the client means focusing on the client's expressed affective and cognitive messages. The worker deals *directly with* the client's concerns and does not veer off into talking *about* the client's concerns or some tangential person or event. That distinction is important.

Rita: I'm afraid Jake might attack me even worse if I tell him I want a divorce.

CW: He did beat you pretty badly. Sam would probably go bananas at that. Jake, your husband, has such a violent temper. [*Talking about the situation and tangentially focusing on Jake.*]

CW: You're feeling some reservations about telling Jake because you really don't want to be beaten up again. [*Dealing with Rita's current feelings and concerns.*]

The latter response is preferred because it stays on target with Rita's feelings and concerns in the here-and-now and because it avoids getting off onto Jake, Sam, or any other third party or issue. The central issue in empathic understanding is to home in on the client's current core of feelings and concerns and communicate to the client (in the worker's own words) the gist of what the client is experiencing.

Nonverbal communication.   Empathic understanding means accurately picking up and reflecting more than verbal messages. It involves accurately sensing and reflecting all the unspoken cues, messages, and behaviors that the client emits. Nonverbal messages may be transmitted in many ways. Body posture, body movement, gestures, grimaces, vocal pitch, movement of eyes, movement of arms and legs, and other body indicators should be carefully observed by the worker. Clients may transmit emotions such as anger, fear, puzzlement, doubt, rejection, emotional stress, and hopelessness by different body messages. Crisis workers should be keenly aware of whether nonverbal messages are consistent with the client's verbal messages. A part of empathic understanding is the communication of such inconsistency to the client who may not be consciously aware of the difference. For example:

CW: [*Observing the way Rita's face lights up whenever she speaks or thinks about Sam.*] Rita, I notice you are talking about all the trouble it is for you to keep seeing Sam on the sly. But your body tells me that those are the moments you live for—that, right now, your only ecstasy is when you're with Sam.

It is important that the crisis worker avoid reading more into body language than it warrants. Communicating empathy in the nonverbal realm is no place for fishing expeditions or long-shot hunches.

The crisis worker's main concern with nonverbal communication, however, involves the worker's own messages. All the dynamics of the client's body language apply to the worker as well. Your nonverbal messages must be consistent with your verbal messages. It would not be empathic or helpful if your words were saying to the client, "I understand precisely what you're feeling and desiring," but your body were saying, "I don't care," or "I'm bored," or "My mind isn't fully focused on what you're saying." Your voice, facial expression, posture—even the office arrangement and environment—must say to the client: "I'm fully tuned in to your world while you're with me. I want to give my total mental and emotional energy to understanding your concerns while you're here. I will not be distracted." If your body can communicate such messages so that they are unmistakably under-stood by the client, then you will have effectively communicated empathy to the client nonverbally, and you will stand a better chance of being helpful.

Silence.   Silence is golden. Beginning crisis workers often feel compelled to initiate talk to fill any void or lapse in the dialogue because they believe they would not be doing their job otherwise. Nothing could be further from the truth. Clients need time to think. To throw up a barrage of questions or engage in a monologue says more about the crisis worker's insecurity in the situation than it does about resolving the crisis. Silence gives the client thinking time—and the crisis worker too.

Indeed, at such times, verbiage from the crisis worker may be intrusive and even unwelcome. Remaining silent but attending closely to the client can convey deep, empathic understanding. Nonverbally, the message comes across: "I understand your struggle trying to put those feelings into words and it's OK. I know it's tough, but I believe you can handle it. How-ever, I'm right here if you need me."

Rita: The last beating . . . I was so ashamed, yet I couldn't seem to do anything except go back to him.

CW: It hurts you not only to get beaten but also that others might find out—which seems even worse. As a result, you don't see any alternatives.

Rita: [*Thinks hard, eyes focused into the distance for more than a minute.*] Yes and no! I see alternatives, but I guess until now I haven't had the guts to do any-thing. I rationalized that something must be wrong with me or that the situation would get better, but it hasn't for five years. It has gotten worse.

CW: [*Silence. Looks at Rita for some 30 seconds while collecting thoughts.*] A couple of things strike me about what you said. First, you've decided to quit blaming yourself. Second, by the fact that you're here now, you've chosen at least one alternative to that five-year merry-go-round of abuse.

In this scene, silence is allowed to work for both the client and the worker. The client needs time to work through her response to the worker and she is unconditionally allowed to do this. The same is true of the crisis worker. The client's comment is synthesized and processed for its full meaning. By reacting immediately, the crisis worker might make less than a potent response. Taking time to digest both the content and the affect of the client enables the worker to formulate a response that is more likely to be on target and helpful.

Communicating Genuineness

Contrary to the thinking of most beginning human services workers, as evi-denced by their behavior, being fully oneself and not some pseudotherapist or mimic of a particular therapist one has heard or seen is an absolutely necessary condition, particularly in crisis intervention. Rogers (1969, p. 228) says it in clear, simple, and succinct terms:

> When I can accept the fact that I have many deficiencies, many faults, make a lot of mistakes, am often ignorant where I should be knowledgeable, often prejudiced when I should be open-minded, often have feelings which are not justified by the circumstances, then I can be much more real.

Rogers's statement means putting on no false fronts but rather being oneself in the relationship and communicating what "oneself" is to the client. In short, it is being honest. The advice to be honest is not simply a platitude. To be honest is to be congruent; it means that the crisis worker's awareness of self, feelings, and experience is freely and unconditionally available and communicable, when appropriate during intervention in a crisis.

Egan (1975, 1982, 1986, 1990) has listed essential components of genuineness that would serve the beginning crisis worker well.

1. *Being role free.* The crisis worker is genuine in life as well as in the therapeutic relationship and is congruent both in experiencing and communicating feelings (Egan, 1975, p. 91).

2. *Being spontaneous.* The crisis worker communicates freely, with tact and without constantly gauging what to say, because such helpers behave freely without being impulsive or inhibited and are not rule bound or technique bound. Worker behavior is based on a feeling of self-confidence (p. 92).

3. *Being nondefensive.* Crisis workers who behave nondefensively have an excellent understanding of their strengths and weaknesses. Thus, they can be open to negative, even hostile, client expressions without feeling attacked or defensive. The crisis worker who is genuine understands such negative expressions as saying more about the client than the worker and tries to facilitate exploration of such comments rather than defend against them (pp. 92–93).

4. *Being consistent.* People who are genuine have few discrepancies between what they think, feel, and say and their actual behavior. Crisis workers who are consistent do not think one thing and tell a client another or engage in behavior that is contrary to their values (pp. 93–94).

5. *Being a sharer of self.* When it is appropriate to the situation, people who are genuine engage in self-disclosure, allowing others to know them through open verbal and nonverbal expression of their feelings (p. 94).

The following dialogue between the crisis worker and Rita demonstrates comprehensively the points both Rogers and Egan make.

Rita: Just what the hell gives? Here I am going crazy and you put it back on my shoulders. You're supposed to help get me out of this mess!

CW: I can see that you're really mad at me because I don't behave the way you think I ought to.

Rita: Well, how can you be such a caring person if you let me hang out there, pushing me to take such risky chances? I could lose everything.

CW: You see me as being a real hypocrite because I'm pushing you to take some action rather than sympathizing with you.

Rita: God knows I could use some . . . and when you act so callously [*Cries.*] . . . you're like every other damn man!

CW: What would I be doing if I were acting in the most helpful way I possibly could, in your opinion, right now?

Rita: Well, I know you can't solve this for me, but I'd sure as hell like for you to point the way or help me solve this.

CW: So, what you're really wanting is to be able to solve this dilemma on your own, and what you're wanting from me is to help you find your own inner choices that are best for you. What I want to do is to help you find those choices. Let's look at your current options right now.

The dialogue aptly depicts the crisis worker owning feelings, using "I" statements, and focusing on the client's emergent concerns rather than allowing the focus to shift to tangential matters or defensive responses of the worker. Such statements allow the crisis worker to retain integrity, squarely face client hostility without becoming hostile in turn, and model a safe and trusting atmosphere in which clients see that it is all right for them to demonstrate angry feelings and still be accepted by the crisis worker. At the same time, the crisis worker stands by and is consistent with a therapeutic approach without being intimidated by or defensive with the client. The crisis worker above all has the self-confidence and congruence to make such statements in a way that is facilitative for the client.

Communicating Acceptance

The crisis worker who interacts with complete acceptance of clients exudes an unconditional positive regard for clients that transcends clients' personal qualities, beliefs, problems, situations, or crises. The worker is able to prize, care for, and fully accept clients even if they are doing things, saying things, and experiencing situations that are contrary to the worker's personal beliefs and values. The worker is able to put aside personal needs, values, and desires and does not require clients to make specific responses as a condition of full acceptance.

Rita: I hate to bother you with all my problems. I know you're married and have never been divorced. You must think I'm a terribly screwed up mess.

CW: I hear your concern and I want you to know that what has happened to you and what you choose to do have nothing to do with my regard for you. What I'm really hoping we can do is to help you arrive at those choices that will best help you get through this crisis and successfully get back in total control of your life.

Rita: I appreciate that very much. But sometimes I wonder whether my running around with Sam doesn't strike you as unwise and immature.

CW: I hope I'm not giving off negative vibes to give you that impression, because your personal preferences have nothing to do with my caring for you. It seems like you really have a concern about my feelings about how you should act.

Rita: Not really. It's just something inside me—that if I were you, I'd be wondering.

CW: So, a source of concern inside you is whether I may evaluate you negatively. What I want you to know is that my esteem for you is not based on what you do.

Even when clients persist in projecting onto the crisis worker negative evaluations or notions such as those expressed by Rita, the worker doesn't have to buy into such notions. If the worker can truly feel an unconditional positive regard for the client, there will be no need for denial, defensiveness, or diversion from the reality of the worker's true feelings. If the worker demonstrates caring and prizing of the client, regardless of the client's situation or status, the client will be more likely to accept and prize himself or herself. That is the essence of acceptance in crisis intervention.

Facilitative Listening

Listening is the first imperative in crisis intervention. When we use the word *listening,* we are applying the term broadly to several important behavioral and communications skills discussed in this chapter. To function in a facilitative way, workers must *give full attention* to the client by

1. focusing their total mental power into the client's world
2. attending to the client's verbal and nonverbal messages (what the client does not say is sometimes more important than what is actually spoken)
3. picking up on the client's current readiness to enter into emotional and/ or physical contact with others, especially with the worker
4. emitting attending behavior by both verbal and nonverbal actions, thereby strengthening the relationship and predisposing the client to trust the crisis intervention process.

One important aspect of listening is for the worker to make initial, owning statements that express exactly what he or she is going to do.

CW: Rita, I can see you're really hurting. So that I can fully understand what's going on and what needs to be done, I'm going to focus as hard as I can on what you're saying and how you're saying it. As well as listening to what you do say, I'm going to be listening for those things that aren't said because they may have some bearing on your problems too. So if I seem to be really concentrating on you, it's because I want to fully comprehend in as helpful and objective a way as possible what the situation is and your readiness to do something about it.

The *second* important aspect of listening is to *respond* in ways that let the client know that the crisis worker is *accurately hearing* both the facts and the emotional state from which the client's message comes. Here we are searching for both the affective and content dimensions of the problem. The crisis worker combines the dilemma and feelings by using restatement and reflection.

CW: As you lay the problem out—the abuse by your husband, the job pressures, the wonderful yet guilt-ridden times with Sam—I get the feeling of an emotional switchboard with all the lines plugged in and even crossed over, and you're a beginning operator who might be able to handle one or two incoming calls, but now you're just sitting paralyzed wishing you'd never taken the job, wondering how you can get out, wanting answers, but having so many problems that you don't even know the right questions to ask.

The *third* facet in effective listening is facilitative responding. It provides positive impetus for clients to gain a clearer understanding of their feelings, inner motives, and choices. Facilitative responses enable clients to feel hopeful and to sense an inclination to begin to move forward, toward resolution and away from the central core of the crisis. Clients begin to be able to view the crisis from a standpoint of more reality or rationality, which immediately gives them a sense of control. Here the crisis worker targets an action.

CW: So, given all the wires running into the switchboard, which ones do you want to pull and which ones do you want to keep plugged in? You've given me all kinds of information about how well you've handled the business up to this crisis point. Look back on how you handled that particular phone line. What worked then that might work now? Using that as an example, can we sort each one of these out and get the circuits plugged in or just say that particular call isn't important right now and unplug the line?

The *fourth* dimension of effective listening is evidenced by the worker's helping clients to understand the *full impact* of the crisis situation. Such an understanding allows clients to become more like objective, external observers of the crisis and to *refocus* it in rational ways rather than remaining stuck in their own internal frame of reference and emotional bias.

Rita: I feel like the whole world is caving in on me. I wonder if I'll ever be able to get out from under all the mess I'm in now.

CW: You're sounding emotionally frozen by what is happening. I'm wondering what would happen if we could step back for a moment and look at it as if we were third-party observers to your situation—as if you were someone else in a soap opera. What would you say to that person?

Rita: Well . . . [*Moment of thought.*] I'd say she's not the first or only one to experience lots of trouble—that things may look horrible now, but that eventually things get worked out—especially if she's lucky and can bear up long enough.

CW: Then looking at it from outside yourself does give you an additional view.

Helping clients refocus is not a solution in itself. It is an extension of the art of listening that may facilitate forward movement when clients are emotionally stuck.

These four aspects of listening don't operate in a fragmented or mechanical way. Such listening requires skill, practice, an emotionally secure listener, and both physical and emotional stamina on the part of the listener. The following dialogue gives a brief but comprehensive demonstration of how effective listening is combined in its many dimensions. The client now is Jean, the daughter of Rita. Don't be perplexed at our shift in clients. One person in crisis may well put a significant other into a crisis situation also. In this instance, Rita's problems have boiled over into her 13-year-old daughter's life.

Jean: I feel put down and ignored by my mother. Every time anything is mentioned about Sam—that's her secret boyfriend—she gets mad and leaves the room. Everything has changed. It's like I'm no longer important to her. I don't know what's happening or what to do.

CW: You're feeling hurt and disappointed, and you're also bewildered by her responses to you.

Jean: [*Crying and very upset.*] I . . . I feel like I no longer count. I'm feeling like I'm in the way. Like I'm suddenly no good . . . I feel like now I'm the problem.

CW: You're blaming yourself even though you're trying to understand what has happened and what you should do.

Jean: [*Crying is slowing down.*] By Sunday night I felt like killing myself. I planned to do it that night. I was feeling abandoned, alone, and hopeless. I just wanted to find some way to end the hurting. I didn't think I could go on another day. I felt like I was no longer her daughter—like she had either disowned me or had been living a lie. I don't know if I can go on.

CW: Even though you were feeling you were at the brink of death, you somehow managed to pull out of it. What did you do and what are you doing now to keep from killing yourself?

Jean: [*Not crying—pondering the crisis worker's last response.*] Well, Marlene and her parents came by. I spent the night with them. That really helped. It was lucky for me that they came by and invited me. They were so kind and understanding. I had a bad night. Worrying about all that stuff. But they, especially Marlene, helped me so much.

CW: Let's see if you can tell me what you have learned from that experience that can help you the next time you feel like killing yourself.

Jean: [*Pause, as if studying the crisis worker's response.*] To get away . . . with someone who cares and understands.

CW: Tell me someone you can contact whenever you feel hopeless and lonely and suicidal so that next time you won't have to depend on luck.

Jean: Well, I'd call Marlene again . . . or my uncle and aunt. They'd be quick to invite me over . . . and there are several friends at school I could call.

[*Dialogue continues.*]

This segment of dialogue contains several of the elements of listening that we have described. It contains accurate reflective listening, open-ended questions, and attention to the client's safety (without asking closed questions, giving advice, or encroaching on the client's prerogatives and autonomy). Also, the crisis worker keeps the focus right on the central core of the client's current concerns, paving the way for the client's forward movement from the immediate crisis toward safer and more adjustive actions. The worker's selective responses are geared toward enabling the client to become aware of and pursue immediate short-term goals. The worker does not digress onto external events, past events, the mother, the secret boyfriend, gathering background information, or conducting long-term therapy.

ACTING IN CRISIS INTERVENTION

As shown in Figure 2-1, the crisis worker's level of action/involvement in the client's world, based on a valid and realistic assessment of the client's level of mobility/immobility, may be anywhere on a continuum ranging from nondirective through collaborative to directive. The appropriateness of alternative coping mechanisms hinges on the client's degree of mobility. Thus, assessment of client mobility is a key concept governing the degree of the crisis worker's involvement.

One of the first things the worker must determine is what event precipitated the crisis. What brought on the disequilibrium? The answer may not be very clear in the client's complex and rambling story. So the worker may have to ask, early in the interview, "What *one event* brought you to seek counseling today?" When you discover the major precipitating event that took away the client's autonomous coping ability, it will likely signal your primary focus with the client. During the worker's *acting* mode (helping clients examine alternatives, plan action steps, and make a commitment), the worker may function mainly in one of three ways: nondirective, collaborative, or directive.

Nondirective Counseling

The nondirective approach is desirable whenever clients are able to initiate and carry out their own action steps. As a general rule, the less severe the crisis, the less directive the crisis worker has to be. The worker uses a great amount of active listening and many open-ended questions to help clients clarify what they really want to do and examine what outcomes various choices might produce. These are some possible questions: "What do you wish to have happen?" "What will occur if you choose to do that?" "What persons are available now who could and would assist you in this?" "Picture yourself doing that—vividly see yourself choosing that route. Now, how does that image fit with what you're really trying to accomplish?" "What activities did you do in the past that helped you in situations similar to this?" These are only a few of the possible open-ended questions the crisis worker may pose. Nondirective questions are geared to a sensitive and accurate identification of the client's current inner feelings, needs, and goals.

In nondirective counseling the worker focuses on the client's inner world, determines that the client has the capability, energy, mobility, and autonomy to make reasonable choices, and facilitates realistic forward movement of the client. The worker does not manage, manipulate, prescribe, dominate, or control. It is the client who owns the problem, the coping mechanisms, the plan, the action, the commitment, and the outcomes. The worker is a support person who may listen, encourage, reflect, reinforce, self-disclose, and suggest. Nondirective counseling assists clients in mobilizing what already is inside them—the capacity, ability, and coping strength to solve their own problems in ways that are pretty well known to them already but that are temporarily out of reach. Here is an example of a nondirective response:

Rita: This is it. I've had the last beating I'm going to take from that jerk! I'm simply going to get myself out of this hell!

CW: You've made a decision to choose a different life for yourself, and you've decided that you are the one who is going to start it.

Collaborative Counseling

The collaborative approach enables the crisis worker to forge a real partnership with the client in evaluating the problem, generating acceptable alternatives, and implementing realistic action steps. When the assessment indicates that the client cannot function successfully in a nondirective mode but has enough mobility to be a partner in the crisis intervention process, the worker is collaborative to that degree. Collaborative counseling is a "we" approach, whereas nondirective counseling is a "you" approach. Consider some typical worker statements in the collaborative mode: "You have asked me where you might find a safe place to spend the night. Let's consider the places we know of around here." "You've come up with a lot of good ideas, but you sound a little confused about which one to act on. Could we put our heads together and make a priority list of alternatives?" Usually the collaborative client's crisis is more severe than that of the fully mobile client. But the collaborative client is a full partner in identifying the precipitating problem, examining realistic alternatives, planning action steps, and making a commitment to carrying out a realistic plan. The collaborative client is not as self-reliant and autonomous as the fully mobile client but does possess sufficient ego strength and mobility to participate in resolving the problem. The worker is needed to serve as a temporary catalyst, consultant, facilitator, and support person. The concept of collaborative counseling is based on the precept that the worker serves as a catalyst to help the client map out immediate action steps in order to get started. The client can then take over, having once achieved a state of precrisis equilibrium. Here is an example of a collaborative response to a client:

Rita: I've thought about going to my mother's or going to the Wife Abuse Shelter, or even calling my school-counselor friend for a place to stay tonight.

CW: Let's examine these three choices and maybe some others available to you that I know of to see which one will best meet your requirements for tonight.

Directive Counseling

The directive approach is necessary when the client is assessed as being too immobile to cope with the current crisis. The crisis worker is the principal definer of the problem, searcher for alternatives, and developer of an adequate plan, and instructs, leads, or guides the client in the action. Directive counseling is an "I" approach. This is an example of a worker-directed statement: "I want you to try something right now. I want you to draw a deep breath, and while you are doing it, I want you to just focus on your breathing. Don't let any other thoughts enter your mind. Just relax and notice how your tensions begin to subside." By using a very directive stance, the worker takes temporary control, authority, and responsibility for the situation.

Rita: I don't know which way to turn. My whole world has caved in. I don't know what I'll do tonight. It's all so hopeless. I'm scared to even think about tonight. [*Rita appears stunned and in a state of panic.*] I don't know what to do.

CW: I don't want you to go home in the state you're in now. I'm going to call Wife Abuse Services and if they have room for you at their shelter, I want you to consider spending at least one night there. Wife Abuse Services has offices and a counseling service at one location and a shelter at a different address, which is unlisted. I don't want you to worry. We have a van that can take you to the shelter. In the morning you may leave the shelter and go talk with the Wife Abuse Services counselors or you can come back and talk with me; but right now my main concern is that you are safe for today and tonight.

There are many kinds of immobile clients: (1) clients who need immediate hospitalization due to chemical use or organic dysfunction, (2) clients who are suffering from such severe depression that they cannot function, (3) clients who are experiencing a severe psychotic episode, (4) clients who are suffering from severe shock, bereavement, or loss, (5) clients whose anxiety level is temporarily so high that they cannot function until the anxiety subsides, (6) clients who, for any reason, are out of touch with reality, and (7) clients who are currently a danger to themselves or others.

In the *real* world of crisis intervention, every crisis worker must deal with some clients who need directive counseling and whose lethality level should be assessed early in the interview. These clients are more apt to be suicidal than the clients who are ready to respond to collaborative or to nondirective counseling. The worker must be able to make a fairly accurate and objective assessment of the client's level of mobility. However, if the worker makes an error of judgment (believing a client to be immobile who in fact is not), no harm is usually done because the client may simply respond by refusing to accept the worker's direction. In most cases of this sort, the worker can then shift into a collaborative mode and continue the helping session. Many times a worker will begin in a directive mode and then shift into a collaborative mode during the session. For example, with a highly anxious client the worker may begin by directing the client in relaxation exercises, which may lower the client's anxiety level to the point where the worker can make a natural shift into a collaborative mode to continue the counseling.

Action Strategies for Crisis Workers

Crisis workers who use the six-step model we have described may begin each session with a nondirective approach and shift to a more directive approach as the ongoing assessment indicates. A number of action strategies and considerations may enhance the worker's effectiveness in dealing with clients in crisis.

Recognize individual differences.   View and respond to each client and each crisis situation as unique. Even for experienced workers, staying attuned to the uniqueness of each person is difficult. Under the pressures of time and exhaustion, and misled by overconfidence in their own expertise, workers find it all too easy to lump problems and clients together and provide pat answers and solutions. Treating clients generically is likely to cost the worker and the client a great deal more in the long run than it saves in time and effort in the short run. Stereotyping, labeling, and taking for granted any aspect of crisis intervention are definite pitfalls.

Assess yourself.   Ongoing self-analysis on the part of the worker is mandatory. At all times, workers must be fully and realistically aware of their own values, limitations, physical and emotional status, and personal readiness to deal objectively with the client and the crisis at hand. Crisis workers need to run continuous perceptual checks to ascertain if they have gotten in over their heads. (See Chapter 12 for a complete description of this phenomenon.) If for any reason the worker is not ready for or capable of dealing with the crisis or the client, the worker must immediately make an appropriate referral.

Show regard for client's safety.   The worker's style, choices, and strategies must reflect a continuous consideration of the client's physical and psychological safety as well as the safety of others involved. The safety consideration includes the safety of the worker as well as the ethical, legal, and professional requirements mandated in counseling practice. The greatest intervention strategies and tactics are absolutely useless if clients leave the crisis worker and go out and harm themselves or others. The golden rule is "When in doubt about client safety, get help." The safety requirement may mean appropriate referral interventions, including immediate hospitalization.

Provide client support.   The crisis worker should be available as a support person during the crisis period. Clients may need assistance in developing a list of possible support persons, but if no appropriate support person emerges in the examination of alternatives, the worker can serve as a primary support person until the present crisis is over. A warm, empathic, and assertive counseling strategy should be used with clients who are extremely lonely and devoid of supports. For example, "I want you to know that I am very concerned about your safety during this stressful time, and that I'm available to help. I want you to keep this card with you until you're through this crisis, and call me if you feel yourself sliding back into that hopeless feeling again. If you call either of these numbers and don't get an answer or get a busy signal, keep trying until you get me. You *must* make contact with *me*. I will be very disturbed if you are in a seriously threatening situation again without letting me become involved with you. I really want to impress upon you my genuine concern for you and the importance of making an agreement or contract to call me whenever your safety is threatened. Will you give me that assurance?"

Define the problem clearly.   Many clients have complicated and multiple problems. Make sure that each problem is clearly and accurately defined from a practical, problem-solving viewpoint. Many clients define the crisis as someone else's problem or as some external event or situation that has happened. Attempting to solve the crisis of some third party (who isn't present) is counterproductive. Pinpoint the client's own problem with the event or situation and keep the focus on the client's central core of concern. Also, attempt to distill multiple problems down into an immediate, workable problem and to concentrate on that problem first. We cannot overemphasize the tenacity with which the worker must avoid being drawn off on tangents by some highly emotional or defensive clients with difficult problems. Consider these exchanges with Rita's husband Jake:

Jake: You don't seem to like me much.

CW: Right now, that's not the issue of importance. What I'm trying to do is help you identify the main source of your problem.

Another example:

Jake: Haven't you ever hit your wife too?

CW: No, but that's not what we're working on now. I'm trying to help us figure out a way for you to avoid fighting with her whenever you first get home each evening.

In both instances the worker stays focused on the client and does not get caught up on side issues such as worker competency, beliefs, and attitudes.

Consider alternatives.   In most problem situations, the alternatives are infinite. But crisis clients (and sometimes workers) have a limited view of the many options available. Through the use of open-ended questions, elicit the maximum number of choices from the client. Then add your own list of possible alternatives to the client's list. For example: "I get the feeling that it might help if you could get in contact with a counselor at the Credit Counseling Bureau. How would you feel about our adding that to our list?" Examining, analyzing, and listing alternatives to consider should be as collaborative as possible. The best alternatives are ones that the client truly *owns*. Take care to avoid imposing your alternatives on the client. The alternatives on the list should be workable and realistic. They should represent the right amount of action for the client to undertake now—not too much, not too little. The client will generally express ownership of an option by words such as "I would really like to call him today." Worker-imposed options are usually signaled by the worker's words, such as *"You need to* go to his office and do that right away." *Beware* of the latter! An important part of the quest for appropriate alternatives is to explore with the client what options worked before in situations like the present one. Many times, the client can come up with the best choices, derived from coping mechanisms that have worked well in the past. But the stresses created by the immediate crisis may keep clients from identifying the most obvious and appropriate alternatives for them. Here the crisis worker facilitates the client's examination of alternatives:

CW: Rita, you say you're feeling frightened and trapped right now and you don't know where to turn. But it sounds like you'd take a step in a positive direction if you could get some of your old zip back. What are some actions you took or some persons you sought out in previous situations when you felt frightened or stuck?

Rita: Oh, I don't know that I've been in a mess quite this bad before.

CW: Well, that may be true. But what steps have you taken or what persons have you contacted before in a mess like this, even if it wasn't this bad?

Rita: Hmm . . . Well, a time or two I did go talk to Mr. Jackson, one of my auto mechanics instructors when I was at the Area Vo-Tech School. He's very understanding and helpful. He always seemed to understand me and believe in me.

CW: How would you feel about reestablishing contact with him whenever you're down again?

Plan action steps.   In crisis intervention the worker endeavors to assist the client to develop a short-term plan that will help the client get through the immediate crisis, as well as make the transition to long-term coping. The plan should include the client's internal coping mechanisms, as well as sources of help in the environment. The coping mechanisms are usually brought to bear on some concrete, positive, constructive action that clients can take to regain better control of their lives. Actions that initially involve some physical movement are preferred. The plan should be realistic in terms of the client's current emotional readiness and environmental supports. It may involve collaboration with the worker until the client can function independently. The effective crisis worker is sensitive to the need of the client to function autonomously as soon as feasible.

Rita: Right now I'd like to just be free of the whole mess for a few days . . . just get off this dizzy merry-go-round long enough to collect my thoughts.

CW: It sounds to me like you really mean that. Let's see if together we can examine some options that might really get you the freedom and breathing space you need to pull the pieces back together.

Rita: I can't really let go. Too many people depending on me. That's just wishful thinking. But it would be wonderful to get some relief.

CW: Even though you don't see any way to get it, what you're wanting is some space for yourself right now—away from work, kids, Jake, Sam, and the whole dilemma.

Rita: The only way that would happen is for my doctor to order it—to prescribe it, medically.

CW: How realistic is that? How would that help you?

Rita: It would call a halt to some of the pressures. The treadmill would have to stop, at least temporarily. Yes, I guess that kind of medical reason wouldn't be so bad.

CW: Sounds like consulting your physician and laying at least part of your cards on the table might be one step toward getting medical help in carving out some breathing space for yourself.

Rita: I think so. Yeah, that's it! That's one thing I could do.

CW: Let's together map out a possible action plan—for contacting your physician and requesting assistance in temporarily letting go. Let's look at *when* you want to contact your physician, *what* you're going to say, and *how* you're going to say it—to make sure you get the results you must have right now.

The crisis worker is attempting to work collaboratively with Rita and to facilitate Rita's real ownership of her plan. The worker also implies a view of Rita as competent and responsible.

Use the client's coping strengths.   In crisis intervention it is important not to overlook the client's own strengths and coping mechanisms. Often the crisis events temporarily immobilize the individual's usual strengths and coping strategies. If they can be identified, explored, and reinstated they may make an enormous contribution toward restoring the client's equilibrium and reassuring the client. For example, one woman had previously relieved stress by playing her piano. She told the worker that she was no longer able to play the piano because her piano had been repossessed. The crisis worker was able to explore with her several possible places where she could avail herself of a piano in times of stress.

Attend to client's immediate needs.   It is important for crisis clients to know that their immediate needs are understood and attended to by the crisis worker. If a client is extremely lonely, attempt to arrange for the client to be with someone. The client may need to make contact with relatives, friends, former associates, or former friends. The client may need follow-up appointments with the crisis worker or referral to another worker, counselor, or agency. The client may simply need to be heard—to ventilate about a loss, a disappointment, or a specific hurtful event.

Use referral resources.   An integral aspect of crisis intervention is the use of referral resources. A ready list of names, phone numbers, and contact persons is a necessity. It is also important for the crisis worker to develop skill in making referrals as well as in working with a wide variety of referral agencies. Many clients need to be referred early to make contact with sources of help regarding financial matters, assistance from social agencies, legal assistance, long-term individual therapy, family therapy, substance abuse, severe depression, or other personal matters. A worker might use referral resources for purposes like these: to obtain emergency eyeglasses for a junior high school student whose family cannot buy them; to get dental care for a child who is suffering excruciating pain and whose family cannot pay; to prevail upon a parole officer to mandate that a specific parolee cease abusing his wife and children; to ensure that a client disabled by an automobile accident receives help for his vocational rehabilitation as well as for his depressed mental state. We have compiled a list of suggestions and cautions that we have found to be useful in working with a variety of agencies. Generally, we find that a breakdown in our communication with agencies follows our having overlooked a few obvious and simple cautions.

1. Keep a handy, up-to-date list of frequently used agencies. Keep up with personnel changes.
2. In communities that publish a directory of human services, have available the most recent edition.
3. Cultivate a working relationship with key persons in agencies you frequently use.
4. Identify yourself, your agency, and your purpose when telephoning.
5. Know secretaries and receptionists by name; use their names when you call. Treat them with dignity, respect, and equality.
6. Follow up on referrals you make.
7. Don't assume that all clients have the skill to get the services they need. Be prepared to assist, to avoid runarounds and bureaucratic red tape.
8. Whenever necessary, go with clients to the referral agencies to assist and to ensure that effective communication takes place.
9. Be sensitive to the client's needs for transportation and child care.
10. Write thank-you messages (with copies to their bosses) to persons who are particularly helpful to you and your clients.
11. Don't criticize fellow professionals or the agencies they represent, and don't carry tales about either workers or agencies.
12. Keep accurate records of referral activities.
13. Remember that police and fire departments are referral resources also.
14. Know frequently used agencies' hours, basic services, mode of operation, limitations, and, if possible, policies such as insurance, sliding scale fees, and so forth.
15. Be aware of any agency services the client is already using.

16. Use courtesy and good human relations skills when dealing with agency personnel. Put yourself in their shoes and treat them as you would like to be treated.
17. Give agencies feedback on how they did; obtain feedback from them, too.
18. Avoid expecting perfection of other agencies.
19. Be aware of sensory impairment in clients, especially in older adults and make those impairments known in referrals.
20. If the client is able to do so, it is a good idea for the client to make the call (this creates a personal link between the client and the referral agency).
21. If the agency has an orientation session, seek to attend and to participate in it.
22. Practice honesty in communicating to referral agencies regarding the status or needs of clients. (Honest and ethical portrayal of the client's needs will build credibility with other agencies.)
23. Obtain permission of the client before attempting to refer.
24. Observe rules of confidentiality and rights of privacy in regard to all clients and fellow workers.

Develop and use networks.   Closely allied with referral is a function we call *networking*. Networking, for us, is having and using personal contacts within a variety of agencies that directly affect our ability to serve clients effectively and efficiently. Although each person in our network is a referral resource, it is the relationship we have with that individual that defines it as a network. Effective crisis workers can't sit behind a desk and wait for assistance to come to them. They must get out into the community and get to know personally the key individuals who can provide the kinds of services their clients require. A personal relationship based on understanding and trust between the worker and vital network persons is invaluable in helping the worker cut through bureaucratic red tape, expedite emergency assistance, and personalize many services that might otherwise not be available to clients.

As crisis workers, we do not operate alone in the world. We are interdependent on one another. Networking permits us to spread the responsibilities among other helping professionals. We mean "helping professionals" in the broadest possible context: lawyers, judges, parole officers, ministers, school counselors, federal, state, and local human services workers, directors and key persons in crisis agencies, business and civic leaders, medical doctors, dentists, police, and political leaders may play important roles in the networking process. The development and use of effective networking is an indispensable function of the successful worker.

Get a commitment.   One of the vital aspects of crisis intervention is getting a commitment from the client to follow through on the action or actions planned. The crisis worker should ask the client to summarize verbally the steps to be taken. This verbal summary helps the worker understand the client's perception of both the plan and the commitment, and it gives the worker an opportunity to clear up any distortions. It also provides the worker an opportunity to establish a follow-up checkpoint with the client. The commitment step can serve both as a motivational reminder to the client and to encourage and predispose the client to believe that the action steps will succeed. Without a definite and positive commitment on the part of the client, the best of plans may fall short of the objectives that have been worked out by the worker and the client.

Step 6, the commitment step, does not stand alone. It would be worth little without the foundation of the five preceding steps. The actions that a client in crisis owns and to which the client commits are derived from solid planning (Step 5), which is, in turn, based on systematic examination of alternatives (Step 4). The three acting steps (Step 4, 5, and 6) are based on effective listening in Steps 1, 2, and 3. All six of these steps are carried out under the umbrella of assessing. Commitment is individually tailored to the specific client crisis situation. The following segment is one example of a crisis worker functioning during the commitment step.

CW: So, Rita, it seems to me that what you've decided to do is to reinitiate some kind of meaningful contact with Mr. Jackson. That seems to be one thing you've decided that might really help right now. So that we're both very clear on what you've committed yourself to doing, would you please summarize how and when you're going to proceed?

Rita: I'm going straight to my office today and phone him at school. I'll either talk to him or leave a message for him to call me. As soon as I talk to him, I'll set up a definite day and time to meet with him.

CW: And when you've set up. . . .

Rita: Oh, yes! And when I've set up my appointment with him I'm going to phone you and let you know how it went.

CW: Good. And in the meantime, you have my number on the card if you need me —especially if the safety of either you or your children becomes jeopardized.

Rita: That's right, and I'll call if I lose my nerve with Sam. I've got to get some space for myself there—at least some temporary space.

Experienced crisis workers are generally able to sense how far and how fast the client is able to act. Usually the client is encouraged to commit to as much action as feasible. If we cannot get her or him to make a giant leap forward, we'll accept one small step in a positive direction. The main idea is to facilitate some commitment that will result in movement of the client in a constructive direction.

COUNSELING DIFFICULT CLIENTS

We are frequently asked by crisis workers, counselors-in-training, counselors in community agencies, and volunteer workers for suggestions for dealing with "difficult" clients. Individuals in agencies that do a lot of crisis intervention as well as general counseling sometimes have to deal with clients who are angry, uncooperative, or less articulate than we would choose them to be. Generally, we are requested to provide specific strategies that a crisis worker may use to help difficult clients effectively, both individually and in small groups (such as mediating with couples or a family in crisis). This brief discussion is intended to speak to this recurring need.

Ground Rules

Prior to the start of the counseling session, one can obtain an understanding and a commitment from clients who are known to be difficult. At the time the appointment is made, the worker can set a tone of positive expectancy. A set of ground rules can be agreed upon at the outset. The ground rules can be structured to help avoid defensive, uncommunicative, defiant, and other problem behaviors before such behaviors actually have a chance to occur in the session.

The ground rules may vary according to the particular situation. We offer a typical set of ground rules for dealing with difficult clients. Workers who must deal with difficult clients regularly may wish to print a set of ground rules to place in the hands of selected client groups at the initial session or prior to the first meeting.

1. We start on time and quit on time; if couples are involved, both parties must be present; we will not meet unless both parties are present.
2. There will be no physical violence or threats of violence.
3. Everyone speaks for himself or herself.
4. Everyone has a chance to be fully heard.
5. We deal mainly with the here-and-now; we try to steer clear of getting bogged down in the past and in blaming others.
6. Everyone faces all the issues brought up—nobody gets up and leaves just because the topic is uncomfortable, and everyone stays for the entire session.
7. Everyone gets an opportunity to define the current problems, suggest realistic solutions, and make at least one commitment to do something positive; at least *one positive action step* is desired from each person present.
8. Everyone belongs, because he or she is a human being and because he or she is here.
9. The crisis worker will not take sides.
10. There will be no retribution, retaliation, or grudges over what is said in the session; whatever is said in the session belongs and stays in the session.
11. The time we spend together is for working on the concerns of persons in the group—not for playing games, making personal points, diversion, ulterior purposes, or carrying tales or gossip outside the session.

12. When we know things are a certain way, we will not pretend they are another way—we will confront and deal with each other as honestly and objectively as we possibly can.
13. We will not ignore the nonverbal or body messages that are emitted— we will deal with them openly if they occur.
14. If words or messages need to be expressed to clear the air, we will say them either directly or with role playing; we will not put them off until later.
15. We will not expect each other to be perfect.
16. In the event the ground rules are broken, the consequences will be discussed in the group. People who comply with the rules will not be denied services because one person disobeys the rules.

The crisis worker may go over the ground rules, in person or over the phone, prior to the first session. If this is not possible, a brief orientation that includes the ground rules is advisable at the start of the first meeting.

Confronting Difficult Clients

In dealing with difficult clients (such as highly emotional or defensive persons, those who deny any involvement in either the problem or the solution, and belligerent individuals) the worker may have to *confront* such behavior directly. We can confront clients with what they are doing by paying particular attention to *nonverbal behavior* and giving immediate feedback: "You're saying one thing but seem to be doing another; look how you're turning away and frowning whenever she says she wants the marriage to last." It is also essential to use good, focused, *open-ended questions* with difficult clients. If the worker is helping a couple, one of whom is uncooperative, the worker must remain neutral. Regardless of how difficult a client is, the worker must not take sides, exhibit frustration, or show preference for one or the other.

There is a possibility that a client may be so difficult that the session may have to be terminated. (This should happen very, very infrequently.) In such a rare case, the worker would openly admit, "We're getting nowhere, so let's adjourn and see if we can figure out a way to try again." The worker might then reword the ground rules. The individuals may have to be seen separately for a while before they are ready to meet as a couple or in the group again. Consultation with a professional colleague for suggestions would be one of the first steps the group leader would take following such an adjournment. Also, we must recognize that we cannot succeed with every client. Sometimes, all we can do is let some of the clients ventilate, admit that we cannot help the situation, and perhaps refer the clients to a different worker, counselor, or agency.

The worker must be prepared to deal with various kinds of difficult clients: the nonverbal (nontalking) person, clients sent by a court order, clients from a particular ethnic or social group who are uncomfortable when talking with or facing a crisis worker, and clients who are "forced" or coerced into coming. The worker uses the utmost empathy when needed. We must also be sensitive to the need for confrontation, assertion, and directive tactics and ready to use them ("I will not permit you to violate our ground rules by attacking her that way"). Role playing may be needed to model appropriate assertion among group members.

In confronting a client who is belligerent and shows the potential for violence, the crisis worker should be sensitive to the possibility of imminent danger inherent in the situation. The worker should focus on attempting to defuse the client's anger as well as ensuring the safety of the crisis worker and others. The potentially violent client is addressed extensively in Chapter 10.

The worker has the option of "staffing," or seeking the expert professional assistance of other highly trained, experienced, and skilled professionals. Often, getting consultatory assistance from a competent professional colleague provides a key to dealing with a specific difficult case. Knowing when to seek professional assistance and supervision ourselves is an important strategy in the referral, networking, and counseling process. We cannot afford to burn ourselves out by taking our clients' problems home with us.

SUMMARY

This chapter has presented an overview of crisis intervention from a practitioner's standpoint by incorporating fundamental counseling skills into a six-step model of systematic helping. Figure 2-1 provided the central organizing focus: facilitative *listening* and *acting* within an overarching framework of *assessing*. The six-step model is an organized and fluid process of applying crisis intervention skills to the emerging feelings, concerns, and situations that clients having any type of trauma might present.

The six steps in crisis intervention serve to organize and simplify the work of the crisis worker. Step 1 explores and defines the problem from the client's point of view. Step 2 ensures the client's physical and psychological safety. Step 3 provides supports for the person in crisis. Step 4 examines . alternatives available to the client. Step 5 assists the client in developing a plan of action. Finally, Step 6 helps the client to make a commitment to carry out a definite action plan.

Assessment of the person and the crisis situation is the keystone for initiating intervention. Assessment techniques such as evaluating the severity of the crisis, appraising clients' thinking, feeling, emoting, and behaving patterns, assessing the chronicity and lethality of the crisis, looking into the client's background for contributing factors, and evaluating the client's resources, coping mechanisms, and support systems were presented and explored.

Listening is a fundamental imperative for *all* successful counseling, including crisis intervention. The chapter described essential components of effective listening and communication, such as the application of effective attending, empathy, genuineness, and acceptance.

Action skills such as nondirective, collaborative, and directive worker strategies, showing consideration for individual differences and client safety, examining alternatives with clients experiencing crises, helping clients plan for and commit themselves to facilitative choices, wise use of referral resources, and techniques for dealing with difficult clients were explored.

Fundamental relationship skills such as attending, listening, communicating, showing empathy and acceptance, exhibiting genuine responses, and ensuring client safety were demonstrated or modeled in excerpts of worker-client dialogue with a client named Rita. The appropriate use of the six steps in the dialogue with Rita provides a thumbnail view of therapeutic counseling in action.

REFERENCES

Cormier, W. H., & Cormier, L. S. (1991). *Interviewing strategies for helpers: Fundamental skills and cognitive behavioral interventions* (3rd ed.). Pacific Grove, CA: Brooks/Cole.

Egan, G. (1975). *The skilled helper: A model for systematic helping and interpersonal relating.* Pacific Grove, CA: Brooks/Cole.

Egan, G. (1982). *The skilled helper: Model, skills, and methods for effective helping* (2nd ed.). Pacific Grove, CA: Brooks/Cole.

Egan, G. (1986). *The skilled helper: A systematic approach to effective helping* (3rd ed.). Pacific Grove, CA: Brooks/Cole.

Egan, G. (1990). *The skilled helper: Model, skills, and methods for effective helping* (4th ed.). Pacific Grove, CA: Brooks/Cole.

Gilliland, B. E. (1982). *Steps in crisis counseling.* Memphis, TN: Memphis State University, Department of Counseling and Personnel Services.

Gilliland, B. E., James, R. K., & Bowman, J. T. (1989). *Theories and strategies in counseling and psychotherapy* (2nd ed.). Englewood Cliffs, NJ: Prentice-Hall.

Rogers, C. R. (1969). *Freedom to learn: A view of what education might become.* Columbus, OH: Chas. E. Merrill.

Rogers, C. R. (1977). *Carl Rogers on personal power: Inner strength and its revolutionary impact.* New York: Delacorte.

CLASSROOM EXERCISES
The Case of Rita

The case of Rita, based on a real situation in our counseling practice, is presented here for you to consider because it clearly demonstrates and emphasizes the six steps in crisis intervention. We suggest that you make notes as you read and reread it. Suppose that you were the crisis worker to whom

Rita had come for help (in person, not on the telephone). As an exercise to discover how well you have learned the six-step crisis intervention model, write a personal narrative description of how you might use the six-step model to help Rita during the initial session you have scheduled with her. (We have also written our description. Please write your description before reading ours, found at the end of this case; then compare your crisis intervention strategies with the narrative we have prepared. Remember, in crisis intervention, there is no one best way. Yours may be as effective as ours, or more so. We hope the exercise will prove instructive for you.)

Rita is a 35-year-old businesswoman. She is a graduate of high school and a post-high school vocational-technical institute. She holds a certificate in auto mechanics. She has never been to a counselor before. She has come to the crisis worker at the suggestion of a close friend who is a school counselor. Rita owns and operates an automobile tune-up and service shop. She employs and supervises a crew of mechanics, tune-up specialists, and helpers. She works very hard and keeps long hours, but maintains some flexibility by employing a manager. Rita's husband Jake is a college-educated accountant. They have two children: a daughter, 13, and a son, 8. The family rarely attends church, and they don't consider themselves to be religious. But they are church members. Their close friends are neither from their church nor from their work.

Rita's presenting problem is complex. She constantly feels depressed and unfulfilled. She craves attention but has difficulty getting it in appropriate ways. For diversion, she participates in a dance group that practices three nights a week and performs on many Friday and Saturday evenings. Rita, Jake, and their children spend most of their Sundays at their lake cottage, which is an hour's drive from their home. Their circle of friends is mainly their neighbors at the lake.

Rita's marriage has been going downhill for several years. She has become sexually involved with Sam, a wealthy wholesaler of used automobiles. She met him through a business deal whereby she contracted to do the tune-up and service work on a large number of cars for Sam's company. Sam's contracts enable Rita's business to be very successful. Rita states that the "chemistry" between her and Sam is unique and electrifying. She says she and Sam are "head over heels in love with each other." She lives with Jake but no longer feels any love for him.

According to Rita, Sam is unhappily married too, and Sam and his current wife have two small children. Rita states that she and Sam want to get married, but she doesn't want to subject her two children to a divorce right now and she's very fearful of her own mother's wrath if she files for a divorce. Sam fears his wife will "take him to the cleaners" if he leaves her for Rita right now. Lately, Sam has been providing Rita with expensive automobiles, clothing, jewelry, and trips out of town. Also, Sam has been greatly overpaying Rita's service contracts, making her business flourish. Jake doesn't know the details of Rita's business dealings with Sam, but he is puzzled, jealous, frustrated, impulsive, and violent. Jake used to slap Rita occasionally. Recently, however, he has become more frustrated, impulsive, and violent. Jake has beaten Rita several times in recent months. Last night he beat her worse than ever. Rita has no broken bones, but she has several bruises on her body, legs, and arms. The bruises do not show as long as she wears pantsuits.

Rita has told her problems only to her school-counselor friend. She fears that her boyfriend would kill her husband if he found out about the beatings. Rita is frustrated because she cannot participate with the dance group until her bruises go away. Rita is feeling very guilty and depressed. She is not especially suicidal, however. She is feeling a great deal of anger and hatred toward Jake, and she suffers from very low self-esteem. She is feeling stress and pressure from her children, from her mother, from Jake, and even from Sam, who wants to spend more and more time with Rita. Recently, Rita and Sam have been taking more and more risks in their meetings. Rita's depression is getting to the point where she doesn't care. She has come to the crisis worker in a state of lethargy—almost in a state of emotional immobility. But Rita has decided to share her entire story with the worker because she feels she is at her "wit's end," and she wouldn't dare talk with her minister, her physician, or other acquaintances. Rita has never met the crisis worker, and she feels this is the best approach, even though she is uncomfortable in sharing all this with a stranger.

I. A Crisis Worker's Narrative

Write your own narrative describing how you would use the six-step model of crisis intervention with Rita. If you are participating in a class, workshop, or other study group, get together with others (preferably in small groups of five to seven persons) to share descriptions of your particular method of crisis intervention.

Following is our own narrative of how we would intervene in the case of Rita. Read this narrative only after you have written your own and met in small groups to discuss your own and others' narratives.

First, I would explore and *define Rita's problem* from her point of view. I would use active listening techniques. I would avoid closed questions. Apparently Rita is feeling trapped because of several situational conditions: her marriage; her relationship with Sam; her own web of unfulfilling activity; and the beatings by her husband, Jake. I would try to identify the one area that precipitated the crisis and immediately focus on that. After Rita's whole story had been fully examined, I might say, "Rita, what one thing caused you to come to see me today?" I would start with that one event or stressor. *Active listening* would bring us to that point.

Second, I would take whatever steps I deemed necessary to *ensure Rita's safety.* From the case data, I assume that Jake does not physically abuse the children, but he might do so. If my assessment indicated that Rita was in imminent danger, I would refer her to Wife Abuse Services and inform her of their shelter options. Other safe places could be explored with Rita to ensure the safety of both herself and her children.

Third, I would offer myself as an immediate *support person.* I would also attempt during the session to develop other viable support persons to whom Rita could turn, especially in an emergency. I would assume that Rita's school-counselor friend is a positive support person, and I would encourage Rita to maintain that relationship as well as explore others.

Fourth, I would encourage Rita to *examine the various alternatives available to her.* I would give special attention to the options that Rita could own and do for herself that would contribute directly to restoring her precrisis level of equilibrium.

Fifth, I would attempt to help Rita *develop a plan of action* that she could own and that would represent a *positive action step* toward her precrisis level of equilibrium. The plan would have to be concrete, positive, realistic, and clearly oriented toward alleviating her crisis. If her stress level were high, I might immediately use relaxation techniques to assist her through the current stressful and anxious state. This could be one method by which Rita might begin to learn to deal with future stresses as they are encountered in her life.

Sixth, before the termination of the session with Rita, I would try to *get a commitment* from her to carry out some action that would be positive and that would help her restore her equilibrium or make a step toward it. I would ask her to summarize the commitment as a means of helping to so-lidify it in her mind as an immediate objective and to motivate her toward attainment of the stated goal. I would assure Rita of my support and encouragement and make arrangements for the two of us to check back with each other to follow up on her progress.

In terms of problem solving, I would covertly brainstorm two important components while I listened and responded to Rita: (1) I would make a mental list of *adequate situational supports;* and (2) I would make a mental list of *adequate coping mechanisms.* I would not disclose all of these to Rita. The mental options would be available to me to effect referrals or to ask appropriate open-ended questions in helping her to discover the alternatives available to her. I would take care not to impose my own solutions, alternatives, or plans on Rita.

Throughout the crisis intervention session, I would be engaged in assessing Rita's situation. During the listening, safety, and support phases of the session, I would be *active* with Rita. My degree of action would depend on my *assessment* of Rita's mobility or immobility. If Rita were assessed as immobile, I would be quite *directive;* if she were partially mobile, I would be *collaborative.* If she were totally mobile, I would be *nondirective.* From the case data, I assume that Rita is fairly mobile, so initially I would function in a *collaborative* mode. Depending on my own ongoing assessment, I would move toward either directive or nondirective, but I believe I would function largely in the collaborative mode most of the time.

I would certainly avoid asking closed questions. By continuing to focus on Rita's situation with open-ended questions, I would try to get her to concentrate on what she wants to do; that is, I would focus on alternatives. I would hope to get her to consider as many realistic alternatives as possible. I would assist her in brainstorming to identify these alternatives. From a repertory of choices, I would hope that her plan, mentioned in Step 5, would be a sound one that would move her toward attainment and success. The optimum plan would be simple and realistic. I would not be attempting to get her to solve all her situational problems. My first goal would be to help her get the present crisis under control and then work toward having the mobility to independently take charge of her life.

In *problem solving* Rita's case with her, I would start with a list of support persons gleaned from the case data. In crisis intervention, a support person is someone whom the client trusts and who is always available. That person or persons could be an acquaintance, a friend, relative, coworker—anyone who could be called upon to provide temporary comfort, encouragement, or support. In Rita's case, the most obvious support persons would be the crisis worker (myself), her school-counselor friend, her own children, other dancers in her dance group, her "lake" friends, her shop manager and shop employees, and her former vocational-technical instructors. Other possible supports include her mother, her physician, other members of her family, and even former classmates from school. These are the kinds of persons who would be identified and remembered by the crisis worker as possible appropriate supports for Rita to consider. Normally, we recommend using only one or two support persons at a time, not a whole host of people. I would encourage Rita to choose and contact one or two appropriate support persons.

Adequate *coping mechanisms* stored in the crisis worker's mental repertory for possible assistance to Rita could be: leaving Jake the next time he beats her; breaking off the relationship with Sam; setting priorities on the amount of time she is spending on various activities; devising better or different ways to obtain positive attention when she needs it; calling a support person on the phone; calling the Crisis Center or Wife Abuse Services; calling me (the crisis worker); consulting an attorney for legal advice; consulting her physician for a complete physical examination, diagnosis, and advice; initiating marriage counseling with Jake, if he agrees; initiating couples' counseling with Sam, if he agrees; planning ways to spend time with and engage in activities with her school-counselor friend; entering individual counseling on a continuing basis; doing something that is recreational or relaxing for herself, such as working on cars or developing a new dance routine; enrolling in an assertiveness training course to enhance her self-esteem and improve her coping behaviors; wearing tights or colored hose to her dance rehearsals until the bruises heal; and thinking of something innovative or creative that she would enjoy to get away from the turmoil.

In helping Rita (using the six-step crisis intervention model), I would seek to involve Rita in *prioritizing* any of the alternatives, plans, support persons, or coping mechanisms she might wish to pursue. If chosen *action steps* could truly represent Rita's own priorities, the chances of success would be greatly increased. Finally, and most important, I would reemphasize getting Rita to commit herself to one or more of the actions that we collaboratively developed as her plan. I would ask her to summarize her plan so that she and I could agree on what she was committing herself to. I would try to respond to her during the commitment phase in a way in which she would feel supported by me but not *dependent* on me. I would certainly want her to be motivated and predisposed toward success.

II. Crisis Intervention Role Play

Class members form pairs. You will practice two roles: (1) being a crisis worker and (2) reliving a real crisis from your past experience. All sessions must be tape-recorded; to begin each tape, the person serving as crisis worker obtains the client's spoken permission to record the session. The crisis worker practices accurate listening skills: attending, observing, understanding, and responding with empathy, genuineness, respect, acceptance, nonjudgment, and caring. The client relates the past crisis to his or her partner as if the crisis event were being reexperienced in the present moment. When each partner has had an opportunity to play the roles of both crisis worker and client in the laboratory experience, the class regroups for discussion. Here are some possible discussion questions:

1. To you as a client, what aspects of the process were most helpful? What aspects would you like to see improved?
2. To you as a client, what was the most threatening part of the exercise?
3. For you as a worker, what did you perceive to be your strongest and most positive intervention technique?
4. For you as a worker, what did the exercise bring out that you wish to improve upon?
5. What additional skills or learnings do you need to make your next session more successful?

Take the taped session home, listen to it, and in your role as the crisis worker, write a six-step plan for intervention. At the next class meeting, share that plan with the client and obtain verbal feedback from that person.

III. Restatement and Reflection

Most of us would like to improve the odds that we really do accurately interpret clients' messages when they talk to us. There are many hints to aid us in listening to clients. We will deal with two methods in these exercises.

1. *Restatement of ideas.* Make a simple statement in your own words telling the client what you heard him or her say. This helps to be sure that you and the client are talking about the same thing. Example:

Client: I don't think I can go back home tonight—just too many heavy problems for me to handle.

Worker: You don't think you can face what's at home.

2. *Reflection of feelings.* Reflecting feelings means sending the client the message that confirms your understanding of what the client must be feeling. In that way you let the client know you heard him or her and give the client a chance to correct or clarify (you may have received half the message but not all of it). Reflective listening also helps the client see the basis for his or her behavior. Example:

Client: My boss really chewed me out in front of my friends last night.

Worker: Sounds like it really embarrassed you.

To help you learn to make appropriate responses that contain both restatement and reflection, we have prepared a practice sheet (Worksheet 2-1). Do the exercise as directed on the sheet without consulting anyone else. Then obtain feedback from others as the directions indicate.

IV. Open-ended Questions

Asking open-ended questions does not guarantee that every client will respond with full statements. The purpose of this exercise is to help you become aware of how you state your questions so that you can get fuller, deeper levels of response. Decide whether the following counselor questions are closed or open-ended.

1. Do you have a girlfriend?
2. Tell me about your family.
3. How old are you?
4. How did that happen?
5. When will you go?
6. Tell me about school.
7. What happened next?
8. Isn't that a silly choice?

Change the following closed questions to open-ended questions.

1. How long have you been out of work?
2. Can I help?
3. Did you like that story?
4. Are you angry with me?
5. Do you have to hit Sally every time you get drunk?

V. Owning Feelings

Worksheet 2-2 is designed to let you try out owning your own feelings and expressing them in responses that indicate that you are owning them. We

WORKSHEET 2-1   Restatement and Reflection

DIRECTIONS: In your own words write a restatement and a reflection of the client's statement. In small groups, give one another feedback, making check marks under Yes or No to indicate whether others find your responses appropriate.

Client's Statement	Worker's Restatement	Worker's Reflection	Yes	No
1. When he says those hateful things to me I wish I could die.				
2. I don't need her and I frankly don't think I need counseling. She's the one with problems.				
3. You're so wonderful. Nobody else understands me, but you do. I think I love you.				
4. Life is like a roller coaster —up and down. Isn't that kind of the way it is with you?				

WORKSHEET 2-2 Owned Message Practice

DIRECTIONS: Read the situation in the first column. Examine the disowned message in the second column. Then write in the third column an "I" message that indicates you take responsibility for your feelings. The purpose is *not* to resolve the problem, but rather to communicate that you are aware of your feelings and are being honest about them at this moment. In small groups, give each other feedback, making check marks under Yes or No to indicate whether the message indicates owning one's own feelings. If after you have shared your responses, others feel that most of your responses are not "I" messages, please elicit help in restating your message.

Situation	Disowned Message	Owned Message	Yes	No
1. Client has been sulking and acting sad all session.	Come on, now. Stop moping around. Life isn't that bad.	I'm really puzzled. You say things are OK! Yet your behavior doesn't fit with OK.		
2. Macho man brags about beating wife. Has just responded, "Women need to be kept in control."	Well, I wonder if you'd do that to the Raider linebackers.			
3. People complain about client's body odor. (It's bothering you, too.)	James, you really should bathe more frequently.			
4. Cynthia has a reputation for being promiscuous and has talked at some length about it.	We workers feel that talk only leads to acting out behavior.			
5. John is extremely overweight. Wants to lose weight but doesn't seem to be able to stick to a plan.	Face it, John. You're fat. I'm sorry, but that's it. No wonder you can't get dates. Why not try jogging?			

WORKSHEET 2-3   Total Listening Practice

DIRECTIONS: Read the client's statement in the first column. Then write a restatement of the message, a reflection of the message, an "I" message that owns your feelings but communicates acceptance, and an open-ended question that elicits more information. Break into dyads (pairs) and role-play the client and the worker in dialogue beyond initial responses to one of the statements.

Client's Statement	Restatement	Reflection	Owning "I" Statement	Open-ended Question
1. I used to like him as a boss. But he chewed me out today. I hate his guts.				
2. He beat the daylights out of me last night.				
3. Well, I really wonder what life's all about; love, too, for that matter.				
4. You're just like all the rest. You don't really care about me. I think I'll kill myself.				

call such messages *"I" messages*. When we disown a feeling, we usually give someone else the responsibility for it and begin statements with words that refer outside ourselves, such as *"they," you, people,* and *all people.*

VI. Worker-Client Communications

Communication is often not a simple matter. Words come so fast and easily at times that we have our responses formulated in our heads before we hear the full message of the client who is speaking.

Worksheet 2-3 is designed to help you practice (1) attentive listening and (2) formulating responses that communicate acceptance of the feeling behind the message as well as awareness of the message's content. An accepting response combines (1) restatement, (2) reflection, (3) owning one's feelings, and (4) an open-ended question designed to get to the fuller meaning. Thus, Worksheet 2-3 is a culmination of the communications skills you've been practicing.

CHAPTER 3

Crisis Case Handling

CRISIS CASE HANDLING VERSUS LONG-TERM CASE HANDLING

To understand crisis case handling, we must first clearly differentiate between crisis intervention and long-term counseling and psychotherapy. In that regard we can distinguish between what crisis interventionists and long-term therapists do, the principles that undergird the two modes of helping, their objectives, client functioning, and assessment procedures.

Comparison of What Crisis Workers and Long-Term Therapists Do

On first inspection, typical models for long-term therapy do not look radically different from a crisis intervention model. Our own long-term six-step systematic counseling model (Gilliland, James, & Bowman, 1989, pp. 298–302) incorporates problem definition, examination of alternatives, planning courses of action, and obtaining client commitment in much the same operational format as crisis intervention.

However, what is radically different is that in long-term therapy, problem definition, identification of alternatives, and planning are much broader in scope, more methodological, and rely on continuous feedback loops to ascertain effectiveness of intervention. A typical counseling session with a long-term client will review progress since the previous session, collaboratively refine the plan of action if needed, process the content of the session and the client's feelings about it, and then propose a new homework assignment to be tried out prior to the next meeting. Crisis intervention models do not operate on such liberal time dimensions nor problem scope. In crisis intervention, problem exploration, identification of alternatives, planning, and commitment to a plan are all much more compressed in time and scope. What may occur in a rather leisurely fashion over a period of weekly sessions in long-term therapy may commonly occur in one-half to two hours in crisis intervention.

While in long-term therapy a great deal of background exploration may provide the therapist a panoramic view of client dynamics, the crisis worker's exploration typically is narrow and starts and stops with the specific presenting crisis. The long-term therapist's view of alternatives and planning a course of action commonly incorporate psychoeducational processes that seek to change residual, repressive, and chronic client modes of thinking, feeling, and acting. The crisis worker seeks to quickly determine previous coping skills and environmental resources available to the client and use them in the present situation as a stopgap measure to gain time and provide a modicum of stability in an out-of-control situation. Whereas the long-term therapist would view comprehensive personality change as a necessary part of the therapeutic plan, the crisis worker would endeavor to change personality only to the degree necessary for restoring precrisis functioning.

A long-term therapist would look toward a methodological manipulation of treatment variables, assess those variables on a variety of dimensions, and process the outcomes with the client. A crisis worker often uses a "best guess" based on previous experience with what works and does not work with a particular problem. While protocols for treatment in long-term therapy may be quite flexible and induce numerous tryouts of different procedures, crisis intervention is a good deal more rigid and may typically involve set procedures for moving the client from an immobile to a mobilized state.

Finally, assessment and feedback of outcome measures in long-term therapy typically involve a great deal of processing between client and therapist as to the efficacy of treatment. If treatment outcomes are not as expected, a feedback loop is integrated into the model that will allow a return to any of the previous steps. Feedback and assessment in crisis intervention typically occur on a here-and-now basis with emphasis on what changes have occurred in the previous minutes and what the client will do in the next few hours.

Comparison of Principles, Objectives, Client Functioning, and Assessment

There are many approaches to long-term therapy. Although Thorne's (1968, pp. 11–13) approach is dated and somewhat psychoanalytic, it is one of the most comprehensive and eclectic systems we have found. To provide a clear delineation between crisis intervention and long-term therapy, we have contrasted our own model of crisis intervention with Thorne's *principles, objectives, client functioning,* and *assessment* of case handling. Tables 3-1, 3-2, 3-3, and 3-4 contain and illustrate that comparison.

TABLE 3-1   Principles compared

Crisis case handling mode	Long-term therapy mode
1. *Diagnosis:* Rapid triage crisis assessment.	1. *Diagnosis:* Complete diagnostic evaluation.
2. *Treatment:* Focus on the immediate traumatized component of the person.	2. *Treatment:* Focus on basic underlying causes; on the whole person.

TABLE 3-1   Continued

Crisis case handling mode	Long-term therapy mode
3. *Plan:* Individual problem-specific prescription focused on immediate needs to alleviate the crisis symptoms.	3. *Plan:* Personalized comprehensive prescription directed toward fulfilling long-term needs.
4. *Methods:* Knowledge of time-limited brief therapy techniques used for immediate control and containment of the crisis trauma.	4. *Methods:* Knowledge of techniques to systematically effect a wide array of short-term, intermediate-term, and long-term therapeutic gains.
5. *Evaluation of results:* Behavioral validation by client's return to precrisis level of equilibrium.	5. *Evaluation of results:* Behavioral validation of therapeutic outcomes in terms of the client's total functioning.

TABLE 3-2   Objectives compared

Crisis case handling mode (Listed in linear order with a crisis-specific focus)	Long-term therapy mode (Listed in no particular order, but global in scope)
1. *Define problem:* Clarify in concrete terms the issues that precipitated the crisis.	1. *Prevent problems:* More basic than cure. Use preventive procedures whenever possible.
2. *Ensure client safety:* Assess client lethality and provide for the physical and psychological safety of the client and significant others.	2. *Correct etiological factors:* Involves comprehensive treatment of broad-based psychological and environmental factors in both the past and present.
3. *Provide support:* Establish conditions, either by the crisis worker or significant others, whereby the client feels secure and free of threat or abandonment.	3. *Provide systematic support:* Comprehensive measures directed toward improvement of the state of health of the individual.
4. *Examine alternatives:* Provide options for alleviating the immediate situational threat in relation to the crisis.	4. *Facilitate growth:* Treatment should ideally facilitate rather than interfere with natural environmental and developmental processes.
5. *Develop a plan:* Formulate a stepwise procedure using client coping skills, crisis worker expertise, and systemic measures to energize the client to take action.	5. *Reeducate:* Treatment seeks to reeducate and teach new modes of adjustment for lifelong coping.
6. *Obtain commitment:* Obtain agreement as to specific time, duration, and number of activities required to stabilize the client and/or crisis situation.	6. *Express and clarify emotional attitudes:* Major emphasis is on methods of securing emotional release and expression in a permissive and accepting environment.

TABLE 3-2 Continued

Crisis case handling mode (Listed in linear order with a crisis-specific focus)	Long-term therapy mode (Listed in no particular order, but global in scope)
	7. *Resolve conflict and inconsistencies:* Viewed from a psychoanalytic standpoint, therapy aims to help the client achieve *insight* into the causation and the dynamic roots of the behavior.
	8. *Accept reality:* Help the client to *accept* what cannot be changed.
	9. *Reorganize attitudes:* Move the person toward exhibiting a more positive view of life.
	10. *Maximize intellectual resources:* Improve the functions of sensing, perceiving, remembering, communicating, thinking, and self-control.

TABLE 3-3 Client functioning compared

Crisis case handling mode	Long-term therapy mode
1. *Affectively,* the client is impaired to the extent that there is little understanding of his or her emotional state.	1. Client shows sufficient *affect;* manifests some basis for experiencing and understanding his or her emotional state.
2. *Cognitively,* the client shows inability to think linearly and logically. In Ellis and Grieger's (1977) RET system, the event is perceived to cause the feeling—the client illogically believes that the event directly caused his or her internal beliefs or feelings.	2. Client shows some ability to *cognitively* understand the connection between behavior and consequences—between what is rational and irrational.
3. *Behaviorally,* the client is out of control.	3. There is some modicum of *behavioral* control.

TABLE 3-4 Assessment compared

Crisis case handling mode	Long-term therapy mode
1. *Intake data:* Client may not be able to fill out an intake form because of instability or time constraints; a verbal and/or visual evaluation of current maladaptive state may be the only data available.	1. *Intake data:* Client is stable enough to provide in-depth background regarding the problem; lengthy intake form may contain details of the client's total history: family, medical history, drug use, education, therapy background, social history.

TABLE 3-4   Continued

Crisis case handling mode	Long-term therapy mode
2. *Safety:* Crisis worker's first concern is client and others' safety; determining whether client is suicidal, homicidal, or otherwise a danger or threat to someone.	2. *Safety:* Client safety is not the primary focus unless there are clues pointing toward imminent danger to self and others.
3. *Time:* Crisis worker has no time for administering formal instruments.	3. *Time:* The therapist has time to procure a variety of assessment data to confirm or contraindicate the hypothesized problem; total case diagnosis and workups are gathered prior to the development of the treatment plan; personality assessment indexes are generally gathered such as MMPI and Rorschach profiles to compare client functioning against norm groups on standard pathology measures.
4. *Reality testing:* Using simple questioning procedures, the crisis worker must determine whether the person is in touch with reality and how effectively the person is functioning.	4. *Reality testing:* The therapist assumes the client is in touch with reality unless assessment data or other clues indicate otherwise.
5. *Referrals:* Referral resources have implications of immediacy in terms of getting the client to safety and some degree of stability. Examples of referrals might be to the police, paramedics, emergency rooms of hospitals, psychiatric or medical evaluation, immediate support persons, or the person's psychiatrist or physician.	5. *Referrals:* Referral resources have implications for long-term development. Examples of referrals might be to family services, mental health centers, vocational/educational assistance, and job placement services.
6. *Consultation:* Professional consultants who are trained in the diagnosis of pathology are on call for backup purposes.	6. *Consultation:* Consultants and other backup resources are available as needed. Collaboration is normally initiated after consultation with the client and/or the therapist's supervisor.
7. *Drug use:* The crisis worker relies on verbal and visual responses to ascertain the level and type of prescription medication or illicit drug or alcohol usage.	7. *Drug use:* The therapist relies on data from the intake material and on information developed in the normal course of the therapy to ascertain the level and type of prescription medication or illicit drug or alcohol use.

We are now ready to turn our attention exclusively to crisis case handling, the first component of which is assessment of crisis clients at the initial point of contact.

THE TRIAGE ASSESSMENT SYSTEM

As rapid and adequate assessment of a client in crisis is one of the most critical components of intervention (Hersh, 1985), we have given assessment a preeminent place in our crisis intervention model as an overarching and ongoing process. Constant and rapid assessment of the client's state of equilibrium dictates what the interventionist will do in the next seconds and minutes as the crisis unfolds (Aguilera & Messick, 1986). Unhappily, many assessment devices that can give the human services worker an adequate perspective on the client's problem are unwieldy and time-consuming and mandate that the client be in control enough to complete the assessment process or be physically present while undergoing evaluation. While we might gain a great deal of helpful information with an extensive intake form, a background interview, or an in-depth personality test, many times events are occurring so quickly these are unaffordable luxuries.

What the interventionist needs in a crisis situation is a fast, efficient way of obtaining a real-time estimate of what is occurring with a client. Such a tool should also be simple enough that a worker who may have only rudimentary assessment skills can use the device in a reliable and valid manner. Myer, Williams, Ottens, and Schmidt (1991) at Northern Illinois University have formulated a three-dimensional crisis assessment model (see Figure 3-1) and rating scale (see Figure 3-2), the Triage Assessment Form (TAF), an instrument that we believe holds great promise as an aid to performing utilitarian assessment of a client in crisis.

Although simple to use, the TAF is also elegant in that it crosscuts the current affective, cognitive, and behavioral dimensions of the client, compartmentalizes each dimension as to its typical response mode, and assigns numerical values to these modes that allow the worker to determine the client's current level of functioning. These three severity scales represent mechanisms for operationally assigning numerical values to the crisis worker's action continuum in Figure 2-1 (Chapter 2). The numerical ratings provide an efficient and tangible guide to both the degree and the kind of intervention the worker needs to make in most crisis situations. Following are the rationale and examples for each of the scales.

The Affective Domain Scale

No crisis situation that we know of has positive emotions attached to it. Crow (1977) metaphorically names the usual emotional qualities found in a crisis as yellow (anxiety), red (anger), or black (depression). Invariably, these negative emotions appear singularly or in combination with each

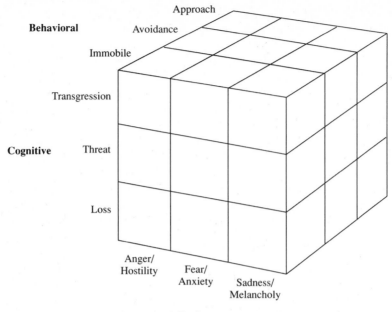

FIGURE 3-1   Three-dimensional crisis assessment model

NOTE: From *Three-Dimensional Crisis Assessment Model* by R. A. Myer, R. C. Williams, A. J. Ottens, and A. E. Schmidt, 1991, De Kalb, IL: Northern Illinois University, Department of Educational Psychology, Counseling, and Special Education.

other when a crisis is present. In their model, Myer et al. have replaced the term *depression,* because of its diagnostic implications, with *sadness/melancholy.* For example, if a client who is suffering from unresolved grief issues and and cannot shake off his or her sadness over a recent divorce is judged to be a 7 on this scale but to have moderate cognitive and behavioral scores, the crisis worker might passively listen while the client mourns, use positive injunctions to build self-enhancement, and help the client start rebuilding his or her social network.

The Cognitive Domain Scale

Ellis has written at length about the part that thinking plays in emotions and behavior (Ellis, 1971; Ellis & Abrahms, 1978; Ellis & Grieger, 1977; Ellis & Harper, 1979). In a crisis situation, the client's cognitive processes typically perceive the event in terms of a transgression, threat, loss, or any combination of the three. These "hot" cognitions, as Dryden (1984) calls them, can take on catastrophic dimensions at the extreme end of the continuum. Such highly focused irrational thinking can cause the client to obsess on the crisis to the extent that little, if any, logical thinking can occur within or beyond the boundaries of the crisis event. The event itself consumes all of the client's psychic energy as the client attempts to integrate it into his or her belief system.

TRIAGE ASSESSMENT FORM: CRISIS INTERVENTION*

©R.A. Myers, R.C. Williams, A.J. Ottens, & A.E. Schmidt

CRISIS EVENT:

Identify and describe briefly the crisis situation: _____
_____
_____
_____

AFFECTIVE DOMAIN

Identify and describe briefly the affect that is present. (If more than one affect is experienced, rate with #1 being primary, #2 secondary, #3 tertiary.)

ANGER/HOSTILITY: _____
_____

ANXIETY/FEAR: _____
_____

SADNESS/MELANCHOLY: _____
_____

Affective Severity Scale

Circle the number that most closely corresponds with client's reaction to crisis.

1	2	3	4	5	6	7	8	9	10
No Impairment	Minimal Impairment		Low Impairment		Moderate Impairment		Marked Impairment		Severe Impairment
Stable mood with normal variation of affect appropriate to daily functioning.	Affect appropriate to situation. Brief periods during which negative mood is experienced slightly more intensely than situation warrants. Emotions are substantially under client control.		Affect appropriate to situation but increasingly longer periods during which negative mood is experienced slightly more intensely than situation warrants. Client perceives emotions as being substantially under control.		Affect may be incongruent with situation. Extended periods of intense negative moods. Mood is experienced noticeably more intensely than situation warrants. Lability of affect may be present. Effort required to control emotions.		Negative affect experienced at markedly higher level than situation warrants. Affects may be obviously incongruent with situation. Mood swings, if occurring, are pronounced. Onset of negative moods are perceived by client as not being under volitional control.		Decompensation or depersonalization evident.

*May not be reproduced without permission.

FIGURE 3-2 Triage assessment form: crisis intervention

Maladaptive cognitions may be generated by the client about intrapersonal, interpersonal, or environmental stimuli. Transgression, threat, or loss may be perceived in relation to physical needs such as food, shelter, and safety; psychological needs such as self-concept, emotional stability, and identity; relationship needs such as family, friends, coworkers, and community support; and moral and spiritual needs such as integrity and values. In the case of a batterer whose irrational belief about his moral right to "whip his wife into shape" marks him at a 9 in psychological and social relationships areas, the interventionist might attempt to depropagandize the client's belief about "ruling the roost," to enhance his threatened weak self-concept, and to diminish the fear he feels of loss of control of his family.

COGNITIVE DOMAIN

Identify if a transgression, threat, or loss has occurred in the following areas and describe briefly. (If more than one cognitive response occurs, rate with #1 being primary, #2 secondary, #3 tertiary.)

PHYSICAL (food, water, safety, shelter, etc.):
TRANSGRESSION ___   THREAT _____   LOSS _____

_____
_____
_____

PSYCHOLOGICAL (self-concept, emotional well being, identity, etc.):
TRANSGRESSION __   THREAT _____   LOSS _____

_____
_____
_____

SOCIAL RELATIONSHIPS (family, friends, co-workers, etc.):
TRANSGRESSION__   THREAT _____   LOSS _____

_____
_____
_____

MORAL/SPIRITUAL (personal integrity, values, belief system, etc.):
TRANSGRESSION ___   THREAT _____   LOSS _____

_____
_____
_____

Cognitive Severity Scale

Circle the number that most closely corresponds with client's reaction to crisis.

1	2	3	4	5	6	7	8	9	10
No Impairment	Minimal Impairment		Low Impairment		Moderate Impairment		Marked Impairment		Severe Impairment
Concentration intact. Client displays normal problem-solving and decision-making abilities. Client's perception and interpretation of crisis event match with reality of situation.	Client's thoughts may drift to crisis event but focus of thoughts is under volitional control. Problem-solving and decision-making abilities minimally affected. Client's perception and interpretation of crisis event substantially match with reality of situation.		Occasional disturbance of concentration. Client perceives diminished control over thoughts of crisis event. Client experiences recurrent difficulties with problem-solving and decision-making abilities. Client's perception and interpretation of crisis event may differ in some respects with reality of situation.		Frequent disturbance of concentration. Intrusive thoughts of crisis event with limited control. Problem-solving and decision-making abilities adversely affected by obsessiveness, self-doubt, confusion. Client's perception and interpretation of crisis event may differ noticeably with reality of situation.		Client plagued by intrusiveness of thoughts regarding crisis event. The appropriateness of client's problem-solving and decision-making abilities likely adversely affected by obsessiveness, self-doubt, confusion. Client's perception and interpretation differ substantially with reality of situation.		Gross inability to concentrate on anything except crisis event. Client so afflicted by obsessiveness, self-doubt, confusion that problem-solving and decision-making abilities have "shut down." Client's perception and interpretation of crisis event may differ so substantially from reality of situation as to constitute threat to client's welfare.

FIGURE 3-2   Continued

The Behavioral Domain Scale

Although we depict a client in crisis as more or less behaviorally immobile, immobility can take three different forms. Crow (1977) proposes that behavior in a crisis occurs in approaching, avoiding, or being paralyzed in attempts to act in the crisis. Although Crow's proposal may seem contradictory to our own on first inspection, it is not. A client may seem highly motivated, either acting out maladaptively toward a specific target or in a random, non-goal-directed manner with no specific target discernible. Oppositionally, the client may attempt to flee the noxious event by the fastest means possible. While a great deal of energy may be expended and the client may look focused, once the crisis goes beyond the client's capacity to

BEHAVIORAL DOMAIN

Identify and describe briefly which behavior is currently being used. (If more than one behavior is utilized, rate with #1 being primary, #2 secondary, #3 tertiary.)

APPROACH: _____

_____

AVOIDANCE: _____

_____

IMMOBILITY: _____

_____

Behavioral Severity Scale

Circle the number that most closely corresponds with client's reaction to crisis.

1	2	3	4	5	6	7	8	9	10
No Impairment	Minimal Impairment		Low Impairment		Moderate Impairment		Marked Impairment		Severe Impairment
Coping behavior appropriate to crisis event. Client performs those tasks necessary for daily functioning.	Occasional utilization of ineffective coping behaviors. Client performs those tasks necessary for daily functioning, but does so with noticeable effort.		Occasional utilization of ineffective coping behaviors. Client neglects some tasks necessary for daily functioning, performs others with decreasing effectiveness.		Client displays coping behaviors that may be ineffective and maladaptive. Ability to perform tasks necessary for daily functioning is noticeably compromised.		Client displays coping behaviors that are likely to exacerbate crisis situation. Ability to perform tasks necessary for daily functioning is markedly absent.		Behavior is erratic, unpredictable. Client's behaviors are harmful to self and/or others.

DOMAIN SEVERITY SCALE SUMMARY

Affective _____

Cognitive _____

Behavioral _____

Total _____

FIGURE 3-2 Continued

NOTE: By R. A. Myer, R. C. Williams, A. J. Ottens, and A. E. Schmidt, 1991. Unpublished manuscript, Northern Illinois University, De Kalb, Illinois.

cope in a meaningful and purposeful manner, we would propose that the client is immobilized, stuck in the particular behavior in a continuous, nonproductive loop no matter how proactive he or she may seem to be. At the extreme end of the continuum, behavior takes on a lethal aspect either in regard to the client or others. Returning to the batterer whose irrational and out-of-control approach to the problem earns him a 10 in the behavioral domain, the crisis worker would be very directive in attempting to teach the client anger management skills to control his violent behavior.

Combining Scales

Since each scale provides a range from 1 to 10, the three scales combined provide a range of 3 to 30. While talking to a client who is having relational problems with her elderly mother, the worker could quickly glance at the three scales and mentally compute a combined summative score. For instance, a total score of 10 on the Domain Severity Scale Summary might be arrived at thus:

1. Client reports somewhat extended periods of oscillating guilt and anger over attempts to persuade her mother to move to a retirement home and her mother's response to her daughter that she might as well be dead if she has to go to an old folks' home. Client feels continuously stuck on the horns of a dilemma. *Affective Scale score = 5*

2. Client reports that she has thought through the situation, considered all the alternatives, and sees this as best for both her and her mother. Continues reasoning even when a guilt trip is laid on her. Does not see this as a loss but rather a gain due to enhanced lifestyle for both parties. *Cognitive Scale score = 2*

3. Client reports one instance of loss of control with mother in these continuing dialogues. Quickly regained control of herself. Has decided to obtain literature from five different retirement centers and have one of her mother's friends invite her for an overnight visit. She is clearly goal-oriented and active. *Behavioral Scale score = 3 Domain Severity Scale total = 10*

The crisis worker would immediately assess this score to be in the minimal impairment range. Affectively, the woman may be reporting a good deal of emotional trauma that oscillates between guilt and anger at attempting to convince her mother to go to a retirement center. However, her thinking is mostly linear and logical in how she is going about doing this and her planful behavior supports her reasoning. The interventionist would probably assume a nondirective stance on the worker action continuum and allow the woman to ventilate her conflicted feelings without attempting to directly intervene in this situation. If the woman had a total score in the moderate to high impairment range of 15 to 21, the worker would assume a more active role and attempt to collaborate with the woman in reaching a resolution of her dilemma. If her score were in the severe impairment to no control range of the high 20s the worker would become much more directive and would probably refer her for medical evaluation and observation.

Comparison with Precrisis Functioning

While it may not always be possible, the worker should attempt to assess the client's precrisis functioning in the same manner. Comparison of precrisis ratings with current ratings enables the worker to gauge the degree of deviation from the client's typical affective, cognitive, and behavioral operating levels. By obtaining this information, the worker can then determine how atypical the client's current functioning is, whether there has been a radical shift in that functioning, and whether such functioning is transitory or chronic. As an example, a very different counseling approach would be used with a chronic schizophrenic suffering auditory hallucinations versus an individual who was experiencing similar hallucinations from a prescription medicine. Such an assessment can be made in one or two questions without having to ferret out a great deal of background information.

In summary, the TAF provides infinite three-dimensional combinations, enabling the crisis worker to evaluate the client and then construct specific interventions aimed directly at areas of greatest immediate concern. The TAF is quick, efficient, easy to learn, and from our own initial research with beginning crisis workers, highly reliable.

NEUROLOGICAL ASSESSMENT

While neurological assessment for psychopathology is beyond the scope of this book and most crisis situations both in terms of immediacy of assessment and the assessment skills of most human services workers, mounting evidence indicates that neurotransmitters play an exceedingly important role in the cognitive, affective, and behavioral functioning of individuals (Kolb & Whishaw, 1990).

For at least three reasons, human neuropsychology can be an important consideration in crisis intervention. First, evidence exists that dramatic changes occur in discharge of neurotransmitters, such as the endorphins, when individuals are involved in traumatic events. These neurological changes may become residual and long-term and have subtle and degrading effects on emotion, thinking, and acting (Burgess-Watson, Hoffman, & Wilson, 1988).

Second, research indicates that abnormal changes in neurotransmitters such as dopamine, norepinephrine, and serotonin are involved in mental disorders that range from schizophrenia (Crow & Johnstone, 1987) to depression (Healy, 1987). Psychotropic drugs are routinely used for a host of mental disorders to counteract such neurological changes. A common problem faced by human services workers is the deranged or violent client who has gone off medication because of its unpleasant side effects or inability to remember when to take it (Ammar & Burdin, 1991).

Third, both legal and illegal drugs have a major effect on mental health. While the way illegal drugs change brain chemistry and behavior has gained wide attention, legal drugs may promote adverse psychological side effects in just as dramatic a manner. Particularly, combinations of nonpsychotropic drugs are routinely given to combat several degenerative diseases in the elderly. At times these drugs may have interactive effects that generate unanticipated psychological disturbances. One has to read no further than over-the-counter books on prescribed drugs to obtain a rather frightening understanding of the psychological side effects prescription drugs can cause.

Therefore, the human services worker should attempt to assess prior trauma, psychopathology, and use, misuse, or abuse of legal and illegal drugs in an effort to determine if they correlate with the current problem. "Talking" therapies do little good when neurobiological substrates are involved. If the human services worker has reason to suspect any of the foregoing problems, an immediate referral should be made for a neurological/drug evaluation.

Given the significance of assessment in case handling, we now turn to three different settings where crises are likely to be handled: on telephone crisis lines, at walk-in facilities, and in long-term therapy settings.

CASE HANDLING ON TELEPHONE CRISIS LINES

The Telephone As a Crisis Tool

"Reach out and touch someone" is a slogan that is particularly appropriate to crisis counseling. The tremendous growth of "hotlines," both in number and in geographical coverage, attests to the fact that people in crisis avail themselves of telephones to solve their personal problems (Haywood & Leuthe, 1980). By picking up the daily newspaper or the telephone directory in any medium-sized city or major metropolitan area, one can quickly find a list of emergency numbers to call for a variety of human services assistance programs. These services may range from a generic crisis hotline to a variety of specialized services. Typically, crisis phone lines are open 24 hours a day, 365 days a year, while other specialized services may operate during regular business hours. There are several reasons for the upsurge in use of the telephone to solve psychological problems:

Convenience. Telephones have become such an easy way of communicating that calling for psychological assistance is a natural extension of "taking care of business." As in the case of battering, most crises do not occur during normal business hours. When help is needed in a crisis, it is needed right now.

Anonymity. Guilt, embarrassment, shame, self-blame, and other debilitating emotions make face-to-face encounters with strangers very difficult, particularly in the immediate aftermath of a traumatic event. Telephone counselors understand that clients have such feelings and are generally not concerned about identifying a client unless a life-threatening emergency is involved. Conversations are usually on a first-name-only basis for both the worker and the client. Thus, a victim of date rape may call a rape hotline and freely discuss her emotions without having to muster the courage to face what may be perceived as a judgmental human services worker.

Control. A great deal of fear, anxiety, and uncertainty occur when a client's life is ruptured by a crisis. The concept of secondary victimization by institutions (Ochberg, 1988) is well known to victims of a crisis who have sought assistance from a social agency and then have been victimized by its bureaucratic callousness. In telephone counseling, the client decides when and if to seek further assistance. At any time during a dialogue on a crisis line, the client may terminate the conversation without fear of recrimination.

Immediacy of access. Most institutions and clinics and many private practitioners use pagers. At our own university, a harried residence hall supervisor who is trying to deal with a distraught student who is suffering from severe homesickness and academic failure can call campus security. The security staff will page a member of the staff of the student counseling center who is the after-hours "beeper keeper." The psychologist will immediately respond to the request for assistance by checking with the residence hall supervisor on the current mental status of the student and will then come to the dorm, talk to the student over the phone, or request additional help from security to transport the student to the city crisis stabilization unit.

Cost-effectiveness. Crisis lines are inexpensive—both for the client and the community. Clients who cannot pay for private therapy or afford transportation can usually avail themselves of a phone. Most community agency hotlines are staffed by volunteers. While the idea of obtaining counseling from a volunteer may seem no better or worse than talking to a bartender or hairdresser, volunteers typically go through a good deal of training in initial point-of-contact mental health counseling. Volunteers have few pretensions about their "professional role" and are often seen by callers as having more credibility than a paid professional because they "do it out of the goodness of their hearts."

Access to support systems. Support groups make extensive use of telephone networks. From Alcoholics Anonymous to support groups for relatives of military personnel in a war zone, telephone support networks have provided constant links to group members between organized meetings.

Avoidance of dependency issues. Dependence on a particular human services worker who may not be readily available is negated by telephone crisis lines. Standard practice in most crisis lines discourages workers from forming lasting relationships with clients so that dependency issues do not arise.

Availability of others for consultation. Crisis lines are seldom staffed by one person. When a difficult client is encountered, other staff at the agency are available for consultation. Further, at least one phone line is reserved for calling support agencies when emergency services are needed.

Availability of an array of services. A vast array of information, guidance, and social services is quickly available via telephone linkages. The specialized services of different agencies and the expertise they offer can provide on-the-spot guidance for emotionally volatile situations. Many an angry mother or father has received "five-minute parenting sessions" from the staff of a metropolitan "parenting line" and short-circuited potential child abuse. In that vein, any crisis hotline should have readily available a list of phone numbers of specialized agencies to which they can refer callers.

Agency proactivity.   While hotlines have been mainly reactive to clientele, as agency philosophy has changed, so has the use of telephones. A family trouble center in one city is closely allied with the police department. On a typical Monday morning, an average of 250 domestic violence reports from the previous week will be delivered by a police officer to the center. Volunteers will immediately start making phone calls to check on the complainants and apprise them of their rights, offer brief phone counseling, invite them in to discuss their problems, or broker services for them with other community agencies (Winter, 1991). In other agencies, where the identity of the client is known, the staff may make periodic calls back to ascertain if the client is still stable or in need of further assistance.

Telephone Counseling Strategies

Conducting crisis intervention over the telephone is a double-edged sword. Although phone counseling offers the advantages just listed, the crisis worker is entirely dependent on the content, voice tone, pitch, speed, and emotional content of the client in generating responses. For many human services workers, it is unsettling to deal with ambiguous client responses and not be able to link body language to verbal content. Further, the worker is entirely dependent on his or her own verbal ability to stabilize the client and has little physical control over the situation. It takes only one experience of having a suicidal client hang up on a worker to understand how frustrating and emotionally draining crisis intervention over the telephone can be. Consequently, a great deal of care and effort needs to be taken in responding to clients. In the following paragraphs we outline an effective telephone counseling strategy.

Making psychological contact.   First, psychological contact needs to be made, and this endeavor takes precedence over anything else the phone worker does. By psychological contact we mean that the worker attempts to establish as quickly as possible a nonjudgmental, caring, accepting, and empathic relationship with the client that will give the worker credibility and elicit the client's trust. Therefore, Step 3, *provide support,* in the six-step model in Chapter 2 becomes the first order of business. It is safe to assume that people who use crisis lines have exhausted or are separated from their support systems. It is a moot point that the crisis worker can make an astute dynamic analysis, synthesize material, diagnose the problem, and prescribe a solution if the client feels no trust in the relationship and hangs up the phone! In establishing psychological contact on the phone, providing support is a first priority and is highly integrated with defining the problem through active listening and responding skills.

The phone worker must be able to react in a calm and collected manner. Thus, the worker's voice must be well modulated, steady, low-keyed with an adequate decibel level, but not high-pitched. Neither should the content of the worker's response be deprecating, cynical, cajoling, or demeaning. While the foregoing may seem obvious, few people realize how their voice sounds or are aware of what happens to their voice level and pitch when they are caught up in a rapidly escalating and evolving emotional event. Further, when the person on the other end of the line is acting out, angry, intoxicated, or otherwise demanding of the worker to "fix things right now," the worker needs a great deal of self-discipline and emotional security to refrain from becoming caustic, judgmental, and demanding.

It is essential that persons who engage in phone work be audio-taped in role-play situations under strenuous simulation conditions and then be given an opportunity with a supervisor to listen to themselves as they attempt to effectively intervene.

Defining the problem.   Once psychological contact is established, the worker attempts to define the problem by gaining an understanding of the events that led to the crisis and assessing the client's coping mechanisms. Open-ended questions on the *what, how, when, where, who* continuum will usually enable the worker to obtain a clear picture of the event itself. However, in assessing the coping mechanisms of the client in a phone dialogue, it may be difficult for the worker to obtain a clear picture of the affect of the client. Thus, it behooves the worker to become more sensitive to the underlying emotional content and to endeavor to reflect the implied feeling content more than might normally be required in a face-to-face encounter. Reflection of feelings is a tough job for most beginning mental health workers, and it is even more difficult in a phone dialogue. Yet, it is absolutely imperative that the worker attempt to reflect feelings, given the inability to make a visual assessment of the client.

One of the real pluses of phone counseling is that the beginning crisis worker can have supportive aides readily at hand without detracting from the counseling session. One useful tactic is to have a reference list of feeling words that cover the gamut of emotions. A second tactic is to have at hand a list of standard questions the counselor can check off to be sure that all areas typically pertinent to the problem are covered. A third tactic is to keep handy a note pad on which the worker can jot down the salient aspects of the events and coping mechanisms the client has employed and make a rapid assessment on the ten-point triage scale presented in Figure 3-2.

Ensuring safety.   During problem definition, the phone worker must be very specific in determining the client's lethality level. If the worker detects the potential for physical injury, then closed questions that obtain information specific to the safety of the client should be asked, and these should be asked not only without hesitation but also with empathic understanding that clearly depicts the worker's overriding concern and valuing of the client. These questions typically start with *do, have,* and *are* and in phone dialogues they should be put directly and assertively to the client. "Do you have a plan to carry out the suicide?" "Are you convinced that it's the only way out?" "Have you ever thought about killing him?" If the answers to any of these questions are yes then the worker must immediately move to directive action steps that are covered in detail in the chapters on suicide and battering.

Making plans. Creating alternatives and formulating a plan are integral to one another in any crisis situation but are even more closely tied together in phone counseling. To alleviate the immediate situational threat, the phone counselor needs to jointly explore alternatives that are simple and clear-cut. Without the benefit of an eyewitness view or an in-depth background of the client, the worker needs to be cautious about proposing alternatives that may be difficult to carry out due to logistical or tactical problems of which the worker is unaware. Alternatives need to be explored in a slow stepwise manner with checks by the worker that the client is able to do the physical and psychological work necessary to complete the task. Role play, verbal rehearsal, and recapitulation of objectives by the client are vital ingredients of a functional plan. No plan should be accepted until the client can reassure the worker that he or she thoroughly understands the plan and has the means to put it into action.

Obtaining commitment. Commitment to a plan of action generated over the phone should be simple, specific, and time limited. If at all possible, the worker should attempt to obtain the client's phone number and call the client back at a preset time to check on the plan or, if the agency accepts walk-in clients, the worker should attempt to have the individual schedule an appointment as soon as possible. If the worker is linking with other agencies, then a phone call should be made to the referral agent to check whether the client has completed the task. While it is preferable to have the client take the initiative in contacting other agencies so that dependence on the worker is not created, it may be that conditions prohibit the client from doing so. In that case, the worker should have no hesitation in offering to make the call.

Types of Regular and Abusive Callers

The foregoing points are textbook examples of how things ought to go in telephone crisis line work. The problem is that the real world seldom functions in such neat and tidy ways. Many callers use the crisis line for reasons other than its intended use. When this happens, the overriding questions telephone workers must pose to themselves are, What is the person getting out of using the crisis line at this time and is it helpful to the person? and How is this person's use of the crisis line at this time affecting its operation? (McCaskie, Ward, & Rasor, 1990). Crisis lines should not cater to every whim, fantasy, deviant behavior, or self-indulgence of callers.

A newspaper article reported that in Sacramento, "a former suicide prevention center volunteer confessed he slit the wrists of a suicidal and depressed chronic caller who had become too demanding. 'He was sucking everything out of me. He antagonized me so that I would kill him.' The volunteer was ordered to stand trial for attempted murder" ("Suicide Counselor," 1991). Regular or chronic callers can be a plague to crisis lines and devour time and energy of staff, which legitimate callers may desperately need (Peterson & Schoeller, 1991). Chronic callers can also be very frustrating to telephone workers because they do not improve (McCaskie, Ward, & Rasor, 1990). These callers can pose a serious morale problem for the volunteers and staff who receive such calls, particularly when the calls become sexually explicit and the deviant fantasies of callers are directed at the crisis worker (Knudson, 1991; Tuttle, 1991).

A counterpoint to this negative view is the approach of the staff at the Lawrence, Kansas, Headquarters Crisis Center, who believe that *chronic* is a negative term and implies these callers will never improve (Epstein & Carter, 1991). All behavior is purposive. If seen in that light, no matter how aberrant or weird the content of the call, it is important to remember that those who regularly use the crisis line do so for a reason—it helps them make it through the day. For these clients, it becomes part of their lifestyle and method of coping.

One of the misconceptions about crisis line counseling is that the majority of calls are from occasional callers who need to get "cooled off, fixed, and sent on their way." It is erroneous to believe that patching up these situational crises is all that the crisis line does or should do (McCaskie, Ward, & Rasor, 1990).

Even though regular callers are not easily handled, they represent a major component of what crisis lines deal with and need to be handled in specific ways that do not end with telephone workers becoming frustrated and clients acting out in order to get their needs met. Therefore, while the term *chronic* is often used in telephone crisis work, we believe it to be somewhat perjorative and agree with the staff at the Headquarters Crisis Center that *regular* better captures the essence of this clientele.

Understand the regular caller's agenda.   Helping people in crisis is different from being nice to them. The agenda of regular callers places the crisis worker in a dilemma. While the worker may feel ethically bound to respond to the caller and the agency's protocol dictates that all calls must be taken, that does not mean that workers need to suffer the abuse and invective leveled at them by such callers. A very real difference exists between what callers may want and what they may need, and helping a caller is generally predicated much more on needs than wants. Often what these regulars want is a reaffirmation that their problems are unsolvable. Thus, they become dependent upon the telephone worker to sustain their problem. Therefore, the worker needs to recognize such patterns and not support them when this blocks progress (McCaskie, Ward, & Rasor, 1990). Telephone workers do themselves and their callers a service when they model that they are not willing to be manipulated or abused and that they value their own needs as highly as they value those of the caller. Generally, if a telephone worker spends more than 15 to 20 minutes with a caller, the client's crisis becomes the worker's crisis (Knudson, 1991).

Given the foregoing admonition, the telephone worker needs to remember that the sameness of the material and the dependency these clients demonstrate day in and day out makes it easy to forecast their repetitious behavior and treat them as bothersome, inept, boring, and unimportant clients. Regular callers may tend to be placed in a stereotypical catchall category because they represent an aggravation to the crisis line. However, the reasons these individuals call are diverse. Identification of specific types is at least as important as identifying the specific caller (Peterson & Schoeller, 1991). From that standpoint, McCaskie, Ward, and Rasor (1990) have constructed brief descriptions of some of the more typical personality disorders of regular callers, their outward behavior, inner dynamics, and strategies for counseling them.

Paranoid. Paranoids are guarded, secretive, and can be pathologically jealous. They live in logic-tight compartments and it is difficult if not impossible to shake their persecutory beliefs. They see themselves as victims and expect deceit and trickery from everyone. The counseling focus is to stress their safety needs.

Schizoid. Schizoids have extremely restricted emotional expression and experience. They have few social relationships and feel anxious, shy, and self-conscious in social settings. They are guarded, tactless, and often alienate others. The counseling focus is to build a good sense of self-esteem through acceptance, optimism, and support.

Schizotypal. Schizotypals have feelings of inadequacy and insecurity. They have strange ideas, behaviors, and appearances. The focus of counseling is to give them reality checks and to promote self-awareness and more socially acceptable behavior in a slow-paced, supportive manner.

Antisocial. Antisocials use others, cannot relate to the needs of society or its rules or regulations, and behave in relation to their own self-gratification with little if any thought of the welfare of others. These clients call only when they are in serious personal trouble. The focus of counseling is to get them to assume responsibility for their behavior and the very real and personal consequences their behavior will undoubtedly incur.

Narcissistic. Narcissistics are grandiose, extremely self-centered, and believe they have unique problems that others cannot possibly comprehend. They see themselves as victimized by others and always have the need to be right. The focus of counseling is to get them to see how their behavior is seen and felt by others, while not engaging in a "no win" debate or argument with them.

Histrionic. Histrionics move from crisis to crisis. They have shallow depth of character and are extremely ego-involved. They crave excitement and become quickly bored with routine and mundane tasks and events.

They may behave in self-destructive ways and can be demanding and manipulative. The focus of counseling is to stress their ability to survive using resources that have been helpful to them in the past.

Dependent. Dependents have trouble making decisions and seek to have others do so—oftentimes inappropriately. Feelings of worthlessness, insecurity, and fear of abandonment predominate. They are particularly prone to become involved and stay in self-destructive relationships. The focus of counseling is reinforcing strengths and acting as a support for their concerns without becoming critical of them or accepting responsibility for their lives.

Self-defeating. Self-defeating types choose people and situations that lead to disappointment, failure, and mistreatment by others. They reject attempts to help them and make sure that such attempts will not succeed. The focus of counseling is stressing talents and the behavioral consequences of sabotaging themselves.

Obsessive-compulsive. Obsessive-compulsives are preoccupied by and fixate on tasks. They expend and waste vast amounts of time and energy on these endeavors. They often do not hear counselors due to futile attempts to obtain self-control over their obsessions. The focus of counseling is to establish the ability to trust others and the use of thought stopping and behavior modification to diminish obsessive thinking and compulsive behavior.

Avoidant. Avoidant types are loners who have little ability to establish or maintain social relationships. Their fear of rejection paralyzes their attempts to risk involvement in social relationships. The focus of counseling is encouragement of successive approximations to meaningful relationships through social skills and assertion training.

Passive-aggressive. Passive-aggressives cannot risk rejection by displaying anger in an overt manner. Rather, they engage in covert attempts to manipulate others and believe that control is more important than self-improvement. The focus of counseling is to promote more open, assertive behavior.

Given the foregoing personality disorders and their agendas, our admonition is still to treat these clients not as types, but as individuals with their own idiosyncratic problems. Knowing the type of a caller should not be an excuse for dismissing her or him or dealing with her or him in a cursory manner.

Rappers. Psychotics and those with personality disorders are not the only regulars who call crisis lines. Other callers may just wish to "rap" or "talk." The question becomes whether time should be spent just listening to someone who only wants to "rap" with no seemingly pressing issues. However, if "lonely" is tacked onto the description of the person, this may change the telephone worker's perception of the productivity of the call. It may also be that the caller is having trouble bringing issues into the open and is testing the waters to muster enough courage to get to the real dilemma. By allowing some leeway in approaching issues but at the same time gently confronting the caller's loneliness or reluctance to get down to business, the worker sets reasonable limits on the conversation and still provides a supportive forum.

Sexually explicit callers. "Call 1-900-LUST, Cindy's lonely and wants to talk to you!" The proliferation of these ads on late-night television and in porn magazines is a sad testimony to the existence of thousands of men whose insecurities, aberrances, and deviance make "sex-talk" a multi-million-dollar business. An even sadder testimony is given by those individuals who use crisis lines for the same purpose. The sexually explicit caller is a particular millstone hung around the crisis line because many female volunteers resign due to frustration caused by frequent sex calls (Fenelon, 1990). Such behavior should not be tolerated by workers and should be terminated as soon as it becomes apparent.

Even though the foregoing types of callers are striving to fulfill their needs, they often pose problems for telephone workers. Following are some techniques to help prepare crisis workers to deal with this sometimes difficult clientele.

Pose open-ended questions.   Appropriate use of open-ended questions can help defuse the problems generated by chronic or regular callers (Epstein & Carter, 1991).

Caller: You people don't know anything. Everything you've told me is a bunch of crap.

CW: What did you expect to gain from this call, then?

Caller: Just to tell you what I think of your lousy service.

CW: If you were me, what would you be doing or saying right now?

These directive questions refocus the problem back to the caller and force movement toward problem solving rather than keeping the worker subjected to condemnatory statements.

Set limits.   When it is apparent that attempts to refocus the problem to the caller are futile, then a time limit should be set (Knudson, 1991).

Caller: You ought to be congratulating me on getting my act together, no thanks to you.

CW: I'm glad you've done something positive since you last called. Now we can talk about your current situation for five minutes. Then I'll have to take another call.

Terminate.   When the caller's behavior escalates to what the worker perceives as abusiveness, the call should be terminated in a clear and firm manner (McCaskie, Ward, & Rasor, 1990).

Caller: You bitch! Don't you dare hang up this God-damned phone!

CW: [*Assertively.*] I'm sorry, but that is language we do not tolerate, so I'm going to another caller now.

Switch.   Particularly with a sexually explicit caller, switching the call to another worker, preferably a male, takes the stimulus thrill out of the situation and makes it very difficult for the caller to bring masturbation to orgasm, which is usually the end goal of such a call (Knudson, 1991).

Caller: I'd love to cover you with honey and lick you all over.

CW: [*Female, calmly and coolly.*] Given your specific problem, I'm going to switch you to Ralph. [*Signals to Ralph.*]

CW: [*Ralph, assertively.*] I understand you have a problem. How can I help you?

If a male is not available, the call should be shifted to a supervisor and terminated. The caller should be told that the worker will hang up and that should be done immediately (McCaskie, Ward, & Rasor, 1990).

CW: [*Supervisor, authoritatively and firmly.*] We are *not* here to answer demeaning remarks. I am going to hang up and we will continue to do so until your behavior changes.

To bait a telephone worker and hold her on the line, sexually explicit callers often externalize their fantasies by reporting some hypothetical significant other's problem in florid detail. When the first hint of this ploy occurs, the worker should interpret the behavior as the caller's own and make the switch (Knudson, 1991).

Caller: I'm really worried about my uncle and his 10-year-old daughter. She's a little doll and he's always giving her these massages in her bedroom and I . . .

CW: [*Interrupts.*] That's out of my area of expertise; please hold the line and let me switch you to our child abuse expert, Ralph.

For a variety of other responses that caringly but firmly deal with the sexually explicit caller, see Vanda Wark's (1984) book *The Sex Caller and the Telephone Counseling Center.*

Formulate administrative rules.   Administratively, crisis lines need to set specific rules to extinguish abusive behavior by doing the following:

1. Limiting number and duration of calls from any single caller.
2. Limiting the topics that will be discussed.
3. Requiring that only specific workers versed in handling abusive callers take such calls.
4. Using speaker phones for on-the-spot consultation.
5. Requiring the caller to establish a face-to-face relationship with an outside worker and allow communication between the therapist and crisis line personnel.
6. Allowing the staff to prohibit calls for a day, a week, or more, if physical threats are made. (Knudson, 1991; McCaskie, Ward, & Rasor, 1990)

The Headquarters Crisis Center of Lawrence, Kansas, uses a tracking log for regular callers that lists their name, phone number, address, style of interaction, major and tangential issues, effective and ineffective response modes, their physician/therapist, medications, support groups, and lethality levels. The log is kept current and available to staff, saving them a great deal of time and energy. This center also has an internal messages notebook labeled "Client Concerns." It contains information about regular callers that workers can quickly read to become updated on the caller's circumstances. It is an effective method to keep staff current and can be used to offer feedback and suggestions to clients (Epstein & Carter, 1991). Staff should be brought together on a regular basis to discuss these callers, plan strategy for them, and make suggestions and voice personal concerns (McCaskie, Ward, & Rasor, 1990).

Finally, it is our own recommendation that supervisors be critically aware of the impact that such callers can have on personnel. Crisis center administrators should be ready, willing, and able to process debilitating emotions that such calls often evoke in workers in a caring, empathic, and supportive manner through regularly planned and emergency debriefing sessions.

Handling the Disturbed Caller

"The behavior of the severely disturbed is primitive, disorganized, disoriented, and disabling. These people are likely to elicit discomfort, anxiety, and outright fear in the observer. These are strange people. These are different people. These are people we lock away in mental institutions pumping them full of strong drugs that turn the mania into docileness" (Greenwald, 1985b). This stereotypical public view of the mentally disturbed quoted in the University of Illinois at Chicago's Counseling Center hotline training manual introduces hotline workers to the mentally disturbed. These are many of the people who call crisis hotlines. On the neophyte phone counselor's first meeting with the disorganized and disjunctive thought processes of the mentally disturbed, all of the training the crisis worker has ever received is likely to go by the wayside.

These callers represent a cornucopia of mental illnesses. They may be delusional and hallucinatory; be unable to remotely test what they are doing, believing, or thinking against reality; be emotionally volcanic or conversely demonstrate the emotionality of a stone; lack insight or judgment about their problems and be unable to relate any linear or logical history of these problems; be so suspicious in their paranoid ideation that they believe even the phone worker is out to get them; be manipulative, resistant, and openly hostile and noncompliant to the simplest requests; not have the slightest idea of appropriate interpersonal boundaries with significant others or the crisis worker; demonstrate obsessive behavior and compulsive thoughts that they continually harp on to the exclusion of any effective functioning; have no meaningful interpersonal relationships with the possible exception of crisis line workers; impulsively place themselves in problematic and dangerous situations over and over; and present themselves in childlike or even infantile ways (Grunsted, Cisneros, & Belen, 1991). Whether these behaviors are biochemically or psychologically based makes little difference. These people are so distanced from our own reality and so threatening that the beginning phone counselor's immediate reaction is to get off the line!

However, if the disturbed client is pictured as a person whose developmental processes have gone terribly awry, then the call may take on structure and sense and become less intimidating. No matter how bizarre the call may be, these primary axioms apply to the caller's behavior:

1. Behavior is always purposeful and serves motives that may be either conscious or unconscious.
2. Behavior is comprehensible and has meaning even though the language used may not.
3. Behavior is characteristic and consistent with personality even though it is exaggerated.
4. Behavior is used to keep a person safe and free of anxiety. (Greenwald, 1985a, p. 1)

The following rules for dealing with disturbed callers are abstracted from a number of crisis hotlines (Epstein & Carter, 1991; Greenwald, 1985a, 1985b; Knudson, 1991; Tuttle, 1991).

Slow emotions down.   Although disturbed callers have many feelings that have been submerged from awareness, it is not the best strategy to attempt to uncover these feelings. The caller is being beseiged by too many feelings and needs to find a way to get them in control. Focusing on here-and-now issues that are concrete and reality-oriented is the preferred mode of operation. Do not elicit more feelings with open-ended questions such as "Can you tell me more about that?" Instead, use calming interventions that force the person to order thinking in small realistic bits of detail.

CW: I understand how scary those thoughts are that keep creeping into your mind and the "things" you think are in the room. What I want you to do right now is look around the room and tell me what is there. Then tell me what happened to start this thinking.

The idea is to slow emotions down. While the worker may acknowledge the feelings, they are not the focus of attention. By breaking up freewheeling ideation into discrete manageable pieces, the telephone worker gives the individual a sense of regaining control. The worker may also bring the caller back to reality from a flashback by asking the client what he or she is doing.

CW: You say you're in that alley and he's assaulting you. Were you smoking a cigarette then? I know you just lit a cigarette a minute ago. I want you to slowly inhale, smell that smoke, and tell me where you are. Now blow the smoke out and see where it goes around the room.

Refuse to share hallucinations and delusions.   If a caller is hallucinating or delusional, the telephone worker should never side with the psychotic ideation.

Caller: Do you see, hear, smell, feel those things?

CW: No! I'm sorry, I don't. I understand right now you do and that's terrifying, but what I want to do is get you some help. So stay with me. What is your [doctor's, sister's, friend's] phone number so we can get some support for you?

Little if any good ever comes of participating in such thinking, and as the delusion increases, it becomes difficult to extricate oneself from it. Yet, grandiose thinking, no matter how bizarre, should not be denied.

CW: [*Inappropriate and sarcastic.*] Come on, now. The CIA isn't really listening to an auto mechanic by electronic eavesdropping. Certainly they've got better things to do than that. Why do you believe that?

CW: [*Appropriate and empathic.*] It's pretty clear that you really believe the CIA is listening to you. When did this start?

The worker affirms the paranoid delusion is real without agreeing to its veracity. By asking a *when* question, the worker is able to start eliciting information that will allow for an assessment of the scope and extent of the paranoia. A *why* question is never appropriate because of the defensive reaction it may elicit in any caller and especially in a paranoid.

Determine medication usage.   If at all possible, the worker should attempt to elicit information as to the use of any medication, amount and time of dosage, and particularly, discontinuance of the medication without consulting the attending physician. Changing, forgetting, or disregarding medication is one of the most common reasons that individuals become actively psychotic (Ammar & Burdin, 1991). Further, having this information will give the worker a better idea of the type of mental disturbance the caller is being treated for. Regardless of the reasons or excuses clients give for not taking medicine, the worker should endeavor to get them to their prescribing physician so medication can be adjusted or reinstituted.

CW: Lemuel, I want you to call up your doctor as soon as we get off the phone. I understand that the medicine gives you a bad taste in your mouth and makes you feel queasy. However, your doctor needs to know that and you need to let her know you're not on your meds.

Becoming familiar with the major tranquilizers, antidepressants, and antipsychotic drugs is important for this work (Pope, 1991). However, given all the different kinds of drugs and their numerous generic and trade names, keeping track of all of them is extremely difficult. The *Physicians Desk Reference* provides information on what these drugs do, how much is generally given, and what the side effects are. No crisis line office should be without a current copy.

Keep expectations realistic.   The telephone worker should keep expectations realistic. The caller did not become disturbed overnight. No crisis worker is going to change chronic psychotic behavior during one phone call. The crisis worker is buying time for the caller in a period of high anxiety and attempting to restore a minimum amount of control and contact with reality. If the caller is trying to "milk" the worker through an interminable conversation, confronting the problem in a direct manner will generally determine whether the caller is lonely or is in need of immediate assistance.

CW: It seems as if this can't be solved and you say you can't wait until tomorrow to go to the clinic. I'm concerned enough that I think we ought to make arrangements to transport you to the hospital right now.

Maintain professional distance.   Calls from severely disturbed individuals may evoke all kinds of threatening feelings in phone workers, leaving them feeling inadequate, confused, and in crisis themselves! Maintaining professional distance when exceedingly painful and tragic stories are related is difficult for the most experienced phone worker. When these feelings begin to emerge, it is of utmost importance for workers to make owning statements about their feelings and get supervision immediately. Passing the line to another worker in no way indicates inadequacy.

CW: Frankly, I'm a bit confused as to what to do. I've done everything I know and I'm tapped out. I'd like to connect you with Irma, who may have some other ideas, while I talk to our director.

As confused and disoriented as disturbed callers may be, they seem to have a sixth sense about sensitive areas in others. Countertransference (the attributing to clients of the therapist's own problems) is not uncommon, and disturbed callers have the potential to unearth the worker's own hidden agendas and insecurities. Strong reactions to these callers in either a positive or negative way should alert the hotline worker that processing and feedback with a coworker or supervisor is needed.

Caller: [*Paranoid.*] I know who you are, when you work on the hotline, and where you live.

CW: [*Inappropriately responding to the threat in a shaky voice.*] What have I ever done to you? I'm trying to help you and you get bent out of shape. I've got a good mind to hang this phone up right now or even call the police. We can trace these calls, you know!

CW: [*Appropriately responding to the implication in a clear, firm, but empathic voice.*] Jacque, those things are not important to what's going on with you right now. What is important is making you feel safe enough to go back to your apartment tonight and go to the doctor in the morning. I understand why you might get upset over my suggesting you see the doctor, but I also want you to clearly understand it's your safety I'm concerned about. So what's making you angry with me?

By deflecting the caller's paranoia and refocusing the dialogue back on the client's issues, the telephone worker directively forces the caller, in an empathic manner, to respond to his own emotional state.

Avoid placating.   Placating and sympathizing do little to bolster the caller's confidence or help move the client toward action.

Caller: [*Depressed.*] I'm just not any good to anybody, much less myself.

CW: [*Inappropriately sympathetic.*] From all you've told me, you've had a really rocky road. Nobody should have to suffer what you have, but things can only look up.

Rather, by empathically responding and exploring past feelings and coping skills when life was better, the telephone worker not only acknowledges the dilemma but also focuses on the client's strengths.

CW: You do sound pretty hopeless right now, but I wonder how you were feeling when things weren't this way, and what you were doing then that you aren't doing now?

Assess lethality.   Many clients who call crisis lines have active suicidal or homicidal ideation. It may seem puzzling that such individuals would call a crisis line when they seem so bent on harming themselves or others. What these callers are doing is trying to put distance between their thoughts and the actions that might result from those lethal thoughts. As much as the callers may avow intentions of lethality, they are still in enough control of themselves to attempt to place a buffer (the telephone worker) between thinking and acting.

Caller: If I can't have him, she sure as hell won't. I'll kill them both, and you, the police, or nobody else can stop me.

CW: Yet, you called here, for which I'm glad. Something is holding you back, and I'd like to know what that something is.

Caller: Well, I'm a Christian, but their sins go beyond redemption.

CW: So as a Christian, you probably think the commandment "Thou shalt not kill" is pretty important. What you're saying is you're about to commit sin, just as they did. How will that help you and how will it look in the eyes of God?

While it may be construed that the telephone worker manipulates the spiritual philosophy of the caller to achieve an end, the major goal of the crisis worker is to disrupt the irrational chain of thinking that is propelling the client toward violence. In that regard, when dealing with the disturbed caller, the overriding thesis is "Save the body before the mind" (Grunsted, Cisneros, & Belen, 1991). Crisis intervention over the telephone with the severely disturbed is clearly not meant to be curative. It is a stopgap measure designed to be palliative enough to keep action in abeyance until help arrives. Whether that help is in the form of getting the police or a mobile intervention team to the site, setting up an appointment for a therapy session the next morning, obtaining a support person, or helping a lonely, depressed person get through the night, the idea is to psychologically hold the disturbed caller's hand until help arrives.

CASE HANDLING AT WALK-IN CRISIS FACILITIES

Unlike contact with the telephone client, who is faceless and anonymous, crisis worker contact with walk-in clients is close-up and personal. We'll describe the types of presenting crises generally seen at walk-in facilities. Then we'll examine how cases are handled at a typical community mental health clinic.

Types of Presenting Crises

Clients who present themselves for crisis counseling at walk-in facilities generally fall within one of four categories.

1. Those who are experiencing chronic mental illness.
2. Those who are experiencing interpersonal problems in their social environment.
3. Those who are experiencing intrapersonal problems in their own development.
4. Those who are experiencing a combination of the three foregoing categories.

Chronic crisis.   Since the federal Community Mental Health Centers Act of 1963, the major responsibility for treatment of the mentally ill has fallen on community mental health centers. While in theory the act was designed to deinstitutionalize patients and return those who are able to functional living, in fact the act has placed many individuals in chronic crisis.

Besides deinstitutionalization of long-term patients in the 1960s, the Vietnam War, increased drug abuse, a rise in crime, fragmentation of families, and a host of other societal ills have caused a tremendous upsurge in the need for mental health services. While originally focused on reintegrating the long-term hospital patient into the community, mental health centers have tended to assign chronic cases a less-than-priority status. The unspoken reason is that these clients are extremely frustrating to mental health providers because they show little progress and are a constant financial and emotional drain on the resources of the agencies that come in contact with them. Many community mental health centers have deemphasized this role and moved more toward dealing with developmental problems of "normal," more highly functioning individuals (Slaikeu, 1990, p. 284). Perhaps more ominously, community mental health centers have been forced due to funding cutbacks to look more to a client's ability to pay as a condition of treatment, which means that those who may be most in need of service may be relegated to a waiting list. Further, because of legal ramifications and funding problems, severely disturbed individuals who are committed to state hospitals typically have very brief stays and are turn-stiled back onto the streets.

The result is that a host of chronically mentally ill individuals who are poorly functioning, impoverished, homeless, victims or perpetrators of crime, and without support systems of any kind are left to fend for themselves. These people often have multiple problems besides a primary diagnosis of psychopathology. They may be noncompliant to treatment, disregard their medication, abuse alcohol and drugs, have other severe physical problems, and be victimized financially, physically, and psychologically by others (Bender, 1986; Nurius, 1984; Pope, 1991). It is easy to see why these individuals often wind up in crisis when understaffed and underfunded mental health clinics (Roberts, 1991, p. 31) and other social services agencies are unable to care for them. The chronically mentally ill are often on a first-name basis with local police and personnel in emergency rooms, mental health clinics, and social services agencies.

Social/environmental crisis.   Chronics are not the only people who avail themselves of, or are brought to, walk-in facilities. Runaways, addicts, battered women, crime victims, survivors of violent events, the sexually abused, the terminally ill, divorcées, the unemployed, and relatives of the chronically physically and mentally ill are some of the many participants in a drama of social crisis that is played out every day and night in mental health clinics, emergency rooms, student counseling centers, social services agencies, and police stations across the country. Many of the precipitating events may be unexpected and sudden and may have an impact far beyond the individual on families and communities, leaving these systems disorganized and out of control. Crises that are generated in the social environment are some of the most potent for mental health workers because of their ramifications across systems and the heightened emotionality and immediacy that accompany them both for clientele and workers.

Developmental crisis.   It used to be thought that development was fixed by the end of the adolescent years. In this view, when a person became physically mature, somehow other aspects of the person were set in concrete and one lived out one's life according to a set script determined by genetic and environmental factors. However, starting with Havinghurst's (1952) and Erikson's (1963) theories of general developmental tasks through the life span and Roe's (1956) and Super's (1957) theories of career development, theory and research have continued to flesh out a series of stages that extend from infancy to old age.

Perhaps two works—one that deals with adult men, *The Seasons of a Man's Life* (Levinson, 1978), and the other with adult women, *Passages* (Sheehy, 1976)—have done more than any others to popularize the notion that people are constantly faced with challenges and tasks as they move through life. Choosing a college, dealing with an unwanted pregnancy, raising children, selecting an occupation, purchasing a first home, job loss and mobility, maintaining a marriage or relationship, physical decline, preparing for retirement, caring for one's parents, and chronic illness and hospitalization are typical tasks that people face as they move from adolescence to old age. Whether individuals are able to successfully transit through these developmental tasks has a great deal to do with how well they face the next stage of living and its tasks. If they are not successful and remain stuck in a particular stage, they become excellent candidates for crisis (Levinson, 1978). In reality, passage through one stage to another invariably involves some degree of crisis and makes growth possible. However, when lack of skills and knowledge, inability to take risks, absence of support systems, or lack of material resources combine with chance factors and pile up, the individual's coping skills become unequal to the task and a developmental crisis is the result. While the crises of these individuals may lack the duration and severity of the crises of the chronically mentally ill or victims and survivors of social/environmental trauma, their sheer numbers impact mental health delivery systems and provide a fertile field for the crisis interventionist.

Combination of types.   The foregoing types rarely occur as such discrete categories. Interaction between types and problems that crisis workers deal with is the rule rather than the exception. Attempting to stabilize a chronic schizophrenic without providing food and shelter, treating a trauma survivor without first working on a drug addiction, or considering vocational exploration without handling the depression of a middle-aged executive who has just lost her job is a waste of valuable time. Crisis workers must be able to assess and prioritize problems as to their immediacy, react swiftly to rapidly changing conditions, understand and move adroitly through social services bureaucracies, and still maintain an empathic and caring attitude toward their clientele without suffering burnout (Intrater, 1991).

Case Handling at a Community Mental Health Clinic

We have chosen Midtown Mental Health Clinic in our hometown of Memphis, Tennessee, as a generic representation of how clients are taken care of who walk into or are brought to a community mental health facility. This clinic's catchment area includes a number of housing projects, the downtown area, the University of Tennessee medical facility, the city hospital, private hospitals that have inpatient psychiatric facilities, the Memphis Veterans Administration Hospital, the Memphis Mental Health Institute (a state psychiatric hospital), the county jail, several halfway shelters for drug addicts and the homeless, the Crisis Stabilization Unit (a short-term mental health inpatient facility) and a variety of other social services agencies. Further, its catchment area has the highest crime rate and incidence of domestic violence in the city, a high percentage of school dropouts, and some of the most impoverished areas of the city.

Along with general and specialized individual and group therapy programs, Midtown provides a variety of services that include alcohol and drug treatment, geriatrics, group living facilities, inpatient day treatment, vocational rehabilitation, mobile mental health teams, child counseling, family therapy, and General Education Diploma programs. It also provides outreach and liaison to a variety of other human services organizations that range from businesses to schools. Counselors, social workers, psychologists, psychiatric nurses, and psychiatrists are affiliated with the clinic and certified or licensed in their specific area of expertise. The clinic is constantly underfunded and understaffed given the many missions it is asked to carry out. Yet, somehow it generally accomplishes what it sets out to do. There are few dull moments at the clinic. The following description of that clinic's case-handling procedures comes from Ron Pope (1991), assistant director of the clinic.

Entry.   Clients may come to the mental health clinic on their own, be brought by relatives or social services agencies, or be taken into custody by the police. At the moment of entry, disposition of the case commences. A person in crisis who walks in or is brought to Midtown may range across the Triage Rating Scale from mildly to severely disturbed. If the person is severely disturbed, a senior clinician is summoned. An attempt is made to remove the client to an isolated office to reduce environmental stimuli and calm the client so that an assessment can proceed. The clinician attempts to obtain a case history. If this is not possible, a visual and verbal assessment by the clinician in regard to information-processing problems, tangential thinking, hallucinations, disassociation, threats to oneself or others, or severe drug abuse is made. If any of these symptoms are present, then a psychiatrist is called to evaluate the client and decide whether hospitalization is warranted.

Commitment.   If the client is so mentally fragmented as to be clearly out of touch with reality or deemed an imminent danger to self or others, commitment to an inpatient mental health facility is made. The individual is asked to voluntarily commit to hospitalization. If the individual is unwilling to do so, an involuntary commitment order may be written by a physician. An officer of the Crisis Intervention Team, a special unit of the Memphis Police Department trained to deal with the mentally ill, is then called to transport the patient. Under no circumstances do mental health workers become involved in transportation, because of safety concerns and the possibility of stigmatizing themselves as punitive agents in the eyes of the patient. Patients may be transported to a private psychiatric facility if they are financially able. If they are indigent, they are taken to the Crisis Stabilization Unit (CSU) or the Memphis Mental Health Institute (MMHI).

Inpatient care.   The CSU is a short-term inpatient facility that keeps individuals for a maximum of three to five days. Examples of types of patients at the CSU are those who attempt suicide, have a violent episode, are off their antipsychotic medication, require drug detoxification, or otherwise are in need of a short-term stay until they can be emotionally stabilized or moved to a long-term facility. The CSU's relationship with Midtown is reciprocal. While Midtown sends clients to the CSU for a short-term respite, it also receives clients from the CSU. Every morning a staff meeting is held at the CSU to discuss the previous day's admissions. Staff members from all local community mental health clinics attend the daily meetings. If a patient falls in the Midtown catchment area, a staff member from Midtown picks the case up. Upon release from the CSU, the case is taken over by Midtown.

MMHI is a full-service psychiatric facility run by the state. Patients at MMHI typically have more severe or chronic problems. If a patient cannot be stabilized at the CSU, then referral to MMHI is made. Midtown also may make direct referrals to MMHI if the CSU is full or the patient is in need of the more comprehensive services provided by MMHI.

Intake interview.   If the individual is coherent enough to provide verbal and written information, an intake interview is started. Following closely the six-step model in Chapter 2, the intake worker first attempts to define the problem, assess for client safety, and apprise clients of their rights. In a patient and methodical manner, the intake worker goes through a standard intake interview sheet. Through open-ended questions and active listening, the worker tries to obtain as comprehensive a picture of the client as possible. The worker also attempts to determine the precipitating problem that brought the client to the clinic. The intake worker must be nonjudgmental, empathic, and caring and must also obtain concrete and specific information from a client who may not be able or willing to reciprocate.

Two critical components are always appraised in this initial assessment: degree of client lethality and drug use. It is a given that crisis situations either involve or have the possibility of acting-out behavior. Therefore, the intake worker evaluates clients in relation to their plans or intent to do harm to themselves or others. Because of the widespread use of prescription and illicit drugs, the worker checks to determine if drugs are involved in the presenting problem. Drug involvement may take a variety of forms:

1. The client may be having negative psychological side effects from drugs prescribed for an unrelated physical problem.
2. The client may have stopped taking prescribed antianxiety or antipsychotic drugs because of their extremely unpleasant physical side effects.
3. Drugs and/or alcohol may have been abused by the client to anesthetize himself or herself against terrifying psychological problems.
4. The client may be addicted to illicit drugs, prescription drugs, or alcohol.

Thus, intake workers need to have a thorough understanding of the *Physicians Desk Reference.* The intake worker must also have a working knowledge of the side effects of "street drugs" because of the high incidence of their use in the Midtown area.

Disposition.   After the intake has been completed, the worker constructs and writes a proposed diagnosis and treatment recommendations. The intake worker discusses the treatment recommendations and possible services with the client. It is then the client's decision to accept or reject services. If services are accepted, the intake worker introduces the client to the therapist who will most likely be in charge of the case. A full clinical team meeting is held to confirm or alter the initial diagnosis and treatment recommendations. At that time a primary therapist is designated and assumes responsibility for the case.

Anchoring.   Clients are never left alone on their initial visit. From their intake interview to disposition to a primary therapist, clients are made to feel a personal interest is being taken in them and their problems. The client is taken and handed over to the therapist who will be in charge of the case. The therapist gives a verbal orientation about what is going to occur for the client. The idea behind this methodical orientation is to demystify the world of mental health, familiarize clients with what their treatment will be, and provide them with a psychological anchor in the form of a real person who will act as their advocate, support, and contact person. Quickly establishing rapport with the primary therapist is helpful in forestalling future crisis and is extremely important to unstable clients given the threatening implications of entering a mental health facility, possible loss of freedom, and the bureaucratic maze of the mental health system. It is also designed to immediately empower clients and make them feel they have taken a step in the right direction.

Once basic needs have been met, the client is given a card with an appointment time and day on it. In many instances, a compeer volunteer is assigned to the client. Compeers are trained volunteers who act as support and socializing agents for clients who do not have friends or relatives to assist and encourage them.

Short-term disposition.   Many crises relate to the basic physical necessities of living, and if that is the case, short-term provisions for food, clothing, shelter, and other necessities are made by the intake worker while the wheels of other social services agencies are set in motion to provide long-term subsistence services. If it is determined that clients are unable to care for themselves, the Tennessee Department of Family Services is appointed as a conservator to handle their money and look after their basic needs. Thus, it is highly important that the intake worker and other staff have a thorough understanding of and ability to access the local social services network.

Long-term disposition.   The intake worker's diagnosis and recommendations are reviewed and evaluated by an interdisciplinary team. If a psychiatric or pharmacological evaluation is deemed necessary, a psychiatrist and a pharmacist conduct an evaluation of the client. If a psychological evaluation is required, a psychometrist evaluates the individual on standardized personality and intellectual measures. Depending on the needs of the client, team members from various specialty units are added. Once the team is complete, objectives and goals are formulated and a therapeutic plan is operationalized. This plan is reviewed on a regular basis and if conditions warrant, it is changed.

Twenty-four-hour service.   Midtown operates 24 hours a day. After regular working hours, telephone relays are linked into the CSU. Any client who calls the Midtown number reaches a trained professional at the CSU. Telephone workers there evaluate the call and make a decision about how to handle the case. Telephone counseling is similar to that of most crisis lines with the exception that workers at the CSU can generally learn the identity of the client and if needed, summon emergency support from the client's therapist or the police.

Mobile crisis teams.   For certain clients, particularly geriatric cases, it may be necessary to make home visits. At other times, when a client is out of control and unwilling or unable to go to the clinic, crisis workers go wherever the client is. With the advent of the police department's Crisis Intervention Team, this need has diminished a good deal in Memphis. However, in many other cities these mobile teams are on call and often follow up after local police departments have contained the situation.

Transcrisis.   The telephone can serve long-term clients who are at transcrisis points in their therapy. Such clients may avail themselves of their therapist by phone for perceptual checks and support. Many times as clients move through developmental stages of therapy, they face new and terrifying aspects of their growth toward mental health. Phone calls to their therapist help dissipate the ambiguity and rapidly oscillating emotions as clients test what are for them risky new behaviors.

TRANSCRISIS HANDLING IN LONG-TERM THERAPY

Clients in long-term therapy are not immune from crisis. Therapy tends to move in developmental stages with psychological troughs, crests, and plateaus. Even though clients have success in meeting therapeutic goals, each new stage brings with it what are seen in many instances to be even more formidable obstacles. The beginning therapist who has seen a client make excellent progress is often in for a rude awakening when the client's progress comes completely undone and behavior regresses to pretherapeutic functioning.

Consider Melanie's present dilemma. Melanie has escaped from an alcoholic marriage and subsequently completed two years of secretarial science at a community college, but she falls apart when she is faced with an interview for a job that she desperately wants.

Melanie: [*Intoxicated over the telephone at 1 AM to her therapist of three years.*] I doon't know. I'mm jes kinda scared. I doon't think I can get through tha' interview. I'mm na sur life'sh wurf living. [*Starts to sniffle.*]

The therapist first makes a rapid assessment of Melanie. Her intoxicated state is entirely uncharacteristic of her work for the past two years with the therapist. Even though Melanie has been depressed before, she has never threatened suicide. Although Melanie is coherent in her slurred speech, the therapist immediately assesses her as high as 8 on the behavioral dimension of the triage scale, and checks her out for safety needs.

TH: Melanie, I'm concerned about your job interview and we'll talk about that, but right now I'm concerned about your physical state. Have you been taking drugs or drinking? If so, how much?

If the client is out of control and in danger because of her drinking, the therapist will get help immediately. If the client is really contemplating suicide, the therapist will move immediately into a suicide prevention mode (see Chapter 4).

TH: Melanie, I know you don't normally get drunk. If you've had more than half a bottle of gin, I think you need to have somebody there right now. I want you to call your sister, and I want her to call me and tell me so. If she can't come, I'll get you and the kids back down to the halfway house for the night, but one way or the other I want to know you're safe.

In this crisis, as in any other, safety needs take top priority.

We'll discuss here a number of crisis situations that might arise in the course of long-term therapy. The six-step model of crisis intervention is an appropriate guide to action in these situations.

Anxiety Reactions

A puzzling aspect of therapy occurs when clients are highly successful in achieving tremendously difficult goals and then are completely undone by a task that to the objective observer does not seem all that difficult. Though it seems cognitively irrational, the fear of failure to achieve this minor goal becomes a self-fulfilling prophecy. The client fears that others will see through her sham of competence and irrationally thinks that any real progress is a delusion. At such times, clients engage in various types of flight behavior. Severe anxiety is one way of escaping the threatening situation.

Melanie: [*Extremely anxious and agitated.*] I hated to call you, but I'm so scared. I've thrown up twice and I've got the shakes. This hasn't happened since I walked out on Bill over three years ago. God, I can't get a grip and I need to do my best tomorrow. I know I'll just blow it. I can't think straight and I can't remember a thing about interviewing. Everything's just running together.

On the triage scale the therapist puts Melanie at a 5 for cognitive threat and a 6 for affective anxiety/fear. If the therapist does not help to diminish the anxiety the potential is that Melanie may move upward to 8–9 on these scales by the time she goes for her job interview the next day.

TH: Just do this for a minute, Melanie. Take a deep breath and let it out slo-o-owly. That's right! Now take another! OK, again. [*Continues in a patient, calm voice for approximately two minutes, taking Melanie through a brief deep breathing exercise to calm her anxiety attack.*]

After the deep breathing exercise, when Melanie has regained some semblance of control, the therapist paces with her through the role play they had conducted the previous session, has her write down her blunders and strong points, discusses those with her, determines that she is receding from her attack, and assesses her now as being between a 2 and a 3 on the subscales. The positive change in current functioning is reinforced and further buttressed by a quick review of the client's other successes.

TH: Now notice the change in your voice. I'll bet you've also calmed down to where you aren't shaking. Did you notice how much more you're in control now? Remember what you're there for. While a lot depends on this for you, you've also done even bigger, more threatening and scary things in your life like getting the hell out of that malignant marriage. Remember! You've become very good in secretarial science. They need you as much as or more than you need them. I want you to put that up as a big sign board in your head, in dayglow pink. THEY NEED YOU JUST AS MUCH AS YOU NEED THEM!

By role-playing the scene, the therapist puts Melanie back on familiar ground and puts the problem back into context—getting a job as opposed to having a free-floating anxiety attack. By marshaling the client's resources and very specifically and objectively reminding her of what her strengths are, the therapist concretizes the vague dread she feels at having to face the interview. The therapist's exhortation about who needs whom is not placating here. It is realistic. Melanie's ego needs to be reminded of these facts so that she will have a positive mental set both toward her personhood and her skills as she enters the interview. Finally, the therapist offers her the opportunity to have a safety net.

TH: Melanie, I think you're ready to get some sleep and go knock their socks off tomorrow. However, if you wake up tomorrow morning and really have some questions or think you need to role-play that interview once more, give me a call. I've got some free time before your interview and we can go over it once more. Now go to bed, get some sleep, and dream about that dayglow pink billboard.

By leaving her with a positive injunction and making time for her the next day, the therapist continues to provide a support system and a security net for Melanie.

Regression

The risk of taking the next step in therapeutic development may become too overwhelming even though clients have been highly successful in attaining prior goals. When clients are overwhelmed, they may regress in their behavior, retreating to maladaptive but familiar ways of behaving, feeling, and thinking.

Melanie: [*Somewhat embarrassed and mumbling in a childlike voice.*] I know what you're going to say, but I was thinking I really couldn't cut this, and Bill made that offer even after I got him arrested that he still loved me and was getting help, and I know he doesn't drink much anymore.

TH: [*Interpreting the dynamics.*] What you're really saying is the prospect of that interview is scaring the hell out of you, and it's so scary that you'd give up three years of hard work and sacrifice to go back to a really lousy, not to mention dangerous, way of living, when you're about to get the gold ring. I'm wondering why you've decided to sabotage yourself now?

By interpreting the dependency needs of the client, the therapist welds regressive thinking to the current threat of becoming independent as manifested in the job interview. Although the client's behavior and affect is not blatant, she is moving insidiously higher on the triage cognitive loss subscale. Left alone, that negative self-talk could convince the client to give up her new self-identity and go back to the long-dead and dangerous marriage.

Melanie: Oh, I just knew you'd say that, but I'm not sure I can do this. I mean a big outfit like United Techtronic.

TH: [*In a cool, clear, no-nonsense, but not condemning, voice.*] Big or small, United Techtronic is not the question. The question is, Are you going to choose to blow this, before you ever see if you can cut it? That's one way of never finding out if you're good enough. You can make that choice, although you've now been making a different one for three years. I'd hope you wouldn't do that—I believe you are good enough—but then it's your choice.

This reality-based approach directly confronts the client with the underlying and unwarranted irrational decision she is about to make and vividly points out how she is attempting to delude herself into buying back into a dependent status and revictimizing herself.

Termination Anxiety

When clients have met their goals for therapy, are fully functioning, and are ready to get back to the business of living their own lives, they may suddenly have terrible problems that only their therapist can solve. Whatever these problems are, it is an excellent bet that they have been told that it's time to terminate or they have figured out termination is about to happen. At such times it is a common occurrence for dependency issues to arise. These problems generally can be resolved by successively approximating the client to termination. For example, instead of every week, the therapist schedules the client every two weeks, then once a month, and then for a six-month follow-up. The other option is clearly discussing the possibility of this issue's arising.

TH: Melanie, I think it's time we discussed your spreading your wings and flying away from here. You landed that job and . . .

Melanie: [*Interrupts.*] But I couldn't have done that without you. You give me the courage to try those things. You've been so wonderful, I just couldn't have done any of this without you. And there's still the problem with the kids and . . .

TH: [*Gently interrupting.*] I appreciate those compliments. They mean a lot to me. Yet, while we've worked together on those things it's been you who's done it, not I. What I want to talk about with you now is some of those fears and really being on your own, like what you just said. That's pretty normal to have those feelings, lots of people do. Sort of like when you left home the first time. I want you to know I'll be here if you need me, but I want you also to know that I think it's time for you to be on your own. I'd like to discuss this with you in today's session.

Crisis in the Therapy Session

One of the scariest times for a therapist occurs when a technique has done its job exceedingly well and the client gains insight or release from a deeply buried traumatic experience—and then completely loses control. This unexpected turn of events can unsettle the most experienced therapist. As this wellspring of affect emerges, it may go far beyond cathartic insight and leave the client in a severe state of disequilibrium.

At this point it is absolutely mandatory to stay in control of the situation and take a firm and directive stance, no matter how frightening the client's actions or how personally repulsive the uncovered material may be. Our own admonition to our students is, "You may feel physically sick, start to break out in a sweat, and wish to be anyplace else but in that room. However, you are the therapist, and after the session is over you can have a world-class anxiety attack if you wish—you probably deserve it—but right now you are going to stick with the client." By demonstrating cool levelheadedness to the client, the therapist is modeling behavior that the client can emulate.

TH: I'm just wondering if the reason you ever got in that abusive marriage is that sometimes your father might have abused your mother and that's what was modeled as the way a marriage ought to be.

Melanie: [*Recoils in a shocked state.*] He never did have intercourse with me.

TH: [*Taken aback.*] I'm not quite sure what you said—"intercourse"?

Melanie: [*Breaking down and sobbing.*] For 12 years that bastard would mess with me and my sister, and Momma knew, she knew and wouldn't do anything about it. [*Completely breaks down.*] I . . . God . . . he beat us if we didn't do . . . he'd make us masturbate him . . . oh Lord . . . how could he . . . I've kept this secret . . . I can't handle this. I should have done something . . . killed him . . . [*Uncontrolled and wracked sobbing and shaking.*]

TH: [*Recomposing herself and gently touching Melanie's arm and quietly talking in a consoling and affirming voice.*] I am truly sorry for uncovering that old wound, but you *can* handle it. You've finally got it out. You lived with that hell as a child and another hell as an adult. You are a survivor.

Psychotic Breaks

Staying calm and cool is even more important when a person is engaging in a psychotic break with reality. No matter how delusional or disassociative the client becomes, the central thesis is that the client can maintain contact with reality and take constructive action.

Manuel: [*Walks into the therapist's office unannounced and unknown.*] I need help, and they recommend you. But no telephones, they listen to me through the telephone. [*Picks up the telephone in a threatening manner.*]

TH: [*In a slow, even voice.*] I need for you to put that telephone down before we go any further. I will help you, but I want you to put the telephone back on the stand. What is your name? We've never had the pleasure of meeting.

Manuel: It's Manuel. [*Hesitates.*] I'm just coming apart, they won't leave me alone.

TH: I understand that, but I need you to put the phone down and keep it together so you can tell me who's after you. Go ahead and sit down and tell me what's bothering you.

Manuel: It's my supervisor. He wants to fire me and catch me stealing so he listens in on my phone conversations, he's in league with Satan and he's probably in this room. I can smell the brimstone. [*Starts to become agitated and mumble about Hell.*]

TH: [*Calmly but in an assertive voice.*] OK! You're having trouble with your supervisor. Now we're getting somewhere. That's good, but stay with me, I personally guarantee Satan is not here. I want to know about your supervisor and how long this has been going on. I also want to get you to a safe place where nobody can hurt you, but to do that I need your help and I need you to stay in contact so I can help you.

Manuel: OK. [*Sits down and starts to talk about his supervisor.*]

The therapist immediately seeks to establish contact by obtaining the client's name while at the same time establishing ground rules for conduct in the therapist's office. When the young man starts to disassociate and talk in an incoherent manner, the therapist directively seeks to keep Manuel in contact with reality by using his grievance with his supervisor as the focus of discussion. The only acknowledgment he gives to evil spirits is his concern for the client's safety. The therapist reinforces the client for staying in contact with him and repeats his request to put the telephone down. Because psychotic clients may have difficulty hearing others due to the intrusive hallucinations assailing them, the therapist slowly and clearly repeats his requests for compliance. By staying in control, the therapist turns a potentially violent situation with an unknown client into a satisfactory resolution.

Manipulative Clients

Most clients attempt to manipulate their therapists during the course of therapy, for a variety of reasons. These reasons may range from avoiding engagement in new behaviors to testing the credibility of the therapist. Clients with personality disorders are the ultimate test of the therapist's ability to handle manipulative behavior and can create severe crises for themselves and the therapist if not dealt with in very specific ways. The borderline personality is the epitome of this group. The reaction of this personality type in therapy is an open Pandora's box of crises, as graphically described by Beck and Freeman (1990) and Chatham (1989).

Presenting problems:

1. A wide variety of presenting problems that may shift from day to day and week to week.
2. Unusual combinations of symptoms ranging across a wide array of neurotic to subpsychotic behaviors.
3. Continuous self-destructive and self-punitive behavior.
4. Impulsive and poorly planned behavior that shifts through infantile, narcissistic, or antisocial behavior.
5. Intense emotional reactions out of all proportion to the situation.
6. Confusion regarding goals, priorities, feelings, sexual orientation, and so on.
7. A constant feeling of emptiness with chronic free-floating anxiety.

Therapeutic relationship:

1. Frequent crises such as suicide threats, abuse of drugs, sexual acting out, financial irresponsibility, and problems with the law.
2. Extreme or frequent misinterpretations of the therapist's statements, intentions, or feelings.
3. Unusually strong, negative, acting-out reactions to changes in appointment time, room changes, vacations, fees, or termination in therapy.
4. Low tolerance for direct eye contact, physical contact, or close proximity in therapy.
5. Unusually strong ambivalence on issues.
6. Fear of and resistance to change.
7. Frequent phone calls to, spying on, and demands for special attention and treatment from the therapist.

Borderlines vacillate between autonomy and dependence, view the world in black-and-white terms, are ever-vigilant for perceived danger, have chronic tension and anxiety, are guarded in their interpersonal relationships, and are uncomfortable with emotions (Beck & Freeman, 1990, pp. 186–187). Because of these personality traits, they are apt to continuously test the therapeutic relationship to affirm that the therapist, like everybody else, is untrustworthy and not capable of living up to their expectations, while at the same time they are desperately craving attention, love, and respect.

From that standpoint, it is important to set clear limits for borderline personalities, structure specific therapeutic goals, provide empathic support, caringly confront manipulative and maladapative behavior, and rigorously stick with these guiding principles (Chatham, 1989). This is easier said than done because of the dramatic kinds of problems and emotions borderlines display. The following dialogue with Tommy, a college student, depicts such problematic behavior:

Tommy: [*Calling the therapist at 2 AM.*] I can't take this any longer. Nobody cares about me. I think I'm going crazy again—all these weird voices keep coming into my mind. It'd just be easier if I got a gun and blew myself away.

TH: If that's the case, then I'm concerned enough about your welfare to call 911 and get the police there immediately to take you to the hospital. If things are that serious, a phone conversation won't get the job done.

Tommy: Well, I didn't say I was going to kill myself right now! You always jump to conclusions. I just couldn't sleep or study because of all these voices and I really need to talk about them.

TH: I'm willing to talk for 15 minutes, but if I don't see you calmed down and functional by that time, I'll feel warranted in calling 911.

By voicing legitimate concern about the client's safety and setting a specific time limit on the conversations, the therapist reaffirms therapeutic control and does not become engaged in a rambling dialogue. The latter would serve nothing other than to reinforce maladaptive client behavior and cause a sleepless therapist to be angry and irritable the next day! No special considerations other than those normally given to any other clients should be given to the borderline.

Tommy: But Dr. James, I really need to change the appointment and see you tomorrow. I've got this research presentation and my group's meeting during our appointment time. Can't you move somebody else around?

TH: I have an appointment with another client at that time, Tommy. As I told you, to reschedule I need to know 48 hours in advance. It wouldn't be fair to him anymore than it would be fair to you if I did that to your regular time.

Tommy: [*Sarcastically.*] You just really don't give a damn about me, do you?

TH: The fact is I do give a damn, and that's why I'm not going to cave in and change the appointment time. We're not talking about rejection here, we're talking about a reasonable policy that I use on everybody. I know lots of times it would be easy for you to believe I'm blowing you off. At times you certainly aren't the easiest client to deal with, but I knew that going in, and I committed to see this through with you. I'll expect you at our regular Thursday time.

The therapist owns both his positive and his negative feelings about the client and directly interprets and confronts the client's underlying fear of rejection (Chatham, 1989). Finally, by reminding the client of his regular appointment, the therapist targets behavior rather than affect. Focusing on behavior is far less problematic than dealing with relational issues either inside or outside therapy because of the client's low tolerance for intimacy (Beck & Freeman, 1990, p. 196).

Treatment noncompliance is par for the course with borderlines.

TH: So how did your assignment go in thought stopping and not arbitrarily categorizing women as saints or prostitutes?

Tommy: Well, I was real busy this week. Besides which, you didn't really make that thought stopping stuff very clear. And then the rubber band reminder on my wrist broke.

TH: [*Frustrated and becoming agitated.*] This is the sixth week I've gone through this with you. You continuously put women in those one-up or one-down positions. Yet you continuously complain that no females are interested in you. How do you ever expect to have an equitable relationship unless you change your thinking?

Tommy: [*Flushed and shouting.*] Oh yeah? You're so perfect? I'll bet your supervisor would like to know the way you verbally harass your clients. Screw you! Who needs therapy or bitches, anyway? They're all sluts anyway. [*Storms out of the room and slams the door.*]

The therapist's frustration may turn to anger if the therapist ascribes malicious intentions to the client's nonperformance, particularly when trying to change the client's black-and-white thinking. Overt frustration often results in reciprocal acting out by the client. The borderline's passive noncompliance is a balancing act between fear of change and fear of offending the therapist through outright refusal to comply with therapeutic requests. When noncompliance is consistently the normative response, the therapist needs to step back from the situation, seek outside consultation, confront these issues openly, and acknowledge freely the client's right to refuse an assignment rather than doggedly proceeding (Beck & Freeman, 1990).

TH: Tommy, I feel really frustrated right now. We've been going at this one assignment for six sessions. Maybe I'm the problem—pushing too fast. On the other hand, I feel you maybe don't want to make me disappointed so you go through the motions. You've always got the right to say no to an assignment, and we can certainly discuss the pros and cons of that. What do you want to do about this assignment?

A favorite ploy of the borderline and other dependent types of clients is to externalize and project their problems onto others. They then attempt to get the therapist to intercede for them by acting as an intermediary or otherwise "fixing" the problem.

Tommy: If you could just write my econ professor a note telling him I'm under your care. I've only missed five classes and he's threatening to flunk me.

TH: School and therapy are separate and I won't get into that.

Tommy: But you know how bad off I've been.

TH: If you are sick enough to miss class, perhaps you should consider an academic withdrawal for medical reasons.

Tommy: Well, I'm not that bad off that I need to quit school.

TH: How has getting others to make excuses for you helped in the past?

In refusing to be used by the client, the therapist avoids a pitfall that would invariably lead to more dependent behavior and the continuation of cyclical self-reinforcing dependent and manipulative behavior.

Finally, the watchword with borderlines and other clients who consciously or unconsciously seek to manipulate the therapist is: remain calm throughout therapy and do not respond to each new crisis as an emergency. The key question therapists must ask themselves is, Who's doing the majority of work here? If the answer is, Not the client! then there is a good chance the therapist is getting manipulated.

The foregoing are a representative variety of problems that may confront therapists as they engage in long-term therapy. While these examples have not included all of the crises a therapist is likely to encounter, they have illustrated typical responses following the six-step model when crisis intervention is needed in long-term therapy. In summary, the following eight points encapsulate the therapist's role when a crisis erupts:

1. Listen closely to client concerns.
2. Assess for safety needs.
3. Make clear owning and assertive statements about the therapist's role in the current dilemma.
4. Interpret defense mechanisms in light of current problems.
5. Concretely and objectively deal with current functioning to the exclusion of other, tangential issues.
6. Speak forthrightly and clearly to the problem in the here-and-now.
7. Take direct, immediate action to restore mobility and equilibrium.
8. Provide an immediate, temporary support system during the crisis.

No matter what one's theoretical orientation, when the potential for crisis arises, most experienced therapists move quickly to help clients control their behavior until equilibrium can be reestablished. When therapy goes awry and leads to crisis situations, a major reason is that the therapist has chosen to disregard the warning signs of impending problems, remain passive, and not be proactive in confronting issues in a caring, supportive manner. Yet, to approach therapy in an action-oriented manner calls for therapists to have a clear notion of client dynamics and an even clearer notion of their own dynamics, particularly in taking well-gauged risks and being able to live with those risks without self-reproach, guilt, or anxiety over being wrong. To do otherwise jeopardizes the therapist's own mobility and equilibrium and puts both the client and the therapist in harm's way.

CONFIDENTIALITY IN CASE HANDLING

One of the benchmarks of crisis is the dramatic onset of potentially violent behavior. While we will deal extensively with the control and containment of such behavior in Chapter 10, a particular admonition to the crisis interventionist is appropriate here in our discussion of case handling. That admonition involves the issues of confidentiality and privileged communication. Confidentiality indicates an explicit promise or contract to reveal nothing about an individual except under conditions agreed to by the source or the subject (Siegel, 1979). Privileged communication is designed to protect confidential information from disclosure in the area of legal proceedings (Dekraii & Sales, 1982). The limits of confidentiality and privileged communication come under scrutiny when a case involves the potential for violent behavior.

Principles Bearing on Confidentiality

Three important principles have a bearing on this issue. Those principles involve the legal, ethical, and moral codes of the helping professions.

Legal principles.   Legally, the clients of certain professionals have the right of confidentiality through privileged communication. Such professionals include pastors, lawyers, medical doctors, and to a lesser extent licensed psychologists, social workers, and counselors. Depending on the type of setting and the geographic locale in which they practice, human services workers have varying degrees of privileged communication in the eyes of the law. Emphatically, volunteers, no matter what agency they work for, do not have such legal protection unless specifically provided by law.

Ethical principles.   Ethical standards do not have the weight of law. While they may closely parallel the law (Thompson, 1983, p. xv), ethical standards are general guiding codes of conduct for a particular profession. Violation of ethical standards may result in censure or in loss of license mandated by the profession's ethics board, but it does not necessarily expose the professional to legal problems. Ethics are general guiding principles of conduct for the particular profession, and only that. Professional associations such as the American Psychological Association, the National Association of Social Workers, and the American Association of Counseling and Development have specific standards that speak to confidentiality. Certainly, standard professional conduct and reasonable level of care dictates that what is said in confidence remains so; otherwise, the human services worker quickly loses credibility with the clientele.

Moral principles.   In the early days of psychotherapy, it was believed that the therapist could remain value-free and suspend moral judgment (Thompson, 1983, p. 1). This view has been vigorously attacked by London (1964), who maintains that no one in the mental health field can define terms such as *health, illness,* and *morality* without reference to morals, nor can they define a proper method of treatment without involving their own moral commitment (p. 5). Although critics may wrangle over the degree to which therapist morals enter into the therapeutic endeavor, they do agree that there is no value-free brand of therapy and thus no morally neutral therapist (Thompson, 1983, p. 3). While moral precepts may vary widely, when one shares problems of a deeply personal nature, common decency dictates that the recipient should keep the confidence of the individual who shares such information.

The Intent to Harm and the Duty to Warn

Given the legal, ethical, and moral principles that uphold a client's right to confidentiality, it's nevertheless true that when the client provides information about the intent to do harm to himself or herself or another person, rules of confidentiality take on an entirely different perspective. The professional is then essentially faced with making a decision about whether to inform the authorities, significant others, or a potential victim of such threats and taking action to ensure the client does not carry them out.

The Tarasoff case (*Tarasoff v. Board of Regents of the University of California,* 1976) is the premier example of a therapist, a supervisory staff, and an institution not adequately dealing with a client threat, and it has reconceptualized professional thinking in regard to confidentiality and the duty to warn a potential victim. The Tarasoff case resulted when a therapist on a university campus was informed by a male client of his intention to murder a young woman. While the intended victim was not specifically identified, the therapist was able to discern who she was but took no steps to warn her of the client's threats. The therapist wrote a letter to the campus police about the client's homicidal ideation, and the client was immediately taken into custody for observation. After evaluation, the client was found rational, and based upon a promise to stay away from the woman, he was released. The supervisor requested the police return the letter and directed that all copies of it and subsequent notes related to the incident be destroyed. Two months later the client killed the woman (Thompson, 1983, p. 167)!

The parents of the woman brought suit against the university, and on appeal to the State Supreme Court of California, the court found for the plaintiff. In this precedent-setting case, the court held that when a psychotherapist ascertains that a threat is neither remote nor idle in its content, the public good demands that disclosure of the threat to a third party outweighs the benefits of preserving confidentiality (Cohen, 1978).

As far as we can ascertain, this finding holds true whether it involves phone counseling, a private therapy session, or working with someone in crisis on a street corner. Based upon the foregoing, the following points are paramount in guiding the human services worker's actions where the clear threat of violent behavior toward another person or the client's self is made.

1. It is a good practice to convey very clearly what you can and cannot hold in confidence and to apprise the client of this before intervention is started (Wilson, 1981). As ridiculous as it may seem, prior to starting a counseling group at a correctional facility we always warn the participants

that we cannot preserve their anonymity if they threaten themselves or others, reveal plans to escape, or attempt to smuggle contraband into or out of the facility. It is noteworthy that we have had to act on this statement more than once!

2. If you are unclear about the implication of a client's threats or unsure about what to do, the cardinal rule is to consult with another professional or an immediate supervisor and keep notes of the consultation (Wilson, 1981). If you are still not sure what to do, consult with another professional. All call-in or walk-in agencies should have a supervisor well versed in dealing with this problem and readily available. Consultation is always advisable (Thompson, 1983, p. 170) and is substantiating protection from legal and ethical problems that may arise, particularly when the threat is not clear. If for some reason another professional is not available, the general rule for determining a clear and present danger is that such a danger is present if a client specifies victim identity ("my husband"), motive ("revenge"), means ("gun"), and plan ("I'll wait for him after work") (Thompson, 1983, p. 83).

3. If the client does concretely state a threat, then you are bound morally, legally, and ethically to take action. It is your duty to warn the victim if you know who it is (Wilson, 1981), unless state statute clearly indicates otherwise. Patiently and emphatically explain your concerns to the client and attempt to get the client calmed enough to get him or her to a place of safety. Tell the client what you are doing and why. Inform the client that you are prepared to hospitalize him or her. Committing a client to a hospital is generally accepted by everyone as far less disruptive and protects the client as well as potential victims. The client is also far less likely to perceive the therapist as another "enemy" and place the therapist on a "hit list" (Thompson, 1983, p. 169). If the client is vehement or acting out, avoid a confrontation. This has now become a matter for the police or security. If neither is immediately available, then get another coworker as a support person to help contain and calm the client until help arrives. In a crisis intervention setting, no worker should ever be alone; cases such as this graphically demonstrate the necessity for having more than one person on duty at the same time.

4. When clear intent to harm is indicated by the client, feeling guilty about breaking confidence has little merit. Your principal duty is to the client, not the relationship, your ethical dilemma, or any other pangs of conscience or second-guessing that may immobilize you from keeping a potential victim out of harm's way (Wilson, 1981). Apprise clients in a supportive and empathic manner of your responsibility to protect them.

5. Threats of legal reprisal by the client should not dissuade the crisis worker from reporting threats against others (Wilson, 1981). There is no legitimacy in threats of reprisal, given the law in most states.

No particular formula applies in these scary situations as to what to say, when to say it, and what degree of action is warranted. In any case involving this severe lack of control, the crisis intervention should be handled with empathy, concern, positive regard, and concreteness. Clients may make many threats in the heat of the moment and have every intention of carrying them out. However, handled in a sensitive and timely manner by the crisis worker, both client and potential victim can be kept from personal harm.

Before signing on as a volunteer or in any professional capacity, find out what the agency's policy is in regard to confidentiality, legal rights, ethical standards, and liability insurance. Finally, state law on confidentiality is variable. It is the therapist's responsibility to know what it is.

SUMMARY

Case handling in crisis intervention is different from long-term therapy. While crisis intervention deals with many of the same components as long-term therapy, crisis work can be differentiated by its emphasis on expediency and efficiency in attempting to stabilize maladaptive client functioning, as opposed to fundamental restructuring of the client's personality. Case handling in crisis intervention emphasizes concern for client safety, brevity in assessment, rapid intervention, compressed treatment time, and termination or referral once equilibrium has been restored.

Because rapid and adequate assessment at onset of the crisis is critical in determining intervention strategies, the Triage Assessment Form enables the worker to determine the client's degree of disequilibrium across affective, cognitive, and behavioral domains without having to depend upon time-consuming background interviews or standardized assessment instruments. Triage assessment represents a unique system of determining the degree of crisis at onset, what progress the client is making during intervention, and how directive the worker's intervention should be.

Case handling in crisis intervention involves three different settings: (1) telephone crisis lines, (2) walk-in facilities, and (3) long-term therapy settings. Telephone crisis lines are efficient, readily available, and inexpensive; they preserve anonymity and provide support systems and informational services. Crisis lines provide immediate access to help and utilize a vast number of trained volunteers and paraprofessionals as crisis interventionists who would otherwise not be available to clients.

Since the Community Mental Health Act of 1963, the major responsibility for treatment of the mentally ill has fallen on community mental health centers. Such centers, along with a wide variety of other community social services agencies, are on the front lines in dealing with crises of chronic mental illness, severe developmental problems, and social and environmental issues that afflict individuals. Because of the wide variety of clientele seeking services, walk-in facilities must have close linkages with other social services agencies, the legal system, and both short-term and long-term mental health facilities. Mental health workers who staff such facilities must have a broad background in dealing with a wide variety of psychological problems and be ready and able to deal with whatever crisis walks in the door.

Clients in long-term therapy may also experience crises as they move through the therapeutic process. These crises may be instigated by situational events in the client's environment, attempts to engage in new, more adaptive behaviors, or past traumatic material that is uncovered in the therapy session. When such crises occur, therapy may degenerate to the point that clients undergo severe traumatic stress and revert to pretherapeutic functioning. At these points in therapy, long-term work must be suspended and the therapist must concentrate on the emergent crisis until the client has achieved success in overcoming the current stumbling block.

In all crisis work, as indeed in all therapy, client confidentiality is a moral, ethical, and sometimes legal requirement. In many instances, crisis workers are faced with the possibility of violent behavior and the need to ensure the safety of clients and significant others. Therefore, when clients disclose an intent to do harm either to themselves or others, the crisis worker has a moral, ethical, and legal duty to take action, break confidence, and warn intended victims, significant others, or legal authorities.

In whatever setting crisis intervention occurs, effective case handling in a rapid and efficient manner is of critical importance and often determines whether the crisis will be resolved or become even more profound. Therefore, crisis workers must have an excellent understanding of their own internal resources and limits, as well as those of the agency and other referral services.

REFERENCES

Aguilera, D. C., & Messick, J. M. (1986). *Crisis intervention: Theory and methodology* (5th ed.). St. Louis: C. V. Mosby.

Ammar, A., & Burdin, S. (1991, April). *Psychoactive medication: An introduction and overview.* Paper presented at the Fifteenth Annual Convening of Crisis Intervention Personnel, Chicago, IL.

Beck, A., & Freeman, A. (1990). *Cognitive therapy of personality disorders.* New York: Guilford Press.

Bender, M. G. (1986). Young adult chronic patients: Visibility and style of interaction in treatment. *Hospital and Community Psychiatry, 37,* 265–268.

Burgess-Watson, I. P., Hoffman, L., & Wilson, G. V. (1988). The neuropsychiatry of post-traumatic stress disorder. *British Journal of Psychiatry, 152,* 164–173.

Chatham, P. M. (1989). *Treatment of the borderline personality.* Northvale, NJ: Jason Aronson.

Cohen, R. N. (1978). *Tarasoff* vs. *Regents of the University of California. The duty to warn: Common law and statutory problems for California psychotherapists. California Western Law Review, 14,* 153–182.

Crow, G. A. (1977). *Crisis intervention: A social interaction approach.* New York: Association Press.

Crow, T. J., & Johnstone, E. C. (1987). Schizophrenia: Nature of the disease process and its biological correlates. *Handbook of Physiology, Vol. 5.* Bethesda, MD: American Physiological Society.

Dekraii, M. B., & Sales, B. C. (1982). Privileged communication of psychologists. *Professional Psychology, 13,* 372–388.

Dryden, W. (1984). *Rational emotive therapy: Fundamentals and innovations.* London: Croom Helm.

Ellis, A. (1971). *Growth through reason.* Palo Alto, CA: Science and Behavior Books; Hollywood, CA: Wilshire Books.

Ellis, A., & Abrahms, E. (1978). *Brief psychotherapy in medical and health practice.* New York: Springer.

Ellis, A., & Grieger, R. (1977). *Handbook of rational-emotive therapy.* New York: Springer.

Ellis, A., & Harper, R. A. (1979). *A new guide to rational living* (rev. ed.). Englewood Cliffs, NJ: Prentice-Hall; Hollywood, CA: Wilshire Books.

Epstein, M., & Carter, L. (1991). *Headquarters training manual.* Lawrence, KS: Headquarters Crisis Center.

Erikson, E. H. (1963). *Childhood and society.* New York: Norton.

Fenelon, D. A. (1990, April). *Recognizing and dealing with the bogus sex caller.* Paper presented at the Fourteenth Annual Convening of Crisis Intervention Personnel, Chicago, IL.

Gilliland, B. E., James, R. K., & Bowman, J. T. (1989). *Theories and strategies in counseling and psychotherapy* (2nd ed.). Englewood Cliffs, NJ: Prentice-Hall.

Greenwald, B. (1985a). *In-Touch Hotline training materials: Coping.* Chicago, IL: University of Illinois at Chicago Circle Campus, Counseling Center.

Greenwald, B. (1985b). *In-Touch Hotline training materials: The disturbed caller.* Chicago, IL: University of Illinois at Chicago Circle Campus, Counseling Center.

Grunsted, V. L., Cisneros, M. X., & Belen, D. V. (1991, April). Working with the disturbed hotline caller. Paper presented at the Fifteenth Annual Convening of Crisis Intervention Personnel, Chicago, IL.

Havinghurst, R. J. (1952). *Developmental tasks and education.* New York: Longmans, Green & Co.

Haywood, C., & Leuthe, J. (1980, September). *Crisis intervention in the 1980's: From networking to social influence.* Paper presented at the annual convention of the American Psychological Association, Montreal, Canada.

Healy, D. (1987). Rhythm and blues: Neurochemical, neuropharmacological, and neuropsychological implications of a hypothesis of circadian rhythm dysfunction in the affective disorders. *Psychopharmacology, 93,* 271–285.

Hersh, J. B. (1985). Interviewing college students in crisis. *Journal of Counseling and Development, 63,* 286–289.

Intrater, L. C. (1991, April). *The effective crisis therapist.* Paper presented at the Fifteenth Annual Convening of Crisis Intervention Personnel, Chicago, IL.

Knudson, M. (1991, April). *Chronic and abusive callers: Appropriate responses and interventions.* Paper presented at the Fifteenth Annual Convening of Crisis Intervention Personnel, Chicago, IL.

Kolb, B., & Whishaw, I. Q. (1990). *Fundamentals of human neuropsychology* (3rd ed.). New York: W. H. Freeman.

Levinson, D. J. (1978). *The seasons of a man's life.* New York: Knopf.

London, P. (1964). *The modes and morals of psychotherapy.* New York: Holt, Rinehart & Winston.

McCaskie, M., Ward, S., & Rasor, L. (1990, April). *Short-term crisis counseling and the regular caller.* Paper presented at the Fourteenth Annual Convening of Crisis Intervention Personnel, Chicago, IL.

Myer, R. A., Williams, R. C., Ottens, A. J., & Schmidt, A. E. (1991). *Three-dimensional crisis assessment model.* Unpublished manuscript, Northern Illinois University, Department of Educational Psychology, Counseling, and Special Education, De Kalb.

Nurius, P. S. (1984). Stress: A pervasive dilemma in psychiatric emergency care. *Comprehensive Psychiatry, 25,* 345–354.

Ochberg, F. M. (Ed.). (1988). *Post-traumatic therapy and victims of violence.* New York: Brunner/Mazel.

Peterson, B., & Schoeller, B. (1991, April). *Identifying and responding to problem and repeat callers.* Paper presented at the Fifteenth Annual Convening of Crisis Intervention Personnel, Chicago, IL.

Pope, R. (Speaker). (1991). *Crisis counseling of the walk-in.* (Videotape Recording No. 6611-91B). Memphis, TN: Memphis State University, Department of Counseling and Personnel Services.

Roberts, A. R. (1991). Crisis intervention units and centers in the United States. In A. R. Roberts (Ed.), *Contemporary perspectives on crisis intervention and prevention* (pp. 18–31). Englewood Cliffs, NJ: Prentice-Hall.

Roe, A. (1956). *The psychology of occupations.* New York: Wiley.

Sheehy, G. (1976). *Passages.* New York: Dutton.

Siegel, M. (1979). Privacy, ethics, and confidentiality. *Professional Psychology, 10,* 249–258.

Slaikeu, K. A. (Ed.). (1990). *Crisis intervention: A handbook for practice and research.* Boston: Allyn & Bacon.

Suicide counselor cuts client's wrists. (1991, May 19). *Memphis Commercial-Appeal,* p. A2.

Super, D. (1957). *The psychology of careers.* New York: Harper & Bros.

Tarasoff v. Board of Regents of the University of California, 551 P.2d 334 (1976).

Thompson, A. (1983). *Ethical concerns in psychotherapy and their legal ramification.* Lanham, MD: University Press of America.

Thorne, F. C. (Ed.). (1968). *Psychological case handling; Vol. 1: Establishing the conditions necessary for counseling and psychotherapy.* Brandon, VT: Clinical Psychology Publishing.

Tuttle, A. (1991). *Advantages and strategies of telephone crisis counseling* [audio tape]. Memphis, TN: The Crisis Center.

Wark, V. (1984). *The sex caller and the telephone counseling center.* Springfield, IL: Charles C Thomas.

Wilson, L. (1981). Thoughts on Tarasoff. *Clinical Psychologist, 34,* 37.

Winter, B. E. (1991, April). *The Family Trouble Center: A pilot program for domestic violence intervention.* Paper presented at the Fifteenth Annual Convening of Crisis Intervention Personnel, Chicago, IL.

CLASSROOM EXERCISES

I. Assessing a Crisis

Adequate assessment is an absolute necessity in effective crisis intervention. In the rapidly changing scene of an active crisis, assessment is difficult, puzzling, and frustrating to beginners. Making a valid assessment during an ongoing crisis is perhaps more an art than a science and comes with practice, making mistakes, obtaining feedback, and plunging in again. This exercise is designed to allow you to try out your assessing skills in the safety of the classroom. It will further allow you to upgrade your skills as you move through the course. Finally, it will provide you with a way to compare the skills you had at the start of the course to your skills at the end.

Divide into groups of seven. Each person chooses one of the following roles: (1) a suicidal client, (2) a battered client, (3) a violent client, (4) a post-traumatic client, (5) a substance-abusing client, (6) a sexual assault victim, (7) a grieving client. Each person will assume the role of one of the foregoing clients for the next class meeting. It is helpful to quickly read the chapter containing the material on the particular client before the next class meeting so you will adequately depict the typical dynamics of the crisis.

At the next class meeting, each person is to role-play the client assigned for approximately five minutes. One other person in the group acts as the counselor. The counselor's role is to elicit enough information so that a domain severity assessment can be made. While the counselor and the client are working with one another, other group members monitor the dialogue and use the Triage Assessment Form in this chapter to assess the severity of the problem in regard to its affective, behavioral, and cognitive components. Write down your thoughts as you systematically go through the form. After each person has completed the role assignment, discuss your respective ratings. Pay particular attention to why you gave the ratings you did and what those ratings imply for any subsequent intervention you might use. Don't worry about trying to be perfect or any lack of knowledge you may have about the problem. Just go ahead and do it! Clearly, there are no wrong answers at this point in your education.

After you have finished, save your notes and ratings. As you move through subsequent chapters, reassemble your group and replay the crisis appropriate to that chapter. The client should attempt to replay the role as closely as possible to the initial rendition. Group members will repeat their triage assessment of the client. You will then pull out your initial ratings and compare them with your current ratings. Group discussion should cover what changes occurred and why members may have rated the person differently from the first time. By reassessing these role plays, you should start to feel more comfortable about making educated guesses in crisis situations.

HANDLING SPECIFIC CRISES: GOING INTO THE TRENCHES

Part Two focuses on applying intervention strategies to several of the currently most prevalent types of crises in the human experience. The purpose of Part Two is to provide crisis workers, counselors, caregivers, and various other professionals with information about the background, dynamics, and intervention methodologies needed to effectively help individuals or groups in crisis. We believe you will appreciate the strong emphasis on the *applied* art and science of crisis intervention.

We have several objectives in mind as we discuss specific types of crises: (1) to provide valid, useful, and interesting material, (2) to deal with areas of current importance in our culturally pluralistic world, (3) to promote sound practice, based on the best available research and theoretical foundations, and (4) to demonstrate a wide number of alternatives available to workers who are in the business of crisis intervention.

Part Two contains a wide array of crisis case illustrations to enhance our descriptions of not only the usual and accepted intervention practices but also many innovative strategies for intervention. It examines suicide, posttraumatic stress disorder, sexual assault, woman battering, substance addiction, and personal loss. The latter includes coping with loss, grief, and the crisis of AIDS. Several central themes pervade these chapters (which often deal with devastating human dilemmas):

1. Some crises are *time limited* and some are *transcrisis* in that the person in crisis may progressively experience severe problems, either deal with or suppress them, and then experience and exhibit repeated responses and symptoms of the same crisis over a period of many years.
2. Crises are characterized by both danger and opportunity.
3. No one set of theories, assumptions, strategies, or procedures is appropriate for intervening in *all* crisis situations; rather, a systematic and eclectic approach is recommended and demonstrated as the preferred mode of helping in a broad assortment of crisis problems and settings.

CHAPTER 4

Suicide

In crisis work the possibility of dealing with suicidal clients is ever present. Thus, in Chapter 2 we emphasized the importance of the crisis worker's continuous awareness and assessment of the level of suicide risk for all clients in crisis. In this chapter we present strategies to help crisis workers strengthen their skills of assessment, counseling, intervention, and prevention. The strategies addressed in this chapter are solidly based upon the concepts, including the six steps in crisis intervention, found in Chapter 2. All of the examples, cases, and exercises are presented with the assumption that workers will understand and use these fundamental crisis intervention concepts in dealing with suicidal clients as well as with clients in any other category of crisis.

BACKGROUND

Although crisis workers may not be able to identify every client having a high suicidal risk and may not succeed in preventing suicide in 100% of high-risk clients encountered, it is possible to provide the kinds of support and intervention that have proved to be helpful to self-destructive persons (Dunne, McIntosh, & Dunne-Maxim, 1987; Fujimura, Weis, & Cochran, 1985; Moldeven, 1988). A wealth of literature on counseling suicidal clients is available (Allen, 1977; Crow & Crow, 1987; Fujimura et al., 1985; Getz, Allen, Myers, & Linder, 1983; Hatton, Valente, & Rink, 1977; Hersh, 1985; Hipple & Cimbolic, 1979; Morgan, 1981; Motto, 1978; Patros & Shamoo, 1989; Phi Delta Kappa, 1988; Ray & Johnson, 1983; Shneidman, Farberow, & Litman, 1976; Wekstein, 1979). Crisis workers who deal with suicidal clients and their families and associates have found that keeping up to date through regular reading is an excellent way of enhancing their knowledge and skill as helpers.

Suicide can strike any family. It is among the top five to ten causes of death in the Western world (Toughy, 1974); it occurs among all segments of the population ("Tidewater Psychiatric," 1985). It is prevalent in all age and racial/ethnic groups. More women than men attempt suicide; men succeed in killing themselves more often than women. The highest risk group for many years has been Caucasian men over 35, but the suicide rate among teenagers and young black males has been dramatically increasing over the past 30 to 35 years (Fujimura et al., 1985; Shneidman et al., 1976). Even though the elderly make up roughly 10% of the total population, 25% of all suicides occur in the over-65 population. Women over 65 have a suicide rate twice that of the total population and men over 65 kill themselves at a rate four times the national norm (Janosik, 1984, p. 153).

The suicide rate among children and adolescents tripled between 1950 and 1985, and suicide is now the second leading cause of death among children and teens (American Association for Counseling and Development, 1985). Berman and Jobes (1991, p. 16) reported that for young people ages 15–24, suicide is the third leading cause of death (following accidents and homicide, respectively). Roberts (1991, p. 219) reviewed research on the prevalence of suicide attempts among all adolescents and estimated that between 10% and 15% of adolescents had attempted suicide. Other data reported by Shaffer, Vieland, and Garland (1990, p. 3154), based on written self-report surveys, estimated that between 9% and 10% of all ninth and tenth graders (mean age, 14 years) had attempted suicide.

According to Shaffer, Bacon, Fisher, and Garland's (1987) review of research on attempters and completers of adolescent suicide, we cannot distinguish among attempters and completers on any demographic or diagnostic criterion except by sex. They reported that females attempt suicide approximately nine times more often than males and that males complete suicide attempts about five times more often than females.

Despite the vast amount of attention being focused on suicide, especially teenage suicide, professionals have a difficult time identifying a common denominator for the cause of so many adolescent suicides ("Teenage Suicide," 1985). Dr. Donald Reay, a Seattle medical examiner, conducted a two-year study on teenage suicides. On the basis of his data, he stated, "We didn't find any outstanding characteristic. . . . In other words, take 100 teenagers and, on the basis of what we looked at, we wouldn't be able to identify a potential suicide victim" (p. 3). Dr. Reay's conclusions substantiate the premise that the mythical "suicidal type" does not exist and underscore the complexity and the difficulty encountered when we attempt to predict, identify, type, assess, and prevent potential suicides in any segment of the population (Phi Delta Kappa, 1988, p. 24). Perhaps the best assumption to begin with is that no two potential suicide situations are ever alike but that there are common threads and clues that are useful in treatment and prevention work with suicidal clients and their loved ones.

DYNAMICS OF SUICIDE

According to Fujimura et al. (1985), two different approaches have been advanced to explain suicidal behaviors: Freud's psychodynamic approach (Allen, 1977) and Durkheim's (1951) sociological approach. In the psychodynamic view, suicide is triggered by an intrapsychic conflict that emerges when a person experiences great psychological stress. Sometimes such stress emerges either as regression to a more primitive ego state or as inhibition of one's hostility toward other persons or toward society so that one's aggressive feelings are turned inward toward the self. In extreme cases, self-destruction or self-punishment is chosen over urges to lash out at others.

In Durkheim's approach, societal pressures and influences are major determinants of suicidal behavior. Durkheim (1951) identified three types of suicide: egoistic, anomic, and altruistic (pp. 152–276). *Egoistic* suicide is related to one's lack of integration or identification with a group. *Anomic* suicide arises from a perceived or real breakdown in the norms of society. *Altruistic* suicide is related to perceived or real social solidarity, such as the traditional Japanese hara-kiri or, to put it in a current context, the episodes of suicidal attacks by Middle East extremist groups. A fourth type of suicide, identified by Fujimura et al., (1985), is *dying with dignity.* This type of suicide is typified by a person's choosing death in the face of an incurable illness.

Characteristics of People Who Commit Suicide

We have often heard statements such as "The suicide makes perfect sense at that particular moment to the person who accomplishes it." What is it about a person's inner dynamics that makes suicide seem sensible? Shneidman (1985) made a substantial contribution toward clarifying suicide when he formulated ten common characteristics present in an individual when the act is accomplished.

Shneidman's (1985, 1987) ten common characteristics are grouped under six aspects of suicide, which he calls *situational, conative, affective, cognitive, relational,* and *serial* (1985, pp. 121–149).

Situational characteristics: (1) "The common *stimulus* in suicide is unendurable psychological pain" (p. 124) and (2) "The common *stressor* in suicide is frustrated psychological needs" (p. 126).
Conative characteristics: (1) "The common *purpose* of suicide is to seek solution" (p. 129) and (2) "The common *goal* of suicide is cessation of consciousness" (p. 129).
Affective characteristics: (1) "The common *emotion* in suicide is hopelessness-helplessness" (p. 131) and (2) "The common *internal attitude* toward suicide is ambivalence" (p. 135).
Cognitive characteristic: "The common *cognitive state* in suicide is constriction" (p. 138).
Relational characteristics: (1) "The common *interpersonal act* in suicide is communication of intention" (p. 143) and (2) "The common *action* in suicide is egression" (p. 144).
Serial characteristic: "The common *consistency* in suicide is with lifelong coping patterns" (p. 147).

This list of characteristics points us toward what makes sense to the individual about to embark on suicide. It is not meant to suggest that all suicides are alike. In using the word *common,* Shneidman is careful to note that suicides, taken together, do reflect similarities. However, he also reminds us that each suicide is idiosyncratic and that there are no absolutes or universals (1985, pp. 121–122).

Myths About Suicide

There are a number of commonly held myths about suicide that the crisis worker should know and take into account while assessing potentially suicidal clients (Fujimura et al., 1985; Shneidman et al., 1976, p. 130). Some of the myths are as follows:

1. *Discussing suicide will cause the client to move toward doing it.* The opposite is generally true. Discussing it with an empathic person will more likely provide the client with a sense of relief and a desire to buy time to regain control.

2. *Clients who threaten suicide don't do it.* This is untrue. A large percentage of people who kill themselves have previously threatened it or disclosed their intent to others.

3. *Suicide is an irrational act.* Maybe so, but nearly all suicides and suicide attempts make *perfect sense* when viewed from the perspective of the persons doing them.

4. *Persons who commit suicide are insane.* Again, not so. Only a small percentage of persons attempting or committing suicide are psychotic or crazy. Most of them appear to be normal people who are severely depressed, lonely, hopeless, helpless, newly aggrieved, shocked, deeply disappointed, jilted, or otherwise overcome by some emotionally charged situation.

5. *Suicide runs in families—it is an inherited tendency.* This may appear, at times, to be true, but suicidal tendency is not inherited. It is either learned or situational.

6. *Once suicidal, always suicidal.* Again, this is untrue. A large proportion of people contemplate suicide at some time during their existence. Most of these individuals recover from the immediate threat, learn appropriate responses and controls, and live long, productive lives, free of the threat of self-inflicted harm.

7. *When a person has attempted suicide and pulls out of it, the danger is over.* This is not true. Probably the greatest period of danger is during the upswing period, when the suicidal person becomes energized following a period of severe depression. One danger signal is a period of euphoria following a depressed or suicidal episode.

8. *A suicidal person who begins to show generosity and share personal possessions is showing signs of renewal and recovery.* Not necessarily so. Many suicidal persons begin to dispose of their most prized possessions once they experience enough upswing in energy to make a definite plan.

Such disposal of personal effects is sometimes tantamount to acting out the last will and testament. Beware of recently suicidal clients who go around distributing their most valued and cherished belongings to friends. Their behavior may be indicative of another form of presuicidal euphoria.

9. *Suicide is always an impulsive act.* Not always. There are several types of suicide. Some involve impulsive actions. Some are very deliberately planned and carried out.

Areas for Assessment

Workers who deal with suicidal clients should assess the presence of warning signs in three areas: risk factors, suicide clues, and cries for help. The reason we urge crisis workers to focus attention on these areas is that most suicidal clients will manifest signs in a number of them. A necessary part of the crisis worker's assessment function is to be able to recognize the client's risk factors, clues, and cries for help.

Risk factors.   Battle (1991), Bernard and Bernard (1985), Gilliland (1985), and Hersh (1985) have identified a number of risk factors that may help the crisis worker in assessing suicide potential. We recommend that the following list be used as a risk-assessment checklist. Whenever a person manifests four or five of these risk factors, that should be an immediate signal for the crisis worker to treat the person as a high risk in terms of suicide potential.

1. Client has a family history of suicide.
2. Client has a history of previous attempts.
3. Client has formulated a specific plan.
4. Client has experienced recent loss of a parent through death, divorce, or separation.
5. Client's family is destabilized as a result of loss, personal abuse, violence, or other problems.
6. Client is preoccupied with the anniversary of a particularly traumatic loss.
7. Client is psychotic.
8. Client has a history of drug and/or alcohol abuse.
9. Client is seriously depressed.
10. Client has a history of unsuccessful medical treatment or recent physical trauma.
11. Client is living alone and cut off from contact with others.
12. Client is coming out of depression or has recently been hospitalized for depression.
13. Client is giving away prized possessions or putting personal affairs in order.
14. Client displays *radical shifts* in characteristic behaviors or moods, such as apathy, withdrawal, isolation, irritability, panic, anxiety, or changed social habits, eating habits, or school or work habits.

15. Client is experiencing a pervasive feeling of hopelessness/helplessness.
16. Client is preoccupied and troubled by earlier episodes of experienced physical, emotional, or sexual abuse.
17. Client exhibits *profound degree of one or more emotions*—such as anger, aggression, loneliness, guilt, hostility, grief, or disappointment—that are uncharacteristic of the individual's normal emotional behavior.

The crisis worker must realize that assessing suicide risk is no simple matter. There are no direct "if–then" connections. Some risk factors are more lethal than others and must be given more weight or attention. Assessment is a complex, ongoing art, science, and skill that requires workers to be alert, attentive, sensitive, caring, and practiced in attending and responding to verbal, behavioral, situational, and "syndromatic" clues. (The latter is Shneidman's term for constellations of syndromes [Shneidman et al., 1976, p .433].)

Strother (1986) states that suicide is the third most common cause of death among persons between the ages of 15 and 24—accounting for more than 5000 deaths per year. She lists (p. 756) the following risk factors for young people in that age bracket:

1. a family history of alcohol and drug abuse
2. family breakdown (destabilized family situation)
3. symptoms of delinquency, aggression, or depression
4. nonspecific crises such as conflict with parents, peers, or school officials
5. impulsive responses to crisis or loss.

Diekstra and Hawton (1987) cite three categories that contribute to adolescent suicide: (1) physical (biological), (2) mental (psychological), and (3) social (sociological). Of the three, they attribute the greater significance to psychological factors and identify three psychological states as indicative of high risk for adolescent suicide: (1) a negative self-concept, (2) a negative picture/expectancy of relationships with others, and (3) negative expectancies of the future (p. 19). Disruption of family and other relationships and love-object loss are cited as frequent antecedents of suicidal behavior (p. 20).

Some crisis centers and practitioners have developed weighted scales for crisis workers to use in assessing clients' suicide lethality. One such instrument, the Scale for Assessment of Suicidal Potentiality (Battle, 1985), is a checklist containing 121 weighted items in the nine risk categories of (1) demographics, (2) symptoms of behavior, (3) stress, (4) resources outside of self, (5) personal and social history, (6) suicide plan, (7) prior suicidal behavior, (8) suicidal communication, and (9) personality features and other clinical signs. Instruments such as the Battle scale are not meant to be highly precise, but they are quite helpful to crisis workers in evaluating and considering all the factors relevant to a client's total risk level.

Suicide clues.   Most suicidal clients, feeling high levels of ambivalence or inner conflict, either emit some clues or hints about their serious troubles or call for help in some way (Shneidman et al., 1976, pp. 429–440). The clues

some of them serious, some of them gestures; (2) had used a wide variety of drugs in her college years—in fact, she had dropped out of college after two years because of drug use and resulting poor academic performance; (3) had a history of episodes of severe depression, loneliness, hopelessness, and helplessness followed by mood swings to euphoric and deep religious activity and commitment; (4) had been hospitalized numerous times for psychiatric care; (5) had experienced a sense of great loss and grief at the divorce of her parents when she was 22 years old; (6) had recently gone into self-imposed isolation and remorse—cutting herself off from friends, family, and coworkers; (7) was feeling a new sense of meaninglessness related to her career—she had been seeking something that she really chose to do (as opposed to working for her father). In relation to point 7, the crisis worker learned that Deborah had, all her life, sought to both appease and oppose her father; that Deborah now worked as a real estate salesperson in her father's firm; that Deborah had obtained her realtor license to please her father, yet constantly blamed him for keeping her bonded to him; that Deborah had both resented and appreciated the fact that her father planned for her to inherit and manage the lucrative real estate brokerage firm at the time of his retirement; that Deborah had vacillated between gratitude for inheriting a lot of money and security and resentment of her father's dominating her and deciding her career for her. Deborah, in tears, was trembling and in a state of acute anxiety.

CW: So, Deborah, I'm picking up that you're right back again at the very brink of death. How specific is your suicide plan this time, and how close are you today —to doing it?

Deborah: Well, I can see you've zeroed right in. I was halfway hoping you wouldn't ask that. Well, I might as well tell you, I've got it mapped out to a T . . . have had for some time now. I'm just going to end the hurting . . . just end it all. . . .

CW: Deborah, when? And how?

Deborah: Simple . . . easy . . . and smooth! I'm gonna do it with exhaust fumes. And I don't know just when. Soon, though . . . very soon.

The crisis worker was having a difficult time remaining calm. Deborah's risk factors and nonverbal clues were too numerous and too lethal to take a chance on making a contract with her and letting her leave. Over Deborah's verbal protests, the crisis worker took the necessary step of contacting Deborah's regular therapist's consulting psychiatrist. The psychiatrist knew Deborah, had treated her on previous occasions, and agreed to meet Deborah and the worker at the hospital.

The crisis worker had correctly assessed Deborah's lethality and appropriately used directive methods to get her to safety and help. That's about all the crisis worker could do when presented with Deborah's lethal situation. Even though the hospital and psychiatric staff did everything they knew to do to help Deborah, she carried out her plan a few weeks later, following her release from the hospital. She killed herself with exhaust fumes just as she had said she would. All the professionals and crisis workers who had known and cared for Deborah were saddened and felt a deep sense of grief and loss. But they did not blame themselves. Few felt guilt. They vowed to go on working with their living clients and learning to be better helpers. They also participated in the postsuicide mental health team meetings both for their own mental health and for documentation and research, so they would know how to deal more effectively with future Deborahs.

Gertrude, Age 61

Gertrude was an eminent and successful primary school principal who had devoted her life to children and the teaching profession. She was exceptionally capable, hardworking, conscientious, and efficient. She was also compulsive and perfectionistic in her work and personal habits. At age 61, Gertrude faced some life and career decisions that she regarded as catastrophic: (1) she had been cured of TB only to discover she had cancer of the colon, and she could not bear to think about her physician's recommendation to accept early retirement; (2) she felt trapped between the two unacceptable choices of continuing to hold the principalship in her debilitating physical condition and becoming the ex-principal who had been forced into early retirement; and (3) she was totally unprepared to alter her whole identity, which had included serving the students, faculty, parents, community, school, and the teaching profession. Gertrude had no family. She had never married because she had devoted all her energies and talents to education. She came to the crisis worker in desperation. The following dialogue took place some ten minutes into the initial interview.

Gertrude: [*In tears.*] It is so hopeless. Why me? Why has God forsaken me? What have I done to cause me to come to this? I don't think I can bear it. [*Sobs. Pause.*] It's so unfair. I have no choice. [*Sobs.*]

CW: You're feeling hurt, hopeless, and vulnerable—and you're looking for better answers and choices than you've been able to find so far.

Gertrude: [*Still in tears.*] I guess I'm just getting too old and cranky to do this job.

CW: Well, Gertrude, I want you to know that I'm glad you have the courage to discuss it. And I don't view you as being old and cranky. What scares me is the desperation and danger you're feeling. You're feeling that, right now, there are no acceptable choices, but what you'd like to find are some choices other than pain and oblivion in your future.

Gertrude: [*Still in tears; nonverbal clues show that she is experiencing acute fear, anxiety, and hopelessness, and has almost given up.*] There is no future. There are no choices. None. None at all.

CW: Gertrude, it sounds to me like you've considered suicide. I feel a need to know your thinking on this subject.

Gertrude: [*Still in tears.*] Oh God! I've thought about that a lot. Toyed with it a lot. And I'll have to admit that it becomes more appealing all the time.

The crisis worker did not suddenly jump to the conclusion that Gertrude was suicidal. As the crisis interview progressed, more and more of the background clues, verbal clues, and nonverbal clues pointed toward suicide. When Gertrude said, "There is no future," the worker immediately judged that her words and her nonverbal signs of desperation must not be ignored or pushed aside. The alertness and forthright response of the crisis worker provided the pivotal point from which to help start Gertrude on her way out of her desperate course toward oblivion. Crisis counseling was followed by medical and psychiatric referrals. Long-term therapy was required to bring Gertrude from the brink of self-destruction to the point where she could come to accept the unacceptable—medical retirement, life away from the school, and steadily deteriorating physical health. The choices in cases like Gertrude's are never simple or easy. Crisis workers, therapists, and medical professionals cannot completely solve problems in such difficult situations. The best they can do is to listen, assess, care, understand, and intervene in ways as objective and appropriate as humanly possible.

Roy, Age 75

Roy had been a farmer all his life. At age 73 he went into semiretirement, turning his land, equipment, buildings, and livestock over to his two sons, who also were career farmers. One year after he began his semiretirement, his wife died. About a year later, he was despondent and could find no purpose in life even though he was in excellent health and had the good fortune of financial independence. The following dialogue occurred after several minutes in the initial interview.

Roy: Well, I never did think I'd be in here talking to you.

CW: Roy, I can understand that. You're obviously very self-sufficient. I'd be curious to know—just what brought you in to talk today?

Roy: That's just it. Nothing. That is, no one thing. But it's everything too. My world has changed. There's nothing left for me. I'm really not needed anymore.

CW: So it's your whole life situation that brings you here. Any one thing? Any one happening or situation in particular that stands out today to make life so meaningless?

Roy: Well, nothing but just pure loneliness—and the fact that my usefulness is over. All my life is in the past.

CW: It's true that you've accomplished a great deal during your life. Right now it sounds like you're feeling that *all* your life is over. And the fact that you've taken the time to come in to talk about it tells me that you're very serious about it. What's different for you now from, say, six months or a year ago?

Roy: Well, now there's really nothing else to live for. A man's got to have some purpose. I've got nothing to go to—nothing to get up for in the morning.

CW: Then the situation sounds so bad and so hopeless for you that it sounds to me like you're considering ending it all. Are you thinking about killing yourself?

Roy: You bet I am! It's a wonder I'm even here now. I've been close to it many times lately.

The crisis worker followed the usual procedure of attempting to discover the specificity of Roy's plan, the time, place, and so on, as a means of assessing Roy's imminent risk. Roy proved to have a definite plan.

Roy: When I do it, I won't be fooling around. I've got a good, stout rope down there in the barn. It will do the job. No doubt about it. That barn loft is high and those beams are sound. There'll be no way to miss. That'll do the job all right. And it will be early in the morning. If I do it, it'll be soon. It'll be at the end of another one of my long, sleepless nights. I'll be the only one around.

In assessing Roy's responses the worker quickly concluded that he definitely exhibited six of the lethality characteristics that Fujimura, Weis, & Cochran (1985) defined as high-risk factors: (1) the plan was definite and readily accessible, (2) the method was irreversible, (3) there was indication of sleep disruption, (4) support persons would not be around, (5) rescue would not be probable, and (6) the most valued possessions had been disposed of. Also, the crisis worker knew that among men Roy's age there are very few suicide gestures or attempts. Older men are more likely to accomplish the act than to merely attempt it (Shneidman, Farberow, & Litman, 1976). The worker knew that this was a life-or-death situation and that there was little time to act. A person as fiercely independent as Roy would not easily go to see a crisis worker or therapist; that person would more than likely go to the barn and hang himself and be done with it! The worker, who managed to get Roy referred for medical evaluation and long-term psychiatric care, felt that it was fortunate that Roy had come in for help in the first place.

Dennis, Age 88

Dennis had a long, productive, and successful career as a carpenter. He and his wife had reared seven children. Dennis had worked until he was 70 and had remained physically alert and healthy until he was 84, at which time he had had a stroke that paralyzed the right half of his body from head to toe. Following his partial recovery and release from the hospital, he had gradually regained a small percentage of the psychomotor control of the impaired right half of his body. His hearing, which had been getting progressively worse over a number of years, had declined to the point where he had a serious hearing deficit. It had become increasingly difficult for him to communicate. He had become feeble and slow at walking, but he refused to use a cane or a walker. Since his seven children were involved in plying their own careers and rearing their own families, Dennis had become totally dependent on his wife, Millie, age 81. Although his wife was in relatively good health and of sound mental status, the situation had become quite serious. Maintaining the household and providing total care for her husband quickly had become a greater responsibility than she was able to assume.

Dennis became more and more withdrawn; he refused to exercise, he refused to go out of the house except to go to the doctor; he became self-conscious about his unsteady pattern of walking; and he soon began to make statements such as "I'm no good to anyone now," "I should have just passed on instead of being left like I am," "People would be better off without me around," and "Someday I may just take that rifle and end it all." At first his wife, children, and grandchildren attempted to refute him and discount such statements. Finally, Dennis was taken to the family physician, who prescribed medication to deal with his suicidal symptoms. Nothing was done to provide psychiatric, psychotherapeutic, or physical therapy treatment. Dennis became even more withdrawn, he slept most of the time, and he lost interest in much of the family activity.

Following one of his verbal expressions of a wish to die, the crisis worker was summoned for a home visit. The worker began by obtaining permission for a private interview with Dennis. The worker was sensitive to Dennis's hearing loss and also judged by Dennis's body language that Dennis would respond to the crisis worker's sitting close and physically touching him. The worker sat very close to Dennis, took him by the hand, and gently stroked the back side of the impaired but sensitive right hand and arm as they talked. The worker used a very loud, clear, calm, and even voice to talk with Dennis. The worker sought to provide clear, nonthreatening, caring messages combined with the gentle physical stroking. Dennis responded positively. The worker provided long periods of time for Dennis to formulate ideas and speak them. (Family members had rarely waited for Dennis to respond. They would ask him a question and, before he was able to respond, would go on to something else. Dennis felt that they ignored him and that he was being treated like a retarded child.) The worker was able to establish good rapport with Dennis.

CW: [*Loudly, while gently stroking Dennis's arm.*] So you are feeling like you aren't being listened to lately, and you really do miss talking to people.

Dennis: [*Long pause; eyes and facial expression show him formulating a response.*] Yeah. They . . . won't . . . wait . . . for . . . me to finish. Some . . . won't wait . . . for me to start.

CW: What you'd like is for someone to let you talk at your own speed. It bothers you for them to "run off and leave you."

Dennis: [*Long pause; tears in his eyes.*] I . . . guess it's hard . . . for them to . . . to talk to me. I . . . have to have time . . . to get it . . . out.

CW: [*Still gently stroking, looking him in the eyes, and waiting for his responses.*] It makes you feel sad, not to be understood. You really want people to take time to hear what you have to say.

Dennis: [*Tears in his eyes; long pause.*] I guess they . . . don't think . . . I . . . have . . . anything . . . worth saying. I'm . . . so . . . old and stove up . . . guess I'm no account now.

CW: Being, as you say, "stove up" doesn't mean you're worth any less. They tell me you've built lots of this town with your own hands. You've accomplished lots of things in your life, which you must be proud of. Tell me something you've done, which really makes you proud you did.

Dennis: [*Long pause; thoughtful; no tears; smiles.*] I've . . . raised . . . helped raise . . . a bunch of fine children. . . . I've been a good dad . . . a good provider.

CW: [*Still gently stroking.*] That's true, I'm sure. I want you to think back to raising those kids. Think back to the happiest times you had with your growing kids, and just imagine you're back there now. Just take your mind back. Tell me exactly what you're doing with them that makes you feel good—a good daddy.

Dennis: [*Long pause; smile; look of intensity and reminiscence.*] We'd all go down to the . . . swimming hole . . . on Sunday afternoon. . . . We took a basket of . . . of sandwiches . . . and melons . . . and a great big ball. We . . . we played games . . . their mother . . . Millie and I . . . we'd play all kinds of games . . . big ones . . . little ones. . . . All the children . . . running, playing, squealing. . . . Yeah, . . . [*Laughs.*] . . . all sorts of games. . . . We had a time! . . . Millie and I . . . we had some good times with those children . . . had a real good time . . . a good life.

The worker continued using what are called *reminiscence techniques* (Ebersole, 1976a, 1976b). Many interesting facets of Dennis's past were highlighted, remembered, and relished: family, carpentry, social life, travel, hardships. His whole life was reviewed and appreciated. These reminiscence techniques (American Association of Retired People, 1986) have been used quite effectively in working with many elderly people—to strengthen their sense of valuing how their life has been lived. The worker went back to see Dennis several times and used the reminiscence technique during a part of each visit. The worker was able to facilitate several productive strategies to help Dennis: part-time help was hired to assist with the daily care of Dennis; physical therapy was prescribed by the family physician to enhance Dennis's muscular functioning; a counselor provided communications skills that the family members could learn, including verbal and nonverbal skills, delayed responding, and touching; and the crisis worker called in a gerontologist, who taught family members how to use the reminiscence technique with their father. The crisis worker did not ignore the suicide threats that Dennis voiced. Along with reminiscence, Dennis was encouraged to talk about his self-destructive feelings. Finally, the family counselor held a group session concerning the suicide issue, after which Dennis never mentioned it again.

Assessing and responding to cries for help from the elderly are difficult and delicate tasks. They normally involve friends, relatives, and support persons from several age groups and disciplines. Workers aren't always successful. Work with the elderly must invariably take into account their age, physical impairments, experiences, and needs. Even though they are unique, they are reachable, responsive, and appreciative. The crisis worker who visited Dennis made a statement that is typical of those who develop a closeness and rapport with the elderly: "I can truly say that I received much more from Dennis than I gave. I was blessed and enriched by the experience. I think I learned more than he did."

INTERVENTION STRATEGIES

Suicide intervention strategies involve "interrupting a suicide attempt that is imminent or in the process of occurring" (Fujimura et al., 1985, p. 612). Since each person and each problem situation is unique, each suicide situation is also unique. There are no clear, simple strategies that are recommended for every case. In the previous section on counseling, we purposely showed the crisis worker moving from assessing to acting. That is the way crisis intervention works—in a fluid, ongoing, emerging process. We now present an encapsulation of some additional strategies that crisis workers might use in continuing to intervene with the representative clients we have described.

Children and Adolescents

In recent years, suicides of children and adolescents have received increasing attention from the public (Allberg & Chu, 1990; Berman & Jobes, 1991; Kalafat, 1990). Here are some strategies and suggestions for anyone (crisis worker or layperson) who comes into contact with a child or adolescent suspected of being suicidal:

1. Trust your suspicions that the young person may be self-destructive.
2. Tell the person you're worried about him or her, then listen to the person.
3. Ask direct questions, including whether the youngster is thinking about suicide and, if so, has a plan.
4. Don't act shocked at what the youngster tells you. Don't debate whether suicide is right or wrong, or counsel the person yourself if you're not qualified. Don't promise to keep the youngster's intentions a secret.
5. Don't leave the youngster alone if you think the risk of suicide is immediate.
6. If necessary, get help from a competent counselor, therapist, or other responsible adult ("Teenage Suicide," 1985, p. E3).
7. Ensure that the youngster is safe and that the appropriate adults responsible for the youngster are notified and become actively involved with the youngster.
8. Assure the youngster that something is being done, that the youngster's suicidal urges are real, and that, in time, the emergency will pass. Advise the youngster not to expect the urges to disappear right away. Rather, apprise him or her that survival is a step-by-step, day-to-day process; that help is at hand; and that calling for help in a direct manner is necessary whenever the suicidal urge gets strong.

9. Assume an active and authoritarian role as needed to protect the person at risk. The youngster may need such directive action to enable him or her to become sufficiently involved with support persons to resume self-responsibility.

10. After the youngster has apparently resolved the high-risk crisis, monitor progress very closely. Many persons have been known to suddenly commit suicide after they seemed to be renewed and strong. Remember that previously depressed suicidal clients may decide to kill themselves once they gain enough energy to do it. Helping persons must continue to be proactive and involved with suicidal youngsters until the apparent danger has definitely subsided (Fujimura et al., 1985, pp. 612–613).

Crisis workers, counselors, and other adults who work with suicidal youngsters must pay careful attention to clues.

CW: Lester, I asked for this conference because I'm worried about you again. I thought you were doing great! And I hoped you could keep it up, but now, frankly, I'm scared to death for you.

Lester: Oh, I'm OK. Things are going great.

CW: [*In a calm, soft, caring, empathic voice—not a lecturing or agitated tone.*] They may seem OK to you, but what concerns me right now is the amount and direction of energy you're spending lately. Your mother is very upset and puzzled because you've given your stereo.to a friend and the principal is livid because you've picked two fights on the way home from school this week. I've noticed that the last two days in the hallways and cafeteria you've been like an entirely different person. I don't know what's behind these observations, but if these things say what they appear to say, I don't think I can leave here today until I can be sure you're safe. I don't want to wake up in the morning and hear that you're dead!

Lester: It's really not anything you should be worried about. I'm OK, really I am.

CW: [*Soft, empathic vocal tone continued.*] Fine, then you can help me feel OK by discussing with me what's going on, because if these observations are even partially true, your actions have really taken an unusual turn. I just want you to know that the clues I'm picking up spell danger, and that I'm as concerned for you as I've ever been. And I need to know that you're safe, even though you say you're OK. I really care about you.

The crisis worker was confrontive and persistent even though it would have been desirable and comforting to believe that Lester was OK. As it turned out, Lester was indeed on the threshold of suicide again. The important thing was that the worker interpreted Lester's unusual and energetic actions as clues that called for help—whether the client overtly called for help or not. It was also fortunate for Lester that the worker acted directively and decisively to intervene in his life again.

Workers must be alert and proactive in checking out clues and intervening whenever and however needed to stem the suicidal plans of youngsters. Suicidal children and adolescents need to know that adults are available who will respond in mature, sensitive, responsible, caring, and skillful ways

(Crow & Crow, 1987; Curran, 1987; Diekstra & Hawton, 1987; Joan, 1986; Patros & Shamoo, 1989; Pfeffer, 1986; Phi Delta Kappa, 1988). Hunt, Osten, and Teague (1991) found that classroom teachers who are sensitive to the emotional changes in and have a close relationship with youth can be primary identification, support, and referral sources for youth who are suicidal (pp. 20–21). Berman and Jobes (1991) found that suicidal adolescents particularly need empathic therapeutic alliances to help them feel affirmed, valued, and understood. No-suicide agreements, decreased isolation, problem-solving intervention, and availability/accessibility of therapeutic supports were also found to be helpful to teens who are self-destructive (pp. 175–197).

There is some evidence that publicity about children and adolescent suicide completions and media programs depicting factual or fictional suicides have been associated with suicide attempts and completion in geographical areas reached by the publicity (Kalafat, 1990, p. 364). Shaffer et al. (1990) reported that among adolescent suicide attempters, "talking about suicide in the classroom makes some kids more likely to try to kill themselves" (pp. 2153–2155). Thus, "postvention" classroom programs designed for suicide education and prevention may be appropriate for the majority of adolescents who are not currently at risk, but may not be appropriate for the at-risk population.

Kalafat (1990) suggested that the contagion concern can be addressed through several suicide education initiatives: (1) television and other media should emphasize responsible behavior and publicize local services such as hot lines; (2) media educational programming should *not* depict actual or fictional suicide methods or completions; and (3) classroom discussions should emphasize coping and appropriate actions and resources (p. 364). Shaffer et al. (1990) pointed out that educational programming may do little to help high-risk adolescents, such as previous attempters. Instead, for high-risk kids, "consideration should be given to alternative techniques that couple more efficient case identification with individualized evaluation and intervention" (p. 3155).

Adults

Intervention in suicidal adult behavior sometimes raises complex philosophical questions about the individual's right to commit suicide (Zinner, 1985, p. 75). For example, does a terminally ill cancer patient have a right to die with dignity through an act of suicide to avoid prolonged pain and suffering? Also, in institutional settings, the worker should be sensitive to the legal and ethical issues that may arise when one adult intervenes in the suicidal behavior of another (Bernard & Bernard, 1980, 1982).

The following discussion of considerations provides both attitudinal and behavioral guidelines for crisis workers who are involved in suicide work with adult clients. Most of these considerations may also apply to younger populations, but they are particularly applicable to intervening with adults. We have incorporated a number of guidance tips from our own repertory along with those of other contributors (Bernard & Bernard, 1985; Gilliland, 1985; Hersh, 1985; Hipple, 1985; Hipple & Cimbolic, 1979; Hipple & Hipple, 1983).

Considerations for crisis workers.   At the beginning of the interview, the crisis worker must establish a sense of rapport and trust right away in order to create a working relationship and provide clients with an anchor to life. It is also important to begin to reestablish in clients a sense of hope and to diminish their sense of helplessness—to take immediate steps to speak and act on the clients' current pain. The worker will want to look for the hidden messages behind the suicidal behavior, trying to discover what the behavior in its simplest form is saying and to whom. In many instances it is necessary to establish stay-alive contracts that provide clients with some concrete and immediate structure. Courtois (1991) cautions that suicidal lethality contracts must not be imposed on clients. Rather, such stay-alive contracts must be mutually agreed upon by both client and crisis worker.

Another area of importance is to help clients discover their ambivalence; part of them may be oriented toward self-destruction and part toward living. The worker can help clients clarify and understand their inner conflicts.

Always, client safety is primary. Even though confidentiality of the suicidal person's communication is important, confidentiality must be reconsidered if a life is at risk. The crisis worker must consider whether important others need to be contacted to gather information, rally community support, or establish a network of support persons interested in and committed to keeping the client alive.

The crisis worker can use history taking to evaluate the client's developmental background and show how the current suicidal crisis evolved. The worker can also determine whether the crisis is situational or systemic; that is, do the roots go deep into the client's personal history? The worker can be as directive, active, or collaborative as the crisis situation dictates. One point to remember is to follow up on missed appointments. The suicidal person must not be ignored. During the crisis interview itself, the crisis worker must be acutely sensitive to the client's verbal or behavioral cries for help. Ignoring these cries may be interpreted by the client as confirmation of a feeling of worthlessness.

The crisis worker should realize that suicidal behavior is a symptom of complex interactions of biological, psychological, and sociological factors. Many clients will respond to cognitive strategies. The worker may assist those suicidal persons to (1) separate thought from action, (2) reinforce expression of affect, (3) anticipate consequences of action, and (4) focus on precipitating events and constructive alternatives.

Crisis workers must be prepared to provide simple, clear-cut, and appropriate referral sources. Clients may need access to a central telephone number for crisis referral. Clients may need a safe place to stay where overnight observation is available. A repertory of referral resources is a necessity if the crisis worker is to be effective with suicidal clients.

Considerations for community and media.   The community and the local media can be instrumental in helping to stem the tide of loss of life by suicide. Martin, Martin, Barrett-Kruse, and Waterstreet (1988) have documented how the total community's commitment is needed to respond to adolescent suicide and, indeed, how public complacency itself may be a serious risk factor. The channels of public information (newspapers, radio, television, newsletters, and other networks) can be used to educate the total population by communicating the essential information, attitudes, and behaviors needed to deal with suicide. Of particular importance is to get across to the community the message that all suicidal behavior (ideation, gestures, threats, or attempts) can result in completed suicides and thus must be taken seriously.

The community and media can establish and support crisis hotlines and advertise suicide and crisis intervention services as a first line of help for troubled persons. They can also ensure that emergency shelters for safe overnight observation and support are available for persons who find themselves in temporary suicidal or severe crisis situations. Another source of help in almost every community is its religious organizations.

The media can serve as advocates to counter the fears, myths, prejudices, and punitive attitudes that may exist toward suicidal persons and their families. The media can have a positive influence by making frequent use of crisis workers to highlight the realities of suicide and to publicize appropriate ways of preventing and responding to suicide.

Considerations for institutions.   Educational, training, and mental health institutions in the community can do much to prevent and respond to the phenomenon of suicide. A starting point is assessing the existing knowledge and attitudes about suicide in the community. Institutions need (1) to become familiar with research, legal, and ethical issues involved in suicides (Bernard & Bernard 1980, 1982) and to disseminate relevant information to the community and its leaders and (2) to engage in research and exchange of data on suicide prevention and intervention. They can sponsor educational programs and transmit information on suicide awareness, risks, prevention, and intervention to the public, to workplaces, and to community agencies. Crisis workers should play a major role in community education programs (Dunne et al., 1987).

Institutions can provide educational leadership to help reduce suicides. Such leadership might result in providing lectures on potential suicides, risks, indicators, gauging lethality, causes, and so forth, in adult education courses and in instructional areas such as counseling, psychology, social work, sociology, home economics, marriage and family therapy, and others. Institutions can also establish peer support groups of persons who have survived suicidal urges and attempts and who are willing to share their knowledge and experience to help others. To a large degree, institutions can also teach and encourage empathic responses to suicidal persons by family, friends, coworkers, and peers.

One of the most important roles that institutions can play is helping to train volunteers, paraprofessionals, and community support persons to deal with suicidal persons. Suicidal persons may be encountered anywhere at any time. A trained citizenry is a great asset. Institutions can also provide a ready mechanism for the hospitalization of the acutely suicidal person. Institutions responsible for suicidal clients should provide for close follow-up of acute cases after discharge from the hospital—for at least 90 days following the high-risk period. And finally, they should provide appropriate procedures for notifying and dealing with family, associates, and friends who were close to the person who completed the suicide act.

Considerations for family, friends, and associates.   The family, friends, and associates of the suicidal person can do many things to contribute to prevention as well as coping with acts of suicide. They can focus on prevention by correcting the alienated lifestyle that cuts off the suicidal person's connectedness with others. Crisis workers can serve an important educational role by assisting families, friends, and associates to learn about and become attuned to the risk factors, cues, and cries for help that suicidal persons generally display in some way.

Family, friends, and associates can provide the suicidal person with permission to live and accept himself or herself: the suicidal person may need to hear directly that he or she is a person of value and worth and therefore deserves to live. They can also help the suicidal person to gain permission to be human—to accept his or her own fallibility and to give up perfectionism. This may mean that people around the suicidal person must learn to deal with the suicidal person's perception of loss and despair without encouraging helplessness or dependency.

Family, friends, and associates who attend to the many cues we have described can help the suicidal person by genuinely and assertively confronting suicidal issues. For instance, they can watch for the suicidal person's preoccupation with an anniversary date of a significant loss, such as the death of a loved one, and intervene in a directive manner if needed. Finally, significant others can help the survivors cope with suicide after it happens. When bereaved groups cannot get past the shock of the suicide and/or exhibit excessive blame or guilt, crisis workers can meet with them and assist them to deal with their grief over the loss.

Some don'ts.   Hipple (1985) has identified some don'ts of suicide management that also serve to supplement the intervention considerations we have listed:

1. Don't lecture, blame, or preach to clients.
2. Don't criticize clients or their choices or behaviors.

3. Don't debate the pros and cons of suicide.
4. Don't be misled by the client's telling you the crisis is past.
5. Don't deny the client's suicidal ideas.
6. Don't try to challenge for shock effects.
7. Don't leave the client isolated, unobserved, and disconnected.
8. Don't diagnose and analyze behavior or confront the client with interpretations during the acute phase.
9. Don't be passive.
10. Don't overreact. Keep calm.
11. Don't keep the client's suicidal risk a secret (be trapped in the confidentiality issue).
12. Don't get sidetracked on extraneous or external issues or persons.
13. Don't glamorize, martyrize, glorify, or deify suicidal behavior in others, past or present.
14. Don't forget to follow up.

Older Adults

All the strategies for helping suicidal clients, from children through adults, are useful for helping older adults, such as Gertrude, age 61, Roy, age 75, and Dennis, age 88. The crisis worker must keep in mind what research into the age factor among suicidal clients has shown: "In general, for both sexes, the intensity of the wish to kill and the wish to be killed decreases with advancing age, while the intensity of the wish to die increases with age" (Shneidman et al., 1976, p. 165). The research indicates that the percentage of failed attempted suicides decreases with age and the percentage of completed suicides increases with age. It would seem that workers may have fewer second chances at helping persons above 60 than they would normally expect among youths and younger adults.

In intervening with older adults, workers should pay particular attention to all forms of verbal and behavioral clues to suicidal risk. The worker's own silent assessment during the interview helps bring to the forefront a special consideration for dealing with older persons. An excerpt from an interview with Roy, age 75 (showing parenthetical worker self-talk), is one example.

Roy: Well, now there's really nothing else to live for. A man's got to have some purpose. I've got nothing to go to—nothing to get up for in the morning.

CW: ("Wow, he's not fooling! I'm remembering his age, his male image, his having disposed of all his property, his wife's death—it's a wonder he's even in here talking about it. I sense how lethal he may be. I'm thankful he's here. I'd better not take any chances now.") Then the situation sounds so bad and so hopeless for you that it sounds to me like you're considering ending it all. Are you thinking about killing yourself?

Roy: You bet I am! It's a wonder I'm even here now. I've been close to it a good many times lately.

CW: ("I've lucked in again! It's a good thing I know that many of these older folks don't play around too long with gestures.") Roy, that really scares me. How about telling me just how you've been thinking of doing it—the method, I mean.

Once Roy had described a specific and lethal plan, the worker's silent self-talk immediately leaped forward.

CW: ("OK, this is it! Look at all these risk factors! I don't need much more clarity than this. I'm lucky he came in. My immediate goal is to make sure we don't find him swinging by a rope in the barn!") Roy, there are several things that I think you and I can do. Let me assure you that I'm thankful you're here talking to me this way. And I want you to know that I'm ready to start right now, working on some definite things with you to reduce the loneliness, the sleepless nights, and the risks to your life. I want you to know that now that you've reached out to me, I'm returning that reaching hand, and together we will work toward making things safer for you.

[*Dialogue continues.*]

Roy's situation was unique. But it contained similarities to problems experienced by many other older persons. The worker's knowledge of risks associated with Roy's age group and sensitivity to Roy's present emotional functioning were key assessment factors in the helping process. The worker's clear and accurate inner self-talk enhanced and facilitated the intervention and referral.

PREVENTION

It is not really possible or desirable to separate and compartmentalize intervention and prevention. For example, most of the treatment considerations listed in the sections entitled "Counseling Suicidal Clients" and "Intervention Strategies" in this chapter are indeed preventive in thrust. The intent of this section is to augment what we have already emphasized in the name of counseling and intervention.

Crisis workers helping suicidal clients are also primary prevention workers. But prevention is the work of everyone. Effective suicide prevention involves comprehensive educational and communications programs designed to touch, influence, sensitize, and educate every segment of society. Since every segment of society is affected by suicides, effective and pervasive prevention must also involve every segment of society. This means taking suicide out of the closet and publicly dealing with all its dimensions in an honest, realistic, and responsible manner. Post and Osteri (1983) have described how support groups that include all suicidal patients and staff in a day hospital can combine the elements of communication, client-staff trust, safety, stay-alive contracts, personal contacts, and individual responsibility to form an effective suicide prevention program.

All of our institutions, as well as individuals, can contribute to suicide prevention (Morgan, 1981; Pretzel, 1972; Shneidman et al., 1976; Wekstein, 1979). The techniques, strategies, and attitudes reflected throughout this chapter can be used in educational institutions, business and industry, the print media, television, radio, churches and religious organizations, governmental and community agencies, and professional offices to help alleviate the pain and loss of life accompanying the phenomenon of suicide ("Horror of Suicide," 1985). As it is in all other plagues to human existence, prevention is the preferred mode of responding to suicidal people (Crow & Crow, 1987; Morgan, 1981).

Shneidman (1987) developed the technique that is commonly called *psychological autopsy* for the purpose of compiling detailed post mortem mental histories following suicides. Psychological autopsies provide some of the most valuable data we have for suicide prevention. On the basis of nearly 40 years of study, treatment, and prevention work with people who have manifested suicidal tendencies, Shneidman states that suicide "is not a bizarre and incomprehensible act of self-destruction. Rather, suicidal people use a particular logic, a style of thinking that brings them to the conclusion that death is the only solution to their problems. This style can be readily seen, and there are steps we can take to stop suicide, if we know where to look" (p. 56).

The most effective means of suicide prevention appears to be educating the general public, mental health professionals, and agency personnel regarding the characteristic thinking and behavior of suicidal persons.

From a societal standpoint, there are compelling reasons why we must prevent suicides: grief suffered by friends and family, financial burden to family and community, societal stigma attached to the family, loss of human talent, and many others. In our early history the laws and social attitudes about suicide were so punitive and restricted by taboo that little help was available to the potential suicide victim. Even though many of our earlier fears and attitudes persist today, we are beginning to realize that suicide prevention is everybody's business.

According to Shneidman et al. (1976), effective prevention begins with the realization that suicide affects everyone: clients, medical staff, family, friends, rich, poor, educated, uneducated, professional, laypersons, persons of status, and persons who are unknown. The optimal starting point in prevention is to sensitize people at all levels of society to the possibility of suicide potential in everybody (p. 439). Since suicide is "democratic" (p. 438) in its occurrence, we must be democratic in our prevention efforts. Coworkers, family, friends, and colleagues can contribute to prevention by not running scared whenever they encounter symptoms of suicidal intention.

We may be prone to overlook suicide clues in high-status persons such as ministers, physicians, politicians, business executives, and the like. But these individuals need and deserve our help just as much as the poor vagrant. Therefore, we must not hold back from becoming a support person or notifying appropriate others when we encounter individuals of any status who are at risk. For example, we might ordinarily tend to overlook the presuicidal message of a well-known professional. Our fear of becoming involved or of embarrassing that person should not impede our willingness to become assertive in assisting that person to examine options and counter constricted thinking (Goleman, 1985).

Shneidman et al. (1976) have identified four methods to effect a reduction in the suicide rate in this country (pp. 145–146):

1. Increase the acumen for recognition of potential suicide among all potential rescuers.
2. Facilitate the ease with which each citizen can utter a cry for help.
3. Provide resources for responding to the suicidal crisis.
4. Disseminate the facts about suicide.

WHEN PREVENTION FAILS

Hipple (1985), Shneidman (1985, 1987), and others recommend post-intervention programs in the case of clients who commit suicide, to assist the survivors to cope, grieve, understand, and become instruments for prevention of future suicides.

An important point for crisis workers to remember is that we cannot prevent all suicides. What do we do when one of our clients takes his or her own life despite our best efforts? The case of Deborah in this chapter provides at least a partial answer. In her case, even though a number of professionals, laypersons, and support persons had worked and hoped for Deborah's survival, they knew that they could not expect to save all clients. Deborah died, but these professionals had done their best. Knowing that, they vowed to learn, by carefully reviewing the case, how to be successful with future Deborahs who would come into their lives. They did not place blame or wallow in their own guilt.

When crisis workers fail to save a suicidal person, they must go home, renew themselves, be kind to themselves and their associates, get some rest and sleep, and awaken with vigor, sensitivity, and resolve. Never forgetting the Deborahs of the world, they must go forward, ready to meet, understand, and help future clients. Even though crisis workers try as much as they can, they cannot be successful 100% of the time. They are not perfect. They are 100% human.

SUMMARY

The phenomenon of suicide is democratic in that it affects every segment of society. It is a serious problem that is on the rise among all groups, especially youth, but the highest risk group is, and has remained for many years,

Caucasian males over 65. Researchers find few common denominators in their quest to identify suicide risk types and to predict and prevent suicide.

In this chapter we have attempted to strengthen crisis workers' knowledge and competency in dealing with suicidal clients by acquainting them with the dynamics of suicide, counseling techniques, intervention strategies, and prevention considerations. Background information, concepts, and applications were provided. It is assumed that the fundamental concepts of crisis intervention found in Chapter 2, including the six steps emphasized there, are an integral part of working with suicidal clients.

Dynamics of suicide are important because crisis workers who deal with suicidal clients need to know that there are several different types and characteristics of suicide. There are many reasons why people kill or attempt to kill themselves and there are differing points of view about suicide among various social, ethnic, and age groups. A thorough knowledge of the dynamics of suicide should sensitize workers to the causes and signs of suicide. A good many myths about suicide complicate the assessment, counseling, intervention, and prevention that workers attempt to do.

Despite the difficulties, however, we now know enough about suicide to be of great help to suicidal people. A great number of risk factors have been identified that serve as danger signals and help to determine levels of lethality. These risk factors are important criteria for both assessing and acting in the realm of suicide intervention. Workers who are sensitized to the dynamics find that suicidal persons often send out subtle but definite clues and/or cries for help. We have provided suggestions for deciphering and assessing the behavioral cues of potential suicide victims.

Examples of counseling with eight different suicidal clients were included to illustrate several techniques that workers might use. Samples of counseling included a wide variety of problems presented by clients whose ages were 11, 14, 17, 21, 27, 61, 75, and 88. The counseling vignettes clearly demonstrated that crisis workers do not have to be expert suicidologists to help clients who are at risk. Rather, the examples showed crisis workers being reasonably knowledgeable and sensitive to the cues and needs of suicidal people.

The intervention strategies we portrayed showed crisis workers being appropriately assertive, directive, and forceful. In work with suicidal clients, workers cannot be passive. We gathered a list of do's and don'ts that pertain exclusively to intervention with suicidal clients. We discussed a number of special considerations for coping with the act of suicide and with suicidal people. In suicide intervention, workers have to consider many environmental and social factors in addition to attending to client safety.

Several ideas were given on the topic of suicide prevention. There is wide agreement that the most effective means of keeping people from killing themselves is education. This is an enormous task because it involves all of society. Preventive suicide education is a continuous process that involves every institution and every mode of communication. Making the general public aware of the dynamics, dangers, cues, myths, and rudimentary techniques for counseling and intervention is the primary goal of prevention.

REFERENCES

Allberg, W. R., & Chu, L. (1990). Understanding adolescent suicide: Correlates in a developmental perspective. *The School Counselor, 37,* 343–350.

Allen, N. (1977). History and background of suicidology. In C. L. Hatton, S. M. Valente, & A. Rink (Eds.), *Suicide assessment and intervention* (pp. 1–19). New York: Appleton-Century-Crofts.

American Association for Counseling and Development (AACD). (1985, September 5). Congress eyes youth suicide; AACD to testify. *Guidepost,* pp. 1, 5.

American Association of Retired People (AARP). (1986). Reminiscence: Thanks for the memory. *News Bulletin, 27* (8), p. 2.

Battle, A. O. (1985, November). Outpatient management of the suicidal adolescent (paper, presentation, and assessment instrument). Symposium on Suicide in Teenagers and Young Adults, University of Tennessee, College of Medicine, Department of Psychiatry, Memphis.

Battle, A. O. (1991, January 19). *Factors in assessing suicidal lethality.* Paper presented at Crisis Center Preservice Volunteer Training, University of Tennessee, College of Medicine, Department of Psychiatry, Memphis.

Berman, A. L., & Jobes, D. A. (1991). *Adolescent suicide: Assessment and intervention.* Washington, DC: American Psychological Association.

Bernard, J. L., & Bernard, M. L. (1980). Institutional responses to the suicidal student: Ethical and legal considerations. *Journal of College Student Personnel, 21,* 109–113.

Bernard, J. L., & Bernard, M. L. (1982). Factors related to suicidal behavior among college students and the impact of institutional response. *Journal of College Student Personnel, 23,* 409–413.

Bernard, J. L., & Bernard, M. L. (1985). Suicide on campus: Response to the problem. In E. S. Zinner (Ed.), *Coping with death on campus* (pp. 69–83). San Francisco: Jossey-Bass.

Courtois, C. A. (1991, August 16). *The self-destructive person and the suicidal bind.* Paper presented at the 99th annual convention of the American Psychological Association, San Francisco, CA.

Crow, G. A., & Crow, L. I. (1987). *Crisis intervention and suicide prevention: Working with children and adolescents.* Springfield, IL: Charles C Thomas.

Curran, D. K. (1987). *Adolescent suicidal behavior.* New York: Hemisphere Publishing.

Diekstra, R. F. W., & Hawton, K. (Eds.) (1987). *Suicide in adolescence.* Dordrecht, The Netherlands: Martinus Nijhoff Publishers.

Dunne, E. J., McIntosh, J. L., & Dunne-Maxim, K. (Eds.). (1987). *Suicide and its aftermath: Understanding and counseling the survivors.* New York: Norton.

Durkheim, E. (1951). *Suicide.* New York: Free Press.

Ebersole, P. (1976a, August). Reminiscing. *American Journal of Nursing, 76,* 1304–1305.

Ebersole, P. (1976b, November-December). Problems of group reminiscing with institutional aged. *Journal of Gerontological Nursing, 2,* 23–27.

Fujimura, L. E., Weis, D. M., & Cochran, J. R. (1985). Suicide: Dynamics and implications for counseling. *Journal of Counseling and Development, 63,* 612–615.

Getz, W. L., Allen, D. B., Myers, R. K., & Linder, K. C. (1983). *Brief counseling with suicidal persons.* Lexington, MA: D. C. Heath.

Gilliland, B. E. (1985, November). Surviving college: Teaching college students to cope (paper and presentation). Symposium on Suicide in Teenagers and Young Adults, University of Tennessee, College of Medicine, Department of Psychiatry, Memphis.

Goleman, D. (1985, October 8). Painful path to suicide studied: Biological factors play role in pushing people to brink. *The Commercial Appeal,* Memphis, Section A, p. 2.

Hatton, C. L., Valente, S. M., & Rink, A. (1977). *Suicide: Assessment and intervention.* New York: Appleton-Century-Crofts.

Hersh, J. B. (1985, January). Interviewing college students in crisis. *Journal of Counseling and Development, 63,* 286–289.

Hipple, J. (1985). Suicide: The preventable tragedy (mimeographed monograph, 25 pp.). Denton, TX: North Texas State University.

Hipple, J., & Cimbolic, P. (1979). *The counselor and suicidal crisis.* Springfield, IL: Charles C Thomas.

Hipple, J., & Hipple, L. (1983). *Diagnosis and management of psychological emergencies; A manual for hospitalization.* Springfield, IL: Charles C Thomas.

Horror of suicide: Young people have a right to know. (1985, September 24). *The Commercial Appeal,* Memphis, Section A, p. 4 (editorial).

Hunt, R. D., Osten, C., & Teague, S. (1991). Youth suicide: Teachers should know . . . *Tennessee Teacher, 59,* 16–21, 29.

Janosik, E. H. (1984). *Crisis counseling: A contemporary approach.* Belmont, CA: Wadsworth.

Joan, P. (1986). *Preventing teenage suicide: The living alternative handbook.* New York: Human Sciences Press.

Kalafat, J. (1990). Adolescent suicide and the implications for school response programs. *The School Counselor, 37,* 359–369.

Martin, M., Martin, D., Barrett-Kruse, C., & Waterstreet, D. (1988). A community response to an adolescent suicide. *The School Counselor, 35,* 204–209.

Moldeven, M. (1988). *Suicide prevention programs in the Department of Defense: A planning aid for mental health, crisis intervention, and hu-*

man resources administrators in the public and private sectors. Del Mar, CA: Moldeven Publishing.

Morgan, L. B. (1981). The counselor's role in suicide prevention, *Personnel and Guidance Journal, 59,* 284–286.

Motto, J. A. (1978). Recognition, evaluation, and management of persons at risk for suicide. *Personnel and Guidance Journal, 56,* 537–543.

Patros, P. G., & Shamoo, T. K. (1989). *Depression and suicide in children and adolescents: Prevention, intervention, and postvention.* Boston: Allyn & Bacon.

Pfeffer, C. (1986). *The suicidal child.* New York: Guilford Press.

Phi Delta Kappa. (1988). *Adolescent suicide.* Bloomington, IN: Phi Delta Kappa Center on Evaluation, Development, and Research, Hot Topics Series.

Post, J. M., & Osteri, E. M. (1983). Sign-out rounds. *Journal of Psychosocial Nursing and Mental Health Services, 21,* 11–17.

Pretzel, P. (1972). *Understanding and counseling the suicidal person,* Nashville: Abingdon Press.

Ray, L. Y., & Johnson, N. (1983). Adolescent suicide. *Personnel and Guidance Journal, 62,* 131–134.

Roberts, A. R. (Ed.). (1991). *Contemporary perspectives on crisis intervention.* Englewood Cliffs, NJ: Prentice-Hall.

Shaffer, D., Bacon, K., Fisher, P., & Garland, A. (1987). *Review of youth suicide programs.* New York: New York State Psychiatric Institute.

Shaffer, D., Vieland, V., & Garland, A. (1990). Adolescent suicide attempters: Response to suicide-prevention programs, *Journal of American Medical Association, 264,* 3151–3155.

Shneidman, E. S. (1985). *Definition of suicide.* New York: Wiley.

Shneidman, E. S. (1987, March). At the point of no return: Suicidal thinking follows a predictable path. *Psychology Today,* pp. 54–58.

Shneidman, E. S., Farberow, N. L., & Litman, R. E. (1976). *The psychology of suicide.* New York: Aronson.

Slaikeu, K. A. (Ed.). (1990). *Crisis intervention: A handbook for practice and research.* Boston: Allyn & Bacon.

Strother, D. B. (1986, June). Suicide among the young. *Phi Delta Kappan,* 756–759.

Teenage suicide (1985, September 22). *The Commercial Appeal,* Memphis, Section E, pp. 1, 3.

Tidewater Psychiatric Institute's SOS sessions help "victims" left behind after a loved-one's suicide (1985, July). *Network* (employee publication of National Medical Enterprise),*15,* p. 3.

Toughy, W. (1974, October 25). World health agency zeros in on suicide. *Los Angeles Times,* pp. 1–3.

Wekstein, L. (1979). *Handbook of suicidology.* New York: Brunner/Mazel.

Zinner, E. S. (Ed.). (1985). *Coping with death on campus.* San Francisco: Jossey-Bass.

CLASSROOM EXERCISES
The Case of Tom

Tom, his wife, Sheila, and his daughter Renee (age 7) live in a small town surrounded by a large agricultural area. Tom is employed as a heavy equipment operator. He likes the outdoors, particularly hunting, and he prides himself on being macho. He was an excellent high school athlete and could have gone to a small college on a football scholarship. But he took a job working for his father and an uncle, married Sheila (who had been his classmate and the high school homecoming queen), and obligated himself with a large mortgage on a home next door to his parents. Tom began to drink heavily, drive fast cars, frequently take risks on the highways, get into fights at taverns, come home late at night, and neglect his physical health. He felt remorseful, guilty, depressed, and suicidal following each fling at a tavern. Sheila and her supervisor at work repeatedly attempted to persuade Tom to see a therapist. Sheila finally prevailed upon Tom to call the tricounty crisis line after she walked into their bedroom at 7:30 PM Saturday and discovered him preparing to shoot himself in the head with his deer rifle. The volunteer crisis worker received the call from Tom later that evening.

Tom: [*In a fearful, tense, and anxious voice.*] I wouldn't have called, but my wife insisted. She caught me trying to shoot myself tonight. Now I'm scared as hell. She sort of demanded that I get help.

CW: Tom, I'm glad you called. You did the right thing when you called, because you can be helped, and I want us to start right now. I can hear the tenseness in your voice. What I want to do first is for you to stay on the line, sit down, and tell me what's happening in your life right now—in the past day or so—that's brought you so close to killing yourself. That's what I want to know first.

Tom: Well, everything. All these pressures. Everybody expecting big things from me, and I'm not really worth a shit! My wife and kid would be better off if I was out of the way, and I would be too. I ain't the happy-go-lucky guy I look like on the surface.

CW: So Tom, you're really down; you've had a very close call, and you're frightened. What happened to cause the stress at this time?

Tom: Well, it's a buildup of lots of things. I'm getting nowhere on a treadmill, And yesterday—it just hit me—I realized I'm a nothing. A dependent kid in a man's clothing. One of my friends I went to high school with has his MBA. Another one owns a car dealership. I'm still working for my daddy—can't get away from Mamma. I'm a dud—a nobody. And I'm stuck. A nobody, going nowhere.

CW: So you're trying yourself, sentencing yourself, and you've nearly executed yourself because you're struck—and you're realizing that what you're really wanting is to be in a successful career, independent from your folks. And it really hurts when you face it head on. You're feeling powerless right now.

Tom: That's it. And Sheila deserves a better man than that! I'm stuck, so she's stuck with me, and I ain't much to look at.

I. Simulated Telephone Interview

Generate a role play to carry the interview forward, with a volunteer taking the role of Tom and another volunteer taking the role of the crisis worker. Place two chairs back to back in the middle of the room to simulate the telephone interview. An audio tape recording of the interview should be made. To make it realistic, Tom and the crisis worker must not be able to see each other. Continue the simulated telephone call with the objective of taking Tom through the six-step crisis counseling model described in Chapter 2. If possible, obtain a realistic commitment from Tom not to kill himself without first meeting with the crisis worker, going to a hospital, or going directly to a therapist. If the person taking the role of the crisis worker gets stuck, have someone else take over and continue the telephone counseling. When the simulated telephone session has been completed, convene the whole group for discussion and suggestions. Time should be taken by the role players to disassociate themselves from the characters they have portrayed during the role play. Here are some questions to facilitate discussion:

1. What were the advantages and drawbacks of the lack of visual contact between the crisis worker and Tom?
2. If this client-worker simulation were repeated, what could you do to improve upon the first session?
3. What other strategies could the worker use?
4. What other alternatives might the worker help Tom to explore?
5. What feelings (frustration, stress, and so on) were experienced by members of the group who were observers?
6. What are the implications and suggestions from the group with respect to helping suicidal clients who call on crisis hot lines?

II. Interview, Take Two

Listen to the tape recording of the simulated telephone interview. Two new volunteers will now repeat the exercise, with the group again considering all six questions. Compare the tape recording of the two sessions.

III. Postintervention Meeting: The Psychological Autopsy

Suppose that the entire group were the tricounty crisis center staff and volunteer workers in a meeting called a week following the telephone interview. The purpose of the meeting is to deal with the death of Tom, who shot himself the following Friday, despite the best efforts of the center, support persons, and other intervention and referral resources. Make a list of the points that need to be addressed and discuss the issues that need to be brought before the combined group. All participants should have opportunities to express their feelings and concerns. Make a list of actions the center might want to take as a result of the experience with Tom.

CHAPTER 5

Posttraumatic
Stress Disorder

If you have ever been in a war, been physically or sexually abused, lived through a tornado or an earthquake, been involved in a bad accident, or experienced a host of other traumas that you were completely unprepared for, this chapter has much to say to you as a consumer of mental health services. If you are aspiring to the mental health professions as an occupation, you will find that posttraumatic stress disorder (PTSD) is coupled to a variety of other mental health problems and should be suspected as a possible agent. While we will speak to immediate intervention after a trauma in Chapter 13, we concern ourselves in this chapter with the long-term residual effects of trauma on survivors.

BACKGROUND

Psychic trauma is a process initiated by an event that confronts an individual with an acute, overwhelming threat (Freud, 1917/1963). When the event occurs, the inner agency of the mind loses its ability to control the disorganizing effects of the experience and disequilibrium occurs. The trauma tears up the individual's psychological anchors, which are fixed in a secure sense of what has been in the past and what should be in the present (Erikson, 1968). When a traumatic event occurs that represents nothing like the security of past events, and the individual's mind is unable effectively to answer basic questions of how and why it occurred and what it means, a crisis ensues. The event propels the individual into a traumatic state lasting for as long as the mind needs to reorganize, classify, and make sense of the traumatic event. Then and only then does psychic equilibrium return (Furst, 1978).

If the individual is able effectively to integrate the trauma into conscious awareness and organize it as a part of the past (as unpleasant as the event may be), then homeostasis returns, the problem is coped with, and the individual continues to travel life's rocky road. If the event is not effectively integrated and is submerged from awareness, then the probability is high that the initiating stressor will reemerge in a variety of symptomological forms months or years after the event. When such crisis events are caused by the reemergence of the original unresolved stressor, they fall into the category of delayed or posttraumatic stress disorder (PTSD).

PTSD is a newborn compared with the other crises we have examined, at least in regard to achieving official designation as such. To understand why this is so, read the following description of an imaginary computer built about 1966. The computer is called the 11-Bravo.

> **11-Bravo:** Military service computer. Basic motherboard installed at Ft. Leonard Wood, Parris Island, and other military programming facilities. Subroutines installed for specialized combat modes at Ft. Benning, Little Creek, and other specialized military programming facilities. Set to run basic and specialized offensive combat files on command. Activated Republic of South Vietnam 1966–1974. Alternate, nonfunctional hacker programs not designed for this computer were emplaced in some 11-Bravos at destination. Surplused after one year run time Southeast Asia. *Warning! Some 11-Bravos have not been deactivated and remain combat operational!* If your family has come into possession of an 11-Bravo that refuses to run on standard civilian mode, take it to the nearest Vietnam Veterans Center immediately for reprogramming.

Our mythical 11-Bravo (military parlance for a combat infantryman) is the major reason that PTSD finally found its way into the third edition of the *Diagnostic and Statistical Manual of Mental Disorders* (DSM-III) of the American Psychiatric Association (1980) as a classifiable and valid mental disorder.

However, PTSD has been in existence for a long time. Probably the first written account of a person who suffered at least the acute version of this disorder was that of Samuel Pepys, the noted diarist of 17th-century England. His diary's account of the Great London Fire of 1666 and his agitated mental state long after the fire would admirably fit the diagnostic criteria listed in DSM-III for PTSD (Daly, 1983). The antecedents of what has been designated as PTSD first came to the attention of the medical establishment in the late 19th and early 20th centuries. Two events serve as benchmarks.

First, with the advent of rail transportation and subsequent train wrecks, physicians and early psychiatrists began to encounter in accident victims trauma with no identifiable physical basis. Railway accident victims of this type became so numerous that a medical term, *railway spine,* became an accepted diagnosis. In psychological parlance, the synonymous term *compensation neurosis* came into existence for invalidism suffered as a result of such accidents (Trimble, 1985, pp. 7–10). Concomitantly, Freud formulated the concept of *hysterical neurosis* to describe trauma cases. He documented symptoms of warded-off ideas, denial, repression, emotional avoidance, compulsive repetition of trauma-related behavior, and recurrent attacks of trauma-related emotional sensations (Breuer & Freud, 1895/1955).

Second, the advent of modern warfare in World War I and World War II, with powerful artillery and aerial bombardment, generated terms such as *shell shock* and *combat fatigue* to attempt to explain the condition of traumatized soldiers who had no apparent physical wounds. Various hypotheses were proposed to account for such strange maladies (Trimble, 1985, p. 8), but Freud (1919/1959) believed that the term *war neurosis* more aptly characterized what was an emotional disorder that had nothing to do with the prevailing medical notion of neurologically based shell shock.

The United States Medical Service Corps came to recognize combat fatigue in World War II and the Korean War as a treatable psychological disturbance. The treatment approach was that combat fatigue was invariably acute and treatment was best conducted as quickly and as close to the battle lines as possible. The idea was to facilitate a quick return to active duty. The prevailing thought was that time heals all wounds, and that little concern needed to be given to long-term effects of traumatic stress. Such has not been the case (Archibald, Long, Miller, & Tuddenham, 1962). Indeed, a notable proponent of establishing the Vietnam Veterans Centers, Dr. Arthur Blank, ruefully commented that when he was an army psychiatrist in Vietnam he felt there would be no long-term difficulties for veterans (MacPherson, 1984, p. 237).

Although PTSD can and does occur in response to the entire range of natural and man-made catastrophes, it was the debacle of Vietnam that clearly brought PTSD to the awareness of both the human services professions and the public. Through a combination of events and circumstances unparalleled in the military history of the United States, veterans who returned from that conflict began to develop a variety of mental health problems that had little basis for treatment in the prevailing psychological literature. This combination of events and circumstances had insidious and long-term consequences that were not readily apparent to either the victims or human services professionals who attempted to treat them. Misdiagnosed, mistreated, and misunderstood, military service personnel became known to a variety of social services agencies that included the police, mental health facilities, and unemployment offices (MacPherson, 1984, pp. 207–330; pp. 651–690).

DYNAMICS OF PTSD

Diagnostic Categorization

PTSD is a complex and diagnostically troublesome disorder. The *Longman Dictionary of Psychology and Psychiatry* and DSM-IIIR provide an encapsulated review of the problem. This is Longman's definition of PTSD (Goldenson, 1984, p. 573):

> An anxiety disorder produced by an uncommon, extremely stressful life event (e.g., assault, rape, military combat, flood, earthquake, death camp, torture, car accident, head trauma, etc.) and characterized by (a) reexperiencing the trauma in painful recollections or recurrent dreams or nightmares, (b) diminished responsiveness (emotional anesthesia or numbing), with disinterest in significant activities and with feelings of detachment and estrangement from others, and (c) such symptoms as exaggerated startle responses, disturbed sleep, difficulty in

concentrating or remembering, guilt about surviving when others did not, and avoidance of activities that call the traumatic event to mind.

The first diagnostic description of PTSD as an identifiable malady occurred in 1980 in the third edition of the *Diagnostic and Statistical Manual of Mental Disorders* (DSM-III) of the American Psychiatric Association. It has since been updated in the 1987 revision of DSM-III (DSM-IIIR). To be identified as having PTSD, a person must meet a number of the following conditions and symptoms (American Psychiatric Association, 1987):

First, the person will have experienced an event that is outside the range of usual human experience and that would be markedly distressing to almost anyone. Examples are a serious threat to one's life or physical integrity; serious threat or harm to one's children, spouse, or other close relatives and friends; sudden destruction of one's home or community; or seeing another person who has been or is being seriously injured or killed.

Second, the traumatic event is persistently reexperienced in at least one of the following ways:

1. recurrent and intrusive distressing recollections of the event.
2. recurrent nightmares of the event.
3. flashback episodes that may include all types of sensory hallucinations or illusions that cause the individual to dissociate from the present reality and act or feel as if the event were recurring.

Stimuli that in some way resemble the past event may precipitate the reexperiencing. Such stimuli may range from the anniversary of the event to a smell associated with it.

Third, the person persistently avoids such stimuli through at least two of the following ways:

1. attempts to avoid thoughts or feelings associated with the trauma.
2. tries to avoid activities or situations that arouse recollections of the trauma.
3. has an inability to recall important aspects of the trauma.
4. has markedly diminished interest in significant activities.
5. feels detached and removed emotionally and socially from others.
6. has a restricted range of affect by numbing feelings.

Fourth, the person will have persistent symptoms of increased nervous system arousal that were not present before the trauma, as indicated by at least two of the following problems:

1. difficulty falling or staying asleep.
2. irritability or outbursts of anger.
3. difficulty concentrating on tasks.
4. constantly being on watch for real or imagined threats that have no basis in reality (hypervigilance).
5. exaggerated startle reactions to minimal or nonthreatening stimuli.

6. physiologic reactivity upon exposure to events that symbolize or resemble some aspect of the trauma such as a person who was in a tornado starting to shake violently at every approaching storm.

Young children too may be symptomatic of these conditions and also have a sense of a foreshortened future in which they see themselves meeting an early death with no marriage, career, or children. Children may also regress behaviorally and lose recently acquired developmental skills such as toilet training or language skills. Their play activities may be overly repetitious and demonstrate themes or aspects of the trauma.

Finally, for a diagnosis of PTSD, duration of the foregoing symptoms must be for at least one month. Delayed onset is specified if the start of symptoms is at least six months after the trauma (American Psychiatric Association, 1987, pp. 247–251). It should be readily apparent from the conditions needed for a diagnoses of PTSD that it is an extremely serious condition. Further, neither the Longman definition nor the DSM-IIIR criteria begin to depict all of the consequences and effects of the disorder that assail the individual and ripple out to significant others in the victim's life.

Conflicting Diagnoses

Given the wide variety of behaviors that characterize the disorder, it is not uncommon for those who suffer from PTSD to have companion diagnoses of anxiety, depressive, organic mental, and substance use disorders (American Psychiatric Association, 1980, p. 237). Further, because of presenting symptoms, PTSD may be confused with adjustment, paranoid, somatoform, and personality disorders. Because of the symptomatology presented, Vietnam veterans with PTSD could be and in most instances were viewed by human services professionals as being inadequate personality types or having long-term character disorders. Very few of the symptoms of PTSD are unique to the disorder. Thus, accurate diagnoses requires careful examination of the sequencing and relationship of presenting problems prior to and after the trauma. Diagnosis of the problem is confounded even more because onset from the time of the stimulating trauma is so variable. Both human services workers and people closely related to victims may find the disorder hard to understand, particularly the delay of onset (Scurfield, 1985, pp. 221–226.) Thus, diagnosis and treatment of PTSD are complicated because there are few "pure" cases and few symptoms are unique to the disorder (Atkinson, Sparr, & Sheff, 1984).

The Question of Preexisting Psychopathology

Being a victim of crime, war, or other types of human cruelty is not the equivalent of being mentally ill. Vietnam veterans who early on sought help from Veterans Administration (VA) hospitals were misdiagnosed or thought to have some preexisting psychopathology or character disorder.

As a result, they were revictimized by a bureaucratic and rigidly conservative mental health system that added psychic insult to psychic injury (Ochberg, 1988, p. 4). It is not surprising that many veterans are rabidly critical of their case handling by the VA. Happily, this state of affairs has changed significantly both in VA hospitals and the armed services. However, there are still many mental health professionals and members of the victims' support system who continue to believe that victims of PTSD might actually be suffering from some other inherent or preexisting malady.

Although there are undoubtedly some people who are more predisposed to stress than others, there is little evidence to suggest that PTSD is activated because of some preexisting psychopathology (Wilson, Smith, & Johnson, 1985, pp. 142–172). Several years ago the collapse of a concrete walkway in a crowded hotel gave us a prime example of how one event may suddenly produce PTSD symptoms. Biographical data gathered following the Kansas City Hyatt Regency skywalk disaster revealed that few survivors had character disorders prior to the event. Yet many were suffering from a variety of presenting symptoms six months after the event itself (Wilkinson, 1983). White (1989) found the same result in a study of burn victims suffering PTSD symptoms. The overwhelming majority of the victims had no past psychiatric history.

Probably the best summing statement about who will and who will not manifest PTSD was made by Grinker and Speigel (1945) in their study of World War II veterans. They concluded that no matter how strong, normal, or stable a person might be, if the stress were sufficient to cross that particular individual's threshold, a "war neurosis" would develop. In short, susceptibility to PTSD is a function of several factors: genetic predisposition, constitution, personality make-up, past life experiences, state of mind, phase of maturational development at onset, social support system before and after the trauma, and content and intensity of the event (Boman, 1986; Foy, 1987; Furst, 1967; Green & Berlin, 1987; Kelman, 1945; Moses, 1978).

Physiological Responses

Exhortations by significant others to victims and survivors of traumatic events to "Get it out of your head!" while fruitless, have a good deal of physiological validity. Researchers have discovered that neurotransmitters, hormones, cortical areas of the brain, and the nervous system play a much greater role in PTSD than was previously suspected (Berga & Girton, 1989; Bourne, 1970; Bower, 1981; Mason, Giller, Kosten, & Harkness, 1988; Ornitz & Pynoos, 1989; Shalev, Attias, Bleich, & Shulman, 1988; Vander-Kolk, 1983, 1984, 1988; Walton, 1985). The underlying thesis is that the brain is much more a "wet" hormonal gland than a "dry" cybernetic computer (Bergland, 1985).

When a person is exposed to severe stress, neurotransmitters, hormones, and specific cortical functions designed to deal with the emergency are activated (Grinker & Speigel, 1945; Selye, 1976). While cessation of the traumatic event may remove the person from danger and no longer require the body's system to function on an emergency basis, if the stress is prolonged, the nervous system may continue to function in an elevated and energized state as if the emergency were still continuing (Burgess-Watson, Hoffman, & Wilson, 1988). These changed physiological states are important because they not only cause individuals extreme physical and psychological duress long after the traumatic event but also imply why people do not "get over" PTSD.

Affective State Dependent Retention

Changed physiological functioning due to traumatic stimuli is important as a building block in Bower's (1981) hypothesis of *affective state dependent retention*. Bower has proposed that since the traumatic event was stored in memory under completely different physiological (increased heart rate, higher adrenal output) and psychological (extreme fright, shock) circumstances, different mood states will markedly interfere with recollection of specific cues of the event. Therefore, the important elements of the memory that need exposure in order to promote anxiety reduction are not accessible in the unaroused state (Keane, Fairbank, Caddell, Zimmering, & Bender, 1985, p. 266) and can only be remembered when that approximate state is reintroduced by cues in the environment (Keane, 1976; Weingartner, Miller, & Murphy, 1977). Thus, the notion that a victim of PTSD can "just forget" or adopt a "better, more positive attitude" does little to effect change in the victim (Keane et al., 1985, p. 266). This proposal has important implications for treatment, particularly with respect to returning the individual to as close an approximation to the event as possible.

Incidence

If PTSD has been with us for so long, what made it finally surface with such profound impact? Quoted in MacPherson (1984, p. 224), Blank states "Long term presence of stress reactions is not unique. They isolated that with World War II veterans. What is unique, however, about Vietnam veterans and stress is the long term persistence in large numbers." The numbers of returning Vietnam veterans that were having some kind of personality disorder went far beyond what statistics would predict. Although a definite number can't be given, various surveys have indicated that approximately half of the 3 million service personnel who served in Vietnam have severe psychological problems (Figley, 1978). Polls taken on selected samples of veterans indicated that from 44% to 61% still have symptoms indicating PTSD and 17% are fully classifiable as PTSD cases (DeFazio, 1978; Fischer, Boyle, & Bucuvalas, 1980). A best estimate indicates that about 800,000 veterans of Vietnam manifest symptoms of PTSD including estimates ranging from 33% to 60% of all combat veterans (Brende & Parson, 1985, p. 1).

Residual Impact

People's basic assumptions about their belief in the world as a meaningful and comprehensible place, their own personal invulnerability, and their view of themselves in a positive light account to a great extent for their individual manifestations of PTSD (Figley, 1985b, pp. 401–402). Even in the most well-integrated people, who have excellent coping abilities, good rational and cognitive behavior patterns, and positive social support systems, residual effects of traumatizing events linger.

An outstanding example of such residual effects is the experience of a retired Marine captain who had seen extensive field duty as a combat infantryman in Vietnam in 1968. The anecdote he related typifies the residual effects in an individual who is psychologically well integrated, is securely employed in a professional job, has a tightly knit, extended family support system, and on the whole enjoys life and has a positive outlook on it.

Chris: I had just gotten home from work late one summer evening. The kids had decided to camp out in the woods down by the creek. A thunderstorm was rolling in and I decided I'd better go down and check on them to see if they were packed in for the night. It had started to rain pretty heavily and there was a lot of thunder and lightning. I pulled on a poncho and got a flashlight, crossed the road, and went into the woods. I don't suppose it was 200 yards to where the kids were camped. Now, I'd grown up running those woods, so I knew it like the back of my hand. However, once I got into the woods things kinda went haywire. I immediately thought, "Get off the trail or you'll get the whole platoon zapped." I slipped off the path and became a part of the scenery. Every sense in my body went up to full alert. I was back in Nam again operating with my platoon and I was on a natural, adrenalin high. Time and place kinda went into suspended animation and I eased through the woods, kinda like standing off and watching myself do this, knowing it was me, but yet not me too. The last thing I remember before walking into the clearing where the kids had their tent set up was that we could have ambushed the hell out of that place. I don't harp and brood on Nam, put it behind me after I got out of the Corps, but that night sure put me in a different place than central Indiana, July 1984. I just couldn't believe that would ever happen. It's a bit unnerving.

Importance of Trauma Type

Catastrophes, when viewed by the public, tend to fall into one category: bad. However, one of the interesting phenomena of PTSD is that there is a marked distinction between natural and man-made catastrophes. Acts of God create far fewer victims of PTSD than do man-made ones. Man-made acts of trauma create even more victims of PTSD when the trauma directly affects the social support system of the family. Children of murdered parents, Holocaust survivors, hostages, raped women, and victims of incest are all strong potential candidates for PTSD. In their study of 26 incest victims, Donaldson and Gardner (1985) found that all but one met clear diagnostic criteria for PTSD (p. 361).

Like Samuel Pepys, survivors of uncommissioned man-made disasters such as the breaking of the Buffalo Creek dam and commissioned trauma like the Chowchilla bus kidnapping clearly carry high potential for PTSD. (The Buffalo Creek disaster occurred when a coal company retainer dam broke during a series of heavy rainstorms. The resulting flood wiped out the residents of the Buffalo Creek valley in West Virginia. The bus kidnapping occurred in the late 1970s when a Chowchilla, California, school bus carrying elementary and secondary school children was hijacked at gunpoint. The children were taken from the bus, driven to a buried truck trailer, and locked in it.) What makes these events so particularly terrible is that they would seem to be tragedies that should not have happened, responsibility for them can be quickly placed, and they clearly violate accepted standards of moral conduct (Figley, 1985a, pp. 400–401). Thus, there exists in any man-made catastrophe the likelihood of posttraumatic psychological problems.

Vietnam: The Archetype

Although the subject matter of this chapter relates to catastrophes of all types, it is still the experience of Vietnam survivors that best manifests what the chapter is about. This is true not only because of the large numbers of Vietnam vets presenting PTSD but also because the conditions necessary to activate PTSD are nowhere more clearly evident. In a comparative analysis of PTSD among various trauma survivor groups, Wilson, Smith, and Johnson (1985) isolated a number of variables that were hypothesized as predisposing to PTSD: degree of life threat, degree of bereavement, speed of onset, duration of the trauma, degree of displacement in home continuity, potential for recurrence, degree of exposure to death, dying, and destruction, degree of moral conflict inherent in the situation, role of the person in the trauma, and the proportion of the community affected. They compared these variables in a variety of trauma survivor groups: Vietnam combat veterans as well as victims of rape, auto accident, armed robbery, natural disasters, divorces, life-threatening illness of a loved one, family trauma, death of a significant other, multiple trauma, and a control group. Veterans were significantly affected in seven of the ten dimensions, with rape victims a distant second in terms of number of predisposing variables present. When the data were transformed to fit precise PTSD criteria, all trauma groups were significantly different from the control groups (pp. 142–172). In plain words, the data suggest that one could not experience a catastrophic event more likely to produce PTSD than Vietnam.

Why was this? Although any war could be construed to produce many PTSD symptoms, the rules of war got changed in Vietnam. First, the average age of the soldier in Vietnam was 19.2, as opposed to 26.0 in World War II (Brende & Parson, 1985, p. 19). Whatever basic training might program into our mythical 11-Bravo computer, a 19-year-old psychologically immature soldier was not mentally prepared for the psychic trauma that awaited him in Vietnam (MacPherson, 1984, pp. 62–63). We'll list a few elements of that trauma.

Hypervigilance.   In Vietnam, there was no front line and no relief from constant vigilance. A 365-day combat tour was exactly that. In comparison to World War II troops, who might be in acute combat situations for a few days or weeks and then be pulled off the line, Vietnam "grunts" spent extended periods of time in the field, and even when they were in a base camp resting for another "hump" in the "bush," they had to be alert for rocket attacks and combat assaults on their position. Hypervigilance became an ironclad rule of survival. Listen to Billie Mac, a composite character of many combat veterans we have interviewed, who will be followed throughout this chapter.

Billie Mac: I was 18 when the plane set down at Da Nang. The crew chief told us to hit the ground running because Da Nang was under a rocket attack. I was scared stiff. Well, Da Nang was heaven, rockets and all, to what later happened. It got a lot, lot worse than that.

Lack of goals.   No territory was ever "won," so there was no concrete feeling of accomplishment. There was a feeling of betrayal by combat troops over a war that had no fixed goals for winning and a command structure that was waging a war of attrition, with "body counts" being the primary way of judging whether a mission was successful (Lifton, 1974; MacPherson, 1984, p. 58).

Billie Mac: We swept that one village at least a half dozen times. Sometimes we'd dig in and dare the NVA to hit us and they did. We lost a half dozen guys in that pesthole. For what? For nothin'. We gave it up and they moved right back in.

Victim/victimizer.   It further compounded the virulent psychological milieu of Vietnam that veterans, unlike most individuals who suffer from PTSD, played two roles—that of victim and that of victimizer. Because both enemies and allies were Vietnamese, a soldier could not distinguish friend from foe, nor could vigilance be relaxed around women or children because of their potential lethality. Because the enemy was Asian and had extremely different cultural values from Americans, it was relatively simple to dehumanize the killing or the maiming of them, particularly when troops saw such things done to their comrades. The nasty way guerrilla war is fought brought out brutality on both sides, and incidents that would normally be considered morally repugnant were committed in the name of staying alive and getting even (Lifton, 1974). Shifts of role from victim to aggressor could occur in seconds (Brende & Parson, 1985, p. 96).

Billie Mac: I couldn't imagine killing a kid or woman. That was true until our medic tried to take care of a kid covered with blood. We all thought he was wounded. When John went over to the dink, he opened up his arms and had a grenade. Blew him and the medic away. Kill them after that? You bet!

Bonding, debriefing, and guilt.   The way the armed services filled units had much to do with lack of a support system within the service itself. Personnel replacements were parceled piecemeal into units. Although this method put rookies with veterans, it was not the best way to bond a unit together. The rotation system also took its psychological toll. Each person did a 365-day tour. "Thirty-two days and a wake-up" or a "one-digit midget" became the watchword for being close to the end of a one-year tour in Vietnam. The stress of being "short" caused men to become very self-preservative and immobilized. Units as a whole were never moved out of combat, and a man who entered combat singly returned singly without benefit of debriefing time. The war was essentially fought in patrol and platoon actions. It was a loner's war, and the soldier who fought alone went home alone (MacPherson, 1984, pp. 64–65). One day a man might be sweating out an ambush in the jungle and two days later be sitting on his front porch back home.

It is no great surprise that returning soldiers who had no transition period from Vietnam to the United States were viewed as "different" and "changed" by their relatives (Brende & Parson, 1985, pp. 48–49). Such rapid transitions out of life-threatening situations, both for the rest and recreation and for DEROS (Date of Expected Return from Overseas), left many with survivor's guilt (Speigel, 1981). They were glad to be out of Vietnam, but felt guilty of betrayal for leaving comrades behind; or they took responsibility when they were away from their units and friends were hurt or killed (MacPherson, 1984, p. 237).

Billie Mac: It was inside of a week from jungle to home. My folks thought it was pretty weird because I put my fatigues on and slept in the woods. I just couldn't take being confined in that house. I had to be able to move. I kept thinking about the guy who took my place as squad leader, Johnson. He was a screw-off. I knew he was gonna get somebody wasted. I needed to be there, but I sure didn't want to be. I immediately got drunk and stayed that way for a long time.

Civilian adjustment.   The rapid change from intense alertness in order to preserve one's life to trying to readjust to a humdrum society made many question where the "real world" was. Further, the returnee's basic belief system would be quickly jarred when, upon his arrival home, he would be greeted with insensitivity and hostility for having risked his life for his country (Brende & Parson, 1985, p. 72). Veterans would quickly find that for all the ability they showed in making command decisions of life-or-death importance and the authority they had over expensive equipment in Vietnam, the onus of having been there relegated them to civilian jobs far below their capabilities (MacPherson, 1984, p. 65).

Billie Mac: Any job I could get stunk. They were all menial and they acted like they were doing me a favor. Hell! I'd made a lot bigger and smarter decisions than anybody I ever had as a boss.

Substance abuse.   The ease with which soldiers could obtain alcohol and drugs to numb themselves and escape mentally from the reality of Vietnam had severe consequences, both in addiction upon return and in the public's growing misconception that veterans were all "drug-crazed baby killers" and were to be shunned because they were too erratic and undependable (Brende & Parson, 1985, p. 72; MacPherson, 1984, pp. 64–65, 221–222).

Billie Mac: Yeah, I drank. Yeah, I shot kids. I drank mainly to try to forget about shooting kids. Anybody who hadn't been there could never understand.

Attitude.   The time period during which a vet served in Vietnam seems to be highly correlated with PTSD. Historically the war can be divided into trimesters. Anyone serving in Vietnam during the last two trimesters, from the time of the Tet offensive to the wind-down in the war, would have, from a psychological standpoint, a much greater reason to question the purpose of being there than those who had served early on. The prevailing attitude of "Nobody can win, so just concentrate on surviving" cynicism was in direct opposition to the "Save a democracy from the perils of communism" idealism of the first trimester (Laufer, Yager, & Grey-Wouters, 1981).

Antiwar sentiment.   The impact of the antiwar sentiment veterans met on their return home cannot be minimized. It is unique to the Vietnam War and found its focal point in returnees. Veterans were spurned immediately on their arrival in the United States, suffered prejudice on college campuses as they came back to school, were left out of jobs because of antiwar sentiments and were disenfranchised from government programs through meager G.I. Bill benefits and government disavowal of physical problems associated with Agent Orange. Perhaps worst of all were the comparisons their fathers made—men who had fought the "honorable" fight of World War II and could not understand the problems their sons suffered in a war that was not black or white but was a dirty shade of gray (MacPherson, 1984, pp. 54–58).

Billie Mac: I tried to talk to my old man about it. He'd been in WW II on Okinawa. Hell, he might as well have been in the Revolutionary War for all he could understand about Nam. He finally got so mad that he told me I was nuts and no damn good. He didn't mean that, but I'll never forget it.

All these factors came together in a sort of generic problem for veterans trying to make meaning out of a situation that was life-threatening and generally considered pointless (Williams, 1983). To survive such a situation called for imposing psychological defense mechanisms that made a fertile breeding ground for PTSD.

Denial/Numbing

As individuals attempt to cope with catastrophes, they become passive (immobile and paralyzed) or active (able to cope with the situation). Individual reactions fall into three major groupings: momentary freezing, flight reaction, and denial/numbing. In the prolonged stress of a combat situation, denial/numbing is the most common response and allows the soldier to cope and live with the experience in three ways: by believing he is invulnerable to harm, by becoming fatalistic, or by taking matters into his own hands, becoming extremely aggressive. Any of these proactive stances allows the victim to get through the trauma and cope with it without losing complete control (Figley, 1985a, pp. 406–408). Typically, survivors of trauma will let down these defense barriers and will have acute stress disorders immediately after the trauma, but will recover. For those who do not, continued emotional numbing and repression can have severe consequences.

Billie Mac: Looking back on it, I can't believe how callous I became. SOP (standard operating procedure) was, "It don't mean nothin', screw it, drive on." This would be right after a B-40 round had blown your buddy's brains all over you. You had to put it behind you to survive. Fifteen years later I have survived, but I wake up to the sound of that incoming round.

Submerging emotions out of conscious awareness does not mean that they are summarily discarded. The price is that emotional numbing left in place and not relieved can generalize to other aspects of one's life and result in later psychological difficulties (Wilkinson, 1983). Shunted into the unconscious for a long time, trigger events in the form of everyday stressors can pile up and cause emotional blowouts when the individual is least prepared for them (Figley, 1985a, p. 408).

Billie Mac: I can't stand the sound of a chopper. Every time I hear one, I want to run. I get the feeling that every time I hear the 5 o'clock traffic chopper, it's gonna circle in, pick me up, and take me to a hot LZ (landing zone).

What the individual needs most is to bring these thoughts into conscious awareness and come to grips with them so they can be resolved. Yet, rather than confronting the intrusive and threatening material, the individual is more likely to deny its existence and use a variety of avoidance responses to escape from the situation (Horowitz, Wilner, Kaltreider, & Alvarez, 1980).

Intrusive-Repetitive Ideation

The other major symptom of PTSD besides denial/numbness is intrusive-repetitive ideation (Horowitz & Solomon, 1975). Intrusive-repetitive thoughts become so problematic for the individual that they begin to dominate existence. Intrusive thoughts generally take the form of visual images that are sparked by sights, sounds, smells, or tactile reminders that bring the repressed images to awareness (Donaldson & Gardner, 1985, pp. 371–372).

Billie Mac: That day at the village when Al got it keeps coming back. I don't go fishing in the bayou anymore. It smells and looks like Nam, and every time I'd go I'd start thing about that village.

Accompanying emotions of guilt, sadness, anger, and rage occur as the thoughts continue to intrude into awareness. To keep these disturbing thoughts out of awareness, the individual may resort to self-medication in the form of alcohol or drugs. Use of alcohol and drugs may temporarily relieve depressive, hostile, anxious, and fearful mood states (Horowitz & Solomon, 1975), but what usually occurs is a vicious cycle that alternates between being anesthetized to reality by the narcotic and experiencing elevated intrusion of the trauma with every return to sobriety. The ultimate outcome is increased dependence on the addictive substance as a method of keeping the intrusive thoughts submerged (LaCoursiere, Bodfrey, & Ruby, 1980).

Billie Mac: The drinkin' is no damn good. I know that, but try going without sleep for a week and knowing every time you nod off that horrible nightmare's gonna come. Then it starts popping up in the daytime and you drink more to keep it pushed back.

Family Responses

Natural disasters leave so few emotional scars because such disasters often strike intact social support systems simultaneously (Figley, 1988). In natural disasters that affect the whole community, everyone becomes a survivor. Family members help each other through the horror of the disaster and there is no blaming the victim (Figley, 1985a, p. 409). One of the keystones for bridging the gap between traumatic events and a return to adequate and wholesome functioning is a strong support system that is most generally based within the family. But when the trauma is intrafamilial and takes the form of child and spouse abuse, those who are most traumatized are most generally the ones who are denied the most social support within the family. Those who should provide the most comfort are the ones who are inflicting the most pain (Figley, 1985a, p. 411).

For Vietnam veterans, social support systems were lacking. The perceptual and cognitive alterations and distortions that accompanied a veteran's return home took place for both the veteran and the family. Issues of sex, responsibility, and fidelity emerged early between victim and family (Brende & Parson, 1985, pp. 46–47). For the veteran, dependency issues arose that tended to alienate and push away those on whom the veteran would be most dependent while in transition from the shock of the traumatic event. Whereas hypervigilance and pervasive suspiciousness were mandatory for survival in a combat zone, they no longer fit at home. This fact made little difference, given the response sets the individual had internalized.

Further exacerbating family relationships is the ingrained tendency in trauma victims to "not feel." Whereas the individual would like to be able to demonstrate feelings of caring and love, experience has taught the victim that exposure of feelings is foolhardy because it invariably makes the victim vulnerable to further pain. These concepts strike at the very heart of what sustains family life—trust. The response of family members is to feel misunderstood, unloved, fearful, and angry. The response is reciprocal and plunges all members deeper into a vortex of family discordance. For veterans, the battle has moved from the field to within themselves and spills over into the rest of the family.

From a family-system perspective, if children, parents, or spouses attempt to regulate the continuing warfare in which the victim is engaging, they will be worn down and out by the effort. The victim may also become so dependent on the stabilizing person (usually the spouse) that the victim's needs breed resentment in anyone else who demands time and effort (usually children). The outcome of this spiral is what the victim may fear most from the support system—rejection. Feelings of guilt, numbing, anger, and loss plague the victim, and the spiral continues ever downward into more inappropriate behavior patterns and ultimate disintegration of the family.

Vietnam veterans are not the only victims bothered with such difficulties. Victims of incest report behavioral and emotional changes involving difficulty with friends, school failure, teenage pregnancy, drug abuse, suicide attempts, sexual acting out, hysterical seizures, intense guilt, rage, anger, and low self-esteem (Donaldson & Gardner, 1985, p. 359). The same is true for rape victims who, if children, may have parents who are psychologically unable to provide support for them, or, if adults, may have a spouse who is unable to respond in supportive ways (Notman & Nadelson, 1976).

In attempting to deal with a family member who has suffered a traumatic experience, other members may experience the stress to the degree that they become "infected" by it (Figley, 1988). Indeed, if other family members have inadequate coping skills, their own problems may escalate to crisis proportions as the victim's reactions to the trauma create stress within the family. Or, if other members of the family have a hidden agenda of keeping the family in pathological homeostasis, they may engage in enabling the victim's disorder much as an alcoholic's family may sabotage attempts at recovery. Finally, family members who cannot deal with the trauma may paradoxically turn on the victim. Sadly, this is too often the occurrence in the case of mothers who deny their spouse's abuse of the children, finally are confronted with the issue by children and family services, and then blame the children for the trouble they have caused!

Danieli (1985, pp. 299–304) has categorized families of PTSD victims into four distinct types. Although the research was conducted on Jewish families that were victims of the Holocaust, the types are generically representative of what those who work with PTSD victims are likely to find. In our own experience the first three types are characteristic of families of Vietnam veterans and the third type is particularly characteristic of those who have been sexually traumatized or suffered abuse.

Victim. Families of the victim type operate from a closed system, having little interaction with outsiders. A high priority is put on physical, nutritional, and material needs. Security is the watchword. Joy and self-fulfillment are regarded as frivolous. All questions concerning the family's well-being are seen as life-and-death matters. There are no adequate outlets for anger, and there is a lot of survivor guilt. There are overprotection of and overinvolvement with all members of the family, which lead children to have problems in establishing meaningful relationships in general and marital relationships in particular. Children get the message that they are not to outdo their parents, and as a result often unconsciously destroy their successes and accomplishments. Children are often used as mediators in such failing families, yet they are generally powerless to effect any meaningful changes.

Fighter. In families of the fighter type, weakness and self-pity are not permitted. Admonitions to build and achieve are predominant. Pride in one's work and accomplishments are given high family status. Relaxation and pleasure are superfluous. Although there is a great deal of mistrust of and little socialization with outsiders, aggression in the form of achievement and standing up for one's rights is encouraged. The avoidance of any dependence on others and the utter contempt for it in themselves and others are barriers to forming any positive peer or marital relationships. Sharing or delegating responsibility is also viewed as an act of dependence. In order to be seen as adequate, children must assume a "hero" identity, oftentimes placing themselves in risky or dangerous situations to prove their worth.

Numbing. The numbing response to trauma engulfs the whole family. Silence is pervasive and emotions are depleted. The family system consumes its energy by engaging everyone in protecting everyone else. Children are left to their own devices in the business of growing up and often look outside the home for role models and mentors. Since numbing is modeled for the children, they adopt the behavior, with the result that they appear less intelligent and capable than they are. Because the family is immersed in the victim role, children are not the central focus and generally believe themselves not to be worthy of attention. Carried over into their adult lives, the response invariably causes them to seek out relationships in which they are "mothered" by the spouse. Because of their inability to assume responsibility, they generally have problems establishing close relationships with their own children or even wanting to have children.

Those who make it. People who make it are persistent and intent on achieving success. They tend to deny their background and particularly the horrifying experiences they have been through. Children of these families respond bitterly to finding out, usually indirectly, about the problems their parents suffered. These families also experience a great deal of denial and are much like "numb" families. The accomplishments of the survivor of the trauma are paramount in the family. Although proud of parental achievements, children feel a good deal of emotional distance from their parents. Parents in this group often use their influence and money to "ease the path" and thus deny children the logical consequences of their actions.

In summary, it should be clear that treating trauma victims also means treating the family.

Maladaptive Patterns Characteristic of PTSD

Summed dynamically, PTSD involves five common patterns: death imprint, survivor's guilt, desensitization, estrangement, and emotional enmeshments.

Death imprint. The traumatic experience provides a clear vision of one's own death in concrete biological terms (Ochberg, 1988, p. 12). Particularly in young victims, the sense of invulnerability is vanquished and is replaced by rage and anger at one's newfound mortality (Lifton, 1975). For veterans in particular, there is a continuing identity with death. The normal boundary between living and dying is suspended. It is not unusual for veterans to describe themselves as already dead. The only way they have of testing the boundary between life and death is to seek sensation, even if it means danger and physical pain (Brende & Parson, 1985, p. 100). Combined with rage reactions, sensation-seeking behaviors put victims squarely on a collision path with law enforcement agencies, employers, and families.

Billie Mac: After every law officer in Mississippi started chasing me, I ditched the car and ran into a woods. They even had bloodhounds after me. I slipped through them like a sieve. It was crazy, but for one of the few times since I've been back I really felt alive. I'd done that a hundred times on patrol.

Survivor's guilt. A second pattern is guilt. Guilt comes in a variety of forms: guilt over surviving when others did not, guilt over not preventing the death of another, guilt over not having somehow been braver under the circumstances, guilt over complaining when others have suffered more, and guilt that the trauma is partly the victim's fault (Frederick, 1980). Most commonly, guilt takes the form of intrusive thoughts such as "I could have done more, and if I had he/she'd still be here," or "If I had just done this or that, it (the trauma) wouldn't have happened." Dynamically, the basis of these thoughts may be relief that the other person was the one to die or the victim was lucky to get off so lightly (Egendorf, 1975).

Billie Mac: I was the only one in my outfit to get out of Tet without a scratch. I wonder why. Why me out of all those people? I've screwed my life up since then. Why did I deserve to get out clean when all those other good men didn't?

For other types of trauma victims, bereavement is closely allied to survivor's guilt. Facilitating grief includes the expression of affect, reconciliation of the loss of a loved one or a missed part of one's life, the ambivalence of not having shared the same fate as others, and moving on to new and meaningful relationships (Ochberg, 1988, p. 10). Since numbing of affect is a major dynamic response to PTSD, it is extremely difficult for survivors to let loose their emotions and grieve.

Desensitization.   A third pattern is desensitizing oneself to totally unacceptable events and then trying to return to a semblance of normalcy in a peaceful world. Feelings of guilt and fear over pleasurable responses to physical violence to others may occur. These feelings may become so acute that the victim conceals firearms for protection against imagined enemies but is simultaneously terrified of the guns and what might happen because of the violence that continuously seethes below the victim's calm outer appearance. These strong bipolar emotional currents that flow back and forth within the individual lead to hostile, defensive, anxious, depressive, and fearful mood states that find little relief (Horowitz & Solomon, 1975).

Billie Mac: I don't hunt anymore. I hate it. Yet this one guy who was my boss didn't
    know how close he came to getting killed. I was within one inch of taking him
    out, I was so hot. It would have been a pleasure, the guy was such an ass.

Estrangement.   A fourth pattern is the feeling that any future relationships will be counterfeit, that they mean little or nothing in the great scheme of things. As the individual attempts to ward off reminders of the experience, severe interpersonal difficulties occur. Because of the vastly different experiences they have undergone, PTSD victims become estranged from their peers and truncate social relationships with them because "they don't understand," and indeed "they" do not. Victimization may also be part of estrangement. From being victimized in the original trauma, to possible secondary victimization by social services, hospitals, and mental health providers, to revictimization by significant others, the survivor is crushed under the weight of dealing with these initial and secondary assaults (Ochberg, 1988). The result is that the individual becomes more isolated from social support systems and develops secondary symptoms that range from neurosis to psychosis (Horowitz & Solomon, 1975).

Billie Mac: I was sitting at my dad's watching TV when Saigon fell. I went nuts and
    trashed the house. What the hell was it all for? That really cooked it with my old
    man. I moved out after that and haven't said anything to him since.

Particularly for victims of sexual abuse, estrangement may take the form of negative intimacy. Invasion of one's personal space and being cause feelings of filthiness and degradation that make reestablishing old relationships or engendering new relationships an extremely difficult ordeal (Ochberg, 1988, pp. 12–13).

Emotional enmeshment.   A fifth pattern is a continuous struggle to move forward in a postholocaust existence but with an inability to find any significance in life (Lifton, 1973, pp. 191–216; Lifton, 1975). Emotional fixation, particularly for veterans, has disastrous effects on family life. Sent to Vietnam as adolescents and exposed to prolonged trauma that the majority of the population will never experience, these victims cannot bring themselves to engage in equitable relationships with their families and friends, nor can their families begin to understand their aberrant behavior (Brende & Parson, 1985, pp. 116–117).

Billie Mac: I can't believe what I've done to my kids. I love them more than anything in the world. At times, I'm the greatest dad in the world, coach the Little League team, take them everywhere. The next minute I'm all over them. I've knocked them around in a rage and that scares the hell out of me. I'm some kind of Jekyll and Hyde and my kids are afraid of me.

Children and PTSD

For children who suffer trauma, much less is known about PTSD. However, case reports of kidnapping (Senior, Gladstone, & Nurcombe, 1982; Terr, 1979), abuse (Green, 1983), animal attack (Gislason & Call, 1982), tornado (Bloch, Silber, & Perry, 1956), sexual abuse (Kiser, Ackerman, Brown, & Edwards, 1988), community violence (Pynoos & Nader, 1988), and murder of a parent (Eth & Pynoos, 1985) suggest that PTSD is a valid disorder suffered by children. Saigh's (1989a, 1989b) research confirms marked personality differences between children classified as victims of trauma and those with phobias.

Lack of full cognitive and moral development causes distinctive differences in how children react to trauma. Preschool children react to trauma with fears and worries, somatic problems, restitutive play, compulsions, regression, separation anxiety, nightmares, and sleep disturbances. School-age children manifest the foregoing symptoms plus fantasies, anger, hostility, belligerence, interpersonal problems, school phobias, chronic sadness, depression, and self-deprecation. Adolescents additionally may experience personality change, apathy, rationalization, anxiety, and acting out. Overall, children's responses are highly variable and are directly influenced by the situation and a variety of other intrapersonal, interpersonal, and environmental variables (Mowbray, 1988).

Terr's (1983) in-depth four-year follow-up on children who were victims of the Chowchilla, California, bus kidnapping substantiates that PTSD does occur with children, although dynamically in somewhat different form. The victims of this trauma were a group of 26 elementary and high school children who were kidnapped together with their school bus, were carried about in vans for 11 hours by their kidnappers, and were buried alive in a truck trailer. Terr's findings suggest that PTSD in children is characterized by denial, intrusion, reenactment, physical responses, displacement, and transposition. Some of these characteristics have been substantiated by other researchers who have studied the effects of various other traumas on children.

Denial.   Terr (1983) found that the children still had specific feelings of traumatic anxiety over the event after four years. When asked to speak about it, children generalized their anxiety from the event to statements like "I'm afraid of the feeling of being afraid." Unlike combat veterans, who might boast about harrowing experiences, the children were profoundly embarrassed by their experience, were unwilling to talk about the event, and shied away from any publicity. They generally voiced feelings of being humiliated and mortified when asked about their experience. Whereas 8 of 15 children had overcome their fear of vehicles such as vans and buses, they still reported occasional panic attacks triggered by unexpected sudden confrontation with stimuli such as seeing a van parked across the street from their house and vaguely wondering if some of the kidnappers' friends had not come back for them.

Eighteen of the children were found to employ suppression or conscious avoidance of the trauma. Parents often aided them in this endeavor, although the two children whose parents encouraged them to talk about the experience were still not spared its residual effects. Their typical response was that they hated the feeling of helplessness they experienced and needed to feel in control of the situation.

All the children could remember almost every second and minute of the contents of the event. However, they were able to remember few, if any, of the emotions or behaviors they experienced during the ordeal. The work production of adults may seriously decline after such an event, but Terr found very little decline in the children's school performance, although Eth and Pynoos (1985, p. 44) believe that continuous intrusion of a traumatic event, evolution of a cognitive style of forgetting, and interference of depressed affect with mental processes very definitely influence school achievement.

Intrusion.   Terr (1983) found that intrusive thoughts did not repeatedly enter the children's conscious thoughts; however, sleep brought very different problems. Whereas a few reported daydreams, the children had nightmares through which ran many repetitious themes of death. The children believed these dreams to be highly predictive of the future and made comments like "I'm 11 now but I don't think I'll live very long, maybe 12, cause somebody will come along and shoot me."

Researchers who have studied children who have witnessed the murder of a parent have found that these children, also, report nightmares with themes of death (Pruett, 1979; Schetky, 1978). Adolescents in particular are brought face to face with their own vulnerability and, in the case of those who have experienced the murder of a parent, report that they will never marry or have children because they fear history will be repeated (Eth & Pynoos, 1985, p. 48).

Reenactment.   The play of children with PTSD is very distinctive because of its thematic quality, longevity, dangerousness, intensity, contagiousness to siblings, and unconscious linkage to the traumatic event (Bergen, 1958; Maclean, 1977; Terr, 1981). The clearly prevalent dynamic is a continuing reenactment of their plight during the trauma (Eth & Pynoos, 1985, p. 42). This thematic play can be characterized as burdened, constricted, and joyless (Wallerstein & Kelly, 1975). For adolescents, reenactment may take the form of delinquent behavior that is similar to that of their adult counter-parts (Eth & Pynoos, 1985, p. 47). Delinquent acts ranging from truancy, sexual activity, and theft to reckless driving, drug abuse, and obtaining weapons are typical of traumatized adolescents (Newman, 1976).

Physical responses.   Physiologically, approximately half the children in the Chowchilla kidnapping manifested physical problems that could be con-strued to be related to the trauma of being held prisoner without food, wa-ter, or bathroom (Terr, 1983). In young children suffering from PTSD, regression may occur and previously learned skills such as toilet training may have to be retaught (Bloch, Silber, & Perry, 1956).

Displacement.   In the Chowchilla survivors, a great deal of displacement of affect occurred, with emotions about the event being shifted to a related time, an associated idea, or another person—particularly the interviewing psychiatrist. Prior to the follow-up interviews, children displayed a variety of displaced behaviors, including the belief by one of the children that the psychiatrist had placed notes posing questions about the kidnapping in her school locker (Terr, 1983).

Transposition.   In the Chowchilla survivors, one of the most profound changes occurred in transposition of events surrounding the trauma. Events that happened after the trauma were remembered as having happened before the trauma (Terr, 1983). Also, there was a general belief that the traumatic events were predictive of what was about to happen to them. (Ayalon, in a 1983 study of victims of terrorism, found a similar effect in children.) Chil-dren attempted to resolve their vulnerability and lack of control by saying they should have listened to the omens and "shouldn't have stepped in the bad luck square." Thus, in PTSD, such distortions of time become part of the child's developing personality and are attempts to take personal responsibil-ity and even feel guilty for events over which they had no control.

Terr's (1983) study indicates that whereas children behave differently from adults in their attempt to resolve the traumatic event, they are no more flexible or adaptable than adults after a trauma, and it would be erro-neous to assume that they "just grow out of the event." Further, these chil-dren did not become toughened by their experience, but simply narrowed their sphere of influence in very restrictive ways to control their environ-ment better.

INTERVENTION STRATEGIES

Intervention in cases of PTSD, like intervention in other types of crises, begins with assessment. For children, the methods of assessment and therapy used are different from those used for adults.

Treatment of Children

Assessment. Early assessment is critical in determining the potential for trauma (Terr, 1979, 1981, 1983) and should happen as soon as possible after the event (Mowbray, 1988, p. 206). Interviewing should involve determining the degree and severity of exposure to trauma and assessing the child's response as it relates to the degree of exposure (Pynoos & Nader, 1988).

Criminal or other legal ramifications are often involved with children who are victims of trauma. If that is the case, the child should be referred to a professional well versed in taking legal testimony such as the police or child welfare workers. Because of the worker's own liability and possible witness status, interviews where legal ramifications are suspected should be taped and comprehensive summaries written. Children should be asked specific and concrete *what, when, who, where,* and *how* questions about their experience. They should be allowed to proceed at their own pace, assured that they were not to blame, and should *always be believed* (Mowbray, 1988, p. 206). This last point is extremely important. Because of adult fear of false accusations, reports by children are oftentimes construed as fantasy or distortions of what really happened. In the overwhelming majority of cases, particularly those involving sexual abuse or assault, this is categorically not true (Salter, 1988).

However, because children submerge their affect and parents are loath to deal with the trauma until it causes severe repercussions in their lives, children are rarely brought in for counseling until behavior has reached crisis proportions (Mowbray, 1988, p. 206). Triage assessment at this time may not reveal that trauma is the underlying agent. In that regard, the crisis worker who works with children should have a good knowledge of both projective and question-and-answer personality inventories that will ferret out the trauma.

Therapy. While Saigh (1987) has reported success using flooding techniques with school-age children, we want to emphatically emphasize that this is a *hazardous* procedure for children and may exacerbate symptoms. Further, nondirective play therapy may also be ill-advised since restitutive play becomes increasingly destructive and serves only to increase anxieties (Terr, 1979).

A safer approach to reenactment of the trauma is the use of guided imagery (Sluckin, Weller, & Highton, 1989) or a variety of play therapy techniques (Landreth, 1987) that include puppets (Carter, 1987; James & Myer, 1987), sand play (Allan & Berry, 1987; Vinturella & James, 1987), poetry (Gladding, 1987), writing (Brand, 1987), music (Bowman, 1987), computer art (Johnson, 1987), drama (Irwin, 1987), and drawing the traumatic event and telling a story about it (Eth & Pynoos, 1985, p. 37). All of these techniques may be controlled and paced by the therapist in consideration of the psychological safety of the child. Play therapy is particularly efficacious because it enables the therapist to enter the trauma on the child's cognitive terms, reduce the threat of the trauma, establish trust, and determine the child's current means of coping and ways of defending against the trauma (Gumaer, 1984). Further therapeutic intervention should most likely be referred to a specialist in child therapy who will help the child face the truth of what happened, rebuild a poor self-image, reconcile feelings of anger, grief, and fear, and provide the child a psychological anchor while support systems are being reestablished in the environment (Salter, 1988).

Assessment of Adults

A variety of personality tests that purport to diagnose PTSD have recently been constructed. Most notable are the Mississippi Scale for Combat-Related Posttraumatic Stress Disorder (Keane, Caddell, & Taylor, 1988), the Combat Exposure Scale (Lund, Foy, Sipprelle, & Strachan, 1984), the Stress Event Test (Olde, Schauer, Garfield, & Patterson, 1987), the Purdue Post-Traumatic Stress Disorder Scale (Figley, 1989), and the Impact of Events Scale (Horowitz, Wilner, & Alvarez, 1979). Established tests such as the Zung and Beck Depression Scales (Keane et al., 1985), the Millon Clinical Multiaxial Inventory (Hyer, Woods, Boudewyns, & Bruno, 1988), the Sixteen Personality Factor, and the Minnesota Multiphasic Personality Inventory (MMPI) (Foy, Sipprelle, Rueger, & Carroll, 1984; Merbaum, 1977; Roberts, Penk, & Gearing, 1982) have generated profiles that attempt to measure PTSD. In addition, the *PK* subscale on the new MMPI-II has been formulated for the specific purpose of diagnosing PTSD (Keane, Malloy, & Fairbank, 1984).

However, conflicting reports of reliability and validity continue to dog instruments designed to assess PTSD (Blanchard, Wittrock, Kolb, & Geradi, 1988; Burke & Mayer, 1985; Cannon, Bell, Andrews, & Finkelstein, 1987; Gayton, Burchstead, & Matthews, 1986; McCaffrey, Hickling, & Marrazo, 1989; Moody & Kish, 1989; Watson, Juba, & Anderson, 1989; Watson, Kucala, & Manifold, 1986). Faking of symptoms has also been detected (Dalton, Tom, Rosenblum, & Garte, 1989; Hyer, Woods, Harrison, & Boudewyns, 1989).

One assessment device that will quickly provide clues to the possible presence of posttraumatic stress disorder is Figley's Traumagram Questionnaire (1990). The questionnaire elicits the number, length of time, and self-reported degree of stress of all previous traumatic experiences and can be easily incorporated into a standard interview format. By plotting the number of events across their length of time on an x-axis and then plotting the degree of stress on a 1 (minimum) to 10 (maximum) scale on the y-axis, the interviewer can quickly gain a graphic representation of the total number, type, and duration of traumas and the degree of stress the client has experienced. This visual representation of previous trauma can provide valuable clues to the presence of PTSD.

The structured interview probably remains the best diagnostic device for determining if a victim has PTSD. Figley's very comprehensive Structured Interview for PTSD (Figley, 1985b, pp. 424–438), although specifically aimed at Vietnam veterans, could be adapted to almost anyone who is suspected of having PTSD. Besides combat-related questions, the interview covers the kind and degree of PTSD symptoms the client is suffering, along with associated features such as depression, anxiety, substance abuse, legal problems, relationship problems, adjustment before the trauma, and a mental status exam. However, the survey is somewhat lengthy and not likely to be used by an intake interviewer unless PTSD symptoms are clearly pronounced.

Any intake interview should allow the client to describe current problems without interference by the interviewer. The interviewer should carefully consider what the client is saying about the problem in comparison with the PTSD criteria listed in the DSM-IIIR. Frequency, duration, intensity, and pervasiveness of symptoms should be carefully noted. Masking but indicating symptoms of PTSD also include substance abuse, violence and aggression, domestic problems, bad employment records, paranoid ideation, auditory or visual hallucination, magical thinking, delusions, and autonomic arousal. Virtually all PTSD victims will report variations on a theme of chronic anxiety and depressive symptoms including sleep and appetite loss, hopelessness, guilt, and suicidal ideation (Keane et al., 1985, pp. 269–277). The interviewer should, with great sensitivity, attempt to discern if there are functional relationships between these symptoms and antecedent events.

A clear distinction between individuals with character disorders and those suffering from PTSD is their affiliative responses. In general, victims of PTSD avoid interpersonal relationships, as opposed to exhibiting the ingratiating gregariousness of a sociopath. PTSD victims have few close friends, prefer being alone, and discuss few intimate details of their lives. Unexpected contact with other people or stimuli reminiscent of the traumatic event may make victims extremely "jumpy" and "edgy" (Keane et al., 1985, p. 270).

The human services worker should never dismiss a report, no matter how trivial it may seem, of involvement in a catastrophic situation (Scurfield, 1985, pp. 238–239). Because PTSD victims may be very reluctant to talk about the trauma they have been through, human services workers should attempt to obtain background information from relatives, coworkers, and any other persons who have personal knowledge of the victim. The personal history is particularly important when substance abuse is involved, because if PTSD is not identified, all the efforts of the worker will not ameliorate the substance-abuse problem.

Our own clinical experience with depressed clients has uncovered many who have suffered sexual abuse as children. We are coming more and more to believe that until ruled out, PTSD should be suspected as a causative agent. However, getting at it may prove extremely difficult, particularly on account of the severe social taboos associated with talking about incestuous and abusive relationships. Therefore, in an initial assessment, even though the interviewer may have a strong hunch that repression of a traumatic event is causing the problem, the causative agent should never be exposed, interpreted, or even guessed at until a high degree of trust has been built (Scurfield, 1985, pp. 238–239).

In the case of Billie Mac, a traumagram assessment shows little if any evidence of traumatic experience prior to Vietnam besides the death of a grandfather to whom he was quite close. However, for the year he was in Vietnam, his traumagram consistently ranks a minimum of 8 although he rigidly controlled his thinking, feeling, and acting in a disciplined manner during combat. He was in major battle after major battle, interspersed with patrols and sweeps. He was the only man out of his original company to walk away physically unscathed after the Tet offensive.

After Vietnam, the traumatic wake continues. Violent episodes with his father, his wife, and his children, scrapes with the law, drunken binges, barroom brawls, prolonged bouts of depression interspersed with manic acting out, alcohol addiction treatment, job loss due to nonperformance, suicidal ideation, plus the standard symptoms of PTSD mark his years since Vietnam with almost continuous crises. There are very few months in the 15 years since his return that he would not rank extremely high on the Triage Assessment Scale. Affectively, he goes far beyond what the situation warrants with large mood swings that cycle through anger, fear, and sadness. There are few instances when he ranks less than 6 on the Affective Severity Scale, and his average is 7.

In the cognitive domain he has suffered physical, psychological, social, and spiritual transgression, threat, and loss. His problem-solving abilities are characterized by self-doubt, confusion, and excessive rumination on Vietnam and his abortive attempts to reacclimate to the civilian world. His severity rating is consistently an 8 to 9, in the "Marked Impairment" range.

Billie Mac's behavior invariably makes the situation worse. He either approaches the situation in a hostile-aggressive manner or avoids it for fear of acting out against others. He is immobilized between these two extremes, and reports of his behavior from significant others indicate that they feel he is erratic, unpredictable, and dangerous. A most conservative estimate places him at a minimum of 8 on the Behavioral Severity Scale. His total scale score is 24, which places him in the lower range of the "Marked Impairment" category. As he presents for treatment, he is in serious trouble, and at times of stress his triage rating scale score spikes into the lethal "Severe Impairment" range.

Phases of Recovery

Brende and Parson (1985, pp. 185–186) have compiled the work of Wilson (1980), Figley (1978), and Horowitz (1976) to construct five phases of recovery in the PTSD victim. These phases directly parallel treatment approaches, and each has its own crisis stage.

1. *The emergency or outcry phase.* The victim experiences heightened "fight/flight" reactions to the life-threatening situation. This phase lasts as long as the survivor believes it to last. Pulse, blood pressure, respiration, and muscle activity are all increased. Concomitant feelings of fear and helplessness predominate. Termination of the event itself is followed by relief and confusion. Questions about why the event happened and what its consequences will be dominate the victim's thoughts.

2. *The emotional numbing and denial phase.* The survivor protects psychic well-being by burying the experience in subconscious memory. By avoiding the experience, the victim temporarily reduces anxiety and stress symptoms. Many victims remain forever at this stage unless they receive professional intervention.

3. *The intrusive-repetitive phase.* The survivor has nightmares, volatile mood swings, intrusive images, and startle responses. Other pathological and antisocial defense mechanisms may be put into place in a futile attempt to rebury the trauma. It is at this point that the delayed stress becomes so overwhelming that the victim is propelled to seek help or becomes so mired in the pathology of the situation that outside intervention is mandated.

4. *The reflective-transition phase.* The survivor develops a larger personal perspective on the traumatic events and becomes positive and constructive, with a forward- rather than backward-looking perspective. The victim comes to grips with the trauma and confronts the problem.

5. *The integration phase.* The survivor successfully integrates the trauma with all other past experiences and restores a sense of continuity to life. The trauma is successfully placed fully in the past.

Neat and orderly progression for the PTSD victim through these stages is the exception rather than the rule. What is more likely to occur is a precipitative crisis far removed in chronological time from the event itself and then a continuing series of crises that escalate until the victim voluntarily seeks help or is forced to seek it. Once intervention occurs, a cyclic pattern of avoidance, recall, recovery, and more avoidance continues until the core issues that gave birth to PTSD are resolved (Figley, 1985a, pp. 402–404). The human services worker can expect a series of crises as this process unfolds.

Initiating Intervention

As disequilibrium from the trauma subsides, some form of reorganization takes place. The reorganized state is either adaptive or maladaptive, and it is important to intervene before maladaptive reorganization occurs (Scurfield, 1985, p. 239); otherwise treatment may become much more difficult (Horowitz, 1976, p. 123). Generally, victims of trauma refuse early intervention because they either see the event as too difficult to deal with or believe that people of good character ought to be able to cope with such events on their own without outside intervention. It is these two faulty assumptions that get victims into the delayed part of the disorder, where most of the treatment population will emerge.

Importance of Acceptance

If we have been relentless in stressing the need for excellent listening and responding skills, congruence, empathy, and genuine positive regard for the client, it is because our experience teaches that these are absolute musts in crisis intervention. Nowhere is this more true than in the case of PTSD victims, where these skills are essential in enabling the human services worker to make a clear and adequate assessment. Given the variety of negative and conflicting emotional baggage the victim brings to the session, it is of paramount importance that the human services worker provide an accepting atmosphere so that the victim can start to recount and encounter the trauma. Disclosure of the trauma is difficult for the PTSD victim, because recounting what has happened may be horrifying and socially unacceptable. Also, open-minded acceptance of the client's story may be extremely difficult for and repugnant to the human services worker, but if therapeutic progress is to be made, nothing less will do (Brende & Parson, 1985, p. 178).

Billie Mac: [*Thinking to himself.*] If I tell about killing that kid what will the counselor think? A baby killer, that's what! Yet, it's bugging the hell out of me. [*Slowly tells the counselor about the incident.*]

HSW: [*Stating personal feelings.*] I know how hard it was for you to talk about that. A part of me wonders how you or anybody could ever kill a child. However, I understand how scared you were, wondering whether he had a grenade, what a moral quandary that put you in, and the guilt and anguish you feel as you recall the incident.

Risks of Treatment

It is also incumbent upon the human services worker to state clearly the risks inherent in treatment. It may be hard to make such statements and to propose a poor prognosis, but it is a safe bet that the victim will silently have pondered many of the same questions. After the initial crisis has passed, and the victim is back to a state of at least semiequilibrium, the human services worker should convey clearly the following risks, as outlined by Brende and Parson (1985, pp. 168–174):

1. There may be only partial recovery; there are no magical cures for this tenacious and pernicious problem.
2. Because of the continuing nature of the crisis, either long bouts with hospitals or weekly trips to the therapist are required and play havoc with keeping a job.
3. As catharsis of the event occurs, it is inevitable that the victim gets worse before getting better. Fear of a psychotic breakdown may occur as the victim learns more about the disorder.

4. As the struggle to find oneself goes forward, personality change may put heavy burdens on interpersonal relationships as significant others see a very different person emerge from the therapeutic experience.
5. Psychic pain may become almost intolerable as the victim reexperiences disturbing memories and emotions that, as they are voiced, may cause rejection by friends and professionals alike.
6. Because of the numerous self-constraints placed upon volatile emotions, the victim may fear that giving vent to those emotions will lead to uncontrolled anger and result in physical harm to others. Because of the hurt suffered, it will also be very difficult for the victim to give up the idea of revenge on both real and imagined perpetrators of the traumatic event.
7. Because of the compartmentalized and constricted lifestyle that follows the trauma, the victim will safeguard against change and may have extreme difficulty following directions and doing what others may suggest, no matter how reasonable and proper. Giving up such maladaptive self-reliance will put the victim at the mercy of others, a seemingly intolerable situation.
8. A great deal of pain will result from coming to accept the world as it is with all its frailties and injustices. In attempting to gain reentry into such an imperfect world, the victim is in danger of losing patience with it and falling back into the vortex of PTSD.
9. Correlative with accepting the frailties of the world is also the acceptance of one's own set of infirmities; bad memories may return; relationships may not always be excellent; others may obtain better jobs for no legitimate reason. Acceptance of oneself, including the guilt, sorrow, and regret that goes with it, is the sine qua non of getting through PTSD, but it may be an extremely difficult and fearsome task that will call for far more courage than surviving the catastrophe itself.

In view of the risks, what kind of help can a victim of PTSD expect, and from where? Because of the large numbers of victims and the agitation and subsequent legislation to fund help for them, let us turn to the Vietnam veteran and the many veterans centers scattered throughout the country for a working treatment model.

THE VETERANS CENTER MODEL OF TREATMENT

Veterans centers provide a variety of services to their constituents, covering all kinds of readjustment counseling. They do crisis intervention, do referral and follow-up on medical disabilities, assist with legal problems, upgrade less-than-honorable discharges, consult with police departments and parole officers, and provide job placement and vocational counseling (Brende & Parson, 1985, pp. 210–211). Most important, the centers and their staff members have been in the forefront in developing therapeutic approaches to PTSD cases.

A key component of the veterans center's attack on PTSD is its multimodal approach, and from this standpoint it probably has material, professional, financial, and other resource advantages, particularly its alliance with VA hospitals, that other mental health facilities lack. However, its therapeutic approach can be instituted with almost any type of PTSD victim, can be used in any setting, and would seem to have particular utility with victims of rape, incest, and child abuse (Donaldson & Gardner, 1985, p. 373). The principal initiating components of this treatment approach are the "rap" or self-help and support group tied in with individual therapy from counselors at the center.

Group work is helpful because of the shared experience, mutual support, sense of community, reduction of stigma, and restoration of self-pride it fosters. Confrontation by peers is more acceptable than confrontation by professionals because it is reality-oriented (Scurfield, 1985, pp. 247–248). Groups also serve an educative function. The terrifying nature of PTSD calls for clearly delineating what is happening and why. Answers to victims' questions such as "What are common PTSD symptoms?" "Why do victims use drugs?" "What are definitions of words like *secret, conscience, anger, helplessness, love,* and *trust*?" How long will it take to get better?" "Am I crazy?" "What do I do in this situation?" "Will I ever be as I was before this happened?" help build a cognitive anchor for the victim.

Individual therapy is used to buttress the supportive atmosphere of the group and to deal specifically with crises idiosyncratic to the victim's life. In both group and individual therapy, it is important that therapists working with the victim keep in close touch with one another (Brende, 1981), for two reasons. First, engaging in both kinds of therapy has the potential to result in therapeutic drainage. Important issues brought up in one setting may not be transferred to the other (Ohlsen, 1970, p. 122). Second, because of the distinct possibility of transference and countertransference issues, it is extremely easy for the individual therapist to get trapped psychologically with such emotionally volatile groups and lose objectivity. Cotherapists that work closely together in planning and coordinating activities are highly beneficial (Brewi, 1986).

Rap Groups

Rap groups were started for veterans in 1970 by Robert Lifton and Chaim Shatan in New York City. Lifton and Shatan were human services professionals who had become disaffected with the Veterans Administration's constant refusal to acknowledge that many Vietnam veterans were suffering from combat-induced psychological problems. Rap groups became the members' own therapy groups, without the benefit of professional psychotherapy. Indeed, the rap group was probably started as a reaction to human services professionals, who had done a generally poor job with veterans in the first place. The veterans' experience with the formal structure of therapy merely augmented their existing anger toward authority (Lifton, 1978;

Shatan, 1978). The outcome of this dilemma was that professionals finally came to recognize the success of rap groups and integrated them into more traditional formats (Walker, 1983).

The human services worker who works with such groups needs some special qualifications. Distrust and suspicion are strong in the early stage of such groups, and human services workers can be expected to be tested over and over again until they have proven themselves to be congruent and trustworthy (Gressard, 1986). Our own experience shows this to be true regardless of whether or not the human services worker has had experiences similar to those of the victim.

Veterans' groups are ideally conducted with veterans as leaders because of the defensiveness and hostility with which most veterans view professionals who have not undergone the Vietnam experience. One could extrapolate this notion to group work with other kinds of trauma victims. The problem is that professionals who have also experienced the trauma are often not readily available. Therefore, the Veterans Center of Memphis has published a list of 12 "rules of the road" for establishing the credibility of nonveterans who work therapeutically with veterans (Memphis Vietnam Veterans Center, 1985).

1. He has the experiential knowledge you don't have; you have the clinical and technical knowledge he doesn't have. Together you can forge a working alliance.
2. Make your desire to understand come across so that considerable experiential gaps are bridged.
3. Realize that the veteran wants you to help him help you understand. In the process, he recreates and reexperiences the sources of the problems and you, by providing the therapeutic climate, gain an in-depth understanding of the Vietnam experience.
4. A female therapist serves as a role model, i.e., a woman who can understand and accept the victim for what he is, which has important effects on the veteran.
5. Clinical experience and expertise with Vietnam veterans is built over time—as your understanding and technical expertise grows, you will be accepted in the group and accepted as the leader despite your lack of direct experience.
6. As a nonveteran, you can challenge the defense of exclusivity, i.e., as one who wasn't there can't understand, thus serving to break through his feelings of isolation and "contamination."
7. Your military combat naivete often helps the veteran to explore and express himself. In his effort to help you understand, he uncovers areas of conflict.
8. At the same time, because of your naivete, you must guard against becoming too involved in Vietnam problems and memories thereby "triggering" situational stress which may need immediate attention and treatment.
9. Realize that moral conflicts will probably be raised for you personally as stories unfold; guard against any display of emotional revulsion to a vet who describes real atrocities. Be nonjudgmental and objective.
10. Guard against overidentification with the vet or hero worship, or you will blunt your problem-solving ability.
11. Expect to need controls and to have to clearly enforce them for your sake and the vet's—don't try to do therapy with a vet who is drunk or "stoned," refuse to be a party to long tirades on the phone, bar all weapons and mean it.
12. Heed the signs of burnout: thinking or talking too much about your clients to others, finding yourself having combat-like nightmares, etc. Step back and evaluate whether you may be too immersed in trying to do too much for too many.

These rules are adaptable to any kind of trauma survivor and the people who work with them *and apply particularly to those who work with adult survivors of childhood sexual abuse.* One further admonition is necessary for any human services worker who would work with trauma victims. Frick and Bogart (1982) identified one of the stages that veterans go through as "rage at their counselor." This stage is important in coming to terms with the traumatic experience. Human services workers may well become the focal point of all the frustration, grief, fear, lost opportunity, confusion, lack of progress, attempts at reconciliation with society, family, and friends that mark the trauma survivor's attempt to reintegrate into the social mainstream. Human services workers need to deal with such anger by owning their mistakes in being insensitive to issues, accepting and reflecting the victim's anger while at the same time not being defensive, containing impulsive responses after being attacked, owning their own anger, and not becoming discouraged and giving up when attacked.

The Therapeutic Sequence

The chronology of events that occurs in therapy for PTSD, while elastic, operates in the following manner. Once a PTSD client is stabilized, the human services worker suggests participation in a group. No demands are made of the individual (Brewi, 1986). The human services worker issues an invitation something like this:

HSW: We've got some guys that meet on Wednesday night to talk about many of the problems you're trying to deal with now. I think you've got a lot in common with them and believe it might be helpful for you to meet them. They've all been in Nam and are trying to come to terms with their experiences there. You don't have to talk if you don't want to, that's up to you. You'll probably feel a lot of different emotions, and some of those aren't going to be too pleasant. However, all of the guys you'll meet have been feeling a lot of the same kinds of things even though they may have different kinds of problems that brought them into the vet center. From that standpoint they all know what you're going through, and while it may get tough, they'll support you and not pass judgment. I'd really like to see you come in.

Once the individual agrees, he comes to the group, which meets for an hour and a half. The group is composed entirely of veterans. The first item is that individuals are asked to introduce themselves by name and unit. This structured event is not just for the purpose of getting into war stories; it also serves to move men psychologically back in time to the starting point of their trauma and to cement the "we-ness" of the group. After introductions, anything on anybody's mind is fair game for conversation.

The group will be composed of "veterans" who have been through many such sessions and "greenhorns" who are at their first meeting. As in any other group, there will be some problem members who are monopolizers, some who are hostile and acting out, scapegoats, socializers, and a constellation of other typical group members (for a complete description of problem clients, see Ohlsen, 1970, pp. 164–192). Occupationally, members will range from lawyers, doctors, carpenters, and electronic technicians to the unemployed, parolees, and hospitalized substance abusers. Topics range from problems of day-to-day living to the government, families, the war, and how all these problems affect them.

The leaders at the Memphis center are two social workers and a clinical psychologist, all with combat time in Vietnam, but they are not group therapists in the truest sense of the word. They are more like participatory members who have been endowed with the task of keeping the group within loose guidelines concerning time, monopolizing the group, facilitating support and responses from the other members, and, in a few extreme instances, acting as empathic but firm sergeants-at-arms. As leaders they must be willing to keep a low profile while group members interact. Their leadership role is subtle rather than directive and requires an infinite supply of patience as the group struggles toward resolution of its problems. If therapy in a classical sense of the word is to occur, it happens much later in the game. A clear distinction between the rap group and the therapy group is that trauma and its expiation are the main focus and not life adjustment. Life-adjustment problems represent another stage in the crisis of this malady and are handled later. The group is large, ranging from 12 to 24 members. The typical rap group starts something like this:

HSW: Hi, everybody. We've got some new people here and because they don't know everybody I'd like you all to introduce yourself and your unit. I'm George McClellan, 25th division, infantryman, Nam 69–70.

Joe: Joe LaDue, First Air Cav, gunner, Nam 67–68.

Ralph: Ralph Novicki, SEALS, Nam 68.

Billie Mac: B. M. Anson, First Marines, infantryman, Nam 68.

Skeeter: Skeeter Schmidt, Rangers, 69–70 Nam.

Lamont: Lamont Stokes, 101st Airborne, radio operator, Nam 70.

[*Introductions continue around the group.*]

HSW: Has anybody got anything that's hot?

Joe: That poem that George read really hit me last week. I sure wish I could put words together like that. Although I still hate what the NVA did, I can respect them as people individually.

A rather lively discussion takes place regarding the poem, whose main theme is that whatever side a soldier is on, he has the same hopes and fears. Some men have resolved their hatred for the North Vietnamese and others have not. The men loosen up and wheel into other issues. One issue is expressing feelings.

Lamont: Hey! Whatcha mean it's too tough to talk, why not put some of that stuff you feeling' down in here?

Joe: I dunno. What've I got to say?

Lamont: Hey, turkey, we listen to everybody in here, don't we!

Joe: Well, yeaah, but . . .

Ralph: No "buts" about it. Why doncha give it a try?

Typically, when one member attempts to do something positive in his life, members leap to his support, sometimes pushing, sometimes cajoling, sometimes confronting, but the support and caring are always there. Another generic problem surfaces, the inability to find a job, particularly for those men who are undergoing therapy.

Lamont: I tell you all I am by God sick of it! I put my butt on the line for this country, I ain't never done nothin' wrong, went to church, enlisted and all that shuck. I hurt like hell from the shrapnel still in me. They say I got no problem over to the VA. It's in my mind. Like hell, it be in my legs. I'm no good at workin', can't keep a job, 'cause my legs, can't get no help from them. I'd like to show them what I could do with an M-60.

Billie Mac: [*Pushes Lamont to tell specifically what happened and then responds.*] Man, I hear that, but if you get off like you are now you're gonna wind up in jail or worse, and I can tell you that's no place to be. I was so down when the wife left that I went off. Oh, yeah, I foxed the cops, but I still wound up in jail. Talk to George or Gene, they've got some clout over there, they can straighten that out.

Lamont: It ain't just the VA, man, it's this whole country that's haywire.

HSW: So the anger goes way beyond the VA, and while we can help you with that, sounds like there's something more eatin' at you.

Billie Mac: Yeah, Lamont! What's stickin' in your craw? You been chewin' on somethin' the last two weeks. What you mad about, man?

Lamont: I dunno. I really dunno. Man, I just get so uptight sometimes I think I'm gonna blow sky high and that scares me pea green, man!

Ralph: [*Gently.*] We've all been there and know how tough it is; you knew it'd get worse before it got better, we all told you that. It's hell. You been talkin' to your counselor?

Lamont: Yeah, I been talkin' to Gene. But it just seems like the more stuff comes up, the worse my leg feels.

Because of the mutual support and resources within the group, lots of suggestions are given about how Lamont can grapple with his emotional turmoil. Lamont's anger is a common thread that runs through many members: anger toward the establishment and particularly toward the VA. Ralph's comments offer no great insight, but they are therapeutic in that they are accepting and understanding of the rage and the trauma Lamont feels. Skeeter, a new member of the group, who has been silent throughout the meeting, finally speaks up in a quiet, trembling voice. He is a doctor, with clean-cut good looks, dressed neatly and conservatively, and on first appearance would seem to have everything going for him. That is anything but the case.

Skeeter: I don't know what kind of help I can get here. I'm a doctor. I'm about to lose my license to practice. I'm also in trouble with the law. I wrote a bunch of bogus prescriptions to subsidize my own coke habit. My wife has cleared out with the kids, says she can't take it anymore. I'm a nervous wreck. I've been coming here for six weeks talking to George. They dried me out at the VA. He finally talked me into coming to the group. I thought I could handle things. The damn dreams are getting worse. I don't know that anybody can help me with this. Christ, I wasn't much in Nam and now I'm nothing here. [*Wipes tears from his eyes.*] I can't handle anything. [*Holds heads in his hands and returns to silence.*]

Skeeter is a very erudite man. However, as he tries to find a starting place to talk, his sentences are strung together in disjointed fashion; to admit his problems to this group, men like those he led as a Ranger captain in Vietnam, is getting close to rock bottom. George has pushed for him to come into the group for quite a while with little success. One might guess that this man, who is so distinctly different from other group members in speech, dress, and occupation, would be greeted with something less than enthusiasm, particularly since he was an officer and most of the group were not.

Ralph: If you could survive for a year in the Nam in the Rangers you can survive this. I mean nobody's poppin' at you with an AK-47.

Skeeter: I don't know, it's like it's all coming undone and I can't stop it.

Lamont: You stayin' off the nose dust and the pills since drying' out?

Skeeter: Yeah, but I dunno about that either—whether I can go on.

Lamont: You've been off for ten weeks ever since the VA cleaned you out and you come here, I'd say that's somethin'. Do it one step at a time. You livin' and you clean. I was savin' this, but I'm gonna say it now. Look at me, man, how screwed up I am, but it's been a year and I ain't been on that crap. [*General applause and some derisive but good-natured catcalls. Lamont smiles.*] You think you no better than me, well, that's a crock. You here now and that took guts, so you got a lot of help. We wiped you officers' noses in Nam, so what's the difference now? [*General laughter from the group.*]

Lamont, who has been vitriolic in ventilating his feelings, switches roles and becomes a support person to Skeeter. In mutual help groups like this, such role shifts are common and the need to become a helper rather than a beneficiary is extremely important (Silverman, 1986). It is indicative of the progress that members of mutual help groups can make toward becoming integrated with the mainstream of living. George, the leader of the group, recognizes this shift and wisely lets Lamont carry the dialogue. George's major contribution, besides summing what has been said, is to reinforce Lamont for his role shift.

HSW: What I hear everybody saying is that while those are some stiff problems, that they've been there, and know what you're going through. You're also doing something right now, even though you may not think so. You've taken three steps in your own right. Going to the VA, coming in here to see me, and then coming into this group. I don't think it could be said any better than Lamont said it. We're here to help each other, and that's what it's all about, man. It makes me proud to be a vet. Thanks, Lamont.

Lamont: [*Smiles sheepishly.*] Aw, man, don't be layin' that shine on me.

Ralph then begins a long-running commentary about a friend who is a mercenary and now is MIA in Afghanistan.

Billie Mac: Well, that's tough. But from what you're saying, you could have saved him, Superman, and now you're taking a guilt trip on that. Ain't we been here before?

Ralph: If I just wasn't stuck in this wheelchair. How could he have done such a stupid thing? No way he couldn't take out a tank on his own and that's how I hear he got it.

Joe: Wheelchair or not, you can't do a thing for him. If he's gone he's gone. I'm not sure what it is for you, feeling guilty, 'cause you've talked about that before with guys who bought it in Nam, angry because of what happened to you to get you in that chair, sorry he got it, or what. You talk about all that crap like it still goes on and don't do much about it now. What about you, man, and your future? We ain't in no war and you ain't gonna go to one unless it's the Handicapped Olympics War.

A heated general discussion ensues, on topics ranging from losing one's buddies to the rightness of Vietnam and government support for it and whether Joe has any right to pick on Ralph in the manner he has.

Joe: Hey, man, you know me better than that! I love you, you big dumb ape, and that's why I said that to you, 'ceptin' you don't wanta hear that about livin' past time when you know that's the truth.

Confrontation is not unusual in these groups. Probably more than in most mutual help groups, at times a great deal of heated discussion and confrontation go on. Although this is not an encounter group, the members are not shy about calling some pretty straight shots. Such confrontations may initially meet with little acceptance or even with hostility, but the underlying trust that has been built up enables such hard-hitting statements to be made with little interference from the leaders.

As the group session closes, each member is given the floor to speak on what has occurred for him personally during the meeting. No one else is allowed to respond to his comments. Summing statements include both reflections about the impact of the discussion on oneself and reinforcing comments to others. Finally, the group rises, joins hands, and has a silent moment of meditation. One of the authors, who has been a practitioner in the helping professions for 20 years, found, in visiting this group, one of the most moving moments of his professional life. The emotionally positive high voltage that flowed through the locked hands of some very tough men was both touching and powerful, and it conveyed far better than words the caring and support each man felt for his comrades.

As each man speaks of his experiences, the human services worker continues to educate the group about what occurs with the disorder. The men learn that traumatic experiences can produce psychological maladjustment in anyone. They come to understand that intrusive imagery, startle responses, rage, anger, and unresolved grief are common and continuing occurrences. They come to see the fear of losing control as a by-product both of training and of closely guarding emotions to keep from experiencing the full onslaught of the disorder, and they realize that it does not mean they are crazy. Although some of the symptoms may never go away, they see men who have gotten better and learn that the condition is amenable to treatment. At the very least, with work, the disorder can be controlled or reduced in severity and frequency of occurrence. Finally, the men are reinforced over and over by leaders and their peers for being strong enough to have experienced what they did and be in the group talking about their problems.

Evidence seems to suggest that victims who have suffered other types of catastrophic intrusion into their lives can profit from support groups such as the veterans center uses. Donaldson and Gardner (1985) report that incest victims quickly gain an intense sense of relief in coming together with other victims in mutual support groups. A typical comment is "No one else understands, but I can come out of the closet here." A Vietnam veteran, when asked where he could be found six months hence, said, "Six months from now . . . come here on Wednesday night 'cause these are the people that care about me." When asked why this was so important, the veteran said, "I don't have to explain anything to anybody here, what it was like, or how I felt if I don't want to, but if I do, they all understand 'cause they been there."

Defining these groups at a deeper level is Foulkes's (1948) comment that such support groups can reinforce each other's normal reactions and break down each other's pathological reactions because they collectively constitute the very norm from which the individuals deviate. As such, members of the veterans' rap group have what one member called very good "crap detectors": "We can smell it immediately when somebody isn't coming clean with us."

The Combat Group

Once a given evening's session has ended, the group is split in two. Some of the men go into what is called the combat group and the others go into the life-adjustment group. Participation in either of the two groups depends on the member's stage of recovery.

Because Vietnam veterans were both victims and victimizers, the combat group serves as a cathartic agent. The group is built along the lines of the small squad units that operated in Vietnam. Each member is asked to recount combat experiences there and reflect upon their impact on him both then and now. The group's purpose is best summarized in the statement of Ralph:

Ralph: I was a SEAL, and this country didn't make anybody better at the jobs of interdiction, murder, mayhem, and efficiently slaughtering the enemy than us. As soon as I arrived in the country, they took us out in the bush and got us blooded. I waited on the trail and we ambushed a group of VC. I mean this wasn't long-range stuff, this was up close and personal. I killed an old man with a Bowie knife. Cut his throat and got his blood all over me. He was the first of many. Sure, he was carrying an AK-47 and I have no doubt that he would have offed me, but I still can't get that old guy out of my mind. I don't know why, but he's the guy I dream about.

Unlike the freewheeling rap group, with its laissez-faire attitude, the combat group is designed specifically to dig up buried emotions. The leaders make conscious attempts to weld the experiences generated by combat into what is happening here and now. Given Horowitz's (1976, p. 115) premise that no stress response syndrome is ever a matter of a single conflicted train of ideational and affective responses, the twists and turns over various content and time frames are probably appropriate and to be expected as the men hopscotch between Vietnam and their contemporary world. Free association is encouraged, and one monologue leads into another. The leader encourages as much detail as possible, seeking clues to long-buried guilt and anger. Such clues may give the human services worker material to use in individual sessions with clients.

For some men, speaking of what has happened to them is extremely difficult. Billie Mac, who has been silent for many weeks in the combat group, finally gets up and, protesting that he has never written anything longer than a postcard, reads the following:

Where Did B. M. Go?

What happened to B. M.—the boy from Mississippi—happy-go-lucky, not a care in the world, who loved life, sports, the sunshine, the rain . . . and everything in the used-to-be-beautiful world. Everyone told B. M., "Go to school. Play sports. Go to college. Make everyone proud of you. B. M., you are one of a kind!" But B. M. decided to do for his country. B. M. wanted to go to war and fight to win . . . to serve his country . . . to make everyone proud of him. B. M. went to war, B. M. killed, massacred, mutilated, burnt, hated—a hate that was like a drunk hate—tore his own heart out a little at a time, time after time.

B. M. fought and survived a war that 127 warriors that went with B. M. didn't. B. M. hated and was cold and mean. B. M. didn't care whether he came home or not. B. M. looked at everyone around him and wondered why the people hated him. Why they were scared of him . . . why they feared the warrior from Vietnam who went to a fight they were scared to fight.

B. M. wanted to love . . . to be loved. It seemed like the world was completely different from him and didn't have the same ideals about life and love.

B. M. became a drunk. He drank to forget the war, the brave warriors who had given their lives in Vietnam, to forget the people that he was living around. To these people B. M. was a cold-blooded murdering S.O.B.—a baby-killing M.F.

B. M. had been taught all his life, "Thou shalt not kill, love thine enemy." B. M. lost his morals. B. M. killed his enemies. B. M. cut the heads off some of his enemies. B. M. cut the ears off and mutilated them. B. M. lost his soul. B. M. is lost to God, to the world—and that B. M. can't be forgiven. He has committed an unforgivable sin to man and God's will. People can say, "Ask God to forgive you, B. M." But B. M. can't forgive himself and can't ask for forgiveness. B. M. feels that if he dies he is going to hell. B. M. has accepted that as part of his life. B. M. has accepted that feeling like someone took his heart out and stomped it into the ground. B. M.'s life is full of hurt and pain. There is not a day in his life that he doesn't feel hurt or hurts the ones he loves.

B. M. just wants to be loved . . . to love himself again; to get rid of that hard feeling deep down inside of his heart. B. M. wants to have peace of mind, to be at peace with himself and his heart. Is it too much for him to ask, to seek, to search for? Is death what it will take for B. M. to finally find peace within himself?

Why can't B. M. get out of all these depressing moods he stays in . . . and cries about nothing when he is driving down the road.

Sometimes B. M. thinks he is a crazy S.O.B. Maybe the people are right. Why can't B. M. keep a job? Because B. M. was a fuckup after he got back from Vietnam. His vengeance and his screwed-up attitude keep him in trouble. B. M. would get so much on his mind and B.M. would keep putting it back inside. The more he put it back, the worse his depression would get until it would erupt in a rage of vengeance, which would always wind up hurting himself or the people he loved. People would say, "Don't worry, B. M., things will get better. We will help you. Now help yourself." If B. M. knew how to help himself, he wouldn't be in the shape he is in. Even the government deceived B. M. They told B. M., "Don't worry, B. M. You go and fight this war for your country and if anything happens we will take care of you." B. M.'s response to this is, "Fine! I will do all I can for my government and my country." But give me my heart and soul back. Make me sleep at night. Make me quit crying. Take this depression away. Help me find a job and help me feel alive again. Give me back what you took from me. B. M. is what you took and I want myself back. I've done everything you wanted of me, so just give myself back to me.

I wish I could give back the lives I have taken from the world, but I know that I can't. I would if I could and I am the one that will have to live with that in my heart throughout eternity.

Upon completing his reading of this cathartic statement, B. M. runs from the group sobbing, goes to the bathroom, and vomits.

B. M. vividly and dramatically illustrates the anguish of PTSD in his writing: anguish from both an intrapersonal and interpersonal standpoint, of guilt he feels within himself for his moral travesties and rage at the travesties visited on him by an impersonal government and an uncaring society; anguish over what he was and is and how he is now attempting to resolve and reintegrate these two vastly different people that were and are B. M. Billie Mac continuously uses his nickname, pointing over and over to himself, but in the third person. Only in the last paragraph does his plea change clearly to subjective, first-person, owning statements. Even these statements are couched in terms of magical thinking—wish fulfillment. This is typical of the kind of self-condemnation that an individual who is both victim and victimizer experiences.

This excruciating piece of writing is an initiating step in the long process that moves from self-condemnation to what Lifton (1973) calls *animated guilt*. Animated guilt enables the victim to start taking responsibility for past actions and start to experience new degrees of personal liberation.

B. M.'s first step, though small, is significant. The self-destructive behaviors of 15 years are starting to give way.

This rather dramatic example of journal writing was done voluntarily, but when clients in a crisis situation will not talk about their experiences, sometimes suggesting that they write down their feelings can be a way of breaking the impasse (Gilliland, James, & Bowman, 1989, pp. 315–317). After Billie Mac returns to the group, the human services worker pursues the idea of keeping a journal (Pearsons, 1965).

HSW: B. M., everybody thought that was great. Could you do some more of that? I mean write those feelings down whenever.

Billie Mac: I dunno. I mean, I just couldn't sleep and I just set down and started in. That was terrible.

Chorus from the group: You're wrong! George wasn't kidding! That was tough! I wish I could have done that! That was great, terrific!

By putting down their thoughts in their own words and then hearing them, victims place the terrible memories at a safe enough psychological distance that they and the human services worker can analyze them (Cienfuegos & Monelli, 1983). Journal writing gives the human services worker a catalyst for encouraging the kind of free association necessary to open the crystallized defenses of the victim who might otherwise never open up and explore the traumatic event (Progoff, 1975).

Yet, as catharsis takes place within the combat group, an outside observer may wonder whether this rehashing of old battles is indeed therapeutic or whether it is a futile grasp to hold on to days of glory that are long past. The litmus test as to the degree of therapeutic benefit derived from the combat group is not so much the stories themselves, but how they are told. As one listens, the vivid detail of fire fights and patrols did not happen twenty years ago. It is as if these men just got off a plane from Vietnam and reentered the "world" yesterday. Being "stuck" in time when the trauma occurred is one of the hallmarks of PTSD, and helping individuals talk about the traumatic events and their feelings about it is critical to finally moving past it.

It is easy to see in some of these men a great deal of ambivalence concerning combat. While suffering horrible events, they were also on an all-time adrenalin high. They agonize over their present situation but continuously retreat into the days when they rose to the sound of gunfire. While they protest that they love their families and wish to change their ways of behaving toward them, one wonders if they love the call of battle even better.

An alternative hypothesis may be advanced. For these men, the combat group is a psychological detoxification process. Addicts who are just coming out of detoxification know full well the agony of not being able or not wanting to remember what happened to them. To come to grips with the buried trauma that helped produce that dependency may be an awesome task. First, as stories are continuously repeated, individuals move from the content of the episode to the emotional baggage that shields the true horror of the event from awareness. Long-buried guilt over what the victim did or did not do begins to emerge. Details that start one way slowly shift until the focus is on the affective reaction of the individual while the event was occurring. Much as the children of the Chowchilla bus kidnapping played "abduction" games over and over again in an attempt to sort through the traumatic event, patience and time are necessary to allow the adult victim to sort through the content of the trauma. As this occurs, the emotions that the altered content preserves begin to see the light of day.

The Life-Adjustment Group

As the guilt and horror of the combat situation are resolved, the men are moved into the life-adjustment group, which may be the more difficult one, and another crisis ensues. It is not enough to bring to light hidden traumatic experiences. The key is to integrate past experiences, to find meaning and new ways of coping, to make atonement not only for oneself but for others, and to find new directions in life (Brende & Parson, 1985, pp. 199–201). The group at this point will diminish and absences will increase. The reason is twofold. First, threatening material will again be covered. Second, action and behavioral change now become mandatory. Moving from the insight gained about what happened in the past to taking that insight and applying it to present time is a giant step, and one that is guaranteed to be rife with crisis. What is now called for is to get on with the business of living. At this juncture, intervention will take many forms, depending on what the particular problems are that the individual faces. Such problems range from serious substance abuse to obtaining salable vocational skills. Most of these problems will be referred to human services workers who are skilled in dealing with the individual's particular problem. The life-adjustment group will serve as a common base in which members can trade success stories and receive reinforcement and encouragement for their efforts.

However, one thread will usually run through the circumstances of all men at this stage. That thread is of vital importance and must be rewoven into the fabric of their lives. It is their family. Whereas any of these men could fight in a barroom brawl and give a good account of themselves, wrestling with the close intimacy of interpersonal problems and the intrapsychic strain under which that puts them is quite another story, particularly with regard to reconciliation with and atonement to family members. The veterans center also makes available a support group for the women close to these men. The group is both educative and cathartic in nature and provides a forum for the women as they struggle to make sense out of what the men in their lives have been going through and what is yet to come. Family support is critical for PTSD victims, and the center makes provision for the inclusion of the family in therapy—although this is often easier said than done.

Family Treatment

If the trauma is unresolved and chronic, its residue will eventually become enmeshed in the victim's interpersonal network (Figley, 1988, p. 91). As reluctant as the victim of trauma may be to seek help, often the family is even more unwilling to participate in the recovery process (Solomon, 1988). Even though the family may be suffering terribly because of the victim's actions toward them and their respondent actions toward the victim and each other, there will be much resistance to change the status quo, even though family members will adamantly maintain that change is needed. As strange as it may seem, while families may be stressed to the limit in adapting to the PTSD victim, they do try to adapt, at times in pathological ways. As the victim changes, the family may be in for a rude awakening and may not be able to make parallel changes.

Therefore, one of the crisis worker's major tasks is assessing the family's willingness to engage in treatment. The family's ability to resolve the crisis is a function of the nature of the event, the family's definition of the event, the resources they can bring to bear on it, the buildup of stressors that led to the event, and the effectiveness of their past and current coping skills (McCubbin et al., 1980). Figley (1988) proposes the following questions as preconditions for treatment:

1. What set of circumstances brought them to treatment?
2. How committed are they as a family to do this?
3. Is there an accurate PTSD diagnosis of one of the members?
4. What is the extent to which family members are suffering?
5. Do they understand that a new method of family relation skills must be established? (p. 95)

Once these questions have been fully explored, the worker's role is both educative and therapeutic. Treatment objectives are to develop and implement an intervention program to deal with both the stress disorder of the victim and assorted family dysfunctions that were in place prior to the event or have developed after the event. Learning about the disorder, dealing with the boundary distortions of intimacy and separation caused by it, alleviating psychosomatic results of rage and grief, urging recapitulation of the trauma, facilitating resolution of the trauma-inducing family conflicts, clarifying insights and correcting distortions by placing blame and credit more objectively, offering new and more positive and accurate perspectives on the trauma, establishing and maintaining new skills and rules of family communication, and initiating new coping and adapting skills as family dynamics change are some of the many tasks the worker will have to tackle (Figley, 1988, pp. 86–88; Rosenthal, Sadler, & Edwards, 1987). The foregoing is a major order and is best dealt with by a referral to a therapist who is a specialist in families and conjoint therapy. However, it is practically a must if the family has any hope of survival as a healthy system, and the crisis worker should understand that at an early point in the therapeutic process the family needs to be apprised of their role in the trauma and urged to become proactive in its solution.

Finally, for the victims, relearning how to be effective members of their families and society calls for the same kind of courage that propelled them into treatment in the first place. However, this time it may be much more difficult because they will be working with the people they need the most and probably have hurt the most.

Individual Intervention

Multiphasic treatment.   Individual treatment goes hand in hand with group work. From crisis stage to crisis stage, a multimodal therapeutic approach is used with heavy reliance on various combinations of behavioral and cognitive-behavioral therapy (Fairbank & Brown, 1987; Scurfield, 1985, p. 250). In the first phase of recovery, the emergency or outcry phase, the major problem is to get the victim stabilized; this means reducing the anxiety and physical responses associated with the trauma. Meditation, relaxation, and biofeedback may be used (Kolb & Mutalipassi, 1982).

In relaxation training and meditation, the human services worker teaches the victim how to relax body muscle groups systematically and to focus calmly on mental images that produce psychic relief of body tensions and stress (Benson, 1976; Wolpe, 1958). Victims learn how to exercise self-control over many of their stresses and anxieties and dampen debilitating physiological responses.

HSW: OK, Billie Mac. Just imagine that you are lying on the beach with that soft warm sand, the calm breeze blowing gently over you, the gentle lapping of the cool, crystal-clear water, and just easily focus your attention on that scene. Now just notice the difference in your body too. Notice the difference between how your muscles feel when they are tense and relaxed. Starting with your legs, just tense them up, feel how your muscles tighten up. Now relax them, and just feel that tightness drop away. Notice the difference and the really pleasant feelings that occur when your muscles are just hanging loose and flaccid. Continue to picture the scene on the beach as your work your way up your body, alternating between tensing and relaxing your muscles. Notice as you continue to do this how you can change the way your body feels and what you can focus on in your mind's eye.

While relaxation alone is helpful in alleviating current symptoms and enabling the victim to regain a measure of emotional and behavioral control, it is also a preliminary step in tackling the cluster of problems so characteristic of PTSD. Through deep relaxation or hypnosis, the client may be moved imaginally back in time to the traumatic event. Regressing the client in this manner is necessary to elevate bad memories of the traumatic event, and the intrusive images that accompany them, to conscious awareness (Brom, Kleber, & Defares, 1989; Kingsbury, 1988; Spiegel, 1989).

Extinguishing intrusive images.   Given the previously discussed neuro-psychological foundations of PTSD, Ochberg (1988) has concluded that PTSD should be viewed first in terms of autonomic nervous system (ANS) arousal and any treatment should take into consideration the physiological aspects of the disorder. Thus, a standing hypothesis for PTSD treatment has evolved that proposes a return of the client to the original state of elevated psychophysiological arousal in order to affect current maladaptive response sets (Malloy, Fairbank, & Keane, 1983). Once the victim has learned how to relax, other therapeutic strategies such as systematic desensitization, flooding, implosion, and Gestalt techniques may be employed to create ANS arousal (Black & Keane, 1982; Crump, 1984; Fairbank & Keane, 1982; Grisby, 1987; Keane & Kaloupek, 1982; Marafiote, 1980; Parson, 1984; Scurfield, 1985; Stutman & Bliss, 1985).

The human services worker continues to work slowly through the relaxation exercises and the mental imagery, continuously reinforcing the client for being able to shift to calm, relaxed scenes and away from the intrusive, anxiety-producing images. Practice for the victim in this and the other techniques to be covered in individual therapy is important. We recommend that sessions be audiotaped so that the victim can practice the procedures at home on a daily basis.

Once the victim has learned how to relax, the second phase of intervention occurs, coincident with the victim's emotional numbing and denial phase of recovery. This phase is concerned with bringing to conscious awareness the traumatic event and the hidden facts and emotions about it that the victim denies (Brende & Parson, 1985, pp. 191–192). A favorite phrase of the Vietnam infantryman, "Screw it, it don't mean nothing," aptly characterizes this stage and what has to be done. In a gentle but forceful way, the human services worker guides the victim, in the here-and-now of the therapeutic moment, to reexperience in the fullest possible detail what occurred in the traumatic experience so that submerged feelings are uncovered and ultimately expunged (Scurfield, 1985, p. 245). While deeply relaxed, the victim is asked to reexperience the terrible events of the trauma, with the injunction that at any time the memories can be switched off and the victim can return to the pleasant image of the beach.

HSW: Now go back to the village and tell me what is happening.

Billie Mac: [*Lying down, relaxed, eyes closed.*] The point man all of a sudden comes under fire and gets popped. I see him get hit. He's lying in the open across a ditch about 100 meters from the tree line. It's really getting hot, a lot of fire from concealed bunkers. They're using him as bait. This goes on for about five minutes, I guess. All of a sudden I decide to go and get him. Me and some other guys just get up and run across the open field to the ditch. We're getting all kinds of fire and out of five of us, only me and Al make it to the ditch without getting dinged. The point man is only about five meters from me, but I can't get at him. [*Billie Mac breaks into a sweat with slight tremors.*] I finally spot where the concealed bunker is that's making it so hot for us. I've got an LAW [light anti-tank weapon] and I get a bead on the bunker and zap it. At about the same time there's an explosion right next to me, a B-40 grenade, I guess, and that's all I remember until I wake up on the medivac chopper. [*Breaks into profuse sweating and major tremors.*]

HSW: All right, just shift out of that scene and back to the beach and just relax. Notice the cool water, the warm sand, the gentle breeze, and just let your muscles relax. [*Billie Mac noticeably relaxes and, with continued directives from the human services worker, returns to a calm, relaxed state.*]

Although the account of the combat situation is fearsome in its intensity, the human services worker suspects that it alone is not responsible for the traumatic reaction. Billie Mac was in many such situations, but this village is the focal point of his nightmares and intrusive thoughts. The human services worker suspects that there is more here than what Billie Mac is revealing, and seeks to slowly peel away the psychological walls that defend the trauma from awareness. The human services worker believes that the recounting of the combat situation, despite having psychological value as a defense mechanism, is probably not historically accurate. The victim has left out certain traumatic parts of the story and the human services worker's job becomes one of trying to fill in the gaps (Horowitz, 1976, pp. 117–118). Having built a very strong rapport and mutual trust with the victim (Keane et al., 1985, p. 291), the human services worker probes into the situation and actively seeks to interpret and clarify the content of the client's story with respect to its potentially overwhelming effect (Scurfield, 1985, p. 245).

HSW: Go back to the village and the ditch right before you take out the bunker. What do you see?

Billie Mac: I see the point man, he's alive, but bad off.

HSW: What are you thinking?

Billie Mac: I've got to get him, but I can't, the fire's too heavy.

HSW: What do you feel?

Billie Mac: Scared, I um . . . I can't seem to do anything . . . the rounds are really coming . . .

HSW: What's happening around you?

Billie Mac: Al keeps yelling, "Take the bunker out with the LAW!"

HSW: Then what?

Billie Mac: I . . . can't . . . do it . . . it . . . I'm terrified. [*Starts to shake uncontrollably.*]

HSW: Stay right with that, Billie. I'm right here.

Billie Mac: Al grabs the LAW, stands up and fires it and—Oh, my God! Get down! Oh, Jesus, the B-40 got AL. He's gone. His blood's all over me . . . I killed him. It was my job and I couldn't do it and I killed Al. [*Breaks into uncontrollable sobbing and shaking.*]

HSW: It's OK! Just erase that scene from your mind and slide back to that warm quiet beach. Just put yourself out of the firefight and back to that beach and relax, just focusing that soft sand in your mind.

As the victim breaks through the defenses that have allowed him to numb and shield the actual events from awareness, the full force of the reality of the incident floods over him, along with the overwhelming feelings of fear, guilt, remorse, and terror that accompany the event. As these thoughts come into awareness, they give the human services worker a much clearer picture of the how and why of phase 2 (denial and numbing) and those of phase 3 (intrusive-repetitive thoughts). The human services worker, using tolerable doses of reminiscence of the event, seeks to push forward into full awareness what the true scene at the event was and not what the victim's mind has fantasized it to be.

HSW: Now shift out of the scene at the beach and go back to the village. The B-40 has just gone off and Al is gone. What happens next?

Billie Mac: I can't remember . . . I don't know . . . I passed out.

HSW: [*Gently.*] Yes, you can. Just think a moment and picture the scene.

Billie Mac: Oh, God! You've got to get the point man now, Al took the bunker out and died doing it. You've got to go get him. I'm up and running, the fire is terrible, it's only 20 feet to him but it's like a mile, I'm so damned scared. [*Breath coming in rapid, ragged gasps.*] I've got him and am dragging him back to the ditch. Bullets are kicking up all around me, I'll be cut in two. He weighs a ton. I get to the ditch and roll him and me into it. I turn him over and . . . Oh, Mother of Mary! He's dead. Why, oh why, didn't I get there sooner? I could have saved him. You puke-faced coward. [*Starts uncontrolled sobbing.*]

HSW: [*Very calmly.*] You are OK. Just shift out of that scene and back to the beach. Just take all the time you need to relax and erase that scene from your mind. Just let the cool breeze blow over you, smell the clean salt air, and enjoy that feeling of being completely relaxed. [*Time passes, and Billie Mac becomes noticeably more relaxed.*] Now I'm going to count up from one to ten and when I reach ten you'll be fully alert and refreshed.

The human services worker does this and brings Billie Mac back to present time. The worker then processes the events of the imagery session with Billie Mac. At this point, the worker uses a more psychodynamic approach, actively intervening in the situation through clarification and interpretation of what the client says.

HSW: So it's not just that terrible fight at the village, but more what you didn't do. You feel as if you were a coward there, and that cowardice cost the life of your friend. It's almost as if all these years you'd been trying to atone for that in the only way you know how. That is, by doing things that would almost guarantee that you die too. The brushes with the law, the uncontrollable rage that winds up in knock-down, drag-out fights, the DWIs, and the suicide attempt.

Billie Mac: I don't know. [*Sobbing.*] I feel so terrible about it. How could I have frozen? It would have been better if I had got killed rather than live with this.

HSW: Yet you did act. You went after the man, and you couldn't know whether a minute or two would have saved his life. It seems as if that minute or two of indecision has caused 15 years of terrible retribution that you can never pay off.

I'd like to suggest that it has been paid with interest and now the time has come to pay the balance. Are you willing to do that?

Billie Mac: [*Shakily.*] I guess . . . although I don't know how much more I can take.

HSW: Remember! We've made it this far. Trust me and yourself. Together we can pull through this.

Even if the human services worker is right on target with his interpretation, getting Billie Mac to integrate the material and also allowing him to reconcile himself to the event are much more difficult matters. Although it can be extremely traumatic for the client, the human services worker will attempt to encourage the client to experience the full range of emotional responses that he felt at the time of the event, as well as how he tried to make sense of it (Donaldson & Gardner, 1985, p. 370). This marks the fourth phase of the crisis, the reflective-transition phase (Brende & Parson, 1985, p. 192). The human services worker will do this by combining behavioral techniques of flooding and thought stopping.

Flooding and implosion.   Flooding and implosive therapy is one of the most effective, if not controversial, techniques for getting rid of the bad memories of PTSD (Cooper & Clum, 1989; Keane et al., 1989; Lyons & Keane, 1989). In flooding and implosion (Stampfl & Levis, 1967), the fear-evoking stimuli are presented continuously. The rationale is that if the victim is literally flooded with anxiety-provoking stimuli for several periods of from one to two hours, the client will discover that there is no basis for fear. Continuously flooding the client causes the stimuli generating the anxiety to be imploded; that is, repeating the response without reinforcement will cause the tendency to perform that response to diminish. As the victim reenacts the trauma, the human services worker puts in the missing pieces of the puzzle and ferrets out all conditioned stimuli buried in memory. The result is that no noxious components of memory will be left to recondition debilitating responses (Keane et al., 1985, p. 265). This technique is a very serious therapeutic endeavor and should not be undertaken by neophytes until they have received supervised training.

Thought stopping.   Thought stopping is a simple but powerful device that enables the victim, with help from the human services worker, to change debilitating, intrusive thoughts to self-enhancing ones. The human services worker initially sets the scene and builds the images until the fear-evoking stimuli are at maximum arousal, and then shouts "Stop!" and replaces them with positive, self-enhancing thoughts (Williams & Long, 1979, p. 285). The human services worker tells the victim that at the point when the intrusive scene is most terrifying, the human services worker will slam a book sharply on the table and state in a firm voice, "Stop! Shift back to the beach!" The victim will be passive throughout the procedure, with the human services worker setting and enhancing the scene. An audio tape of the session is made, and the client is given the assignment of listening to the tape and then using the procedure whenever the intrusive images occur.

HSW: Now erase the beach scene and come back to the village. You're in the ditch. Bullets are snapping angrily over your head. Smell the stench of that ditch, feel death all around you, eagerly licking its chops. You can almost see the grim reaper there. Feel the frightening aspect of that scene. You'd like to run away, but there's nowhere to run. Oh, what a fool you were to ever make the dash out here in no-man's-land. Look back and see your squad members shot up, contorted in pain, with the blood and dirt covering them. Peek over the ditch and see the point man, he's in terrible pain, screaming for help, but there's a blizzard of fire coming from the bunker. It's certain death to stick your head above the dike. Feel the conflict. You want to do something, you know you've got to take the bunker out, but you are paralyzed. You can smell the fear in you, sweating out of your pores. Look at Al, he expects you to do something, you're the squad leader, but you can't. Feel Al's stare. Listen to him yelling, "Take the bunker now, man." Your fingers are glued to the LAW. Feel Al grab the LAW. Watch him as he stands up in that dreadful hail of death and fires the LAW into the bunker, and in the next instant see the explosion and the dirt fly as the B-40 round hits and Al disappears in the flame and smoke. Smell the smoke of cordite and the sheared copper odor of blood. Enhance those images—hear, smell, feel, see, taste that terrible moment. It's all there now as it really was. [*Billie Mac is writhing in the reclining chair.*] NOW STOP! [*Slams book down on desk.*] Shift away.

Billie Mac: [*Screaming.*] I can't do it!

HSW: Yes, you can! Just slide out of that and into that soft warm sand. Stay with that beach scene, smell the salt air, the cool breeze, and know that you can do that any time you want. Notice the difference in how your body feels, what goes through your mind. Just enjoy that feeling of knowing you can move into that scene.

This sequence is repeated over and over until the victim is able to switch volitionally from the intrusive image to the relaxing one with ease.

Gestalt techniques.   The Gestalt techniques of reaching into the victim's past and bringing to conscious awareness what Gestalt practitioners call "unfinished business" is particularly helpful in draining the pustulant affect that infects the event (Scurfield, 1985, p. 246). For Billie Mac this technique will take a different twist and will be the last part of the crisis, that of making atonement, penance, and restitution (Horowitz & Solomon, 1975).

HSW: The empty chairs in front of you represent various people. Al, the point man, other members of your squad that got hit on that day in the village. I want you to tell them what you felt about what you did. I may move to one of the chairs or have you take their place. Right now I want you to imagine Al in that chair over there. What are you going to say to him?

Billie Mac: I'm . . . so sorry. I froze. I shouldn't have done that. I killed you and I can't ever forget that.

HSW: [*Takes the chair of Al.*] Hey, man, what about that time at Chu Lai, and the A Shau valley? You didn't freeze then. You saved my bacon then. Remember how I froze? You didn't say squat. You think you're perfect?

Billie Mac: You were my best friend and I let that happen. It was my job. [*Sobs.*]

HSW: [*As Al.*] You think you got a corner on the market. Everybody was scared. I just did it. You gave me back my life a half dozen times. I'll never forget that. You did well by me, buddy. I got no regrets.

Billie Mac: Jesus, I miss you, I loved you so damn much.

HSW: [*As Al.*] Then remember the good times we had. That R & R in Bangkok, when we took the town apart. Those are the parts I remember. I love you too, buddy, but it's time we were done with that village. There's no forgiving to be done. You did your part plenty. It's time for you to say good-bye to me. [*The HSW gets up and goes over and takes Billie Mac into his arms and hugs him. Billie Mac weeps, releasing a flood of emotion.*]

For each man in the squad, the scene is replayed. Sometimes Billie Mac takes the role of the other man, and sometimes the human services worker does. Each piece of unfinished business is slowly and patiently worked through until Billie Mac has reconciled accounts with each person who was there on that terrible day. Clearly, Billie Mac goes through a painful but necessary grieving process that must take place if he is to put the event behind him (Brende & Parson, 1985, p. 105). As Billie Mac makes atonement for that day long past, and the trauma is expunged, the human services worker seeks to pull him to the present time and help him move forward with his life. Intensive intervention slacks off and the victim may then go through a series of booster sessions on an "as needed" basis, with a minimum of a booster session once a month for three to four months (Balson & Dempster, 1980). This point marks the fifth, or integration, phase of the crisis.

Helping Other Victims

One way survivors move from the tightly wrapped intrapersonal world of agony they have lived in to a more self-actualized and healthy interpersonal focus is to use their experience to help other victims (Lifton, 1973, pp. 99–133). Listen to two veterans, one a volunteer and one a professional in the human services field.

Jim: I'm in the group not because of what happened in Nam. I'm pretty much through that. A year's worth of the VA and some excellent help from other people got me over being nuts. I'm here because I owe those folks and maybe, I'm not sure how, to pay some back for what I got.

George: Why did I become a social worker at the vet center? Because I'd been in Nam, hassled with my own stuff, and thought I knew something about it and could help other people. Frankly, I think I've done about all I can here, and I believe I'm ready to start something else professionally. I'm going back to school and would like to concentrate on working with kids.

For both of these men, the ghosts of PTSD have been exorcised. They have integrated all aspects of the traumatic experience, both the positive and the negative. They know pretty clearly who they were before, during, and after the event. They have accepted responsibility for their own actions, as imperfect as those actions may have been at the time, and have made atonement for any guilt they carried (Scurfield, 1985, p. 246). George, in particular, manifests a forward view. Trauma changed his life dramatically. He grew from it and became a human services worker who dealt with the very problem he had conquered. He is now ready to move forward into other areas of human services. He has become more than a survivor. He has become a full-fledged member of the human race again, and though it may seem a meaningless platitude to some, he is a better person for it.

SUMMARY

Posttraumatic stress disorder (PTSD) has multiple symptoms and for that reason is often confused with a variety of other disorders. Its basis is maladaptive adjustment to a traumatic event. The disorder is both acute and chronic. In its chronic form it is insidious and may take months or years to appear. Its symptoms include, but are not limited to, anxiety, depression, substance abuse, hypervigilance, intrusive-repetitive thoughts, sleep disturbance, poor social relationships, suicidal ideation, and denial and numbing of the traumatic event. Both natural and man-made disasters may be responsible for PTSD, but it is far more likely to occur in victims who have been exposed to some man-made disaster that should have been prevented and is beyond accepted moral and societal bounds.

PTSD has probably been in existence as long as humankind has been rational enough to personalize the disasters that assail us. However, it was the debacle of the Vietnam War that brought it enough publicity to become a classifiable malady. The psychologically virulent milieu that was Vietnam became a breeding ground for trauma, which found its way back to the United States in an estimated 800,000 service personnel who have PTSD or related disorders.

Slow to recognize the disorder, human services professionals did little to ameliorate problems returning veterans suffered. Self-help groups were started by veterans when they had no other place to turn. Through lobbying efforts by such men as Dr. Arthur Blank, Vietnam Veterans Centers were set up throughout the United States. Along with other mental health professionals who had been grappling with the problems of veterans and other victims of trauma, staffers at the centers began developing treatment approaches for PTSD. Most notable of the techniques have been the rap groups developed at the veterans centers, which are a combination of support and therapeutic catharsis groups. Continuing treatment includes both group and individual intervention that is multimodal in nature. That treatment currently continues at Veterans Centers across the country and includes individuals who were involved in the recent Gulf War. Realizing the potential long-term mental health problems for individuals who have been exposed to combat, the Veterans Centers are now open to men or women who have been involved in any combat theatre. Hopefully, we have learned something from the debacle of Vietnam and that its dark legacy of mass mental health problems are a one-time occurrence for the United States.

Research and treatment of PTSD has taught us that many other trauma victims do not just "grow out" of their trauma and that time doesn't heal all wounds. Victims of trauma, especially of those types that originate in familial or severe sexual abuse, are prime candidates for PTSD. Bringing PTSD into the light of day has also disclosed many victims who were previously unknown to the mental health professional or were thought to be suffering from other kinds of disorders.

If PTSD has taught the human services one thing, it is that no traumatic experience should ever be dismissed in a cursory manner and that any initial assessment of a crisis client should investigate the possibility of a traumatic event buried somewhere in the client's past. Assessment and intervention are particularly difficult when the traumatic event is of a familial or sexual nature. A great deal of finesse and skill is necessary to uncover and treat such problems because of clients' reluctance to talk about socially taboo subjects or the feeling that a person, especially a man, should have the intestinal fortitude to bear up under the trauma. From what we now know, the latter assumption is patently false; under the right circumstances, anyone can fall victim to PTSD.

Interest in both cause and cure of PTSD has initiated a tremendous upsurge in research in the past few years. An excellent, comprehensive summary and discussion of PTSD may be found in the Brunner/Mazel Psychological Stress Series. For any human services worker who would like more firsthand information from practitioners, the Veterans Centers scattered throughout the United States are an excellent resource.

REFERENCES

Allan, J., & Berry, P. (1987). Sandplay. *Elementary School Guidance & Counseling, 21,* 300–306.

American Psychiatric Association (1980). *Diagnostic and statistical manual of mental disorders* (3rd ed.). Washington, DC: Author.

American Psychiatric Association (1987). *Diagnostic and statistical manual of mental disorders* (3rd ed., rev.). Washington, DC: Author.

Archibald, H. C., Long, D. M., Miller, C., & Tuddenham, R. D. (1962). Gross stress reaction in combat—a 15 year follow-up. *American Journal of Psychiatry, 119,* 317–322.

Atkinson, R. M., Sparr, L. F., & Sheff, A. G. (1984). Diagnosis of posttraumatic stress disorder in Viet Nam veterans: Preliminary findings. *American Journal of Psychiatry, 141,* 694–696.

Ayalon, O. (1983). Coping with terrorism. In D. Meichenbaum and M. Jaremko (Eds.), *Stress reduction and prevention.* New York: Plenum.

Balson, P., & Dempster, C. (1980). Treatment of war neurosis from Vietnam. *Comprehensive Psychiatry, 21,* 167–176.

Benson, H. (1976). *The relaxation response.* New York: Avon.

Berga, S. L., & Girton, L. G. (1989). The psychoneuroendocrinology of functional hypothalamic amenorrhea. *Psychiatric Clinics of North America, 12,* 105–116.

Bergen, M. (1958). Effect of severe trauma on a four-year-old child. *Psychoanalytic Study of the Child, 13,* 407–429.

Bergland, R. (1985). *The fabric of the mind.* Victoria, AU: Penguin Books Australia.

Black, J. L., & Keane, T. M. (1982). Implosive therapy in the treatment of combat related fears in a World War II veteran. *Journal of Behavior Therapy and Experimental Psychiatry, 13,* 139–165.

Blanchard, E. B., Wittrock, D., Kolb, L. C., & Geradi, R. J. (1988). Cross-validation of a Minnesota Multiphasic Personality Inventory (MMPI) subscale for the assessment of combat related post-traumatic stress disorder. *Journal of Psychopathology and Behavioral Assessment, 10,* 33–38.

Bloch, D. A., Silber, E., & Perry, S. E. (1956). Some factors in the emotional reaction of children to disaster. *American Journal of Psychiatry, 113,* 416–422.

Boman, B. (1986). Early experiential environment, maternal bonding and the susceptibility to post-traumatic stress disorder. *Military Medicine, 151,* 528–531.

Bourne, P. G. (1970). Military psychiatry and the Vietnam experience. *American Journal of Psychiatry, 127,* 123–130.

Bower, G. H. (1981). Mood and memory. *American Psychologist, 36,* 129–148.

Bowman, R. P. (1987). Approaches for counseling children through music. *Elementary School Guidance & Counseling, 21,* 284–291.

Brand, A. G. (1987). Writing as counseling. *Elementary School Guidance & Counseling, 21,* 266–275.

Brende, J. O. (1981). Combined individual and group therapy for Vietnam veterans. *International Journal of Group Psychotherapy, 31,* 367–378.

Brende, J. O., & Parson, E. R. (1985). *Vietnam veterans: The road to recovery.* New York: Plenum Press.

Breuer, J., & Freud, S. (1955). Studies on hysteria. In J. Strachey (Ed. and Trans.), *The standard edition of the complete psychological works of Sigmund Freud* (Vol. 2, pp. 1–10). London: Hogarth Press. (Original work published 1895.)

Brewi, B. (Speaker) (1986). *Crisis intervention with the Vietnam veteran* (Cassette recording No. 9). Memphis: Department of Counseling and Personnel Services, Memphis State University.

Brom, D., Kleber, R. J., & Defares, P. B. (1989). Brief psychotherapy for posttraumatic stress disorders. *Journal of Consulting and Clinical Psychology, 57,* 607–612.

Burgess-Watson, I. P., Hoffman, L., & Wilson, G. V. (1988). The neuropsychiatry of post-traumatic stress disorder. *British Journal of Psychiatry, 152,* 164–173.

Burke, H. R., & Mayer, S. (1985). The MMPI and the post-traumatic stress syndrome in Vietnam era veterans. *Journal of Clinical Psychology, 41,* 152–156.

Cannon, D. S., Bell, W. E., Andrews, R. H., & Finkelstein, A. S. (1987). Correspondence between MMPI PTSD measures and clinical diagnosis. *Journal of Personality Assessment, 51,* 517–521.

Carter, S. R. (1987). Use of puppets to treat traumatic grief. *Elementary School Guidance & Counseling, 21,* 210–215.

Cienfuegos, A. J., & Monelli, O. (1983). The testimony of political repression as a therapeutic instrument. *American Journal of Orthopsychiatry, 53,* 43–51.

Cooper, N., & Clum, G. A. (1989). Imaginal flooding as a supplementary treatment for PTSD in combat veterans. A controlled study. *Behavior Therapy, 20,* 381–391.

Crump, L. D. (1984). Gestalt therapy in the treatment of Vietnam veterans experiencing PTSD symptomatology. *Journal of Contemporary Psychotherapy, 14,* 90–98.

Dalton, J. E., Tom, A., Rosenblum, M. L., & Garte, S. H. (1989). Faking on the Mississippi Scale for Combat-Related Posttraumatic Stress Disorder. *Psychological Assessment, 1,* 56–57.

Daly, R. J. (1983). Samuel Pepys and post-trauma stress disorder. *British Journal of Psychiatry, 143,* 64–68.

Danieli, Y. (1985). The treatment and prevention of long-term effects and intergenerational transmission of victimization: A lesson from holocaust survivors and their children. In C. R. Figley (Ed.), *Trauma and its wake: The study of post-trauma stress disorder* (pp. 295–313). New York: Brunner/Mazel.

DeFazio, V. J. (1978). Dynamic perspectives on the nature of combat stress. In C. R. Figley (Ed.), *Stress disorders among Vietnam veterans* (pp. 36–37). New York: Brunner/Mazel.

Donaldson, M. A., & Gardner, R., Jr. (1985). Diagnosis and treatment of traumatic stress among women after childhood incest. In C. R. Figley (Ed.), *Trauma and its wake: The study of post-trauma disorder* (pp. 356–377). New York: Brunner/Mazel.

Egendorf, A. (1975). A Vietnam veteran rap group and themes of post-war life. *Journal of Social Issues, 31,* 111–124.

Erikson, E. (1968). *Identity, youth, and crisis.* New York: Norton.

Eth, S., & Pynoos, R. S. (1985). Developmental perspective on psychic trauma in childhood. In C. R. Figley (Ed.), *Trauma and its wake: The study of post-trauma disorder* (pp. 36–52). New York: Brunner/Mazel.

Fairbank, J. A., & Brown, T. A. (1987). Current behavioral approaches to the treatment of posttraumatic stress disorder. *Behavior Therapist, 10,* 57–64.

Fairbank, J. A., & Keane, T. M. (1982). Flooding for combat-related stress disorders: Assessment of anxiety reduction across traumatic memories. *Behavior Therapy, 13,* 499–510.

Figley, C. R. (Ed.). (1978). *Stress disorders among Vietnam veterans.* New York: Brunner/Mazel.

Figley, C. R. (1985a). From victim to survivor: Social responsibility in the wake of catastrophe. In C. R. Figley (Ed.), *Trauma and its wake: The study of post-trauma stress disorder* (pp. 398–416). New York: Brunner/Mazel.

Figley, C. R. (Ed.). (1985b). *Trauma and its wake: The study of post-trauma stress disorder.* New York: Brunner/Mazel.

Figley, C. R. (1988). Post-traumatic family therapy. In F. M. Ochberg (Ed.), *Post-traumatic therapy and victims of violence* (pp. 83–113). New York: Brunner/Mazel.

Figley, C. R. (1989). *Helping traumatized families.* San Francisco: Jossey-Bass.

Figley, C. R. (Speaker). (1990). *Post-traumatic stress disorder: Managing bad memories in individuals and family systems* [National teleconference]. Talahassee, FL: Florida State University, School of Social Work.

Fischer, V., Boyle, J. M., & Bucuvalas, M. (1980). *Myths and realities: A study of attitudes toward Vietnam era veterans.* Washington, DC: Lou Harris Associates.

Foulkes, S. H. (1948). *Introduction to group analytic psychotherapy.* London: Heineman.

Foy, D. W. (1987). Premilitary, military, and postmilitary factors in the development of combat-related posttraumatic stress disorder. *Behavior Therapist, 10,* 3–9.

Foy, D. W., Sipprelle, R. C., Rueger, D. B., & Carroll, E. M. (1984). Etiology of posttraumatic stress disorder in Vietnam veterans: Analysis of premilitary, military, and combat exposure influences. *Journal of Consulting and Clinical Psychology, 52,* 79–87.

Frederick, C. (1980). Effects of natural vs. human-induced violence: Evaluation and change. *Services for Survivors,* pp. 71–75. Minneapolis Medical Research Foundation, Inc./NIMH, Mental Health Services Development Branch.

Freud, S. (1959). Introduction to psychoanalysis and the war neurosis. In J. Strachey (Ed. and Trans.), *The standard edition of the complete psychological works of Sigmund Freud* (Vol. 5). London: Hogarth Press. (Original work published 1919.)

Freud, S. (1963). Introductory lectures on psychoanalysis XVII. In J. Strachey (Ed. and Trans.), *The standard edition of the complete psychological works of Sigmund Freud* (Vol. 16). London: Hogarth Press. (Original work published 1917.)

Frick, R., & Bogart, M. L. (1982). Transference and countertransference in group therapy with Vietnam veterans. *Bulletin of the Menninger Clinic, 46,* 429–444.

Furst, S. S. (1967). A survey. In S. S. Furst (Ed.), *Psychic trauma.* New York: Basic Books.

Furst, S. S. (1978). The stimulus barrier and the pathogenicity of trauma. *International Journal of Psychoanalysis, 59,* 345–352.

Gayton, W. F., Burchstead, G. N., & Matthews, G. R. (1986). An investigation of the utility of an MMPI posttraumatic stress disorder subscale. *Journal of Clinical Psychology, 42,* 916–917.

Gilliland, B. E., James, R. K., & Bowman, J. T. (1989). *Theories and strategies in counseling and psychotherapy* (2nd ed.). Englewood Cliffs, NJ: Prentice-Hall.

Gislason, I. L., & Call, J. D. (1982). Dog bite in infancy: Trauma and personality development. *Journal of the American Academy of Child Psychiatry, 21,* 203–207.

Gladding, S. T. (1987). Poetic expressions: A counseling art in elementary schools. *Elementary School Guidance & Counseling, 21,* 307–311.

Goldenson, R. M. (1984). Post-trauma stress disorder. *Longman dictionary of psychology and psychiatry.* New York: Longman.

Green, A. (1983). Dimensions of psychological trauma in abused children. *Journal of the American Academy of Child Psychiatry, 22,* 231–237.

Green, M. A., & Berlin, M. A. (1987). Five psychosocial variables related to the existence of Post-Traumatic Stress Disorder symptoms. *Journal of Clinical Psychology, 43,* 643–649.

Gressard, C. F. (1986). Self-help groups for Vietnam veterans experiencing post-traumatic stress disorder. *Journal for Specialists in Group Work, 11,* 74–79.

Grinker, R. R., & Speigel, J. P. (1945). *Men under stress.* Philadelphia: Blakiston.

Grisby, J. P. (1987). The use of imagery in the treatment of posttraumatic stress disorder. *Journal of Nervous and Mental Disease, 175,* 55–59.

Gumaer, J. (1984). *Counseling and therapy for children.* New York: Free Press.

Horowitz, M. J. (1976). *Stress response syndromes.* New York: Aronson.

Horowitz, M. J., & Solomon, G. F. (1975). A prediction of delayed stress response syndromes in Vietnam veterans. *Journal of Social Issues, 31,* 67–80.

Horowitz, M. J., Wilner, N., & Alvarez, W. (1979). Impact of Events Scale: A measure of subjective stress. *Psychosomatic Medicine, 41,* 209–218.

Horowitz, M. J., Wilner, N., Kaltreider, N., & Alvarez, W. (1980). Signs and symptoms of post-trauma stress disorders. *Archives of General Psychiatry, 37,* 85–92.

Hyer, L., Woods, M. G., Boudewyns, P. A., & Bruno, R. (1988). Concurrent validation of the Millon Clinical Multiaxial Inventory among Vietnam veterans with posttraumatic stress disorder. *Psychological Reports, 63,* 271–278.

Hyer, L. A., Woods, M., Harrison, W. R., & Boudewyns, P. A. (1989). MMPI F-K indexes among hospitalized Vietnam veterans. *Journal of Clinical Psychology, 45,* 250–254.

Irwin, E. C. (1987). Drama: The play's the thing. *Elementary School Guidance & Counseling, 21,* 276–283.

James, R. K., & Myer, R. (1987). Puppets: The elementary counselor's right or left arm. *Elementary School Guidance & Counseling, 21,* 292–299.

Johnson, R. G. (1987). Using computer art in counseling children. *Elementary School Guidance & Counseling, 21,* 262–265.

Keane, T. M. (1976). *State dependent retention and its relationship to psychopathology.* Unpublished manuscript, State University of New York at Binghamton.

Keane, T. M., Caddell, J., & Taylor, K. (1988). Mississippi Scale for Combat-Related Posttraumatic Stress Disorder. Three studies in reliability and validity. *Journal of Consulting and Clinical Psychology, 56,* 85–90.

Keane, T. M., Fairbank, J. A., Caddell, J. M., Zimmering, R. T., & Bender, M. E. (1985). A behavioral approach to assessing and treating posttrauma stress disorder in Vietnam veterans. In C. R. Figley (Ed.), *Trauma and its wake: The study of post-trauma stress disorder* (pp. 257–294). New York: Brunner/Mazel.

Keane, T. M., Fairbank, J. A., Caddell, J. M., & Zimmering, R. T. (1989). Implosive (flooding) therapy reduces symptoms of PTSD in Vietnam veterans. *Behavior Therapy, 20,* 245–260.

Keane, T. M., & Kaloupek, D. G. (1982). Imaginal flooding in the treatment of post traumatic stress disorder. *Journal of Consulting and Clinical Psychology, 50,* 138–140.

Keane, T. M., Malloy, P. F., & Fairbank, J. A. (1984). Empirical development of an MMPI subscale for the assessment of combat-related posttraumatic stress disorder. *Journal of Consulting and Clinical Psychology, 52,* 888–891.

Kelman, H. (1945). Character and the traumatic syndrome. *Journal of Nervous and Mental Disease, 102,* 121–153.

Kingsbury, S. J. (1988). Hypnosis in the treatment of posttraumatic stress disorder. An isomorphic intervention. *American Journal of Clinical Hypnosis, 31,* 81–90.

Kiser, L. J., Ackerman, B. J., Brown, E., & Edwards, N. B. (1988). Posttraumatic stress disorder in young children: A reaction to purported sexual abuse. *Journal of the American Academy of Child and Adolescent Psychiatry, 27,* 645–649.

Kolb, L. C., & Mutalipassi, L. R. (1982). The conditioned emotional response: A sub-class of the chronic and delayed stress disorder. *Psychiatric Annals, 12,* 969–987.

LaCoursiere, R. B., Bodfrey, K. E., & Ruby, L. M. (1980). Traumatic neurosis in the etiology of alcoholism: Vietnam and other trauma. *American Journal of Psychiatry, 137,* 966–968.

Landreth, G. L. (1987). Play therapy: Facilitative use of child's play in elementary school counseling. *Elementary School Guidance & Counseling, 21,* 253–261.

Laufer, R., Yager, T., & Grey-Wouters, E. (1981). Post-war trauma: Social and psychological problems of Vietnam veterans in the aftermath of the Vietnam War. In A. Egendorf, C. Kadushin, & R. S. Laufer (Eds.), *Legacies of Vietnam* (Vol. 1). Washington, DC: U.S. Government Printing Office.

Lifton, R. J. (1973). *Home from the war: Vietnam veterans—neither victims nor executioners.* New York: Simon & Schuster.

Lifton, R. J. (1974). "Death imprints" on youth in Vietnam. *Journal of Clinical Child Psychology, 3,* 47–49.

Lifton, R. J. (1975). The postwar war. *Journal of Social Issues, 31,* 181–195.

Lifton, R. J. (1978). Advocacy and corruption in the healing profession. In C. R. Figley (Ed.), *Stress disorders among veterans* (pp. 209–230). New York: Brunner/Mazel.

Lund, M., Foy, D., Sipprelle, C., & Strachan, A. (1984). The Combat Exposure Scale: A systematic assessment of trauma in the Vietnam War. *Journal of Clinical Psychology, 40,* 1323–1328.

Lyons, J. A., & Keane, T. M. (1989). Implosive therapy for the treatment of combat-related PTSD. *Journal of Traumatic Stress, 2,* 137–152.

Maclean, G. (1977). Psychic trauma and traumatic neurosis: Play therapy with a four-year-old boy. *Canadian Psychiatric Association Journal, 22,* 71–76.

MacPherson, M. (1984). *Long time passing: Vietnam and the haunted generation.* New York: Doubleday.

Malloy, P. F., Fairbank, J. A., & Keane, T. M. (1983). Validation of a multimodal assessment of posttraumatic stress disorders in Vietnam veterans. *Journal of Consulting and Clinical Psychology, 51,* 488–494.

Marafiote, R. (1980). Behavioral strategies in group treatment of Vietnam veterans. In T. Williams (Ed.), *Post-traumatic stress disorders of the Vietnam veteran* (pp. 49–70). Cincinnati: Disabled American Veterans.

Mason, J. W., Giller, E. L., Kosten, T. R., & Harkness, L. (1988). Elevation of urinary norepinephrine/cortisol ratio in posttraumatic stress disorder. *Journal of Nervous and Mental Disease, 176,* 498–502.

McCaffrey, R. J., Hickling, E. J., & Marrazo, M. J. (1989). Civilian-related post-traumatic stress disorder: Assessment-related issues. *Journal of Clinical Psychology, 45,* 72–76.

McCubbin, H., Joy, C., Cauble, E., Comeau, J., Patterson, J., & Needle, R. (1980). Family stress and coping: A decade review. *Journal of Marriage and Family, 43,* 855–872.

Memphis Vietnam Veterans Center. (1985). *The nonveteran helper.* Unpublished pamphlet of the Memphis Vietnam Veterans Center.

Merbaum, M. (1977). Some personality characteristics of soldiers exposed to extreme stress: A follow-up of post-hospital adjustment. *Journal of Clinical Psychology, 33,* 558–562.

Moody, D. R., & Kish, G. B. (1989). Clinical measures of the Keane PTSD scale. *Journal of Clinical Psychology, 45,* 542–546.

Moses, R. (1978). Adult psychic trauma: The question of early predisposition and some detailed mechanisms. *International Journal of Psychoanalysis, 59,* 353–363.

Mowbray, C. T. (1988). Post-traumatic therapy for children who are victims of violence. In F. M. Ochberg (Ed.), *Post-traumatic therapy and victims of violence* (pp. 196–212). New York: Brunner/Mazel.

Newman, C. J. (1976). Children of disaster: Clinical observations at Buffalo Creek. *American Journal of Psychiatry, 133,* 306–312.

Notman, M., & Nadelson, C. (1976). The rape victim: Psychodynamic considerations. *American Journal of Psychiatry, 133,* 408–412.

Ochberg, F. M. (Ed.). (1988). *Post-traumatic therapy and victims of violence.* New York: Brunner/Mazel.

Ohlsen, M. M. (1970). *Group counseling.* New York: Holt, Rinehart & Winston.

Olde, C. C., Schauer, A. H., Garfield, N. J., & Patterson, T. W. (1987). Preliminary steps in development of a screening instrument to assess posttraumatic stress disorder. *Journal of Counseling and Development, 66,* 104–105.

Ornitz, E. M., & Pynoos, R. S. (1989). Startle modulation in children with posttraumatic stress disorder. *American Journal of Psychiatry, 146,* 866–870.

Parson, E. R. (1984). The reparation of the self: Clinical and theoretical dimensions in the treatment of Vietnam veterans. *Journal of Contemporary Psychotherapy, 14,* 4–56.

Pearsons, L. (1965). *The use of written communications in psychotherapy.* Springfield, IL: Charles C Thomas.

Progoff, I. (1975). *At a journal workshop.* New York: Dialogue House Library.

Pruett, K. R. (1979). Home treatment of two infants who witnessed their mother's murder. *Journal of the American Academy of Child Psychiatry, 18,* 647–657.

Pynoos, R. S., & Nader, K. (1988). Psychological first aid and treatment approach to children exposed to community violence: Research implications. *Journal of Traumatic Stress, 1,* 445–473.

Roberts, W. R., Penk, W. E., & Gearing, M. L. (1982). Interpersonal problems of Vietnam combat veterans with symptoms of post-traumatic stress disorder. *Journal of Abnormal Psychology, 91,* 444–450.

Rosenthal, D., Sadler, A. G., & Edwards, W. (1987). Families and post-traumatic stress disorder. *Family Therapy Collections, 22,* 81–95.

Saigh, P. A. (1987). In vitro flooding of childhood posttraumatic stress disorders: A systematic replication. *Professional School Psychology, 2,* 135–146.

Saigh, P. A. (1989a). A comparative analysis of the affective and behavioral symptomatology of traumatized and nontraumatized children. *Journal of School Psychology, 27,* 247–255.

Saigh, P. A. (1989b). The validity of the DSM-III posttraumatic stress disorder classification as applied to children. *Journal of Abnormal Psychology, 98,* 189–192.

Salter, A. C. (1988). *Treating child sex offenders and victims.* Newbury Park, CA: Sage Publications.

Schetky, D. H. (1978). Preschoolers' response to the murder of their mothers by their fathers. *Bulletin of the American Academy of Psychiatry and Law, 6,* 45–47.

Scurfield, R. M. (1985). Post-trauma stress assessment and treatment: Overview and formulations. In C. R. Figley (Ed.), *Trauma and its wake: The study of post-trauma stress disorder* (pp. 219–256). New York: Brunner/Mazel.

Selye, H. (1976). *The stress of life.* New York: McGraw-Hill.

Senior, N., Gladstone, T., & Nurcombe, B. (1982). Child snatching: A case report. *Journal of the American Academy of Child Psychiatry, 21,* 579–583.

Shalev, A., Attias, J., Bleich, A., & Shulman, H. (1988). Auditory evaluation of nonalcoholic, drug-free posttraumatic stress disorder patients. *Biological Psychiatry, 24,* 522–530.

Shatan, C. (1978). The emotional content of combat continues. In C. R. Figley (Ed.), *Stress disorders among Vietnam veterans* (pp. 43–52). New York: Brunner/Mazel.

Silverman, P. R. (1986). The perils of borrowing: Role of the professional in mutual help groups. *Journal of Specialists in Group Work, 11,* 68–73.

Sluckin, A., Weller, A., & Highton, J. (1989). Recovering from trauma: Gestalt therapy with an abused child. *Maladjustment and Therapeutic Education, 7,* 147–157.

Solomon, Z. (1988). The effect of combat-related posttraumatic stress disorder on the family. *Psychiatry, 51,* 323–329.

Speigel, D. (1981). Vietnam grief work under hypnosis. *American Journal of Clinical Hypnosis, 24,* 33–40.

Spiegel, D. (1989). Hypnosis in the treatment of victims of sexual abuse. *Psychiatric Clinics of North America, 12,* 295–305.

Stampfl, T. G., & Levis, D. J. (1967). Essentials of implosive therapy: A learning-theory-based psychodynamic behavioral therapy. *Journal of Abnormal Psychology, 72,* 496–503.

Stutman, R. K., & Bliss, E. L. (1985). Posttraumatic stress disorder, hypnotizability, and imagery. *American Journal of Psychiatry, 142,* 741–743.

Terr, L. C. (1979). Children of Chowchilla: Study of psychic trauma. *Psychoanalytic Study of the Child, 34,* 547–623.

Terr, L. C. (1981). "Forbidden games": Post-traumatic child's play. *Journal of the American Academy of Child Psychiatry, 22,* 221–230.

Terr, L. C. (1983). Chowchilla revisited: The effects of psychic trauma four

years after a school-bus kidnapping. *American Journal of Psychiatry,
140,* 1543–1550.

Trimble, M. R. (1985). Post-traumatic stress disorder. History of a concept.
In C. R. Figley (Ed.), *Trauma and its wake: The study of post-trauma
stress disorder* (pp. 5–14). New York: Brunner/Mazel.

VanderKolk, B. A. (1983). Psychopharmacological issues in posttraumatic
stress disorder. *Hospital and Community Psychiatry, 34,* 683–691.

VanderKolk, B. A. (Ed.). (1984). *Posttraumatic stress disorder: Psychological and biological sequelas.* Washington, DC: American Psychiatric
Press.

VanderKolk, B. A. (1988). The biological response to psychic trauma. In
F. M. Ochberg (Ed.), *Post-traumatic therapy and victims of violence*
(pp. 25–38). New York: Brunner/Mazel.

Vinturella, L., & James, R. K. (1987). Sand play: A therapeutic medium
with children. *Elementary School Guidance & Counseling, 21,* 229–238.

Walker, J. I. (1983). Comparison of "rap" groups with traditional group
therapy in the treatment of Vietnam combat veterans. *Group, 7,* 48–57.

Wallerstein, J. S., & Kelly, J. B. (1975). The effects of parental divorce:
Experiences of the preschool child. *Journal of the American Academy of
Child Psychiatry, 14,* 600–616.

Walton, J. (1985). *Brain diseases of the nervous system* (9th ed.). Oxford:
Oxford University Press.

Watson, C. G., Juba, M. P., & Anderson, P. E. (1989). Validity of five combat scales. *Psychological Assessment, 1,* 98–102.

Watson, C. G., Kuchala, T., & Manifold, V. (1986). A cross-validation of the
Keane and Penk MMPI scales as measures of post-traumatic stress disorder. (1986). *Journal of Clinical Psychology, 42,* 727–732.

Weingartner, H., Miller, H., & Murphy, D. L. (1977). Mood-state-depen-
dent retrieval of verbal associations. *Journal of Abnormal Psychology,
86,* 276–284.

White, A. C. (1989). Post-traumatic stress. *British Journal of Psychiatry,
154,* 886–887.

Wilkinson, C. B. (1983). Aftermath of a disaster: The collapse of the Hyatt
Regency steel skywalk. *American Journal of Psychiatry, 140,* 1134–
1139.

Williams, C. C. (1983). The mental foxhole: The Vietnam veteran's search
for meaning. *American Journal of Orthopsychiatry, 53,* 4–17.

Williams, R. L., & Long, J. D. (1979). *Toward a self-managed life style* (2nd
ed.). Boston: Houghton Mifflin.

Wilson, J. P. (1980). Conflict, stress, and growth: Effects of the war on
psychosocial development. In C. R. Figley & S. Leventman (Eds.),
Strangers at home. New York: Praeger.

Wilson, J. P., Smith, W. K., & Johnson, S. (1985). A comparative analysis of
PTSD among various survivor groups. In C. R. Figley (Ed.), *Trauma
and its wake: The study of post-trauma stress disorder* (pp. 142–172).
New York: Brunner/Mazel.

Wolpe, J. (1958). *Psychotherapy by reciprocal inhibition.* Stanford, CA: Stanford University Press.

CLASSROOM EXERCISES
The Case of Ann

Ann Wotachek is a 44-year-old woman who is currently enrolled in a graduate human services program at a state university. She has been an excellent but quiet student throughout her academic coursework. She is now in her last semester and is currently enrolled in a practicum experience at a local family services facility that deals largely with child abuse. A phone call from the on-site supervisor to her practicum coordinator reveals that Ann is having trouble with her clientele.

Specifically, Ann becomes very defensive and hostile toward any parent whose child may have been abused. She becomes overly sympathetic with the child and is not effective in her intervention. The problem has progressed to the point that she becomes argumentative with her on-site supervisor over whether parents should even be treated or not. Ann's angry contention is that parents should immediately be jailed.

When she meets with her university supervisor, careful probing leads her supervisor to believe that Ann herself was abused in some way as a child. Reflection of this hunch brings a tearful and cathartic response from Ann. She reveals that she was raped by a stranger when she was 9 years old, beaten severely, and left for dead. She survived the ordeal, only to be blamed by her mother for what happened.

Further exploration indicates that Ann has many unresolved feelings of guilt and rage over the incident of 35 years ago, particularly in regard to her mother's vindictive response to the trauma. Her one attempt at marriage failed within six months of the wedding and she refuses to talk about it at all. She has no male friends, has not dated since her marriage 20 years ago, and has only one female friend. She states that she is extremely lonely but feels so alienated that she just can't make friends. Any relationship with a man is absolutely out of the question. She reveals that she has been in therapy before and that it has done absolutely no good. Ann oscillates between depression and inappropriate verbal rages. At present, she is extremely depressed because she feels that her last chance at making something of herself is about to meet with failure. Yet in almost the same breath she attacks the supervisor because she questions whether Ann should continue in the same practicum setting.

Ann also indicates that she has had trouble sleeping at night ever since she started the practicum. Her sleep disturbance is due to nightmares about her mother, now dead, who is accusing her of being sexually promiscuous. Her supervisor suspects that she is a victim of PTSD and suggests that she get in touch with a local therapist who specializes in cases of sexual abuse. Somewhat reluctantly, Ann agrees to go.

I. Using Gestalt Techniques to Resolve Unfinished Business

With the class divided into pairs, one person assumes the role of Ann or, if male, the role of a sexually abused boy. The other person, enacting the interventionist's role, places an empty chair opposite the victim. The chair will contain the victim's mother. The victim will conduct a conversation with the mother about the traumatic event. The interventionist may feel free to have the victim change chairs and assume the mother's role. The interventionist may also feel free to sit in the chair and assume the role of the mother or sit in the client's chair and have the victim be the mother.

The focus in this exercise is on release of feelings. The interventionist should steer away from analysis of content and concentrate on the emotional issues of the role play. Consistent and timely processing of feelings is important. After the victim has spoken to the empty chair and vice versa, the interventionist should pose a processing question on the order of "How did you feel when you said that?" After approximately ten minutes, the partners switch and repeat the process. Whenever both partners have concluded their Gestalt enactments, they should verbally disassociate themselves from the roles they have played. When the role play is finished, return to a large group circle and discuss what happened. Questions to be discussed may include:

1. How contrived did the exercise feel?
2. Did the role play become more realistic as it progressed?
3. What makes this an effective technique to use with victims of PTSD?
4. How do your own feelings come into play as you assume the role of Ann?
5. What alternatives can you think of that would get at the anger Ann feels toward her mother?
6. Is it important to get at such feelings, or should the interventionist concentrate on the symptoms that are currently hindering Ann's performance?

An admonition to the instructor is important in this exercise. It has been our experience that one or more class members may have had a real-life experience similar to that expressed by the character. The instructor should circulate among the pairs and keep a sharp eye out for members who become highly agitated or depressed during the exercise. Individual deprogramming or referral to a mental health professional may be necessary for those who have had such experiences and who experience a traumatic reaction to the exercise.

II. The Interventionist's Role in Support Groups

As a supplementary activity, read the articles in the *Journal of Specialists in Group Work,* May 1986. This special issue is entirely devoted to the support-group concept. After reading the issue, discuss the following questions:

1. What should the role of a human services professional be in the support group?
2. Does the human services worker have to have been a victim of trauma in order to be effective in such groups?
3. How do support groups fit in with overall intervention?
4. What kinds of support groups do you know about that operate in your geographic locale?
5. How does one go about getting into such groups?

CHAPTER 6

Sexual Assault

BACKGROUND

On April 23, 1992 the American public received some startling news regarding rape and sexual assault ("Two Rape Surveys," 1992). The findings of a comprehensive study by D. Kilpatrick and C. Edmunds, funded by the National Institute on Drug Abuse, indicated that 683,000 American women were raped in 1990 and that 12.1 million women had been raped at least once during their lives. In addition, the government-funded National Women's Study showed that about 62% of the rape victims had been sexually assaulted when they were minors, with 29% having been assaulted when they were under the age of 11.

The study clearly dispelled the common myth that most women are raped by strangers. Almost 8 out of 10 of the rape victims knew their attacker. More were concerned about other people finding out about the rape and their name being made public than were worried about getting pregnant or contracting VD or AIDS from their attackers. Nine percent of the women were raped by husbands or former husbands, 11% by fathers or stepfathers, 10% by boyfriends, 16% by other relatives, and 29% by friends or acquaintances. These disturbing statistics clearly document the fact that rape and sexual assault is one of the most serious and tragic crises in America today.

There is abundant evidence to suggest that crises resulting from sexual abuse are different in nature, intensity, and extent from other forms of crisis (Burgess & Holmstrom, 1985; Finkelhor, 1979, 1984, 1987; Hartman & Burgess, 1988; Kelly, 1988; Williams & Holmes, 1981). How the crisis affects an individual depends on many variables. Age, race/ethnicity, family background, cultural and religious mores, community attitudes, type of abuse experienced, length of time and intensity of victimization, attitudes about sex roles, attitudes of family and support persons following disclosure/discovery of the abuse, and effects of policy or legal proceedings following disclosure/discovery of the abuse all influence the trauma of a sexual assault (Williams & Holmes, 1981). Crisis intervention with survivors of sexual abuse incorporates the basic principles of the six steps discussed in Chapter 2.

One survivor may appear to take sexual assault in stride, whereas another person subjected to a similar experience virtually falls apart. One individual may work through the crisis rather quickly, and another may suffer varying degrees of debilitation for a long period of time. Many survivors experience long-term residual effects, which Hartman and Burgess (1988) have delineated as *rape trauma* or *sexual trauma.* Frazier and Borgida (1985) have reported that many psychologists now classify rape trauma as a particular example of posttraumatic stress disorder, as defined in DSM-IIIR (American Psychiatric Association, 1987).

Any person may at one time or another be the victim of sexual abuse (Molmen, 1982, p. 12). Although the majority of victims are children and females under 30 (Amir, 1971; Bass & Thornton, 1983), sexual assault survivors have been identified among males and females from every segment of the population—children, adolescents, adults, and older adults (Williams & Holmes, 1981).

For many years the phenomena of rape and other forms of sexual abuse received attention mainly as crimes. They were largely the purview of law enforcement and the legal system. The predominant societal response was punitive—directed at the attacker. Because of increased public awareness through consciousness raising by the media, the feminist movement, and a host of writers such as Amir (1971), Brownmiller (1975), and A. B. Davis (1985), public concern has shifted to helping the survivors of sexual abuse.

Programs, centers, and agencies for helping survivors of sexual abuse have been established in most cities. Telephone hot lines and rape crisis centers are now within reach of the majority of the population. Listings of resources and agencies to assist survivors throughout the country have been compiled by a number of persons, such as Bass and Thornton (1983), Benedict (1985), Grossman and Sutherland (1983), and Townley (1985). Survivors can also acquire information and assistance through crisis hot lines, community mental health centers, or emergency line 911. In most cities, persons needing help can look in the telephone directory under "Rape" or call the local number of the Department of Human Services. Almost any practicing nurse, psychologist, social worker, certified counselor, or other human services worker can refer survivors and their families to appropriate sources of assistance.

Definition of Rape

There are many definitions of rape. Some are based on legal constructs; some are derived from other sources. We prefer to use Benedict's (1985) definition of rape as "any sexual act that is forced upon you" (p. 1). Brownmiller (1975) distinguishes between most legal definitions and what she refers to as a woman's definition. The legal definition of rape as "the forcible perpetration of an act of sexual intercourse on the body of a woman not one's wife" (p. 380) is seen as much too narrow and protective of male supremacy. Brownmiller's preferred definition from a woman's perspective is that rape is "a sexual invasion of the body by force, an incursion into the private, personal inner space without consent—in short, an internal assault from one of several avenues and by one of several methods [that] constitutes a deliberate violation of emotional, physical, and rational integrity and is a hostile, degrading act of violence" (p. 376). That definition appears to encompass the whole scope of rape, as well as other forms of sexual abuse/misuse.

Literature on Rape and Sexual Abuse

We have derived seven fundamental assumptions about rape and sexual abuse from the literature on rape and the findings of representative sources. These fundamental assumptions underlie this chapter.

1. *Rape is not sex.* Rape, incest, sodomy, digital or object penetration of the vagina or anus, forced oral sex, forced fondling, forced masturbation, and other forms of sexual abuse or misuse are acts of aggression, violence, force, or the willful exercise of power, dominance, or control over other persons, rather than expressions of sexuality (Benedict, 1985, pp. 5–12; Burgess, 1985; Carnes, 1983; Colao & Hosansky, 1983; Fortune, 1983; Geiser, 1979, pp. 14–19; Hursch, 1977; Janosik, 1984, p. 268; Katz & Mazur, 1979; O'Brien, 1983; Sussman & Bordwell, 1981; West, Roy, & Nichols, 1978). Walker (1989) identifies pornography as one aspect of sexual abuse, and husband-wife sexual assault as rape—a criminal act (p. 124).

2. *Rape is an uninvited act.* There is overwhelming evidence that survivors seldom invite or provoke sexual assault. People do not ask for or deserve the various negative feelings or emotions that result from rape and other forms of sexual abuse/misuse. These emotional responses may include a feeling of fear of death or serious injury, panic, terror, degradation, humiliation, helplessness, violation, being overwhelmed, shame, guilt, anger, denial, blame, betrayal, disbelief, loss of control, rage, loss of self-esteem, and immediate or delayed trauma. In the case of sexual assault, the survivor's ensuing negative emotions are brought on directly by the act of sexual abuse itself (Benedict, 1985; Brownmiller, 1975; Burgess & Holmstrom, 1974, 1985; A. B. Davis, 1985; Ellis, 1983; Frazier & Borgida, 1985; Geiser, 1979, pp. 26–31; Grossman & Sutherland, 1983).

3. *Rape can happen to anyone.* Contrary to common opinion, survivors of rape and other forms of sexual abuse/misuse include persons of all ages, races, cultural backgrounds, social groups, and sexes and sexual preferences (although most rapes are committed on females)—from young children through older adults. Most of the recorded rapes of men have occurred in penal institutions, although such assaults may occur anywhere. Men are more reluctant to report rapes than are women (Bass & Thornton, 1983; Benedict, 1985; Burgess, 1985; Colao & Hosansky, 1983, p. 17; Russell, 1982; Williams & Holmes, 1981). Recently, date and acquaintance rape (Harrison, Downes, & Williams, 1990) and husband-wife rape (Walker, 1989, p. 124) have been reported with growing frequency.

4. *Rapists come from every segment of society.* People who rape and commit other forms of sexual abuse/misuse have been identified in every stratum of society—from judges to messenger boys, from weaklings to muscular types, from vagrants to corporate executives, from husbands and fathers to strangers, from known friends or relatives to unknown intruders (Benedict, 1985, pp. 9–10; Burgess, Groth, Holmstrom, & Sgroi, 1978; Burgess & Holmstrom, 1979; Greer & Stuart, 1983; Groth & Birnbaum, 1979; Hursch, 1977; Kempe, 1984; Medea & Thompson, 1974, pp. 29–36; Rada, 1978; Russell, 1982; Sanford, 1980; Sussman & Bordwell, 1981; Townley, 1985, pp. 80–91).

5. *The incidence of sexual assault has been underreported.* The literature describes rape and other types of sexual offense as being a widespread social problem of epidemic proportions. That statement is based on *reported* levels of assault. What is more disturbing is that the literature consistently estimates that "fifty to ninety percent of all rapes or attempted rapes go unreported" (Sussman & Bordwell, 1981, p. 15). The research indicates that suspects are apprehended in about 5% of the cases and that prosecutors obtain convictions in less than 3% of these cases. Most of the reports on rape and sexual assault record only specific age categories. Most instances of incest and molestation are never reported. The vast majority of crime survey reports do not report sexual abuse of children under the age of 12 (Bass & Thornton, 1983; Benedict, 1985, pp. 186–192; Brownmiller, 1975, p. 175; Geiser, 1979, pp. 9–10; Medea & Thompson, 1974; Sussman & Bordwell, 1981, p. 15; Townley, 1985, p. 24).

6. *Nearly all perpetrators of sexual abuse/misuse are men; most survivors are women and children.* Sexual assault and abuse/misuse in all their many forms are predominantly male crimes. Most research indicates that males between the ages of 18 and 35 inflict 99% of the sexual assaults in the United States (Medea & Thompson, 1974; Plummer, 1984, p. v; Townley, 1985, p. 162).

7. *The recovery of survivors of sexual assault/abuse/misuse is enhanced by the empathic help and understanding of the persons close to them.* Whether the survivor's support persons be family, friends, associates, medical or legal personnel, crisis workers, or long-term therapists, the important ingredients in the helping relationship are acceptance, genuineness, empathy, caring, and nonjudgmental understanding. The literature uniformly supports treating the person as a positive, recovering survivor who deserves empathy and support—not as a person who is suspect and blamed for being stupid enough to get raped. The fact is that the assault is considered a crime caused by a violent attacker. The person assaulted emerges alive and should be admired, encouraged, accepted, and helped to recover as soon as possible (Benedict, 1985; Colao & Hosansky, 1983; Gil, 1984; Grossman & Sutherland, 1983; Groth & Stevenson, 1984; James & Nasjleti, 1983; Karpel & Strauss, 1983; Knopp, 1982; Mayer, 1983; McCombie, 1980; Renshaw, 1982; Sanford, 1980).

DYNAMICS OF RAPE
Psychosocial and Cultural Dynamics

Rape is a complex phenomenon. Sussman and Bordwell (1981) interviewed convicted rapists and have vividly demonstrated that each rapist's reasons for assault are individual. Yet the vast majority of rapes have to do with the power relationships between men and women (p. 12). Somehow the contemporary sociocultural milieu produces some males who feel such absence of power and control in their lives that they develop a need to "take it" (control). These males come to believe that it is their "right" (p. 5) and proceed to rationalize and justify their behavior even though they have invaded and taken by force the very essence of another person's life and body. The rapist's justification for committing this ultimate act of humiliation and degradation comes down to forcing the person to submit. Since most survivors are females and children, it is largely a concept of adult male supremacy, even though adult males are themselves sometimes raped. The notion of male supremacy has its roots deep in our cultural history, which has, for centuries, equated the property rights of men with access to and control of the bodies of women, children, and others who are perceived as dependents (Brownmiller, 1975).

Social factors.   Baron and Straus (1989) characterize rape as a social phenomenon and theorize four different causes: gender inequality, pornography, social disorganization, and legitimization of violence. *Gender inequality* relates economic, political, and legal status of women in comparison to men. *Pornography* reduces women to sex objects, promotes male dominance, and encourages or condones sexual violence against women. *Social disorganization* erodes social control and constraints and undermines freedom of individual behavior and self-determination. *Legitimization of violence* is the support the culture gives to violence, as portrayed in the mass media, laws permitting corporal punishment in schools, violent sports, excessive military expenditures, and so on.

Particularly in the Western world, aggression and domination are portrayed as accepted male characteristics, while peacefulness and submission are deemed appropriate for females. These attitudes and values are woven into our social fabric. Brownmiller (1975) and others have documented a part of the history of rape as a psychosocial means by which the victors in wars reward themselves and humiliate their vanquished foes. The wholesale rape and killing of helpless women and children represents the ultimate vulnerability and defeat of a people. It likewise represents the ultimate humiliation and subjugation of a person. Whether it is inflicted on hundreds, as reported in war, or on one person, the purpose is quite similar—the use of unrestrained power to force the vanquished into total submission.

Societal attitudes about rape have long impeded survivor advocacy. In recent years, improved communications, wider reporting, and better research information have tended to improve the lot of the survivor. However, additional negative dimensions have been added, such as the complicating effect of the automobile (increased mobility), the accelerated maturation rate of children and adolescents, population concentration in urban centers, emergence and acceptance of violence in the visual media, greater amounts of personal leisure time, and more discretionary money to spend (Amir, 1971; Brownmiller, 1975).

Cultural factors.   Our cultural heritage has apparently lagged behind our technological and social patterns. Despite factors such as industrialization, population mobility, birth control, the feminist movement, employment of women outside the household, smaller families, higher divorce rates, single-parent families, blended families, relaxed moral codes, and higher economic standards of living, our attitudes about sex, sexuality, and sexual assault have been slow to change (Williams & Holmes, 1981). One example of this cultural lag is the persistent belief that rape is a crime committed for sex (Benedict, 1985; Brownmiller, 1975). The list of myths about rape is long, and these myths are only the tip of the iceberg of problems contemporary culture faces in dealing with rape and other forms of sexual abuse/misuse (Benedict, 1985).

Personal and Psychological Factors

Personal and psychological factors unique to men affect both their decision to assault and the way the assault is carried out (Amir, 1971; Groth & Birnbaum, 1979; Williams & Holmes, 1981). Factors unique to women tend to affect their responses to rape and their recovery process (Amir, 1971; Benedict, 1985; Williams & Holmes, 1981). The male offender

1. acts hostile, aggressive, condescending, and domineering even though he often feels weak, inadequate, threatened, and dependent
2. believes he should act strong, courageous, and manly
3. lacks the skills to make his point in society
4. may be *angry*—the angry rapist is likely to use more violence and force than is needed to compel the individual to submit and is likely to threaten, beat, and revile the person
5. may need to exercise *power*—the power rapist is likely to use the assault situation to prove to himself and to the person that he is powerful, omnipotent, and in total control
6. may show *sadistic* patterns—the sadistic rapist frequently uses extreme violence and often mutilates or murders the individual.

The female who is assaulted

1. fears for her life
2. may respond by exhibiting no emotions—appearing unaffected
3. feels humiliated, demeaned, and degraded

4. may suffer immediate physical and psychological injury as well as long-term trauma

5. may experience impaired sexual functioning

6. may blame herself and feel guilty

7. may experience difficulty relating to and trusting others—especially men

8. may experience fantasies, daydreams, and nightmares—vividly reliving the assault or additional encounters with the assailant—or may have mental images of scenes of revenge

9. may feel intense anger or hatred toward the assailant

10. will never be the same, even though most survivors, over time, develop ways to recover, cope, and go on with their lives

11. may be fearful of going to the police or a rape crisis center

12. may be reluctant to discuss the assault with members of her family, friends, and others because of the risk of rejection and embarrassment.

Myths About Rape

Social and cultural myths about rape have received much attention in the literature on sexual abuse. Benedict (1985, pp. 5–12) has incorporated society's most prevalent and harmful myths into five broad categories.

1. *Rape is sex.* The notion that rape equals sex is perhaps the most destructive myth of all. If we believe that rape is sex, then it follows that rape doesn't hurt (physically or psychologically) any more than sex. We can even believe that the survivor enjoys and is erotically stimulated by it. The fact is that rape is no joke. Rape is violence, torture, and a life-threatening event. It is utterly humiliating. It is robbery of another person's essence by personal assault. Rape is *wrong, inexcusable,* and a *horrifying* crime (Sussman & Bordwell, 1981).

2. *Rape is motivated by lust.* Groth and Birnbaum (1979) believe that the motivation for rape is most likely to be power, anger, revenge, control, frustration, or sadism. Benedict (1985) reports that some men may come to associate sex with violence, thereby viewing women not as human beings but as objects of prey and viewing sex as an act of power (p. 8).

3. *Rapists are weird loners.* No such contention can be supported by the research. Rapists come from every walk of life (Amir, 1971; Medea & Thompson, 1974, pp. 29–36). The rapist could be the man next door, a charming businessman, a laborer, a relative, a transient, or anyone else.

4. *Women provoke rape.* Sussman and Bordwell (1981) have clearly shown that what the survivor does prior to the rape has little, if anything, to do with the rapist's decision to assault. Although most rapists deny that they are rapists, rationalize that women provoke it, or deny that the sexual assaults are rape, there are virtually no documented cases in which women have lured men into raping them. It is true that many women are unlucky enough to be in the wrong place at the time of the assault or are otherwise

out of reach of assistance. However, being vulnerable is never a cause or a reason to be raped.

5. *Only bad women are raped.* This myth is one of the most blatant examples of a "blame the victim" attitude (Brownmiller, 1975). This myth is taken to mean that, if the woman has a "bad" reputation, the rape is justified. Brownmiller's point is that a person's alleged reputation has nothing to do with whether she deserves to be raped. Rape is rape! Whether the person is a professional hooker or a minister should make no difference. Neither deserves to be assaulted and both are entitled to equal protection and treatment.

It is not easy or simple to eradicate or even to refute these five myths in society at large. Even when people mentally come to understand the fallacies of the myths, many individuals hold negative residual attitudes, derived from the myths, that color their language, beliefs, and behavior. Evidence of this crops up everywhere—from our jokes and cartoons to our judicial decisions. There is a critical need for rape prevention programs that target potential or actual perpetrators (Lee, 1987) and demolish the myths. It is necessary that we, as a society, reeducate and reorient ourselves concerning these myths if we are ever to break the cycle of injustice that we have perpetrated in the whole area of sexual abuse/misuse (Benedict, 1985).

DYNAMICS OF SEXUAL ABUSE OF CHILDREN
Recent Historical Dynamics

According to Finkelhor (1984), several factors have contributed to the emergence of child sexual abuse as a problem for society. Resolution of the problem has been championed by the women's movement, the children's protection movement, and a coalition of groups with successful experience in promoting social issues (p. 3). It has recently been established that the sexual abuse of children is a worldwide problem and not one confined to the United States (pp. 5–6). The rate of abuse has grown with the advent of widespread divorce, remarriage, and easy conjugal pairings and dissolvements (increasing the amount of exposure of children to stepfathers, boyfriends, and lovers of children's mothers) (p. 7). Rapid change in sexual norms has accompanied an erosion of traditional, externalized sexual controls, aided and abetted by popular pornography, portraying children as sex objects (p. 8). The sexualization of life, which has become prevalent in the media, has led to new, increased, and heightened expectations. Such expectations, faced by many men who are locked into situations in which they feel a sense of sexual deprivation, have led to the abuse of children by men seeking alternatives for their sexual gratification (p. 9). An additional factor proposed by Finkelhor (1984) is that women have become less willing to live in subservient, passive, childlike roles. Some men, threatened by the assertiveness of women, have turned to children as compliant sex partners (p. 9).

Finkelhor (1979) reports that sexual deviance and victimization are more likely to emerge in families characterized by a high degree of social isolation. Such deviance has been observed in isolated Appalachian families as well as in some cities and suburbs. In fairly self-contained communities, the tolerance of sexual deviance, such as incest, may be passed on from generation to generation (pp. 25–26). Finkelhor also identifies role confusion and fear of abandonment as sources of the sociopathology of child abuse (pp. 26–27). He concurrently reports a positive correlation between the isolated circumstances of those in extreme poverty and the incidence of incest and sexual abuse.

Phases of Child Sexual Abuse

The dynamics of rape apply to the whole scope of sexual abuse-misuse. There are some additional dimensions that crisis workers should consider when dealing with situations involving children. According to Murphy (1985), reporting on the dynamics of sexual abuse developed by Sgroi (1982), the behavior of the abuser may be traced through five phases: (1) engagement, (2) sexual interaction, (3) secrecy, (4) disclosure, and (5) suppression. These phases apply to both intra- and extrafamilial abuse.

Engagement phase.   The abuser's objective in the engagement phase is to get the child involved in sexual activity with the abuser. Both access to the child and opportunity (privacy) are needed if the abuser is to be successful. Therefore, if we were looking for possible instances of unreported abuse, we would identify times and situations when the potential abuser and the child were alone together. We must also look for different strategies that two different types of abusers (child molesters and child rapists) may employ (Murphy, 1985, p. 1).

Molesters tend to use *enticement* and *entrapment* to get the child engaged in sexual activity. *Enticement* may include deceit, trickery, rewards, or the use of adult authority to tell the child in a matter-of-fact way that the child is expected to participate. *Entrapment* is used to manipulate the child into feeling obligated to participate through traps, blackmail, and so forth. Molesters may make pornographic pictures or video tapes and convince the child that there is no other choice than going along with the secret activity and may also seek to impose guilt by making the child feel responsible for the abuse (Murphy, 1985, p. 1).

Child rapists use *threat* (particularly the threat of harm) or the imposition of superior physical *force* to engage the child in the abusive activity. Typically, the rapist will threaten to kill or injure the child or someone dear to the child or threaten to commit suicide himself, convincing the child that he or she will be blamed for the rapist's death if the child resists or reports the rape. In using superior force, the rapist may simply overpower the child, restrain the child by tying him or her, give the child drugs or alcohol, or physically brutalize the child into submission (Murphy, 1985, p. 1).

The vast majority (about 80%) of abusers use the first two strategies—enticement and entrapment. Abusers tend to repeat their engagement patterns and show little tendency to move from nonviolent to violent strategies. Molesters are apt to consistently entice or trap children, whereas child rapists tend to use threat or force almost exclusively. The strategy used by the abuser is an important issue in treatment because survivors typically wonder throughout their lives why they permitted it to happen (Murphy, 1985, p. 1).

Sexual interaction phase.   Types of abuse may include (blatant or surreptitious) masturbation (the abuser may masturbate prior to making physical contact with the child), fondling, digital penetration, oral or anal penetration, dry intercourse, intercourse, forcing or coercing the child into touching the abuser's genitals, forced prostitution, and pornography. Children may be coaxed into cooperation, not consenting, because abusers—as adult authority figures—often command, engage, or enlist cooperation from the child. Children lack the maturity, experience, and age to be able to consent, but they may cooperate because of their subservient status (Murphy, 1985, p. 2; Plummer, 1984, p. 145).

Secrecy phase.   Abusers communicate to children that others must not discover the sexual activity. The objective of abusers is to continue the activity. This necessitates avoiding detection and maintaining access to the child while continuing the abuse. The techniques for maintaining the secrecy may involve incorporating "rules" or "games," implicating the child in the activity, and setting the child up to be responsible for keeping the secret (Bass & Thornton, 1983; Murphy, 1985, p. 2).

Disclosure phase.   Sometimes the abuser is discovered accidentally. At other times the abuse is disclosed intentionally by the child or someone else. Intentional disclosure is usually made by the child. Frequently, intentional disclosure enormously complicates the abuse because parents and others refuse to either face it or believe it. Accidental discovery may come as a result of such consequences as pregnancy, VD, sexual acting out, promiscuity, and physical trauma. The way the abuse is disclosed can affect the child's self-esteem and reaction to treatment. For instance, disbelieving adults sometimes respond by blaming and punishing the child—and allow the sexual abuse to continue (Molmen, 1982, pp. 35–36; Murphy, 1985, p. 2).

Suppression phase.   The suppression phase may begin as soon as disclosure takes place. Suppression may be attempted by the abuser, the child, parents, other family members, professionals, the community, or an institution. There are many reasons for suppression: fear of publicity; fear of reprisal; to protect the reputation of a family, an abuser, or an institution;

to avoid prosecution; to avoid responsibility; to protect the child; to avoid embarrassment; to avoid the kinds of confrontation and intervention required to deal effectively with the difficult and sensitive situation; and fear of getting involved.

Survival phase.   On the basis of our own experience and the reports of a number of other writers (Besharov, 1990; Kendrick, 1991), we have added a sixth phase, the survival phase. It is during this phase that we recommend implementation of strategies for helping the child and the family to respond to and recover from the abuse as much as possible. Phase 6 includes stopping the abuse, providing needed medical and psychological treatment for the child, and helping the significant others close to the child to overcome the trauma, fear, anger, and despair caused by the abuse (Benedict, 1985; Grossman & Sutherland, 1983). It also involves preventing further abuse (Bass & Thornton, 1983; Colao & Hosansky, 1983; Plummer 1984; Townley, 1985) and prosecuting and/or getting counseling for the abuser (Benedict, 1985). There appears to be a growing need for facilities to care for child sexual-abuse survivors and their families. According to Carter (1986), only 20% to 25% of abused children receive any treatment or protection. She reports that additional treatment centers are needed for detecting and treating children who are survivors of both physical and sexual abuse (p. 42).

In summarizing the dynamics of child sexual abuse, it appears that abusers and pedophiles—adults who have an abnormal sexual desire for children—are able to carry on their activities because children are largely powerless and vulnerable and because families and society are reluctant to face and deal with the realities of the abuse.

DYNAMICS OF SURVIVORS
OF CHILDHOOD SEXUAL ABUSE

With the passing of the Vietnam era, we might erroneously conclude that PTSD has seen it heyday—given the same terrible errors in national judgment are not repeated. However, what the discovery of PTSD as an identifiable malady has done is lead investigators to examine other traumatized populations aside from veterans. While the occasional headline sensationalizes a mother throwing her one-year-old in a dumpster, the untold story of child abuse involves the adult survivors of childhood physical and, more particularly, sexual abuse. The incidence of child sexual abuse reported in nonclinical population studies reviewed by Salter (1988) ranges from 8% to 38% for females and 3% to 11% for males. A very conservative estimate by Wyatt and Powell (1988) puts the number of child sexual abuse cases *reported* at 200,000 a year.

However, it was not until the mid-1970s that child sexual abuse began to appear on the agendas of child welfare and mental health professionals (Finkelhor et al., 1986, p. 10). On first inspection this may seem puzzling, since early studies by Terman (1938, 1951) and Kinsey, Pomeroy, Martin, & Gebhard (1953) found a large percentage of women had suffered childhood sexual abuse, and Hamilton (1929) and Landis (1956) found comparable percentages in males. (The average found in these early studies ranged from 20% to 39% of populations sampled.) Yet, the cultural taboo against incestuous relationships and the cultural valuing of the sanctity of a man's home make disbelief and denial of these high percentages easily understood. Even Kinsey debunked his own percentages by preaching against the mass hysteria that such wild accusations could cause and could not understand why children should be disturbed by sexual abuse (Kinsey, Pomeroy, Martin, & Gebhard, 1948). Numerous studies from the 1950s (Gordon, 1955; Rascovsky & Rascovsky, 1950), sixties (Revitch & Weiss, 1962; Weiner, 1962), seventies (Virkkunen, 1975), and eighties (Mohr, 1981) dismiss the pedophile as essentially harmless and young girls as playing out seductive and enticing roles in sexual liasons à la Freudian oedipal dynamics. In direct contrast, Herman (1981) has convincingly demonstrated that the theories of Freud as applied to incest are completely wrong. Whether the former studies were conducted to support an outmoded Freudian view of aberrant sexual behavior, showed sins of omission in methodological design, denied the existence of behavior that went against one of society's most important taboos, or supported a sexist patriarchal view, they have little relevance in contemporary America. Because this position totally ignores the child's experience, the power differential between adults and children, and the potential for exploitation (Courtois, 1988, p. 166), we believe it to be patently false and dangerous.

Dynamics in Adulthood

The aftermath of childhood sexual abuse cuts a wide traumatic swath for adult survivors of it (Kreidler & England, 1990). Study after study has found that a significant number of female psychiatric patients were sexually abused as children (Briere & Runtz, 1987; Coons, Bowman, Pellow, & Schneider, 1989; Craine, Henson, Colliver, & MacLean, 1988; Lindberg & Distad, 1985). These survivors consistently demonstrate the symptoms of Vietnam veterans, in addition to compulsive sexual behavior, sadomasochistic sexual fantasy, sexual identity issues, and loss of sexual interest (Briere & Runtz, 1987; Craine, Henson, Colliver, & MacLean, 1988). Female survivors also experience an increase in rape and wife battery in adulthood (Coons et al., 1989) and, like veterans, are prone to use alcohol and drugs to submerge bad memories from awareness and engage in suicidal ideation and attempts (Kovach, 1986; Rew, 1989). Male survivors of the childhood sexual abuse fair no better and report essentially the same symptoms with concomitant sexual orientation ambiguity, mistrust of adult males, homophobia, and body image disturbances (Myers, 1986).

Dynamics in Childhood

Manifestations of PTSD do not just spring forth full-blown in adulthood. Sexually abused children are significantly higher on specific PTSD symptoms than physically abused and other psychiatrically hospitalized children (Deblinger, McLeer, Atkins, & Ralphe, 1989; Wolfe, Gentile, & Wolfe, 1989). Additionally, these children have a wide variety of other problems that include concentration difficulties, aggressive behavior, social withdrawing, somatic complaints, overcompliance, depression, antisocial tendencies, behavioral regression, poor body image/self-esteem, hyperactivity, suicidal ideation, and extreme, generalized fears (Conte & Schuerman, 1988; Justice & Justice, 1979; Sgroi, Porter, & Blick, 1982). Abused children typically either internalize the trauma and become withdrawn and depressed or externalize the trauma and become aggressive and angry. While the foregoing symptoms may be indicative of numerous disorders of childhood, the following are not and are rarely ever found with any stressor other than sexual abuse (Salter, 1988, pp. 230–235).

Sexually abused children come early to school and stay late and are rarely, if ever, absent. They barricade themselves in their rooms or otherwise hide and attempt to seal themselves off from their assailants. They engage in inappropriate and persistent sexual play with peers. They have a detailed and age-inappropriate understanding of sexual behavior. They have physical and somatic symptoms with overlaying sexual content. They may engaged in excessive, compulsive, and even public masturbation. They may approach other adults sexually. Small children may act out sexually with real or stuffed animals. Teenagers may run away and engage in prostitution. These behaviors provide a template with which varying patterns of psychopathology seen in adult survivors are drawn (Goodwin, 1988).

Family Dynamics

The incestuous family may operate much like an alcoholic or battered family in developing a series of messages or rules that pivot around denial, duplicity, deceit, role confusion, violence, and social isolation (Courtois, 1988, p. 45). Children receive messages such as:

1. Do not show feelings, especially anger.
2. Be in control at all times; do not ask for help.
3. Deny what is happening and do not believe your own senses/perceptions.
4. No one is trustworthy.
5. Keep the secret because no one will believe you anyway.
6. Be ashamed of yourself; you are to blame for everything.

Typically, there is intergenerational transmission of sexual abuse and other severe maladjustment in the family such as battering or alcoholism. Incestuous fathers will display inordinate amounts of jealousy and paranoia over their daughters' dating and relationships with other males and attempt to rigidly control behavior through threats and intimidation (Salter, 1988, p. 237). Abusive fathers are controlling tyrants who erect a facade of respectability in the community. However, because of their sensitivity to power, when confronted with their abuse, they become meek and contrite (Herman, 1981, p. 178).

Mothers are often oppressed and economically dependent, abused by their mates, and products of incestuous families themselves (Courtois, 1988, pp. 54–55; Herman, 1981, pp. 178–179). Mothers may be physically or mentally disabled, causing the eldest daughter to take on the role of "little mother," which extends to fulfilling the father's sexual demands (Herman, 1981, p. 179). While some mothers may confront the abuse once they discover it, many others engage in denial and helplessness, and when confronted with the reality of the situation may revictimize the child by physical or verbal abuse (Salter, 1988, p. 209). While war may be hell, the sexual abuse of children undoubtedly occupies a deeper level of Dante's *Inferno,* and its continuing emergence into the public eye from behind closed doors means that the crises and transcrises associated with PTSD will continue unabated.

INTERVENTION STRATEGIES

Rape and other forms of sexual assault cover a broad spectrum of abuse and require a wide variety of crisis intervention strategies. The conceptual basis for the intervention strategies is the six-step model that was discussed in Chapter 2. We will present three more-or-less representative cases to illustrate various kinds and stages of crisis work.

Rape and Battery: The Case of Jeanette

Jeanette is a 50-year-old teacher. She has been living alone in a small house since the younger of her two children went away to college two months ago. Jeanette was divorced seven years ago. When she returned home from the store at 9:30 PM last evening, she was met, as she emerged from her car in her driveway, by a gunman in his middle 20s. She dropped a small bag of groceries and some items from her purse as she was abducted at gunpoint and forced into the gunman's car, which was parked on the street. Jeanette was beaten, driven away to an isolated area several miles from her home, raped, beaten again, robbed, and abandoned, bleeding and bruised, with her clothing in shreds. She was weak and dazed, but was able to find her way to the nearest house, where she called for help. Now Jeanette is experiencing physical and emotional trauma. She is amazed at herself for being alive, because she believes the attacker meant to kill her.

Immediate aftermath. There are situations in which the most helpful and appropriate immediate response from a crisis worker is empathy and assurance that the survivor is still alive. Jeanette's rape is a case in point.

Jeanette: I spent most of the night in the emergency room. It was horrible—the rape. I don't know how I came out alive and without any broken bones. He intended to kill me. Part of the time I was in a daze. I don't know what came over me. I must have blacked out. I don't know how long I lay out there alone after he left me. I certainly didn't fight back or protest.

CW: Jeanette, I'm so proud of you for the way you handled it. You did whatever it took to stay alive. You saved yourself, and that took courage. Whatever you did, whether it was blacking out or offering no protests, was right, because it preserved your life, and that's the important thing right now.

Jeanette: Well, that's probably a good way to look at it. Right now, I'm tired—exhausted. I thank the Lord I'm here. I feel like I'm in a sort of twilight zone. Maybe part of me did die. I'm feeling so alone and vulnerable.

CW: So you're needing rest and comfort now. After what you've been through, I can see how you would be feeling like you're in a twilight zone. My concern for you right now is that you'll be able to get some rest in a safe and comfortable place. Where would you feel safe in resting the rest of today and tonight?

Jeanette: I don't know. Home, I guess, but . . . [*Pause, with apprehensive look.*]

CW: But you'd like someone there with you whom you really trust and feel comfortable with. Who might that be in this locale?

Jeanette: Well, my sister. I'd want her there with me. She's the only one I can think of. I don't think I can go into that driveway by myself today. There's no way I'd go there after dark by myself.

The crisis worker's intuition is right when she guesses that the place of safety and comfort for Jeanette would be her own home but that the frightening part would be getting past the place in her driveway where she was abducted. The crisis worker is also correct in reassuring Jeanette for her actions, which brought her out alive.

An important issue for rape survivors is control. Jeanette has experienced an emotionally draining loss of control to the attacker, and she needs to be reassured that that loss of control is neither total nor permanent. She did what she had to do to survive, and that took courage. It is important to her for others to recognize her and give her credit. Whatever small amount of control she has, she can build upon as a basis for beginning her long journey toward recovery. Also, the crisis worker does not impose on Jeanette a place for resting or an accompanying person of trust and understanding. These immediate choices are both derived from Jeanette and are undoubtedly more appropriate than any of the choices the crisis worker might have generated or insisted that Jeanette take.

The following three months.   During the three months following a sexual assault, the survivor such as Jeanette

1. may need continuing medical consultation, advice, or treatment; she may experience soreness, pain, itching, nausea, sleeplessness, loss of appetite, and such
2. may have difficulty resuming work; the added stress of the sexual assault may create too much stress in the workplace
3. needs to have people reach out to her, listen to her, and verbally assure her—not shun her or fear continuing to relate to her
4. needs the acceptance and support of family and friends
5. may have difficulty resuming sexual relations and needs understanding without pressure
6. may exhibit unusual mood swings and emotional outbursts, which others will need to understand and allow
7. may experience nightmares, flashbacks, phobias, denial, disbelief, and other unusual effects
8. may go into depression, which may be accompanied by suicidal ideation.

Support persons can be of optimal help during this phase of recovery. They may assist survivors of sexual assault by

1. understanding and accepting the survivor's changed moods, tantrums, and so on, and allowing her the freedom to act them out
2. being available, but not intruding—while supporting the survivor through encouraging her to regain control and to recover her life
3. ensuring that she doesn't have to go home alone (without overprotecting her)
4. realizing that recovery takes a long time and lots of hard work
5. allowing her to make her own decisions about reporting the rape and prosecuting the assailant
6. leaving it up to her to decide whether she wants to change jobs or places of residence
7. responding to her in positive ways, so that she does not sense that the crisis worker blames her for "letting it happen" or that the crisis worker feels she is not capable of taking care of herself
8. allowing her to talk about the assault to whomever she wishes, whenever she wishes, but not disclosing the assault to anyone without her prior consent
9. showing empathy, concern, and understanding without dominating her
10. recognizing that she will likely suffer from low self-esteem (finding ways to show her she is genuinely valued and respected)
11. recognizing that her hurt will not end when the physical scratches and bruises are gone—that her emotional healing will require a long time
12. trying to find ways to help her trust men again—assisting male associates (friends, coworkers, brothers, and her father) to show tolerance,

understanding, and confidence. It is detrimental to her for male support persons to exhibit and express myths about rape. Typically, men have more difficulty understanding rape than women.

13. trying to find ways to encourage female coworkers, friends, sisters, and her mother to believe in her and not avoid her or avoid talking with her openly about the rape

14. including her children, if she has children, in all considerations concerning help toward emotional recovery

15. referring her to sexual assault support groups for survivors and family members. Support groups can be of enormous help. Many YWCA Rape Crisis Centers and National Organization for Women (NOW) chapters have support groups.

16. realizing that the survivor's husband, partner, or lover may develop symptoms similar to those of the survivor (nightmares, phobias, rage, guilt, self-blame, self-hate, and such) and may need help similar to that needed by the survivor herself

17. encouraging the survivor's husband or lover to give her time to recover, free from pressure, before resuming sexual activity and to let her know he is still interested in her, still desires her, but that former patterns of sex life will be resumed at her own pace. It is important for a husband or lover to talk this out openly with her, to clear the air for both parties.

Child Sexual Abuse: The Case of Susie

Susie, age 8, is the middle child in the family. She, her brother, age 11, and a 5-year-old sister live with her mother and stepfather, whom her mother married nearly two years ago. Susie's mother, Allene, and father divorced when the youngest child was about 1 year old. Susie's stepfather started off by fondling her. This went on for several weeks. Although she was bewildered, scared, and intimidated, no one else knew about the activity. Recently, while everyone else was out of the house, her stepfather raped her. He threatened to kill Susie, Allene, and her sister if she told anyone. The following morning Susie confided in her brother, who in turn told Allene what had happened. Allene found Susie's bloody undergarments, took Susie to the hospital, and had the stepfather arrested. Allene plans to file for divorce and to prosecute him.

Immediate aftermath.   In cases where there is physical injury, the survivor will need immediate medical evaluation and care. Susie's mother, Allene, deals with that and several other important concerns.

Allene: This has been a horrifying ordeal. I've stayed in the room with Susie all night. She's sleeping comfortably now. She's under sedation. I won't know the extent of her physical damage until all the tests are in. I'm afraid it's pretty bad, though. It's been a living hell. A nightmare!

CW: You've certainly been through a lot in the last few hours. And you've done a remarkable job of taking care of Susie. Your concerns about her injuries are certainly justified. You're obviously a very good mother who has suddenly been thrust into this—nothing you or Susie did caused it. It was perpetrated upon her and you. Our unit is here to assist you in any way we can. We want to provide someone to be with you and Susie, if you need us, during these critical hours of your hospital stay, as well as providing aftercare and follow-up counseling if needed.

Allene: I appreciate it. Everything happened so fast! I don't know how I managed without falling apart. It's like a wild dream—an ugly nightmare. I don't know how I'll handle it when the dust settles. I'm so mad—I could just kill him! I feel like I've been raped too. There's so much on me right now. I don't know if I'm capable of bearing up under all that's got to be done. Damn, damn, damn that man! Excuse me, I shouldn't blow up like that.

CW: That's all right. You have a perfect right to be angry and to say it. It's good that you care enough to be upset, and it's good to see you direct your anger at him—the real cause of Susie's hurt and your anger. Both of you deserve better treatment than he gave you, and no child asks to be raped.

Allene: That's right. I trusted him! And he took advantage of her. She was helpless—a helpless child. I've got to show her where I stand on this. First, I'm going to take good care of her, and then I'm going to send that louse to jail for good!

Allene shows a variety of legitimate concerns. The crisis worker permits her to express her anger, isn't threatened by Allene's outburst, encourages her to keep owning and expressing her feelings, and lets her know that neither she nor Susie was to blame for the assault. That strategy is important in letting Allene know that she can be in control and that the worker believes in her, without the worker's jumping in and expressing the anger for her.

Six months or more after: family crises.   Discovery of an incestuous relationship will throw the entire family into crisis. The father faces loss of what has become an addictive behavior, possible criminal sanctions, loss of his family, and social stigmatization. The mother finds herself torn between her husband and daughter. The daughter may find herself discredited, shamed, punished, and still unprotected (Herman, 1981, p. 183). The worker will also face a crisis in deciding what to do and whether or not to believe the child's story. However, discovery of child sex abuse is no different from discovery of any other physical abuse *and state law mandates that it must be reported* (Sandberg, Crabbs, & Crabbs, 1988). It is a criminal activity and should be dealt with in that manner. For those workers who are unsure of themselves, it may be reassuring to know that fewer than 5% of complaints of child sexual abuse are false. Conversely, it is not uncommon for children to retract their complaints under pressure from the family (Goodwin, 1982). Therefore, until clearly proven otherwise, *the child's allegations should be accepted as valid, and the worker's primary consideration should be reporting the abuse to child protective services and obtaining safety for the child* (Sandberg et al., 1988).

Because the behavior is both criminal and addictive, treating the problem via family therapy is fruitless. What is called for is immediately referring the problem to and cooperating with local family services and law enforcement agencies (Sandberg et al., 1988). It then becomes much more possible to remove the father from the home through a court order. Removing the child from the home has negative ramifications because it may be construed as banishment and may also serve to strengthen parent bonds against the child. The child needs assurance that she is not to blame for the incest; she should be praised for her courage and clearly told that she is helping, not hurting, her family and will not be abandoned even if she retracts her story (Herman, 1981, pp. 184–185).

Offenders.   While it may be extremely difficult for human services workers who are enraged and repulsed by incest and pedophilia to accept the idea that offenders should be given any consideration other than removal from the family and jail time, treatment should be made available. The offender is engaged in addictive behavior, and for many offenders, it is treatable (Pithers, Kashima, Cumming, & Beal, 1988). As in the case of any other addiction, though, rarely is voluntary treatment effective. Treatment mandated by court order and revocation of probation for termination of treatment or relapse are legal sanctions that increase the likelihood of compliance (Herman, 1981, p. 186). Although treatment of child sex offenders and the various crises they experience is a very specialized therapeutic modality that is beyond the scope of most crisis workers and this book, Salter's (1988) *Treating Child Sex Offenders and Victims* is an excellent and comprehensive work on the subject and we recommend it for those interested in issues of offender treatment.

Support and therapy groups.   Offenders, mothers, and older victims alike can profit from support and therapy groups composed of their peers. Support and therapy groups are extremely important because participants find they have and can discuss mutual problems, are less stigmatized and isolated, and have the opportunity to see that other members are successfully moving past the addiction and trauma (Herman, 1981, p. 186; Salter, 1988).

For offenders, the group breaks down cognitive distortions, isolation, secrecy, and denial, and promotes treatment compliance (Salter, 1988, p. 112). For mothers, the notion of entering a support/therapy group may be highly threatening. However, it is quite possibly the only way they will be able to get their families back together. Mothers should be told that fact in plain and simple terms and highly encouraged to join such groups. Groups for spouses enable members to come to terms with doubts of their own womanhood, regain a sense of control and empowerment in themselves and their families, reduce blame and guilt in themselves, and restore mother-daughter bonds (Brittain & Merriam, 1988; Salter, 1988, p. 211).

For victims, groups provide a number of potential positive outcomes and help them to move from victim to survivor. Though victims may be reluctant to participate, they should be encouraged to do so, although not all victims may be ready or immediately able to participate in groups. Education as to what the group is about, who the members are, confidentiality issues, what kinds of problems members are working on, and the safety and support of the group format are critical components in assessing, selecting, motivating, and committing survivors to group work (Courtois, 1988, pp. 253–262). Courtois (1988, pp. 245–249) lists the following benefits of group treatment for survivors of childhood sexual abuse:

1. The individual's sense of shame, stigmatization, and negative self-image is reduced by meeting other survivors who appear "normal."
2. Commonality of experience raises members' consciousness about incest wherein the experience becomes more normalized and may be seen from an interpersonal and sociocultural perspective rather than an "only me" perspective.
3. The group serves as a new "surrogate" family where new behaviors and methods of communicating, interacting, and problem solving can be practiced in a safe, accepting, and nurturing environment.
4. The group allows for safe exploration and ventilation of feelings and beliefs that have been denied and submerged from awareness.
5. Childhood messages and rules that were generated within the abusive environment can be challenged and dissected to determine how they still influence the survivor's maladaptive behavior patterns.

Individual therapy for children.   Assessment includes thorough documentation of the abusive events for possible legal use. Using anatomically correct dolls helps confirm what actually occurred in the abuse. No specific measures currently exist for measuring the effects of psychological abuse in children, although a complete psychological evaluation may be useful in gauging the child's overall level of functioning (Wheeler & Berliner, 1988, p. 235). The previously mentioned behavioral indicators of childhood sexual abuse and PTSD criteria for children are currently the best indicators that sexual abuse has occurred.

Initial intervention techniques call for managing the crisis of disclosure and the resulting fear and anxiety that follow. Affirmation and validation are critical in regard to what has happened, what is happening, and what will happen to the child, the offender, and significant others.

Our admonition in the PTSD chapter on *not* using flooding techniques with children holds even more firmly with sexual abuse. Because small children are not fully developed cognitively, cognitive-behavioral techniques commonly used with adult survivors are also not efficacious. Yet, anxiety about and fear of the abusive events and the abuser need to be reduced, and doing this calls for reexposure to the trauma. This work is best accomplished by use of play therapy, where the child is given puppets, dolls, and drawing materials to safely distance himself or herself from the trauma. By gently and directively encouraging reenactment and discussion through the safety of the play material, the therapist may enable the child to gradually extinguish fear and anxiety feelings (Wheeler & Berliner, 1988, p. 237).

As with adults, anger and grief are emotional by-products of sexual abuse. Venting of these feelings should be encouraged, particularly when most adults are not comfortable with them and may attempt to repress such feelings when children exhibit them (Wheeler & Berliner, 1988, p. 237). Drawing, painting, modeling clay, sand play, writing, and learning to verbalize emotions are all therapeutic vehicles to ventilate angry feelings and loss. Play techniques can also give the child a renewed sense of empowerment by allowing play figures to be acted on and thus can reduce longstanding feelings of helplessness. Punching a Bobo doll out or picking up a play telephone and calling the police can give children a sense of control in a situation where they have little (Salter, 1988, p. 215). Along with relaxation and other stress-reduction measures, these same play techniques can be used to teach the child to control anger when the child constantly acts out with peers or significant others.

Education.   Education about adult sex offenders and sex itself are important for children since they will have little if any knowledge of why or what has happened to them. Children need to know that it is the adult and not the child who made the mistake. Where physical injuries resulted, children need to have these explained and need to be told that their bodies will be OK. Many children believe that others will be able to tell by looking at them. Children need to know that while they may feel different, sexual abuse does not make them look different.

Cognitively, children have little understanding of sexual functions. Typically they will not initiate questions about sex, but when workers initiate education about sex through slides or books, children will respond with their own questions. Every child who has been sexually assaulted needs some type of sex education and information on what the assault means (Salter, 1988, pp. 217–218).

An adjunct to sex education is educating sexually abused children as to what is and what is not sexually appropriate behavior. Sexual abuse has a high potential for creating misconceptions about sexually acting out. If this is a problem, workers need to modify children's thinking by teaching them internal inhibitions and external controls for socially acceptable behavior. Since physical contact boundaries have been altered for sexually abused children, the worker needs to model what appropriate behavior is. A typical manifestation of such behavior is a child who is physically intrusive in the worker's office by getting into drawers, sitting on the worker's lap, moving objects without permission, and so on. These actions go beyond normal childhood curiosity, and limits should be established in a gentle but firm manner with regard to what is and is not acceptable behavior (Wheeler & Berliner, 1988, p. 243).

Assertiveness training may be seen as more a preventive measure to keep children out of harm's way than a remedial measure for sexually abused children. Yet, sexually abused children have learned to be compliant to deviant requests and clearly need to learn how to "Just say NO!"

(Salter, 1988, p. 219). Since abused children are at greater risk for revictimization, teaching them cues and warning signs is important so that future abuse may be avoided (Wheeler & Berliner, 1988, p. 242).

Ambivalence often accompanies sexual abuse where a loved one is concerned. Initial feelings of anger may be replaced by feelings of ambivalence toward the offender, particularly when ramifications of the abuse spill over into the family. Being glad the offender is out of the house and feeling guilty about him being gone are common feelings. Therefore, while the child is encouraged to ventilate feelings the worker should be receptive to other emotions that are not always congruent with the abuse and the offender (Salter, 1988, p. 221).

Prevention.   Preventive approaches in schools can probably do much to ameliorate child sexual abuse by equipping children to deal effectively with it before it happens (Vernon & Hay, 1988). However, public paranoia about any kind of school-based sex education probably precludes this from happening on any widespread basis in the near future. The April 1988 issue of *Elementary School Guidance and Counseling* provides an excellent and comprehensive list of resource materials, books, and organizations, and critical reviews of curricula and teaching aids that would be helpful to anyone engaged in working with physically or sexually abused children.

Adult Survivors: The Case of Pearl

Pearl was sexually abused by her stepfather regularly from ages 8 through 15. For 20 years she suppressed all memories and emotions related to the abuse, which had included fondling, digital penetration, and intercourse. Now, at age 35, she has regained her memory of the abuse and is experiencing severe symptoms of delayed rape trauma syndrome. Her marriage is breaking up; her career is in shambles; her communications and relationship with her three children are adversely affected by her personal turmoil; her rage toward her stepfather and her anger toward her mother have robbed her of her self-respect and her affection toward her parents, who live across town from her. Her only daughter, the middle child, has recently reached her eighth birthday, and Pearl is deeply obsessed with her daughter's safety. Pearl feels a great deal of guilt, shame, remorse, and loss of self-esteem. For several years she has been experiencing suicidal ideations, and since the recovery of her memory of the abuse these ideations have seriously intensified.

Assessment.   Particularly for older women who suffered childhood sexual abuse under severe societal and family strictures of secrecy and denial, the abuse will be disguised and repressed. Often they may have been under the care of mental health professionals and been diagnosed with a variety of mental illnesses ranging from schizophrenia to depression and borderline personality. Presenting problems are typically depression, anxiety, disassociation, and compulsive disorders (Courtois, 1988). Although the client may present as competent, responsible, mature, and otherwise capable, these characteristics are a facade for underlying emotional problems. Cognitively, affectively, and behaviorally, abuse victims may present themselves in a bipolar manner, rigidly adhering to one end or the other of the continuum—"I'm great" or "I'm terrible"—or rapidly oscillating between the two (Courtois, 1988).

Triage assessment of these individuals can be problematic, to say the least. At one moment they present as affectively calm and controlled, perhaps to the point of rigidity. At the next moment because of some real or imagined slight, particularly in interpersonal relationships, they may become extremely labile with angry tirades or uncontrolled crying and then offer profuse, guilt-ridden apologies for their behavior. Cognitively, they may present themselves as competent and perceptive thinkers and then, when faced with a stimulus that causes a flashback or intrusive image, completely disassociate themselves from present reality and respond in a confused, disjointed manner. Behaviorally, such individuals may run the gamut of DSM-IIIR diagnostic categories—and then appear perfectly appropriate! If there is any key to making an accurate assessment of adult survivors of childhood sexual abuse, it is their consistent inconsistency across triage dimensions. The astute crisis worker who is struggling to make an assessment where such inconsistency is displayed should consider childhood sexual abuse as an operational hypothesis.

A crisis will invariably initiate therapy; as in other forms of PTSD, the crisis may not seem related to a past traumatic event. During the intake interview, if some of the common symptoms of PTSD are revealed, then childhood sexual abuse should become suspect as a causative agent and further assessment should target it as a possibility. If PTSD due to childhood sexual abuse is suspected in an adult, the crisis worker should immediately make plans to refer the client for a comprehensive psychiatric assessment after the initiating crisis is contained.

Pearl initially presented at a community mental health center with suicidal thoughts and actions. At intake she showed the counselor cuts she had inflicted on herself with a box cutter. She was disassociative and saw herself "out of her body" as she drew the knife up and down her arms. She had also cut off her parakeet's head, although she was extremely remorseful about its death and could not imagine why she would have done such a terrible thing. She currently was depressed and saw no reason for living. The counselor rated her overall on the Triage Assessment Form at 27, instituted a stay-alive contract with her, and referred her to a psychiatrist for evaluation and medication. After several false starts and stops at counseling, Pearl finally admitted the real issue, that she was abused sexually and physically as a child by her stepfather and the abuse was denied by her mother.

Treatment of adults.   While treatment considerations for the adult survivor of childhood sexual abuse are still being formulated and investigated, a major component of therapy is to use a posttraumatic stress treatment model like the one described in Chapter 5. In that regard, assessment for PTSD has been underutilized with incest victims (Courtois, 1988, p. 150). However, Finkelhor (1987) proposes that the trauma of childhood sexual abuse goes beyond other causal agents of PTSD because of the unique dynamics of traumatic sexualization, social stigmatization, betrayal of trust by loved ones, and powerlessness of children.

It appears that a group of survivors who have successfully learned to cope with delayed trauma can be more effective in helping survivors who are stuck than most of the other strategies. Probably the best treatment is to provide a combination, placing the survivor both with a support group and with a specially trained female therapist (T. B. Davis, 1985).

Discovery and admission.   For survivors of childhood sexual abuse, particular problems arise in the therapeutic process that do not arise with victims of other traumatic experiences. If the client is otherwise in crisis and childhood sexual abuse is suspected, incest material should not be explored immediately because of the likelihood of compounding the present crisis through decompensation, regression, or disassociation. Client safety is paramount and should always be a primary or conjoint consideration with exploration of the incest (Courtois, 1988, p. 173). At the time the client chooses to own the trauma of incest, the potential for crisis rises exponentially. The worker needs to be very sensitive to the client's admission, gently encouraging the client to disclose the incest and directively and positively affirming the client for doing so.

Pearl: [*Apprehensively.*] I don't know what you'll think about this. But I guess I can trust you. I just can't live with this anymore. [*Pauses.*]

HSW: [*Suspecting from previous indicators what is coming.*] Whatever it is, I can see how deeply troubling it is and how difficult it must be. I am here to listen and try to understand. Whatever it is, I want you to know that you will still be the same Pearl and that person is not going to be any different in my eyes. I hope what I've just said makes it easier to get it out for you.

Pearl: [*Starts sobbing.*] This is really bad.

HSW: [*Softly touching her arm and speaking gently.*] I'm guessing this is about something that somebody did to you or that happened to you, and it's OK, really OK to talk about it.

Pearl: I had sex with my stepfather. [*Relates a long history of sexual and physical torment by her stepfather and real mother, with the counselor listening and empathically responding.*]

Pearl: [*Gently weeping.*] I know you're a counselor and all but you must think I'm horrible.

HSW: I understand how terribly difficult that was. I also want you to know that I believe what you said. I don't think you're horrible at all. What I think is that you were a victim and that you are a survivor of those terrible things that shouldn't have happened and did. I want to correct one thing you said. You did not have sex with your stepfather. You were 12 years old and had no choice. He had and forced sex on you. That's a big difference. Now I want to give you an idea of what is happening to you, why these bad memories keep coming back, and what they do to disrupt your life.

Psychoeducation. Psychoeducation about the role that PTSD plays in incest trauma is important at this point because it can help allay clients' fears that they are "different," "dirty," "mentally ill," and such, and offers the assurance that PTSD is responsive to treatment. Education about PTSD also removes the mystique, confusion, and "craziness," and anchors present maladaptive behavior as purposive and reasonable given the survivor's traumatic history. It also allows the client to feel that something can be done through treatment (Courtois, 1988, p. 173).

HSW: [*After an explanation and showing Pearl the DSM-IIIR PTSD classification.*] So you are not "nuts." Those are the reasons these things are currently happening. We can treat this. It is a long road, and at times it is going to seem as if things are getting worse instead of better. We will have to go back and dig into those memories and they are going to be painful. I want you to think about this because it is not an easy task. It is something you will need to choose. If you choose to do so, I want you to know that we'll go through this together. [*The counselor then explains what the treatment procedures will be and answers questions the client has about different components of the treatment.*]

Validation. As the client starts through the process of therapy, numerous transcrisis points will occur as long-buried trauma is brought back to awareness. In an active, directive, continuous, and reinforcing manner, the human services worker

1. validates that the incest did happen, despite denial of this fact by significant others; the client is not to blame, it is safe to talk about it, and the worker does not loathe the client for having been a participant
2. acts as an advocate who is openly, warmly interested in what happened to the survivor as a child and makes owning statements to that effect
3. reinforces the resourcefulness of the victim to become a survivor
4. provides a mentor/reparenting role model to help with childhood developmental tasks that were missed. (Courtois, 1988, pp 167–170)

Extinguishing trauma. When we speak of extinguishing trauma we are referring to effecting psychological extinction; that is, facilitating the reduction or loss of a conditioned response as a result of the absence or withdrawal of reinforcement. In practical terms, this means the reduction or loss of both Pearl's negative beliefs about herself and her debilitative behaviors that were responses to her childhood sexual abuse. The crisis worker sought to extinguish Pearl's negative beliefs and behaviors by systematically leading her to mentally refute her erroneous perceptions that she was responsible, culpable, or guilty, and had her reframe her previous beliefs to help her gain a new insight that she was an innocent victim and can now view herself more realistically as a guilt-free survivor. The crisis worker's procedures and dialogue with Pearl in the preceding sections on "Discovery and admission" and "Psychoeducation" are examples of strategies to extinguish trauma such as those experienced by Pearl.

When working through traumatic events, the client will experience a dramatic increase in affective and autonomic arousal (Ochberg, 1988). The human services worker must be very careful to provide palatable doses of the traumatic material that do not exceed the client's coping abilities (Courtois, 1988, p. 174) and promote a crisis within the therapy session. Careful processing with the client prior to and after each session of extinguishing and reframing traumatic memories is important in preventing such crises.

HSW: Let's take a look at what we did today.

Pearl: I'm pretty scared. I didn't remember a lot of that stuff until we dug that memory up.

HSW: That's pretty typical. Any reasonable person would bury that stuff. If you really start to feel like you're losing it, I want you to call me.

Pearl: [*Later that evening, calling.*] I really hate to disturb you, but I've really got this urge to start cutting myself. I'm also having thoughts about killing my pet bird. They're starting to get pretty real.

HSW: [*Very directively.*] Do you feel like you're losing it enough that you need to be hospitalized?

Pearl: I don't know. Maybe if I just talk this through.

HSW: OK. Remember what I said about this being rough. What you went through today brought back a lot of old memories and some ugly fresh ones. That's normal. It's nasty, but it is normal. Now I want you to think of how we changed that scene, how you told yourself all those negative things about yourself being dirty and no good, and what the reality of that scene is. [*A dialogue ensues that recaps the day's events. Pearl is able to regain control, and after a 20-minute dialogue is able to feel secure enough to relax and go to bed.*]

The worker should be aware that extinguishing one traumatic event does not lessen the fear and trepidation of moving on to other events. This is particularly true in the case of adult survivors of childhood sexual abuse, who may experience increased intrusive behavioral symptoms and regress to former maladaptive behaviors even though they are making good progress in erasing bad memories (Cogdal & James, 1991). Clients may appear to be getting worse instead of better—which is threatening and scary for both client and worker.

The worker should be prepared for this contingency, apprise the client of its likelihood, and affirm it is totally acceptable for the client to check in with the worker if these symptoms and behaviors reemerge between sessions. The worker's role when this happens is to be understanding, affirming, and calming. Constant validation is important because many clients will be discouraged at the length of treatment, afraid and angry over revitalization and extension of the traumatic experience's "life," and flee from therapy (Courtois, 1988, p. 177).

Cognitive restructuring.   Reframing negative and distorted beliefs about one-self is critical in allowing the client to separate the fact and fiction of an abusive childhood (Courtois, 1988, p. 181). While imaginally flooding an abusive childhood scene, clients paste mental billboards under the scene (Cogdal & James, 1991). These billboards typically deliver all of the myths and distorted messages that the abuser gave in addition to the client's own childhood negative self-talk.

HSW: [*With the client deeply relaxed, eyes closed.*] Picture that videotape, the bed-room, the "game," him making you get on him and suck his "peter," almost strangling as you do so. Feel the pain and the disgust. But he makes you keep doing it until he gets off, and the semen is running all over, sticky and wet. Notice the messages underneath that scene. "This is what fathers do to educate their daughters to become women." "You aren't a good daughter if you don't do this." "I'll kill you if you don't keep our secret." Feel the confusion, the fear, and the repulsion as you do this. Put those messages in big block letters under-neath that scene. Do you see them?

Pearl: [*Eyes closed and body twisting.*] Yes!

HSW: Freeze that scene and the billboards. Take a snapshot of it. Let it develop. Hold it in your hands.

The client is then asked to destroy the image along with the negative parental injunctions and her own negative self-injunctions (Cogdal & James, 1991).

HSW: Now I want you to get rid of that scene. It is in your past and it is gone, so now get rid of it from your memory also. Do that now and tell me what is happening.

Pearl: I set a match to it. It is burning, it's a hugh fire now with yellow, sick-smelling smoke.

HSW: Let it burn.

Pearl: It's just a crisp cinder now, all gone.

HSW: All gone? Is there anything else you want to do with it?

Pearl: CRUSH IT!

HSW: Do it! What's happening?

Pearl: I'm grinding it up with my bootheel. It's nothing, he's nothing.

HSW: Fine. Now relax and slip back into that soft, cool mountain glade. Just relax and feel the tranquillity, calmness, and peacefulness.

The client then replays the scene, but this time substitutes positive, self-enhancing counterinjunctions based on the facts and not the fictional mes-sages of the event. The worker guides the image and reframes the father in a truer psychological image (Cogdal & James, 1991).

HSW: Go back to the bedroom with him now. Picture the scene, but change it. See him as small, very small, weak. He is a small selfish pouting boy, dressed up in a man's pajamas. He looks ridiculous. Put these billboards under the scene. "The only people he has power over are little girls." "It is his fault this is happening."

"It is WRONG!" "It is criminal!" "I should have felt confused, fearful." "I had the right to feel that way!" "I also have the right to be *angry* about it." "*No*body has the right to do that. *No*body!" Now freeze that picture and snapshot it. Let it develop. Look at it. What are you feeling and thinking?

Pearl: [*Yelling.*] You asshole! You bastard! You are gone from my life, you puke! You lied to me, you scared me to death and kept at it. You used me because you were afraid of everybody else. I was the only one you could use, you scumbag. You've got no power over me now, you pissant, or my memories. You are history!

HSW: I want you to save that picture. Put it someplace safe in your memory, and every time that image starts to come back, pull out the picture and look at it. See that scene for what it really is, and see those billboards, flashing. Have you got it?

Pearl: Yes. I've got it.

HSW: How do you feel?

Pearl: Better, relaxed, relieved maybe.

Catharsis.   Like Vietnam veterans, survivors of childhood sexual abuse have developed excellent coping skills to deny and numb feelings. Recognizing and labeling feelings is of utmost importance in helping clients give voice to shunted emotions and warded-off feelings. Pearl's bitter and angry emotions are not unlike those of Vietnam veterans as they relive and extinguish bad memories. Developmentally, clients have to literally relearn and identify their emotional states. In our own work with survivors we use a sheet of faces with different emotions and feeling words attached to them to help clients label their emotions. Far from seeing this exercise as childish, clients report that they pull out and use these sheets on a daily basis to validate their present emotional state.

Grief resolution.   Beginning to recognize past, buried feelings is to start on the road to acknowledging feelings of anger and rage, as Pearl does in the preceding dialogue. These feelings will ultimately end in sadness and grieving for the loss of a happy childhood, her loss of who she might have been without the trauma, and the loss of a psychologically healthy family instead of the malevolent one she grew up in (Courtois, 1988, p. 181). It is likely to be one of the most painful stages as the client comes to grips with the reality that there is no retrieving the past or changing it and that attempts to do so are fruitless. It is only the future that holds promise for her, and she can control only that (Courtois, 1988, p. 181; Hays, 1985).

Grieving and resolution, particularly with perpetrators of the abuse, is another transcrisis point in therapy.

Pearl: I had a call from my mother last night. I wanted to be assertive with her and tell her how I felt, like I had worked out in group. But when it came down to it I just couldn't. I haven't got the guts. [*Starts crying.*] I'll never get rid of this. Why couldn't she have been different? Why does she still try that stuff of browbeating me? Wasn't what she did enough?

HSW: You have every right to feel sad that she wasn't or still isn't what you'd hope a mother might be. I wish she could change, but I have my doubts. So if she won't, what will you do?

Pearl: I guess she won't. I guess I'll just kiss her off.

HSW: You survived with her battering you and you've survived for ten years without her. Perhaps it's time you did say good-bye. [*Patiently lets Pearl silently weep.*]

Changing behavior through skill building.   While coming to terms with past trauma and stopping maladaptive present behavior are critical to the adult survivor, changing behavior to more self-determining choices is the major end goal of therapy. The vacuum left by the removal of bad memories and the psychic energy previously expended to maintain control of those memories is not easily filled. Reeducation is necessary, and the worker may assume a teaching role in transmitting basic life skills such as communication, decision making, conflict resolution, and boundary setting. (Courtois, 1988, pp. 181–182). From that standpoint the therapist should not be unsettled by what may be some rather strange and personal questions.

Pearl: Er, ah, I was just wondering, Dr. James, how you treat your kids. I mean, if they act up do you ground them, or what? What do you talk about at dinner? And do you and your wife ever argue?

While such questions may be construed as intruding on the private life of the worker or attempts by the client to shift focus from her problems, it is important to answer these questions as honestly and succinctly as possible, without shifting the focus away from the client's personal concerns. The client is testing her perceptions against the most valid and stable validity check she currently has—her therapist. For that reason, it is important to urge survivors to join therapy or support groups so that new behaviors can be tested out and discussed with peers.

SUMMARY

Sexual abuse affects all segments of society. Individuals from every developmental age, sexual, and racial/ethnic group and sociocultural stratum have been represented among survivors. The vast majority of sexual assults are perpetrated upon women and upon children of both sexes. Sexual abuse/misuse may occur in many forms: unwanted or forced penile, digital, or object penetration of the vagina, anus, or mouth; fondling; forced or entrapped prostitution; pornography; obscene phone calls; or any forced, unwanted, tricked, or entrapped sexual activity.

Rapists and other sexual abusers are nearly always males who come from all walks of life. Most abusers appear to perceive individuals they attack as objects of prey rather than as persons. Abusers display a variety of pathologies. They usually assault not out of lust or desire for sexual gratification, but out of a perceived need to control, exert power over, punish, vanquish, defeat, hurt, destroy, degrade, or humiliate others. Typically, abusers deny, minimize, and/or rationalize their behavior to the extent that they themselves rarely define their attacks as abuse. Instead, they usually charge that the survivor asked for, deserved, or caused the abusive activity.

In recent years the public has become more aware of the phenomenon of rape and other forms of sexual abuse, and increased awareness appears to have ushered in a greater sensitivity to and advocacy for the rights and needs of survivors. The helping professions have provided many additional programs for assisting survivors: crisis intervention, research, counseling, medical services, long-term mental health care, new laws and legal advocacy, more vigorous efforts to prosecute offenders, and more sympathetic and proactive news media. However, much remains to be done in the arena of sexual assault. There remains a pressing need for society at large to understand better the dynamics of sexual abuse and the needs of survivors and their families. There is a great need for society to overcome a number of long-standing myths about rape and other forms of sexual abuse. There is a need for better reporting and improved police and legal responding. There is a need for survivors to accept counseling and not to blame themselves. And, there is a need for survivor's families, friends, and coworkers to be willing and able to respond to survivor's with openness, genuineness, acceptance, understanding, and respect, all of which are key attitudes or conditions for nurturing recovery from the debilitating trauma and effects of sexual assault.

In treating either children or adult survivors of childhood sexual abuse, the potential for becoming emotionally involved because of one's own shock and rage at the horrible physical and psychological trauma perpetrated on helpless children is exceedingly high. The potential for burnout is also exceedingly high. If you have been repulsed by what you have read in this chapter and some of the language in the dialogues, imagine what occurs for people who work daily with this problem. Of all the crises described in this book, we believe that child sexual abuse is the most potent in generating subjective emotional responses in human servicers workers that are not conducive to client welfare. We hold this to be true whether the worker is male or female. For female workers, their anger at offenders may not be shared by the victims and their repulsion may make them reluctant to explore actual details of sexual encounters. For males, incest victims may become sexually arousing or the worker may side with the offender (Herman, 1981, p. 191). For workers of either sex, involvement in reparenting roles increases the potential for emotional transference and countertransference issues to arise. Our many years of work with children have taught us to seek consistent cross-consultation and supervision with other professionals when counseling children with sexual abuse problems. We are also aware that we could not work with this group day in and day out without suffering rapid burnout. Finally, because of the many abuses we have seen perpetrated on children, we doubt that we would be very effective in treating child sex offenders. We urge others who aspire to work in this arena to look very carefully at these personal and professional issues.

REFERENCES

American Psychiatric Association. (1987). *Diagnostic and statistical manual of mental disorders* (3rd ed., rev.) Washington, DC; Author.

Amir, M. (1971). *Patterns in forcible rape.* Chicago University of Chicago Press.

Baron, L., & Straus, M. A. (1989). *Four Theories of rape in American society.* New Haven: Yale University Press.

Bass, E., & Thornton, L. (Eds.). (1983). *I never told anyone: Writings by women survivors of child sexual abuse.* New York: Harper & Row.

Benedict, H. (1985). *Recovery: How to survive sexual assault—for women, men, teenagers, their friends and families.* Garden City, NY. Doubleday.

Besharov, D. J. (1990). *Recognizing child abuse: A guide for the concerned.* New York: Free Press.

Briere, J., & Runtz, M. (1987). Post sexual abuse trauma: Data and implications for clinical practice. *Journal of Interpersonal Violence, 2,* 367–379.

Brittain, D. E., & Merriam, K. (1988). Groups for significant others of survivors of child sexual abuse: A report of methods and findings. *Journal of Interpersonal Violence, 3,* 90–101.

Brownmiller, S. (1975). *Against our will: Men, women, and rape.* New York: Simon & Schuster.

Burgess, A. W. (Ed.). (1985). *Rape and sexual assault: A research handbook.* New York: Garland.

Burgess, A. W., Groth, A. N., Holmstrom, L. L., & Sgroi, S. M. (1978). *Sexual assault of children and adolescents.* Lexington, MA: Lexington Books.

Burgess, A. W., & Holmstrom, L. L. (1974). Rape trauma syndrome. *American Journal of Psychiatry, 131,* 981–986.

Burgess, A. W., & Holmstrom, L. L. (1979). *Rape: Crisis and recovery.* Bowie, MD: Robert J. Brady Co.

Burgess, A. W., & Holmstrom, L. L. (1985). Rape trauma syndrome and post traumatic stress response. In A. W. Burgess (Ed.), *Rape and sexual assault: A research handbook* (pp. 56–60). New York: Garland.

Carnes, P. (1983). *The sexual addiction.* Minneapolis, MN: CompCare Publications.

Carter, K. (1986, January 3). Pediatrics: Chicago hospital converts vacant unit into cost-effective child abuse ward. *Modern Healthcare, 16,* 42–45.

Cogdal, P. A., & James, R. K. (1991, August). *Combinatorial technique to treatment of adult incest survivors.* Paper presented at the American Psychological Association convention, San Francisco, CA.

Colao, F., & Hosansky, T. (1983). *Your children should know. Teach your children the strategies that will keep them safe from assault and crime.* New York: Berkeley Books.

Conte, J. R., & Schuerman, J. R. (1988). Research with child victims. In G. E. Wyatt & G. J. Powell (Eds.), *Lasting effects of child sexual abuse* (pp. 157–170). Newbury Park, CA: Sage Publications.

Coons, P. M., Bowman, E. E., Pellow, T. A., & Schneider, P. (1989). Post-traumatic aspects of the treatment of victims of sexual abuse and incest. *Psychiatric Clinics of North America, 12,* 325–335.

Courtois, C. A. (1988). *Healing the incest wound. Adult survivors in therapy.* New York: Norton.

Craine, L. S., Henson, C. E., Colliver, J. A., & MacLean, D. G. (1988). Prevalence of a history of sexual abuse among female psychiatric patients in a state hospital. *Hospital and Community Psychiatry, 39,* 300–304.

Davis, A. B. (1985, November 10). Fears follow sex abuse victims. *The Commercial Appeal.* Memphis, Section G, pp. 1–3.

Davis, T. B. (1985, October 10). Adult females who have been victimized by childhood incest and sexual abuse: Assessment and treatment techniques (Lecture). Counseling Psychology Seminar, Department of Counseling and Personnel Services, Memphis State University.

Deblinger, E., McLeer, S. V., Atkins, M. S., & Ralphe, D. (1989). Post-traumatic stress in sexually abused, physically abused, and nonabused children. *Child Abuse and Neglect, 13,* 403–408.

Ellis, E. (1983). A review of empirical rape research: Victim reactions and response to treatment. *Clinical Psychology Reviews, 3,* 473–490.

Finkelhor, D. (1979). *Sexually victimized children.* New York: Free Press.

Finkelhor, D. (1984). *Child sexual abuse: New theory and research.* New York: Free Press.

Finkelhor, D. (1987). The trauma of child sexual abuse: Two models. *Journal of Interpersonal Violence, 2,* 348–366.

Finkelhor, D., Araji, S., Baron, L., Browne, A., Peters, S. D., & Wyatt, E. G. (1986). *A sourcebook of child sexual abuse.* Newbury Park, CA: Sage Publications.

Fortune, M. M. (1983). *Sexual violence: The unmentionable sin.* New York: Pilgrim Press.

Frazier, P., & Borgida, E. (1985). Rape trauma syndrome evidence in court. *American Psychologist, 40,* 984–993.

Geiser, R. L. (1979). *Hidden victims: The sexual abuse of children.* Boston: Beacon Press.

Gil, E. (1984). *Outgrowing the pain.* Palo Alto, CA: Consulting Psychologists Press.

Goodwin, J. (1982). *Sexual abuse: incest victims and their families.* Boston: John Wright.

Goodwin, J. (1988). Post-traumatic symptoms in abused children. *Journal of Traumatic Stress, 1,* 475–488.

Gordon, L. (1955). Incest as revenge against the pre-Oedipal mother. *Psychoanalytic Review, 42,* 284–292.

Greer, J. G., & Stuart, I. R. (Eds.). (1983). *The sexual aggressor: Current perspectives on treatment.* New York: Van Nostrand Reinhold.

Grossman, R., & Sutherland, J. (1983). *Surviving sexual assault.* New York: Congdon & Weed.

Groth, A. N., & Birnbaum, H. J. (1979). *Men who rape: The psychology of the offender.* New York: Plenum.

Groth, A. N., & Stevenson, T. M. (1984). *Anatomical drawings for use in the investigation and intervention of child sexual abuse.* Newton Center, MA: Forensic Mental Health Association.

Hamilton, G. V. (1929). *A research in marriage.* New York: Albert & Charles Boni.

Harrison, P., Downes, M., & Williams, D. (1990). Date and acquaintance rape: Perceptions and attitude change strategies. *Journal of College Student Development, 32,* 131–139.

Hartman, C. R., & Burgess, A. W. (1988). Rape trauma and treatment of the victim. In F. M. Ochberg (Ed.), *Post-traumatic therapy and victims of violence* (pp. 152–174). New York: Brunner/Mazel.

Hays, K. F. (1985). Electra in mourning: Grief work and the adult incest survivor: *Psychotherapy Patient, 2,* 45–58.

Herman, J. (1981). *Father-daughter incest.* Cambridge, MA: Harvard University Press.

Hursch, C. J. (1977). *The trouble with rape.* Chicago: Nelson-Hall.

James, B. J., & Nasjleti, M. (1983). *Treating sexually abused children and their families.* Palo Alto, CA: Consulting Psychologists Press.

Janosik, E. H. (1984). *Crisis counseling: A contemporary approach.* Belmont: Wadsworth.

Justice, B., & Justice, R. (1979). *The broken taboo.* New York: Human Services.

Karpel, M. A., & Strauss, E. S. (1983). *Family evaluation.* New York: Gardner Press.

Katz, S., & Mazur, M. (1979). *Understanding the rape victim.* New York: Wiley.

Kelly, L. (1988). *Surviving sexual violence.* Minneapolis: University of Minnesota Press.

Kempe, R. S. (1984). *The common secret: Sexual abuse of children and adolescents.* New York: W. H. Freeman.

Kendrick, J. M. (1991). Crisis intervention in child abuse: A family treatment approach. In A. R. Roberts (Ed.), *Contemporary perspectives on crisis intervention* (pp. 34–52). Englewood Cliffs, NJ: Prentice-Hall.

Kinsey, A. C., Pomeroy, W. B., Martin, C. E., & Gebhard, P. H. (1948). *Sexual behavior in the human male.* Philadelphia: Saunders.

Kinsey, A. C., Pomeroy, W. B., Martin, C. E., & Gebhard, P. H. (1953). *Sexual behavior in the human female.* Philadelphia: Saunders.

Knopp, F. H. (1982). *Remedial intervention in adolescent sex offenses: Nine program descriptions.* New York: Safer Society Press.

Kovach, J. (1986). Incest as a treatment issue for alcoholic women. *Alcoholism Treatment Quarterly, 3,* 1–15.

Kreidler, M. C., & England, D. B. (1990). Empowerment through group support: Adult women who are survivors of incest. *Journal of Family Violence, 5,* 35–41.

Landis, J. T. (1956). Experiences of 500 children with adult sexual deviation. *Psychiatric Quarterly Supplement, 30* (part 1), 91–109.

Lee, L. A. (1987). Rape prevention: Experiential training for men. *Journal of Counseling and Development, 66,* 100–101.

Lindberg, F. H., & Distad, L. J. (1985). Post-traumatic stress disorders in women who experienced childhood incest. *Child Abuse and Neglect, 9,* 329–334.

Mayer, A. (1983). *Incest: A treatment manual for therapy with victims, spouses and offenders.* Kalamazoo, MI: Learning Publications.

McCombie, S. L. (1980). *Rape crisis intervention handbook.* New York: Plenum.

Medea, A., & Thompson, K. (1974). *Against rape. A survival manual for women: How to avoid entrapment and how to cope with rape physically and emotionally.* New York: Farrar, Straus & Giroux.

Mohr, J. W. (1981). Age structures in pedophilia. In M. Cook & K. Howells (Eds.), *Adult sexual interest in children* (pp. 41–53). New York: Academic Press.

Molmen, M.E.M. (1982). *Avoiding rape: Without putting yourself in protective custody.* Grand Forks, ND: Athena Press.

Murphy, W. D. (1985, October). The dynamics and phases of sexual abuse (Mimeographed, 3 pages). Sexual Abuse Treatment Project, Department of Human Services, University of Tennessee, Memphis.

Myers, M. F. (1986). Men sexually assaulted as adults and sexually molested as boys. *Archives of Sexual Behavior, 18,* 203–215.

O'Brien, S. (1983). *Child pornography.* Dubuque, IA: Kendall/Hunt.

Ochberg, F. M. (Ed.). (1988). *Post-trauma therapy and victims of violence.* New York: Brunner/Mazel.

Pithers, W. D., Kashima, K. M., Cumming, G. P., & Beal, L. S. (1988). Relapse prevention: A method of enhancing maintenance of change in sex offenders. In A. C. Salter (Ed.), *Treating child sex offenders and victims* (pp. 131–170). Newbury Park, CA: Sage Publications.

Plummer, C. A. (1984). *Preventing sexual abuse: Activities and strategies for working with children and adolescents.* Holmes Beach, FL: Learning Publications.

Rada, R. T. (1978). *Clinical aspects of the rapist.* New York: Grune & Stratton.

Rascovsky, M. W., & Rascovsky, A. (1950). On consummated incest. *International Journal of Psychoanalysis, 31,* 42–47.

Renshaw, D. (1982). *Incest: Understanding and treatment.* Boston: Little, Brown.

Revitch, E., & Weiss, R. G. (1962). The pedophiliac offender. *Diseases of the Nervous System, 23,* 73–78.

Rew, L. (1989). Long-term effects of childhood sexual exploitation. *Issues in Mental Health Nursing, 10,* 229–244.

Russell, D. E. (1982). *Rape in marriage.* New York: Macmillan.

Salter, A. C. (1988). *Treating child sex offenders and victims: A practical guide.* Newbury Park, CA: Sage Publications.

Sandberg, D. N., Crabbs, S. K., & Crabbs, M. A. (1988). Legal issues in child abuse: Questions and answers for counselors. *Elementary School Guidance & Counseling, 22,* 268–274.

Sanford, L. T. (1980). *The silent children: A parent's guide to prevention of child sexual abuse.* New York: McGraw-Hill.

Sgroi, S. M. (1982). *Handbook of clinical intervention in child sexual abuse.* Lexington, MA: Lexington Books.

Sgroi, S. M., Porter, F. S., & Blick, L. C. (1982). Validation of child sexual abuse. In S. M. Sgroi (Ed.), *Handbook of clinical intervention in child sexual abuse* (pp. 39–79). Lexington, MA: Lexington Books.

Sussman, L., & Bordwell, S. (1981). *The rapist file: Interviews with convicted rapists.* New York: Chelsea House.

Terman, L. M. (1938). *Psychological factors in marital happiness.* New York: McGraw-Hill.

Terman, L. M. (1951), Correlates of orgasm adequacy in a group of 556 wives. *Journal of Psychology, 32,* 115–172.

Townley, R. (1985). *Safe and sound: A parent's guide to child protection.* New York: Simon & Schuster.

Two Rape Surveys Contrast (1992, April 24). *The Commercial Appeal.* Memphis, TN: Memphis Publishing Co., p. A4.

Vernon, A., & Hay, J. (1988). A preventative approach to child sexual abuse. *Elementary School Guidance & Counseling, 22,* 306–312.

Virkkunen, M. (1975). Victim-precipitated pedophilia offenses. *British Journal of Criminology, 15,* 175–180.

Walker, L. E. (1989). *Terrifying love: Why women kill and how society responds.* New York: Harper & Row.

Weiner, I. B. (1962). Father-daughter incest: A clinical report. *Psychiatric Quarterly, 36,* 607–632.

West, D. J., Roy, C., & Nichols, F. L. (1978). *Understanding sexual attacks.* London. Heineman.

Wheeler, J. R., & Berliner, L. (1988). Treating the effects of sexual abuse on children. In G. E. Wyatt & G. J. Powell (Eds.), *Lasting effects of child sexual abuse* (pp. 227–247). Newbury Park, CA: Sage Publications.

Williams, J. E., & Holmes, K. A. (1981). *The assault: Rape and public attitudes.* Westport, CT: Greenwood Press.

Wolfe, V. V., Gentile, C., & Wolfe, D. A. (1989). The impact of sexual abuse on children: A PTSD formulation. *Behavior Therapy, 20,* 215–228.

Wyatt, G. E., & Powell, G. J. (Eds.). (1988). *Lasting effects of child abuse.* Newbury Park, CA: Sage Publications.

CLASSROOM EXERCISES

I. Counseling Simulations in Small Groups

The instructor constructs one-page scenarios of one or more sex-abuse-victim situations. The cases in this chapter may be used as models for developing the scenarios. A realistic source is recent newspaper accounts of rapes and sexual assaults. The class is divided randomly into task groups, which will conduct their own crisis intervention sessions simultaneously, rather than before the whole class. One person enacts the role of survivor and one the role of crisis worker, and the remaining persons are observer/evaluators. Only the survivor in each group is given a copy of a sexual-assault scenario. The survivor will need a few minutes to read and get into the mood to enact the role. Then the survivor and crisis worker enact a crisis intervention session.

For a specified length of time, the survivors are interviewed by the crisis workers in the groups, with the observer/evaluators taking notes. The instructor will circulate around the room, briefly looking in on each group as it engages in its crisis intervention session. The crisis worker in each group is instructed to be as helpful as possible, incorporating the strategies suggested in this chapter into the six-step crisis counseling model learned in Chapter 2.

Whenever the instructor calls "time" to conclude the crisis intervention sessions, a few moments should be reserved for observer/evaluators to provide constructive feedback to their respective groups. Some suggested guidelines for observer/evaluators are these questions:

1. What verbal responses and nonverbal behaviors did the crisis worker exhibit that appeared to be most helpful to the survivor?
2. What verbal responses and nonverbal behaviors (if any) appeared to be the least helpful or to elicit negative responses from the survivor?

After each observer/evaluator has had an opportunity to provide constructive feedback in the respective groups, each task group is allowed a brief period of discussion and a period for the survivor to disassociate from the role. The survivor can "derole" by taking a moment to tell other members of the task group, "This is the reason I am not the person I portrayed in that scenario," or make a similar statement of disengagement from the role played. The exercise should be concluded by providing an opportunity for one observer/evaluator from each group to share a one-minute summary statement (of that particular group's experience) with the entire class.

CHAPTER 7

Woman Battering

BACKGROUND

In this chapter, the terms *wife, husband, spouse,* and *marriage* are often used in the historical sense of a conjugal relationship. Certainly, physical abuse is not limited to husband-and-wife relationships. Indeed, single, separated, and divorced women are actually at greater risk for battering than married women (Stark & Flitcraft, 1987). Therefore, it should be clearly understood that the concepts discussed in this chapter apply to partners or people involved in any established current or former relationship. *Battering, abuse,* and *assault* are often used interchangeably in the literature. In this chapter, *battering* indicates any form of physical violence perpetrated by one person on another and most typically includes a life-threatening history of injury and psychosocial problems that entrap a person in a relationship. *Abuse* is a more general term that indicates that physical violence is only one weapon in an armory of coercive weapons. *Abuse* denotes the unequal power relationship within which the assault occurs and further suggests that a presumption of trust has been violated. *Assaultive behavior* can include not only harmful acts against a person but also both verbal and behavioral threats to significant others, pets, or property. *Domestic violence* subsumes any act of assault by a social partner or relative, regardless of marital status (Stark & Flitcraft, 1988).

Incidence of Domestic Violence

In current usage, "rule of thumb" means a measure or guideline based on an educated guess, particularly in the carpentry or masonry trade. However, the origins of this expression are not so innocuous. For "rule of thumb" in the original sense refers to a passage in British common law that allowed a husband to beat his wife with a rod no thicker than his thumb so as to spare her permanent physical injury (Davidson, 1977, p. 18). The history of wife beating in Western society goes as far back as the patriarchal system. Whereas an assault on or rape of another man's wife caused and still causes immediate and severe legal punishment and moral outrage, abuse by a man of his own wife is quite another story (Pleck, 1987).

Common law in the United States early acknowledged the right of a man to chastise his wife for misbehavior without being prosecuted for doing so (*Bradley* v. *State of Mississippi,* 1824). Indeed, the law's attitude toward wife beating to the current day is aptly summarized in the case of the *State of North Carolina* v. *Oliver* in 1874. The court ruled that "if no permanent injury has been inflicted, it is better to draw the curtains, shut out the public eye, and leave the parties to forgive and forget." Although laws have changed, there is little doubt that for much of the legal justice system the North Carolina comments still prevail in the contemporary scene. Okun (1986) reports a 1982 Kansas case where a convicted batterer was sentenced to buy his battered wife a box of chocolates (p. 9). The implications of such "blind" justice are ominous.

There is no more anxiety-provoking call for a police officer than a domestic disturbance call. More police die as a result of intervening in domestic violence calls than in any other type of crime (Resnik, 1976, p. 9). Further, domestic disturbance calls far outnumber other types of police calls in which the possibility of violence exists (Benjamin & Walz, 1983, p. 63). And violence does exist, in a big way. Approximately one-fourth of all murders in the United States occur within the family and one-half of those are spouse killings (Margolin, 1979, p. 13).

The national crime survey *Intimate Victims: A Study of Violence Among Friends and Relatives* (U.S. Department of Justice, 1980) found there were about 3.8 million incidents of violence among intimates during the four-year period of the survey. Of this number, 616,000 were between spouses or ex-spouses. In terms of those acts of violence that would be considered wife beating, the national family violence survey revealed that 1 woman in 22 was a victim of abusive violence in the 12 months prior to the interview. In Straus, Gelles, and Steinmetz's (1980) study of married couples that closely modeled the population as a whole, the incident rate of violent behavior was 16% in the target year and 28% across the span of the marriage. If that number is extrapolated across the population of the United States, the number of abused women would be in excess of 8 million (Stark & Flitcraft, 1988, p. 117).

What those statistics translate into is criminal assault, criminal offenses against the family, and murder. The 1990 *Uniform Crime Report* for the United States listed the following statistics. Overall murder was up 9% over the previous year. Of the 4399 women murdered in 1990, 30% were killed by husbands or boyfriends, as opposed to 4% of all male homicides being perpetrated by girlfriends or wives. Given the dangers to and/or unwillingness of women to file complaints against their abusers, and understanding that the following number reflects all types of arrests for family problems, in 1990 there were an estimated 85,800 arrests for crimes against one's family (FBI, 1991).

One of the major reasons that much domestic violence is not reported is the medical system. Only 1 abused woman in 20 who seeks medical services is properly identified (Stark, Flitcraft, & Frazier, 1979). Kurz and Stark (1987) reported that while 75% of the battered women they studied volunteered information that they had been abused, the problem was acknowledged by clinicians in only 5% of the cases. Using a trauma screen, they found that the single most common cause of a female injury brought to medical attention was abuse. Sixteen percent of all female injury patients are battered women, while auto accidents account for only 11% of female injuries admitted to the hospital (Rosenberg, Stark, & Zahn, 1986). Finally, one-third of all rape occurs in battering relationships (Stark et al., 1979). To counter the abysmal record of the medical profession in identifying battering, Antonia Novello, surgeon general of the United States, has joined with the American Medical Association's Physicians Campaign Against Family Violence in calling for training and sensitivity from doctors in spotting victims of domestic violence, questioning patients in a caring way, and referring them to support services (Coleman, 1991). Clearly, the consciousness level of the medical profession needs raising.

Current Approaches to Battery

Despite the long and current history of wife abuse, it has been only since 1974 that a consistent and planned systematic approach to the problem has evolved. Erin Pizzey's book *Scream Quietly or the Neighbors Will Hear* (1974) was responsible for the start of the first women's shelter in England. Subsequently, in the United States, the National Organization for Women, along with grassroots organizations such as the Massachusetts Coalition of Battered Women Service Groups, has come to the forefront in developing funding sources, shelters, support groups, organizing and training manuals, and legislation for battered women.

Media attention about the severity of the problem has raised public consciousness. From a cover picture and the first major article on battering in the August 1976 issue of *Ms.* magazine to a current Rex Morgan M.D. comic strip story line on battering to numerous television documentaries and talk shows to the dramatic and shocking television movie *The Burning Bed,* media coverage has attracted attention, changed public perspective, and removed some of the cloak of secrecy from domestic violence.

Such increased public awareness and the efforts of feminist and other citizen's groups resulted in formation of the National Coalition Against Domestic Violence to promote a national power base for battered women (Capps, 1982). This group has exerted a good deal of social and legislative pressure to combat the problem of domestic violence. One outcome has been a shift in police procedure and law enforcement. In many cities a police call to a domestic dispute where battering is involved now results in a mandatory arrest, and if convicted, the batterer is mandated by the court to participate in counseling and anger management programs or else to go to jail as an alternative (Shupe, Stacey, & Hazlewood, 1987). Since instigation of this policy in Ontario, Canada, there has been a 2500% increase in arrests for domestic assault (Edwards, 1989, p. 192).

Further, stories like those of Francine Hughes (subject of *The Burning Bed*), who suffered prolonged and severe beatings by her husband and who finally killed him by pouring kerosene around his bed and setting it on fire have had an impact on the courts by challenging legal precedents and assumptions about homicide and self-defense (Edwards, 1989). Indeed, psychologist Dr. Lenore Walker's (1989) book *Terrifying Love* is a chilling and eye-opening account of her experiences as an expert witness in murder trials of battering victims who have killed their assailants.

There appears to be some positive effect from raised public consciousness, more stringent laws regarding battering, the shelter movement, and court-mandated counseling for batterers. In their ten-year follow-up study of family violence in 1985, Straus and Gelles (1986) found an overall decline in husband-to-wife violence of 6.6%. What is more significant is that severe husband-to-wife violence (battering) decreased by 26.6%. However, what is perplexing is that wife-to-husband violence has increased to a rate as high as that of husband-to-wife violence in the 1985 study. Clearly, a great deal of violence by women against men is retaliatory or in self-defense. However, it is not something to be dismissed because of even greater violence by husbands. Indeed, almost all shelters for battered women now have policies designed to deal with the high rate of child abuse and some are also facing up to the problem of wife-to-husband violence (Straus & Gelles, 1986). Still, the rate of couple violence had only diminished from 160 to 158 per 1000 in the ten-year span, a rate that is still extraordinarily high.

While efforts to research and address the issue of domestic battering and abuse are expanding rapidly, the problem continues to spiral out of control. As an example, one of the most critical areas is the provision of a safe shelter for women who wish to escape from their assailants. The number of shelters has grown from zero in 1975 to over a thousand today. Funding for these shelters has been supplemented by the Social Security Administration's program for the temporary housing of neglected and abused children, Law Enforcement Assistance Administration grants, community funding sources such as United Way, social agencies such as the YWCA, and state taxes on marriage licenses (Pleck, 1987). Yet, these efforts do not begin to address the scope of the problem. As of 1991 there appears to be little change in the incidence of domestic violence. Crisis workers from hot lines, shelters, addiction programs, and family services that we talked to at the 1991 Crisis Convening (James & Gilliland, 1991) all perceive an increase in domestic violence. Shelters across the country are continuously full beyond capacity and must turn people away. If reports from the Memphis Police Department's Family Trouble Center (Memphis Police Department, 1991) are representative of the rest of the country, then we are experiencing no decrease in battering or abuse.

DYNAMICS OF WOMAN BATTERING
Psychosocial and Cultural Dynamics

The overarching dynamic behind women battering is male supremacy. It is the natural result of a long-term sexist, paternalistic social order that rewards aggressive behavior in men but expects women to be passive and submissive (Benjamin & Walz, 1983, p. 65). Combined with the emergent status of women outside the home, this tradition has produced a volatile mix of personality dynamics. The flash point of such a mix occurs when the man who lives the traditional male image of chief breadwinner and director of the family perceives himself as losing power in the conjugal relationship.

The question of power is the fuse that ignites this explosive mixture. The women's position is to obey, conciliate, perform traditional domestic duties, and, in general, be subservient. Any attempt to establish herself in her own right is likely to be met with punishment for overstepping her bounds (Benjamin & Walz, 1983, pp. 74–77). Violence, though, is not something that develops only in families. It involves a complex interplay of social, cultural, and psychological factors. At least 20 distinct theories on battering of women have been identified (Okun, 1986). The following 6 theories encapsulate past and present thinking about the causes of battering.

Masochism. Psychoanalytic theory, which holds masochism to be the primary motivating factor in abusive relationships, is now mostly obsolete in the scientific community. There is no empirical research to substantiate the notion, still popularly held, that erotic enjoyment of pain through battering is a trait found in abused women (Okun, 1986; Stark & Flitcraft, 1988). From a feminist point of view, this theory held sway for a long time because the male-dominated field of psychiatry found it a convenient pigeonhole for a troublesome problem. Until interest in the problem was generated in the 1970s, little research was presented to refute the idea.

Coercive control. Morgan (1982) has used the term *conjugal terrorism* to describe a tactic akin to brainwashing and political terrorism where violence or the threat of violence is used to break the resistance of the victim and bend her to the will of the terrorist (batterer). Typical brainwashing and terrorist tools such as social and physical isolation, torture, sleep deprivation, malnourishment, dictating use of one's time, bondage, false confessions, and denouncing and belittling of the victim to significant others are all standard operating procedures of abusers to enhance the victim's dependency on them.

Cultural reinforcement. Sociological theories cover a wide gamut of specific theories that are psychosocially and culturally bound. These theories range from finding the roots of violence in the culture at large down to the family unit. Societal attitudes about the legitimate use of violence to achieve personal ends have their roots in a tradition of perceived "national interest." As a nation, we promote and glorify the controlled use of aggression for protection, law and order, self-defense, and national interest (Benjamin & Walz, 1983, pp. 64–66). Force is a major resource in maintaining the existing social structure and projecting national presence. This notion has been extended to the family by at least implicit permission of the state. For the state, the family is the basic disciplinary agent—family over individual, male over female, adult over child. Control is direct, continuous, personalized, and an efficient way of keeping intact the past social order of the state (Capps, 1982). When males are incapable of demonstrating their supposed superior status through other skills or abilities, they still have the resource of physical force to maintain their dominant position.

Our cultural heritage goes far back in aiding and abetting the family as a cradle of violence and learned aggression for the male. Supported by the Judeo-Christian ethic, "Spare the rod and spoil the child" can easily be translated into the same homily for "the wife." Given the excellent role models of learned aggression that such long-standing messages and behaviors imply, it is not too difficult to see that families in which this principle is carried out become excellent training grounds for violent behavior (Gelles, 1972, p. 10). Evidence substantiates the hypothesis that the cycle of violence continues: males from such families mature and practice similar behavior on their spouses (Steinmetz & Straus, 1973). Between what is modeled in families and the extremely violent role models presented in the media, it is little wonder that violence occurs in the home.

However, it is not just a "Rambo" mentality or a twisted, misapplied religious philosophy that is used to support domestic violence. As upheld for many years by courts of the land, the privacy of one's home and the guarantee of that privacy under the Fourth Amendment has much to do with not intruding in others' private affairs and the reciprocal expectation that one's own private affairs will likewise not be violated (Straus et al., 1980). Finally, society's rose-colored romantic view of a perfect Norman Rockwell family Thanksgiving gathering in some happier past time and its unwillingness to acknowledge the family as a violence-prone group contributes much to the denial of domestic violence. That denial translates into little if any preventative or educative measures about domestic violence.

Learning theory.   Learning theory approaches operate on the principle that both perpetration and acceptance of physical and psychological abuse is conditioned and learned behavior. These theories have much to say about why batterers obtain reinforcement for battering and why women stay in a battering relationship. Foremost among these theories is Lenore Walker's (1984, 1989) theory of learned helplessness, which she adapted from animal studies conducted on random, noncontingent punishment. Applied to battering in particular, the theory proposes that battered women do not leave abusive relationships because they have been conditioned to believe they cannot predict their own safety and that nothing they or anyone else does will alter their terrible circumstances. While on the surface, this view of battered women's coping ability may seem at best pathetic and at worst assinine, it should be remembered that when these women have previously sought help in getting relief from their battering, they generally will have had a long history of outright refusal of services, denial of their abuse, and secondary victimization of them by family, the police, the judiciary, mental health and social services, and medical staff and facilities (Stark & Flitcraft, 1988).

Walker (1984, 1989) has proposed a number of factors in childhood and adulthood that are building blocks for learned helplessness. Childhood factors include witnessing or experiencing battering, sexual abuse, or molestation, health problems or chronic illness, stereotypical sex roles, and rigid traditionality. Such experiences teach the child that external, autocratic, and oftentimes whimsical forces dictate outcomes. In adulthood, factors that are instigated by the batterer include an emergent pattern of violence, sexual abuse, jealousy, overpossessiveness, intrusiveness and isolation, threat of harm, observed violence toward others, animals, or things, and alcohol or drug abuse. The more these factors are apparent, the more likely the stage will be set for random and dramatic violence that has little connection to any clear or rational stimulus. Given these conditions, the victim cannot escape the noncontingent punishment.

The term *helplessness* has caused a great deal of furor from feminists because they see this pejorative term as casting women in a victim role with few resources or little empowerment. However, according to Walker (1989), women are not helpless in the standard sense of the term. What learned helplessness does mean is that battered women choose behavioral responses that have the highest predictability of causing them the least harm in the known situation. Although through prior conditioning they may be unable to leave, within the situation they control it as effectively as they can (pp. 50–52). Because of the extreme and often lethal violence that occurs when these women attempt to leave and the lack of social support in making any attempt, it is understandable that a "Better the devil I know!" philosophy predominates for many abused women.

Exchange theory.   Exchange theory (Gelles & Cornell, 1985) is a variant of a learning theory approach. It proposes that batterers hit people because they can. As long as the costs for being violent do not outweigh the rewards, invariably violence as a method of control will be used. Particularly when social control agents such as the police, criminal charges, imprisonment, loss of status, and loss of income are not used as negative sanctions that increase the cost of the behavior, batterers will continue to batter. Sexual inequality in regard to size, financial resources, and social status allows batterers to become violent without fear of retribution. The private nature of the family also reduces the potential for outside agencies to intervene. To do so with any degree of success often means breaking the family up, a drastic measure that courts are loath to take. While there may be loss of status in the larger society for being a child or wife beater, there are certain subcultures where aggressive and violent behavior are proof of being a "real man." Finally, exacting "costs" on a woman to pay for her supposed "sins and transgressions" is in and of itself satisfying to the batterer. (pp. 120–125).

Feminist theory.   Feminist theory views social phenomena as determined by the sexist, patriarchal structure of our society and battering as merely one outcome of a structure that allows rape, incest, prostitution, foot binding, and a host of other sexist restrictions to keep women in servile positions (Schechter, 1982; Stark & Flitcraft, 1988). A strict feminist view categorically separates woman battering from other forms of intrafamily violence or at the most sees the other forms of family violence as a by-product of how women are brutalized (Okun, 1986; Pleck, 1987). The feminist view also holds that until women are seen as other than subservient, compliant victims, little will change. The feminist view strongly opposes professionalization of services to battered women because institutionalizing services merely means that women are put under another yoke of the sexist society (Schecter, 1982).

While each of these theoretical stances has merit, to this point none has proven itself to completely explain the phenomenon of battering. Certainly, there is much to be said for a feminist perspective that is couched in paternalistic sociocultural terms. If it had not been for the feminist movement's willingness to take on battering as a social issue, it would probably still be "behind drawn shades." There is also clear evidence from our bulging prison population that certain people will attempt to get away with anything they can with little regard to the expense of others as long as they believe they can escape the consequences of their actions. Likewise, evidence exists that there are legions of individuals with personality disorders who would think nothing of manipulating anyone in any manner to satisfy their insatiable narcissistic or dependency needs. There is also clear evidence from a national perspective that Teddy Roosevelt's admonition "Speak softly and carry a big stick!" is extremely effective and has trickled down to the family unit. Finally, it is hard to argue against the contention that the founding fathers' belief that "a man's home is his castle" has much to do with society's refusal to intervene in the sacrosanct realm of the home.

Psychological Factors

Psychologically, both parties to a battering situation have certain identifiable characteristics. Men in a battering relationship

1. demonstrate excessive dependency and possessiveness toward their women—although they deny it

2. are unable to express any emotion except anger and generally have poor communication skills where emotional issues are concerned
3. have unrealistic expectations of their spouses and idealize marriage or the relationship far beyond what realistically may be expected
4. have a lack of self-control and, paradoxically, set up rigid family boundaries for everyone else
5. are alcohol or drug abusers
6. were abused as children or saw their mothers abused
7. deny and minimize problems, particularly battering, that they generate in families
8. emotionally cycle from hostility, aggressiveness, and cruelty when they don't get their way to charm, manipulation, and seductiveness when they do
9. may be characterized as jealous, denying, impulsive, self-deprecating, depressive, demanding, aggressive, and violent

(Barnett, Pittman, Ragan, & Salus, 1980; Finkelhor, Gelles, Hotaling, & Straus, 1983; Ganley & Harris, 1978; Gelles & Cornell, 1985; Mott-MacDonald, 1979; Okun, 1986; Shupe et al., 1987; Symonds, 1978; Walker, 1984, 1989)

Encompassing the foregoing factors of abusing men are four general personality patterns: the controller, the defender, the approval seeker, and the incorporator (Elbow, 1977).

1. *The controller.* The individual uses threats and force to get his way. Women are regarded as objects. There is little or no emotional reciprocity. Violence occurs when he feels unable to control his wife. Halleck (1976) has cast this personality pattern as an extremely dangerous, criminally violent individual who may be described as narcissistic, immature, and sociopathic. Total dominance is the end product; therefore, killing one's partner is a distinct possibility since death of one's partner represents ultimate control over her.

2. *The defender.* This individual is insecure and afraid of being hurt. Such a man is able to feel strong only if his mate continuously clings to and depends on him. His spouse may punish him for being aggressive toward her—particularly by withholding sex. To render her nonpunitive and powerless so that he will not be vulnerable to attack, he may resort to violence.

3. *The approval seeker.* This individual has high expectations of himself but low self-esteem. His self-esteem is contingent on acceptance and approval by others. The prospect of losing a mate for any reason is highly threatening because such a loss would confirm his low regard for himself. As a result, he will do anything, including becoming violent, to keep his self-esteem intact.

4. *The incorporator.* This individual cannot see himself as a whole person without incorporating his mate into his persona. By doing so he gains from his mate a degree of self-validation. Fear of losing her results in ego deterioration, which must be avoided at all costs. In extreme cases, this

male is so dependent that if his mate threatens to leave, he may kill her and/or himself.

Women in a battering relationship

1. have a lack of self-esteem as a result of being told over and over that they are stupid, incompetent, and otherwise inadequate
2. experience a lack of control and little confidence in their ability to take any meaningful steps to improve their marriage
3. have experienced a history of abuse that leads them to accept their role as victim, or saw their mothers abused and accept it as their lot
4. are so ashamed that they hide their physical and emotional wounds and become socially and emotionally isolated
5. lack personal, physical, educational, and financial resources that would allow them to get out of the battering situation
6. are extremely dependent and are willing to suffer grievous insult and injury to have their needs met
7. have an idealized view of what a relationship should be and somehow feel they can "fix or change" the man
8. do not have good communication skills, particularly in regard to asserting their rights and feelings
9. learn stereotyped sex roles and thus feel guilty if they do not adhere to a rigid patriarchal system
10. are unable to differentiate between sex and love and believe that love is manifested through intense sexual relationships

(Barnett et al., 1980; Benjamin & Walz, 1983; Finkelhor et al., 1983; Gelles & Cornell, 1985; Ibrahim & Herr, 1987; Okun, 1986; Walker, 1984, 1989).

In one way or another, all the concepts we've just enumerated have to do with power. Whether its presence or absence is perceived or real makes little difference because the outcome—abuse and battering—is the same. To chalk wife battering up to something other than this basic encultured dynamic is not valid. If men acted on impulse or some other drive, they would beat up their bosses, secretaries, friends, or neighbors as often as their mates and children. Only in a conjugal relationship do many men generally believe in and exercise their ability to coerce and abuse their spouses and children (Hart, 1980).

Stressors

If power is the fuse, then stress is the match that lights the fuse. As the idealized image of the relationship breaks down and environmental stresses build up, couples become engaged in an ever-upward spiral of violent interaction (Barnett et al., 1980). When the social system does not provide a family member with sufficient resources to maintain his or her position, tension rises, and physical force is often used as a means of trying to stabilize the situation (Steinmetz & Straus, 1974, p. 9).

Although not generic to all battering, a variety of factors that seem to appear over and over in domestic violence have been compiled by Barnett et at. (1980, pp. 7–9), Benjamin & Walz (1983), Finkelhor et al. (1983), Gelles & Cornell (1985), Okun (1986), and Walker (1984, p. 51). These factors may be introduced by the batterer to control the situation, may occur as a product of the relationship itself, or may be environmentally introduced from outside the relationship.

1. *Geographic isolation.* Because of geographic location, the victim has no friends near who can provide a support system. A farm woman who cannot drive is an example of the worst case: literally being marooned and held captive by an abusive husband.

2. *Social isolation.* Because of extreme emotional dependence, the woman expects all needs to be met by her partner and has no significant others to turn to when she is assaulted.

3. *Economic stress.* When a woman is unemployed or underemployed, has inadequate housing, is pressured by creditors, and cannot feed and clothe her children by herself, she becomes human chattel to her abusive partner.

4. *Medical problems.* Long-term, chronic medical problems for either spouse or children exact tremendous financial and emotional cost.

5. *Inadequate parenting skills.* A lack of knowledge of parenting skills and conflict over parental roles can lead to situations that start as minor disciplinary problems and escalate into violence in the family.

6. *Pregnancy.* Ranging from heralding an unwanted child through creating anxiety over providing for the new baby to arousing jealousy over a wife's attention to a newborn, pregnancy is an especially acute crisis point for potential abuse.

7. *Family dysfunction.* A veritable kaleidoscope of problems causes dysfunction in the family. Some of these problems are related to age and number of children, presence of stepchildren, loyalty conflicts, death, desertion, and career change.

8. *Alcohol and drug abuse.* Chemical dependence serious enough to cause economic chaos and severe emotional disturbance characterizes addictive families and has spin-offs that commonly include spouse abuse. The insidious problem with alcohol and drugs is that they are often used as an excuse for behavior (battering) that is normally prohibited by societal norms and standards.

9. *Educational and/or vocational disparity.* When a female in a relationship has higher educational attainment or higher vocational status than the male, this may raise questions of adequacy and responsibility with both parties. Further, if the man is unemployed and the woman is employed, the man has a great deal of time to brood on his inability to function as the head of household, which is extremely demeaning to males already suffering from feelings of inadequacy. Particularly for men with low self-esteem, this may breed violent confrontations.

The Cycle of Violence

Barnett et al. (1980) have schematically represented the phases leading to the explosion of violence in the family. Walker's (1984) cycle theory of violence closely parallels these phases and her research supports the theory (p. 95).

Phase I.   Tranquillity prevails. The relationship may have been characterized as calm to this point, with no previous violent incidents, or a period of calm may follow an earlier violent episode.

Phase II. Tension starts to build. A variety of stresses impinge on the relationship. They may come in combination or singly from the common group we have already mentioned. However, there is no reduction of tension and the situation grows more strained.

Phase III. A violent episode occurs. The episode may range from harsh words to a severe beating. At this phase, communication has broken down and the situation is out of control.

Phase IV. The relationship takes on crisis proportions. A variety of options becomes available.

   A. The abuser becomes remorseful and asks forgiveness. Sooner or later the victim forgives the abuser and calm is restored.

   B. The abuser is not remorseful and feels his control over the situation has been established. The victim gives in and relinquishes control, and calm is restored.

   C. The victim takes new action. Within this option are two possibilities: the abuser negotiates the situation, and, given that the negotiation is agreeable to the victim, calm is restored; or the abuser rejects the new action and a crisis state continues.

It is at this last point, in which no possibility of resolution exists, that the victim is most likely to seek help by referring herself to a wife abuse center. If effective assessment and intervention do not occur when the violence emerges (Phase II), the likelihood that the violence will recur and will be of greater intensity is dramatically increased (Barnett et al., 1980, p. 34).

Myths About Woman Battering

The following myths encapsulate numerous arguments used by those who would submerge, camouflage, and diminish battering (Gelles & Cornell, 1985; Heppner, 1978; Massachusetts Coalition of Battered Women Service Groups, 1981; Okun, 1986; Pagelow, 1977; Stark & Flitcraft, 1988; Straus et al., 1980).

   1. *Battered women overstate the case.* Any person who has contusions, lacerations, and broken bones is not overstating anything. In any other instance such outcomes are referred to as assault and battery.

   2. *Battered women provoke the beating.* While some women may be

classified as the stereotypical "nag," there can certainly be many significant others in a man's life who fit into the "nag" category. Yet such people do not get assaulted with the regularity that wives do.

3. *Battered women are masochists.* If such women did have masochistic tendencies they would find a variety of ways to suffer pain that would not be exclusive to an abusive mate.

4. *Battering is a private, family matter.* When beaten women are disenfranchised from their homes, and the children of battering relationships learn the pathological roles a battering father models, battering transcends the home and becomes society's problem.

5. *Alcohol abuse is the prime reason for wife abuse.* Although alcohol plays a part in many cases of abuse, it may be only an excuse for, and not the cause of, violent behavior.

6. *Battering occurs only in problem families.* The dynamic representation of stress factors that assail families shows that any family at any given point may be classified as "problem."

7. *Only low-income and working-class families experience violence.* Members of those socioeconomic classes do come to the attention of the police and welfare agencies to a much greater degree than middle- or upper-class members, but statistics from wife abuse shelters indicate that battering has no class boundaries.

8. *The battering cannot be that bad or she would not stay.* The host of personal factors that tie the women to the relationship militate heavily against simply picking up and leaving.

9. *A husband has patriarchal rights.* What a man does in his own family is not his own business when the emotional overflow of what he does spills over into the community. No amount or kind of justification from the Bible or any other authority—be it person, institution, or book—can excuse spouse abuse.

10. *The beaten spouse exaggerates the problem to exact revenge.* Reporting a beating—whether committed by a total stranger or one's spouse —is no exaggeration. If revenge were the motive, there would be a host of ways of going about it that would be far less traumatic than calling or showing up at a wife abuse shelter.

11. *Women are too sensitive, especially when they are pregnant.* If a person is too sensitive who objects to being kicked in the stomach or vagina, thrown down a flight of stairs, or hit in the face with a lamp, then we would suppose that everyone is overly sensitive.

12. *Battering is rare.* The statistics reported in this chapter clearly indicate otherwise. Family violence is endemic in society.

13. *Battering is confined to mentally disturbed or sick people.* It appears that less than 10% of family violence is caused by mental illness. While continued physical and psychological abuse may cause many victims to suffer serious emotional distress and posttraumatic stress disorder, they did not enter the relationship "sick." Further, most perpetrators are not mentally ill by any DSM-IIIR definition.

14. *Violence and love cannot coexist.* Strange as it may seem, violent families may still love one another. Although the threat of violence may hang heavy, violence does not occur all the time. This paradoxical aspect is most problematic because children in such families grow up believing you hit the people you love.

Realities for Abused Women

Why, then, do women stay in an abusing relationship? For those who have no experience with violence in a relationship, it is an easy thing to say, "Throw the bum out!" or "I wouldn't tolerate that, I'd call the cops and have you arrested!" or "Forget you, nobody does that to me, I'm leaving!" In actuality, most women who are in battering relationships do leave, and this in itself is a courageous act because it is one of the most dangerous things a woman can do. The batterer tends to do poorly on his own and would often rather kill or die than be separated from the woman, because he is more terrified of abandonment than violence or punishment (Walker, 1989, p. 65). It is remarkable that a number of women do leave given their clear understanding that lives hang in the balance—their own, those of their children, and even the batterer's.

Most women leave a battering relationship an average of three to six times, but do so with varying degrees of permanency (Dobash & Dobash, 1979; Walker, 1979). The following reasons for staying in the relationship have been gleaned from a number of researchers (Benjamin & Walz, 1983; Conroy, 1982; Gelles, 1976; Okun, 1986; Pagelow, 1981; Walker, 1979, 1984, 1989), and these realities have nothing to do with the myths we've just examined.

1. The woman has a fear of reprisal or of aggravating the attacks even more.
2. Even though the situation may be intolerable for the woman, her children do have food, clothing, and shelter.
3. The woman would suffer shame, embarrassment, humiliation, and even ridicule if her secret got out.
4. Her self-concept is so strongly dependent on the relationship and perceived social approval that leaving would be very destructive to her.
5. Early affection and prior love in the relationship persist and, by staying, the woman hopes to salvage them.
6. If financially well off, the women is unable to forego a reduction in her financial freedom.
7. In the cyclic nature of abuse, her mate may not be terrible 24 hours a day, seven days a week. There may be good times when a lot of caring and tenderness are professed and shown. The victim may tend to forget the batterings and remember only the good times.
8. Early role models of an abusive parent may lead her to believe that relationships exist in no other way.

9. The woman may hold religious values that strongly militate against separation, divorce, or anything less than filial subjugation to the man's wishes.
10. The woman may be undereducated, have small children to raise, and have no job skills.
11. She may be kept so socially, physically, geographically, and financially isolated that she has no resources of any kind to help her get out.
12. She may be so badly injured that she is unable physically to leave.
13. She may believe the man's promise to reform.
14. She may be concerned for children who are still at home.
15. Love or sorrow at the mate's professed inability to exist without her may impel to stay.

We believe that strong social and psychological forces serve to rationalize and deny some very complex dynamics with which few people or social institutions are willing to grapple. As a result, any woman who attempts to break free of a battering relationship will most likely meet active discouragement from the church, police, courts, welfare agencies, legal services, family, and friends (Gelles & Cornell, 1985, p. 78; Schuyler, 1976, p. 489; Stark & Flitcraft, 1988; Walker, 1989). Secondary victimization may result by labeling battered women as hysterical, depressed, schizophrenic, alcoholic, child neglecters and abusers. Such labeling may provide professionals with "reasons" to do things to battered women ranging from overmedication with psychotropic drugs to sending them to jail and removing their children from the home. Any one of the revictimizations by well-meaning or not-so-well-meaning institutions all undermine assertiveness and reinforce submissiveness and compliance, which in turn increases vulnerability to abuse (Stark & Flitcraft, 1988; Walker, 1989). It is little wonder that a woman making her first call to an abuse center may be taking only an initial step in a series that sometimes goes on for years before she can make a complete break from the battering relationship.

INTERVENTION STRATEGIES

Throughout our discussion of the intervention process, we will be speaking of the crisis worker in the feminine gender. After careful consideration, both from a review of the literature and from dialogues with wife abuse workers, we believe that men are likely to be unsuccessful as wife abuse workers. This is true for two reasons. First, the trauma that battered women undergo at the hands of their mates tends to generalize to all men. Dealing with battered women is a difficult enough task without having to wade through issues involving fear of the crisis worker. Second, the crisis worker must be an advocate, but at the same time not allow the client to manipulate the situation. Many battered women have learned to relate to men in a charming and seductive way. Thus, a great deal of extra time may be needlessly spent in teaching battered women how to relate to a male worker in positive and nonseductive ways (Walker, 1979, p. 76). Whereas one long-term goal of therapy may be teaching such women more equitable relationships with men, it is not the goal of crisis intervention.

Assessment

Assessment of battered women by personality measures is somewhat confounding and contradictory to what one might logically expect. One never really knows whether the personality factors found in battered women were present before they were battered or are the result of the victimization (Gelles & Cornell, 1985, p. 71). However, Walker (1989, p. 105) reports that as the battering progressively becomes worse, Minnesota Multiphasic Personality Inventory (MMPI) profiles will also change notably. Using the MMPI, Rosewater (1982) found that the profiles of battered women appear to be similar to those of other emotionally disturbed individuals. However, investigation of subscale inconsistencies indicated battered women to be different from others who have serious mental illness. This is an important distinction that debunks the notion that most battered women are unstable. As an example, battered women may have real reasons to be fearful about their safety, and such fears are not indicative of paranoid ideation (Walker, 1984, p. 75).

Walker's (1984) in-depth study of the personality constructs of battered women sheds some interesting light on how they perceive themselves. Contrary to popular notions that such women would assume a subservient, conservative sex role, she found battered women to be highly liberal in their sex-role views and saw themselves as much more liberated than controlled. Further, such women did not see their male counterparts as more powerful than they were, but rather saw themselves as equals in the battering relationship. It might also be expected that these women would have extremely low self-esteem. To the contrary, battered women were found to have highly positive views of themselves. However, these women were subject to depression and became more depressed after they left the battering relationship than while they were in it (pp. 77–83). This last point has important transcrisis ramifications for the crisis worker and indicates that resolving initiating events is only one component of the intervention process.

Overall, battered women present many of the symptoms of posttraumatic stress disorder and can be placed for diagnostic purposes within the PTSD category of the DSM-IIIR (American Psychiatric Association, 1987). Indeed, Walker (1989, pp. 48–49) proposes Battered Woman Syndrome as a subcategory of PTSD.

Sadly, many in the helping professions still confuse the effects of domestic abuse with symptoms of other diagnoses, make unfounded diagnoses without checking symptoms, and institutionally revictimize the battered woman though inappropriate medication and therapy. It is extremely important to be aware of these masking symptoms. Stark and Flitcraft (1988) report that 19% of all battered women attempt suicide, 38% are diagnosed as depressed or having another situational disorder, and 10% become psychotic. Compared to nonabused women, they are 5 times more likely to attempt suicide, 15 times more likely to abuse alcohol, 9 times more likely to abuse drugs, 6 times more likely to report child abuse, and 3 times more likely to be diagnosed as psychotic or depressed.

Although face-to-face encounters with battered women are the exception rather than the rule for crisis workers, the more that the foregoing symptoms appear on intake interviews, the more the human services worker should suspect that battering is involved. If possible, a cross-check of medical injuries where no clear cause is presented and the injuries are fairly continuous should lead the human services worker even farther down the road to a battering diagnosis. It should not be expected or assumed that the woman will voluntarily relate her abuse or condemn her abusive partner.

Walker (1984, p. 122) has one major rule of assessment that supersedes all others and to which we strongly subscribe: when a woman calls or comes in to report a battering, believe her and start intervention immediately. It is a safe bet that whenever a battered woman seeks help, she is not carrying out the act as some impetuous, hysterical, spur-of-the-moment way to get back at her mate. Battered women refer themselves only after their problems have become exceedingly serious. Walker (1984, p. 26) found that only 14% of battered women surveyed would seek help after a first incident, 22% would seek help after a second incident, and finally, 49% would seek help only after a series of incidents had taken place.

Given the length of time that passes and the degree of severity of the crisis that typically is reached before help is sought, triage assessment of the battered woman should look first and foremost to her safety and the safety of significant others such as her children. We can assume that a battered woman making an initial call to a crisis line will be at the extremely high end of the assessment scale. She will be behaviorally out of control because of the beating she has just incurred. She will be affectively out of control because of the trauma she has just suffered and the threat of more to come after her assailant wakes up from his drunken stupor or comes back home. Cognitively, she may be just holding together and not be far from disassociating from the terrible reality of her situation.

Of all the dilemmas a crisis telephone worker faces, this is one of the worst. While the threat of further injury or death to the woman may be extremely high, unless the crisis worker feels danger is imminent and can get the woman to give her name and address so that a 911 call can be made, the best the crisis worker can do is offer short-term assistance to help ease physical pain and calm the emotional state of the client. Even then the crisis worker may have raging internal debates about what to do. If she helps get the client to a safe place, will that only enrage her mate even more? Is the woman really ready to make such a move? What assets does the battered woman have so that she can leave? What are her debits? That is why the worker should carefully go over each area, making sure that all pertinent information and all possibilities of available action have been carefully considered. No other type of crisis we commonly deal with presents as critical a need for comprehensive yet fast assessment.

It is also worth remembering that if given a call back in a week, the client may be going through a honeymoon phase and seem not to have a care in the world, only to turn around later at the next battering and beseech the crisis worker to help her. These situations that oscillate from extreme need one day to little if any need the next can make workers cynical and uncaring if they do not carefully manage their stress levels. Yet such ambivalence is more typical than not as clients slowly come to grips with the risks and realities of leaving the situation or quite possibly facing death there.

Components of Intervention

As a call comes into the wife abuse center and the crisis worker picks up the phone, the assessment process begins with active listening. The crisis worker immediately has to be concerned with a variety of roles. She not only must be a good listener but also must be supportive, facilitative, and concerned with the caller's safety and must act as an advocate (Barnett et al., 1980, p. 44).

Listening. Facilitative listening and responding are crucial. The victim must know that the crisis worker understands and accepts her present situation in a nonjudgmental, non-value-laden way. Only then will the battered woman be able to open up and share her feelings about her predicament (Heppner, 1978). The crisis worker also immediately reflects that she understands the difficulty and urgency of the situation by positively reinforcing the battered woman for calling and taking a first step toward resolving her problem.

CW: You did the right thing by calling. No matter how bad it seems and what terrible things have happened, you've made a big step on the road to straightening it out. We're here to help and we'll stick with it as long as it takes.

Victim: I . . . I . . . don't know. It's gone on so long. I feel so ashamed. I don't know what to do! It's so confusing.

CW: I understand how you feel and how difficult it was to make this call. The hurt, the fear, the uncertainty of it all. So start anywhere you want. We won't do anything unless *you* decide it's best for you. Right now, though, so I can get a good idea of what your situation is, I want to listen to what you have to say. I'll listen for as long as it takes, so take your time and tell me what's happened.

Supporting. The caller is given both explicit and implicit permission to ventilate. The free flow of the victim's anger, hurt, fear, guilt, and other debilitating feelings may take from a few minutes to two hours to an ex-

tended period of months. Supportiveness means empathizing but not sympathizing with the victim. Many victims are only partially mobile and any
action steps they take may be months away from happening. Thus, support
of a victim does not mean intervention on a one-shot basis. The crisis
worker may have to exert an excruciating amount of patience over a long
period of time as the victim slowly moves toward making a decision to take
action. No matter how bad the victim's situation looks to the worker, only
the victim herself can decide when she is ready to take action to alleviate
her traumatic situation (Dagastino, 1984).

CW: OK! I understand it's a hard decision to make—getting out. Your marriage has
had some good times and you'd really like to hang onto that part of it, even
though the beatings are happening more often. You say you want some time to
think about it. That's OK! It's your decision and we'll help whenever you
need us.

Breaking away from a battering relationship is a slow developmental
process. The crisis worker cannot move the victim any faster than she is
willing to go. The crisis worker must be acutely aware of being manipulated
into becoming sympathetic to the victim's needs and attempting to "fix"
things for her. Many times the victim will project anger onto the police, a
minister, or other significant persons. The victim at some point needs to see
that displacement and shifting of responsibility to others is not going to
solve the problem. The crisis worker must be aware of this possibility and
not get trapped into proposing external remedies.

The victim is actually demonstrating what Heppner (1978) calls the
"wishing and hoping syndrome." The victim wishes the situation would
change, that her spouse would treat her the way he used to, and hopes the
crisis worker can effect a change in her husband. However, cessation of
battering by the abuser rarely happens without legal or therapeutic intervention (Dagastino, 1984). Under no circumstances should the crisis
worker attempt to rescue the victim by talking to the husband. It is dangerous and takes responsibility and autonomy away from the victim. Instead,
the conversation should be redirected away from what can be done to "fix"
the husband and toward what the victim is now able to do.

CW: While I hear you wanting me to come and straighten your husband out and
make things the way they were, I can't do that. I wish I could, but I'm not a
marriage counselor. If you think marriage counseling would work, I can give
you some names of people who do that. What I can do is help you make some
decisions about what you want to do right now.

A typical response to the crisis worker's refusal to fix the problem is
anger.

Victim: You're no damn help at all. You're just as bad as the rest. You're a horrible
counselor. I'm gonna have to go back to him and he'll kill me just because you
wouldn't do anything.

Because abuse workers do not want to lose clients, such ploys often rub a raw nerve in the worker and propel her to do something she may later regret. The worker should understand that she is working not merely with a battered woman but with the whole woman. If she responds to only the battered part, it will be very difficult for her not to become overly sympathetic with the victim. This approach may salve the wounded pride of the worker but will do little to help the victim in the long run. The crisis worker should realize that when a victim doubts the worker's ability, she is also doubting her own ability. She is probably looking for a way to resume the relationship and may be displacing her own incompetence to make changes by blaming the worker (Dagastino, 1984).

The best response the crisis worker can make is not to be confrontive but to be empathic, realizing that right now the woman is looking for a way to go back to her mate.

CW: I'm sorry you're angry with me because I won't talk to your husband. I realize the frustration you feel. Yet I'm also not like the others who'll tell you how to act and what to do. What I'd most like to do is to help you move off dead center because I feel you're really wanting to take some kind of action. If you don't believe you're quite ready to do that, OK. You have our phone number and I want you to know I'd be happy to sit down with you at any time and together we can work on a plan of action you want to take.

The excerpt typifies the response of a crisis worker who is being supportive yet not taking over for the victim. The crisis worker must do her best to give power and control to the battered woman, from the initiating interview to entering a shelter and finally being on her own. Usually abuse victims have not been independent to any degree and quickly fall back into a dependent state. If the crisis worker keeps foremost in her mind that the woman she is now talking to is ultimately going to have to be her own defender and protector, then the crisis worker is not likely to fall into a sympathy trap. The crisis worker who becomes angry or engages in denouncing or criticizing the husband is making a fundamental mistake. She may provoke the victim to defend the violent husband and to attack the crisis worker (Dagastino, 1984).

Facilitating.   To facilitate the movement of a victim to action takes a great deal of tenacity and patience. Typically the crisis worker will have to deal with feelings of dependency, ambivalence, and depression, which are all clear-cut signs of the client's immobility. Overarching these immobilizing feelings is the learned helplessness we referred to earlier. Steinmetz (1978) has suggested that the passive victim of abuse is much like the victim of brainwashing. She is isolated from support systems, her only validation of self-worth comes from her captor, and the inconsistent, contradictory, and threatening treatment interspersed with kindness leaves her alone with her feelings of anxiety, fear, guilt, and shame. To generate movement of the victim, the crisis worker strongly reinforces the victim's attempts at rational decision making, self-control, and statements of personal power (Heppner, 1978).

CW: You said that you couldn't do anything, but that's not true. You called here, didn't you? When you first started talking you were crying uncontrollably and now you're speaking in a rather level, controlled voice. I also notice a lot of "I" statements, which say to me you're starting to take responsibility. Maybe you don't know it, but those are all signs that you're starting to feel some personal power for the first time in a long while, and I think that's great!

Ambivalence about the situation is predominant in most women who seek help from wife abuse centers. Ambivalence is particularly strong with regard to the husband who, after beating his wife, apologizes, showers her with gifts, and tells her what she wants to hear and what society leads her to believe. The message is that if women remain married and stay in the home and mind their husbands, everything will be fine (Conroy, 1982). Consequently, even though the victim knows something is terribly wrong, there is still an extremely powerful pull to try to hold the relationship together. To deal with this ambivalent state the crisis worker cycles between asking open-ended questions and reflecting and clarifying the victim's feelings. The questions that follow, and their variations, represent effective means of helping the victim to begin to examine previously denied feelings and thoughts.

CW: What were you thinking and feeling while he was beating you?

Victim: It was like I was standing off to the side watching a movie of this. It was like this can't really be happening, especially to me.

CW: So that's how you cope with it. Kind of separating yourself from the beating, as if it's happening to someone else.

Victim: Yes, I guess I've done it that way for a long time. I'd go crazy otherwise.

CW: What is your understanding of why you're being battered?

Victim: I don't know. I guess I'm just not a good wife.

CW: You're not living up to his expectations, then. How about your own?

Victim: I'm not sure. I mean, I've never thought of that. It's always been what he wants.

CW: How do you cope with the beating other than just kind of separating yourself from the situation when it happens?

Victim: I try to do what he wants, but when it starts to build—the tension—I just try to stay out of his way and be nice, although I know sooner or later I'm gonna get it. I dread the waiting. Actually sometimes I push the issue just to get it over with. I know he'll always apologize afterwards and treat me nice.

CW: So you do what he wishes even though you know the bottom line is a beating. Yet because of the anxiety you may even push things to get it over with. Seems like you're willing to pay a steep price to get his love back.

Victim: When you say that, I can't believe I'm letting this happen to me. What a fool . . . a stupid fool!

CW: Then you feel foolish about paying that price. What's keeping you in the relationship?

Victim: God! I don't know. Love! Honor! Obey! The kids. The good times. Martyrdom. I don't have a job and I'm pregnant again. Even then, it's no good, but I stay. I've got to get out. This is nuts. He'll wind up killing me.

Using open-ended questions, restatement, and reflection, the crisis worker relentlessly hammers at the victim's faulty and illogical perception of the abusive situation. In assessing the situation, the worker tries to gain an understanding of the victim's interpretation of what being battered means to her. Only by looking and listening through the victim's eyes and ears can the crisis worker form an accurate perception of what steps to take and how she will operate on the nondirective-to-directive continuum of intervention.

Women who have been abused also have in common the feeling of depression. Invariably, once a victim has related the details of the assault, her affect becomes flat. Depression has taken over. The victim is like a rat that gets shocked at both ends of a Skinner box. She is wrong whatever she does and becomes frozen and immobilized. Beneath the depression is a volcano of residual anger that is trying to find an outlet. The crisis worker's job is to help move the victim out of her depressed state and let the angry feelings out (Dagastino, 1984). This is the first step toward taking action.

CW: As you relate the details it sounds like you're reporting it but not living it. I wonder if that's a typical way you hold it in . . . control it.

Victim: I guess . . . if I really thought about it, I'd kill the SOB. How could the bastard do this to me?

CW: How does it feel to let some of those angry feelings out?

Victim: Scary! I'm really scared I would kill him if I got the chance.

CW: That is a legitimate feeling after what you've been through, but that won't get you where you want to go. Let's take a look at some of the alternatives between killing and being killed.

In summarizing the facilitation of the victim's movement from an immobile to a mobile state, the Massachusetts Coalition of Battered Women Service Groups (1981, pp. 25, 67) has made these points. We agree with them in totality.

1. *Be real.* Don't hide behind a role. You are what you are. To pretend to be something else makes the crisis worker false and uncreditable in the eyes of the victim.

2. *Set limits.* The crisis worker is not Superwoman. Owning feelings of puzzlement, anger, stupidity, tiredness, and so forth allows the crisis worker to stay on top of the game. Nowhere is it written that a crisis worker has to become a victim. If the worker is tired, is taking on a lot of anger, and cannot work it through with the victim, she should own the feelings, ask for

time out, and get out of the situation until the problem can be gone over with a fellow professional and a fresh start can be made.

3. *Give the victim space and time to "freak out."* Remember that the victim is experiencing a flood of emotions that have been building over a long period of time. Knowing that anger is one step on the way to becoming her own person can be reassuring and empowering to the victim. Give her time to ventilate before settling down to a plan of action.

4. *Allow the victim to go through the pain, but stay with her.* A crisis worker's first response may be to become a psychological crutch because the victim is so fragile that she cannot hold together. If the crisis worker remembers that the victim has been down a long road of pain and is just now beginning to experience that pain, she will realize that the victim possesses a lot of staying power. Belief in the victim's ability to get out of the mess she is in is of overriding importance.

5. *Maintain eye and ear contact.* Both nonverbal and verbal responses of the victim are important; they tell the crisis worker whether what the victim is saying is congruent with what she is doing. Reading nonverbal responses may be difficult over the phone, but the worker needs to be aware of intonations, pauses, and sighs. How something is said may be as important as what is said. Also, what is not said may be as important as what is said.

6. *Be respectful and nonjudgmental.* The victim's actions must be carefully separated from the victim herself. What the victim does may be asinine. That does not mean the victim is an ass.

7. *Restate and reflect the victim's thoughts and feelings.* Simple as this sounds, it is often extremely difficult. There is no greater therapeutic help than manifesting these skills.

8. *Set priorities together.* Two heads are better than one. This is why the crisis worker is there. If the victim could handle the problem alone, she would. Likewise, the wife abuse worker is not in business to run the victim's life for her.

9. *Look at options.* Brainstorming can uncover a variety of previously hidden ideas and actions.

10. *Stay away from whys.* Asking *why* a person does something like staying in a battering relationship is an open invitation to philosophizing, rationalizing, and intellectualizing. These are all detours away from dealing with the real issue, the person's situation at that particular time. Further, a *why* question often leads the victim, rightly or wrongly, to assume she is being judged. When a victim feels she is being judged, she is apt to respond in defensive ways that do little to help her or her situation.

11. *Give the victim time to experience catharsis, but do not let her get stuck in self-pity.* The client needs to accomplish movement, and the crisis worker needs to move gently from nurturing emotional release to helping the client start to make plans, however small, concerning her own predicament.

12. *Touch the victim.* Both verbally and nonverbally, the worker must show she remembers that most victims are isolated psychologically. To

touch deeply a feeling the victim is struggling with and, indeed, to lean over and touch the victim's hand in an appropriate and empathic way may be worth much.

13. *Get back to the victim.* No matter whether the battered women says, "I guess I can make it now," get her phone number and call a few days later to make sure she is getting along all right. Many abused women are so embarrassed by their plight and their own self-assessed stupidity that they cannot bring themselves to make another call and admit they have failed again.

14. *Peer supervision and feedback are essential for wife abuse workers.* The intensity of wife abuse is such that few, if any, crisis workers can remain totally objective all the time. Cross-supervision by trusted coprofessionals keeps the worker on track, reduces personal stress, and helps avoid burnout.

Ensuring safety.   The crisis worker's first job is to determine how critical the situation is (Walker, 1984, p. 122). All the listening and responding skills known to humanity are of little use if the victim has multiple fractures or if her spouse has threatened to come back and kill her. The crisis worker calmly and cautiously makes an assessment of how bad the situation is. Does the victim need and want medical attention, shelter, a place to send her children, a way out of the house if her husband returns? All these questions are posed in a measured, deliberate way to avoid adding to the panic the victim already feels. Although the situation may be critical and the best alternative may be for the victim to come directly to the shelter, the crisis worker has to remember that the women cannot be forced into making that choice. This does not mean, however, that the worker cannot make such a recommendation.

CW: From what you've said, it sounds like the situation is pretty bad. Bad enough that you might consider leaving and coming to the shelter.

Because of a fear of the unknown, the victim may balk at this alternative (Dagastino, 1984). Patiently, the crisis worker explains the role and function of the shelter, answers any questions the victim has, and tries to allay her fears. If, after all this, the victim is still unwilling to make a decision, the worker does not push the issue. The worker shifts attention to other critical needs of the victim. How physically abused is the client? Is this the first time she has been abused or is this the latest in a continuing series of abusive events? In either case, how severe has the abuse been? Are her feelings hurt, or is her body injured?

Even though most women insist the beatings are random, there may be a subtle correlation between environmental events and occurrence of abuse (Heppner, 1978). All the foregoing questions are important in determining a baseline of what is going on with the victim. It is this kind of information the worker must have to be of the most assistance, both in getting the victim the help she needs immediately and in assessing what long-term help may be needed.

In initially reporting the battering, victims often appear to feel that it is an isolated incident and not abuse. They refuse to see it on an ever-escalating continuum. They delude themselves with the belief, "He really does love me, and if I'm a better person, it'll never happen again."

As the crisis worker intervenes, she should be aware that such incidents are not isolated. Indeed, there is a consistent pattern leading up to the climax of battering (Walker, 1984, p. 24). The crisis worker endeavors to lay that pattern out so that the victim sees it not as isolated but as continuous and predictable. Seeing the pattern is particularly important when the victim is not sure whether to leave or stay.

CW: As you tell me about it, I hear a sort of pattern. For about a week he gets surly, starts criticizing the way the house looks, the way you look, the food you cook, and your control over the kids. Those criticisms start out mild, but become more severe until you finally have had enough and say something to the effect that he ought to take more responsibility if he doesn't like things. That winds up with your getting beat up. As you report that, I wonder if you can look back and see how the situation has repeated itself.

Victim: Well, I don't know. I really think it was different this time. I mean this was the first time I needed emergency treatment. He was really sorry afterward. I don't know.

CW: OK. Granted the beating was more severe, but I believe from what you're saying that there's a very definite pattern to it. What's different is that the pattern seems to be repeating itself more frequently and it's getting more intense.

Many times the client may be highly immobile and may not even hear the question, so the worker may need to pose it again (Dagastino, 1984).

CW: When did he say he'd be back and what'd he say he'd do?

Victim: I just don't know whether to take it anymore. I love him, but I'm really scared.

CW: OK, I understand you are afraid, but I need to know how much time we've got and what threats he made.

By gently guiding the victim back to immediate and pressing issues, the crisis worker keeps the session on track but does not deny the emotional hurt and confusion the victim is experiencing.

By the time the battered woman becomes desperate enough to make the call for help, she does not have time to be analyzed, nor does she have time to go into all kinds of self-analysis. What she does need is some behavioral action-oriented techniques she can use on a short-term basis (Walker, 1979, pp. 75–77). The crisis worker's major task is to get the victim back to a semblance of equilibrium and control. This is accomplished by attempting to get the abused woman to commit to some plan, however small. By just knowing and having a plan, the victim is able to regain some composure and feel that she has obtained some control over the situation. The whole focus of the conversation is to prepare her to get through that one day. At this time, the worker does not worry about tomorrow or any other time.

Tomorrow, the worker may call the victim and talk about the next day. If the worker attempts to deal with future events that extend beyond a week, the victim gets lost (Dagastino, 1984).

Because of the flood of critical needs the victim faces, the worker must realistically judge which needs may require immediate action and which ones can be deferred. To help make sense of the heavy flow of information, the crisis worker writes down what the victim tells her so that she can quickly identify and prioritize the very practical concerns that are pressing in on the victim. Issues such as getting enough money for the children's lunch the next day may be just as important as taking care of a broken nose, and the worker will need to remember this. By calmly, clearly, and concisely feeding back to the victim her written summary, the crisis worker takes the victim step by step through a review of her most critical needs. In doing so, the worker shows the victim that although she has many problems, they are not insurmountable. By dissecting the crisis in this manner, the worker assures the victim that her problems can be broken down and managed (Dagastino, 1984).

CW: Here are all the things I hear happening to you right now. No wonder you're feeling paralyzed; anyone in that situation would feel the same. You've said you have no job, the children don't want to leave, and that he might kill you. Let's take them one at a time and sort through each problem and put them back together.

A careful examination of the woman's fears about these problems, how they need to be prioritized, and the options she has in dealing with them is extremely important. Until the abused woman can confront such fears openly, she cannot begin developing strategies to deal with her problems (Heppner, 1978).

CW: You're afraid to leave because you feel sure he will come after you when he comes back, and you're not sure what he might do, so that causes tension to build. Yet I really believe if we make a plan right now you'll feel better, even if you don't have to use it.

If the victim states that she does not know what to do, the crisis worker immediately looks at the two basic alternatives—staying and leaving. A considerable amount of exploration time is given over to the possible options in each of the two alternatives. A key ingredient is determining the level of danger at home. Is the husband really going to act out, or is the fear of his acting out propelling the woman into making the call? To learn what has happened before, the crisis worker asks questions such as "When he's gone out and gotten drunk before, what has he done? Has he torn up the house, beat you or the kids? What has he done?" From the answers, the crisis worker gains a realistic assessment of the danger level of the situation. If the victim is unwilling to leave the house, then the crisis worker role-plays the scene of the drunken spouse returning home. Assuming the role of the abuser, the worker goes through, in a systematic way, each situation of potential confrontation and then discusses the potential positive and negative outcomes of the victim's attempt to handle the confrontation (Dagastino, 1984).

CW: [*In role.*] Hey, honey! Come on into the bedroom. I need you real bad.

Victim: [*Typical response.*] I can't stand having sex with you when you are drunk.

CW: [*As self.*] Now, look at how you responded to that. When you shut him off like that, he gets angry, right? What could you do or say differently? How could you change things? How about turning the tables so he had no desire for you at all? What'd happen if you had a facial on and your hair up in curlers, and had on a frowzy housecoat? While that might not make you very alluring, would that turn him off?

By looking at options and posing alternative ways of behaving, the worker attempts to provide coping techniques that may defuse the crisis. By the time the worker is done, the victim is feeding back a plan, point by point, either for staying in the house or for moving out. Having an escape plan is critical (Walker, 1984, p. 122).

CW: All right! You've figured out how to get out of the house. You'll keep the back door open. You've given the kids a note to go over to the neighbors. You've got our number and you know you can get to your car, parked out back, and get to a phone booth and call us.

In summary, both short- and long-term safety depends on helping abused women take action steps rather than remaining immobilized. Wife abuse crises are different from other types of crises in this respect. For many victims, it may not be a question of returning to a precrisis equilibrium. The equilibrium was never there in the first place. Therefore, for many women, taking first, tentative steps toward action is likely to be extremely frightening, confusing, and full of trepidation.

The following points seem worthwhile for crisis workers to know and understand in helping abused women make such decisions and take action (Massachusetts Coalition of Battered Women Service Groups, 1981, pp. 25, 67).

1. Help women think and act on their situation by providing legitimate reinforcement for their efforts.
2. Help women figure out what they want by providing a sounding board for examining ideas and alternatives.
3. Help women to identify feelings that prevent them from making decisions.
4. Be honest. The worker cannot tell a person what to do, but can clearly state from her own life how the situation would affect her.
5. Help women to do things for themselves, but do not let them become dependent on the worker.
6. Know and offer resources from which battered women can get specific kinds of assistance: spell out who, what, where, when, and how.

7. Help women gain a sense of self-confidence and ability to take care of themselves.
8. Be challenging. Support women, but do not be afraid to push them toward a decision-making point.
9. Be open to choices. Each woman has control over her life; the crisis worker must not attempt to assume control for clients.
10. Hear and understand what women have to say, particularly if it does not run parallel to the worker's own beliefs, attitudes, and outlooks.
11. Build on the commonalities that women, particularly battered women, share, but recognize the worth of the individual differences of each person.
12. Assess lethality. "I'm fed up and whipped" may really mean "I'm ready to commit suicide."

The following wife abuse worker's response to a battered woman who after two hours of talking on the telephone still could not make up her mind about what to do, aptly illustrates application of the 12 points just made.

CW: I understand your mixed feelings of wanting to stay and wanting to leave; also the constant fear you live with while waiting for the next time, maybe even wishing it would happen quickly so the tension will ease off. But my guess is that tension reduction only occurs for a short period and then starts to build all over again. I also understand that you feel like you're locked into this, but there are some alternatives, which we have gone over. I want you to pick at least one of those, whichever seems best for you, and do it. I won't take no for an answer. Do something that will make you feel better right now. Go take a hot bath if that'll help and don't spare the bath oil. I think it would be safer for you to come to the shelter right now, but if you don't really feel you can do that, I understand. However, if you feel the tension start to rise and feel like you just can't take it anymore, I want you to promise to call back here. I won't take no for an answer. Whatever, I'll call you tomorrow afternoon to see how things are going. What would be a good time?

Advocacy.   Because battered women have been isolated for much of their lives, they generally have little knowledge of alternatives open to them. This is especially true with respect to their rights and options with both legal and welfare systems. Therefore, a major responsibility of the crisis worker is to know not only the formal but also the informal workings of these mono-lithic systems. Understanding the laws and how to weave through bureau-cratic obstacles and how to cut through the red tape that is often put in the way of someone seeking help from the system is of paramount importance. The wife abuse worker who excels has an excellent networking system that she can tap into and get immediate help for a variety of problems. Further, the competent crisis worker will know how the game in each system is played and will know how to bend the rules to get help for the victim. (For an excellent summary of advocacy, see Chapter 4, "Advocacy—Welfare and Legal," in *For Shelter and Beyond: An Educational Manual for Working* *with Women Who Are Battered* [Massachusetts Coalition of Battered Women Service Groups, 1981], and *Battered Women* [Moore, 1979]).

Transcrisis perspective.   All of the foregoing intervention procedures cannot be accomplished in a 20-minute phone call. Even minor crises may require two or three calls to get the client stabilized, in touch with her feelings, and into some semblance of preabuse equilibrium. The crisis worker is not providing a short-term elixir that merely calms the victim and then blithely sends her on her way. What is being provided is a blend that not only deals with the immediate crisis but also has a long-term application. Many battered women need to go through a complete reeducation process about who they are and what they can do. This process should not be hurried even if it takes a year to accomplish the goal. One of the most difficult problems in dealing with battered women is that they have lived at such peak energy levels for such long periods of time. Battered women seem never to come down from their state of anxiety and frenetic tension.

In response to this continuing high-pitched state of emotional existence, a crisis worker must be prepared to deal with emotional brushfires that occur frequently and last for extended periods of time. Indeed, the transcrisis of the battered woman does not end when she gets off the phone and decides to come to the center or go to the shelter. The initiating interview or hot line call is only the first part of the crisis resolution. Other and probably more severe crises will continue to plague the victim.

Ibrahim and Herr's (1987) work with battered women who were involved in a group counseling format that concentrated on vocational exploration and economic independence is an excellent example of a transcrisis point. When these women reached the stage of vocational implementation, ready actually to go out into the world of work and test their skills, they experienced all kinds of threatening and anxious feelings and became immobile and paralyzed. Fifteen two-hour sessions of intensive support by the group leaders were needed to help the women work through this stage!

CENTER AND SHELTER

A center and a shelter are generally two different entities within a wife abuse program. The center deals with telephone and on-site, short-term crisis intervention and counseling. The shelter is a longer-term facility where women and their families can stay for short or extended periods of time. A comprehensive program will have both a center and a shelter and will be staffed around the clock with a 24-hour hot line and an open-door policy for walk-ins (Barnett et al., 1980). There will be tie-ins to other social services agencies: police, free or sliding-scale legal services, hospitals, medical staff and mental health facilities, mobile crisis teams that provide transportation for abuse victims, and direct links to emergency housing facilities with follow-up services (Benjamin & Walz, 1983, p. 83). Such a comprehensive program is the ideal. In reality, shortages of funds and personnel make the ideal a rarity.

The typical shelter is linked to the wife abuse center and is well publicized, but for security reasons its location may not be made public. For the same reason, it will be well patrolled by the police and will be secure. Staffed by both professionals and volunteers, it will have adequate cooking, sleeping, bath, child- and infant-care facilities for a number of families, and funds for clothing, food, and transportation (Langley & Levy, 1977). It should also provide a variety of counseling services to assist women to ventilate feelings, explore alternatives, and make immediate plans for what they will do next (Benjamin & Walz, 1983, p. 84). This ideal, again, is a rarity.

Counseling Women at Shelters

Women who enter the shelter fit into two categories: those who are unsure about leaving the battering relationship and those who have made a definite commitment to leave it (Dagastino, 1984). Women who fall into the first category need to be monitored on an hour-by-hour basis and are the more critical of the two categories. The crisis worker maintains constant contact with these women and reinforces them for having had the courage to come to the shelter.

CW: I'm glad you made it. I know it took a lot of courage.

CW: [*10 minutes later.*] Getting settled in? Come on with me, there's some other women I would like you to meet.

CW: [*2 hours later.*] How are things going? Got the kids settled in? They're great-looking children. Want to have a cup of coffee and talk?

Vacillation between going back and staying is characteristic of these women. The longer the women stay at the shelter, the greater is the probability that they will not return to their mates (Hilbert & Hilbert, 1984). However, until women can recover their self-esteem and come to understand that they are not the cause, they are at risk to leave and go back (Schutte, Bouleige, Fix, & Malouff, 1986). The worker does not try to force women to stay at the shelter, but does try to get them to take some psychological "time out" to review their situation in a more objective way (Dagastino, 1984).

Juanita: I'm all mixed up. I don't know if I'm wrong or not. I'm Catholic and I'm Hispanic. Women in my family just don't walk out of a marriage. But I'm really scared right now and the church and my family both say we just need to work things out, but I really think he'll kill me.

CW: Let's assume you're taking a one-day vacation so you can get some rest before you go back and deal with it. It's fine if you want to go back home, but do this much for me—just take it easy for a while. I can see that you're physically all right and not hurt, and I'm relieved. This is a great time to talk about what you can do when you go back and it is a good time to make some concrete plans.

The shelter worker checks repeatedly with the new arrival and reinforces her decision to come. She conveys her concern for the victim and with the help of other women in the shelter, sees that the victim and her family are settled. The focus is on the here-and-now. During the first few hours of the victim's separation from her abuser, the worker will probably have to be very directive. Few women, at this time, have the ego strength to stand on their own and need an abundance of support and help. The objective is to keep the victim moving, thinking, and acting so that she is preoccupied and does not have time to let fear, guilt, or any other debilitating and anxiety-ridden emotions overcome her. Domestic chores such as cleaning and cooking seem to be particularly helpful in this regard. In all instances, the worker should be carefully attuned to the victim's needs. Some may find help sitting, talking, or crying with a worker or a group of other women. Others may be so exhausted that they need to go to bed and sleep. Whatever the victim needs, the worker should be adaptable to those needs and flexible enough to change as circumstances demand (Dagastino, 1984).

Shelter dynamics.   A variety of positive dynamics occur at shelters. There is substantial support from other women who have experienced the same kind of trauma. This enables victims to begin gaining the courage to face people, recovering their lost self-esteem, and learning that the beatings were not their fault (Schecter, 1982, pp. 55–60).

Wife abuse shelters are not vacation spas where one's every whim is catered to. Although an abundance of caring and sharing occurs, women who live in shelters are encouraged to start trusting themselves to make decisions. Part of the decision-making process includes determining what is best for the shelter. This is not an easy task. Limits have to be set with respect to pets, children, cooking, and so on (Schecter, 1982, pp. 63–64). Women get bored, boss each other around, miss their men, miss sex (pp. 55–60), and have problems relating to people from different ethnic and racial backgrounds and sociocultural milieus (Massachusetts Coalition of Battered Women Service Groups, 1981, p. 28).

Victim: Getting used to a shelter is overwhelming. You like it, but you don't want to be there 'cause it isn't home. You've got to put together all your psychological know-how in getting along with different types of people. Wondering if you're going to make it, especially when you see all the pain and confusion and don't know whether it's yours or theirs or what, and hoping nobody finds out you're here. Trying to be understood and feeling like you are a blabbermouth here when you couldn't talk at home. Trying to look forward and all the time wanting to forget . . . wanting to forget . . . wanting to forget (Schecter, 1982, pp. 59–60).

At a shelter everything is not always as it seems. Many women who come to the shelter are extremely dependent and exceptionally adept at manipulating the workers there (Walker, 1984, p. 126). A statement like "You really understand—you've made my whole life better" is reinforcing to the worker, but she is actually being manipulated. The women is using the house and the worker as a security blanket and is not making any progress toward getting out on her own (Dagastino, 1984). The wise shelter worker comes to see the manipulation for what it is, a refusal to take responsibility for oneself and a shift from dependency on an abusive husband to dependency on a caring shelter worker (Weincourt, 1985). Gently but firmly, the worker extinguishes such behavior.

CW: I appreciate what you said, and I appreciate your wanting to cook my dinner and all other things you want to do for me. Yet I believe your time and mine could be better spent working on getting you set up in an apartment and looking for a job.

Grief. Besides being dependent, many women go through a grieving process. They talk about their furniture, homes, vacations, and so forth, as they relive their past. There are a lot of *yes, buts* as workers start to confront them with making a new future. As victims shift from a depersonalized view of their situation to depression over it, the process can be extremely frightening to a shelter worker unless she knows that this, too, is another step in the transcrisis that battered women go through (Dagastino, 1984). The woman's grief often puzzles those trying to help her. Many human services workers may be threatened by these feelings and deny the woman's need to mourn by concentrating on dealing with concrete aspects of the woman's dilemma such as providing food, clothing, and housing. Her grief can be understood, however, if one asks the question, "For what is she mourning?" In most cases, she has defined herself in terms of her relationship with the batterer, and if that relationship ends, she feels as if she has lost everything—including her sense of self (Turner & Shapiro, 1986). She clings quite tightly to the dreams she has for the relationship—including the expectations with which she entered into it. When the relationship ends, she must come to terms with the fact that these dreams will never materialize. Therefore, she is not grieving so much for what was, but for what she hoped could have been (Spanno, 1990).

Juanita: I wanted this to work so much. We could have had it so good, but I couldn't take him beating on me and the kids too. What went wrong with that good-looking, happy couple in this picture? He was so handsome and so good to me in the beginning. Then it just slowly went to hell and now this. [*Weeps while slowly turning over in her hands a wedding picture that she brought with her to the shelter.*]

CW: It's really hard to say good-bye to all those things that were and might have been. It must hurt even more than the beatings to know that all those hopes and dreams won't come to pass.

Juanita: It tears my heart out, but I know I did the right thing. Sooner or later he would have killed me or the kids in one of his rages. It's so weird! I still love that SOB.

CW: The grief you're feeling is as real as if a close friend or a relative had died. Perhaps even more tragic because when this relationship died, a part of you died with it, Juanita. The part of you who struggled out of the barrio, went to college, got an education, made a success out of herself, married the perfect man, and then with all those expectations dashed because of the way he treated you and the children.

Juanita: I can't let that stop me. Nothing else did, I made the right decision coming here. I also made the right decision getting a warrant on him. Maybe that last act of love will get him the help he needs or the jolt he needs to wake him up so he doesn't do it to somebody else.

CW: As you say that, I see so much determination coming through the tears. I also see a new, different, stronger person as you say those farewells, as tough as they are.

A woman who has been involved in an abusive relationship needs to grieve and to have her grief validated. The crisis worker does this while reinforcing that although there is now an altered future, it has potential to be a good one. It is through this process that the battered woman can come to see the relationship for what it really was—abusive. The crisis worker will make a very bad therapeutic mistake if she expects the woman to rejoice. If she is expected to rejoice for leaving and is discouraged from feeling her sense of loss and expressing it, she may never confront the truth about the relationship. The end result may well be a return to the partner or one just like him (Spanno, 1990).

Depression.   Depression comes in many guises. Many women who come into the shelter sleep much of the time. On first appearance, they may seem to be lazy. Actually, they may be going through a stage of trying to regroup their psychic energy. The worker's task becomes one of trying to help them move past their inactivity, but not by pressuring them or taking them on a guilt trip (Massachusetts Coalition of Battered Women Service Groups, 1981, p. 27).

CW: I've noticed you pretty much sticking to your room and sleeping a lot. I was a little concerned and was wondering how you were feeling. I wonder if you've had a chance to talk to anyone about how you feel since you got here.

Juanita: I feel so guilty. It seems like I have slept ever since I've gotten here and the other women have been so good to take care of the kids. I'm not really like this, I just don't seem to have any get-up-and-go. I'm really sorry to be so much trouble.

CW: What you are doing is exactly what you should be doing, getting your energy back. You burned a tremendous amount of it making the decision to get out and get here. The other women have felt the same way so they understand. In a few days you'll do the same for somebody else. If you want to talk we're here. If you want to rest, that's just fine too. The main thing is you're safe and that's what's important right now.

Terror.   For many women, a stress-related syndrome similar to agoraphobia arises after they have been in the shelter for a while (Massachusetts Coalition of Battered Women Service Groups, 1981, p. 27). They may have extreme and unexplainable attacks of terror that are touched off by seemingly innocuous incidents. These incidents greatly restrict their activities and new freedom. The fear of their mates, the fear of their predicament, the fear of their separation from a definable past, and the fear of an undefinable future can all cause the onset of terror. Under no circumstances should the shelter worker allow it to continue. Victims must be encouraged and helped step by step to pull themselves away from the security blanket of the shelter and out into the real world. Such progress may take place in very small, slow steps, but the steps must be taken. As women take these steps, they receive very specific, positive reinforcement for what they have accomplished, enabling them not to fall back into learned helplessness but instead to take responsibility for their behavior (Weincourt, 1985). Invariably, victims will not be able to see that they have done much of anything, or they tend to diminish their successes.

CW: I know you're still scared to death to go down and talk to them at Federal Express about that job. It's a big step, but a week ago, you couldn't walk down to the grocery store and now you're dong that fine. So let's take it a step at a time. Look at what you overcame. We can go through the job interview, play it a step at a time, talk about those steps right here where it's safe, and give you a chance to really become confident about going down there.

Those who have decided to leave.   The second category of women who come to the shelter are in for a long haul and are not going back to the battering situation. For women who are in for the duration, the crisis worker deals with immediate specifics such as finding a place to live, financial aid, and child care. Emotional support has a low priority because these women are so busy that all they want and need is very practical advice and help. These women are very different from those experiencing acute crisis because they are highly motivated to change their lives. They are much easier to work with because they have made a decision to get out of their domestic pressure cooker (Dagastino, 1984).

For all women who come to wife abuse centers and shelters, a continuing and pervasive problem is their inability not only to say they will not be beaten but also to own that statement behaviorally (Dagastino, 1984). The whole thrust of this type of transcrisis work is to teach victims to view themselves as survivors dependent only on themselves, and to realize that the traumas they have been forced to deal with are not unique to them, but rather are political issues with deep sociocultural roots that all women have to deal with either directly or indirectly (Schecter, 1982, p. 66).

Follow-Up

Once women leave the shelter, they should be provided with follow-up. As immediate demands are relieved, the emotional impact of their decision should be dealt with over the long term. These women are urged to go for counseling with the idea that no one can be beaten even once without suffering some psychological damage. It is not uncommon for a woman to be so busy getting her act together that her emotional reactions are delayed. The victim may be out on her own, well established, and watching television at the time that she experiences a sudden emotional breakdown. The crisis worker apprises the victim of what to expect in the way of emotional aftershocks. Such residual psychological trauma seems to be particularly characteristic of women who initially appear to be very much in control (Dagastino, 1984).

CW: Even though you feel like you've made the break from your husband, don't be surprised if later on you get depressed and really feel like you need and miss your husband. That's to be expected. We know that and we're here to help then too!

Indeed, in the worst of scenarios, the victim may become lonely, forget about the terrible abuse she suffered in the past, invite her ex-mate over for dinner, and get beaten up again. Therefore, in following up with the victim, the crisis worker should understand that there may be relapses and that the victim may fall into old ways of behaving. Thus, crisis workers not only may have to check up on their clients but also may have to be indirect about it so the women do not become dependent on them (Dagastino, 1984).

CW: Hello, Jane. Just called to see if you've been able to make that appointment for counseling at the Human Services Clinic. I know it's hard to get in there at times and thought if you hadn't, I could call the clinic and we'd have one of the people here drive you down and help you get started.

If the victim volunteers to enter therapy, the worker continues to check on her until she has really settled into her therapy and is mobile. The crisis worker continues to be a support system until the victim is well connected to a long-term support source, and only then will the crisis worker fade from the victim's life.

Counseling Children at Shelters

Many times children are lost in the shuffle of domestic violence, but as research has indicated, all too often the violence they watch or experience themselves has ripple effects that carry over into their adult lives. Hughes and Barad (1982) found that when children were removed from the violence to the safety of a shelter, their anxiety level decreased significantly although their behavior problems did not decrease nor did their self-esteem increase while in residency at the shelter. It is interesting that this study also found that mothers rated their children's behavior significantly more negatively than did staff members. The implication is that carry-over effects from a punitive home situation do not self-extinguish just because the women have escaped the battering situation. Indeed, if women return to their mates, abuse of children is likely to continue. If they do not, it is likely to be reduced (Giles-Sims, 1985).

Clearly, an intervention strategy should be developed to break the cyclical nature of violence across generations. Hughes's (1982) brief intervention strategy includes intervention with children, mothers, schools, and shelter staff members. Her model is comprehensive in that it provides individual counseling; initiates group meetings for peers, siblings, and family; teaches parenting skills to mothers; establishes a liaison with school personnel; and trains shelter staff members in child advocacy and child development issues.

COURTSHIP VIOLENCE

To believe that only women who are partners in a conjugal relationship are victims of violence is to be badly mistaken. Studies on courtship violence estimate that it occurs in anywhere from 22% to 67% of courtship relationships and cuts across college, high school, and nonschool dating populations (Burcky, Reuterman, & Kopsky, 1988; Cate, Henton, Christopher, & Lloyd, 1982; Henton, Cate, Koval, Lloyd, & Christopher, 1983; Makepiece, 1981, 1983). A conservative estimate is that violence occurs in approximately 25% of courtship relationships. Even more ominous, in a study of high school students by Burcky et al. (1988), dating violence affected girls as young as 12. These researchers also found that assaultive behavior was not just shoving and pushing. Among those experiencing dating violence, 37.5% reported that the minimum assaultive behavior was being punched, and approximately 9% reported having been assaulted with a gun or knife! It is noteworthy and perhaps presages the future of these relationships that the percentage of violence found closely parallels that found in samples of married couples (Straus et al., 1980; Straus & Gelles, 1986).

What is astounding is that Henton et al. (1983) found that 25% of victims and 30% of offenders she interviewed in courtship assaults interpreted the violence as a sign of love! As Gelles and Cornell (1985) so aptly put it, this is a very scary extension of elementary schoolyard courtship where a boy's shoving a girl means that the boy likes her.

While we are not encouraging everyone to go off to be monks and nuns, we do propose to young women and men reading this book that you take very seriously dating behavior that increasingly turns from verbal arguments into physical confrontation. Research study after research study indicates that violence invariably escalates the longer people are in an abusive relationship. To think that people will give up violent behavior for "love" or any other reason is to think wrong. Worse, to think that one has the power to get a partner to give up an addictive behavior like battering is patently false—as witnessed by the land-office business in substance addiction programs.

While Burcky et al. (1988) offer specific recommendations to counselors for education and intervention, there is little indication that high school counselors or college student development personnel are highly aware of or know what to do about the problem (Bogal-Allbritten & Allbritten, 1985). In that regard, the best directive we can offer to anyone who is physically assaulted even once in a dating relationship, no matter how great the love, how great the good times, how great the sex, how many flowers, apologies, and promises to change are given after an initial assault, *get out of the relationship now!* No battered woman we have met yet, set out with the intention to go with or marry someone who would beat her. However, by letting such behavior occur early in courtship, many battered women unwittingly set the stage for some terrible consequences of their early tolerance.

If you have assaulted someone in a dating relationship, *get help now!* By assaulted we don't necessarily mean that you put the person in the hospital. It may have been a series of hard shakes, a shove or two, or a slap in the heat of an argument or a moment of jealousy. While you can easily rationalize this behavior away, the chances are good that this behavior will increase in the future. Besides the harm you do to someone you profess to love, the changes in the law and increased judicial sensitivity to battering mean that you will probably spend some time in jail if you are convicted of an assault on your girlfriend. If your school counselor doesn't know anger management techniques, there are therapists who do. The following section on treating batterers will give you an idea of what you need to look for in a therapist and the final section provides references to books on anger management.

TREATING BATTERERS

Given what has previously been stated in this chapter about society's historical views of battering, abusive men have had little to fear in regard to consequences for their actions and even less reason to change their behavior. However, with the rise of women's shelters and the unveiling of battering as a major societal problem, class action suits have been brought in New York City and Oakland, California, to give battered women equal protection under the law. During the early 1980s, the Coalition for Justice for Battered Women in San Francisco was instrumental in getting police to redefine how they handle domestic disputes and how the district attorney prosecutes domestic assault cases (Sonkin, Martin, & Walker, 1985, p. 25). Police do not mediate but arrest, and district attorneys do not dismiss but prosecute. In short, batterers need to realize that domestic violence is a punishable crime (Sonkin et al., 1985, p. 41), and in more and more cities and states it is becoming exactly that.

While arrest may serve as a deterrent to battering (Gondolf, 1984; Sherman & Berk, 1984), many communities have adopted a diversion program modeled along the lines of the program that the Coalition for Justice for Battered Women in San Francisco helped create to treat adjudicated batterers. In our own community of Memphis, an adjudicated batterer will be given a choice: come to anger management group for 12 weekly two-hour sessions or go "11–29" (11 months and 29 days in the county penal farm). Grudgingly, approximately 75% of the batterers opt for the anger management program; about 25% hope they won't be found by the police after an arrest warrant is issued for them upon failure to appear at the police department's Family Trouble Center.

Certainly, most batterers, particularly those adjudicated to do so, do not willingly come to a treatment program, nor are they willing to admit that they have problems. Men who enter counseling for abuse often manifest outright denial, minimization, or justification and projection of blame to escape owning their abusive behavior (Shupe et al., 1987, pp. 26–28).

Denying batterer: I never touched her. Sure, I'd been drinking a little and we had an argument. She must have fallen because she was pretty drunk too! [*The complainant had three broken teeth, a fractured jaw, and two broken ribs, plus numerous contusions, cuts, and abrasions.*]

Minimizing batterer: Well, I might have pushed her when we were arguing at the top of the stairs, but I'd never hit her. [*The complainant had a broken nose, a bruised kidney, and two black eyes from the "push."*]

Projecting batterer: Listen, she ain't no rose. She gives as good as she gets. Besides, I got some rights, like dinner when I get home from work, instead of a drunk sittin' in front of the TV suckin' on a drink. She deserved a lesson! She always gets the kids to stick up for her. [*Both the woman and her two children were treated at an emergency room for contusions and lacerations from being whipped with a power cord.*]

While individual counseling, partner counseling, and partner counseling in groups have been attempted with some success (Shupe et al., 1987, pp. 26–27; Tolman & Bennett, 1990), the prevalent mode of counseling for batterers is mainly court-ordered group counseling. Besides being financially, time-, and staff-efficient, groups provide opportunities for social learning and retraining that would be nearly impossible in individual or couple therapy (Adams & McCormick, 1982). The group also provides a support system for what are typically emotionally isolated individuals and enables these men to start to learn how to depend on others in times of stress.

Treatment Goals

Giving anger management top priority reduces the risk of serious injury or death and makes other individual and/or family therapy goals more easily attained. Meeting the following secondary goals as well, as proposed by Sonkin et al. (1985, pp. 90–93), makes long-term change more likely:

1. decreased psychological isolation and development of interpersonal support systems
2. increased feelings of personal control and power by other than violent means
3. increased feelings of self-esteem

4. increased responsibility for behavior
5. increased awareness of the danger of violent behavior to both others and themselves
6. acceptance of the consequences for violent behavior
7. increased awareness of violence in society in general
8. development of communication skills
9. development of stress-reduction skills
10. development of assertiveness skills
11. development of the ability to empathize with their partners
12. increased understanding of the relationship between violence and sex-role behavior
13. development of control over alcohol and/or drug use.

To accomplish the foregoing, most groups have a combination of anger management, stress reduction, communication skills, and sex-role resocialization components (Gondolf, 1985; Sonkin et al., 1985; Tolman & Bennett, 1990). Therapeutically, most programs use some form of cognitive-behavioral approach that deals with batterers' irrational thinking and provides techniques to restructure maladaptive cognitions (Kriner & Waldron, 1988; Saunders & Hanusa, 1986; Tolman & Bennett, 1990). Programs typically are psychoeducational structured learning experiences with some time reserved for role play, discussion, and processing of concepts and ideas (Edleson & Syers, 1990; Scales & Winter, 1991). Coleaders are generally used so that they might model together the types of behaviors the batterers need to learn, and any interactions between one leader and a member can be facilitated by the other group leader (Sonkin et al., 1985, p. 98). Groups typically meet once a week for two hours and range from 8 to 32 sessions, with 12 sessions being optimal (Tolman & Bennett, 1990). Before a batterer is inducted into a group, an intake interview should be conducted to obtain a profile of the battering behavior, incidence of other psychological problems, and motivation to participate in counseling.

Assessment

The Conflict Tactics Scale (Straus, 1979) has been the only instrument used on any wide scale to measure intrafamilial conflict. The scale looks mainly at physical means used to resolve conflicts, does not adequately account for verbal abuse, and entirely ignores the emotional, social, sexual, and economic forms of abuse. It also does not look at power differential—one of the key ingredients in domestic violence (Poynter, 1989). It certainly was not meant to nor does it predict who will be violent, or who, after being arrested or completing counseling, will recidivate. While a variety of personality, self-concept, and trait-type tests have been used to attempt to determine profiles of batterers (Sonkin et al., 1985, p. 88), to this point in time, no instrument we know of will do those things with any degree of reliability or predictive validity.

Both Gondolf (1985) and Hastings and Hamberger (1988) have developed typologies of batterers based on clusters of demographic, personality, and abuse variables. Gondolf labeled his three clusters as sociopathic, antisocial, and typical batterers. The sociopathic group (7%) are by far the most violent and are most likely to have been arrested previously. The antisocial group (41%) are also extremely abusive but are less likely to have been arrested. The typical group (52%) is consistent with Walker's (1979) cycle of violence and are likely to be contrite and apologetic after battering incidents. They generally have never been arrested. While Hastings and Hamberger have labeled the three groups they isolated as borderline, narcissistic/antisocial, and dependent/compulsive, they have essentially the same makeup as Gondolf's. Understanding these differential profiles is important from the standpoint of the kinds of client responses that might be expected in treatment and the kinds of structure and consequences that might need to be applied.

Intake Interview

It would seem wise to provide a comprehensive intake interview to assess the batterer's psychological status and motivation, and also to provide information on what he might expect from a counseling group (Sonkin et al., 1985; Tolman & Bennett, 1990). First, an assessment of lethality should be conducted both for suicidal and homicidal ideation and/or behavior. As paradoxical as it may seem, many batterers are so dependent on their partners that the thought of being without them is worse than death, so suicide and murder may become viable and realistic options. There are apparent relationships between lethality and a number of factors common in battering relationships, such as frequency of violent incidents, severity of injuries, threats to kill, suicide threats by the woman, length and incidence of the batterer's drug use, frequency of intoxication, and force or threatened sexual acts (Sonkin et al., 1985, p. 73).

A fast assessment of the history of the violent relationship would seek details on the first, last, worst, and typical episode to provide a comprehensive profile of the kind, degree, and length of abuse. Assaults and violence on other family members, previous criminal activity, violence outside the home, increased social proximity of victim, attitudes toward violence, life stresses, general mental functioning, physical health, and physical and emotional isolation provide important background information on the potential for future violent behavior. The more these indicators appear, the more likely the client is to engage in lethal behavior (Sonkin et al., 1985, pp. 75–83).

One test that should always be given is an alcohol screening test with follow-up interview questions. Determining alcohol abuse is important for two reasons. First, numerous studies have shown *chronic* alcohol abuse to be a strong predictor of more violent behavior (Tolman & Bennett, 1990). Second, any individual who is under the influence of a mind-altering substance needs to get dried out first, In the program at the Memphis Family Trouble Center (FTC), anybody appearing intoxicated or under the influence of a mind-altering substance is asked to leave and obtain help for their drug problem (Winter, 1991). Failure to present clear evidence of help means probationary status has been violated, and the batterer's probation officer is immediately notified. While such stringent enforcement may seem harsh, we agree with the FTC staff and do not recommend under any circumstances working with a "wet" individual in any kind of therapy.

It should be remembered that these men are in crisis, and appropriate measures should be taken to ensure the safety of everyone. Case staffing and consultation with other professionals should be conducted before individuals who have the potential for violence of these men are admitted into a group. During intake interviews, these men should be given clear messages about expectations inside and outside the group and what the consequences of inappropriate behavior will be. For instance, at the FTC, threats of violence or intimidation against group members or leaders are not tolerated and are grounds for expulsion. While no police officer ever attends an anger management group at the FTC, there is a police substation immediately adjacent to the center, and an emergency alarm will summon help immediately. All participants are aware of this. Finally, there is evidence that clients who are apprised of the procedures, purpose, and goals of the group are less likely to drop out and less likely to recidivate (Tolman & Bennett, 1990).

Motivation

Motivation is contingent upon a number of variables. Men who are younger, less educated, have lower incomes, were abused as children, and are minorities drop out at a significantly higher rate (Tolman & Bennett, 1990) than those who are older, have no arrest record, are better educated, employed, have more children, and were more likely to have witnessed but not been abused themselves as children (Demaris, 1989; Grusznski & Carrillo, 1988). Given these demographic predictors, most individuals who come to the kinds of counseling programs that crisis workers operate do so because of external pressure, either through the court system or in an attempt to gain back their partner. While the hope is that the individual will come to participate and buy into the program because of the intrinsic value for himself, introduction to the program should indicate that there are clear consequences for not attending. The FTC introduces court-ordered participants to its program by specifically detailing its scoring system—which awards points for being on time, discussion, and homework—and how many of these points it will take to graduate. Counselors also apprise clients of what behaviors will not be tolerated and what will happen as a consequence if participants choose to violate the rules. Tolman and Bennett (1990) report that structured groups tend to be more effective, and it appears from the FTC's low attrition rate (10%) that the threat of having probation revoked and spending up to a year in jail is a strong external motivator for obtaining the points necessary to complete the program. Over the long haul, though, the basic question remains to what degree the individual is willing to take responsibility for and change his behavior (Sonkin et al., 1985, p. 85).

Group Stages

Groups typically move through three stages. In the first few sessions the common theme is "I don't really need to be here." Therapists need to confront members' denial gently and with high levels of empathy to allow members to adjust to the group setting and also keep denial to a minimum. As the group coalesces and individuals become invested at a surface level, one-upmanship in the form of "I'm sicker than you are" starts to appear with self-diagnoses of mental illness. Exaggerated descriptions of past abusive incidents are used as a way to gain attention, prestige, and control in the group. At this stage the therapists become much more confrontive and disputational of absolutistic, all-or-none, black-or-white thinking. The therapists now ask the group to start working on reframing thoughts that had previously started them on the road to abusing their partners and reformulating thoughts that had previously resulted in abusive responses to their partners. In the third stage, "I have choices," members become more aware of their own alternatives for handling thoughts, emotions, and behavior in daily living. Advice giving decreases as members move toward supporting and listening to each other (Kriner & Waldron, 1988).

While providing education on various components of battering, the crisis worker oscillates between confronting and supporting group members. Open-ended questions and reflective responses are standard counseling techniques to obtain information and establish trust. However, these facilitative techniques assume an open and honest relationship, with a desire on the client's part to change. They are not conducive to facilitating the start-up phase of a group of hostile and anxious batterers. Therefore, a combination of both open-ended and closed questions and supportive and confrontive statements is needed to break through defense systems, reflect threatening feelings, and reframe irrational thinking (Sonkin et al., 1985, pp. 64–65).

CW: [*Indirectly confrontive.*] How did you come to be here?

Batterer: I sorta hit my wife.

CW: [*Directly confronting the minimization with a semi-open question.*] I don't understand "sorta"! What do you mean?

Batterer: [*Projecting and blaming.*] I mean she made me mad. She was running her mouth, so I had to hit her.

CW: [*Confronting all-or-none thinking.*] You say "had" as if there were no options other than to smack her.

Batterer: Not really—she was really being a bitch!

CW: [*Proposing consequences and obtaining facts.*] So your choice for stopping her bitching was breaking her jaw. That choice also got you arrested. What happened?

Batterer: She swore out a warrant and I got sent to jail.

CW: [*Confrontive closed question.*] Had you ever been in jail before?

Batterer: Lord no!

CW: [*Empathically reflecting feeling.*] I'm betting that was a scary experience.

Batterer: You better believe it, there were some bad dudes in there, I didn't know if I was gonna get out of there in one piece.

CW: [*Reflecting feeling and exploring affect.*] So you were feeling pretty alone and helpless. I'm wondering how you're feeling right now?

Batterer: Madder than hell that I got to be here.

CW: [*Closed question that seeks to elicit defensive responding.*] Do you understand why you're here?

Batterer: [*Projecting.*] 'Cause she swore out a warrant on me.

CW: [*Confronting projection by making client own behavior.*] No! You are here because you put your wife in the hospital by beating her. That's criminal assault. The judge gave you a choice and you are still free to exercise it. You may come here to 12 group sessions for men who have battered. You have the opportunity to learn some things here that may help you with future relationships and that may also keep you out of harm's way in the future. Or you may walk out of here right now.

Batterer: That's not much of a choice.

CW: [*Confronting batterer with consequences of his behavior.*] Maybe not, but it's more of a choice than you gave your partner.

The responses are typical of a batterer's way of defending himself with denial, externalization of blame, and black-and-white kinds of statements that give little consideration to behavioral options and long-term consequences of behavior. The crisis worker gently but firmly wades into the client's defense system while at the same time attempting to establish rapport. This is not an easy job.

A Typical Twelve-Session Group

The following is an abbreviated version of a typical 12-session group counseling format for batterers. The content of the course is taken from the FTC anger management program. The counselor dialogue is abstracted from Betty Winter (1991), director of the program and facilitator of numerous anger management groups.

Session 1.   A great deal of anger is ventilated over being arrested and adjudicated to the program. Participants question the credential of the leader in less than polite and civil ways. They are mad and hostile about being there.

The crisis worker starts the group by sitting in the middle of it and letting the group interview her. She responds to any professional and personal questions she deems appropriate.

CW: [*After giving qualifications.*] One of my major credentials is that I get angry a lot, but I've never been arrested for it. Now that I've given you my credentials, I'd like you to give me your credentials, the ones that got you here. I'd like each of you to pair off and I'd like for each of you to share what caused you to get here with one another. Then I'd like you to report back to the group.

By putting herself at risk with this group and letting them interview her, the crisis worker leads into turning the tables. It is very difficult for these "macho" men not to own up to what brought them here when a woman can face up to their nasty interrogation.

A good deal of assessment is done in the first session. The Attitudes Toward Women checklist, the Conflict Tactics Scale (Straus, 1979) the Family Environment Scale (Moos & Moos, 1974) and the Michigan Alcohol Screening Test (Selzer, 1971) or Substance Abuse Subtle Screening Inventory (Miller, 1983) are given for research and counseling purposes. A major opening for discussion and bringing feelings out into the open is the Attitudes Toward Women checklist. What the members say about this will give the leaders much material with which to work.

The rules of attendance and conduct are reviewed, and positive and negative consequences of appropriate and inappropriate behavior are explained. Such a didactic set of rules may sound very much at odds with counseling. However, for many of these individuals it will be the first structure they have experienced since high school, so they will need to know very clearly what is expected of them. Second, the major purpose of this counseling is corrective and remedial. It is counseling within the criminal justice system. If psychological growth occurs it is beneficial, but it is also clearly an added dividend. The hoped-for result of counseling is that these men will not batter again and will not come to the attention of the justice system. As a result, initially trust is not high, and in these early sessions the issue is met head-on by the therapist.

CW: I don't expect you to share everything in this group. Take some time to see how safe you feel in here. While what you say will be held in confidence within the bounds of the legal and ethical standards I've talked about, you're undoubtedly feeling pretty victimized by the system right now. Nobody will force you to say anything you don't want to.

Paradoxically, the admonition to not trust probably does much to establish trust and breaks down some barriers and paranoia about the group. The group is given an explanation of what taking an anger time-out is and is given a homework assignment of taking practice time-outs at home. They also must explain what they are doing to their partners and why they are doing it. Finally, the concept of choices is introduced.

CW: You'll think this is crazy, but you did have a choice in coming here. If you don't like what we're about you can leave. [*Gets up, walks to the door, and opens it.*] Of course, you will have chosen to violate your probation terms and will probably go to jail.

Batterer: That's no damn choice.

CW: Granted, it's not a good choice, but it is a choice, just like what got you here. Battering was a bad choice, but it was one you made. During the course of the time we're here we'll be looking at a lot of those choices you make.

Most of these men do not realize that when they do something they are making choices. They further don't realize the variety of choices open to them. The concept of decision making and choosing wisely will be woven throughout the 12 sessions. Another key component of the group is instituted in the first session: dyadic interaction, "that pairing crap" as participants call it. Men are immediately paired off and start working with one another in pairs. They then may speak to the total group about the other person or report back to the group on what they have learned. Pairing off starts to generate closeness and bonding of the group. It also conveys early on that there is interest in hearing their story. Homework using the time-out procedure is given.

Session 2.   The time-out assignment is discussed. Participants start looking for physical anger cues and are asked to write down the signs as a homework assignment. Their lists are used to construct a group list of warning signals. The difference between anger as an emotion and violence as an action is discussed. Basic stress management skills and relaxation techniques are taught and practiced. Each man is given the opportunity to tell his story of what got him to anger management. The men are accepted as they are. No evaluation or judgment is made of the truthfulness of the story, the degree and kind of violence, or the personalities involved. A homework assignment that combines the use of relaxation techniques with recognition of physical cues of anger is given.

Session 3.   Physical anger cues are discussed. The leader presents Walker's (1979) cycle of violence and asks members to determine where they are on the continuum. The idea is to make them aware of this cycle and its commonality to all relationships, both at home or in the workplace, and to help them gain some dynamic insight into their own behavior and that of their partners as they go around in this destructive cycle. Clients are apprised of the difficulty of getting out of the cycle because of how long it has happened and its familiarity. As an example, even though the female doesn't like being beaten, she knows the rules of this game and may attempt to pull the male back into it when he started changing the rules. Homework involves adding up the financial cost of battering. Members are to write down all the real and hidden monetary costs incurred from their violence.

Session 4.   The financial consequences of battering are covered. While it may seem somewhat base to put the trauma of battering in such mercenary terms, few batterers have stopped to think of its cost. Costs vary, but it is not uncommon for a group to average a minimum of $10,000 per man in financing his anger.

CW: Add up all the money you've spent on lawyers, work time lost, furniture broken, hospital bills, bail, fines, motel rooms, not to mention divorce proceedings and alimony as a direct or indirect result of violence. What could it have bought you? Wouldn't it be great to never have to spend another dime on your anger? You see, learning to control your anger will make you money. How many of you would be against that?

Time is also spent on the characteristics and dynamics of victims. These characteristics and dynamics paradoxically start to fill in some of the dynamics of batterers because they have also become victims, albeit of their own behavior. Indeed, once they can start to see themselves as victims, they gain insight into how their victims feel. This is the start of empathic understanding for these men.

CW: Add up all the emotional costs: the guilty, angry, hurt, depressed, dependent, hopeless, helpless feelings. Wouldn't it be great to never have another lousy feeling like that? How does that fit with your partner's notions of being a victim of you? Is there any difference between how your partner may feel about you after a beating and how you feel about the court system?

The recurring theme of choices is the basis for the next homework assignment. Members are asked to write down three bad choices and three good choices they have made in their relationships.

Session 5.   Good and bad choice making is discussed. Irrational thinking and the maladaptive behavior resulting from it are introduced. Cognitive behavioral techniques from Albert Ellis's (1990) *Anger: How to Live With It and Without It* are illustrated. Specific emphasis is placed on absolutistic thinking and *should, must,* and *ought* statements. Discussion focuses on how these statements get constructed, what environmental cues set up "musturbatory" thinking, and how irrational, self-defeating thoughts and subsequent maladaptive behavior are tied together.

A violence and abuse assessment is made of the family of origin. Members are asked to respond to questions such as "Did your father hit your mother?" "How were disagreements handled?" "How did you feel about your parents?" "How were you disciplined as a child?" "How do all those events that you learned from early childhood carry over into your present family?" "How do you feel about that?" "How do those irrational beliefs spoken to earlier in the session operate in conjunction with the behavior that was modeled for you and you learned as a child?"

Members are given didactic instruction on how transgenerational violence occurs. Processing the following discussion questions generally will result in a shocking and nasty insight, because the very thing the batterers hated most about their own fathers they may now be perpetrating on their children.

CW: What was your feeling as a child in regard to the abuse you saw? How do you suppose your kids are affected by your violent behavior? Do they feel any different than you did? Guess at their feelings and what they might be thinking about you and why they might feel and think that way.

The homework assignment is to start changing members' ways of responding to stressful situations by

1. watching out for environmental cues that start musturbatory thinking
2. using cooler cognitions, such as "It'd be nice, convenient if XYZ happened, but it doesn't *have* to happen"
3. positively reinforcing children and using time-out procedures with them.

Session 6.   Focus for the sixth session is on feelings. Homework discussion centers on any different responses they saw in their family as they tried to use cooler, more positive approaches and how members felt about those responses. Many of the members will be incredulous and confused by the changes they see. Participants are asked to list several positive and negative feelings they have. Usually most of them will have a great deal of difficulty with this task, because they have never had to identify any feelings they have. Feelings generally get lumped into two categories, angry and happy. A lecture is given on how men are taught at a very early age to stuff their feelings and not acknowledge them as real.

CW: Why it is important to be able to recognize how you feel? To be able to really know yourself and to be able to communicate better?

Outcomes from denying feelings are discussed. Not only might one wind up under arrest and in anger management, but also there are physical costs such as alcoholism, ulcers, and heart attack. Examples are given from Stoop and Arterburn's (1991) *The Angry Man: "Why Does He Act That Way?"* This session is very difficult because members will be asked to share feelings —a very threatening experience for most of them. Leader statements like the following are designed to minimize the threat.

CW: Although there are risks, when you tell someone how you feel you become vulnerable and you also become a lot more real. You become much more lovable and find it is easier to love when you tell someone how you feel. You need to be prepared for them to do the same and understand that there is the possibility of feeling some pain and hurt from what is said. You don't tell someone your feelings just to get their sympathy. You share your feelings with significant others as a way of taking care of yourself, so you don't have to stuff feelings anymore until they finally boil over and get you in trouble or hurt you.

Outcomes may be very dramatic as men start to talk about their feelings, relive their experiences as children, and grapple with feelings of guilt, helplessness, dependency, and insecurity that they have had since child-hood. It is not uncommon for some highly charged emotional catharsis to occur at this point and, as these feelings emerge, for some strong bonds to form as men start, for the first time, to share deeply but closely held feelings with another person. The homework assignment involves the construction and use at home of three sentences using positive feelings and three senten-ces using negative feelings.

Session 7. The attempt to convey verbally both positive and negative feel-ings is discussed and leads into issues of power and control. Power and control are the focus of the session, discussed in relation to faulty belief systems. The facilitator looks for common themes in the men's stories as they talk about times when they felt powerful and powerless. It is interest-ing that many of these men who are physically strong may feel extremely powerless when they are dealing verbally with others and may admire other verbally fluent and erudite men as really strong and powerful. They also can become very frustrated when they are being "outtalked" in a relationship and can regress to their only way of regaining power and control—violence.

CW: When you allow someone else to push your button, who is in control? How do you use anger as a control tool? Abuse is a last-ditch effort to gain control back in a relationship. Why is that so? Do you believe that you try to get power and control only when you feel you don't have any? If power and control are the bottom line, do abuse, anger, and battering get the job done for you? If they really do get the job done, then why do you still have to rely on them?

Closely allied with different ways of obtaining power and control are the concepts of aggressiveness and assertiveness. Because of their inability to use words in powerful ways, most of the participants have difficulty mak-ing clear assertions about what their wants and needs are. Further, they have an overriding fear that they will be rejected if they ask for something, and their insecurity does not handle rejection well at all. As a result, they use aggression to meet their needs. The group is taught how to construct assertion statements and given an assignment of using them at home.

Session 8. The most difficult part of an assertion statement for the group is the "I" or owning part. "I" or assertion statements and "you" or aggression statements are put up on the board so members know what they sound like, how they differ, and what can happen when each is used. Each member is asked to formulate a problem in terms of "I" and "you" statements and practice with a partner.

CW: "I" statements mean taking responsibility for yourself and your feelings. How many of you would really like to do that? How does a person react when "I" statements are used?

Because jealousy is so common to most of the stories that brought members here, time is devoted to retelling the original story using the skills they have learned in their eight sessions. As these stories are reprocessed, other feelings undergirding the jealousy begin to surface. Hurt, betrayal, insecurity, lack of trust, dependency are all threatening feelings that are denied and replaced by jealousy, which allows placement of blame on the partner for "transgressions" and thus allows the batterer a face-saving way of not having to deal with his own problems.

Batterer: I hate to admit it, but all that stuff makes sense. Still and all, I don't believe I can trust her.

CW: Maybe you know she can't trust you so you don't trust her. Could you use some of those "I" statements and discuss it with her and no matter what she said not use "you" statements?

Homework is given to name a time in their lives when jealousy turned to violence. The members are also asked to mentally substitute a new feeling every time they start to feel jealous and to report back on their experience.

Session 9. Jealousy assignments are processed. Because alcohol and drugs play a predominant role in the vast majority of battering incidents, members are educated about how the problem applies to battering: specifically, that alcoholism and drug abuse is not necessarily the cause of battering but does release inhibitions enough that batterers can give themselves permission to become violent.

Batterer: Hell, I couldn't bring myself to beat her until I got a six-pack down. Then I could do it just fine and not think a thing about it.

Results of the Michigan Alcohol Screening Test (Selzer, 1971) or the Substance Abuse Subtle Screening Inventory (Miller, 1983) are given to each participant. Alcohol and drugs are discussed from the perspective of losing control. Participants are shown how alcohol or drugs can be a trigger for violent behavior and an excuse for making violent behavior acceptable. Use of alcohol and drugs as a way to handle anger and frustration from environmental sources is discussed. (Most of the serious alcohol and drug abuse problems will have already been referred to addiction programs.)

Session 10. Sex is an overriding concern because of all the myths that surround it. Much of the need of the batterer to feel superior, confident, and capable is tied to sex and his manhood. Many times, particularly with young female leaders, members will say things and use language designed to shock and embarrass the leaders. While X-rated language for the sake of X-rated language is not tolerated, some leeway is given for the street vernacular that is commonly used. The ability of group leaders, particularly young women, to weather the language goes a long way toward establishing their credentials with these men.

Batterer: So she wouldn't give me a blow job so I smacked her. That's part of earning her keep, to blow my pipes, man!

CW: [*Young female graduate student.*] So forcing oral sex on her keeps you in control. I wonder if the way you said that isn't designed to shock and embarrass me and kinda control me through verbal sex like you control her physically through sex.

Batterer: Hey, I thought we was supposed to be talking about the real stuff in here.

CW: [*Very calmly, with eyes leveled at the batterer, avoiding the taunt.*] I'm wondering how you'd like it if Harold [*240-lb. ironworker in the group*] were to request oral sex of you, and if you didn't comply, start pounding on you, particularly in your groin. Do you start to get some of the feelings your partner would get? I wonder if you can respond to that? [*The group nod their heads in agreement.*]

The many myths that hold men up to impossible Hollywood "stud" standards are discussed and debunked. For many men, this will be the first valid information they have ever received about sexual behavior. They will typically experience relief after being told that no man could live up to some of the performance expectations they have self-propagandized for themselves. The equity of sexual relationships is discussed. Homework assignments focus on irrational and negative thoughts men generate for themselves in their sexual relations. They are asked to watch for and write down some of their unrealistic expectations of themselves. They are also asked to attempt to use assertion statements when asking for sex. Finally, they are asked to pick one of the subjects already covered in the group and be prepared to teach a review on it next session.

Session 11.   Each group member picks one of the major topics from the foregoing sessions and teaches it. Discussion centers on a review of the issue from the standpoint of the effect it has had on the member and what those issues now may mean for other members. Many members may have stage fright at being responsible for "teaching." The crisis worker is extremely supportive and reinforcing of their efforts. Taking responsibility for teaching the concepts is important in validating that the participants have learned and can transmit that knowledge to others. After having done this, many of the men will feel good enough about their capabilities to volunteer to return to colead another anger management group. The homework assignment is to put everything they have learned into operation and return next time to finalize their game plan for not recidivating.

Session 12.   Postassessments are given. Participation, homework, and attendance points are posted. Reflections and feelings are given about the group. A "Good, Bad, and Ugly" exercise is given.

CW: If you had to tell the judge anything about this program, what would it be? What did you like best and least? What would you like to see changed? What techniques seemed to work for you and what didn't?

Members then discuss how they are putting their comprehensive anger management plans into action. They also indicate the strengths they now see in themselves and some of the pitfalls they will have to watch out for. Depending on how cohesive the group has become, it is not uncommon for the men to bring food, exchange phone numbers, and have a graduation party for one another.

While the group format is structured so that the major components of battering and the ways to stop it are covered, group leaders have a great deal of discretion in timing and sequencing of the material. In some groups, more emphasis may be given to one issue than another. Groups may spend more or less time in processing.

Program Success

Do programs work? Overall, batterers report that anger management programs help them gain control of their anger, enable them to communicate better with their partners, and reduce their violence. Shupe et al. (1987) found that battered women in approximately seven out of ten cases reported that physical and sexual violence stopped after their partners went through an anger management program. When violence did recur after the men graduated from these programs, it was almost always remarkably reduced. Relationships were also improved and many women who had not attended indicated that they had picked up pointers that their partners brought home from the sessions (pp. 113–117).

While most men come to counseling angry and hostile because they are pressured or required to be there, the majority report that they learn from and even come to enjoy the camaraderie of the group (Scales & Winter, 1991). The majority of outcome studies of battering groups have found positive outcomes. Increases in self-esteem (Kriner & Waldron, 1988) and assertiveness (Douglas & Perrin, 1987); decreases in depression and anger (Hamberger & Hastings, 1986), jealousy and negative attitudes toward women (Saunders & Hanusa, 1986), and overall psychological symptoms (Hawkins & Beauvais, 1985); reduction in both self-report and corroborated physical and psychological abuse on postcounseling follow-up (Edleson & Syers, 1990; Poynter, 1989); and more cohesive, expressive, and less conflictual family life (Poynter, 1989) have all been found in a variety of studies involving battering groups with different cultural, racial, and socioeconomic backgrounds. Whether the programs truly change their participants or whether they work in other ways, as graphically described in the following excerpt, it is evident that men who complete an anger management or battering program do not come to the attention of the police on a reported basis nearly as often as those who have nothing happen to them.

Batterer: Man, I ain't never gonna beat up on a woman again. Nothing will ever make me go through this shit twice! (Shupe et al., 1987, p. 103).

IF YOU ARE IN AN ABUSIVE RELATIONSHIP

We finish this chapter by offering some advice to any women or men who may be involved in an abusive relationship. If you are being victimized in an abusive relationship, the following points summarizing Bowker's (1986) advice from 1000 battered women in her book *Ending the Violence: A Guidebook Based on the Experiences of 1000 Battered Wives* (p. 110), may be of help:

1. Obtain a divorce or separate and see a lawyer.
2. Get counseling for yourself and/or the batterer.
3. Secure help immediately; don't let the pattern become established.
4. Be independent and raise your self-esteem.
5. Tell others about the violence; keep no secrets.
6. Be firm with the batterer.
7. Call the police to arrest the batterer, file charges, and follow through on the prosecution.
8. Ask friends and neighbors for help.
9. Go to a battered women's shelter.
10. Go to women's groups and women's therapists.

If you are physically and mentally abusive and believe you have a problem with your anger, we would suggest seeking out an anger management group. While Edleson and Syers (1990) found self-help to be much less effective than groups in reducing violence, we understand that it may be a very big step to commit to such a group when you are not forced to do so. It may also be that there is no group available in your area. Given the caution about how effective self-help might be, we recommend two contemporary books on anger management: *Dr. Weisinger's Anger Management Work Out Book* by Hendrie Weisinger (1985) and *Learning to Live Without Violence* by Daniel Sonkin and Michael Durphy (1982).

SUMMARY

Battering has deep roots in the psychological, sociological, and cultural makeup of the United States and in many other countries that go back to the beginnings of their patriarchal systems. Battering is pervasive through all socioeconomic levels of society and knows no ethical, racial, or religious boundaries. Dynamically, battering may be seen as having much to do with the concept of power. A variety of stressors that insinuate themselves into a relationship can escalate relational problems to violence.

Domestic violence is sequential, developmental, and dynamic. The situation of the battered woman is unlike many other crises in that it is trans-crisis in nature; that is, it is cyclic, reaching many peak levels over extended periods of time. For a variety of reasons, it is the rare woman who leaves a violent relationship for good after the first battering. Continued and increased violence over a period of years is the typical pattern of battering relationships.

In the last decade, crisis lines, shelters, and programs for battered women and their children have grown exponentially across the United States. Courts and law enforcement agencies have become much more proactive in protecting the rights of these women. However, the number of battered women still far exceeds the capacity of human services to effectively deal with them in comprehensive ways.

In the complex arena of domestic violence, there are no simple answers. Each case and each situation must be handled as unique. Different victims will feel, think, and behave differently at different times. One of the most frustrating components of intervention with women who are victims of domestic violence is their seeming inability to extract themselves from the terrible situations they face. Providing counseling in such trying circumstances calls for a great deal of empathic understanding. It is clear that no one can or should tell a victim that she must leave a battering situation. Only the victim is qualified to decide when she is ready to take action. The worker's job is to help keep the client as safe as possible, provide options and, working patiently with the victim, help her explore alternatives and choose a plan of action.

Recently, the focus on domestic violence has shifted to include treatment of the batterer. Anger management groups for batterers are starting to appear throughout the country. Typically sent to such groups by court order, batterers learn to understand the factors that lead them to violence, learn to recognize and communicate their feelings, and learn to avoid or stop confrontations which lead them to act out their feelings in violent ways.

Finally, a very bothersome aspect of the concerned citizens and professionals who work with family problems such as child abuse, incest, teenage pregnancy, drug abuse, and domestic violence is that often they specialize in their own particular arena and don't look at the family in its totality or the family as a component of a larger system. Rather, they tend to stay on their own "turf," sometimes guarding it zealously. This isolation has caused infighting over decreasing funding for research and program development, duplication of effort, and bureaucratic red tape created by competing agencies and special interest groups. We in no way disparage the efforts of each of these actors, and we particularly applaud the feminist movement for agitating, lobbying, raising public consciousness, and instigating legislative efforts on the behalf of abused women in particular, and women's rights in general. However, the continued disintegration of the family has broad ramifications not only for the individuals within it, but also for society as a whole. We agree with David Finkelhor (Finkelhor et al., 1983), one of the most noted researchers on family violence, when he calls for unity among researchers and practitioners in endeavoring to form a unifying theory and unified approach to research and practice in combating the awesome problems families are currently experiencing. In that regard this chapter would seem symptomatic of a malaise that reaches very deeply into many segments of contemporary society.

REFERENCES

Adams, D., & McCormick, A. (1982). Men unlearning violence: A group approach based on the collective model. In M. Roy (Ed.), *The abusive partner* (pp. 170–197). New York: Van Nostrand Reinhold.

American Psychiatric Association. (1987). *Diagnostic and statistical manual of mental disorders* (3rd ed., rev.). Washington, DC: Author.

Barnett, E. R., Pittman, C. R., Ragan, C., & Salus, M. K. (1980). *Family violence: Intervention strategies* (DHHS Publication No. OHD 580-30258). Washington, DC: U.S. Government Printing Office.

Benjamin, L., & Walz, G. R. (1983). *Violence in the family: Child and spouse abuse* (Report No. EDN00001). Washington, DC: National Institute of Education. (ERIC Document Reproduction Service No. ED 226–309).

Bogal-Allbritten, R. B., & Allbritten, W. L. (1985). The hidden victims: Courtship violence among college students. *Journal of College Student Personnel, 26,* 201–204.

Bowker, L. H. (1986). *Ending the violence: A guidebook based on the experiences of 1000 battered wives.* Holmes Beach, FL: Learning Publications.

Bradley v. *State,* 1 Miss. 156 (1824).

Burcky, W., Reuterman, N., & Kopsky, S. (1988). Dating violence among high school students. *The School Counselor, 35,* 353–358.

Capps, M. (1982, April). *The co-optive and repressive state versus the battered women's movement.* Paper presented at annual meeting of Southern Sociological Society, Memphis.

Cate, R. M., Henton, J. M., Christopher, F. S., & Lloyd, S. (1982). Premarital abuse: A social psychological perspective. *Journal of Family Issues, 3,* 79–90.

Coleman, B. C. (1991, October 17). Campaign targets domestic violence. *The Commercial Appeal,* p. A6.

Conroy, K. (1982). Long-term treatment issues with battered women. In J. P. Flanger (Ed.), *The many faces of family violence.* Springfield, IL: Charles C Thomas.

Dagastino, A. (Speaker). (1984). *Crisis intervention series: Helping abused women in wife abuse centers and shelters* (Cassette Recording No. 4–1). Memphis: Memphis State University Department of Counseling and Personnel Services.

Davidson, T. (1977). Wife beating: A recurring phenomenon throughout history. In M. Roy (Ed.), *Battered women: A psychosocial study of domestic violence.* New York: Van Nostrand Reinhold.

Demaris, A. (1989). Attrition in batterers' counseling: The role of social and demographic factors. *Social Service Review, 63,* 142–154.

Dobash, R. E., & Dobash, R. (1979). *Violence against wives.* New York: Free Press.

Douglas, M. A., & Perrin, A. (1987, July). *Recidivism and accuracy of self-*

reported violence and arrest. Paper presented at the Third National Conference for Family Violence Researchers, University of New Hampshire, Durham.

Edleson, J. L., & Syers, M. (1990). Relative effectiveness of group treatments for men who batter. *Social Work Research and Abstracts, 26,* 10–17.

Edwards, S. M. (1989). *Policing domestic violence: Women, the law, and the state.* London: Sage Publications.

Elbow, M. (1977). Theoretical considerations of violent marriages. *Social Casework, 31,* 515–523.

Ellis, A. (1990). *Anger: How to live with it and without it.* New York: Carroll Publishing Group.

Federal Bureau of Investigation. (1991). *Uniform crime report for the United Sates, 1990.* Washington, DC: U.S. Government Printing Office.

Finkelhor, D., Gelles, R. J., Hotaling, G. T., & Straus, A. A. (Eds.). (1983). *The darkside of families.* Beverly Hills: Sage Publications.

Ganley, A. L., & Harris, L. (1978, August). *Domestic violence: Issues in designing and implementing programs for male batterers.* Paper presented at the annual meeting of the American Psychological Association, Toronto. (ERIC Document Reproduction Service No. ED 167 871)

Gelles, R. J. (1972). *The violent home: A study of physical aggression between husbands and wives.* Beverly Hills, CA: Sage Publications.

Gelles, R. J. (1976). Abused wives: Why do they stay? *Journal of Marriage and Family, 38,* 659–668.

Gelles, R. J., & Cornell, C. P. (1985). *Intimate violence in families.* Beverly Hills, CA: Sage Publications.

Giles-Sims, J. (1985). A longitudinal study of battered children of battered wives. *Family Relations Journal of Applied Family and Child Studies, 34,* 205–210.

Gondolf, E. (1984). *Men who batter: Why they abuse women and how they stop their abuse.* Indiana, PA: Domestic Violence Study Center, Indiana University of Pennsylvania.

Gondolf, E. (1985). Fighting for control: A clinical assessment of men who batter. *Social Casework, 65,* 48–54.

Grusznski, R. J., & Carrillo, T. P. (1988). Who completes batterers' treatment groups? An empirical investigation. *Journal of Family Violence, 3,* 141–150.

Halleck, S. L. (1976). Psychodynamic aspects of violence. *Bulletin of the American Academy of Psychiatry and Law, 4,* 328–335.

Hamberger, L. K., & Hastings, J. E. (1986, August). *Skills training for treatment of spouse abusers: An outcome study.* Paper presented at the meeting of the American Psychological Association, Washington, DC.

Hart, B. (1980, June). Testimony at a hearing before the U.S. Commission on Civil Rights, Harrisburg, PA.

Hastings, J. E., & Hamberger, L. K. (1988). Personality characteristics of spouse abusers: A controlled comparison. *Violence and Victims, 3,* 31–47.

Hawkins, R., & Beauvais, C. (1985, August). *Evaluation of group therapy with abusive men: The police record.* Paper presented at the meeting of the American Psychological Association, Los Angeles.

Henton, J., Cate, R., Koval, J., Lloyd, S., & Christopher, S. (1983). Romance and violence in dating relationships. *Journal of Family Issues, 4,* 467–482.

Heppner, M. J. (1978). Counseling the battered wife: Myths, facts, and decisions. *Personnel and Guidance Journal, 56,* 522–525.

Hilbert, J. C., & Hilbert, H. C. (1984). Battered women leaving the shelter: Which way do they go? A discriminate function analysis. *Journal of Applied Social Sciences, 8,* 291–297.

Hughes, H. M. (1982). Brief interventions with children in a battered women's shelter: A model preventive program. *Family Relations Journal of Applied Family and Child Studies, 31,* 495–502.

Hughes, H. M., & Barad, S. J. (1982). Changes in the psychological functioning of children in a battered women's shelter: A pilot study. *Victimology, 7,* 60–68.

Ibrahim, F. A., & Herr, E. L. (1987). Battered women: A developmental life–career counseling perspective. *Journal of Counseling and Development, 65,* 244–248.

James, R., & Gilliland, B. (1991, April). *Future directions of crisis intervention.* Paper presented at Crisis Convening XV, Chicago, IL.

Kriner, L., & Waldron, B. (1988). Group counseling: A treatment modality for batterers. *Journal of Specialists in Group Work, 13,* 110–116.

Kurz, D., & Stark, E. (1987). Health education and feminist strategy. K. Yllo & M. Bograd (Eds.), *Feminist perspectives on wife abuse.* Beverly Hills, CA: Sage Publications.

Langley, R., & Levy, R. C. (1977). *Wife beating: The silent crisis.* New York: Dutton.

Makepeace, J. (1981). Courtship violence among college students. *Family Relations, 30,* 97–102.

Makepeace, J. (1983). Life-events stress and courtship violence. *Family Relations, 32,* 101–109.

Margolin, G. (1979). *Conjoint marital therapy to enhance anger management and reduce spouse abuse.* Los Angeles: University of Southern California Psychological Research and Service Center.

Massachusetts Coalition of Battered Women Service Groups (1981). *For shelter and beyond: An educational manual for working with women who are battered.* Boston, MA: Red Sun Press.

Memphis Police Department. (1991). *Summary of monthly uniformed patrol calls: Domestic violence summary.* Memphis, TN: Author.

Miller, G. (1983). *SASSI: Substance Abuse Subtle Screening Inventory.* Bloomington, IN: SASSI Institute.

Moore, D. M. (Ed.). (1979). *Battered women.* Newbury Park, CA: Sage Publications.

Moos, R. H., & Moos, B. (1974). *Family Environment Scale.* Palo Alto, CA: Consulting Psychologists Press.

Morgan, S. M. (1982). *Conjugal terrorism: A psychological and community treatment model of wife abuse.* Palo Alto, CA: R & E Research Associates.

Mott-MacDonald, L. (1979). Report on the Belmont Conference on Spouse Abuse. Washington, DC: Center for Women Policy Studies.

Okun, L. (1986). *Woman abuse: Facts replacing myths.* Albany, NY: State University of New York Press.

Pagelow, M. D. (1977). *Battered women: A new perspective.* Berkeley, CA: University of California Press.

Pagelow, M. D. (1981). *Woman battering: Victims and their experiences.* Beverly Hills, CA: Sage Publications.

Pizzey, E. (1974). *Scream quietly or the neighbors will hear.* London: Penguin Books.

Pleck, E. (1987). *The making of societal policy against family violence from colonial times to the present.* New York: Oxford University Press.

Poynter, T. L. (1989). An evaluation of a group programme for male perpetrators of domestic violence. *Australian Journal of Sex, Marriage, and Family, 10,* 133–142.

Resnik, M. (1976). *Wife beating: Counselor training manual.* Ann Arbor, MI: NOW Domestic Violence Project.

Rosenberg, M. L., Stark, E., & Zahn, M. A. (1986). Interpersonal violence: Homicide and spouse abuse. In J. Last & J. Chin (Eds.), *Maxcy-Roseneau: Public health and preventive medicine* (pp. 1399–1426). New York: Appleton-Century-Crofts.

Rosewater, L. B. (1982). *An MMPI profile for battered women.* Unpublished doctoral dissertation, Union Graduate School. Ann Arbor, MI.

Saunders, D. G., & Hanusa, D. (1986). Cognitive-behavioral treatment of men who batter: The short-term effects of group therapy. *Journal of Family Violence, 1,* 357–372.

Scales, K., & Winter, B. (1991, April). *Anger management for spouse abusers: The interpersonal transaction group.* Paper presented at Crisis Convening XV, Chicago, IL.

Schecter, S. (1982). *Women and male violence.* Boston: South End Press.

Schutte, N. S., Bouleige, L., Fix, J. L., & Malouff, J. M. (1986). Returning to partner after leaving a crisis shelter: A decision faced by battered women. *Journal of Social Behavior and Personality, 1,* 295–298.

Schuyler, M. (1976). Battered wives, an emerging social problem. *Social Work, 21,* 488–491.

Selzer, M. L. (1971). Michigan Alcohol Screening Test: The quest for a new diagnostic instrument. *American Journal of Psychiatry, 127,* 1653–1658.

Sherman, L. W., & Berk, R. A. (1984). The specific deterrent effects of arrest for domestic assaults. *American Sociological Review, 49,* 1261–1272.

Shupe, A., Stacey, W. A., & Hazlewood, L. R. (1987). *Violent men, violent couples.* Lexington, MA: Lexington Books.

Sonkin, D., & Durphy, M. (1982). *Learning to live without violence.* San Francisco: Volcano Press.

Sonkin, D. J., Martin, D., & Walker, L. E. (1985). *The male batterer: A treatment approach.* New York: Springer.

Spanno, T. K. (1990, April). *Eclipse of the self: The grief of the battered women.* Paper presented at Crisis Convening XIV, Chicago, IL.

Spencer, J. T., & Helmreich, R. (1972). The Attitudes Towards Women Scale: An objective instrument to measure attitudes towards the rights and roles of women in contemporary society. *Catalog of Selected Documents in Psychology, 2,* 66–67.

Stark, E., & Flitcraft, A. (1987). Violence among intimates: An epidemiological review. In V. B. Van Hasselt, R. L. Morrison, A. S. Bellack, & M. Hersen (Eds.), *Handbook of family violence.* New York: Plenum.

Stark, E., & Flitcraft, A. (1988). Personal power and institutional victimization: Treating the dual trauma of women battering. In F. M. Ochberg, (Ed.), *Posttrauma therapy and victims of violence* (pp. 115–151). New York: Brunner/Mazel.

Stark, E., Flitcraft, A., & Frazier, W. (1979). Medicine and patriarchal violence. The social construction of a "private" event. *International Journal of Health Services, 9,* 461–493.

State v. *Oliver,* 70 N. C. 60, 61–62 (1874).

Steinmetz, S. K. (1978). Wife beating: A critique and reformulation of existing theory. *Bulletin of American Academy of Psychiatry and the Law, 6,* 322–334.

Steinmetz, S. K., & Straus, M. A. (1973). Family as a cradle of violence. *Society, 10,* 50–56.

Steinmetz, S. K., & Straus, M. A. (Eds.). (1974). *Violence in the family.* New York: Harper & Row.

Stoop, D., & Arterburn, S. (1991). *The angry man: "Why does he act that way?"* Dallas, TX: Word Publishing.

Straus, M. A. (1979). Measuring intra-family conflict and violence: The C.T. Scale. *Journal of Marriage and Family, 41,* 75–88.

Straus, M. A., & Gelles, R. J. (1986). Societal change and change in family violence from 1975 to 1985 as revealed by two national surveys. *Journal of Marriage and Family, 48,* 465–479.

Straus, M. A., Gelles, R. J., & Steinmetz, S. (1980). *Behind closed doors: Violence in the American family.* Garden City, NY: Anchor/Doubleday.

Symonds, M. (1978). The psychodynamics of violence-prone marriages. *American Journal of Psychoanalysis, 38,* 213–222.

Tolman, R. M., & Bennett, L. W. (1990). A review of quantitative research on men who batter. *Journal of Interpersonal Violence 5,* 87–118.

Turner, S. F., & Shapiro, C. H. (1986). Battered women: Mourning the death of a relationship. *Social Work, 31,* 372–376.

U.S. Department of Justice. (1980). *Intimate victims: A study of violence among friends and relatives.* Washington, DC: U.S. Government Printing Office.

Walker, L. (1979). How battering happens and how to stop it. In D. Moore (Ed.), *Battered women* (pp. 59–78). Beverly Hills, CA: Sage Publications.

Walker, L. (1984). *The battered woman syndrome.* New York: Springer.

Walker, L. E. (1989). *Terrifying love: Why battered women kill and how society responds.* New York: Harper & Row.

Weincourt, R. (1985, March). Never to be alone: Existential therapy for battered women. *Journal of Psychosocial Nursing, 23,* 24–29.

Weisinger, H. (1985). *Dr. Weisinger's anger management work out book.* New York: Quill.

Winter, B. (Speaker). (1991). The Family Trouble Center anger management program (Videocassette recording #6781-A-91). Memphis, TN: Memphis State University Department of Counseling and Personnel Services.

CLASSROOM EXERCISES
The Case of Joyce

The following is a typical case of an abused wife. Joyce is a 34-year-old woman who has been married ten years. She has three children, all under 10 years old: Sheena, age 9; Jack, age 6; and Beth, age 2. Her husband is a prominent attorney. The family presents an ideal picture of an upper-middle-class family. They live in a fashionable suburb. The husband has been successful to the extent that he has been made a full partner in a large law firm. The family is very active in church, the country club, and various other social organizations. Joyce is an active member of several charitable, civic, and social groups. Joyce's initial call to the wife abuse center was vague and guarded. She expressed an interest for "another woman" in regard to the purpose of the center. After she had received information and an invitation to call back, a number of weeks elapsed. Joyce's second call occurred after receiving a severe beating from her husband. This is a segment of that conversation.

CW: [*Answering phone.*] Wife abuse center. May I help you?

Joyce: I feel terrible calling you so many times, but I've gotta have help right away. [*Sobbing.*]

CW: OK! Tell me what's happened that you need help now.

Joyce: Well, last night he beat me worse than ever. I thought he was really going to kill me this time. It had been building up for the past few weeks. His fuse was getting shorter and shorter, both with me and the kids. It's his work, I guess. Finally he came home late last night. Dinner was cold. We were supposed to go out and I guess it was my fault . . . I complained about his being late and he blew up. Started yelling that he was gonna teach me a lesson. He started hitting me with his fists . . . knocked me down . . . and then started kicking me. I got up and ran into the bathroom. The kids were yelling for him to stop and he cuffed Sheena . . . God, it was horrible! [*Wracked with sobs for more than a minute. CW waits.*] I'm sorry, I just can't seem to keep control.

CW: After all that I think anyone would be insane if they weren't feeling out of control. Right now, I'm concerned about your and your children's safety. Do you need medical attention? A safe place to come and stay, like right now?

Joyce: No . . . I guess I'm OK . . . I guess . . . I don't know. Then, he broke down the door and started in again and the next thing I knew Sheena was wiping blood off my face with a washcloth and he'd left.

CW: What do you want to do now?

Joyce: Well, I was going to get a divorce but when I went to see a lawyer a couple of years ago I thought I'd lose the children if I went through with it. So I just figured I'd put up with it. [*Voice trembles.*] I'd rather die than lose the children. I was afraid he might kill me, too.

CW: Did he ever threaten you?

Joyce: No, but somehow I just thought he would. Besides, when I went to our minister he told me to pray about being a better wife and I just felt like maybe he was right. So there wasn't any help from him or anyone else. I just felt so bad and guilty, too. I mean, he provides a good home and all. Kids go to the best schools. Even my best girlfriend says, "It's no big deal—he could be a womanizer or a drug addict." Besides, it'd really be a scandal if everybody found out. I just didn't have any place to turn. What can I do? [*Begins sobbing again.*]

I. Simulated Telephone Interview

In small groups of five or six, one person takes the role of Joyce and one person takes the role of the crisis worker. The remaining group members are observers. The crisis worker picks up where the telephone dialogue left off, following the six-step model discussed in Chapter 2. Pursue the crisis intervention session through to gaining a commitment, if possible, from Joyce. At the conclusion of the intervention, the observers will provide feedback to both crisis worker and client. These are typical discussion questions:

1. Did the crisis worker *really* hear what the victim was saying, both verbally and nonverbally?
2. What did the crisis worker do to attend to the client's safety and security needs?
3. What evidence indicates that the client understood and owned realistic options?
4. What typical dynamics did you see occurring—denial, guilt, fear, rationalization, withdrawal, and so on—in the victim? How did the crisis worker handle them?

5. Did the crisis worker attempt to impose solutions or alternatives on Joyce?

After these questions have been discussed, all those who played the role of Joyce should have the opportunity to disassociate themselves from the simulated role. They each make a statement to members of the group, explaining why they are *not* Joyce and noting ways in which they are personally different from that person. Typically we say, "Word your statement in such a way that all of us who observed will never again associate you with that role." Then we call for a round of applause from the group for the persons doing the role play.

II. Simulated Support Group

Five or six female volunteers from the group take the roles of abused wives who are now in residence at the wife abuse shelter. Either the instructor or a volunteer crisis worker from the group conducts a short session of a support group for abused wives. Use a "fishbowl" arrangement—that is, the support-group players are seated in the center of the room. Role players should draw upon their own experience and reading of this chapter to make the exercise as realistic as possible. During the process the crisis worker will want to focus on these issues:

1. the effects of being transplanted from one's home to crowded conditions of living in a socioeconomically and ethnically diverse group of women
2. the desire to reestablish contact with the husband even though the consequences may be extremely negative (particularly note any dependency needs)
3. bringing to the surface and dealing with the dynamic responses of victims, including disbelief, denial, fear, anger, negotiation, pride, striving for independence, and resolution
4. typical problems such as employment, finances, child care, transportation, legal aid, food, clothing, permanent shelter, schooling for children, and vocational skills
5. what each abuse victim wants to do over the long term.

Following the role-playing session, discuss questions like these: How does the crisis worker act as facilitator of solutions to these problems? Does she let group members take responsibility or is she responsible for them? How does she resolve conflict? How does she respond to group members who exhibit overt helplessness and dependency? Again, after the discussion the role players should disassociate themselves from their roles and receive a round of applause.

CHAPTER 8

Chemical Dependency:
The Crisis of Addiction

BACKGROUND

"Wine is a mocker, strong drink is raging" (Proverbs 20:1). "At the last it biteth like a serpent, and stingeth like an adder" (Proverbs 23:32). These biblical verses depict the continuing saga of drugs and addiction with which humankind has struggled over the ages. Efforts to treat the problem of substance abuse go back at least to the Romans, who attempted aversive conditioning of drunkards by placing spiders in the bottom of wine cups (J. W. Smith, 1982, p. 875).

Whole economies have been founded on drug use. The United States has been no shirker in this regard. The discovery that an acre of corn could be made much more salable by turning it into alcohol played a dominant role in developing the economies of colonial New England and the early American frontier. How striking the demand for and the problem of alcohol became in colonial America is eloquently described by Asbury (1950, pp. 3–19), who documented the prodigious gallonage manufactured, the drunkenness extant in the population, the belief that alcohol could cure everything from hangnails to consumption, and its use to alleviate a life of drudgery.

In 1785, nearly everyone in the United States would have thought the idea of abstinence to be ludicrous, but by 1835 a temperance movement "demonizing" alcohol was in full swing (Levine, 1984). The effort to "keep a devil out of the mouth of America" culminated in the Volstead Act and ratification of the Eighteenth Amendment to the Constitution, which brought prohibition to the country in 1920 (Asbury, 1950; Edwards, 1985). What this "Noble Experiment" did was allow the rampant growth of organized crime, which provided a thirsty public with bathtub gin, Canadian whiskey, and moonshine. The Twenty-First Amendment repealing prohibition in 1933 is a large legislative memorial to the futility of trying to prohibit a drug, and in a social perspective it has much to say about what a society believes to be good or evil.

In view of contemporary issues of addiction, it seems that we do not learn the lessons of history very well. The expansion of smuggling, underground drug factories, and domestic cultivation of illicit drugs continues.

The illicit drug trade is so lucrative that conservative estimates rank it only behind Exxon, the nation's largest corporation, in profits of some $80 billion a year (W. F. Smith, 1982). The New York City special narcotics prosecutor calculated the drug trade in New York City alone to be a $45-billion-a-year business that retains 10,000 full-time and between 100,000 and 300,000 part-time employees. These figures rank illegal drug distribution only behind the retail and manufacturing industry as New York City's biggest employer (Goode, 1984, p. 51).

Legal drugs are also big business. The total retail amount spent yearly on alcoholic beverages in the United States has remained fairly constant at around the 1989 rate of $67 billion or about $270 per person (U.S. Department of Commerce, 1991). Considering these figures, it is not too difficult to understand why economic motivation was one of the forces that helped repeal prohibition. An assessment of how bad the problem is gets lost in the exponential numbers that are attached to alcohol use. It is estimated that somewhere between one-half to two-thirds of the population use alcohol regularly, and 10% of those may be classified as alcoholic (Goode, 1984; U.S. Department of Commerce, 1991). Per-capita consumption of all intoxicating beverages has hovered at the 38-gallon mark for the last ten years (U.S. Department of Commerce, 1986; 1991). What makes this statistic astounding is that one-third of the population drinks 95% of the output (Olson & Gerstein, 1985, p. 13).

Drug abuse is especially important in the social context of what various special interest groups think should be done about it. Big business, law enforcement, the judiciary, religious organizations, human services providers of all types, the medical establishment, legislatures, journalists, educators, family members of alcoholics, and survivors of victims of drunk drivers—all have a vested interest in either providing, controlling, or eradicating intoxicants. Whereas every one of these principals may agree that abuse is a problem, reaching a unified decision on how to handle the problem is about as likely as winning the grand prize in the state lottery.

Sociocultural Determinants

Social and cultural attitudes have been widely reported to be major determinants of both drug-use patterns and how different professions view the problem of addiction (Doweiko, 1990, pp. 143–162). The society and the cultural background of an individual seem to have a great deal to do with what kinds of pharmacological and extrapharmacological effects will occur with use of addictive substances. Taking alcohol as an example, at a 0.40% blood alcohol content (BAC) most people pass out, and that is generally construed to be the LD-50 level—the level of intoxication at which about half of the people will die from an overdose (Goode, 1984, p. 62). Physiological outcomes are much the same for everyone having that BAC. However, psychological outcomes are very different as the user progresses to a 0.40% BAC level. Whereas one person with a BAC of 0.10% may want to

fight a whole motorcycle gang, another may be the caricature of the garru-
lous, happy drunk, and another may sit stone-faced and bother no one.

It is a chemical fallacy that a specific dose of drug Z will invariably
cause effect A in a user. What does seem to be true is that set and setting
have a great effect on the behavior of the drug user. *Set* can be defined as the
mental and emotional state of the user, including expectations, intelligence,
personality, feelings, and so on. *Setting* refers to the social and physical
environment of the user at the time of use. It can be defined as immediate
surroundings, such as a living room as opposed to a bar, or, in a broader
context, can be the legal and religious perspective of the country (Goode,
1984, p. 35).

Set and setting define which situations are appropriate for drug use and
which are not. Nowhere is this clearer than in the fallacious belief that alcohol automatically releases inhibitions. In a comprehensive study of a number of tribes who have very different beliefs about what is appropriate and
inappropriate behavior, MacAndrew and Edgerton (1969) found that people would not automatically lose their inhibitions and violate norms due to
ingestion of alcohol unless the particular culture permitted it. Further,
when a member of one culture was placed in a different cultural setting, that
person might act in extraordinary ways when drinking that were very different from his own societal norms (Heath, 1985, p. 470).

A Unified View of Chemical Dependency

Much remains to be discovered about the crisis of addiction. But according
to Doweiko (1990), many researchers in the medical and mental health
fields recognize that either directly or indirectly, complications involving
chemical dependency are the most common problem presented for treatment. Even though the patient's treatment may be initiated because of an
injury in an automobile accident, a perforated ulcer, a dysfunctional marriage, or a host of other stated physical or emotional causes, the underlying
disease of addiction occurs more often than any other etiology. The problem is enormously complicated by the fact that among all these presenting
problems, medical and mental health professionals frequently do not recognize, diagnose, or report that chemical addiction is connected to the presenting malady. Doweiko additionally states that medical and mental
health professionals rarely receive adequate training to recognize and deal
with the widespread effects of chemical dependency (pp. 5–6).

Researchers and practitioners who are knowledgeable about the issues
have recently tended to assert that addictive behaviors spring from a common disease core. Robertson (1988) has suggested that compulsive use of
all chemicals springs from a single addictive core. Doweiko (1990) reports
that mental health professionals now tend to move away from classifying
alcoholism as separate from other addictions. Rather, he implies that when
people who are dependent on any substance easily switch addictive
chemicals, a single disease of addiction probably underlies all their compul-

sive behaviors, and these behaviors have a common neurochemical foundation (p. 2).

Alcohol: Number One

We debated long and hard over which drug to choose in order to demonstrate crisis intervention procedures with drug abusers. The choice of potential abusive agents available today is much like a cafeteria menu. In attempting to compose a generic drug abuser for this chapter, we were tempted to select one of the more glamorous drugs. Cocaine addiction was high on the list because of the large amount of publicity it has received, its fast addiction time, potentially destructive physical and psychological outcomes, its tremendous cost, vigorous attempts by law enforcement to stop it, and its lethality (there are few old cocaine addicts because they just do not live that long). However, after much discussion, we believe that alcohol is still the best drug to illustrate what happens in the crisis of addiction. There are several reasons for our choice.

1. *Duration.* Alcohol has a clear history in the United States, both in its use and in attempts to contain it. Starting with the temperance movement in the 19th century, followed by the founding of Alcoholics Anonymous (AA) in the 1930s and the birth of the National Institute of Alcohol Abuse and Alcoholism (NIAAA) in 1971 to coordinate the federal government's attempt to provide research, public education, and treatment (Costello, 1982, p. 1197), alcohol continues to play a great role in how our society attempts to deal with drug abuse.

2. *Legality.* There are only limited conditions under which one can go to jail for possession. Even for people caught under those conditions, the social acceptability of alcohol plays an important part in determining punishment.

3. *Widespread use.* Given that alcohol is legal, figures support the contention that it continues to be the most abused drug. Beasley (1987) reported that between 10 and 15 million people in the United States are alcoholics, and that another 10 million are "on the cusp of alcoholism" (p. 21). An additional 30 to 40 million Americans were reported by the American Psychiatric Association (1985) to be indirectly affected by alcoholism through family ties to either an alcoholic or a victim of an alcoholic. Even though there are an estimated 500,000 known heroin addicts (Peluso & Peluso, 1988; Siegel, 1989) and perhaps 2 million Americans who are dependent on cocaine (Peluso & Peluso, 1988), alcohol remains the most prevalent drug used by addicts. According to Franklin (1987), an astounding 85% of all drug addiction is to alcohol.

4. *Financial cost.* Because of time lost from the job, splitting of families, expenditures on the substance, hospital care, education, law enforcement, and judicial and correctional expenditures, the indirect financial cost of alcoholism may be greater than that of any other public health issue

(Costello, 1982, p. 1197). Nace (1987) reported that as early as 1983, alcoholism *alone* cost Americans more than $116 *billion* annually in direct medical costs and indirect losses such as reduced work productivity.

5. *Psychological cost.* If one believes only a part of the literature on codependency, adult children of alcoholics, and family systems, the psychological trauma that afflicts members of an alcoholic's family is appalling. Family members left in the wake of an alcoholic's slide into chronic addiction represent a tremendous pool of maladaptive psychological dynamics and coping mechanisms that reach beyond the family into the total fabric of society (Ames, 1985). Olsen (1987) reported that 38 million children have been adversely affected by their alcoholic parents, and the American Psychiatric Association (1985) estimated that 3 million children and adolescents were addicted to alcohol. Data uncovered by Newcomb and Bentler (1989) indicated that by early adolescence, 56% of teenagers have used alcohol at least once and that by their senior year that figure had grown to 92%.

6. *Physical cost.* Although physical ramifications of continued alcohol abuse may not be nearly as sudden and shocking as those of overdoses of "crack," PCP, heroin, cocaine, or amphetamines, continued and chronic abuse of alcohol leads to a wide variety of physical health problems that include but are not limited to delirium tremens, liver and pancreatic disease, Korsakoff's syndrome, reproductive and sexual dysfunction, poor fetal development, endocrine disturbances, gastrointestinal irritation, respiratory failure, heart disease, reduced immunity, cancer, and malnutrition (Pattison & Kaufman, 1982a).

In absolute terms, alcohol leads the list as an agent in acute physical problems associated with drug overdose. Emergency room reports of the early 1980s indicated that 19% of emergency admissions were due to use of alcohol alone or in combination with other drugs, and fatal overdoses of alcohol accounted for 17% of emergency room deaths related to drug abuse (Drug Abuse Warning Network, 1983). These data *do not* include chronic conditions, accidents, or assaults related to alcohol abuse. According to Beasley (1987), the late 1980s saw no improvement in the level of emergency treatments attributable to alcohol abuse. Beasley also observed that the medical treatment of alcohol and drug addictions, combined with the various psychiatric consequences of these addictive disorders, accounted for some 40% of all hospital usage in the United States in the late 1980s. As of 1989, there were 7,642 profit and nonprofit drug treatment facilities in the United States (U.S. Department of Commerce, 1991).

Alcoholism also has severe and profound effects on the unborn. While much publicity is given to the horror of "crack" babies who are born going through withdrawal, fetal alcohol syndrome causes a lifetime of problems for children whose mothers drank heavily during pregnancy. Severe birth defects that range from mental retardation to disfigurement and organ defects are hallmarks of the syndrome. One of the highest incidences of fetal alcohol syndrome is among Native Americans: an average of 2.2 children are affected per 1000 live births, and in one area of Alaska the rate was 250 per 1000 live births (Backover, 1991).

7. *Links to crime.* The high cost of illegal recreational drug use inextricably links these drugs to crime involving theft. Whereas these drugs are notoriously tied to agitated and violent behavior (particularly in those who are coming off depressants and need another fix or are pumped up on stimulants), alcohol is still a major contributor to violent behavior that is responsible for many assaults and murders (MacDonald, 1961; Pernanen, 1976; Shupe, 1953). Further, and contrary to popular opinion, property crime offenders also have high percentages of alcohol use (Collins, 1980; Shupe, 1953).

8. *Implication in accidents.* About half of all highway deaths in the United States and Canada are alcohol-related (Canadian Commission of Inquiry into the Nonmedical Use of Drugs, 1973, pp. 393–395; National Commission on Marijuana and Drug Abuse, 1973, pp. 28–32). Highway deaths involving alcohol have been responsible for the loss of more American lives than all those lost in all the wars in which the United States has fought (Goode, 1984, p. 60). In single-car accidents involving fatalities, 70% of male and 40% of female drivers had BACs of 0.10% or higher (Ray, 1983). Haberman and Baden (1974) found that one-third of victims of falls and pedestrian fatalities had BACs of 0.10% or higher. Victims of drowning (41%), fire (58%), stabbing (68%), and shootings (40%) all had BAC levels of 0.10% (Goode, 1984, p. 61).

9. *Reality that alcohol is a drug.* There is no biochemical aspect of alcohol use that is different from what most would consider drug use. Doweiko (1990) calls alcohol a drug that produces differential *physical* and *behavioral* tolerances between chronic and occasional drinkers (p. 23). An important distinction between alcohol and other drugs is the arbitrary view of society, which does not define people who drink as drug users (Goode, 1984, pp. 5, 55). Doweiko (1990) reported that all chemical dependency is both underrecognized and underreported, particularly the abuse of alcohol (pp. 5–6).

10. *Use in combination with other drugs.* The addiction picture in the United States is changing. Very few "pure alcoholics" exist (Doweiko, 1990, pp. 10–13). Maxwell (1986) reported that most persons who become addicted use a variety of other drugs in addition to alcohol (p. 6).

11. *Embroilment in controversy.* Controversy surrounds the issues of both the etiology of alcoholism and its treatment. One of the most significant issues about alcoholism is defining exactly what it is. Is it clearly a disease, or is it "dis-ease" with one's ability to cope? Treatment issues spin off this controversy and pit AA and recovering alcoholics against professionals in the field of medicine, psychology, sociology, and anthropology. Alcoholism is one of the few health problems about which beliefs are so embedded in the popular health culture and so strongly held that they influence both patients and practitioners. As a result, a number of models have developed to explain its existence.

Models of Addiction

Very few programs for treatment of chemical dependency adhere to any one model of addiction; most use a compilation of many models. Currently there is no single, clear-cut model or treatment approach based on theory or research that holds sway over another. The debate over the efficacy of these models continues and serves to define competing schools of thought rather than facilitating agreement among proponents. The best that can be said about this current state of affairs is that the field of chemical-dependency treatment is in a preparadigmatic period: one in which all the facts that could possibly pertain are likely to seem equally relevant (Shaffer, 1986). It is our position that each one of the models has worthwhile components. Doweiko (1990) uses the term *final common pathway* to advise that each of the theories of drug addiction contains an element of truth and efficacy (pp. 160–161). We take an eclectic approach and hold that at present *no one model is better and each has utility in treatment.* Following is a brief summary of each of the major models.

Disease model. In the disease model of addiction, drug use is seen as an aberrant condition afflicting otherwise healthy people, and exposure to the drug is seen as leading to physiological addiction. Through a sequence of internal events, alcoholics lose control of their drinking behavior (Jellinek, 1960). With increased use, more and more alcohol is needed to meet physiological needs. When use ceases or is reduced, the drug reaches too low a level for the tolerance that has been created, the person goes into withdrawal, and physiological craving leads to continued use (Oetting & Beauvais, 1986). Jellinek (1946, 1952) postulated that certain types of alcohol users could be classified as ill and were suffering from a progressive disease that could be divided into phases. The World Health Organization's (1952) and the American Medical Association's (1956) acceptance of a diagnostic framework for alcohol abuse as a disease has lent much credibility to the disease model.

Genetic predisposition model. The genetic model proposes an inherited and transmitted predisposition to become a substance abuser (Cadoret & Gaith, 1978; Cotton, 1979; Goodwin, 1979; Schuckit & Rayses, 1979; Vaillant, 1983; Vaillant & Milofsky, 1982). Research studies found that adopted children of an alcoholic parent, monozygotic twins of an alcoholic parent, and children from multiproblem families with an alcoholic parent were four to five times as likely to become alcoholics as children from comparable groups who had no alcoholic parents.

Gateway model. The gateway model proposes an orderly progression from one drug to another and particularly applies to young people as they move into heavier and heavier drug use (Dupont, 1984; Hamburg, Kraemer, & Jahnke, 1975). Only after trying beer will the person move to whiskey, then to marijuana and pills, and finally to PCP, cocaine, and heroin (Oetting & Beauvais, 1986).

Prescriptive model. The prescriptive model suggests that alcoholism begins in self-prescription and physician prescription of alcohol and other drugs as tranquilizing agents to relieve acute or chronic pain symptoms (Blume, 1973; Pattison & Kaufman, 1982b, p. 11). Cases fitting the prescriptive model are rather rare.

Psychoanalytic model. This model posits that certain pathological personality traits established early in childhood predispose the individual to alcoholism (Barry, 1974; Zwerling, 1959). Spotts and Shontz (1980) traced the obsession with a particular drug to specific flaws in early development and demonstrated how the action of that drug meshed with the resulting personality.

Behavioral learning model. Drinking is caused and maintained by the association of alcohol intake with positive rewarding experiences, according to the behavioral learning model. Habituation is progressively strengthened by repetitive use of alcohol to combat anxiety and alleviate stress (Pattison & Kaufman, 1982b, p. 12).

Sociocultural models. Sociocultural models examine factors external to the individual. The environment is seen as a chief contributing factor and is inclusive of demographic and ethnographic variables such as race, age, socioeconomic status, employment, education, social norms, religion, crime rates, belief systems, consumption rates, drinking behavior, and so on. All of these may be considered as possible determinants of alcoholism. In its emphasis on environmental factors, this approach empirically challenges the disease model (Heath, 1978; Lukoff, 1980).

Lifestyle model. In the view of this model, the rewards of living in an altered state of consciousness outweigh all other costs of a destructive, drug-dependent lifestyle. For the people described by the lifestyle model, a drug-free existence is no existence at all (Pattison & Kaufman, 1982b, p. 12).

Peer-cluster model. This model links drug use to small groups of people, including pairs such as best friends or boyfriend-girlfriend, who share beliefs, attitudes, values, and a rationale for drug use. Drug use plays an important role in group membership and identification (Oetting & Beauvais, 1986).

Psychosocial model. The psychosocial model proposes that a constellation of factors involving an individual's personality, environment, and behavior are interrelated and organized so as to develop a dynamic state designated as *problem-behavior proneness.* These variables define both the personal problems and the social environments that may underlie involvement with drugs—the greater the level of drug use, the greater the level of deviance (Jessor, Chase, & Donovan, 1980; Jessor & Jessor, 1977).

AA and the Model Controversy

The major division of thought about models of alcoholism segregates the disease model from all the other models, which propose chemical dependency as something other than biologically based. At the center of this controversy have been the treatment principles of AA, therapist credentials, research funding, and third-party payments by health insurance companies.

AA.   AA bases its approach to alcoholism on the disease model. One of the abiding principles of AA has been the insistence that there is a permanent change in the alcoholic's biochemistry and that willpower and insight as the essential forces for change are useless. The disease model communicates hope and implies that only one part of the alcoholic is disabled. It is psychologically efficacious because it reduces the guilt, confusion, and self-doubt about moral worth and lack of willpower that might otherwise plague the alcoholic (Stuckey & Harrison, 1982, p. 871).

For AA, the disease basis of alcoholism may be compared with diabetes. Certainly diabetes is a permanent condition, but by watching their diet, diabetics can contain their level of blood sugar within normal limits. The analogy is clear that if the alcoholic remains abstinent, then his or her body will not be affected. Just as there is no such thing as an ex-diabetic, there is also no such thing as an ex-alcoholic. Thus, in the disease concept, the alcoholic is always "recovering" (Bissell, 1982, p. 811). This concept has been systematized in AA's 12-step program to recovery (Stuckey & Harrison, 1982, p. 866).

Model's shortcomings.   Although AA has been highly effective, the disease model of alcoholism on which it is based is open to question. Alcoholism as a disease or an illness is not well defined in the health professions (Chrisman, 1985, p. 15), and 40 years after Jellinek's first proposal that specific types of alcoholism fit a disease model, what that disease is remains vague and uncertain (Ames, 1985, p. 24). A true disease model must also reject the influence of situational factors on alcohol consumption (Peele, 1986), and there is a growing body of knowledge questioning the appropriateness of a disease model, which would imply orderly progression of symptoms, concepts of physiologically based craving, loss of control, and the choice of abstinence as the only acceptable goal of treatment (Marlatt & Donovan, 1982, p. 560). Finally, persons who abstain from drinking for a number of years are no less likely to relapse into alcoholism than persons who have been chemically dependent and then drink moderately for a number of years. It would seem that both abstinence and nonproblem drinking can be maintained over long periods of time, and neither precludes the possibility of relapse (Sobell & Sobell, 1978, pp. 19–20).

Credentials.   The fact remains that the AA approach works for many, many recovering alcoholics. One key to its success may be that it consists of recovering alcoholics helping recovering alcoholics. Many recovering addicts view with suspicion therapists who have not suffered from alcoholism. While this parochial thinking is akin to saying that to be effective, medical doctors must suffer from the diseases they treat, it's true that many traditionally trained therapists from universities and medical schools have had little coursework or practical experience in addictions and automatically debunk AA treatment approaches and philosophy with little basis other than, "It's not scientific!" Historically, traditional techniques that professionals have used in addiction treatment have had a dismal record of enabling patients to beat addiction in comparison to AA and its participants. And many "professional" therapists have been accused of being in denial themselves in regard to their own codependent behaviors and inability to acknowledge they also may have addictive personalities and behaviors. Their rationalization that it's the client's resistance and not the treatment approach or therapist effectiveness that is the problem leaves many clients, particularly those who have suffered relapses, not overly impressed by therapeutic credentials (Schaef, 1986, pp. 7–9).

One reason for the number of conflicting views of what alcoholism is and how to treat it may have to do with competition for funding. Since the advent of the NIAAA and the provision of money for research, education, and treatment, the field of drug abuse treatment has grown exponentially. Because AA had been the principal actor until the NIAAA arrived on the scene, it would prove little for others to attempt entrance into the abuse field singing the same theoretical song and playing the same treatment tune as AA. Therefore, to obtain recognition, other theoreticians proposed alternate approaches to the disease model. No research evidence exists to support this cynical view; nevertheless, our subjective opinion, based on numerous dialogues with experts in the field, is that there is some truth to this controversial viewpoint.

A related point about the controversy over models is that until the time that treatment of substance abuse became a paying proposition, few professionals cared to be bothered with it. The field was left largely to the volunteer efforts of AA. Those individuals within AA had seen all too clearly the ineptitude with which professionals had attempted to handle them or dismissed their abuse problem outright. However, with the advent of payments from insurance companies to health care providers for the treatment of drug addiction, hospitals and health care professionals became highly interested in the problem, as evidenced by a dramatic increase in the number of drug dependence treatment units throughout the country. We find it intriguing that most "cures" in such units take 28 days, the exact time span covered by many insurance programs. As a result, it is not surprising that when professionals entered the field they and their theories were greeted with suspicion and hostility by AA (Rosenberg, 1982, pp. 802–809).

Given this controversy, it is little wonder that clinicians do not endorse the findings of researchers, and this situation further impedes efforts at teaching and training in addiction fields (Shaffer, 1986). This is a sad state of affairs. We would hope that movement toward rapprochement, which now appears to be under way between more moderate elements in the field, will continue and will result in a systematic, eclectic paradigm of theory and treatment that uses the best of all models and discards the worst. It is from this complex, conflicted, commingled, and convoluted perspective that we present this chapter.

Definitions

Many definitions are coined in an attempt to adequately describe those who get into trouble with drugs. To facilitate the reading of this chapter, we list the following commonly used terms in alphabetical order.

Abuse. The chronic, recurrent misuse of chemicals (Lawson, Ellis, & Rivers, 1984, p. 37). Abuse occurs when there is a pathological use of the substance and a minimal duration of disturbance of at least one month. *Pathological use* may be variously defined as referring to intoxication throughout the day, inability to cut down or stop use, restriction of use to certain times of the day, need for the drug to enable daily functioning, and physical complications arising from intoxication. The duration requirement is that signs of disturbance must occur throughout the month and sufficiently frequently for a pattern of pathological use to become apparent (American Psychiatric Association, 1987, pp. 165–185).

Addiction. A cellular change that occurs with the increased use of most depressant drugs. The primary clinical features are the development of tolerance and the development of withdrawal symptoms upon the removal of the drug (Lawson, Ellis, & Rivers, 1984, p. 37).

Alcoholism. A highly complex condition characterized by preoccupation with alcohol and loss of control over its consumption so that intoxication results if drinking is begun; by chronicity; by progression; and by a tendency to relapse. It is associated with physical disability and impaired emotional, occupational, and/or social adjustment as a result of persistent use (Shearer, 1968, p. 6).

Chemical dependent. Any person who has a dependence on drugs such that the substance governs his or her life to the extent that it severely impairs the ability to function psychologically and/or physically (Lawson et al., 1984, p. 37). Currently the "in" term for a person receiving treatment for a drug problem.

Codependent. Any significant person in the chemical dependent's life, such as spouse, parent, lover, or child, who is enmeshed in the chemical dependency (Maxwell, 1986, p. 7) and is characterized by extreme preoccupation with and dependence (emotional, social, and sometimes physical) on a person or object. Eventually this dependence on another person becomes a pathological condition that affects the codependent in all other relationships (Wegscheider-Cruse, 1985, p. 2).

Contradependent. Any significant person in the chemical dependent's life, most particularly a child, who acts to prevent being emotionally hurt by defensiveness, self-sufficiency, isolation, and acting out (Hogg & Frank, 1992).

Dependence. Physical or psychological reliance on someone or something. Physical dependence is the inevitable result of the pharmacological action of some drugs, given sufficient time and dosage quantity. Psychological dependence occurs in users who have a strong urge to alter their state of consciousness through the use of a chemical. This mental state may be the only factor involved, even in cases of the most intense craving and perpetuation of compulsive abuse. These two types of dependence may occur independently or in combination with one another (Lawson et al., 1984, p. 37).

Drug. A psychoactive substance that has a direct and significant impact on the processes of the mind with respect to thinking, feeling, and acting. The term *drug* is a cultural artifact and a social fabrication because it denotes something that has been arbitrarily defined by certain segments of society as a drug (Goode, 1984, p. 15).

Enabler. A codependent who, by first rejecting and then tolerating the chemical dependency, furthers its progression in the dependent. Maintenance of the relationship is more important than the problem of chemical dependency (Maxwell, 1986, p. 103).

Habituation. The degree to which one is accustomed to taking a certain drug. A habituated user can and will take more of a drug than a first-time experimenter (Goode, 1984, p. 33). Defined in regard to an addictive/dependent state, it is imprecise and ambiguous (Pattison & Kaufman, 1982b, p. 9).

Misuse. Use of a chemical with some adverse physical, psychological, social, or legal consequence (Lawson et al., 1984, p. 37).

Use. The intake of a chemical substance into the body with the goal of somehow altering one's state of consciousness (Lawson et al., 1984, p. 37).

These definitions do not nearly convey the power that chemical dependence holds over people. The comments of two chemical dependents we know paint a striking picture of what being addicted and chemically dependent really means.

Federal correctional incarcerate (alcohol and cocaine addict): Think of the best sex you ever had. Man! Think how great that feeling was. I mean the best and greatest. Well, that ain't nothin' compared to shovin' that spike in your arm and getting that first rush. That's why I do it.

University professor (recovering alcoholic): When you get stressed out, there may be a number of things you do to get over it. You may go out and jog, pray, meditate, have a fight with your wife, chop wood, and so on. The problem with that is the payoff is variable. It may or may not work. When I get stressed out I drink. My way works *all* the time and *every* time. It's invariable. I know what will happen before I do it. It is absolutely dependable in taking the pain away. Beat that!

DYNAMICS OF ADDICTION

Defense Mechanisms

Drug abusers offer examples of all of the defense mechanisms one might find in a text on abnormal psychology. Gordon, a recovering alcoholic we will follow throughout the rest of this chapter, is a composite, displaying these maladaptive defense mechanisms.

Denial. Alcoholism is often called the "disease of denial" (Lawson et al., 1984, p. 36). Denial is the emotional refusal to acknowledge a person, situation, condition, or event the way it actually is (Perez, 1985, p. 5). Addicts are deniers par excellence of the reality of their situation.

Gordon: Real men handle their problems. I'll handle mine. I've had a lot of problems lately. Sure I like a drink. Do a lot of business that way. Most of my friends drink. I get loaded every once in a while, but so would you if you had the pressures I do right now.

Displacement. Alcoholics find many targets on which to unload their problems. Displacement is the venting of hostility on a person or object, neither of whom deserves it (Perez, 1985, p. 6).

Gordon: Yell at my wife? You betcha. Always griping at me for not being at home. Hey! I provided a great living, then when I really needed her support because of the pressure at work, she'd just whine more.

Fantasy. Alcoholics use fantasy to escape from a variety of threatening circumstances and emotions. They escape boredom with the job, anxiety in coping with relationships, and frustration over career progress by retreating to a drug-induced euphoria. That euphoric state is far more rewarding than the real world and one to which the alcoholic feels compelled to return again and again (Perez, 1985, p. 6).

Gordon: Having a drink takes the edge off. I mean, you can just relax and put it out of your mind for a while—the job, the old lady, everything. I can really get it together and plan the next big project.

Projection. Alcoholics often attribute motives within themselves to significant others. Sensitivity, suspiciousness, and hostility toward others are outward manifestations of the distancing, estrangement, and lack of communication that characterize the alcoholic (Perez, 1985, p. 6).

Gordon: Amy never did love me. Oh, she loved the house, the club, and the private schools for the kids, and all that. I finally figured that out and told her that straight to her face!

Rationalization. Alcoholics make all kinds of excuses to support their addiction and their felt inadequacies of acting and behaving (Perez, 1985, p. 6).

Gordon: By God! I had severe back problems from doing the engineering on that sorting machine. Hell! Even the doctor gave me a prescription for the pain. That machine made this company. It had to get finished. What's wrong with taking a couple of pops at midnight? It made my back quit aching. I got it done.

Intellectualization. Alcoholics speak in generalizations or theoretical terms in an impersonal manner and thereby remove themselves from hurtful feelings (Maxwell, 1986, p. 65).

Gordon: They say I drink too much. Well, I've done some extensive reading on the subject and I certainly don't fit the category of a drunken bum. What do they know, anyway? They're not doctors.

Minimizing. Alcoholics play down the seriousness of the situation (Maxwell, 1986, p. 64).

Gordon: This is just temporary. I got a little out of line. No problem. I'll just have to watch things a little closer.

Reaction formation. Reaction formation occurs as a defense against perceived threat and is one of the most harmful defense mechanisms because it distances dependents from their true feelings. Addicts constantly fear rejection and go out of their way to find it—even if it is not there (Perez, 1985, p. 11).

Gordon: Those kids of mine, too. The little ingrates. Gave them everything. Lisa just stares at me. Mark even said I didn't love him because I missed a lousy soccer game. He sure didn't miss his personal computer I got him. No time for the old man 'cause he was too busy himself. That kid never loved me. Always took up for his mom.

Regression. Alcoholics are often immature and narcissistic, with resulting behavior similar to that of emotional prepubescence. The behavior is intended to manipulate, control, and get one's way. Temper tantrums, sulking, and pouting are all common forms of regression (Perez, 1985, p. 6).

Gordon: There was no use talking to her, so I just clammed up. Wouldn't support me in the business. Me apologize? She's the one who ought to apologize! I'm not saying one word to her until she does.

Repression. Alcoholics deal with threatening and hurtful events by burying them in unconscious memory (Perez, 1985, p. 7). When sober, alcoholics repress the dependency needs and angry feelings that accompany them, and they remember nothing of the personality and behavior changes that occur when they are intoxicated (Zimberg, 1982, p. 1002).

Gordon: Warnings about my job performance? No way! They just dropped it on me one day. Things were fine up to that point! The same with the family. No warning! No nothing! They just up and leave. I never touched a hair on their head!

These defense mechanisms are far different from those of the average neurotic. They may be extremely intrusive into others' lives: grossly inconvenient, inexcusable, objectionable, and socially undesirable. The chemical dependent's defenses are sometimes primitive and regressive. They may personify the alcoholic as a self-centered and dependent person. Unlike the neurotic, some alcoholics suffer no discomfort and may not be motivated to change. The two major components of a sociopathic personality—having no conscience and being excessively egocentric—can dominate in the chemical dependent (Perez, 1985, p. 9). Arrogance, grandiosity, and omnipotence at the expense of others are the kinds of personality traits that sometimes predominate in alcoholics (Goodwin, Crane, & Guze, 1971; Guze, Goodwin, & Crane, 1969; Guze, Tuason, Galfield, Stewart, & Picken, 1962; Maxwell, 1986, pp. 64–70) and there is indication of these traits in prealcoholics (Loper, Kammeier, & Hoffman, 1973).

Also enmeshed in the hostile and angry feelings of the alcoholic is depression (Hoffman, 1970; Kristianson, 1970; Speigel, Hadley, & Hadley, 1970). Alcoholics perceive that they are beset by an uncaring world. When floods of guilt come pouring through the walls of drug abusers' defenses, they are overwhelmed by an inability to take any kind of reasonable control over their lives and undo the damage they have done to themselves and significant others. The cyclical battering alcoholics take between having no conscience and having an overpowering one is draining and leaves little psychic energy for anything but depression when they start sobering up.

In a worst-case scenario, the defense mechanisms of most chemical dependents serve one goal and one goal only: to support, nurture, and help feed the one god in the addict's life, the drug. Nothing else matters. The drug becomes an ultimate and demanding taskmaster. No service is given to anything else until its needs are fulfilled. Feeble attempts to control it are marked by guilt and remorse, but those feelings are niggardly in comparison with the urge to get "fixed" (Stuckey & Harrison, 1982, p. 868).

Gordon: I can't understand how things got this way. We used to have a great family. Yeah! I hate thinking about it. When I get to thinking about it, I feel rotten. Well, you can't function on the job with that kind of cloud hanging over you, so I'd have a drink and I'd feel better. Four or five and you can forget it all. But what else was I to do under all that?

Enabling and Codependency

When a family is enmeshed in addiction, the crisis is compounded, and a strange phenomenon occurs. In an attempt to keep the family in equilibrium, members will first reject and then begin to tolerate the addict. To keep the family in homeostasis, various members unconsciously assume roles that not only keep the system on an even keel but also enable the addict to fall further into the addiction (Ford, 1987, pp. 16–17; Perez, 1985, p. 19).

The marital relationship becomes highly competitive, with the alcoholic's dependency needs counterbalanced by the spouse. Being forceful, blunt, active, and domineering are ways that the spouse seeks to retake control of the situation. However, neither alcoholic nor spouse gains dominance, and this continuous warfare results in each blaming the other for the family's problems (Kaufman & Pattison, 1982a, p. 667). By attempting to maintain the system, even though it is extremely pathological, family members become codependents. They also manifest many of the *maladaptive* and *unconscious* defense mechanisms that their addicted counterparts have. We have used the responses of Amy, Gordon's wife, to illustrate these defenses, which immobilize the family system.

Suppression. Codependents may suppress the problems the addict brings to the family by maintaining a "stiff upper lip" and not allowing their emotions to surface (Maxwell, 1986, pp. 78–79). This is a defense of quiet desperation and is based on the hope that some miraculous change will occur in the dependent.

Amy: I made a commitment when I got married that it was for keeps. He was probably an alcoholic when we got married, but a contract is a contract. In sickness and health and all that.

Disassociation. For those who disassociate themselves from the problem and repress it, their perception of events is drastically altered by putting the problem aside. Disassociation means distancing the problem emotionally and sometimes geographically (Maxwell, 1986, p. 80).

Amy: When it got really bad I'd make sure the kids were busy doing something and then I'd throw myself into the club work. That kept my mind off his problem. The best two weeks of my life every year would be going back home to my parents. I'd take the kids and we could get away.

Repression. Repression of events takes disassociation a step further. By burying hurtful events in unconscious memory, codependents avoid having to grapple with the terrible feelings that accompany those events (Maxwell, 1986, p. 82).

Amy: I mean he's horrible all the time when he's bombed, but what he actually says I'm not real sure. He's real nasty, but I can't quite put my finger on what he actually does.

Escape to therapy. Seeking therapeutic assistance may be another form of escape for codependents. A lot of catharsis may occur in therapy, but little real change is considered because it would also mean that the codependents would have to face reality and make some serious changes away from the maladaptive coping patterns that they have established (Maxwell, 1986, p. 82).

Amy: If somehow he could just change. I don't know, maybe you could talk him into coming here. I know that I at least get a little peace of mind from coming to these sessions.

Intellectualization. Codependents use intellectualization to keep themselves distanced from the hurtful affect. In attempting to keep the system in balance, they are obsessive-compulsive in planning and attending to details. They spend a great deal of time thinking about and attending to the problem without ever feeling much about it. By compulsively paying attention to the many details of these events, intellectualizers order their outward world but do nothing about their inner turmoil (Maxwell, 1986, pp. 83–84).

Amy: It's exhausting, but I've figured out when he's really going on a bender. So I plan activities down to the last detail to keep everybody busy and out of his way. The parties are the worst because I've got this whole ritual laid out so that he won't get angry. It really takes some planning to keep things in balance then. By putting together a stepwise plan I can keep it down to a dull roar.

Displacement. By displacement, a codependent moves feelings off the focal point of the problem, the addict's behavior, and moves it to less frightening and hurtful subject matter (Maxwell, 1986, p. 86).

Amy: I've been reading about this new vitamin therapy, and I'm really concerned Gordon's going to get sick because he's so run down. I've been giving him all kinds of good information on this and even got him an appointment with this M.D. who practices holistic medicine.

Reaction formation. As the alcoholic becomes more and more irresponsible, a typical reaction for the codependent is to become more and more responsible. In actuality, this assumed responsibility for the family is focused directly on the alcoholic. The only safe way for the codependent to stay in the relationship is to give in and submerge the anger he or she feels. Reaction formation is ideally suited to this situation because alcoholics, no matter how much they express their independence, are among the neediest people in the world. Taking over for the alcoholic, codependents "save" the marriage and the family by behaving in ways exactly opposite to their internal feelings about the situation. Instead of expressing their true feelings toward the addict's behavior, the codependents appear to accept it (Maxwell, 1986, pp. 88–90).

Amy: The family has to keep going. That's why I'd take those plans for him when he couldn't make the plane and call in sick for him. I know he said some terrible things to me and the kids, but he really didn't mean them. He wouldn't act that way when he was sober.

By denying their own needs in reaction formation, codependents forestall indefinitely their ability to change the situation. This defense overextends the codependent in every conceivable way and can lead to physical or emotional breakdown. In the latter stages of alcoholism, codependents may resort to the very immature defenses of passive aggression and hypochondriasis (Maxwell, 1986, pp. 88–90).

Passive aggression. By being late, forgetting, starting arguments and then leaving, overspending, and the implied threat of suicide the codependent keeps everyone in a state of uproar (Maxwell, 1986, pp. 91–94).

Amy: I don't know what's come over me. I've watched the money so carefully over the years. Gordon's still getting a paycheck, but I just can't seem to get bills paid and we're getting duns from creditors.

Hypochondriasis. The defense of hypochondriasis converts anger into physical complaints. This is an extremely effective punishment of others because no matter how much consolation they receive, codependents obtain attention by this defense mechanism, and they don't give it up without a struggle (Maxwell, 1986, pp. 94–95).

Amy: [*Weeping.*] I'm sorry for breaking down like this. It's just with everything else I keep getting these terrible migraines. They knock me flat for a day at a time, and then I get behind and can't handle all the other stuff and wind up bawling.

The typical response to the chemically dependent person is first to reject and then to tolerate the objectionable behavior. This marks a person as an enabler (Maxwell, 1986, p. 103). In the early phases of enabling there is denial and rationalization that the behavior will improve, and the enabler takes responsibility and assumes guilt for the alcoholic. In the middle phases the enabler becomes hostile, disgusted, and pitying and becomes preoccupied with protecting and shielding the alcoholic. In advanced phases, the enabler's feelings of extreme hostility, withdrawal, and suspicion become generalized to the total environment. In the final phases, responsibility for and quarreling with the alcoholic become all encompassing. Outside interests and maintenance of self are disregarded in all-consuming attempts to keep the system and the alcoholic stabilized (Kaufman & Pattison, 1982b, pp. 1022–1024).

Each of these phases is for naught. Chemically dependent persons listen to nothing. They respect only action, and only when that action threatens to interrupt their dependency in some way. Only when enablers decide to stop rescuing dependents and let them start to suffer the natural consequences of their actions will there by any change in the dependents' behavior (Stuckey & Harrison, 1982, p. 870).

Children in Alcoholic Families

Children raised in homes where open communication is practiced and consistency of lifestyles is the norm usually have the ability to adopt a variety of roles dependent on the situation. Children growing up in alcoholic homes seldom learn the combinations of roles that mold healthy personalities. They become locked into roles based on their perception of what they need to do to survive and bring some stability to their lives in a chaotic family (Black, 1981, p. 14). The following generic roles of children who live in alcoholic families have been profiled by Black (1981) and Wegscheider-Cruse (1989). While these roles are stereotypical and no child can be so neatly categorized, they do represent common themes of personality patterns in such families. Although these roles are individually adaptive for children who live in addictive homes, the primary purpose of these roles is to maintain the rigid and dysfunctional homeostasis of the addictively enmeshed family (George, 1990, p. 76).

The acting-out child.   The acting-out child is the stereotypical troubled child of an alcoholic family. The acting-out child is the one who comes to the attention of school administrators, police, and social services. The problems these children create should not be too surprising given that their parents are excellent role models for learning unacceptable behavior. These children have extremely poor self-images and attempt to enhance themselves by rebellious, attention-seeking behavior. While other children learn how to repress or depress problem areas, acting-out children use unacceptable forms of behavior to say, "Care about me" or "I can't cope." While other children either draw positive attention to themselves or escape attention, the acting-out child gets negative attention by inappropriate means. Socially, these children generally gravitate toward peers who have equally low self-esteem and are prone to engage in delinquent behavior. They are the individuals who fill correctional facilities, mental health institutions, and chemical dependency units in hospitals. Termed "the scapegoat" by Wegscheider-Cruse (1989), they enable the addiction by becoming another stressor that can serve as an excuse for substance abuse and also by focusing the family's anger and energy away from the addict and onto themselves (Black, 1981, pp. 25–27).

The responsible child.   The oldest child is most likely to be a very responsible child or family hero (Wegscheider-Cruse, 1989). This is the little adult who takes care of the alcoholic, the spouse, and the other children. In attempting to care for the family, the responsible child enables the alcoholic by providing her or him more time to drink. Not only are they highly responsible to the family, they are also highly responsible in their academic and extracurricular endeavors. Outwardly, they appear as stalwart and outstanding young men and women who are successful in much that they do. Heros learn to completely rely on themselves, because adults can neither be depended upon nor are they astute or sensitive enough to provide direction for their lives (Black, 1981, pp. 17–20).

The adjuster.   The adjuster is the middle or younger child. Called "the lost child" by Wegscheider-Cruse (1989), the adjuster follows directions, handles whatever has to be handled, and adjusts to the circumstances, however dysfunctional they may be. The adjuster outwardly appears to be more flexible, spontaneous, and somewhat more selfish than others in the home. These children don't feel, question, get upset, or act in any way to draw attention to themselves. They just handle the situation. They enable the alcoholic by not being a "bother." Typically, the adjuster is academically average in school and consequently doesn't draw any negative or positive attention. Socially, this child doesn't take leadership roles and is generally a loner (Black, 1981, pp. 21–23).

The placater.   The placater is usually the youngest child, who comforts everybody in the family and makes them feel better. Also known as "the family mascot" (Wegscheider-Cruse, 1989), this child thinks that by making family members feel better, he or she can divert attention from the problem and it will subside or go away. The placating child may operate in three distinctive patterns.

First, the placater may act the clown and distract the family through humorous antics. Socially these people may be the life of the party, but have few close friends because they discount everybody's feelings as a stress reduction mechanism. Academically, if placaters defuse stress by humor, such antics may land them in trouble with their teachers. Socially, they may also be in the middle of everything but accomplish little in the bargain (George, 1990, pp. 72–76).

The placating child may also assume a role of sympathetic counselor to the rest of the family. Highly sensitive to the needs of others, this child may be the apologist for the family's behavior and attempt to apply psychological balm to the emotional wounds other members of the family suffer. Such sensitive characteristics are well rewarded at school, where such children are praised for their compliant, helpful, and sharing qualities. The placater abets the alcoholic by distracting the family from being forced to come to grips with the constant conflicts they are engaged in (Black, 1981, pp. 23–25).

The placater or mascot may also assume the "sick" role in the family through manifestation of continuous and sometimes severe psychosomatic illnesses. This overprotected child becomes the illness focal point for the family, and enables the chemical dependency by deflecting the family focus on sickness away from the addict (George, 1990, p. 76).

To keep the foregoing dysfunctional family roles operational, iron-clad family rules must be followed.

Family Rules in Alcoholic Families

There is a clear method to the madness of the foregoing roles, and in addictive families, unspoken rules are learned very quickly if one is going to survive. In the parlance of substance abuse programs, families of addicts have a metaphorical pink elephant sitting in the living room that everybody sees, that everybody walks around, and that nobody acknowledges. The presence of this elephant makes children think there is something wrong with them, since nobody else seems to be much concerned with the elephant (the addictive behavior) or at least isn't acknowledging it. What is even more disconcerting is that these children tend to believe that everyone else lives in an idyllic Cleaver or Huxtable family. Yet, this is certainly not the Bill Cosby show, and to make things liveable in the grim reality of addictive families, children have to adopt the following rules to survive (McGowan, 1991).

Don't talk.   Because of the denial of alcoholism in an alcoholic family, seldom are any of the children/problems recognized and the family problem—alcoholism—is never discussed. One does not talk about the real issues. By ignoring or rationalizing the addictive behavior, family members hope to make it go away. If one does talk about it, then bad things happen (Black, 1981, pp. 33–37).

Lisa: Early on, Dad would be throwing up in the sink in the morning. Mom would just say he was sick. It scared me 'cause I thought he had, like, cancer or something, and he was gonna die. Every time I'd ask a question about it, she'd just blow me off or get mad at me.

Don't trust.   The single most important ingredient in a nurturing relationship is honesty. No child can trust or be expected to trust unless those around him or her are also open and honest about their own feelings. One should never trust that parents will be there emotionally, psychologically, or even physically for a member of an addictive family. To trust means to have faith and confidence in another person and to feel safe when in their care. These vital ingredients are generally missing in the home of an alcoholic. Children not only cannot depend on the alcoholic, but they also may not be able to depend on the other enabling parent because he or she is so busy trying to meet the alcoholic's needs and will minimize, rationalize, or blatantly deny that certain events are taking place (Black, 1981, pp. 39–45).

Mark: Even though it's a long way to the ball park, I always plan on riding my bike. Dad says he'll take me but he works late a lot and can't get home on time. Sometimes Mom has to take care of him when he's sick, or she doesn't feel well herself. So I just always plan on getting myself there for practice and the games.

Don't feel.   Members of addictive families have a well-developed denial system in regard to feelings—particularly one's own feelings. If one starts discussing feelings about incidents surrounding the addictive behavior, they are either dismissed or ruthlessly suppressed. Members quickly learn that vocalizing feelings of fear, guilt, anger, sadness, embarrassment, and other hurtful feelings just brings more pain to the family. While these feelings are shunted aside and submerged in the maladaptive roles family members assume, they are experienced over and over in addictive families and do not go away when one gains adulthood and leaves the addictive family of origin (Black, 1981, pp. 45–49).

Mark: I really wish Dad and Mom could have been there to see me get most valuable player, but Lisa was, and my coach told me how proud he was of me, and then the whole team went to his house for ice cream. Well, it wasn't that big a thing anyways . . . just a Little League championship.

Don't behave differently.   Any attempt to shift roles within the family is not allowed because this would turn the system topsy-turvy. If role vacancies do occur, they must be quickly filled by other members of the family (George, 1990, p. 79).

Lisa: Oh yeah! I tried to be Little Miss Goody Two-Shoes, the perfect kid. Got good grades in school, went out for the volleyball team, dated "nice" guys and was a "nice" girl. But I got yelled at anyways so forget that. I might as well get yelled at for having fun.

Chemical dependency is not to blame.   Assigning blame to people, things, and situations outside the family is typical of the denial of personal responsibility for one's actions that pervades a chemically dependent family. While the addict may receive some severe judgment by the rest of the family, family members believe that it is fate that keeps an iron grip on the family's misery.

Amy: I know he can be such an SOB, but it's been the lot of the Chung women to marry that kind of guy for three generations now. I swear my younger sister married a clone of Gordon. It just runs in the family, I guess.

Certainly, the trauma experienced by children who live and survive in chemically dependent families would seem bitter enough. However, the trauma and the crises of childhood in a chemically dependent family do not end with an escape from home or maturation into adulthood. The traumatic wake of being reared in a chemically dependent family often ripples into adulthood in the form of a variety of transcrisis events that might seem on first glance to have little reason for being and no discernible links to one's family of origin.

Adult Children of Alcoholics

In the 1980s a new phenomenon gained a great deal of publicity and attention in therapeutic settings and became a darling of the media talk shows. In the past, the primary focus of treatment of alcoholism was on the addicted person. Even with family system approaches, family members were seen as enablers and any intervention with the family was aimed at understanding the part their enabling played in the progression of the disease and educating them as to how they might support or sabotage treatment of the addict. Rarely were family members seen as the primary recipients of treatment for their own codependent and personal problems arising from the addiction (Schaef, 1986, p. 6). Given a best estimate that there are about 28 million children of alcoholics in the United States (Lewis & Williams, 1986, p. v) and that one out of every six families is affected by alcoholism (Black, 1981, p. 3), it is not difficult to understand why a treatment approach that focuses on the codependents themselves would quickly gain a great deal of notoriety and credibility.

The zealotry that sometimes assails the chemical dependency field is not missing here. As reported by Schaef (1986) in her review of the codependency literature, Wegscheider-Cruse (1984) believes that 96% of the population of the United States is codependent and Larsen's (1983) predictions indicate a potential number of codependents larger than the current population of the United States! Schaef goes on to say that the addictive process is a generic, underlying disease syndrome that is endemic in the basic culture and most individuals (p. 39). While there is much to be critical of in current society and while many addictive behaviors are rampant within it, we are not ready to commit everyone to a therapeutic program to rid them of codependence. In the popular self-help literature, almost every problem of identity development or impulse control has been associated with codependency (Hogg & Frank, 1992). At the same time, many of the characteristics attributed to adult children of alcoholics (ACOAs) are not necessarily unique to them (McGowan, 1991). Although there is a constellation of behaviors that *appear* to classify a group known as ACOAs, there is no substantive empirical research to prove this is so. At this date much has been written about codependency, yet little has been proven. It is with this qualifier that we introduce the ACOA in crisis.

Facts.   There is clear evidence that three facts relate to ACOAs (Black, 1981, p. 105; Schafer, 1989; Woititz, 1983, p. 103):

1. Alcoholism runs in families. Rarely is a case seen in isolation. There may be generational skips, but alcoholism is invariably found in the extended family of the alcoholic.
2. Children of alcoholics run a higher risk of developing alcoholism than children in the mainstream of the population. Males are four times as likely and females are three times as likely as their peers from nonalcoholic families to become alcoholic.
3. Children of alcoholics tend to marry alcoholics. Rarely do they go into the marriage with that knowledge, but the phenomenon occurs over and over.

While ACOAs drink with the belief that "It'll never happen to me because I've seen it and I didn't like it and I'd never become what my parents were," the facts are contradictory. ACOAs comprise approximately 60% of all patients in chemical dependency programs. They also show up as collaterals of those being treated for addictive disorders and appear in excess frequency among criminal justice offenders, mental health clientele, and hospital patients (Liepman, White, & Nirenberg, 1986, p. 39).

Feelings.   Upon reaching adulthood the majority of children of alcoholics continue to experience problems related to trust, dependency, control, identification, and expression of feelings. They are people-pleasers who are not able to trust their feelings or instincts about others. They have difficulty saying no and may be manipulated by others and extend themselves beyond any reasonable human capacity (George, 1990, p. 85).

ACOAs often experience an overwhelming sense of fear. Most particularly, the fear of abandonment is predominant and intensifies from childhood. These fears are episodic in that extreme high and low mood swings are experienced and are manifested either by clinging behavior or an inability to form meaningful relationships. Fear of the unknown keeps ACOAs immobilized behaviorally, cognitively, and affectively. Because they have learned to stuff feelings so well as children, ACOAs have a fear of confrontation and seldom argue or fight, even when their emotions are boiling over. Fear results in a tendency for ACOAs to discount their own perceptions and not have the courage to check out other people's perceptions (Black, 1981, p. 116; George, 1990, p. 86)

Anger is seldom acknowledged by the ACOA. The anger of being powerless when adults could have done something breeds resentment. Because the ACOA as a child was seldom if ever allowed to acknowledge or display anger, it is a feeling that is often repressed, twisted, and distorted in the ACOA. It is a feeling that is invariably denied, yet manifests itself in a variety of ways such as overeating, depression, psychosomatic illness, and passive-aggressive behavior toward others. Seldom if ever does anger come out in confrontive ways. ACOAs learned long ago that such displays cause more problems than they solve (Black, 1981, p. 115; George, 1990, p. 86).

Guilt is a tenacious feeling that ACOAs may hold onto for 10, 30, or even 60 years. The guilt may be over a range of things, from wishing parents would die, to not doing enough for the family, to running away from the problem. If no resolution with or confrontation of a parent occurs before death, the guilt may lead to more severe disturbances (Black, 1981, p. 120; George, 1990, p. 86).

Effects of childhood roles.   Dynamically, the adaptive roles that ACOAs take on in childhood may follow them into adulthood. Heros become extremely responsible adults who are scared to death of losing control. Because they punched back their own feelings as children, they particularly have difficulty with sharing feelings and become wildly out of control and have few places to turn when things go awry. To have fun means to temporarily lose control of oneself. Responsible ACOAs had little fun as children and they have little ability to enjoy life as adults. The idea of loss of control is intolerable. As a result, heros have to be in charge, stay in one-up positions, and allow no room for equal relationships. For the responsible ACOA, alcohol can remove the stress and anxiety of always retaining rigid control (Black, 1981, p. 123; George, 1990, p. 89).

For the ACOA lost child, life is a perpetual roller coaster. They perceive themselves as having few alternatives because when forced to make commitments based on logical and linear thinking, they have few mental resources to call on. They have never learned that choices are available to them, because they have never had to make a decision; they have merely adjusted to changing conditions. They associate with others who are as emotionally closed as they are, because this limited association is the only one that is safe. They find mates who are chaotic representatives of their former childhood experiences. These ACOAs live in constant agitation because their comfort zone consists of perpetuating childhood roles of adapting to inconsistent people. They know how to handle chaotic situations by adjusting. The problem is that these relationships are insubstantial because no one takes responsibility for making decisions. The result is a person who is lonely, depressed, and isolated socially. Alcohol can give these people a false sense of power and control. Making decisions and talking about real issues become easier with alcohol (Black, 1981, p. 85; George, 1990, p. 89).

Placaters are experienced by others as nice people because of their attempts to please others. They are adept at diverting attention from themselves; otherwise they'd have to deal with their own pain (Black, 1981, pp. 23–25). These ACOAs have always been so responsible for others that they have lost the ability to take care of themselves and their own needs. Chemical dependents are perfect marriage partners for these individuals because they can continue their loving and supportive role that they perfected in their alcoholic family of origin. The comic placater as an adult is the life of every party but of no use in an emotional maelstrom. The psychosomatic version of the placater draws sympathy and attention, but never focuses on any issues of change that would allow for a more fulfilling and productive life. Finally, the placater who is always sensitive to and supportive of others actually does little to help others confront the dilemmas they face. As a result, placaters make excellent enablers (Black, 1981, pp. 59–61; George, 1990, p. 90).

Finally, acting-out children may experience life as adults in two operating modes. First, they may continue to rebel, but in more sophisticated and dramatic ways. Their rebellion extends out from the family into society. They lack education and job skills, have anger control problems, marry early, and produce illegitimate children. In law enforcement terms, they graduate from misdemeanors to felonies. They are prime candidates to have severe addiction problems and also suffer from mental health problems. They are the stereotypical bad apples that live on the edge of society or are outcast from it (Black, 1981, pp. 62–63; George, 1990, p. 89).

If the acting-out child assumes the scapegoat role, as ACOAs they become everyone's doormat because they are incapable of standing up for themselves. They allow themselves to be used and abused by others. Indeed, they become excellent candidates to marry into or work in abusive relationships. Their low self-concept makes them prime candidates for chemical dependency because of the false sense of well-being it provides (George, 1990, p. 89).

Potential problems.   Many ACOAs are seen as valuable members of both their families and society, and indeed they are. Yet, in adulthood these ways of surviving often lead to unhealthy and extreme patterns of coping that draw them into problems with substance abuse, marrying someone who becomes an abuser, or having an unusual number of personal problems in their adult years (Black, 1981, pp. 16–17). Woititz (1983) has compiled a chilling summary of potential problems ACOAs are likely to face. ACOAs

1. guess at what "normal" is
2. are procrastinators supreme

3. lie when it would be as easy to tell the truth
4. judge themselves without mercy
5. take themselves too seriously and have little fun
6. have difficulty with intimate relationships
7. overreact to changes over which they have no control
8. constantly seek approval and affirmation
9. feel they are different from other people
10. are superresponsible or irresponsible
11. are loyal even when the loyalty is undeserved
12. are impulsive.

Multivariate Diagnosis

Although we agree with Maxwell (1986, p. 33) that treatment approaches to drug abuse should be based on dealing with the abuse first, we also believe that treatment should be geared toward the individual and his or her particular circumstances. A therapeutic approach for a 45-year-old housewife who anesthetizes herself in front of the soap operas with a pitcher of martinis every afternoon may be quite different from one for the 16 year old who has been doing street drugs with his peer group (Lawson, Ellis, & Rivers, 1984, p. ix). Not only do setting events contribute to how treatment is carried out, but also the particular personality constellation, demographics, learning history, ethnicity, social support systems, term of abuse, sex, age, and drinking systems determine the behaviors of the alcoholic and dictate specific treatment (McCrady, 1982, p. 682).

Age, culture, environment, and sex are not the only variables that must be taken into account in formulating intervention plans with the chemically dependent. It has only been in the past decade that human services professionals have come to understand that chemically dependent clients also may have underlying mental health problems (Doweiko, 1990, p. 190). Estimates vary, but it appears that up to 50% of all alcohol and substance abuse problems mask other psychiatric problems (Brown, Ridgely, Pepper, Levine, & Ryglewicz, 1989; Carey, 1989; Graubart, 1991). If that figure is correct, then many chemical dependency programs are not really dealing effectively with underlying problems since little understanding or emphasis is placed on individual psychological dynamics outside the parameters of the dependency (Graubart, 1991). The emphasis of treatment has been more on behavioral techniques dealing with control of the problem than on resolution of underlying mental health problems. Hence, the focus has been on relapse prevention, which has not been highly effective with such individuals (Graubart, 1991). One classical example of this problem has been the attempt to treat PTSD sufferers for their chemical dependency problems only. They may be dried out for a while, but the nightmares and sleeplessness that PTSD causes will invariably drive them back to self-medicating to get some sleep.

Dual-diagnosis clients also may use a system of "floating" denial, talking of their psychiatric problems with drug addiction workers, while talking about their drug abuse with mental health workers (Doweiko, 1990, p. 191). Besides dual-diagnosis clients' own attempts to sabotage treatment, many times when standard operating procedures for mental health facilities and dependency treatment programs come together, there are conflicting treatment philosophies, only adding to the confusion of the dual-diagnosis client (Doweiko, 1990, p. 192). While other types of mental disturbance should always be looked for as possible causative agents of the addiction or occurring concurrently with it, no mental health problems that we know of can be dealt with effectively while a person is abusing chemicals. From that standpoint, the primary rule is to get the person detoxified first (Rado, 1988).

Our own theoretical approach, backed by a great deal of reported research (Pattison & Kaufman, 1982b, p. 13), is that alcoholism is a multivariate construct and implies the following (pp. 13–14):

1. There are multiple patterns of use, misuse, and abuse that may be denoted as a pattern of alcoholism.
2. There are multiple interactive etiological variables that may combine to produce a pattern of alcoholism.
3. All persons are vulnerable to the development of some type of alcoholism problem.
4. Treatment interventions must be multimodal to correspond to the particular pattern of alcoholism in a specific person.
5. Treatment outcomes will vary in accordance with specific alcoholism patterns, persons, and social contexts.
6. Preventive interventions must be multiple and diverse to address diverse etiologic factors.

INTERVENTION STRATEGIES

Crisis in a substance abuser's life rarely manifests itself as a one-time occurrence. The abuser's life is characterized by both transcrisis and transcrisis points. Generally, the transcrisis is related to the whole problem of addiction. Transcrisis points are related to the recurrent crises in the abuser's everyday life that seem to erupt in spontaneous ways whenever the person encounters stressors and that are rarely identified as being rooted in the greater underlying transcrisis of addiction. Typically, transcrisis points erupt in a series of what may appear to be single crises from time to time.

In this chapter we portray crisis workers dealing with both the transcrisis and transcrisis points. The six-step model explained in Chapter 2 applies to all phases of substance abuse work. In addition to the six-step method, effective intervention with abusers almost always requires clients to become highly involved in a number of other methodologies, including treatment groups such as those associated with family systems therapy, AA, or comparable specialized treatment groups. It is from the vantage point of both transcrisis and transcrisis points and a broad variety of intervention strategies that we deal with crisis work with addictive clients.

Assessment

The assessment of chemical dependence is a complex task, but it is critical in formulating differential diagnoses, specific outcome goals, and valid treatment modalities (Kaufman & Pattison, 1982b, p. 1091). The DSM-IIIR of the American Psychiatric Association (1987) devotes an entire section of 21 pages to substance abuse disorder (pp. 165–185). This includes diagnoses that refer to maladaptive behavior associated with more or less regular use of the substance. The categories covered are alcohol, amphetamines, cannabis, cocaine, hallucinogens, nicotine, opioids, phencyclidines, sedatives, polysubstances, and not otherwise specified dependence or abuse. Each category is divided into dependence and abuse classes. Acute and chronic systemic effects are found under substance-induced organic mental disorder and include another 41 pages of disorders (pp. 123–163). Clearly, the reason for alloting this large amount of space to substance abuse is the large part it plays in much of the mental health business that occurs in the United States.

While a biochemical test will be a fairly reliable and valid indicator of the presence or amount of drugs in a person's system, breathalyzers being one familiar assessment device, it will not tell us whether a person is an occasional user, an abuser, or a full-blown addict. Let us turn then to the old standby of assessment techniques, the paper-and-pencil test.

Psychometrics. A wide variety of personality tests have been used in attempts to characterize an alcoholic personality (Knox, 1976). A prototype is the MacAndrew Alcoholism Scale, from the Minnesota Multiphasic Personality Inventory (MMPI). The MacAndrew has been fairly successful in predicting alcoholism and a general tendency toward addiction (Greene, 1980; Knox, 1980). The MMPI itself has been used to predict an addictive personality. An addictive profile is characterized by moderate to severe depression, obsessive-compulsive trends, poor impulse control, anxiety, irrational fears and phobias, irresponsibility, immaturity, and acting out (Forrest, 1984). The MMPI has the additional distinction of having validity scales that can uncover faking and lying. Another self-report inventory that specifically targets substance abuse but is camouflaged as to its purpose is the Substance Abuse Sterile Screening Inventory (SASSI). It has subscales that allow the examiner to use a series of decision rules to determine if the individual is a chemical abuser (Miller, 1983). The Alcohol Use Inventory is another psychometric device that has demonstrated utility in measuring the psychological, social, marital, and family factors affecting alcohol use (Wanberg, Horn, & Foster, 1977). A major problem with these and other personality tests, though, is that they are unstable over time. The alcoholic may have very different scores and configurations prior to and after detoxification (Knox, 1976). These and other tests have general use in determining personality types of abusers, but no absolute pattern of personality has yet been found that covers all types of alcoholism (Mendelson & Mello, 1979).

Direct psychometric methods are related to alcoholic behavior and use. Prototypical are the Michigan Alcohol Screening Test (MAST), which asks questions about alcohol consumption and drinking behavior; the Alcadd Test, which measures drinking in terms of regularity, preference over other activities, loss of control, rationalization of use, and emotionality (Ornstein, 1976); the Twenty-Question List from Johns Hopkins, which asks individuals about the effects that drinking has on their lives, and the Problem Drinker Scale (Vaillant, 1983), which can identify life problems associated with drug use. Finally, the Cocaine Addiction Self-Report (Gold, 1984) is distinctive in that it very clearly and chillingly tells individuals what scores and test items mean in relation to the progress of their dependence.

There are also adolescent inventories that screen for drug abuse. The Personal Experience Screening Questionnaire is a group screening test to determine whether substance abuse is a factor in emotional, behavioral, or academic problems. It covers problem severity, psychosocial risk of personal and environmental problems associated with adolescent substance abuse, drug use history, and validity scales. The Adolescent Alcohol Involvement Scale is another screening device that considers the teenager's shorter history of use, means of procurement, and drinking acquaintances.

Triage assessment.   As should be well understood by now, all of the foregoing assessment devices have one major problem. They are self-reports, and as such, their reliability and validity are highly questionable. It should be clear that what drug abusers have to say about their dependency in regard to the severity of their problems should be highly suspect (Knox, 1982, p. 58).

In any assessment of chemical dependents, the crisis worker should follow two rules that Doweiko (1990, p. 214) has proposed and we believe should be chiseled in granite. First, always seek collateral information. A spouse's or an employer's response to a MAST may be very different from the alcoholic's. Second, until proven otherwise, always assume deception. For example, alcoholics will invariably attempt to minimize their use, while cocaine and opiate addicts may exaggerate their use to impress others. Given the foregoing warning, the crisis worker should attempt to obtain information from as many different sources as possible before attempting to make a valid assessment of a chemical dependent (Doweiko, 1990, p. 215).

From that standpoint, triage assessment is often difficult because little of what the drug addict says can be believed. Until chemical dependents have hit rock bottom, they will cover their figurative and literal drug tracks behaviorally, cognitively, and affectively in self-defeating efforts to deny to themselves and others the control that the drug exercises over them. A rule of thumb that many of our coworkers in chemical dependent treatment programs use in interviews about consumption of alcohol should give a vivid illustration of what we are talking about. Whatever an alcoholic reports as the amount used should be doubled to arrive at a very conservative estimate of the real amount used!

Diagnostic intake.   A comprehensive clinical assessment of a chemical dependent will cover biological and psychosocial components of the problem and will include a complete medical workup. Whatever the diagnostic system used, one question overrides all others, and that is: Does the diagnosis help the individual and does it provide information necessary to treatment (Lawson et al., 1984, p. 44)? Toward that goal, one of the better intake formats we have seen is the Continuous Data Questionnaire (CDQ) (Poley, Lea, & Vibe, 1979). Combined with a complete medical workup and psychometric measures, the CDQ provides an extensive and intensive profile of the client. The CDQ specifies treatment stage, alcohol use, work/education background, family system, social-recreational-community involvement, adjudication, personality and emotional development, physical and sexual health, motivation, and a comprehensive section for the intake worker's conclusions.

The CDQ accomplishes a number of important tasks. First, it monitors a client at many points in the treatment process. Second, it is not concerned with drug issues to the exclusion of other problems. Its comprehensiveness allows the worker to obtain information on a variety of areas that may need remediation. Third, the CDQ gives a historical perspective to make an excellent analysis of what treatment goals need to be established and how those goals are being met. In sum, the CDQ or a similar intake device is of critical importance in providing the worker with a road map of the treatment process.

Assessment by the worker.   We believe that the worker's ability to retrieve, analyze, and synthesize clinical information is crucial to making a valid assessment and subsequent treatment decisions. An initiating interview to determine drug abuse is unlike many other exploratory interviews because the defense mechanisms of the chemical dependent will be granite hard, and the worker must be aware that these defenses will do all they can to safeguard the abuser's secret.

Analysis starts by monitoring the verbal defenses of the client. Hedging, minimizing, seduction, changing the subject, projecting onto significant others, and refusal to speak directly about oneself in the here-and-now are defenses all clients may manifest. However, these are extremely pronounced in the alcoholic. For example, ruminating on past drinking episodes and drinking friends should not be viewed as innocent, idle nostalgia, but rather suggests that the person has not learned to fill the social void in his or her life left by giving up the abusing agent and while physically detoxified is not psychologically detoxified (Perez, 1985, pp. 34–37).

Behavioral assessment includes such simple procedures as noticing whether there is alcohol on the client's breath. Chewing peppermint or gum and heavy use of cologne or perfume may be attempts to mask alcoholic odors. Physical appearance of an alcoholic may include facial puffiness, a red nose, sudden weight gain, a glazed look or a hunted, fearful aspect, shaking, rigid attending and listening or a very casual, laid-back approach (Perez, 1985, pp. 34–37). Having conducted the intake assessment, the worker should write a summary in narrative form that includes all the points we have discussed in the CDQ.

Assessment of spirituality.   A major component of triage assessment for chemical dependency that is different from assessment in any other crisis situation is a careful analysis of the individual's spiritual resources. This analysis has little to do with religion: it does not mean the number of times the individual attended church, the amount of money put in the collection plate, or pages of the Bible read per day. Modern science tends to sneer at something so subjective and archaic as "spirit." Yet, in so doing, it denies our uniqueness, for humans are distinct from all other creatures in regard to our spirituality. Unfortunately, society has trouble accepting a disease of the spirit as being a real disease. Clearly, the success of the spirituality-based self-help organizations AA and Narcotics Anonymous (NA) in helping addicts to achieve and maintain sobriety should lend some validity to the importance of spirituality in assessment and treatment (Doweiko, 1990, pp. 163–165).

No paper-and-pencil test or specific interview questions can tell which percentile a person belongs to in regard to spiritual resources in comparison to some norm group. Since the spiritual disease of addiction is self-centered absorption to the exclusion of anything or anybody else, spiritual assessment should focus on the degree to which the individual is willing to change basic belief systems to continue use. It should focus on the narcissistic desire to change life from what it is to "how I want it and how it must be." It should also focus on the despair and hopelessness that addicts feel and the emptiness in their lives that they attempt to fill through their addiction. A very simple way that the crisis worker can do this is to listen for, count, and categorize the defense mechanisms detailed in this chapter that the addict uses to stay behaviorally, cognitively, and spiritually blind.

While the 12 steps of AA may be discounted by empiricists, we are aware of very few people who have come to grips with their addiction without admitting their powerlessness over the drug, giving themselves over to a higher power, and taking deep and painful stock of their soul. Therefore, in triage assessment we believe that the spirituality of the chemically addicted should be given a good deal of emphasis and diagnosis and treatment goals should routinely incorporate it in program planning.

An example: Intake analysis and summary of Gordon Brand.   Gordon Brand was seen after initial admission for polydrug overdose. Stage of treatment is initial assessment. The date is March 15, 1987. The client is a 42-year-old male Caucasian who was brought to St. Polycarp by the paramedics for treatment of a drug overdose. BAC was 0.37% on admission with evidence of Quaalude® ingestion. Gordon was comatose on entry and was in intensive care for three days.

Chemical use. Preferential drug is alcohol. Over the past three months, Gordon reports consuming a bit less than a pint of whiskey per day, although this quantity is subject to scrutiny because of client's defensive responses. Drinking is continuous and Gordon does not remember when he was last abstinent. Drinking has been with peers from work and alone at home. Lately drinking has been mostly by himself. Valium was prescribed by Gordon's family physician for "stress" and Gordon has used it rather extensively for a number of years, especially when he was trying to "cut down" alcohol use. His only experience with Quaaludes was immediately prior to admission, and he maintains this was a "terrible mistake" and he will not use them again.

His social drinking behavior includes the three-martini lunch, stopping at a local bar after work, and numerous parties that are social/business in nature. His ability to control alcohol use is rated by himself as neither difficult nor easy and the seriousness of his problem is probably underrated because of his extensive and intensive denial system. Gordon's wife is an occasional user of alcohol, but tends more to abstinence.

Educational and vocational background. Gordon is a college graduate with a degree in mechanical engineering and a master's in business administration. He is employed as director of internal operations by United Tectonics. His income is approximately $100,000 a year, with numerous perquisites. He reports no absences from work due to alcohol or drug-related problems, but does report he has missed approximately 20 days of work in the last two months due to "intestinal problems" and generally feeling "unwell." His best estimate of being late to work is 10 times during the last month. He indicates he is moderately satisfied with his job, but says he would be extremely satisfied if the company president "would get off his back and leave him alone." He rates his job performance as quite good and says it would be excellent if he were not currently ill.

He is not sure how much money he owes at present because "that was always his wife's job," but believes besides a house note of $1750 and two car notes of $850 he pays "about $1500 a month on credit cards." Cost of drinking is "peanuts." He is not sure how much outstanding debt he has, but vaguely remembers his wife saying something about bills being overdue.

Family status. Gordon currently resides with his wife and children in an upper-middle-class subdivision and has lived there for the past eight years. He relates that he used to love his wife a great deal, but now gets along poorly with her. He maintains that he gets along moderately well with his children, Lisa and Mark, although "they side with their mother on most things." Prior to the last two months he often (several times a week) did things with his family. He believes his family is very important to him but is extremely angry that his wife is not more supportive. He also feels he is extremely important to his family, but states this in economic terms: "All I'm good for is to bring home a paycheck." He does not handle arguments with his wife well and "clams up" after initial exchanges. His dealings with his children are much the same, and he reports, "They don't listen to me and are rebellious."

Social involvement. He reports having many business acquaintances, but no real friends. Gordon has been involved with a number of charitable and service organizations in the community, until the last couple of years, when he got so involved in work that he could not do those things anymore. He enjoyed service activities, particularly with the Boys' Club. His recreational pursuits are "tinkering" in his shop at home, fishing and hunting, and reading military history.

Judicial involvement. Aside from being found by the police passed out in his car, he has no prior arrest record. He reported one domestic disturbance call when he and his wife were arguing, but smoothed that over with the officer who responded to the call.

Health. His physical and mental health have been average to poor. He last saw a doctor about six months ago and was told that he had the beginnings of major health problems, "something to do with my guts and stress," but he is not quite sure what it was. He has been taking an antacid for the problem. He has "fallen down" on his eating habits because of both stress and a nervous stomach and only occasionally eats regular, well-balanced meals. He averages about 5 to 6 hours' sleep a night and uses alcohol and Valium to help him get to sleep, particularly when he is under stress. He has never been in the hospital for other than minor medical problems. He has never considered suicide, but states it is not the worst thing in the world. His sexual health is poor. He has no strong sexual urges, has not had or cared to have sex in a long time, and had been very unsatisfied with his sex life, but now is neither satisfied nor unsatisfied.

Gordon presents the appearance of a man coming out from addiction. After he was stabilized for his overdose he slept for the better part of three days. His withdrawal symptoms were severe enough that he was given phenobarbital to ease the pain of withdrawal. His appearance is sallow and wan. He is overweight and his muscle tone is poor, with his flesh sagging over his body. As he sits in the intake interview he has a hunted look to his eyes and is constantly wringing his hands when he is not chain smoking. His agitation is further demonstrated by pitched up and accelerated speech patterns.

Personality profile. His personality and emotional development are rated moderately low in responsibility to self and others, very low in self-worth and general feeling of well-being, high on anxiety and depression and neither high nor low on initiative, sociability, assertiveness, and hostile aggression toward others. He is more tense than relaxed, more critical than tolerant, more depressed than happy, more nervous than calm, more unfriendly than friendly, more unforgiving than forgiving, and much more sickly than healthy. The MacAndrew supports this self-analysis and the MAST indicates he is a heavy alcohol abuser.

Motivation. He is ambivalent about changing. Although he can articulate goals, they are generally nonspecific, such as "straightening things out at home and work." His rating of present attempts to accomplish these tasks is that they are very unsuccessful, and he rates as moderately important a goal to stop abusing alcohol "for a while." His most desirable use of alcohol would be to drink socially, "because drinking alone really isn't all that good and probably helped get me here in the first place." He believes no one is interested in his problems "except to get on my back."

Corroboration. Follow-up includes checking with Gordon's employer, wife, and doctor. Their story is a good deal different from what Gordon reports. Mr. Fredricks, the president of United, indicates that Gordon was one of his best employees until about three years ago, when his drinking got steadily worse and his performance declined. At first, Mr. Fredricks said nothing about the drinking, because Gordon still had a performance rating that was superior to those of most other members of the staff—drunk or sober. Later, Mr. Fredricks gave him some fatherly advice about his problem, which Gordon ignored. Three months ago, the advice turned into a warning about absences and poor performance. Mr. Fredricks now feels that unless Gordon dries out and takes care of his problem, termination is imminent. Mr. Fredricks also agreed that Gordon had been such a valuable employee that the company would pick up any cost for treatment that insurance did not cover. The employer agreed to support and coordinate efforts with the hospital. Analysis of employer cooperation in regard to chemical dependency treatment is excellent.

Gordon's wife Amy supports his employer's analysis of the problem. His drinking has steadily escalated to the point that the family has become completely dysfunctional. She and the children are terrified of Gordon when he is drunk, which is most of the time. He has become an isolate from his family and only relates to them when he wants something. Any mention of his drinking causes severe arguments and then a period of sullen hostility. Amy also reports serious financial problems, saying that they are behind on the house and car notes and owe credit card accounts of $7000. Two months ago Gordon got drunk, became violent, and threatened her. The police intervened in the situation and Gordon left the house. She threatened to obtain a restraining order on Gordon, but relented after he promised to remain sober and be the husband and father he used to be. He kept his vow for two weeks, then he started drinking even more heavily. She states that she is near a nervous breakdown and has a number of physical complaints that are probably due to the stress of trying to deal with Gordon for so many years. She is "sick" of it and is thinking of filing for divorce. She did agree to come to the hospital for an interview if Gordon agreed to treatment. General analysis of the home situation is that it is extremely poor and may not be redeemable.

A call to Gordon's doctor indicated that he had given Gordon a severe upbraiding six months ago about his drinking and stated that he would no longer give him prescriptions for Valium. He had recommended at that time that Gordon seek immediate inpatient treatment for severe alcohol abuse. He also told Gordon that he was having liver, pancreas, and intestinal problems due to alcohol and that if he kept drinking he was going to be in critical trouble in short order. Gordon became hostile and told his family doctor of 15 years that he didn't know what he was talking about and wasn't much good if he couldn't give him some tranquilizers for the stress he was experiencing.

Spirituality. Gordon was reared in a strict fundamentalist church, but left it during college because they were "real blue noses who never had any fun." He later tried a more liberal church, attending fairly regularly with his wife in the early years of their marriage, but quit attending that church because they were "pretentious asses." Aside from his nonattendance of any organized religious services, Gordon is spiritually bankrupt with the exception of the spirits he drinks. The only deity he acknowledges and attends to comes in a bottle. Any relationship that presently exists between he and a higher power is in name only, "Well sure I believe in God." He is alone, helpless, and hopeless in a hostile world.

Conclusions. General analysis of interviews with Gordon, his boss, his wife, and his doctor is that Gordon shows clear signs of chemical dependency (alcohol) across physical, psychological, and social components of his life. He denies that he has a problem with alcohol and has put in place strong defense mechanisms to shield him from the reality of the situation. He is in extreme peril of losing his job, his family, and quite possibly his life. He is in need of immediate inpatient treatment. Recommendations after case staffing with the chemical dependency unit were

1. that Gordon be apprised of the seriousness of his physical condition
2. that Gordon be apprised of the likelihood of keeping his job
3. that Gordon be apprised of the perilous state of his marriage
4. that Gordon fully experience the crisis he is in and that workers gain his agreement to undergo treatment in the chemical dependency unit
5. that if he agreed to undergo treatment, his family be contacted with the proposal that they also undergo treatment as codependents
6. that if he agreed to treatment, particular goals be established for a comprehensive rehabilitation plan
7. that controlled drinking is not an option due to the seriousness of his physical problems and the failure of his previous self-managed attempts to quit.

What It Takes to Be a Chemical Dependency Worker

Brill (1981, pp. 61–70) makes a number of points in regard to what it takes to be a world-class chemical dependency worker. These workers

1. need to be aware of their own underlying biases about drug use and users
2. should understand their own personal needs and feelings regarding power and dependency prior to becoming involved in the field
3. must possess skill in communication and in fully accepting a wide range of behaviors and personalities
4. must be trained in a number of treatment modalities
5. must be able to deal with challenges by clients who are adept at intimidating, testing, challenging, rationalizing, provoking, and trapping therapists
6. must be prepared to deal with dishonesty, cover-ups, illegal activities, and other forms of deviant behavior
7. must develop skill in dealing with a continuing saga of client crises, which tends to put workers in a bind between rejecting the client and assuming responsibility for solving the crisis, thereby engendering dependency
8. must be prepared to confront an unmotivated family support system in which treatment is often a long, drawn-out process (characterized by relapses, regressions, and dashed hopes for a rapid cure)
9. must find ways to deal with clients who cannot tolerate success—for any one of a variety of reasons, some drug users engage in self-defeating behaviors whenever an important attainment becomes imminent
10. must be competent in dealing with drug users even if their clients relapse and come to a treatment session high on drugs
11. must learn and practice ways to deal with resistant clients who are sent by a court, parole officer, or other authority
12. should be aware that drug users will employ seductive tactics: tell the worker what the worker wants to hear; present a pleasant, agreeable front; imitate the worker's favorite jargon; diagnose themselves and corroborate what the worker has been saying; confirm that they have made great progress as a result of the worker's help where all others have failed—all of which usually mask the client's underlying rage and hostility
13. must deal with clients who want to talk only about drugs and their drug exploits, to the exclusion of any meaningful work in solving their problem
14. must realize that many clients will drop out of treatment when it seems that the treatment is beginning to be effective; that the irregular and inconsistent pattern of contact is endemic to drug users; that clients tend to disengage from treatment when things are going well and return when there is a new crisis.

For example, Carolyn and Ray, two counselors on the treatment staff of St. Polycarp assigned to Gordon, manifest these characteristics. They can be loosely described as the good-guy/bad-guy team. Carolyn is a recovering alcoholic who is direct, assertive, and confrontive. At times, she uses self-disclosure about her own dependency so that the client can't get away with saying, "Nobody knows the trouble I've seen." She has a high degree of credibility even though, as residents on the unit say, "She's meaner than a snake when you try and con her." She is also a good model. The alcoholic can look at her as a peer and say, "If she can get through this, so can I," and "Here is a tough, competent person who has been where I am, and if that's true, then there's hope for me" (Graham, 1986).

Ray is more nondirective and unconditionally accepting. His stock in trade are the basic skills of empathic listening and responding. His job is to build a healthy, trusting, relationship and focus on the client's positive attributes, to promote faith in the client, and to help the client come to his or her own self-realizations about the problem. Ray is also a model in that he is a professional who is not an alcoholic. Clients cannot reject treatment on the basis that "they're just a bunch of burned-out boozers here."

Another reason that Carolyn and Ray operate as a team is that drug users are the most manipulative group of clients we know. Clients may con one person, but they will have a much more difficult time conning two people. Carolyn and Ray run constant perceptual checks with one another. One of them might be wrong, but the two of them together seldom are. Teaming is also a support mechanism for the workers. Working with drug addicts is one of the toughest jobs in therapy. By acting as a team they have far less chance of burning out (Parker, 1986).

Crisis Points

Clients who are addicted will have used drugs to shield themselves from all kinds of hurtful feelings, thoughts, and behaviors. Once this shield is taken away, all the problems will tend to converge like an accordion, and clients will be assailed from all sides at once. The very reasons that the alcoholic drank in the first place will return in condensed, magnified, and more powerful ways. Each instance will present a crisis point for clients. As a result, the whole therapeutic inpatient treatment program may be seen as trans-crisis in nature. Successfully jumping one hurdle generally means getting ready immediately for the next one and the next one after that.

The first crisis to be dealt with is getting the client motivated to dry out. Working with a "wet" person is impossible, because all the person is interested in is getting "fixed" (Parker, 1986). To get the person to detoxify means creating enough of a crisis that the person voluntarily agrees to stay. The best way to do this is by attacking the client's vulnerable points. For Gordon, there are two: his job and his health.

Carolyn: Hello, Gordon. I'm Carolyn and this is Ray. We're from the chemical dependency unit and we'd like to talk with you.

Gordon: Well, that's fine, but I don't know why you're talking to me. I made a dumb mistake and took some pills I shouldn't have, but that won't ever happen again.

Carolyn: Maybe not. But from your intake interview and the problem that got you here, we think you very seriously need to consider coming over to the chemical dependency unit.

Gordon: I really need to get out of here and get back to my job. It's hanging by a thread as it is.

Ray: We understand how concerned you are about your job. We've talked to your employer, Mr. Fredricks, and he understands the situation. He's willing to support you if you go into treatment.

Gordon: [*Angrily.*] I'll bet! That SOB used to be my best friend. He'll use me being a drunk to give me the axe. That's all the excuse he'd need.

Carolyn: He may be the biggest SOB in the state. But he cares about you and has offered you a choice. He believes that if you don't seek help from us, then you're not going to have a job at all. He also said you'll have your same job when you finish treatment. I have him outside and I want you to hear it with your own ears. [*After a lengthy conversation, Mr. Fredricks leaves.*]

Gordon: He really means it. My God! No job. What'll I do?

Ray: Look at it this way. You know you've got some pretty severe physical problems. What difference will a few days make? You meet your commitment to your boss, and you're also someplace where your physical problems can be monitored. It's a no-lose deal.

Gordon: I'm no drunken bum!

Ray: We understand that, but I'm wondering if this statement rings true: that drinking at times produces results you dislike.

Gordon: Yes. I could say that.

Ray: Seems like it would be worth your time to find out a bit more about that. What's a few days' difference one way or the other?

Gordon: I've never been in the hospital before; this is the first time.

Ray: I understand how scary that must have been, waking up and not knowing how you got here in the first place. I also know you're smart enough to know when something's haywire.

Gordon: But going into a dryout ward. It's like I can't handle my problems.

Ray: I'd guess that going into treatment would seem like a sign of weakness, but I'd like to point out that if anything else was wrong with you it would be a sign of mature and healthy thinking to get it taken care of, wouldn't it? You have a serious illness here that needs help.

Carolyn: If you had cancer, would you try to do surgery on yourself? You do want to get better in regard to your health problems, don't you? The doctor told you how serious your physical problems are, didn't he? That you have liver, pancreas, and severe intestinal problems and that if they're not taken care of you will most likely die. Do you believe he's putting you on, or is that what you want? Notice your hands right now. They're shaking so hard you couldn't hold a pencil and write your name.

Gordon: I can too.

Carolyn: Go ahead and do it then. [*Hands Gordon the pencil and paper.*]

Gordon: [*Attempts to write down his name and produces an illegible scrawl that wobbles across the page.*]

Carolyn: In all honesty, is that your typical signature?

Gordon: [*Voice breaks.*] I . . . no, it isn't. I'm . . . I'm sick.

Carolyn: Yes, you are! That's why we're concerned about you and want you to come into the program.

Gordon: [*Downcast but still defiant.*] OK. I'll give it a try, but I'm not promising anything. If I don't like it, I'll leave.

Ray: That's all we ask. Now let us tell you in general what your treatment is going to be. We want you to know what's going to happen so you can help us plan what'll be most effective for you.

Creating a crisis for Gordon.   The human services workers are creating a crisis for Gordon. They are not above putting the client in a corner to get him to stay and will do all they can to motivate him to do so. Very few clients will be self-motivated to change their abusing behavior (Lawson et al., 1984, p. 67). Outside motivation must often be used. In this case it is Gordon's job and his health. For most male alcoholics, their job is critical, and it is the last part of their environment to suffer. There are two major reasons for this. First, to lose one's job is to admit failure to handle the problem. A job is at the core of one's self-esteem, and to lose that is to admit that the chemical dependent has hit rock bottom. Second, without a job, there is no money to keep up one's supply of the addictive substance (Parker, 1986; Trice & Beyer, 1982, pp. 955–956). Such coercive measures may be more effective than those attempts that do not use employer intervention, and appear to have better outcomes than employees who volunteer for treatment without employer pressure to enter treatment or be terminated (Adelman & Weiss, 1989).

Balancing confrontation about poor job performance is an empathic and genuine concern for Gordon's health that specifically tells him that someone now cares what happens to him. The confrontation is firm, but not blaming (Huberty & Brandon, 1982, p. 1082). The information reported is factual and not judgmental. By alternating between the two approaches, the workers seek to set the stage for Gordon through a combination of fear for his life and hope through treatment.

While creating the crisis, the workers avoid directly confronting or accusing Gordon of being an alcoholic. Early attempts to make clients confess to their addiction will likely lead to very defensive behavior. Although the word *manipulate* has an ugly connotation, in a sense all therapists manipulate their clients to positively increase the chances of successful therapy (Lawson et al., 1984, p. 77). The facts of Gordon's case indicate that he is in serious, if not lethal, trouble. The first ten days of treatment are going to be the most difficult, and throughout this time, one of the workers' major tasks will be to keep Gordon from leaving against medical advice (Parker, 1986).

Using family intervention to create a crisis. While Gordon's case is clearly one of "hitting bottom" in addiction parlance, Vernon Johnson (1980; 1986) and the Johnson Institute (1972) have developed a family intervention model that involves carefully coaching family and friends in a supportive group confrontation of the chemical dependent in language he or she clearly understands. This creates a severe crisis for the chemical dependent and the family. It is not something that is done on the spur of the moment, out of frustration, or with malice and intent to punish the chemical dependent's transgressions (Doweiko, 1990, pp. 230–231).

The ingredients for creating such a crisis must be planned and rehearsed beforehand with a professional in the chemical dependence field who is well-versed in such an intervention. As many family members and significant others as possible should be present to combat the denial, bargaining, and promises to change that are sure to be a part of the addict's defense system. At a very minimum, at least two or more caring persons— four or more would be ideal—who are willing to be honest about what they see in the addict's behavior should be present. Significant others such as a boss, a minister, coworkers, and close friends should be involved to support the family with their factual presentations. Each of the interveners should be willing to undergo formal training and education about the illness of addiction. They should also be willing to accumulate and write down specific data about the self-destructive behavior of the addict, rehearse what facts they will report and how they will report these facts with a professional, and then commit to caringly confront the addict with these facts (Johnson, 1986).

Individual confrontation with addicts is futile because of their superior ability to deny, threaten, cajole, plead, and otherwise subvert attempts to interfere with pursuit of their addiction. Therefore, support and corroboration of accounts is important in pinning the addict down. A suggested treatment plan, well formulated and oriented to specifics, is an essential element in the intervention; otherwise, the process will degenerate into a bitch session. Finally, very clear consequences of separation and detachment from the addict are detailed and followed through on if the offered treatment is refused. This is not an attempt to bluff the addict into treatment or an empty threat that may have been used before. Logical consequences of actions and the commitment to follow through on those actions should be calmly and specifically detailed (Johnson, 1986).

The human services worker's role in this endeavor is to first provide support and educate family members about how the crisis setting is created. The worker then helps the family assemble the most powerful and influential people in the addict's life and teaches them how to collect facts of the addict's behavior and how to confront the addict with those facts in a caring manner. During the intervention, the worker acts as a facilitator by coordinating each person's intervention, gently confronting the addict with his or her attempts to defend himself or herself, provides a point-by-point listing of the symptoms of addiction that the intervention has detailed, and then confronts the addict with the choice of undergoing treatment or of having the family and friends detached from the addict. If the addict agrees, then the worker indicates what the treatment options are, that the addict's bags are packed, and that a car is waiting to take him or her to the treatment center. If the foregoing is not done in a coordinated and united manner, the prospects for a successful intervention are minimal (Doweiko, 1990, 233–234; Johnson, 1986; Wegscheider-Cruse, 1985). In no instance do we believe that a family should attempt this on their own without first consulting a professional substance abuse worker.

Wegscheider-Cruse (1985, pp. 20–21) has also proposed this intervention with codependents and ACOAs. This is perhaps even more difficult than cracking the denial system of the addict. Not only do codependents resist change in themselves, but they are also unwilling to let others get well, so they have even more reason to deny their problems and behavior. The codependent will make up excuses for the dependent and will minimize and rationalize problems. Confronted with the hard facts, the codependent "yes, buts" the confronters. As with the chemical dependent, the interveners must be willing to separate from the codependent if commitment to treatment is not forthcoming.

Detoxification

After a client has committed to treatment, the next step is detoxification. In the case of Gordon, once he has agreed to go into the unit, he is transferred to a private room close to the nurses' station and completes his detoxification. Important to this process is that being "undrunk" should not be confused with being detoxified. Detoxification is a very serious medical process, depending on how badly addicted the alcoholic is. Although the procedure may seem to run counter to the goal of detoxification, Gordon is given phenobarbital to allow him to avoid the severe pain accompanying withdrawal. Detoxification is not a character-building experience, so there is no need for him to hurt while going through it. About three days are necessary to get the effects of alcohol out of his system. During that time, Gordon is allowed to sleep as much as possible, eat a well-balanced diet, and watch TV. If he is up to it, other clients who have gone through detoxification will come in and talk with him. The others do not come to proselytize, but to let him know that as tough as it is, they made it through this preliminary crisis stage and so will he (Parker, 1986).

Henry (another patient): Hi! My name's Henry Schultz. I'm another patient here. Ray thought you might be up for some company.

Gordon: Man, I'm glad to talk to somebody. This is tough, I guess I was strung out.

Henry: It is tough! I went through it three weeks ago. I guess you could use a drink, huh?

Gordon: Brother, could I!

Henry: Yeah, I know. That's not gonna get easier for a while either, they make you come face up to it here. It's no piece of cake, but they really care about you. I just wanted to tell you I'm here if you want to talk. I'm not gonna tell you not to drink or judge you about what you've done and nobody else will either. I've gotten into AA in a big way, and it's really been a help.

Gordon: I don't know about that, spilling your guts and all. I don't think I could do that.

Henry: I thought the same thing. Lay my soul bare in front of a bunch of drunks, no way! But it's easier than you think. Especially when you meet the people. Hell! There's all kinds of people in it, some big shots, little shots, but all of us are not-so-hot shots when it comes to drinking. [*The conversation continues for a good bit, with Gordon asking all kinds of questions about treatment and about Henry's drinking problems, and guardedly discussing himself.*]

This initial dialogue with one of the other clients is important because it safely lets Gordon consider what the possibilities for recovery are, provides a peer as a resource, gives him a role model, and establishes at least one relationship within the therapeutic community (Parker, 1986).

Treatment Goals

Polcin (1992) has proposed that any comprehensive treatment program has three distinct phases with comprehensive treatment goals and methods:

Phase 1: Orientation and education. The goal is to engage clients and families in the treatment process.

Phase 2: Addressing core issues that are related to dependency. Clients are expected to address emotional issues in counseling and multifamily groups and examine how their behavior on a day-to-day basis in the treatment milieu reflects core issues.

Phase 3: Leaving the community. This includes going to AA, practicing the tools they have learned in treatment, becoming more acutely aware of relapse triggers, and processing separation events. A continuing care agreement is worked out with the client, the counselor, and the family.

After Gordon's assessment and detoxification, but prior to going into treatment, Carolyn and Ray carefully go over treatment goals with Gordon. His treatment plan contains a comprehensive set of goals. Each was developed from his assessment plan, which identifies a specific debilitating condition, a goal to alleviate that condition, and a set of specific objectives for attaining the goal. Here are two sample goals.

1. *Gordon's drinking goal.*
   Condition: Excessive consumption of alcohol. Gordon has difficulty meeting the demands of his work and social responsibilities without drinking.
   Goal: Eliminate the consumption of alcohol.

Objectives: Gordon will
a. eliminate the intake of alcohol both during working hours and after working hours every day, including the weekend
b. express his feelings and choose positive coping behaviors, which he will employ to deal with stress-producing persons, events, or situations
c. demonstrate for 28 days of inpatient treatment and 6 months' aftercare that he is able to cope successfully with persons, events, and situations at work and at home that trigger anxiety and avoid the use of alcohol to reduce that anxiety
d. use the group and St. Poly's staff as a source of support and strength in attaining the goal of eliminating alcohol consumption by actively participating in group, helping other people attain their goals, and committing himself to accepting help and support from others in working on his own goals.

2. *Gordon's emotional and social goal.*
Condition: Gordon either withdraws from interaction or inappropriately acts out with others, including his own family, when he is stressed.
Goal: Emit appropriate emotional and social responses while in the presence of others who may produce stress, including his own family.
Objectives: Gordon will
a. engage in nondrug conversation with a staff member at least twice each day and with a peer at least three times each day during inpatient treatment
b. carry on at least one nonargumentative discussion with each family member (Amy, Mark, Lisa) during each visit during inpatient treatment
c. during aftercare, carry on at least two nonargumentative discussions per day with Amy and at least one such discussion per day with both Mark and Lisa
d. engage in a minimum of one social activity (game room, gym, horseshoe pit, lake area, dancing, or such) during inpatient treatment
e. engage in a minimum of two social activities (in absence of alcohol) with his family during six months of aftercare—activities to be planned by family as a group.

Formulating comprehensive treatment goals reflects a multimodal approach that recognizes and addresses biological, psychological, and social aspects of addiction (Frances, 1988). Currently, the drug treatment community seems to be moving in the direction of using multimodal approaches that incorporate several different models and reflect the increasing recognition and support through research (Adelman & Weiss, 1989) that chemically dependent clients require a broad-based approach because of the various needs presented by them (Polcin, 1992). The major advantage of the multimodal approach is that the variety of needs that the chemically dependent present can be better accommodated. The approach is based on the premise that chemical dependency involves social, familial, behavioral, medical, psychological, and spiritual factors and that to be effective, treatment must recognize and address each of these.

Multimodal treatment at St. Polycarp is based on the therapeutic community model, which emphasizes both abstaining from alcohol and addressing emotional factors of drug use. The therapeutic community perspective views drug abuse as a disorder of the whole person reflecting problems in conduct, attitudes, values, moods, and emotional management (De Leon, 1989). Emotional issues are addressed primarily in terms of how they are reflected in behaviors and attitudes in the therapeutic milieu. At the center of the therapeutic community is involvement with one's peer group. Through involvement with each other, chemical dependents learn how to manage emotional issues effectively, practice new, more adaptable behaviors, confront and support each other appropriately, and take responsibility for themselves (Polcin, 1992).

Treatment Schedule

To help clients attain treatment goals, the treatment schedule at an inpatient drug treatment center is rigorous. For example, Gordon is going to be very busy with his day once he comes out of detoxification. He will be up at 7:00 every morning. He is responsible for getting his room clean, showering, and dressing. Before breakfast he will meet with his small group and read and discuss the daily passage from the *Twenty-Four Hours a Day* book (Alcoholics Anonymous, 1985). From 9:00 to 10:30 every morning he will be in a small group. This group will deal with value clarification, assertion training, enabling behavior, anger, and a variety of other topics that fuel the fires of alcoholism. From 10:30 to 12:00 Gordon will be in a small therapeutic group that will look specifically at each member's maladaptive coping skills and defense mechanisms. After lunch, from 12:30 to 1:30 he will be in an occupational therapy group that will allow him to use his hands as well as his mind. From 1:30 to 2:30 he will be in a physical therapy group to get his body back in shape. Both of these afternoon activities are for the specific purpose of teaching him to substitute positive addictions for the negative one of alcoholism. He will then be allowed time for a shower and a bit of leisure. From 3:30 to 4:30 he will learn about the AA "Big Book" (Alcoholics Anonymous, 1976). From 4:30 to 5:30 he will have an individual session with his counselors to review his progress, set goals, and obtain homework assignments. After dinner, from 6:00 to 8:00 he may either be in a family therapy session, attend an AA meeting, listen to a speaker on addiction, or view an educational video tape. After this he will have reading and journal writing to complete. By 11:00 he will be dead tired and ready for bed.

Cramming the day with all these activities fill two purposes. First, a great deal of learning needs to take place in the short time available. Each activity is designed to furnish part of this reeducation process. Second, there is usually very little structure in the lives of chemical dependents. The therapeutic community and its activities teach them to live responsibly. By being on time, taking care of their rooms, and completing their assignments, they reengage in responsible living and relearn to make commitments and keep them (Parker, 1986).

The Treatment Group

The format for our demonstration of intervention procedures will be the treatment group. There are a number of reasons why groups are preferable in treating addiction. First and foremost, the relationship skills of chemical dependents are typically wretched. Chemical dependents desperately need positive social interaction to replace isolated self-involvement with their chemical seducer (Lawson et al., 1984, p. 122). Belonging, acceptance, affection, social interaction, nonuniqueness, equality, and development of a new self-concept are all relationship needs that can best be met by the treatment group (Dinkmeyer & Muro, 1979). Specific outcomes of the treatment group (Corey & Corey, 1977; George & Dustin, 1988; Ohlsen, 1970) include

1. learning more effective social skills through feedback from others
2. gaining support for new behaviors by reality testing in a safe environment
3. encouragement of experimentation and risk taking through modeling by others
4. recreation of the world outside, with all its diversity and problems
5. providing opportunity for honest feedback by peers rather than "know-it-all" professionals
6. learning through emotional closeness of others
7. having a safe environment to self-disclose about threatening issues and being accepted by others while doing so
8. productive tension that propels and promotes change
9. increased focus on here-and-now events rather than past activities
10. making an emotional investment not only in oneself but also in other members
11. imparting facts and information about chemical dependence and salient aspects of its effects
12. regaining a sense of humor
13. instilling hope.

Inpatient treatment at St. Polycarp consists of several kinds of group work: group therapy, group education, multiple-family therapy, AA group meetings, community groups, and aftercare groups. Usually there are from six to ten members in the group. Group members represent a heterogeneous mix of sex, age, and race. This mix occurs by design, because the staff wants the unique problems of each member to surface. Addicts have severe blind spots for their own defenses but not necessarily for each other's. Thus, the diversity of members should allow them to be able to see through the defense mechanisms of their peers, confront these blind spots, and help their peers accomplish treatment goals (Ohlsen, 1970, pp. 109–110). For brevity's sake we will introduce four representative members of Gordon's group.

Alice is a 55-year-old Caucasian housewife who had been finishing off her afternoon in an alcoholic haze of martinis. Her children have left and she is now an "empty nester." Her husband and children had denied her drinking until she was involved in an auto accident, left the scene, and was picked up driving while intoxicated. She was remanded to St. Polycarp by a judge.

Liz is a 35-year-old African-American nurse. She was in charge of an intensive-care unit. She burned out on the job and was caught raiding the pharmaceutical cabinet. She yo-yos between depressants (alcohol and pills) to take the pain of the job away and amphetamines to get her "up" for her job. She is on suspension and in danger of losing her job and her license.

Manuel is a 24-year-old suspended bank guard whose father died an alcoholic when Manuel was 11. His Chicano background dictates a macho image that says, "I take care of and handle everything," including alcohol and pills—which he did not handle. He is single and has used alcohol and pills since he was a teenager.

Ruth is a 41-year-old Caucasian who was sexually abused repeatedly by her stepfather when she was a teenager. She married at 18, had two children, and was divorced at 23. She has worked as a bookkeeper for a construction company for the past ten years. She has had several short, fruitless liaisons with men. She has been an alcohol abuser since her teenage years. She got drunk, took some sleeping pills, and turned the gas on in her apartment. The paramedics brought her to St. Polycarp.

Learning Relationship Skills

Relationship skills occupy center stage in the first few meetings of a group. As Brill (1981, p. 129) indicates, during the initial phases of a group, the group leader should provide support and structure, setting the stage for group members to develop trust and cohesiveness. Videotaping is important to this endeavor and is typically used throughout the sessions. The use of videotaping is a powerful tool for assessment, feedback, and therapeutic purposes, catching in pictures and words the dysfunctional defense systems the clients build for themselves (Brill, 1981; Hay & Nathan, 1982; Sobell & Sobell, 1978).

During session 2 with his group, Gordon's poor relationship skills are evident. Despite Gordon's stated desire and willingness to interact positively with other clients and to work on his own addiction in the group, this initial dialogue shows typical difficulties during early developmental phases of the group. Gordon's long history of denial and lack of communication of feelings, trust, and personal needs carries over into the early group sessions.

Gordon: Nothing against the rest of you here, but I really don't understand the reason for putting me in here with such heavy abusers. Ray, how was I chosen for this group anyway?

Ray: You don't see yourself fitting in?

Liz: Yeah, Gordon, you think your boozing's different from ours. Looks to me like you're Mr. High and Mighty and we're a bunch of gutter bums.

Alice: Afraid we've got your number? Still denying what you are. Boy, have you got something to learn!

Carolyn: What I see happening here is basically a lack of trust in this group. That's not only an important issue for here but for outside as well. What I want to do is turn on the video and go back over the introductions and the individual goals you'd all set for yourself that we did in our first session. They may help us all begin to see this group as a unified whole with common needs.

Accepting Responsibility

Clients learn to retake control over their lives, but this is not always easily done. Listen to Gordon as he confronts responsibility during session 3.

Gordon: What gripes me is they treat you like kids around here. Do this, go there, learn that!

Alice: Do you know why we're supposed to do that? It's because we need to know those things if we're going to be any good when we get out.

Gordon: That's fine, but I'm an adult and I can read this on my own.

Liz: Have you? And if you did, could you get anything out of it?

Gordon: I don't know who you are to talk about responsibility. They nailed you for raiding the pharmacy cabinet, didn't they?

Carolyn: When you unload on Liz, that's a neat way of getting the load off your back. If you could make us as angry at you as you feel toward everybody else, then you'd be justified in telling us all to buzz off.

Gordon: She asked for it. We're talking about all the Mickey Mouse stuff like cleaning up your room and so forth. If that's helping me with my drinking problem, I'll kiss your foot.

Manuel (Gordon's roommate): Maybe if you'd paid more attention to the Mickey Mouse stuff and not the booze you wouldn't be here now. Every morning I got to say something about living in a pigsty. If you were that sloppy I'm surprised you still got that big buck job.

Gordon: Oh! Now it's my work. I'll have you know I carried my load at work and I sure as hell don't see what making my bed's got to do with getting back on track.

Ray: When the others say those things to you, it's hard to believe you aren't responsible. Hence, you react angrily to them. While you were highly responsible and capable in the past, it's tough and hurts to be confronted with the fact that you're having trouble keeping up now.

Gordon: That's not right, I . . .

Ruth: Then what is right, Gordon? Sure it's not fun. It's not supposed to be a vacation. You've got 24 more days here. You haven't been responsible for a long time is what the others are saying, and now you pull the same thing with us.

Gordon: What do you want from me? You all sound just like my wife.

Ray: It's the same old tune you're hearing from them, and it makes you angry when you have to take on responsibility, so you'll show them.

Manuel: If he can't even get his bed made, he's not showing me much.

Gordon: I'll show you all!

Carolyn: It's not a question of showing them anything. It's a question, I think, of having the courage to show yourself.

Gordon: I don't know. It scares the hell out of me. I'm not sure what I can do anymore.

Ray: When you say it that way, I think we all understand. It's not just the simple things like making a bed or reading the assignment. It's the scary feeling of doing something you haven't done for a long time and wondering whether you'll fail again.

If Gordon can find enough fault with the treatment center, the staff, or their practices, and get them to respond in the same manner, he will be "justified" in his stance and also justified in returning to alcohol. This rebellious attitude is met by the therapist with empathy and some interpretation. Confrontation would be inappropriate and would place the locus of control too far outside the client—it would put control of his sobriety into the hands of someone else (Wallace, 1978, p. 38). When he answers the other group members in caustic ways, the workers respond empathically to the persons attacked, and when Gordon is attacked, the workers respond in supportive ways to him, casting hypotheses about how he feels now and how it may generalize to others who have attacked him (Ohlsen, 1970, pp. 116–129). By not reinforcing such dependent behavior, but reinforcing Gordon when he takes responsibility on his own shoulders, the workers provide a model for reassuming independence (Blume, 1978, p. 71).

Alice: [*Weeping.*] I know it sounds silly, but that damn wood sculpture I've been working on in art therapy is terrible. I can't get it right. It's just like everything else in my life.

Gordon: Ah, look, Alice. I used to do that as a hobby. If you wouldn't mind I could maybe give you a hand. I know how frustrating it can be.

Manuel: Hey, man! That's the first time you ever said you'd do anything for anybody. You feelin' OK?

Gordon: It's no big deal.

Ray: Yet I think Manuel's got a point. It's good to see you care about Alice. Offering to help her says you're taking on responsibility for someone else, something you haven't been able to do in a long time. Now if we can just get you to make Manuel's bed. [*General laughter, Gordon included.*]

Getting Past Denial

In adults a rigid, nonmodifiable, and repeated use of denial is a defense that is usually associated with psychotic disorders and addiction. As long as it is intact, the client cannot feel concern with doing anything constructive about his or her illness (Maxwell, 1986, p. 176). It is the glue that holds a shattered self-esteem together. The most difficult task of the worker is to lessen the denial and encourage increased self-awareness and disclosure while at the same time keeping anxiety at minimal levels (Wallace, 1978, p. 32).

In the treatment of alcoholism, two levels of denial exist. The first is the denial of the presence and magnitude of a drinking problem (Blume, 1978, pp. 68–69). Continued denial specifically associated with drinking is a poor prognosis, and the chemical dependent who continues to use denial is not likely to stay sober. The second level is denial of long-standing life problems. While it may sound antithetical to recovery, denial of serious life problems other than drinking is an appropriate defense mechanism early on in treatment. This is so because those are the stressors that probably triggered drug use in the first place. To break down defenses in these areas would put more stress on the system, increase anxiety, and set the client up for failure (Chalmers & Wallace, 1978, p. 262).

Confrontation

As Adler (1956, p. 396) says, "It is not enough to be a friend of mankind, a benevolent counselor. Such counseling simply makes life agreeable for the client; the counselor praises the client, all the time believing that the counselor will arrive at results through the charm of his or her personality." When heavy denial and its defensive consorts are encountered, confrontation is probably the most potent and dangerous weapon the worker has (Lawson et al., 1984, p. 125). The use of confrontation as a therapeutic technique needs to be carefully considered. Putting a resisting and denying client on the "hot seat" is a questionable practice for a variety of reasons. First, other clients may viciously attack the client and in the process force compliance or make a scapegoat of the client. Second, focusing only on the one client may permit other members in the group to become less involved. Third, dependent clients are excellent at seducing others into taking responsibility through advice giving (Ohlsen, 1970, pp. 127, 168).

The purpose of confrontation is not to vent personal frustration, impose belief systems contrary to those of the client, or act in punitive ways (Lawson et al., 1984, p. 101). Critical in the confrontation is the worker's emotional astuteness and competence in determining the correct moment to confront (Perez, 1985, p. 164). A main ingredient in successfully confronting a client is trust, which is essential for the confrontation to carry the most therapeutic weight.

A principal characteristic of confrontation is its challenge. The challenge is embedded in a question so that an immediate feeling response is evoked. A second characteristic of confrontation is that it is direct and action-oriented. The client is constantly placed in new roles and situations calling for a response. Explored in a sensitive, perceptive manner, these new roles and situations enable a client to be aware of discrepancies between behaviors and intentions, feelings and messages, and insights and actions (Dinkmeyer, Pew, & Dinkmeyer, 1979, p. 110). Confrontive statements can be hooked to reflective and interpretive statements. They also are generally connected with an owning statement, one that says clearly that "I," the counselor, own this. If the client denies the statement, then the confrontation is redirected: "OK, if that's not you, then what is you?" Confrontations are generally made in the form of a demand and are linked to alternatives. Confrontation catches a client in a contradiction and asks the client why he or she behaves in such a contradictory manner. Used judiciously and altered to fit the dilemma, confrontation can be extremely helpful in jarring clients out of old response patterns (Shulman, 1973, p. 198). There are five major areas of confrontation:

1. experiential: a response to any discrepancy perceived by the worker
2. strength: focused on the client's resources, especially if the client does not recognize them
3. weakness: focused on the client's liabilities or pathology
4. didactic: clarification of misinformation or lack of information
5. encouragement to action: pressing the client to act on his or her world in a constructive manner and discouraging a passive attitude toward life.

Experiential, strength, and encouragement should be used most frequently, with much less reliance on exploiting the client's weaknesses (Lawson et al., 1984, p. 103).

Confrontation is always used in relation to behaviors and never used to attack a client's personhood. Many confrontations will be paradoxical, will be enlarged to farcical dimensions, and will have humor attached so that the client may clearly see the ridiculousness of the behavior called into question. For example, during session 5 with his group, Gordon is confronted by both workers and group members as a way of cracking his denial.

Gordon: It's easy for you to say I shouldn't go drinking with the guys after work. You just can't do that and stay on the inside track.

Carolyn: [*Catching the discrepancy.*] So if you don't do what they want, you're out. Yet the very act of continuing to drink has almost put you out. Do you see the discrepancy there?

Gordon: Yes, but I've got to be a team player. Can't let those young sharks get ahead.

Manuel: [*Calling the question.*] Ahead of what?

Carolyn: [*Creating an exaggerated image.*] Picture this, Gordon. You're a little minnow swimming around in a martini glass with all these big hungry fish circling you, but you're so goofy from that vodka ocean that you swim right into their jaws. How does that fit?

Gordon: [*Chuckles.*] OK. I'll accept that. If only there was some way to get out of that double bind.

Ray: [*Proposing action.*] What would happen if you did exactly the opposite of what you've been doing? That is, just turn that martini lunch down. Become one of the sober sharks instead of the drunken minnows? How could you do that?

Gordon: I don't know. *[Lamely.]* Then I wouldn't be a regular guy.

Ruth: [*Drawing the paradox.*] Yeah. You've been a regular guy, all right. That's with a three-martini lunch. Why don't you put a half-dozen down? Then you'd be Superman. I thought I was Superwoman when I did that crap and you see me now.

Gordon: [*Sullenly.*] Now, wait a second! I didn't mean that. [*Turns to Carolyn.*] That's not true. How can she say that? We're supposed to be helping each other. How can you let her attack me?

Carolyn: [*Redirecting.*] Then what did you mean? [*Placing a demand with a reflection.*] I understand how that hurts, but I also believe that when you try to get me to support you and imply that I'm a lousy counselor if I don't, I'd just be playing into that game of "poor me." What will you do instead? [*Proposing alternatives.*] You have some choices. You can sit and sulk, you can be dependent and ask me to take your part, or you can use your considerable strength and make a clear assertive statement back. Which will it be?

Alice: [*Creating an image.*] See how you get yourself? You want to be so darn independent, yet you continuously say, "Come and hold me, look what a poor child am I." I get this picture of a big baby in a crib and it's full of empty bourbon bottles and you nestled in there.

Gordon: By God that isn't true. I'm not a baby. Life's been a bitch.

Carolyn: [*Commiserating overbearingly.*] Yep! Life's that way. It's rotten, cruel and unusual punishment. Wouldn't it be wonderful to make everybody responsible for your drinking put on hairshirts and roll around in cinders. That would pay them back for all the harm they've done to you.

Gordon: People just don't understand me, and that includes all of you. I'm gonna leave this stinkin' place.

Carolyn: [*Avoiding a trap.*] I'd not like to see that happen, but what they're doing is confronting your own ways of fooling yourself and attempting to get you to see the strengths you've got. If I get them off your back, you don't have to be responsible. If I don't, you leave and I'm at fault. Either way you'd have an excuse for continuing to blame somebody else. [*Attributing the projection.*] It seems as if you'd like me to get into the same kinds of double binds you put yourself in. [*Owning.*] So if you believe I'm not much of a counselor because of that, it's certainly your privilege.

Gordon: [*Rocks back in chair.*] I do that? Damn! I guess maybe I do.

Some of the responses may seem to put Gordon on the hot seat, but the other members are willing to own that they too have been where Gordon is now. The confrontations point to the affective, cognitive, and behavioral discrepancies in Gordon's life, not to the totality of Gordon, the person. The confrontations are exhortations to action. The group is pushing Gordon to make changes in his life, particularly in regard to the way he denies and defends his drinking behavior.

Disrupting Irrational Mental Sets

According to Ellis (1987), it is not an event itself but our belief about that event that causes us to feel and act in certain irrational ways. By starting to think "insane" thoughts about what people or events "should," "ought," "must" do or be to make it a perfect world, chemical dependents become victims of their irrational thoughts about the events. By putting such irrational statements up in the billboard of their minds, chemical dependents can easily fall back into hurt, rejected feelings and manifest these feelings in behavior designed to pay back the persons or events that intrude into their self-centered universe. It is extremely important to catch chemical dependents as they begin to build these billboards, because this kind of thinking is what starts a chain of events that can ultimately build up to another drinking episode. The key to stopping this "insane" thinking is teaching the person to recognize the cues that appear antecedent to the negative feelings and subsequent bad behavioral outcomes. Once these cues are picked up, then new, rational statements can be manufactured to replace the old, debilitating ones that underlie beliefs.

For example, in Gordon's treatment, a videotape of session 6 was used as the focus for group therapy in session 7. Session 6 had examined the events and behaviors that brought each client to St. Polycarp. The group viewed excerpts of session 6 that were selected by the group leaders to vividly recreate and model each individual's unique addictive situation and to stimulate and uncover each member's defense mechanisms. Clients first portrayed themselves; then, after a discussion of defense mechanisms commonly used by chemical dependents, members exchanged roles and attempted to model what the other's defenses appeared to be.

Manuel: Man, those were tough. Liz played me to a T! I also thought Alice really hit Gordon's nail on the head too!

Ray: How he first rationalizes, and then when things really get hot, regresses.

Gordon: Before I saw that videotape I would never have believed it! But there I was. Rationalizing my drinking by telling myself I was "sick" when I couldn't make it to work because I was hung over or still smashed. Boy, was that sad! And then with my doctor about my health. Just throwing a fit. Alice role-played me so well, it was as if she'd been there. It made me sick to watch that. What a jerk!

Ruth: What about that preadolescent stuff, "I'll take my ball and go home," see how Liz did that with the doctor routine. It was just like yesterday with the family therapy. I didn't know whether that was your mother or wife, the way you were manipulating her and sulking like a kid who didn't get any candy.

Gordon: [*Angrily.*] What do you mean, acting like a kid? Why don't we take a look at how you act around that teenager of yours?

Liz: Look at what you just did, Gordon. You're regressing right now!

Alice: That videotape didn't lie. Don't you see how you get into that? It's weird that you can see the rationalizing, but kick up your heels when we call you on the regression.

Carolyn: Remember the work we did on cueing in our verbal and nonverbal behavior the other day. Notice what feelings you get when your defense mechanisms kick in and what thoughts go through your head to get that going. [*Gordon looks at videotape again.*]

Gordon: [*Sheepishly.*] Maybe I was acting like a kid. Maybe I wasn't connecting that stuff you call cueing to my real life.

Carolyn: Right here we have a good example of how you might begin to use that cueing. When Ruth confronted you just a minute ago, what messages went through your mind to cause you to react angrily and then attack her—rather than looking at yourself?

Gordon: The first thing that flashed through was, "You're just like my wife." She's always implying I'm not capable of acting like an adult. She makes me crazy when she does that.

Carolyn: Using Gordon as an example, what cues did we teach you all to recognize and what did we learn to do to counteract our irrational thinking as well as our behavior?

Ruth: First off, Gordon needs to recognize that as one of those stop signs you were talking about. Anytime that he relates to the old ways he behaved toward Amy and hears, "I'm not good enough," he needs to see that as a warning sign that he's kicking in a lot of that old dependent put-down crap.

Manuel: He also could change "she" to "I" 'cause it's really him and his beliefs about what she said. He allows that to happen.

Alice: He could make an assertive statement out of it, like, "I understand how you might feel that way, but right now I'm feeling like I'm behaving pretty straight with you and it hurts me that you'd feel I haven't changed."

Cueing provides Gordon with psychological stop signs. These are not easy to see, especially when, in the heat of the moment, it is all too easy to revert to years' worth of programmed thinking. Cueing is like any other new skill and will take much practice and feedback before the client is able to "rewire" his or her thinking.

Carolyn: I want you all to list out your cues for those predicaments that make you crazy, angry, depressed, and so on in your logs. Then let's work on building new belief statements. Monitor yourself as we work together and see if you can catch yourself before others do. If you feel a bit odd when you put those new statements in and say them, then you're on the right track.

If clients cannot catch the insane messages they send themselves, then other physiological or affective responses may work as cues. Sweating hands, a lump in the throat, and a palpitating heart may be good physical cues. The flush of anger, the chagrin of embarrassment, and the gloom of despair may be good affective cues.

Overcoming Environmental Cues to Drink

Sobell and Sobell (1978) have done significant work in demonstrating how setting events reinforce the desire to drink. In their therapeutic experiments they have rigged elaborate sets that include complete taverns. Subtly but surely, settings and the events that occur within them provide powerful cues to respond in particular ways. Returning to a world that is filled with potent environmental cues to drink strains the newfound coping skills of the recovering alcoholic to the limit and can create another crisis point.

Putting chemical dependents in role plays and imaginal sets in groups will work effectively in helping them recognize and manipulate environments that are powerfully reinforcing of their chemical dependency. By learning how to use cognitive restructuring (McMullin & Giles, 1981), imaging (Neisser, 1976), coping thoughts (Cormier & Hackney, 1987), emotive imagery and covert modeling (Cormier & Cormier, 1985), and stress inoculation (Meichenbaum, 1985), clients are able to armor themselves against the negative setting events that they will inevitably encounter.

In session 10 of Gordon's treatment group, the group constructs and role-plays a setting event that portrays Gordon getting into his car after a very stressful day at work, which has been interrupted by phone calls from home saying that Mark has been suspended from school because he was found with a marijuana cigarette in his possession. Gordon watches as Manuel plays the part.

Manuel: [*As Gordon, talking to himself as he guns the car out of the company lot.*] Jesus Christ! Everything was supposed to be better. If this is better, screw it! Work sucks! The president is on my back again. Produce! Produce! Produce! That's all I hear. And now Mark! I suppose that's my fault too. Amy sure laid that one on me while going nuts over the phone. That's what I got to look forward to when I hit the door. Hey, there's the Olde English Inn coming up over the hill. My favorite watering hole, those dark oak booths and overstuffed chairs. Man, do they make a mean Manhattan in there. I can just smell that aroma. I'll bet some of the old crowd's still there too, and Roxie, my favorite bartender. They sure never gave me any flak. Glad to see me. It's happy hour too! Man, are my hands sweating, I'm shaking too. I've got to settle down. Two for the price of one. To hell with it. I'll just have one and go. It'll take the edge off before I hit the door and have to deal with Amy and Mark. [*Manuel turns the car into the inn parking lot.*]

Ray: OK! Now, that's not a pretty scene, but we know that there are going to be times just like that. The world isn't perfect, and you're going to run into problems like that, feel those lousy emotions, and those tempting places like the Olde English Inn are going to be there just waiting for a day like that. What are you going to do, Gordon?

Gordon: All right. Let me put my plan into action. My positive self-statements will be, "I don't care how rough it's been at work, I did a helluva job today. The boss always gripes like that around the end of the month so don't take it personally." My stress inoculates will be a number of things. First, I'll put Mozart on the tape deck, that's calming and reminds me of being on the banks of Lake Zurich just watching the sailboats glide by. Yeah, I'm already relaxed. Behaviorally, I can practice my breathing skills, just taking deep easy breaths and letting all that stress flow right out my nose. While I'm doing that, I can see my jogging shoes and sweats waiting for me by the back door at home.

I can replace my negative thoughts about home by saying, "I would have come in and blustered and stormed around and grilled Mark, generally raised hell and then sulked. That didn't do a damn bit of good except get me stressed out even more. I know I can think clearer and more rationally after I've worked out. I'll ask Amy to go for a jog around Audubon Park. I can feel that sweat pouring out of my body, cleaning it out. I can feel my body, hard, lean, coordinated, just like a fine machine, just rolling along, eating up the miles. That'll feel good."

Now here comes the inn over the hill. I'm starting to think how easy it'd be to just turn in there. I can feel my hands getting sweaty, and my throat's dry. I put my thought stopping into gear, "STOP THAT! Switch. Think what your sagging, pulpy body was after you got through with a bout in there, turkey! You couldn't stumble to the john without gasping for air. God, were you ever a sorry sucker."

To cue myself to how good I now feel, I'll flex my leg and feel that hard thigh muscle, a great tactile cue to remind me how far I've come, and I'm not giving that up. Reviewing my self-talk, I can say, "Yeah, Roxie and the inn were a great place to get quietly smashed, but that was then. Looking at the place in broad daylight, it's shopworn, and I've got real oak in my study instead of that fiberboard, ersatz stuff in there. Ha! I'll bet the boys look a little shopworn too after today. Further, I never really liked that sweet smell of a Manhattan, always covered it with a cigarette. I don't want that crap. There's nothing like a V-8, and only 10 calories too. Then what I want is to get out and run."

I also know that after I get back from jogging I can use all the communication skills I've learned here. No ranting and raving. It's a bitch about Mark, but I don't need to catastrophize over it. I can handle that, and I'll take the time to handle it. My family's the most important thing in the world to me, and I'm not just paying lip service to it, I'm living it! Press the accelerator down and go on by with no regrets.

By taping and practicing these new mental images over and over with the assistance of the workers and the group, Gordon learns how to use a wide variety of positive coping mechanisms to get by this potentially dangerous environmental set. This is not a one-shot exercise. It will take Gordon a great deal of practice to reprogram himself to ignore those old cues that set him up to drink.

Treating the Family

The attitudes, structure, and function of the family system have been shown to be perhaps the most important variables in the outcome of treatment. If the system changes from enabling to more adaptive behavior, it may sustain improvement and change in the alcoholic (Kaufman & Pattison, 1982a, p. 669). However, this is easier said than done because, paradoxically, if the alcoholic makes a commitment to stop drinking, the maladaptive family may become so threatened that it does everything in its power to reinstitute the homeostasis of alcoholism. In the case of Gordon, several hypotheses support this idea. If his drinking ceased, one or more family members might attempt to sabotage his sobriety; Amy might undermine the treatment to ensure that Gordon's drinking recurred so she could retain control. The drinking may represent a cover to distract attention from underlying relationship conflicts. Gordon's alcohol use may have been a stabilizing rather than a disruptive influence on the family's lifestyle and represented attempts to deal with family issues that could not be confronted during sober periods.

From the perspective of the codependent, the vehemently denied but enabling statement translates into something like, "If I get you fixed, then I can let go, and you can take care of me and I won't have to be responsible ever again! But I can't really risk that, because I really want the power of control, without having to take responsibility for that power." The threat of disturbing such a tenuous family equilibrium creates a crisis of substantial proportions, and it is one of the most difficult situations with which the worker must deal.

At St. Polycarp, members of the family are not allowed to see the client for the first ten days of treatment. The only interaction between the staff and the family in this early stage is to obtain a social history. Families are kept away from the chemical dependent for fear that they may try to sabotage treatment efforts in a bid to return the recovering addict to his or her addiction (Parker, 1986).

Amy: [*On the telephone.*] Carolyn, I know you said that we wouldn't be allowed to come see Gordon until we first came together in family therapy, but his folks have flown in from Chicago and I was wondering if we couldn't just bring them out for a while. He sounded pretty good when I talked to him on the phone. The kids really miss him, too.

Carolyn: I understand how his parents must be concerned, but as I told you when we took the social history, these first few days are critical to Gordon's assuming responsibility for getting well. As I told you then, it's awfully easy to fall back into old ways of behaving. You wouldn't want the work we've done so far to come undone, would you?

Amy: Well . . . of course not. But what will I tell Gordon's parents?

Carolyn: Tell them the truth. That Gordon's been dependent on other people a long time. He's got to handle this himself for a bit longer.

The worker lays a guilt trip on Amy. This may be construed as manipulation of the rankest type, but the chances for sabotage are too great, even though the client's family may have badgered the client to go into treatment in the first place. Indeed, if Amy feels that Gordon is getting better, this may cause a great deal of anxiety for her. If she has been a "supermom," she may be afraid that in his newfound strength Gordon may usurp her place in the system. Alcoholics may also play this game by complaining that their family really needs them (Parker, 1986).

Gordon: [*On the fourth day of treatment.*] Look, I've got the booze out of my system. I really need to get out of here.

Carolyn: We discussed that when you agreed to come into the program. You'll see your family with me next week in therapy.

Gordon: [*Adamant.*] My family really needs me! By God! You don't want me to see them. Just because you don't have a family, trying to stick it to me. [*Sarcastic.*] Hell, you couldn't get a man again if you were covered with gold dust!

Carolyn: [*Calmly.*] It would be neat if you could blame me for all that's gone on in your family over the years, but it won't wash. They also needed you when you were a drunk for the last four years.

Gordon: [*Pleading, promising, and whining.*] Look. I've really learned my lesson this time. I haven't even wanted a drink since I've been at St. Poly's.

Carolyn: [*Assertively.*] I don't listen to that. I don't need any promises, and you don't need to make any. We operate like AA, one day at a time. This is the fourth day you've been sober. Tomorrow we'll work on five. That's the way it is.

Gordon: [*Screaming.*] Listen you cold, merciless bitch. I can leave here any damn time I want to.

Carolyn: [*Calmly and calculatedly.*] If screaming is your way of getting me to cave in, that won't work either. If you leave against medical advice, and that's what it is, you are signing your death warrant. Is that how you will help your family?

Gordon: [*Whining.*] You don't trust me.

Carolyn: You're right about that. You haven't earned my trust yet. You can earn it by doing your level best in this program. Show me you want to stay sober and that'll go a long way toward it. Leave and you'll end up dead inside of a year. I want you to clearly understand, physically dead. So if you've become so responsible, make the choice. If you stay here I'll do everything in my power to help you get back to your family in good shape. If you leave there's nothing I can do for you. So choose.

The worker experiences a wide range of the client's manipulations. She turns Gordon's ploys against him in calm, factual, and confrontive ways. She will not take on any of the client's responsibility for getting well other than to say she'll work with him, nor will she accept any of the client's residual emotions that he tries to project onto her. The worker is not above painting a very grim picture of the client's future when he threatens to leave. Her primary mission is to keep him in treatment, and Carolyn will use her considerable manipulative skills to do that when necessary.

Family options.   Families like Gordon's have three options: (1) keep doing what they have been doing, and nothing changes, except for the worse, (2) detach and emotionally distance themselves from the alcoholic, and changes may occur for the better, or (3) separate and physically distance themselves from the alcoholic, and changes may also occur for the better. Although paradoxical to what one might assume to be the closeness and caring the alcoholic's support system ought to demonstrate, choices 2 or 3 are the most supportive ways significant others can act toward an alcoholic.

The alcoholic must understand that significant others will no longer tolerate the addictive behavior and the harm that it does to them. While such choices undoubtedly may breed crisis, this in no way means the people in the support system have given up. Choices 2 and 3 indicate that the family members will become responsible for themselves rather than trying to change the alcoholic. If the family can say, "We prefer that you not kill yourself, but we won't let you kill us, so you must make a choice as we have," this is an excellent start on the road to recovery (Kaufman & Pattison, 1982b, p. 1026). Even if both codependents and dependent agree to change, there should not be explicit or implicit assumptions that family ties will be fully reconstituted. While long-term nurturing of all system members is ideal, such positive interactions will not happen overnight. Each individual member first has to get intimate with himself or herself before trying to do so with the alcoholic. Any attempts to reassume responsibility for the alcoholic, no matter how well intended, have a high probability of enabling and promoting a relapse (Maxwell, 1986, p. 209). Avoidance of enabling behavior and assumption of responsibility are difficult, as Gordon's first family therapy session shows.

Family therapy session.   The primary task of the worker in the family is to detect and penetrate the defense systems the family has set up to keep things stable. Almost without exception, alcoholic families will have real trouble expressing feelings and communicating with one another (Maxwell, 1986, pp. 205–206). By keeping a low profile in the beginning, the worker lets the pathology of the family emerge (Parker, 1986). As Carolyn sits quietly, Gordon, Amy, Lisa, and Mark exchange stilted pleasantries and defensive comments, punctuated by long, awkward silences. As soon as the worker obtains an adequate assessment of the family's dynamic interaction, she becomes involved.

Amy: Now, I don't want you to worry about anything. I talked to your boss and he assured me the company is behind you 100%.

Gordon: That's great!

Carolyn: Amy, I'd like you to notice what you just did. You decided to take care of Gordon. What about your own feelings about carrying the load?

Amy: I just didn't want him to worry about his job. I know how much he's put into it.

Carolyn: Yes, but what about your feelings?

Amy: It just seems to me that Gordon should concentrate his efforts on getting better, don't you think?

Carolyn: Do you see what you're doing? I've asked you twice to speak to your feelings. Yet each time, you take responsibility for Gordon. You talk about him and not yourself. You pose a question that asks for my agreement. And you shift to events rather than dealing with your feelings. How does that strike you, Gordon?

Gordon: Er, I don't know. I guess Amy ought to express how she feels.

Carolyn: How do you feel?

Gordon: I think we probably don't do enough talking about our feelings.

Carolyn: That's right, but how do you feel?

This short exchange graphically demonstrates the tremendous difficulty the two adults have in expressing feelings to one another. They adroitly shift off this topic in a variety of ways. One very subtle way to avoid direct confrontation about feelings is to send a messenger. Of course, the messenger has to be very careful how the news is delivered; otherwise, he or she may get psychologically murdered in completing the task.

Amy: Lisa, tell your father what Grandpa and Grandma had to say.

Lisa: Ah, they said they were real sorry they didn't get to see you, and hoped you get well. They'd have really liked to stay and come here today, but Grandpa had to get back to Chicago for a meeting.

Carolyn: I wonder why you asked Lisa to tell Gordon that. My guess is that's a touchy subject about his parents leaving. Does your mom often ask you to do that?

Lisa: You bet! You do that all the time, Mom. Whenever you've got something you think'll cause a ruckus, you always send me to tell Dad 'cause you think he'll take it from me. Then I'm the bad guy. I hate it!

Carolyn: So you see, there's another way of getting around dealing with feelings. Send somebody else and let them deal with it, because feelings are risky, scary, and hard to handle.

Amy: Lisa has always been the apple of her dad's eye. She's always had a way with him.

Carolyn: Excuse me for picking on you right now, Amy, but what were you just doing?

Amy: I was talking about Lisa and her relationship with her dad.

Carolyn: That's right! You were talking *about* her, not *to* her. What would happen if you said that straight out? You might risk getting a feeling response back.

Lisa: Mom, you wouldn't like that. You always tell me to bear up when I try to talk to you about my feelings, and that goes for you too, Dad! Mom, you're too worried about what's going on with Dad's drinking to care about me, and Dad, you're too worried about getting a drink to listen, and if it wasn't booze it was work. Is it any wonder this family's screwed up?

Carolyn: Great, Lisa! Lisa's raised some pretty hot issues. Any feelings about them?

Gordon: [*Looking at Carolyn.*] I guess I just didn't realize I wasn't being the father I could be to her. I didn't realize I was doing that. I'm sorry.

Carolyn: Gordon, do you want me to be your messenger to Lisa?

Gordon: No!

Carolyn: Then don't tell me, but tell her that.

Amy: Well, I just know Mark doesn't feel that way. A real little trooper. He's kept a stiff upper lip through all this, kept up his grades and done everything around the house, plus made his own spending money mowing yards.

Carolyn: Amy, it is interesting that you find it difficult to feel for yourself, yet can tell others how they feel and even answer for them. What I'd like to do now is give each one of you an assignment for next time that specifically gets at what problems I see with communication in this group. Mark, since you didn't say anything today, I want you to write a letter to each member in the family telling each how you feel about him or her. Lisa, I'd like you to wear a big paper heart next time, and every time somebody doesn't respond directly to you or speak to their feelings, I'd like you to tear a piece of your heart off. Amy, in the codependency group I want you to solicit direct, feeling responses from people. I'll give you the questions to ask. Gordon, I want you to write down some of the feelings you had in here today into a script, and then take it back to the group and we'll role-play it on the videotape.

The major task is teaching all the family members to express their feelings in an open and honest way. Debilitating communication patterns are pointed out over and over to all family members who engage in disruptive communications. It is noteworthy that no mention is made of Gordon's drinking by anyone except Lisa. This conspiracy of silence still continues even after Gordon is in a chemical treatment unit and the whole family is in therapy for the problem. As Parker (1986) says, "There's a big, pet, pink rhinoceros [alcoholism] sitting there in the middle of the family, but everybody circles around it as if it didn't even exist, and it just keeps getting bigger and bigger and taking up more space." This problem will need to be reflected by the worker, for the sooner the alcoholism is brought into the open, the quicker the family can start building a new communication system.

Another issue is Mark, who has remained silent throughout the session. Invariably there is someone who can be extremely helpful in changing the system (Kaufman & Pattison, 1982b, p. 1031). Mark may have a great deal to do with changing the family network. Lisa is also a potent member of this system. The worker early on acknowledges her strength and reinforces her for clear, directional feeling responses—a rarity in this family. Finally, to facilitate communication, tasks may be assigned within the session as homework.

Comprehensive family treatment. While the family is not ultimately responsible for the chemical dependent's choice to use or stay dry, its behavior certainly influences the outcome. As a result, comprehensive treatment goes beyond abstinence and looks at improving family functioning. However, what type of treatment occurs for the family is of critical importance. Schaef (1986) has criticized typical family therapy as focusing exclusively on the chemical dependent and the enabling behavior of family members while excluding consideration of their own problems. Unwittingly, this treatment approach replicates the sick chemically dependent family with most attention focused on the substance abuser, next on the spouse, and finally on the children. Schaef extends this criticism to Al-Anon, where much of the focus is on how to live with an alcoholic rather than understanding and dealing with codependency (pp. 5–6).

Assuredly, family members adopt patterns of behavior to maintain the stability of the system along with much fear of and resistance to changing the status quo. This fear and resistance extends into the crisis that brings them into therapy. However, these defenses are more open during a crisis and, at that time, the worker can be firm and supportive by bringing in all family members to explore the problem and label the chemical dependence openly (Cable, Noel, & Swanson, 1986, p. 73).

There are three major advantages to family therapy if it is conducted with a view to helping the whole family. First, the family can confront the chemical dependent's addiction and can support his or her attempt to move into recovery. Second, the family learns how substance abuse is related to other patterns of family life such as roles, rules, and patterns of communication and may become aware of how they play a part in keeping others in the system in thrall to it (Cable et al., 1986, pp. 73–74). Third, and perhaps most important, the children can be educated as to the part they play in the dysfunctional system (Liepman et al., 1986, pp. 56–57).

Therapy for children.   Whenever therapeutic assistance is sought or recommended for the family, it should not be surprising if children are resistant, because they will feel it is the chemically dependent parent who needs help and not them. The therapist's legitimate and sincere explanation is that while this is the chemical dependent's problem, it is also a family problem and the children in particular deserve special attention (Black, 1981, p. 102). Cable et al. (1986) have listed nine common treatment goals for children of alcoholics:

1. assessing the children's situations and needs
2. providing support for the children
3. providing accurate, nonjudgmental information about alcoholism
4. correcting the children's inaccurate perceptions that they are the cause or reason for their parent's drinking
5. helping the children to focus on their own behavior by giving them a sense of control and the perception of being able to make responsible choices; and, if necessary, helping them to learn how to have fun
6. helping the children learn how to cope with real situations that may arise because of the parent's alcohol abuse—for example, if the parent passes out
7. reducing the children's isolation and helping them to share their dilemma with other children in similar situations
8. reducing the children's risk of developing substance abuse or alternately treating the children's substance abuse
9. enlisting the family and/or other support system to reinforce the children's gains (p. 69).

While school-based education about chemical dependency and its effects on families through such programs as CASPAR (1978) are effective, for children who are going through the crisis of a family member's addiction or recovery, Alateen, family therapy, or specialized codependent-child counseling groups are critical treatment components. Children learn in these groups about the disease concept so they can stop feeling guilt over the alcoholic behavior of their parents, realize which of their family rules and roles are healthy and unhealthy, understand they are not alone in their misery, and discover that there are alternate ways to cope with their problems other than the maladaptive ones taught by their families (Liepman et al., 1986, pp. 56–57). *The bottom line is that the emotional issues of all children raised in chemically dependent homes need to be addressed because all children are affected.* Finally, as a critical adjunct to treating children, all members of the affected family should be urged to participate in therapy. If certain members of the family refuse to participate in therapy there is danger of undermining it (Liepman et al., 1986, p. 55).

Radical attempts to restore the old family system.   As the masking behaviors that support the codependency are stripped away, it may be expected that more and more radical attempts will be made to restore the old system. In Gordon's case, a very traumatic experience from a multiple-family session that occurred the day before session 17 illustrates this dramatically. Ten minutes before the end of the multiple-family session, Amy announced that she was so distraught she was thinking of suicide. This threw things into an uproar and necessitated an individual suicide intervention with Amy that lasted two hours after the group session. Gordon, who had been attempting to deal with some of his feelings with Amy, was paralyzed and shocked into submission. This therapeutic material was immediately brought back to the group.

To help Gordon deal with this ploy, an "alter ego" exercise was videotaped. An alter-ego routine is done by having members of this group stand behind each seated role player and verbally state the potent (but unspoken) self-thoughts and self-talk that they perceive to be going on inside the role player's head.

Carolyn: [*Role modeling Amy.*] Gordon, I understand you wanted to talk to me about what happened in the family session yesterday.

Ruth: [*Taking the role of Amy's alter ego, standing behind Carolyn, with her hands resting gently on Carolyn's shoulders.*] I don't like this one little bit. But I really got him, the bastard.

Gordon: [*Avoiding eye contact and stammering.*] Yes . . . I was disturbed about the way you brought up the suicide stuff . . . without me knowing about it.

Ray: [*Taking the role of alter ego of Gordon, standing directly behind Gordon, with his hands resting gently on Gordon's shoulders.*] This is scary as hell! I'd like to kill her myself. I'm struggling like crazy to stay straight and she pulls that number. I want to tell her what I really feel about that. But I can't. I've got to protect her and me, so don't run your mouth. But I'm feeling betrayed too! Why am I feeling so paralyzed?

Carolyn: [*Role modeling Amy.*] Dear, I really didn't mean it the way it looked, it just came out. I couldn't help it. They said to get our feelings out. This whole mess is . . . I just want to get well and for us to be just like we used to be . . . right after we were married.

Ruth: [*As alter ego of Amy.*] I've got to cover this up, put it back on him. Let him wallow in it and see what he's done to me. It's payback time.

Gordon: [*Looking Carolyn straight in the eyes.*] Look, I feel lousy about what I've done in the past. But there's nothing I can do about it now. When you pull that kind of stunt it's just the past all over again. It hurts like hell when you do that. What I want to do is cut through all that phony baloney we've put on each other. I don't feel like it was ever anything but that. What I'm concerned about is right now. I'm scared to death I'm not gonna cut this, and I need you to understand that. I don't believe I'll break, whatever happens. You don't have to act helpless or self-destructive to keep me in line or earn my love. You've got that already and you'll have more of it, the better both of us get. By the way, you still haven't talked about how you feel.

Group: [*Cheers.*] All right, Gordon! Way to go!

Ray: [*As alter ego of Gordon.*] Holy cow! I don't believe I did that. I spilled the beans, told her how I felt. I thought I'd throw up. I was so scared, but I didn't. Maybe I have got what it takes to get out of this. I feel good. I really feel *good*! [*Breaks from role.*] How did that go, Gordon?

Gordon: [*Smiling from ear to ear.*] That's the first time in years, maybe ever, I said stuff like that. And you alter egos are right. I do feel good. If that had happened before I came here, it'd be a sure bet I'd have started drinking. There may be something else that sets me off, but I don't believe it'll be from keeping my feelings shut up now.

Ray: Could you now do that with Amy?

Gordon: It'd still be scary, but yes. I think, no, I *feel* like I can.

By bouncing submerged feelings off Gordon, the alter egos attempt to make crystal clear what the hidden messages are that drive the codependent and dependent. Given the opportunity to bring these agendas into the open, dependents and codependents can construct self-enhancing, positive, feeling-based, coping statements that untangle the snares and traps they set for one another. Although difficult and risky, constructing these kinds of statements is absolutely necessary to forming new and equitable relationships in a drug-free family system.

Aftercare

At St. Polycarp, the aftercare program requires that the client attend meetings two evenings a week for at least six months following dismissal from inpatient treatment. To address the issues of codependency and enabling activities, workers attempt to ensure that all significant family members also participate (McCrory, 1987). The objectives of aftercare are (1) to provide ongoing education and information needed to maintain sobriety, (2) to create an environment in which natural and healthy social-influence patterns reinforce positive behaviors and self-esteem, (3) to establish an ongoing group of caring, accepting, empathic, genuine, trusting individuals who serve as an extended family, among whom the individual can always feel safe and understood, and (4) to serve as the first line of safety any time a crisis occurs. The aftercare safety line may need to extend to one of the most difficult crises the drug dependent faces—the euphoria that often accompanies recovery and the distrust and cynicism of family members—in the new and strange home that no longer has the pink elephant of drug addiction sitting in the living room.

Euphoria.   Maxwell (1986, p. 229) refers to recovery euphoria as a reaction formation. Gordon used euphoria as a highly sophisticated defense to replace the immature defenses that he had used during his active chemical dependency. Almost immediately after he left inpatient treatment, Gordon changed to a rabid proselyte. He made AA and being the completely responsible parent and husband his whole life. He became an all-knowing, all-responsible, didactic, forceful autocrat who smothered his family, directing the life of Amy, Mark, and Lisa. Although he was overbearing, his family was so afraid that confronting his behavior would send him back to drinking that they walked on eggshells. In fact, when such reaction formations occur, family members may resent the dependent's sober behavior so much that they secretly wish he or she would return to drinking. Only through some tough family aftercare was Gordon's overdose of perfectionism and righteous recovery brought under control.

Carolyn: Gordon, a moment ago you described how frustrated you have been because Mark clams up and withdraws from you, and you also spoke to the fact that now Lisa seems to be even more resentful of you than when you were drinking. Notice how Mark is slumped back in his chair and Lisa is sitting with arms and legs crossed as you discuss how exasperated you are.

Gordon: I can't understand it. Dinner is supposed to be our time together. Right after I got out of inpatient treatment we were really communicating. But that's all changed lately. They've started shutting me out again. I love them and I want what's best for them. I just want to make it up to them for being the lousy dad and husband I was for so long. Why are they locking me out?

Carolyn: Mark, what are your feelings as your dad is relating his frustration?

Mark: [*Shedding tears.*] I'm mad at him . . . because nothing I say is right and everything I do is either wrong or not good enough.

Lisa: Yeah. I wish sometimes you were drinking again. At least then you left us alone.

Amy: Gordon, the kids are finally saying what we've all been feeling at home. Your personality is so overpowering since you quit drinking that none of us can come up to your standards. And AA, as good as it is, has become the center of our universe. Don't misunderstand, I don't want you to drink again, but there's just got to be something in between. We're worn out. We just need a normal life. We don't need you as Superman. Lord knows, I pulled that long enough.

Gordon: I don't know what to say. I just wanted to make things up to you. I don't know what to do!

Carolyn: This whole thing you're experiencing is not uncommon. As problematic as it is, it's a good sign and sort of a stage of development on the road to recovery. Understand it for that and we can work on it just like we have the other hot spots that have come up.

Blind spots.   Carolyn keyed in on Gordon's euphoria and took steps during the aftercare session to help the whole family deal with the issue. Such euphoric responses should be carefully monitored in aftercare settings because they may literally drive significant others to return to enabling behavior.

Further, zealous immersion in programs such as AA is also fraught with peril. For some people, organizations such as AA no longer fulfill a support function, but rather become a platform for airing the recovering chemical dependent's self-indulgence. Based on the premise that the recovering alcoholic now knows all the answers and will gladly tell them to anyone who will listen, this presumptive stand may indicate that the individual has lost perspective on what the essence of a support group is about and is building up to drink. In short, the rules of the road that the individual rigidly espouses to others no longer hold for the individual, and this self-centered view may become a lethal one in regard to drinking. Upon the first sign that others may not share the recovering chemical dependent's viewpoints, the person may fall from these dizzying heights, become depressed and angry, and have a relapse.

Role changes.   One of the major difficulties that exists in aftercare is continuance of therapy by the family. The family is so euphoric over the cessation of drug use, that they believe that everything else will go back to "normal" because the worst is behind them. They also believe that only the drug abuse and its immediate effects impacted them, and now that it has ceased, they will no longer feel any adverse effects (Black, 1981, pp. 99–101). In actuality, much of the work of the family is just starting. Recovering parents may find that children resent their attempts to reclaim the parental roles they have abdicated. To expect the responsible child to just "mess around and play" is likely to cause all kinds of rebellious behavior in that child (McGowan, 1991). Reshaping and realignment of roles to create healthy family relations will take a great deal of work and may be one of the most difficult crises the family faces.

Validation of feelings.   As the chemical dependent starts recovery, children start to reexperience feelings. It will be a strange new phenomenon that they will probably resist because of fear of change. These children will have trouble playing dolls and superheros when they have had to take care of mother and help get her dressed or remove a smoldering cigarette from the hand of a passed-out father. They also may find it difficult to cry, laugh, cease being fearful, or get angry. Fearfulness needs to be validated as all right. Children need to know that becoming angry will not lose their parents' love or drive them back into substance abuse. They also need to have their anger acknowledged as appropriate and not discounted—particularly by the parent in recovery (Black, 1981, p. 82).

To summarize the major task of aftercare, if the chemical dependent, aside from performing his or her jobs inside and outside the home, is concentrating almost solely on maintaining chemical freedom, he or she is doing about all that needs to be done. If codependents, aside from jobs inside and outside the home, are focusing on themselves rather than on the dependent, then they are doing all that needs to be done (Maxwell, 1986, p. 234).

Gordon: [*In family therapy session, six months after inpatient treatment.*] One thing strikes me now. I guess I went 180 degrees in the other direction. I was as rigid in my abstinence as I was in my drinking. I was so damned afraid that I'd fall off the wagon, and I think everybody else around me was too, that if I didn't go hog wild in trying to be the best recovering alcoholic there ever was, and the best father and husband there ever was, I'd go right back to being a drunk. The truth is I was still scared to death and so was everybody else. It's taken some time, but I now realize that I'm just about average. I sure keep going to the AA meetings and I'm ready to help anyone else, but I don't have to stand out on a street-corner looking for drunks. I'll probably always need a support group, and while that bugs me at times, I know there are things that bug everybody else, and that's OK. I guess I'd rate myself as an average father and husband. We still have problems, and I guess that doesn't make me much different from any other guy. And the best part about that is it feels just fine.

Relapse

Relapse is a crucial issue for the family and the recovering dependent that is likely to take on crisis proportions sometime during recovery. Percentages of persons who relapse has been calculated to be as high as 37% in the first year (George, 1990) to 90% over time (Svanum & McAdoo, 1989). Any aftercare program needs to discuss the distinct possibility of this happening, the warnings signs of building up to reusing, and how the recovering dependent and family should respond to signs, chemical slips, or a major relapse (Cable et al., 1986, p. 74).

Denzin (1987) proposes that relapse is a complex social act that occurs in four phases: (1) permissive thinking—for example, not going to an AA meeting, (2) use of a drug—for example, just one snort at a social occasion, (3) serious use—that is, getting high or drunk, (4) seeking help. Marlatt and Gordon (1985) discuss relapse as issuing out of a series of minidecisions that form a chain of high-risk cognitions and behaviors that allow relapse to occur and are most likely when the individual is in a negative emotional or physical state or under social pressure.

Three components are critical as crisis intervention techniques in getting the addict away from conditions where relapse may occur. First is understanding the warning signs that lead up to a return to chemical use. George (1990) has listed 51 relapse symptoms that range from "doubting my ability to stay sober" to "convincing myself I'm cured." All of these signs start with the typical "stinkin' thinkin' " of chemical dependency and should serve as immediate cognitive signals and cues that the dependent is starting to head toward trouble. While memorizing George's list may seem a bit much, aftercare should certainly cover a constant check of these cues and the family should certainly be aware of them and what they may betoken.

The second component, once cues are recognized, is the immediate use of the kinds of cognitive techniques previously illustrated with Gordon to stop irrational thinking dead in its tracks and replace negative mental billboards with cognitive stop signs and positive counterinjunctions. Rehearsal and role playing are excellent techniques the worker can use to model how the potential setting events and negative cognitions that set the dependent up for a relapse can come together (Marlatt & Gordon, 1985; Meichenbaum, 1985).

The third component is the use of support systems such as family, AA sponsors, and therapists as resources that enable chemical dependents to stay honest with themselves about their problems and their recovery by constantly assessing with significant others the symptoms of relapse and their ability to avoid those symptoms (George, 1990, p. 182). In AA terms, they "are working the program."

Finally, Schuckit (1984) suggests that fewer than 2% of those individuals with drinking problems can safely return to social drinking, although it is undoubtedly 100% of alcoholics who either believe or wish they could (Doweiko, 1990, p. 250). For any alcoholic who suggests a return to social drinking to a crisis worker, it should be quickly pointed out that the odds are from 50 to 100 to 1 against his or her being able to handle it and that is clearly the "stinkin' thinkin'" that helped get the alcoholic in trouble in the first place. From our own experience in working with the chemically dependent, we believe that Schuckit's statistics are very optimistic.

INTERVENTION WITH THE ACOA

While McGowan (1991) has criticized the ACOA movement as at times cultlike and providing a convenient excuse on which to blame all of one's shortcomings and problems, nevertheless, ACOAs seem to experience a commonality of problems that follow them from their family of origin into adulthood (Black, 1981; Lewis & Williams, 1986; Schaef, 1986; Seixas & Youcha, 1985; Wegscheider-Cruse, 1985; Woititz, 1983). To illustrate the steps of intervention with ACOAs, let us move forward two years after Gordon's hospitalization and look at his daughter Lisa, who has just walked into a counselor's office at the university counseling center.

Assessment

Lisa's intake questionnaire indicated drug use, low grades, poor relationships with males, depression, and low self-concept. Subsequent follow-up testing indicated moderate depression, borderline drug abuse, and an extremely low self-concept on both intra- and interpersonal dimensions. Lisa's initial appearance is of a willowy ash blonde who is pretty, dressed immaculately in the current "in" clothes.

As she meets the counselor she is smiling, gregarious, and forthright, which is in stark and puzzling contrast to her self-report and her test scores. The counselor is Dr. Maxine Robertson, an expert in addictions, who has been assigned the case based on Lisa's borderline McAndrews Alcoholism Scale and her self-report of drug abuse and overdose. Lisa comes straight to the point.

Lisa: I'm scared to death. I don't know what's happening to me. When I came to State I was determined not to make the same mistake I made at Tech. I almost flunked out of there. I did real well here the first semester. Good grades and worked 20 hours a week and was in the Young Democrats and real active in a sorority and a good social life. But now it's all falling apart and I feel terrible and look even worse and then there was the other night.

Dr. Max: This is a tough question right off the bat, but it's made out of concern. Were you feeling bad enough to kill yourself?

Lisa: [*Emphatically.*] No way. I'm down in the dumps, but not that down.

While it may seem tedious by this point in your reading, we never take overdoses or any other "accidents" for granted. The human services worker *must* check out the possibility of suicide. Once she is assured that it was an accident she moves forward.

Dr. Max: Tell me about the drugs that you put down on your intake sheet.

Lisa: I don't know what came over me, I mean I drink some beer and wine, and I've smoked a little Mary Jane, but I took some speed because I needed to study all night, and then I drank some, and got into a terrible fight with Ron, my boyfriend, and I guess I got pretty weird, and then I passed out, and the next thing I knew they had me over at McKinley Hospital waking me up. It was really scary, and the residence hall director was worried after she brought me back and suggested I come over here. My parents don't know anything about this, and I don't want them to know, it's too much like what happened to Dad and I don't want Mom to worry. [*Her veneer and composure breaks and she starts to sob vigorously.*] God! I'm such a mess. I'm ugly, stupid, can't get it together. What's the use?

At the least, Lisa is currently a polydrug experimenter, which does not bode well for possible addictive behavior. She also provides the worker significant information when she links her behavior to her father's. The worker makes an open-ended lead to allow Lisa to illuminate the source of her affect.

Dr. Max: [*Hands Lisa a tissue.*] Is the sobbing about feeling guilty about letting your parents down, or anger at yourself, or sorrow for your father's problems, or what? I'm not real clear.

Lisa: [*Sniffling.*] I . . . don't know. All of that and more. I mean, I love my dad and mom, but I hated the drinking and now here I am. Worse—the kinds of guys I go out with, like Robbie. God! He's in engineering just like Dad. The only time he ever unwinds is when he's had a few beers. He's like all the rest of the guys I've gone out with except smarter, maybe. Real macho types, actually big babies. I attract them like a magnet. If there was one in a room of thousands, he'd find me, and I always fall for the jerk. Seems like all I ever do is take care of him. Jesus! I even wash his clothes and iron them. Then when I want some help from him, no dice. He'd left after we had that fight and went drinking at a club across the state line. He didn't even know I'd been in the hospital. Then I wind up apologizing for the fight, but he decided to break up anyway. I can really pick 'em, can't I?

A clear pattern of an oldest child taking on heroic dimensions is starting to emerge, along with a placating component that nonassertively apologizes for someone else's bad behavior. While ACOAs don't have some special biorhythms that send electomagnetic waves out to other addictive personalities, long and well-developed personality patterns fit like virus proteins into cell walls. Indeed, these people do have a great ability to find partners who will cause them grief. The worker reflects on Lisa's merry-go-round of poor male relationships.

Dr. Max: So there seems to be a pattern of relationships where you give a lot and don't get much back, and it kinda reminds you of how things were at home? You seem pretty angry about that pattern.

Lisa: I guess, I dunno. I mean, I don't have the foggiest notion about what a regular family's like unless you call Dad throwing up every morning and Mom holding his head in the sink and calling in to work for him, and him falling into the Christmas tree and knocking it over on Christmas Eve normal. Yeah, I am sorry for that all right. I don't know why Mom didn't divorce him. Yet here I am just spinning my wheels and not doing anything like Mom. Yeah, you could say I'm angry—at me, though, for being so dumb.

What Lisa says is true of her knowledge of relationships. To her, the male relationships she has had, while one-sided and not fulfilling, follow the blueprint of what she saw at home. She has little idea about what relationships that are not dependent and enabling look like. She also brings up a well-learned message from her past as a discount. The worker response to the discount is a first step in extinguishing Lisa's negative perception of herself.

Dr. Max: The fact is you are doing something. You came here of your own free will. Nobody put a gun to your head.

Lisa: It wasn't easy. I just feel so bad about myself. I had to do something.

The worker continues her exploration of Lisa's father. While this may seem like an invitation for the client to externalize and regress to the past, the therapist is trying to build a connecting link in a dynamic way between past and present behavior.

Dr. Max: Tell me about what happened to your dad.

Lisa: Well, uh, like he has a drinking problem and wound up in like the hospital, but I mean I'm not like him, he got blasted for long stretches and stayed that way. Almost caused a divorce a couple of years back, but he's OK now.

As the counselor gently explores Lisa's use of alcohol and other drugs, the dynamics of her family of origin, and her current functioning in school, a clear picture emerges of a young woman who has codependency problems. She has served both as hero and scapegoat in her family, with some placating thrown in for good measure. A straight-A student in high school and one of the most involved girls in her class with extracurricular activities, she still was criticized by her father. Her redoubled efforts occasioned only brief comments of "That's more like it!" from her father and acknowledgement of her work around home and taking care of her younger brother, Mark, by her mother. What got her a lot of attention was her contradependent behavior of getting into verbal battles with her father over her choice of friends, particularly boyfriends, and late hours and occasional drinking parties.

Her relationships with her boyfriends have the earmarks of a reenactment of her family of origin. Her contemporary use of alcohol and drugs puts her on the edge of abuse. In her own way, she has bottomed out. Her trip to the hospital has jarred her into an awareness that she has more than boyfriend and self-image problems. Her life is in crisis and although she appears to own some of her feelings in an open and honest way, denial is a major component of her defense system. She has gotten out of control, and for the hero, that is a worst-case scenario.

Education

Given what the counselor now knows, she decides to intervene.

Dr. Max: I'd like for us to work together on some of those problems, particularly your self-concept. I'd like to give you a book to read between now and next week. It's called *Choicemaking* by Sharon Wegscheider-Cruse and it has some stuff in it that will be helpful to you.

Lisa: What's it about?

Dr. Max: It's about families and particularly children who grew up in alcoholic fam . . .

Lisa: HOLD ON! I'm not an alkie like my old man.

Dr. Max: Lisa, I want to be straight with you. No, you're not chemically dependent yet, but you're headed there. Look at the signs—a blackout, no parties or dates without booze, ready availability through friends who smoke marijuana and can get ups and downs easily. You took a test that puts you right on the line. [*Shows Lisa her MacAndrews score.*] Furthermore, both your past experiences and present ones are telling me you may have walked out of that alcoholic family, but it hasn't left you yet. [*Briefly explains the hero and scapegoat roles.*] Finally, as much as you may hate to hear it, the research says you're a high risk coming out of an alcoholic family, and your recent behavior suggests that you are even more at risk. I'm guessing that a lot of what you did in therapy focused on your dad getting better and not quite so much on you.

The primary thrust of therapy for the ACOA is to provide education. Information about *whats* and *whys* are extremely important to ACOAs who have little idea that the alcoholic family of origin could still be exerting such a profound influence on them.

Lisa: Well kinda, like they did do some stuff with Mark and me, but they didn't say any of the stuff you just told me. It's scary . . . and I guess I probably don't really want to hear about it . . . denial, huh? Yeah, I know that word big time. OK! I'll read the book.

Dr. Max: I am also wondering if you'd be willing to think about joining a group here along with individual counseling.

Lisa: I don't think I want to talk about this to anyone. I went through Alateen for a year. I hated that. They made us go through that for Dad's drinking problem and his rotten behavior to us, like we were responsible for his being a jerk or we needed sympathy.

Dr. Max: This is not an Alateen or Alanon group. While there are a number of students in the group who have issues with chemical dependency, this is also a standard counseling group. Students like yourself with all kinds of nitty gritty problems. We cover a lot of different issues and a number of yours would fit nicely. I do ask each member, before they go in, to commit to work on a problem, help other members with their problems, and commit to confidentiality. You said you were a risk taker—what do you have to lose?

Lisa: Well, OK, I guess it won't kill me.

The Counseling Group

Education about her codependency is necessary, but it is not sufficient. Lisa's movement out of codependency will not occur just by reading her way out of it and talking to a therapist about codependency dynamics. She will need to experience surrender and emotional healing before the codependency is expunged. A group of her college peers will be a safe proving ground for her personal development. Besides providing a sounding board and support system for one another, such counseling groups can help develop what Wegscheider-Cruse (1985, p. 133) calls a sense of responsibility and separateness. By developing her own individuality through sharing and receiving feedback from the group, Lisa's self-worth will grow. The group will also help her come to grips with lousy relationships and provide her with ideas on how to inoculate herself against dependency-eliciting males in particular.

The group will also provide her with the support she needs as she commits to giving herself choices for the future instead of living bound to the past. She will have to surrender her need to be protective and controlling. She'll also have to continue caring, give up enabling or denying, not regret the past, fear less, and give up guilt and inadequacy (Wegscheider-Cruse, 1985, p. 146). Along with individual counseling, the group will provide the emotional support she needs to move toward being neither codependent or contradependent, but interdependent (Hogg & Frank, 1992).

Extracting a Commitment to Abstain

Dr. Max: I want you to commit to one more thing. I want you not to drink for one week. You said you were sick of the way you were operating, so for one week, I'd like you to take it a day at a time. I know you don't care much for the AA stuff, but I'd like your word and commitment on that.

Lisa: Well, my social life is down the tubes, and I could use the homework time, so I guess I can be a hermit for a week. You'd trust me to do that on my word alone?

Dr. Max: Should I not? Are you telling me that's impossible for you right now?

Lisa: Oh, no. I can do it and I appreciate you for trusting me. It's just that I can't trust people very much.

Lisa's compliance is typical of a responsible and placating ACOA. Her inability to trust may mean a number of perceptual checks with the therapist, and perhaps the acting-out side of her will test some of the limits to which she so compliantly agrees. The therapist is aware of all this as she extracts the commitment to abstain. The therapist also knows that attempting to extract a promise to go to an AA meeting would probably push Lisa away from counseling. However, a responsible ACOA who gives her word will usually stick by it even though it may be difficult. In the not-too-distant future, the therapist will start to encourage Lisa to become more assertive, not only with others but with the therapist as well. For the present, though, Lisa needs information, emotional support, and to not use drugs, and those are the three critical ingredients of an initial crisis intervention with the ACOA.

Pitfalls

Finally, Wegscheider-Cruse (1985) proposes that the recovery process for the codependent, like for the chemical dependent, is continuous and believes that there are certain pitfalls that the recovering codependent must constantly guard against. She lists the following:

1. *Defiance.* Even though one may intellectually accept codependency, anger about the injustices done may poison any growth.
2. *Secret recovery.* Suffering is not noble, and as the individual moves into recovery, successes toward individuation should not be kept a secret; otherwise, the old belief systems will not be expunged.

3. *Emotional binges.* During the process of replacing emotional numbness with emotional catharsis, the codependent who has not had any experience with handling emotions may become fixed on a continuous discharge of emotions, to the exclusion of making any effective behavioral changes.

4. *Avoiding change.* Recognizing and feeling the need to change occurs on cognitive and affective levels. Making the change calls for action behavior. It is scary to do this and easy to rationalize why action doesn't need to be taken right now.

5. *Living by mottos and frameworks.* If the codependent does not play an active role in recovery, but is rather a passive receptacle, all the therapy, literature, and workshops will do little good (pp. 152–154). The danger signs that indicate the codependent is dropping back into old familiar habits are also listed by Wegscheider-Cruse and include fatigue, workaholism, dishonesty, self-pity, frustration, impatience, relaxing the recovery program, setting unreachable goals, forgetting gratitude, and self-righteousness (p. 155). Knowing these danger signs is important to heading off new crises. Keeping constant perceptual checks with and listening to trusted others is important as a safeguard against the denial that is always too readily available to the codependent.

SUMMARY

The crisis of addiction is unique among all crisis categories. It is full of complexities, controversies, and contradictions. The prognosis for cure is poor because the condition is beset with multiple transcrisis points. A person may appear to be cured, only to relapse later into a drug episode more severe than before.

We have summarized several models of addiction, which attribute the problem to inherited, environmental, social, biological, chemical, or psychological causative factors. It appears that each of the models is partially correct and partially incorrect in ascribing causality.

In terms of dynamics, it seems that there are many types and degrees of addiction. The most prevalent and puzzling dynamic revolves around the concept of psychological denial. The chemical dependent tends to deny adamantly that there is addiction and to deny that any problem exists related to the addictive behavior. Family, friends, and even bosses frequently become a part of the denial system and unknowingly contribute to the addict's difficulties by becoming enablers. The treatment and rehabilitation of clients is enormously complicated when significant others reinforce the narcissistic and sociopathic behavior of the chemical dependent by abetting the dependency.

The stabilization of an addictive crisis is difficult in that it usually requires, first, that the dependent become aware that he or she needs help, and second, that the person have some motivation to seek help. To that end, reasoning with the dependent about the problem is generally useless. Most often, direct confrontation and the generation of a crisis of significant proportions by some significant other such as an employer or spouse are the only ways to propel a drug abuser to treatment.

It is clear that a multimodal approach is needed to help addicted persons through the crises they face. Competent medical supervision and counseling are needed from the detoxification phase through aftercare. Group counseling is a primary operating mode because peers who are themselves recovering addicts are highly effective in breaking down denial systems of fellow chemical dependents. Extensive use is made of family, friends, employers, and support groups such as Alcoholics Anonymous, to supplement what professional caregivers can do for clients.

Adult children of alcoholics (ACOAs) have become an emergent treatment group during the 1980s. As with Al-Anon and Alateen, ACOA support groups have sprung up across the country. Like many of the components of drug addiction and treatment, there are conflicting views and controversy surrounding ACOAs. Whether problems ACOAs experience stem from identifiable maladaptive personality constructs as a result of having lived in alcoholic families or whether their substance abusing parents are excuses for current maladaptive functioning is part of a continuing debate. At the very least, though, these clients need information about the dynamic effects of being reared in an alcoholic home, emotional support as they come to grips with past and present problems, and education about their own high risk status for addiction.

At present, there is no known permanent cure for chemical dependents. Following stabilization, clients must work and practice coping skills and the "one day at a time" philosophy of AA for the remainder of their lives to prevent a relapse.

REFERENCES

Adelman, S. A., & Weiss, R. D. (1989). What is therapeutic about inpatient alcoholism treatment? *Hospital and Community Psychiatry, 40,* 515–519.

Adler, A. (1956). *The individual psychology of Alfred Adler: A systematic presentation in selections from his writing.* Ed. H. L. Ansbacher & R. R. Ansbacher. New York: Harper & Row.

Alcoholics Anonymous. (1976). *Alcoholics Anonymous* (3rd ed.). New York: Anonymous World Services, Inc.

Alcoholics Anonymous. (1985). *Twenty-four hours a day.* Garden City, MN: Hazeldein.

American Medical Association. (1956). Hospitalization of patients with alcoholism. *Journal of the American Medical Association, 162,* 750.

American Psychiatric Association. (1985). Research on mental illness and addictive disorders: Progress and prospects. *American Journal of Psychiatry, 142,* Supplement A.

American Psychiatric Association. (1987). Diagnostic and statistical manual of mental disorders (3rd ed., rev.). Washington, DC: Author.

Ames, G. M. (1985). American beliefs about alcoholism: Historical perspectives on the medical-moral controversy. In L. A. Bennett & G. M. Ames (Eds.), *The American experience with alcohol: Contrasting cultural perspectives* (pp. 23–40). New York: Plenum.

Asbury, H. (1950). *The great illusion: An informal history of prohibition.* Garden City, NY: Doubleday.

Backover, A. (1991, May). Native Americans: Alcoholism, FAS puts a race at risk. *AACD Guidepost, 33,* 1, 3.

Barry, H. (1974). Psychological factors in alcoholism. In B. Kissin & H. Begleiter (Eds.), *The biology of alcoholism: Clinical pathology* (Vol. 3, pp. 53–108). New York: Plenum.

Beasley, J. D. (1987). *Wrong diagnosis, wrong treatment: The plight of the alcoholic in America.* New York: Creative Infomatics.

Berry, E. R., & Boland, J. P. (1977). *The economic cost of abuse.* New York: Free Press.

Bissell, L. (1982). Recovered alcoholic counselors. In E. M. Pattison & E. Kaufman (Eds.), *Encyclopedic handbook of alcoholism* (pp. 810–820). New York: Gardner Press.

Black, C. (1981). *It will never happen to me.* Denver, CO: M.A.C.

Blume, S. (1973). Iatrogenic alcoholism. *Quarterly Journal of Studies on Alcohol, 34,* 1348–1352.

Blume, S. B. (1978). Group psychotherapy in the treatment of alcoholism. In S. Zimberg, J. Wallace, & S. B. Blume (Eds.), *Practical approaches to alcoholism psychotherapy* (pp. 63–76). New York: Plenum.

Brill, L. (1981). *The clinical treatment of substance abusers.* New York: Free Press.

Brown, V. B., Ridgely, M. S., Pepper, B., Levine, I. S., & Ryglewicz, H. (1989). The dual crisis: Mental illness and substance abuse. *American Psychologist, 44,* 565–569.

Cable, L. C., Noel, N. E., & Swanson, S. C. (1986). Clinical intervention with children of alcohol abusers. In D. C. Lewis & C. N. Williams (Eds.), *Providing care for children of alcoholics: Clinical and research perspectives* (pp. 65–80). Pompano Beach, FL: Health Communications.

Cadoret, R. J., & Gaith, A. (1978). Inheritance of alcoholism in adoptees. *British Journal of Psychiatry, 132,* 252–258.

Canadian Commission of Inquiry into the Nonmedical Use of Drugs. (1973). Ottawa: Information Canada.

Carey, K. B. (1989). Emerging treatment guidelines for mentally ill chemical abusers. *Hospital and Community Psychiatry, 40,* 341–342, 349.

CASPAR Alcohol Education Program. (1978). *Decisions about drinking.* Cambridge, MA: CASPAR.

Chalmers, D. K., & Wallace, J. (1978). Evaluation of patient progress. In S. Zimberg, J. Wallace, & S. B. Blume (Eds.), *Practical approaches to alcoholism psychotherapy* (pp. 255–279). New York: Plenum.

Chrisman, N. J. (1985). Alcoholism: Illness or disease. In L. A. Bennett & G. M. Ames (Eds.), *The American experience with alcohol: Contrasting cultural perspectives* (pp. 7–22). New York: Plenum.

Collins, J. (1980). *Alcohol use and criminal behavior: An empirical, theoretical, and methodological overview.* Research Triangle Park, NC: Research Triangle Institute.

Corey, G., & Corey, M. S. (1977). *Group process and practice.* Pacific Grove, CA: Brooks/Cole.

Cormier, L. S., & Hackney, H. (1987). *The professional counselor: A process guide to helping.* Englewood Cliffs, NJ: Prentice-Hall.

Cormier, W. H., & Cormier, L. S. (1985). *Interviewing strategies for helpers: Fundamental skills and cognitive behavioral interventions* (2nd ed.). Pacific Grove, CA: Brooks/Cole.

Costello, R. M. (1982). Evaluation of alcoholism treatment programs. In E. M. Pattison & E. Kaufman (Eds.), *Encyclopedic handbook of alcoholism* (pp. 1179–1210). New York: Gardner Press.

Cotton, N. S. (1979). The familial incidence of alcoholism. *Journal of Studies on Alcohol, 40,* 89–115.

De Leon, G. (1989). Psychopathology and substance abuse: What is being learned from research in therapeutic communities. *Journal of Psychoactive Drugs, 21,* 177–188.

Denzin, N. K. (1987). *The recovering alcoholic.* Newbury Park, CA: Sage Publications.

Dinkmeyer, D. C., & Muro, J. (1979). *Group counseling: Theory and practice.* Itasca, IL: F. E. Peacock.

Dinkmeyer, D. C., Pew, W. L., & Dinkmeyer, D. C., Jr. (1979). *Adlerian counseling and psychotherapy.* Pacific Grove, CA: Brooks/Cole.

Doweiko, H. E. (1990). *Concepts of chemical dependency.* Pacific Grove, CA: Brooks/Cole.

Drug Abuse Warning Network (DAWN). (1983). Data from the Drug Abuse Warning Network statistical series, Quarterly Report, Provisional Data Series G, No. 12 (July–September). Rockville, MD: National Institute on Drug Abuse.

Dupont, R. L. (1984). *Getting tough on gateway drugs.* Washington, DC: American Psychiatric Press.

Edwards, G. T. (1985). Appalachia: The effects of cultural values on the consumption of alcohol. In L. A. Bennett & G. M. Ames (Eds.), *The American experience with alcohol* (pp. 131–146). New York: Plenum.

Ellis, A. (1987, January). *Employee assistance training workshop: A rational-emotive approach.* New York: Institute for Rational-Emotive Therapy.

Ford, B. (1987). *Betty: A glad awakening.* New York: Doubleday.

Forrest, G. G. (1984). *Intensive psychotherapy of alcoholism.* Springfield, IL: Charles C Thomas.

Frances, R. J. (1988). Update on alcohol and drug disorder treatment. *Journal of Clinical Psychiatry, 49,* 13–17.

Franklin, J. (1987). *Molecules of the mind.* New York: Dell.

George, R. L. (1990). *Counseling the chemically dependent: Theory and practice.* Englewood Cliffs, NJ: Prentice-Hall.

George, R. L., & Dustin, D. (1988). *Group counseling: Theory and practice.* Englewood Cliffs, NJ: Prentice-Hall.

Gold, M. S. (1984). 800-Cocaine. New York: Bantam Books.

Goode, E. (1984). *Drugs in American society.* New York: Knopf.

Goodwin, D. W. (1979). Alcoholism and heredity. *Archives of General Psychiatry, 36,* 57–61.

Goodwin, D. W., Crane, J. B., & Guze, S. B. (1971). Felons who drink. *Quarterly Journal of Studies on Alcohol, 32,* 136–148.

Graham, D. (Speaker). (1986). *Denial, dependency, and codependency in drug treatment programs.* (Cassette Recording No. 8–1). Memphis: Department of Counseling and Personnel Services, Memphis State University.

Graubart, A. V. (1991, April). *The two faces of Eve/Ed: Dual diagnosis (Alcoholism/substance abuse and psychiatric disorders).* Paper presented at Crisis Convening XV, Chicago.

Greene, R. L. (1980). *The MMPI: An interpretative manual.* New York: Grune & Stratton.

Guze, S. B., Goodwin, D. W., & Crane, J. B. (1969). Community and psychiatric disorders. *Archives of General Psychiatry, 20,* 583–591.

Guze, S. B., Tuason, D. W., Galfield, D., Stewart, M. A., & Picken, B. (1962). Psychiatric illness and crime with particular reference to alcoholism: A study of 223 criminals. *Journal of Nervous and Mental Disease, 134,* 512–521.

Haberman, P. W., & Baden, M. M. (1974, March). Alcoholism and violent death. *Quarterly Journal of Studies on Alcohol, 35,* 221–231.

Hamburg, B. A., Kraemer, H. C., & Jahnke, W. (1975). A hierarchy of drug use in adolescence: Behavioral and attitudinal correlates of substantive drug use. *American Journal of Psychiatry, 132,* 1155–1163.

Hay, W. M., & Nathan, P. E. (Eds.). (1982). *Clinical case studies in the behavioral treatment of alcoholism.* New York: Plenum.

Heath, D. B. (1978). The sociocultural and model of alcohol use: Problems and prospects. *Journal of Operation Psychiatry, 9,* 56–66.

Heath, D. B. (1985). American experience with alcohol: Commonalities and contrasts. In L. A. Bennett & G. M. Ames (Eds.), *The American experience with alcohol: Contrasting cultural experiences* (pp. 461–480). New York: Plenum.

Hoffman, H. (1970). Depression and defensiveness in self-descriptive moods of alcoholics. *Psychological Reports, 26,* 23–26.

Hogg, J. A., & Frank, M. L. (1992). Toward an interpersonal model of codependence and contradependence. *Journal of Counseling and Development, 70,* 371–375.

Huberty, J. D., & Brandon, J. C. (1982). Nonmedical alcohol detoxification. In E. M. Pattison & E. Kaufman (Eds.), *Encyclopedic handbook of alcoholism* (pp. 1076–1085). New York: Gardner Press.

Jellinek, E. M. (1946). Phases in the drinking history of alcoholics. *Quarterly Journal of Studies on Alcohol, 7,* 1–88.

Jellinek, E. M. (1952). Phases of alcohol addiction. *Quarterly Journal of Studies on Alcohol, 13,* 673–684.

Jellinek, A. M. (1960). *The disease concept of alcoholism.* New Haven, CT: Hillhouse Press.

Jessor, R., Chase, J. D., & Donovan, J. E. (1980). Psychosocial correlates of marijuana use and problem drinking in a national sample of adolescents. *American Journal of Public Health, 70,* 604–613.

Jessor, R., & Jessor, S. L. (1977). *Problem behavior and psychosocial development: A longitudinal study of youth.* New York: Academic Press.

Johnson Institute. (1972). *Alcoholism: A treatable disease.* Minneapolis, MN: Author.

Johnson, V. E. (1980). *I'll quit tomorrow.* Minneapolis, MN: Johnson Institute.

Johnson, V. E. (1986). *Intervention: A professional guide.* Minneapolis, MN: Johnson Institute.

Kaufman, E., & Pattison, E. M. (1982a). The family and alcoholism. In E. M. Pattison & E. Kaufman (Eds.), *Encyclopedic handbook of alcoholism* (pp. 662–672). New York: Gardner Press.

Kaufman, E., & Pattison, E. M. (1982b). The family and network therapy in alcoholism. In E. M. Pattison & E. Kaufman (Eds.), *Encyclopedic handbook of alcoholism* (pp. 1022–1032). New York: Gardner Press.

Knox, W. J. (1976). Objective psychological measurement and alcoholism: Review of the literature, 1971–72. *Psychological Reports, 38,* 1023–1050 (Monograph Suppl. 1-V38).

Knox, W. J. (1980). Objective psychological measurement and alcoholism: Survey of the literature, 1974. *Psychological Reports, 47,* 51–68 (Monograph Suppl. 1-V47).

Knox, W. J. (1982). The professionals: The issue of alcoholism. In E. M. Pattison & E. Kaufman (Eds.), *Encyclopedic handbook of alcoholism* (pp. 795–801). New York: Gardner Press.

Kristianson, P. A. (1970). A comparison study of two alcoholic groups and control group. *British Journal of Medical Psychology, 43,* 161–175.

Larsen, E. (1983). *Basics of codependency* [Audiotape]. Brooklyn Park, MN: E. Larsen Enterprises.

Lawson, G. W., Ellis, D. C., & Rivers, P. C. (Eds.). (1984). *Essentials of chemical dependency counseling.* Rockville, MD: Aspen Systems Corp.

Levine, H. (1984). The alcohol problem in America: From temperance to alcoholism. *British Journal of Addiction, 79,* 109–119.

Lewis, D. C., & Williams, C. N. (Eds.). (1986). *Providing care for children of alcoholics: Clinical and research perspectives.* Pompano Beach, FL: Health Communications.

Liepman, M., White, W. T., & Nirenberg, T. D. (1986). Children in alcoholic families. In D. C. Lewis & C. N. Williams (Eds.), *Providing care for children of alcoholics: Clinical and research perspectives* (pp. 39–64). Pompano Beach, FL: Health Communications.

Loper, R. G., Kammeier, M. L., & Hoffman, H. (1973). MMPI characteristics of college freshman males who later became alcoholic. *Journal of Abnormal Psychology, 82,* 159–162.

Lukoff, I. F. (1980). Toward a sociology of drug use. In D. J. Lettieri, M. Sayers, & H. W. Pearson (Eds.), *Theories on drug abuse: Selected contemporary perspectives* (NIDA Research Monograph No. 30). Rockville, MD: National Institute on Drug Abuse.

MacAndrew, C., & Edgerton, R. B. (1969). *Drunken comportment.* Chicago: Aldine.

MacDonald, J. (1961). *The murderer and his victim.* Springfield, IL: Charles C Thomas.

Marlatt, G. A., & Donovan, D. M. (1982). Behavioral psychology approaches to alcoholism. In E. M. Pattison & E. Kaufman (Eds.), *Encyclopedic handbook of alcoholism* (pp. 560–577). New York: Gardner Press.

Marlatt, G. A., & Gordon, J. R. (Eds.). (1985). *Relapse prevention.* New York: Guilford Press.

Maxwell, R. (1986). *Breakthrough: What to do when alcoholism or chemical dependency hits close to home.* New York: Ballantine.

McCrady, B. S. (1982). Marital dysfunction: Alcoholism and marriage. In E. M. Pattison & E. Kaufman (Eds.), *Encyclopedic handbook of alcoholism* (pp. 673–685). New York: Gardner Press.

McCrory, J. (Speaker). (1987). *Aftercare and co-dependency in drug treatment programs* (Cassette Recording No. 8-4). Memphis: Department of Counseling and Personnel Services, Memphis State University.

McGowan, S. (1991, October). Effects of parental alcoholism. *AACD Guidepost,* pages 1, 8, 10.

McMullin, R. E., & Giles, T. R. (1981). *Cognitive behavior therapy: A restructuring approach.* New York: Grune & Stratton.

Meichenbaum, D. (1985). *Stress-inoculation training.* New York: Pergamon Press.

Mendelson, J. H., & Mello, N. K. (Eds.). (1979). *The diagnosis and treatment of alcoholism.* New York: McGraw-Hill.

Miller, G. (1983). *SASSI: Substance Abuse Subtle Screening Inventory.* Bloomington, IN: SASSI Institute.

Nace, E. P. (1987). *The treatment of alcoholism.* New York: Brunner/Mazel.

National Commission on Marijuana and Drug Abuse. (1973). *Drug abuse in America: Problems in perspective. The technical papers of the second report of the National Commission on Marijuana and Drug Abuse.* Washington, DC: U.S. Government Printing Office.

Neisser, U. (1976). *Cognition and reality: Principles and implications of cognitive psychology.* San Francisco: W. H. Freeman.

Newcomb, M. D., & Bentler, P. M. (1989). Substance use and abuse among children and teenagers. *American Psychologist, 44,* 242–248.

Oetting, E. R., & Beauvais, F. (1986). Peer cluster theory: Drugs and the adolescent. *Journal of Counseling and Development, 65,* 17–22.

Ohlsen, M. (1970). *Group counseling.* New York: Holt, Rinehart & Winston.

Olsen, M. (1987, March 17). *Life quest: Hidden addicts, the nature and impact of addictive behavior* [Documentary]. ABC Television Network.

Olson, S., & Gerstein, D. R. (1985). *Alcoholism in America: Taking action to prevent abuse.* Washington, DC: National Academy Press.

Ornstein, P. (1976). The Alcadd Test as a predictor of post-hospital drinking behavior. *Psychological Reports, 43,* 611–617.

Parker, C. (Speaker). (1986). *Alcoholic inpatient treatment* (Cassette Recording No. 8-2). Memphis: Department of Counseling and Personnel Services, Memphis State University.

Pattison, E. M., & Kaufman, E. (Eds.). (1982a). *Encyclopedic handbook of alcoholism.* New York: Gardner Press.

Pattison, E. M., & Kaufman, E. (1982b). The alcoholism syndrome: Definitions and models. In E. M. Pattison & E. Kaufman (Eds.), *Encyclopedic handbook of alcoholism* (pp. 3–30). New York: Gardner Press.

Peele, S. (1986). The "cure" for adolescent drug abuse: Worse than the problem? *Journal of Counseling and Development, 65,* 23–24.

Peluso, E., & Peluso, L. S. (1988). *Women and drugs.* Minneapolis, MN: CompCare.

Perez, J. F. (1985). *Counseling the alcoholic.* Muncie, IN: Accelerated Development.

Pernanen, K. (1976). The biology of alcoholism. In B. Kissin & H. Begleiter (Eds.), *Social aspects of alcoholism* (Vol. 4, pp. 42–57). New York: Plenum.

Polcin, D. L. (1992). A comprehensive model for adolescent chemical dependency treatment. *Journal of Counseling and Development, 70,* 376–382.

Poley, W., Lea, G., & Vibe, G. (1979). *Alcoholism: A treatment manual.* New York: Gardner Press.

Rado, T. (1988). The client with a dual diagnosis—A personal perspective. *Alcohol Quarterly, 1,* 5–7.

Ray, O. (1983). *Drugs, society, and human behavior* (3rd ed.). St. Louis: C. V. Mosby.

Robertson, J. C. (1988). Preventing relapse and transfer of addiction. *EAP Digest, 8*(6), 50–56.

Rosenberg, C. M. (1982). The paraprofessional in alcoholism treatment. In E. M. Pattison & E. Kaufman (Eds.), *Encyclopedic handbook of alcoholism* (pp. 802–809). New York: Gardner Press.

Schaef, A. W. (1986). *Co-dependence misunderstood—mistreated.* San Francisco: Harper & Row.

Schafer, C. (1989, March). Many adults face memories of alcoholic home. *AACD Guidepost,* pages 1, 8, 25.

Schuckit, M. A. (1984). *Drug and alcohol abuse: A clinical guide to diagnosis and treatment* (2nd ed.). New York: Plenum Press.

Schuckit, M. A., & Rayses, V. (1979). Ethanol ingestion: Differences in blood acetaldehyde concentrations in relatives of alcoholics and controls. *Science, 203,* 54–55.

Seixas, J. S., & Youcha, G. (1985). *Children of alcoholism: A survivor's manual.* New York: Harper & Row.

Shaffer, H. (1986). Observations on substance abuse theory. *Journal of Counseling and Development, 65,* 26–28.

Shearer, R. J. (1968). *Manual of alcoholism of the American Medical Association.* Washington, DC: American Medical Association.

Shulman, B. (1973). *Contributions to individual psychology: Selected papers of Bernard Shulman.* Chicago: Alfred Adler Institute.

Shupe, L. (1953). Alcohol and crime. *Journal of Criminal Law and Criminal Political Science, 44,* 661–664.

Siegel, L. (1989, January). Want to take the risks? It should be your choice. *Playboy,* p. 59.

Smith, J. W. (1982). Treatment of alcoholism in aversion conditioning hospitals. In E. M. Pattison & E. Kaufman (Eds.), *Encyclopedic handbook of alcoholism* (pp. 874–884). New York: Gardner Press.

Smith, W. F. (1982, Summer). Drug traffic today—challenges and response. *Drug Enforcement,* pp. 2–6.

Sobell, M. B., & Sobell, L. C. (1978). *Behavioral treatment of alcohol problems: Individualized therapy and controlled drinking.* New York: Plenum.

Speigel, D., Hadley, P. A., & Hadley, R. G. (1970). Personality test patterns of rehabilitation center alcoholics, psychiatric inpatients, and normals. *Journal of Clinical Psychology, 26,* 366–371.

Spotts, J. V., & Shontz, F. C. (1980). A life theme of chronic drug abuse. In D. J. Lettieri, M. Sayers, & H. W. Pearson (Eds.), *Theories on drug abuse: Selected contemporary perspectives* (NIDA Research Monograph No. 30, pp. 59–70). Rockville, MD: National Institute on Drug Abuse.

Stuckey, R. F., & Harrison, J. S. (1982). The alcoholism rehabilitation center. In E. M. Pattison & E. Kaufman (Eds.), *Encyclopedic handbook of alcoholism* (pp. 865–873). New York: Gardner Press.

Svanum, S., & McAdoo, W. B. (1989). Predicting rapid relapse following treatment for chemical dependence: A matched subject design. *Journal of Consulting and Clinical Psychology, 34,* 1027–1030.

Trice, H. M., & Beyer, J. M. (1982). Job-based alcoholism programs: Motivating problem drinkers to rehabilitation. In E. M. Pattison & E. Kaufman (Eds.), *Encyclopedic handbook of alcoholism* (pp. 954–978). New York: Gardner Press.

U.S. Department of Commerce, Bureau of the Census. (1986). *Statistical Abstract of the United States* (106th ed.). Washington, DC: U.S. Government Printing Office.

U.S. Department of Commerce, Bureau of the Census. (1991). *Statistical Abstract of the United States*. (111th ed.). Washington, DC: U.S. Government Printing Office.

Vaillant, G. E. (1983). *The natural history of alcoholism: Causes, patterns, and paths to recovery*. Cambridge, MA: Harvard University Press.

Vaillant, G. E., & Milofsky, E. (1982). The etiology of alcoholism: A prospective viewpoint. *American Psychologist, 37,* 494–503.

Wallace, J. (1978). Critical issues in alcoholism therapy. In S. Zimberg, J. Wallace, & S. B. Blume (Eds.), *Practical approaches to alcoholism psychotherapy* (pp. 31–46). New York: Plenum.

Wanberg, R. W., Horn, J. L., & Foster, F. M. (1977). A differential assessment model for alcoholism: The scales of the Alcohol Use Inventory. *Journal of Studies on Alcohol, 33,* 512–543.

Wegscheider-Cruse, S. (1984). Codependency: The therapeutic void. In *Codependency: An emerging issue* (pp. 1–19). Pompano Beach, FL: Health Communications.

Wegscheider-Cruse, S. (1985). *Choice-making for codependents, adult children, and spirituality seekers*. Pompano Beach, FL: Health Communications.

Wegscheider-Cruse, S. (1989). *Another chance: Hope and health for the alcoholic family* (2nd ed.). Palo Alto, CA: Science and Behavior Books.

Woititz, J. G. (1983). *Adult children of alcoholics*. Pompano Beach, FL: Health Communications.

World Health Organization. (1952). Expert committee on mental health, alcoholism subcommittee. Second report. (World Health Organization Technical Service Report No. 18). In H. Milt (Ed.), *Basic handbook on alcoholism*. Fairhaven, NJ: Scientific Aids Publication.

Zimberg, S. (1982). Psychotherapy in the treatment of alcoholism. In E. M. Pattison & E. Kaufman (Eds.), *Encyclopedic handbook of alcoholism* (pp. 999–1010). New York: Gardner Press.

Zwerling, I. (1959). Psychiatric findings in an interdisciplinary study of 46 alcoholic patients. *Quarterly Journal of Studies on Alcohol, 20,* 543–554.

CLASSROOM EXERCISES

I. Addictive Behaviors

All of us have addictions, whether they be drinking alcohol, eating chocolate, gambling on blackjack, buying plaid sport coats, overspending on credit cards, or reading the sports page at breakfast. Anything that we start out wanting and not necessarily needing, but end up either psychologically or physically craving, may be considered addicting. Such addictive behaviors may be as simple as not being able to pass the candy bar machine to attending every Memphis State basketball game—no matter what!

With the class divided into pairs, each person discusses a behavior around which the person seems to plan his or her life (at least in small part). For example, one of the authors of this book does just fine without coffee and cigarettes in the morning until he gets to work. Immediately upon hanging his coat up and setting his briefcase down, he picks up his cup and heads for the coffee pot. Nothing, and we mean absolutely nothing, happens until that first cup of coffee goes down along with a cigarette. It's all downhill after that, and he consumes numerous cups of coffee and cigarettes until he goes home from work. There, he drinks no more coffee, but does put away some antacid.

Each student will isolate such a behavior and then commit to refraining from that behavior for one day. Keep a one-day journal listing your thoughts, feelings, and behaviors as you sweat out the day in abstinence. At the next class meeting, report on the difficulties you faced in forgoing your addiction for a day. This exercise should give individuals a small bit of empathy for the person who has a serious chemical dependency.

II. Denial

Once you have discussed in class what addictive behavior does to you, separate again into pairs. One person takes the part of the interventionist and the other that of the client. Role-play for about ten minutes. The client will engage in denial that the addiction is a problem, using any of the defense mechanisms described in this chapter. The interventionist's task is to crack the denial system of the client by using the confrontational skills listed in the chapter. Audiotape the role play and then reverse roles. Each member will listen to and critique the role play in regard to both denial and confrontation of the denial. Return to the large group and discuss what each member learned from the experience. Questions may include the following:

1. How difficult was it for the worker to confront the client?
2. What kinds of feelings did both client and worker have as they carried the role play forward?
3. Did the worker confront the specific addicting behavior, the defense used to shield it from awareness, or the total personhood of the client?
4. Did the worker feel insecure or threatened while attempting the confrontation?
5. Did the client feel threatened, or was he or she able easily to fend off the worker's attempts to break down the denial?

III. Psychological Blind Spots

Assume that for people to become addicted to drugs they must have psychological blind spots that keep them from becoming aware of their addictive tendencies and shield them from acknowledging the harmful effects of their addiction, both to themselves and to their loved ones. In small groups, each person is to identify, write down, and then share with the group what might be some of the blind spots they have with respect to the addiction discussed in the first exercise. As if they were significant others in the person's life, the other members of the group brainstorm and expand upon these blind spots. Finally, the group will devise strategies for convincing the person that he or she has the blind spot and needs to take preventive steps that would safeguard against letting a habit turn into a full-blown addiction.

CHAPTER 9

Personal Loss:
Bereavement and Grief

BACKGROUND

To be human in the world as we know it is to experience loss. Some obvious major losses precipitate emotional trauma in individuals, which results in crisis. Some losses are relatively minor, cause no crisis, and are not so obvious; yet minor losses may also exact an emotional toll that the individual can ill afford to pay. Examples of major losses are the death of a loved one, the breakup of a close relationship, separation, and divorce. Some not-so-obvious or minor losses are loss of job, loss of money, moving to a different residence, illness (loss of health), changing schools or teachers, being robbed, and attainment of success (loss of striving) (Colgrove, Bloomfield, & McWilliams, 1976, p. 2).

Recovery from a major loss, such as the death of a child, parent, or spouse, may require several years. Reconciling oneself to minor loss, such as breaking a favorite dish or a wall hanging, may require only a few moments or hours (Colgrove et al., 1976, p. 16). During our normal growth and development, we experience many minor losses and a few major ones. But, according to Freeman (1978), the inevitable coping with numerous losses that we must learn to do, plays an important role in our emotional development (p. 16).

The objective of this chapter is to provide a general survey of ways in which crisis workers may help clients understand and cope with losses. The concepts and skills described in the six-step model in Chapter 2 undergird the helping strategies we recommend for workers to use in helping people experiencing a crisis of personal loss. There are many helpful interventions available to crisis workers whose clients present problems of grief and bereavement (Hughes, 1988, p. 77; Osterweis, Solomon, & Green, 1984, pp. 215–279; Rando, 1984, pp. 75–117; Schneider, 1984, pp. 207–271). Crisis workers may prepare themselves to assist grieving clients by remembering that *all* crises can eventually be reformulated within a context of growth (Schneider, 1984, pp. 207–227). "Reformulated within a context of growth" refers to the healthy resolution of grief by bereaved individuals—attaining the ability to abstract meaning from a previously totally destructive event and emerging with greater strength, self-trust, and sense of freedom than they had before (p. 208).

The ultimate growth toward coping with loss occurs when the griever comes to grips with his or her own mortality (Rando, 1984, pp. 2–7). The final loss—death—is the conclusive stage in our development (Schoenberg, 1980, pp. 24–28). All living things go through stages of birth, growth, and death. All human losses—great or small—are increments in the journey through life. As Buscaglia (1982) so dramatically put it in *The Fall of Freddie the Leaf,* " . . . no matter how big or small, how weak or strong. We first do our job. We experience the sun and the moon, the wind and the rain. We learn to dance and to laugh. Then we die" (p. 16).

Loss can be great or small, but it is always personal. Coping with loss—overcoming, healing, and recovering—is also personal. Crisis workers and counselors have many ways of helping people in grief (Lane & Dickey, 1988). But since no one else can overcome grief, heal, or recover for a person, the development of strategies for helping an individual cope with loss is perhaps the most difficult interventional area crisis workers encounter. Crisis workers should come to terms with their own mortality and be currently past their own periods of grief before entering into the role of caregiver to clients suffering from debilitating losses (Rando, 1984, pp. 430–444).

DYNAMICS OF BEREAVEMENT

Cultural Dynamics

According to Rando (1984), each culture develops its own beliefs, mores, norms, standards, and attitudes toward death. Groups with differing backgrounds within a culture have vastly different attitudes toward death. But Rando states that "for all societies there seem to be three general patterns of response: *death accepting, death defying, or death denying*" (p. 51, italics added).

Kübler-Ross (1975) writes that our culture seems to believe that "death has become a dreaded and unspeakable issue to be avoided by every means possible" and that it may be "that death reminds us of our human vulnerability in spite of our technological advances" (p. 5). Becker (1973) documents how the fear or denial of death in the United States constitutes a fundamental factor in human behavior. His contention is that much of what people do in terms of cultural and scientific advancement is designed to avoid facing the finality of death. Becker further asserts that human beings have an innate fear of death, which leads them to try to transcend death through erecting hero systems and symbols. These systems and symbols may be observed in many shapes and forms—from monuments to presidential libraries, to tombstones, to this book! They may be manifested even in the choice of one's profession. Kübler-Ross (1981) reports that there have been studies indicating that doctors tend to choose medicine as a career because of an inordinate fear of death. And medicine is dedicated to defeating death" (p. 128).

Schoenberg (1980) describes how societal mores and attitudes toward life, death, and dying in the United States have changed over the years. As the country shifted from a rural to an urban orientation and lifestyle, there has been a shift from a death-defying culture to a death-denying culture (pp. 51–56). Whereas farm families (children and adults alike) usually came in contact with birth, life, and death of animals as well as people, individuals in the cities rarely encountered dead animals or dead people. People in rural communities cared for their own dying relatives and friends. They prepared the corpses for burial and dug the graves by hand. They laid out the bodies of the dead in the parlor and commemorated the lives of the departed; then they buried them in the family or community cemetery. That is quite a contrast to the way funerals are managed today.

The social organization of bereavement as well as the social reaction to the loss of the loved ones has changed partly because of shifts in age-specific mortality patterns (Osterweis et al., 1984). In former times, adult life expectancy was short and infant mortality was high. Epidemics and famines frequently wiped out large numbers of people. Communities were small and close-knit. Death was taken personally by everyone in the community and mourning rituals were communitywide events (pp. 199–200).

In modern times, the bereavement process has tended to become standardized because of laws, regulations, and the development of specialists who carry out the laws and regulations. Death usually occurs in a hospital or nursing home. Frequently the deceased is an older individual who has been out of the mainstream of community activity for a number of years; as a result, deceased persons are not as widely known as they were in their younger years. Mourning has tended to move out of the home and into funeral parlors and hospital chapels. Laws affecting the role of funeral directors and the policies of employers have influenced the ways society mourns. Workplaces have established rules governing the time employees can take off from work following the death of a close family member or loved one. Many institutional constraints on behavior have tended to impose social uniformity upon the previously diverse patterns of grief and bereavement. Grief that follows a death has become institutionalized (Osterweis et al., 1984, pp. 201–202), but such institutionalization is not necessarily negative. For example, some funeral homes offer professional grief counseling programs for their clientele and communities (Riordan & Allen, 1989).

The sociocultural changes that occurred between the 1930s and 1980s brought important changes in reliance on such helping roles as physicians, nurses, psychologists, social workers, counselors, rehabilitation specialists, and related workers (Schneider, 1984, p. ix). Changes in divorce rates, career development, aging patterns, birth-control and child-rearing practices, marriage stability, population mobility, and information dissemination have greatly affected people's lives—including the way society views and deals with stress, loss, and grief.

Conceptual Approaches to Bereavement

The human response to loss has been a subject of interest and study for many years. Theoretical perspectives have been developed during this century by individuals representing a wide range of disciplines. Of 18 models of response to bereavement we have studied, we will summarize 2. The first is the Kübler-Ross (1969) model, which is probably the most popular and best-known model. The second is the Schneider (1984) model, which is the most comprehensive model we have seen. These two models provide a representative conceptual view of the dynamics of the human response to loss.

The Kübler-Ross model. In her five-stage model, Elisabeth Kübler-Ross (1969) outlines the human reactions or responses that people experience as they attempt to cope with their own imminent deaths. Her concepts have also been applied to the process of grief and bereavement following most personal losses. The model is a general conceptual framework that does not purport to be applicable in every detail to every patient. It was developed for the purpose of providing ways for dying patients to teach caregivers and families how patients feel and what they need.

Stage 1: Denial and isolation. The typical response to the first awareness of one's own terminal condition may be something like "No, it cannot be me. There must be a mistake. This is simply not true." Kübler-Ross (1969) regards initial denial as a healthy way of coping with the painful and uncomfortable news. She states that "denial functions as a buffer after unexpected shocking news, allows the patient to collect himself and, with time, mobilize other, less radical, defenses" (p. 35). During this stage the patient may generate a temporary protective denial system and isolate himself or herself from information or persons that might confirm the terminal condition. Or the patient may become energetic in garnering proof and support from others that death is not going to occur.

Stage 2: Anger. The second stage is characterized by a "why me?" pattern. Persons in this stage cannot continue the myth of denial, so they may exhibit hostility, rage, envy, and resentment in addition to anger. Kübler-Ross reports that families and staffs find it quite difficult to deal with people during the anger stage (p. 44). The patient's anger is a normal adaptation. It is a desperate attempt to gain attention, to demand respect and understanding, and to establish some small measure of control. The patient's anger should not be taken personally by staff or family members. Such expressions of anger and hostility toward other people, the world, or God appear to be typical ways that patients use to try to cry out for love and acceptance.

Stage 3: Bargaining. During the third stage, patients bargain with physicians or bargain with God for an extension of life, one more chance, or time to do one more thing. This is another period of self-delusion, hoping to be rewarded for promises of good behavior or good deeds. It is a normal attempt to postpone death. Rather than brushing aside the patient's bargaining, the sensitive caregiver should listen to the concerns that underlie the behavior. The patient may need to deal with guilt or other hidden emotions.

Stage 4: Depression. Whenever the medical condition, the physical proof, bodily appearance, and evidence of the senses force the patient personally to admit that the prognosis is, indeed, terminal, a sense of loss ensues. Most patients are confronted with many losses as a result of impending death: career, money, loved ones, and possessions, in addition to life itself. It is normal for depression to set in. Kübler-Ross (1969) identifies two kinds of depression in the terminally ill: (1) reactive depression and (2) preparatory depression (p. 76). The first is a reaction to the irrevocable loss; the second is an inner emotional preparation to give up everything. Patients in preparatory depression should be responded to with love, caring, and empathy, using few or no words. Attempts by caregivers to cheer the patient up will only interfere with the person's preparatory grieving.

Stage 5: Acceptance. Patients who have traveled through the previous four stages may reach the point at which they are tired, weak, finished with their mourning, reconciled to their loss, and acceptant of their situation. This stage is characterized by a quiet, peaceful resignation. It is not a happy stage. It is a time in which patients draw into themselves. It is a time when patients do not need conversation or large crowds. Family members and caregivers should show love and support by simply being present, sitting in silence, holding the patient's hand, or calmly responding to the patient's needs or requests. Patients in the fifth stage should be provided with treatment to make their lives as pain free and comfortable as possible.

The Schneider model.   John Schneider (1984) developed a comprehensive eight-stage model, which he calls "The Process of Grieving." It is a holistic, growth-promoting model designed to nurture as much personal growth as possible within a context of stress, loss, and grief. The Schneider model of grief integrates people's physical, cognitive, emotional, behavioral, and spiritual responses to loss. Schneider's concept of loss includes "internal events, systems of belief, and the processes of growth and aging as well as the easily recognized losses, such as death and divorce" (p. x).

Stage 1: The initial awareness of loss. The initial impact of a loss is generally a significant stressor causing a threat to the body's sense of homeostasis (Schneider, 1984, p. 104). The holistic dimensions of this initial awareness stage typically include physical, behavioral, emotional, cognitive, and spiritual dimensions. Shock, confusion, numbness, detachment, disbelief, and disorientation are only a few of a variety of behaviors, emotions, or feelings that the individual may experience as a normal adaptive response to the realization that a significant loss has occurred.

Stage 2: Attempts at limiting awareness by holding on. Holding on means concentrating one's thoughts and emotional energy, for a period of time, on whatever positive aspects of the loss one can recognize and making use of whatever inner resources or hopes one has to immediately stave off immobility and disequilibrium. Holding-on strategies are normal processes that the individual adopts in order to try to use coping behaviors that have worked in the past to cope with loss, frustration, stress, and conflict. This stage has the effect of providing time to put the present loss into perspective, renew energies, and limit feelings of helplessness and despair (Schneider, 1984, pp. 120–122). Some of the behaviors, emotions, and feelings accompanying holding on are muscular tension, sleep disturbance, independence, replacement search, belief in internal control, yearning, ruminations, euphoria, bargaining, and guilt.

Stage 3. Attempts at limiting awareness by letting go. Letting go is described by Schneider (1984) as recognizing one's personal limits with regard to the loss and turning loose "unrealistic goals, unwarranted assumptions, and unnecessary illusions. This stage enables people to separate themselves from dependency or attachment to the lost person or object, paving the way for future adaptive behaviors and attitudes" (pp. 137–138). A few of the characteristic behaviors, emotions, and feelings that may occur during letting go are depression, rejection, disgust, anxiety, shame, pessimism, self-destructive ideation, cynicism, forgetting, and hedonism. During Stage 3, people may decide to give up their formerly held ideals, beliefs, and values.

Stage 4: Awareness of the extent of the loss. Schneider (1984) describes the awareness stage as the one most readily recognized as mourning—the most painful, lonely, helpless, and hopeless phase through which the loss sufferer goes (pp. 161–162). The individual may experience a flooding of consciousness, feelings of deprivation, and extreme grief and may feel defenseless in coping with the reality of the loss. A few of the typical behaviors, emotions, and feelings observed in sufferers are exhaustion, pain, silence, aloneness, preoccupation, sadness, loneliness, helplessness, hopelessness, absence of future time, existential focus, emptiness, and weakness.

Stage 5: Gaining perspective on the loss. The normal function of the perspective-gaining stage is described by Schneider (1984) as reaching a point of accepting that what is done is done and providing the bereaved persons with a time to make peace with their past. This gaining of perspective may take two forms: "(1) discovering the balance of the positive and negative aspects of the loss, including how the bereaved has grown as well as what is permanently gone; and (2) gaining perspective on both the extent and the limits of responsibility for the loss, the bereaved's own and that of others" (p. 190). A few of the typical behaviors, emotions, and feelings that people experience during the stage of gaining perspective are patience, solitude, acceptance, forgiveness, openness, reminiscence, healing, and peace.

Stage 6: Resolving the loss. Schneider (1984) states that "grief has been resolved when the bereaved can see and pursue activities unconnected with the loss without it being a reaction against (letting go) or identifying with (holding on) the lost person or object" (p. 205). Stage 6 is a time of "self-forgiveness, restitution, commitment, accepting responsibility for actions and beliefs, finishing business, and saying good-bye" (p. 206). Some characteristic behaviors, emotions, and feelings of Stage 6 are self-care, relinquishing, forgiveness of self and others, determination, and peacefulness.

Stage 7: Reformulating loss in a context of growth. Schneider (1984) views the reformulation of loss as an outgrowth of resolving grief. When grief is faced and experienced through to resolution, it may provide the motivational impetus for personal growth by reminding people of their "strengths and limits, mortality, and the finiteness of the time they have" (p. 226). The reformulation stage of grief focuses on "(1) discovering potential rather than limits; (2) seeing problems as challenges; (3) being curious again; and (4) seeking a balance between the different aspects of self" (p. 226). Some of the observed behaviors, feelings, and emotions accompanying Stage 7 are enhanced sensory awareness, assertion, spontaneity, patience, integrity/balance/centeredness, recognition of illusions, curiosity, and increased tolerance for pain.

Stage 8: Transforming loss into new levels of attachment. The stage of transformation is an integration of the physical, emotional, cognitive, behavioral, and spiritual aspects of the person—as an integral part of the process of reformulation to higher levels of understanding and acceptance of the loss. Transformation does not end the cycles of loss and grief; but the process makes it possible for people to approach life "with greater openness and the willingness to surrender more readily the necessity of structure in life" and release energies that create new strength (Schneider, 1984, p. 248). It is perhaps ironic that out of life's greatest loss may emerge a reformulation and transformation that produce a greater capacity for growth than before. The transformational stage is accompanied by such behavioral, feeling, or emotional dimensions as awareness of interrelationships, unconditional love, creativity, wholeness, deep empathy, end of searching, and commitment.

Types of Loss

People may encounter many different types of loss that produce stress, trauma, and/or grief. We have identified several types that crisis workers may encounter. It is not our purpose to provide crisis intervention techniques for dealing with every specific type of loss. What we want to show here is that loss covers a broad scope and that certain fundamental helping skills and strategies apply in a generic way to helping individuals suffering from loss.

Death of a spouse.   The death of a spouse is one of the most emotionally stressful and disruptive events in life. It is experienced by more than 80,000 people each year (Shucter, 1986). There are many more women survivors (widows) than men (widowers), and the bereaved spouse typically faces a number of problems and stages of bereavement alone (Kübler-Ross, 1969). In addition to the immediate shock and stress, many survivors face serious personal, emotional, economic, social, career, family, and community problems (Johnson, 1977; Osterweis et al., 1984, pp. 71–75; Rando, 1984, pp. 144–149).

Shucter (1986) identifies six dimensions in the spousal grief process: (1) emotional and mental responses to the loss, such as shock, anger, or guilt, (2) ways of coping with the pain of bereavement, (3) ways of continuing a relationship with the deceased, (4) changes in how people function socially, at work, and medically, (5) changing relationships with family and friends, and (6) the changing identity of the survivor. Typically the loss of a spouse is an emotionally overwhelming event, ranked on a life-event continuum as the most stressful of all human losses (Osterweis et al., 1984, p. 71). Facing a completely new and unfamiliar set of problems alone, during a period of intense bereavement, constitutes enormous adjustment problems for most surviving spouses.

Death of a child.   The death of a child is a major life crisis for parents (Edelstein, 1984; Hansen & Frantz, 1984, pp. 11–26; Kübler-Ross, 1983; Kushner, 1983; Wass & Corr, 1985). Every parent is unique in terms of needs, history, personality, coping style, relationship to others, social concerns, and family situation. Therefore, every parent suffers the loss of a child somewhat differently. The death of a child is traumatic for parents, whether it occurs as stillbirth or sudden infant death syndrome (SIDS) or follows accident or illness in adolescence or young adulthood (Osterweis et al., 1984, pp. 75–79). It is equally traumatic for aged parents to lose their children who may be middle-aged or older. Regardless of the ages of parents or children, the death of a child is always a major loss. The child's age, suddenness of death, circumstances of the death, and family situation affect the bereavement and adjustment of parents, family, relatives, and friends (Rando, 1984, pp. 367–415).

Bereavement following a suicide.   Death as a result of suicide is accompanied by numerous negative cultural messages and meanings. Therefore, the loss of a loved one because of suicide is doubly stressful (Edelstein, 1984, p. 21; Rando, 1984, p. 150). Grieving loved ones left behind by a suicide may refer to themselves as "victims" because, in addition to the emotional stress of the death itself, the survivors must also deal with burdens such as social stigma, guilt, blame, a search for the cause or meaning, unfinished business, and perceived rejection wrought by the suicide (Rando, 1984, pp. 151–152).

The "real victim" of suicide is said to be not the body in the coffin but the family and other loved ones (Hansen & Frantz, 1984, p. 36). Osterweis et al. (1984) report that survivors of the death of a loved one by suicide are thought to be more vulnerable to physical and mental health problems than grievers from other causes of death (p. 87).

The nature and intensity of the survivor's bereavement depend on various factors, such as the survivor's cultural values, survivor's relationship with the deceased, age and physical condition of the deceased, the nature of the suicide, and the survivor's personality characteristics and mental health (Osterweis et al., 1984, p. 88). According to Stone (1972), seven emotional states may constitute a typical adaptation pattern in the bereavement process of surviving loved ones in the case of death by suicide. These states, which resemble stages of the Kübler-Ross model, are shock, catharsis, depression, guilt, preoccupation with the loss, anger, and reality (p. 27).

Bereavement in childhood.   Studies by Gudas (1990) suggest that signs and symptoms of behavioral and psychological difficulty occur differently between bereaved preschool and school-aged children. Older children, with concepts of permanence of death and personalization of their own mortality, experience more anxiety, depression, and somatic symptoms than younger children (p. 7). But younger children also experience profound reactions to loss and may display feelings of sadness, anger, crying spells, feelings of remorse and guilt, somatization, and separation anxiety (pp. 1–2).

An essential dynamic in understanding childhood grief is that the emotions and reactions of children differ from those of adults because of developmental considerations (Bertoia & Allan, 1988; Osterweis et al., 1984, pp. 100–101). Children's cognitive, affective, and behavioral responses must be approached not in terms of adult perspectives but in terms of each child's understanding and developmental stage (Rando, 1984, pp. 157–162). Children are especially vulnerable during periods of major loss because their inexperience and their undeveloped personalities can easily lead to confusion and misinterpretation of events and lack of grieving (Schoenberg, 1980, p. 200). Such childhood misinterpretation can lead to the development of pathological disorders in adulthood (Bertoia & Allan, 1988, p. 33). Since children's personalities are growing and absorbing social stimuli at a very rapid and concentrated rate, care must be taken to provide reassurance and support during family bereavement (Schonfeld, 1989). They may ask the same questions over and over about the loss, not so much for the factual information but for reassurance that the adult view is consistent, that the story has not changed, and that the grieving adults and children are safe. Children need to hear, over and over again, the simple, truthful, reassuring words of adults who are relatively secure and who show genuine concern for the children's feelings (Osterweis et al., 1984, p. 100).

Some people believe that children should be shielded and protected from exposure to death and loss. The research suggests, however, that bereaved children will make healthier adjustments to loss if they are informed about the loss truthfully and actively (Osterweis et al., 1984, pp. 99–127; Rando, 1984, p. 155; Schoenberg, 1980, pp. 151–154). Even though children during the bereavement process may exhibit behavioral responses that adults may interpret as "not caring" or "not understanding," children should be permitted to proceed with mourning at a level and pace appropriate to their development. Medvene (1991) suggested that psychological disturbance resultant from the loss of a parent can be allayed through group work that establishes in the griever "a sense of community where feelings, memories, images, pictures, poems, and thoughts about the death experience could be acknowledged and shared" (p. 5).

Bereavement in adolescence.   Hansen and Frantz (1984, pp. 36–47, 62–72) describe adolescents who are in bereavement as needing to be included (involved) in the family's grief, while at same time needing periods of privacy. Many times the adolescent may feel excluded, for example, at the sudden death of a grandparent. Other bereaved family members may erroneously assume that the adolescent's perceptions of events are the same as those of the adults. At such times adolescents may not know how to behave because they do not have a sufficient understanding of death, of the circumstances of the death, or of the appropriate mourning role. Adolescents may feel a deep sense of pain, fear, guilt, helplessness, and grief, yet they may not know how to express or feel comfortable in expressing these emotions. Adolescents in grief need to be given understanding, information, and private time. They need opportunities to be included in discussions, planning, mourning, and funeral and commemorative activities (pp. 62–67).

Guerriero-Austrom and Fleming (1990), researching the effects of sibling bereavement on adolescents, found that physical and emotional symptoms fluctuate over time, showing the most severity at 6 to 12 months following the sibling death and emerging again at 18 to 24 months. Females exhibited more death anxiety and health-related problems than males. Adolescent grief reactions were documented as long as three years following the death of the sibling but were not necessarily debilitating or pathological, suggesting that counseling immediately following loss, while appropriate, may not be enough. Teenagers may benefit from counseling as long as three years following the sibling death. The research clearly indicates that one cannot put a time limit on the grief process (p. 11).

Separation and divorce.   About 50% of all marriages end in divorce (Schwed, 1986, p. C7), and this breakup in marriages is an epidemic that is ripping the United States apart (Pauley, 1986). It is devastating to adults and children alike. The crisis of separation and divorce often places children in untenable positions, causing them to feel confused, insecure, fearful, trapped, angry, unloved, and guilty. The adult parties are also adversely affected. According to Johnson (1977), the most common experience that marriage partners have regarding separation is intense and disturbing fear and emotional turmoil. Such fear and turmoil are described in the following passage (Johnson, 1977, p. 50):

> The feeling of being overwhelmed by unfamiliar, unexpected, and frightening emotion is normal; the fear of being totally unable to meet new and even old

responsibilities is normal; the fear of losing complete control is normal. While a very few of those who experience these fears do succumb to serious emotional difficulties, the overwhelming majority do not; and in most, if not all, cases of mental breakdown, the central precipitating cause is fear itself.

Separation is almost always experienced as a loss. Even when the separation is desired and sought, it precipitates a sense of frustration, failure, loss, and mourning. Johnson (1977) says that facing and mourning the loss, rather than denying it, can be both healing and constructive (p. 55).

Schneider (1984) reports that persons suffering from loss due to divorce or widowhood "show significant and consistently higher vulnerability to almost every major physical and mental disorder, particularly to heart disease" (p. 19). The phenomenon of separation and divorce is a widespread and complex contributor to loss in today's world. Colgrove et al. (1976) advise that surviving and healing, following such loss, begin by recognizing and facing the loss immediately and doing the mourning now (pp. 1–2).

Death of a pet.   Bereavement over the death of pets has become a phenomenon of concern in recent years (Downs & Walters, 1986; Nieburg & Fischer, 1982). Downs and Walters reported that more and more people seem to be forming strong bonds of affection and attachment with their pets. When pets die or suffer terminal illness and have to be "put to sleep," the owners may suffer grief, guilt, and other emotional reactions similar to those experienced at the death of human family members. Even when the death of a pet does not constitute a devastating event, it is nonetheless an emotionally sobering time (Bahrick & Sharkin, 1990). The death of a pet may provide a naturally occurring opportunity for adults in the family to introduce children to the concept and experience of death and dying (Koocher, 1975; Nieburg & Fischer, 1982; Schoenberg, 1980, pp. 203–204).

Bereavement in the elderly.   From a developmental standpoint, bereavement among the elderly is compounded by decreases in sensory acuity, general decline in health, and reduced mobility. Having a lower income and fewer support persons available to them than in their younger years also represent changes that may affect them. The elderly generally experience more losses than their younger counterparts: loss of relatives and friends; loss of job, status, and money; loss of bodily functions and abilities; and loss of independence and self-respect (Freeman, 1978, p. 116). The most profound and devastating loss that the elderly may encounter is the loss of a spouse (Schoenberg, 1980, pp. 211–214). It is not known whether age, as such, affects the cognitive and behavioral aspects of adult bereavement. It does appear that advancing age tends to correlate with a decrease in coping strategies. But it is not known whether this decrease is related to one's greater awareness of impending death, decrease in physical stamina and function, or other factors (Schoenberg, 1980, pp. 221–223).

Schoenberg (1980, p. 230), summarizes four conclusions that may be drawn from the literature on bereavement and age:

1. The elderly present more somatic problems than psychological problems.
2. There is no indication that the intensity of grief varies significantly with age.
3. A small amount of evidence suggests that grief among the elderly may be more prolonged than among younger people.
4. Elderly people tend to be lonelier and to have far longer periods of loneliness than their younger counterparts.

With the relative numbers of elderly continuing to increase as people live longer, crisis workers and other caregivers face an ever-increasing need to study gerontology. Certainly the elderly must be both understood and prized by those who help them in their times of grief, as well as in other adjustment concerns.

AIDS: A Modern Dilemma

During the 1980s, a startling new plague emerged. The acquired immune deficiency syndrome (AIDS) crisis shocked the health care world as the mysterious disease took its rapid and phenomenal toll of suffering and death. The AIDS virus, human immunodeficiency virus (HIV), is spread mainly through intimate sexual contact and needle sharing and is transmitted to babies born to infected mothers. Sometimes babies born with HIV positive convert (return to) negative after 18 months when their mothers' antibodies disappear (Dagastino, 1991). During the early eighties, transmission of the virus through contaminated blood supplies was a frequent occurrence. What was first widely reported to be a disease afflicting mainly gay men soon was identified as a disease that can infect anyone, prompting Dr. C. Everett Koop, surgeon general of the United States from 1981 to 1989, to assert that "AIDS should not be used as an excuse to discriminate against any group or individual" (Koop, 1990, p. 29). Indeed, AIDS proved to be nondiscriminatory. It was soon afflicting every segment of society: the gay and lesbian community (Blumenfeld & Raymond, 1988), babies born with AIDS (Kübler-Ross, 1987), children and adolescents (Kübler-Ross, 1987; Mantell & Schinke, 1991; Minton, 1991; Savin-Williams & Lenhart, 1990), needle-sharing drug users (Christ, Moynihan, & Gallo-Silver, 1991; Des Jarlais, Friedman, & Woods, 1990; Galea, Lewis, & Baker, 1988), prostitutes (Campbell, 1990), the elderly (Coleman, 1991), women (Kübler-Ross, 1987; Worth, 1990), and the prison population (Kübler-Ross, 1987).

By the middle 1980s it was clear that HIV infection and disease were important personal, social, and medical issues (Miller, 1990, p. 187), and that every segment of society has a vital interest in developing appropriate and positive strategies to cope with the AIDS epidemic (Alyson, 1990, pp. 7–8). The epidemic has become one of our largest sociopolitical and health care concerns (Kübler-Ross, 1987, p. 4); consequently, people living with AIDS (PLWA's) and HIV infection, as well as families of these people, emerged as critically important populations for crisis workers to address and help.

INTERVENTION STRATEGIES

This section on crisis intervention focuses on the types of grief we have identified. One case example and intervention techniques for each type of grief are presented. Use of the triage system is illustrated only for the first case, death of a spouse. Even though we have omitted mention of triage assessment in the other cases, it is just as applicable to them.

Intervention strategies for helping people who are suffering major losses may include, at one time or another, all the known systems of counseling and other techniques of assisting. The concepts and skills that are basic for these strategies are those discussed in Chapter 2. Both long-term and short-term grief work are applicable strategies. Grief work may be enhanced through interdisciplinary teamwork, but empathic listening to the bereaved and their families appears to be the single most useful skill or strategy available to crisis workers (Osterweis et al., 1984; Rando, 1984; Schneider, 1984; Schoenberg, 1980). Studies by Balk (1990) confirm the value of empathic listening. He found that bereaved college students identify "attentive listening and presence" as being the most helpful to grievers and "avoidance" as being the least helpful. Hughes (1988) believes that the grieving client's expectations are crucial in facilitating the healing process. Hughes stated that the therapist's expectations are "always communicated (directly or subtly) to the client, and that clients heal when they are 'informed' by the therapist that they are never helpless victims but instead are powerful and capable of healing themselves" (p. 77).

The Crisis Worker's Own Grief

Schneider (1984) reminds us that "it is not possible to be a facilitator of the growth aspects of bereavement if the helper is not also experiencing growth in relation to personal losses" (p. 270). The knowledge and perspective gained from one's own growth following grief should serve as a quiet reservoir of strength for workers. But the worker's own grief experience should not be projected or imposed on clients. Both Rando (1984) and Schoenberg (1980) challenge caregivers to come to grips with their own personal and professional attitudes toward death, grief, and bereavement before venturing into helping relationships with clients who are in grief. According to Rando (1984), there are several reasons why caregivers should ensure that their own grief and attitudes about grief are not allowed to intrude upon their helping relationships with others (pp. 430–435).

Emotional investment in the client. A certain degree of emotional investment in clients is normal and needed. Overinvestment in those whom they help may require crisis workers to expend an inordinate amount of energy on their own grief responses in cases of dying and bereaved clients.

Bereavement overload. If the worker forms close bonds with several clients, the emotional load may involve too many risks and grief responses on the part of the worker. A series of client losses may cause the worker to experience bereavement overload or burnout. Workers can deal with their own bereavement overload provided that they are aware of it while it is happening to them and that they act upon their internal signals to get help and/or take steps to effect their own renewal before several client losses get them down.

Countertransference. Sometimes crisis workers who are engaged in grief work with others find that such work awakens their own feelings, thoughts, memories, and fantasies about losses in their own lives. Workers who experience such countertransference will be severely impaired in helping others. To deal with countertransference, caregivers who regularly work with loss-related clients should be involved in peer supervision, case staffing, psychological autopsies, and debriefing groups for reduction of emotional overload caused by constant involvement with client grief.

Emotional replenishment. Caregivers in the area of grief and bereavement work must take special care to minister to their own emotional needs. To do this, caregivers need support systems to provide for their physical, emotional, and psychological wellness; they themselves need to have regular access to empathic listeners for the purpose of sharing their own feelings; and they need the reinforcement from others that they, the caregivers, are valued. The knowledge that they are helping clients is not sufficient in itself. Emotional replenishment involves both taking care of oneself internally and having environmental supports from significant others—a supervisor, friends, family, colleagues—and meaningful physical and emotional activities.

Facing own mortality. Work with clients who are dying and/or grieving brings risks of many stressors. One of the important aspects of such work is that it may arouse existential anxiety over one's own death. Support groups, supervision, in-service training, and reading are suggested coping mechanisms. Spiritual growth activities are worthwhile alternatives for many caregivers.

Sense of power. Caregivers, like all other people, need a sense of power or control. Working with clients in dying, grief, and bereavement may cause workers to identify vicariously with the losses of their clients. Such identification may result in a sense of loss of power or control on the part of workers. Strategies for preventing feelings of loss of power are essentially the same as those recommended for dealing with countertransference.

Tendency to rescue. Crisis workers may have selected their respective professions because they have an inner need to "rescue" or save people from distress. It is essential that workers relinquish the rescue fantasy.

Death of a Spouse

Stuart Wynn, a machinist, age 44, his wife Kate, a bookkeeper, age 42, and one daughter, Anne, a high school senior, age 18, were a stable, middle-class family living in a quiet middle-class neighborhood in a large city. On her way to work one morning aboard a city bus, Kate Wynn suffered a severe stroke and was taken by ambulance to a hospital emergency room. A neighbor, who was also aboard the bus Kate was riding, phoned Stuart at work, and Stuart rushed to the hospital. Kate was placed in an intensive care unit but never regained consciousness after the stroke. She lived only 24 hours, leaving Stuart and Anne stunned and in a state of grief. As far as Stuart knew, Kate had been in good health and had had no medical history to indicate that she might have a health problem.

The case of Stuart is an example of immediate short-term crisis intervention. The first intervention session was a very brief meeting that included only the crisis worker and Stuart. The second meeting, approximately 20 minutes later, was also a short-term intervention session that featured a meeting between Stuart and his daughter and a multidisciplinary team consisting of the crisis worker, the attending physician, a psychiatric nurse, and the hospital chaplain. These initial short-term sessions were aimed at providing

1. empathic understanding and acknowledgement of the special problems related to Kate's sudden death
2. assurance to Stuart and Anne that all appropriate emergency medical measures had been attempted in efforts to save Kate
3. emotional support for both Stuart and Anne by the worker and by the other members of the multidisciplinary team
4. time alone with Kate's body prior to its being picked up for autopsy
5. referral resources that Stuart needed immediately to make arrangements for the funeral, notification of kin, and other matters
6. information about autopsy rights and procedures, in case Stuart requested it (which he did)
7. contact with the family minister, at Stuart's request.

On the Triage Assessment Form, the worker mentally computed Stuart's profile: Affective—5 (emotionally shocked but substantially under control), Cognitive—3 (thought processes affected by the crisis but under volitional control and congruent with reality), Behavioral—8 (minimally able to perform tasks relevant to his wife's death), Total—16 (moderate impairment). The crisis worker proceeded to work in a collaborative mode with Stuart. If the total on the triage assessment had been in the 20s, the worker would have intervened in a far more directive stance. Despite the sudden death of his spouse, at that moment Stuart was maintaining psychological equilibrium; it was only later that the impact of the loss would catch up with him and he would experience severe affective, cognitive, and behavioral impairment. But for the moment he could cope, even though the help of crisis intervention was needed and welcomed.

Intervention strategies provided and issues explored with Stuart during the days and weeks immediately following Kate's burial were these:

1. *Individual counseling and intervention.* Issues of loneliness and bereavement related to Kate's absence. Implications for regaining equilibrium and going on with his life. Emotional supports for Anne. Identification of functions and roles in the family that were previously carried out by Kate and that must be reevaluated or reassigned. Review of either Kübler-Ross's or Schneider's stages of grief and assurance that Stuart would, in time, reformulate the loss. Grief work regarding the new identity—without Kate. It was now "I, Stuart," instead of "us—Stuart and Kate." Identifying and dealing with Stuart's areas of vulnerability created by Kate's death. Assessment of ways to remember and use the positive strengths of Kate's life in a healthy and growth-promoting way for both himself and Anne.

2. *Spouse-survivor support group work.* Assessment of overall implications of Stuart's widowerhood, such as loss of social connections. Group-generated alternatives available to Stuart and others who had recently experienced the death of a spouse. Suggestions and guidance from the support group on Stuart's responses and single-parenting role with regard to Anne, his 18-year-old daughter. Referral to other groups, organizations, and institutions offering assistance and support appropriate for Stuart's particular situation. Group focus on ways to cope with the loneliness and other emotions brought on by the absence of one's spouse.

During the first contact with Stuart at the hospital, on the afternoon of Kate's sudden death, the crisis worker met individually with Stuart. The following segment illustrates a part of the first intervention session with Stuart.

CW: [*Holding Stuart's hand.*] Stuart, I realize your wife's death has been sudden and overwhelming to you. I want you to know that I am here to help you with whatever you need done. [*Silence. Still holding Stuart's hand.*] I'll be with you and assist you in whatever way I can. [*Silence. Still holding Stuart's hand.*]

The crisis worker's assessment is that Stuart's emotional status is one of shock, denial, or disbelief.

Stuart: This is so unreal! I just can't believe she's gone. It's such a sudden blow to me. Right now my main thought is Anne—our daughter. She just got here. I guess right now what I want is to make sure she's OK. I want to find out if she wants to see her mother before they take her away from the hospital.

CW: So you're needing to talk with Anne—and it's pretty urgent that you see her right away. Let's see if we can find her.

A few moments later.

Stuart: [*Accompanied by Anne.*] We want to be with Kate—to be alone with her some before they take her away. Can you arrange for us to do that?

CW: Yes, we'll arrange for that right now.

Stuart: One other thing. I'm afraid we're going to be in a pretty heavy way after we've seen her. Could you arrange for us to sit in the chapel a while after we get back? And is there a chaplain around who could be with us for a few moments?

CW: I'll phone Chaplain Myer again. He's aware of Kate's death and he said he'd be available any time, if you want him. I'll go with you and leave you alone with Kate's body and then, when you're ready, I'll go with you to the chapel.

The work with Stuart was immediate and intense. During the first hour, provisions were made for a brief individual session with Stuart, private time for Stuart and Anne in the hospital chapel, and a multidisciplinary team session with Stuart and Anne. Definite provisions for follow-up work were established for helping Stuart and Anne during the following days and weeks. The crisis worker's immediate concern was to deal with Stuart's initial phase of grief, which corresponded with Kübler-Ross's (1969) first stage of denial, isolation, shock, and disbelief. The worker's primary goal was to help Stuart, an hour at a time and/or a day at a time, deal with the loss of Kate.

The worker kept in mind that as time evolved, the emergent stages of anger, bargaining, depression, and acceptance would need to be faced. But, for the moment, the short-term intervention focused on Stuart's need to deal with his first stage of grief. The worker was also sensitive to allowing Stuart to become aware of his own loss. There was never a thought or attempt to try to manage, defer, speed up, or otherwise intrude upon Stuart's grief process. Short-term grief work, in Stuart's case, was more a supportive way of being than overtly doing. Initial grief work is as much attitude on the part of caregivers as it is behavior.

Some two weeks later, after initially taking the death in stride, Stuart was hit with the full impact of the loss of Kate. The daughter, Anne, was similarly impacted and stressed. Stuart's grief and his feeling of helplessness regarding emotional support for his daughter accompanied a rapid escalation of his observed Affective (8), Cognitive (8), Behavioral (7), and Total (23) triage assessment score. This latter assessment brought on an immediate referral of Stuart to a long-term therapist for grief work. Such a rapid escalation is a frequent occurrence among clients who have experienced the loss of a loved one. Crisis workers should be alert to such a possibility following any crisis involving sudden loss.

Death of a Child

Brad Drake, age 34, a rural postal carrier, and his wife Helen, age 30, had twin sons, Herbert and Hubert, age 6. Late one afternoon, while Brad was doing the chores at the barn behind their house and Helen was preparing supper, Hubert attempted to cross the highway in front of their house and was struck by an automobile. The parents rushed Hubert to the hospital 22 miles away, but the child was pronounced dead on arrival. The death of Hubert left them feeling a deep sense of grief, hurt, bewilderment, guilt, powerlessness, psychological immobility and vulnerability, and searching for answers and meaning.

Approximately two weeks following Hubert's burial, Brad and Helen together sought counseling. The crisis worker saw them together immediately following the intake interview. The worker decided that crisis intervention could provide three interrelated but equally important things for Brad and Helen: (1) facilitate the release of their grief energy, (2) reassure them that their feelings were normal, and (3) put them into communication with other grieving parents. These goals of intervention, described by Hansen and Frantz (1984, pp. 21–22), formed the basis for starting grief work with Brad and Helen Drake. The intervention strategies with the Drakes provided

1. empathic understanding and acknowledgement of Brad and Helen's grief related to Hubert's sudden death
2. an opportunity for both parents to talk about their grief, about Hubert, about Hubert's accidental death, about the good times and feelings Hubert had brought into their lives, and about their feelings since Hubert's death
3. a chance to shed tears, which both Brad and Helen did
4. exploration of previously unidentified and unspoken anger and guilt
5. assessment of the family's needs related to grief work and tentative plans for continuation of the work begun during the initial session.

The case of Brad and Helen is an example of long-term intervention. The strategies provided and issues explored with Brad and Helen during the days and weeks following Hubert's burial were as follows:

1. *Couple counseling and intervention.* The impact of the death on the twin brother, Herbert, and appropriate parental handling of Herbert. Continuation of grief work through talk, tears, expressions of guilt and anger, reminiscence and commemoration of Hubert's life, redirection of energies toward the family and creative work together, and a regular exercise program. Reassurance of Brad and Helen that they were not going crazy. Affirmation that they were the best parents they could be; that their parenting should not be blamed for the accident. Assessment of family problems and potentials. Assessment of marital relationship following the death of Hubert and exploration of ways to cope with the effects of the bereavement on the marriage. Reassurance of Brad and Helen that the grief and pain will continue for a long time and that this is normal; that they'll always have memories of the loss; that they will, in time, let go of the pattern of holding onto their grief and move on; that there is no set timetable for them to finish their grieving.

2. *Parent-survivor and support group work.* Involvement of Brad and Helen in a group whose common focus is the loss of a child. Group-supported talk, reminiscence, sharing, grief, tears. Making contact with other bereaved parents for mutual support by phone in addition to group meet-

ings. Bringing parents together so that the newly bereaved can be helped by parents who are further advanced in the grieving process than Brad and Helen.

3. *Reading and media helps.* Provision of books, other reading material, films, and other audiovisual material about bereavement in children and youth, as well as in parents. (The booklet *Death Education: A Concern for the Living,* by Gibson, Roberts, and Buttery [1982], is a good source.) Putting the parents in touch with interventional supports such as parental self-help bereavement groups (Bordow, 1982; Dickens, 1985; Schiff, 1977).

The first crisis intervention session with Brad and Helen was rather emotionally low-key, compared with later sessions, because both parents were still in a stage of denial and isolation. The crisis worker noted that they exhibited signs of being physically and emotionally drained; they vacillated between moping and benign circumspection, but showed no indication of movement to the later stages of anger, bargaining, or depression. The crisis worker's goal was not to facilitate their advancement to a later stage of grief; rather, the aim was to understand their current inner concerns and to provide them with opportunities to identify and express their immediate and deep feelings openly.

CW: I sense that you are both feeling drainage of your emotional energy—like you're stuck there and cannot seem to move on.

Brad: Yes, stuck is the word. But I need this time. I don't want to rush or be rushed. [*Silence.*] I guess we're in unknown and uncharted territory.

CW: It is very important not to hurry yourself or to be hurried.

Helen: We've just about stopped talking about it. We've become two lonely recluses in the same house. That worries me.

CW: Helen, what would you like to be doing right now, instead of being stuck and isolated?

Helen: I'd like to be more open. I'd like to know what's going on with Brad, and I'd like to be able to share feelings—even though they may be sad.

The worker was attempting to respond in a way that would allow both parents the autonomy to experience their current state of bereavement and, at the same time, encourage them to open up and provide mutual support. Open communication was viewed as important in terms of their grief as well as their relationship. The worker was successful in helping both of them share their concerns, which, in turn, enabled them to move on to other issues of importance to them.

Brad: We just don't know where to turn. We take our religion seriously and we've talked to our minister. That doesn't seem to help us. I keep on asking, "Why, why, why?"

Helen: We know the story of Job and such as that. We know tragedy strikes anywhere and anybody. Still, we don't know—we can't see—that a God of love or a God of justice can condone or permit the life of a good and innocent child like that to be snuffed out. I'm amazed at myself for talking like that. But my words are nothing compared to my thinking since this happened. I'm thinking I may be going insane or something.

CW: Helen, you're not going insane. You're responding in a way that makes perfect sense to me. You have both lost the most important and precious gift a mother and father can lose. It is natural and normal for you to experience unusual feelings and grief. You're doing a very good thing by talking openly about your thoughts and feelings. That's why I'm glad you came and reached out to me today. Nobody can erase your hurt or bring your son back, but I will help as best I can.

Later in the same session, the crisis worker has facilitated their release of grief energy and suggested that they contact a local, ongoing support group.

Brad: I'm glad we came today. We would like to come in again. The group of parents you spoke about is a good idea. I think we need that now, and we are going to need it more.

Helen: We didn't know about Compassionate Friends. I'll call them this afternoon. It's good to know that such a group exists. It sounds like a wonderful thing.

CW: I think you will both be glad you discovered Compassionate Friends. I'm truly glad you came, and I'll look forward to seeing you again. Here's my card, in case you want to call me. And don't forget your books.

Helen: Thank you, so much. It sounds like the books you recommended will be especially helpful for us.

Helen was referring to Staudacher's (1987) paperback book titled *Beyond Grief* and Kushner's (1983) paperback titled *When Bad Things Happen to Good People.* The two books combine to represent comprehensive guidelines for surviving the death of a loved one. They are appropriate for both the bereaved and the helping professional because both volumes are readable, objective, positive, comforting, and professionally written. The crisis worker was employing a strategy of bibliotherapy (Ellis & Abrahms, 1978, p. 123), which is an effective way of providing information, reinforcement, and supports through reading and other media that pertain to specific client concerns. The worker was also providing verbal and nonverbal warmth and understanding and attempting to model open communication to encourage them to strengthen their own mutual supports at home. The worker kept the focus on their current concerns, not intruding or imposing extraneous demands on them.

The fact that Brad and Helen returned for follow-up grief work, made a commitment to become involved in a support group, and accepted relevant reading material indicated to the worker that the objectives for intervention were being attained. The worker continued to meet with Brad and Helen while they were also attending the parent support group. The support group provided discussions, resource persons, and readings on several aspects of grief and bereavement, such as the major phases of grief (Tatelbaum, 1980), psychological perspectives (Smith, 1985), and individual and social realities (Stephenson, 1985). Brad and Helen reported that the readings helped them to discuss their loss more openly—both in the group and at home.

Bereavement Following a Suicide

Leah Nichols, age 54, manager of a branch bank, returned home from work Friday evening and discovered her son, Ronnie, age 24, dead from a gunshot wound. Ronnie had left a suicide note where he had apparently killed himself in his bedroom. Leah's husband, a college professor, had been dead (of heart failure) about a year, and she and Ronnie had lived in the family home. Ronnie's other siblings, Brenda, age 31, Richard, age 27, and Larry, age 22, were married and living in cities scattered about the region. Ronnie had been a warm, friendly, loving, and lovable person who had never married or dated much. He was highly sensitive and was given to mood swings from deep depression to euphoria. He had expressed suicidal ideations since his elementary school years and had been under psychiatric care since his adolescent years. But in recent months he had appeared to be gaining in maturity and had gotten off his medication. Ronnie was employed at a local bookstore, where he was regarded as friendly and dependable. Everyone who knew him liked him. Leah's grief was heavy and painful, but she felt she should set a controlled and circumspect image for the other three siblings and other friends and relatives.

Intervention strategies provided and issues explored with the Nichols family during the days and weeks immediately following Ronnie's suicide were these:

1. *Individual counseling and intervention.* Assessment of the impact of Leah's having lost her husband to heart failure and a son to suicide in such a brief time frame. Opportunities for Leah to release her grief energy. Assessment of Leah's medical and psychological vulnerability. Brief therapy for siblings when appropriate and needed.

2. *Family systems therapy.* Facilitation of the family's release of grief energy. Focus on the value and impact of Ronnie's life as well as his death. Exploration of and dealing with residual guilt among family members. Group search for meaning and understanding of Ronnie's suicide. Assessment and addressing of anger, blame, rejection, unfinished business, and stigma encountered by family members. Facilitation of family decisions and actions to commemorate Ronnie's life. Helping family members to become reconciled to the fact that Ronnie chose death and helping family members reformulate his death within a context of their own growth.

Individual crisis counseling following Ronnie's suicide was provided for Leah. The individual follow-up grief work with her dealt with a good many issues that are common in suicide work: denial, guilt, bargaining, and depression. The issue of Leah's martyrdom came out during an individual session approximately three weeks following Ronnie's funeral.

Leah: My kids think I'm holding back. They say I'm too stoic, too unaffected, or too aloof. They think my lack of showing emotions is not normal—not healthy.

CW: What do you think?

Leah: I don't know. I guess I believe somebody has to keep the lid on—keep a steady head during all this. I haven't wanted to trouble any of them with my problems. Their daddy's death, then Ronnie's. They've had enough without me dumping my grief on them.

CW: What are you saying, at a deep level, below the surface, right now?

Leah: I guess I am saying I'm hurting and that I have a need to weep, to feel the impact of the loss of Ronnie, too. I guess my actions have looked pretty cold and strange to them. I guess I've been trying to protect them—to keep them from hurting.

CW: What will it do for you to keep them from hurting?

Leah: Make me a martyr, I guess. I don't know what else it could be.

The crisis worker was not attempting to steer Leah to any particular conclusion. Rather, the questioning strategy, a combination of techniques from reality therapy, rational-emotive therapy, and Gestalt therapy, was used to help Leah home in on her own world. This crisis intervention technique would be ineffective if the worker were trying to analyze or identify pathology in Leah's behavior. Diagnosing, prescribing a cure, and managing Leah's recovery for her would have also been inappropriate.

Leah: I really had no notion I was playing the martyr when I came in here today. The kids could see something I couldn't see. I'm too close to it, I guess.

CW: What do you want to see happen now?

Leah: I want to get rid of it. I don't need it. The kids don't need it. I want to put it behind me.

CW: How are you going to put it behind you?

The worker continued to use reality therapy techniques (Glasser, 1965) to ascribe autonomy and responsibility to Leah. Leah's stability and mobility were assessed to be excellent. She had the power and the motivation to take the lead, on her own, and to exercise independent judgment and choices. Individual counseling with clients following a suicide may make use of any therapeutic modality that is appropriate for the client. The interview with Leah featured several different modalities, under an overall umbrella of the six steps in crisis intervention described in Chapter 2.

Group work was also used in the case of Leah. At approximately the same time as the individual session with Leah, the manager of the bookstore where Ronnie had worked requested a session between the crisis worker and the entire bookstore staff. The manager said that the employees were having a hard time becoming reconciled to Ronnie's suicide. One group session was conducted. Every employee of the bookstore attended and participated in the group session. The crisis worker facilitated the crisis group work by using the following format, with the employees sitting in a circle in a conference room:

1. The worker made a brief introduction, outlining the purposes and structure of the meeting.
2. Starting with the bookstore manager, each participant was given an opportunity to verbalize how he or she wished to remember Ronnie and to identify his most positive attribute.
3. During the second round, each employee was given an opportunity to take care of unfinished business with Ronnie and to verbally say goodbye to Ronnie.
4. The crisis worker summarized the content and feelings that the group had expressed. Then the crisis worker ended the session by (a) affirming the legitimate grief expressed by the group, (b) absolving the group of guilt and responsibility for Ronnie's death, (c) honoring the attributes and memory of Ronnie's life by a period of silent meditation, asking all persons present to imagine themselves saying good-bye and letting go of Ronnie, and (d) giving permission for each person to end the stage of acute grief at the conclusion of the meeting.

The crisis worker used a format that is useful in many crisis group settings—especially in a group whose concern is loss and grief. A variation of this group technique would be appropriate with a variety of groups representing a family, a fraternal group, the employees in a workplace, a school group, or a church group (any group dealing with a loss-related crisis).

What the worker did with the bookstore staff, in relation to Ronnie's suicide, was to tap into the power and cohesiveness of the group to nurture group restoration of the equilibrium of individual members. The worker's assessment was that the group norm was stuck in a stage of denial, isolation, and guilt. The group session was a powerful one. Although it appeared to the crisis worker that each member was ready to let go of Ronnie and move on toward positive growth, the worker invited members to come in for individual follow-up. In this case, none was requested.

Bereavement in Childhood

Elmer and Irene Kirk, ages 36 and 38 respectively, were spending all the time, energy, and money they could in their attempts to cope with the terminal illness of their son, Charles, 5 years old. After a year of being in and out of the children's research hospital, Charles sensed that he did not have long to live, but Elmer and Irene were attempting to make Charles's remaining days as happy and meaningful as Charles's physical condition would permit. Their only other child, Corine, age 8, felt sad, bewildered, lonely, and neglected.

The whole family was consumed with grief the day Charles died. In addition to grief, Corine suffered from guilt. She felt guilty because she had dared to wish within herself for several months that Charles's illness would just end and get it over. Somehow Corine believed that her wish had contributed to the death of her brother. She also felt guilty because she was alive and didn't deserve to live as much as Charles.

Intervention strategies provided and issues explored with the Kirk family during the days and weeks immediately prior to and following the death of Charles were the following:

1. *Individual counseling and intervention.* Assessment of Corine's concept of death. Recognition that Corine will react to the loss in her own way and that Corine and her parents may receive a great deal of valuable help from Corine's school counselor (Bertoia & Allan, 1988). Ensuring that Corine has opportunities to participate actively and learn the medical facts relating to Charles's terminal illness in a truthful and realistic manner. Use of child-centered counseling approaches in helping Corine deal with and refute her guilt feelings related to her brother's death: child-centered approaches to include the use of puppets, artwork, sand play, and psychodrama. Assessment of the impact of Charles's death on both parents and Corine. Including Corine in the funeral plans and commemorative activities. Providing opportunities for each family member to release grief energy. Assessment of the impact of Charles's illness and death on the marriage and provision of individual therapy for Elmer and Irene as needed.

2. *Family systems therapy.* Assessment of the family's stress level and coping resources. Provision of opportunities for the family together to explore the important issues related to Charles's death: the meaning, the good times and memories, guilt, blame, anger, rejection, and unfinished business. Focus on Corine: ensuring that she knows that she is loved and that the time and energy that Elmer and Irene have devoted to Charles in no way diminished their love and devotion to Corine. Discussion of feelings openly and honestly, keeping in mind the developmental capacity of Corine. Ensuring that all family members have permission to mourn openly. Assuming that Charles's death will have a lasting impact on Corine and will be manifested through her play, her fantasy life, and her relationship to both Elmer and Irene.

Crisis intervention strategies with children are different from strategies employed with adults because children are not miniature grownups. Children respond to counseling or teaching in a different way from adults. Typically they learn more through concrete, tactile, enactment, and model-observation modes than through listening to lectures.

A number of versatile child-centered approaches are available and appropriate for use in crisis intervention:

1. Puppets can help children use a total range of abilities for learning and communicating ideas (touching, talking, hearing, seeing, enacting, sharing) (James & Myer, 1987).

2. Artwork is effective in allowing children alternative modes of expression, so that they are not bound only to the written or spoken word (Gumaer, 1984).
3. Sand play provides creative and participatory modes, wherein children are not bound to written or spoken communication, are less inhibited, and are more prone toward creative self-expression (using sand as a safe and familiar medium) (Vinturella & James, 1987).
4. Psychodrama allows children to observe, enact, self-disclose, question, experience, and learn in a protected environment (Gumaer, 1984).

Using puppets in crisis counseling with Corine, the worker was able to help her dispute her irrational and magical belief that her covert wish had caused her brother's death. During two previous sessions with the crisis worker, Corine had developed a great deal of trust in the worker and considerable facility and ease in using the raggedy puppets. At the third session, there were five puppets: Raggedy Ann, Raggedy Billy (Raggedy Ann's dying brother), Raggedy Mom, Raggedy Dad, and Raggedy Doctor.

CW: [*Holding Raggedy Billy and Raggedy Mom—Raggedy Billy speaking*]. Mommy, Mommy, Ann said I'm dying because she had bad thoughts—she wished I would die, so you and Daddy could leave the hospital and come back home.

CW: [*Holding Raggedy Billy and Raggedy Mom—Raggedy Mom speaking.*] Oh, Billy! Wishing someone is dead can *never, never* make it happen! Your sister Ann has a perfect right to wish for this hurting and sickness to end. She is so lonesome for Mommy and Daddy and for you, too. It's normal for her to wish this sickness were ending. But Ann should never feel bad or guilty just because she wished something. Remember, *wishing* doesn't make it happen!

CW: [*Holding Raggedy Billy and Raggedy Mom—Raggedy Billy speaking.*] Mommy, I wish I could see my sister Ann. I'd like to tell her it's OK.

CW: [*Holding Raggedy Billy and Raggedy Mom—Raggedy Mom speaking.*] Oh, Billy, my dear son! [*Smack—Raggedy Mom kisses Raggedy Billy.*] I love you and I love Ann. Here comes your sister now. Why don't you talk to her? She's in the hospital to visit you.

CW: [*Holding Raggedy Billy and Raggedy Mom—turning toward Corine, Raggedy Billy speaking.*] Hi, sister Ann. I'm glad you came to the hospital to see me. I wanted to tell you how much I love you and how much I will miss you when I die. I want you to know that you should not worry about the wishes and thoughts you had. My disease is making me die. Your thoughts cannot make me or anyone else die. I want you to know it's all right. I love you, Mom loves you, and Daddy loves you. We will always love you.

Corine: [*Holding Raggedy Ann and Raggedy Dad—Raggedy Ann speaking.*] I'm sorry. I wish you wouldn't die. I'm very, very sorry. I hope you don't die.

CW: [*Holding Raggedy Billy and Raggedy Mom—Raggedy Mom speaking.*] Oh, Ann, we all hope he doesn't die. But I'm afraid he will. Then we will all be sad together. We will miss him. But we will have to learn to live without Billy when he's gone. We will still love him. But we will have each other and love each other. We will never blame you or ourselves for his death. His death will be caused by his sickness, not by your thoughts or wishes nor by my thoughts or wishes.

The segment is an example of puppet dialogue in child-centered crisis counseling. The crisis worker was using a variety of theoretical approaches: rational-emotive, behavioral, and Gestalt therapies. Though the segment cannot reveal all the preparatory work and dialogue that preceded and followed this brief encounter, it provides some idea of how versatile and effective puppetry can be. The crisis worker was focusing on only one dimension of bereavement during childhood—Corine's guilt feelings. But there are few, if any, dimensions of childhood bereavement that cannot be effectively dealt with through play media.

Corine's grief work could have been processed with equal effectiveness by a crisis worker skilled in using artwork, sand play, or psychodrama. Any concern or issue related to childhood grief can be approached through child-centered methods. What we want to emphasize is that intervention with children must be handled differently from adult intervention and that it is absolutely necessary for crisis workers who help children to be highly trained and knowledgeable in child-centered counseling techniques.

Bereavement in Adolescence

An accident following the prom in early May resulted in the deaths of four Cedar Grove High School students: Phil, age 16, the driver of the car; Jerry, age 17; Lucille, age 16; and Velma, age 17. The whole school and the entire community were distraught with grief and sadness. The families were in a state of shocked bereavement. A group of seven classmates at school, representing the four youngsters' closest friends, appeared to be stuck in their grief. Even after the commemoration program in the auditorium was concluded, the group did not feel they could resume their school activities or daily lives without further grief work. Shirley, Lee, Peggy, and Bryan, all 17, and Eddie, Sheila, and Cynthia, all 16, requested the help of the school counselor in reaching some understanding and resolution of their feelings of anguish and grief.

These were the intervention strategies provided and issues explored with the adolescents by the school counselor during the days and weeks immediately following the burial of the four teenagers killed in the automobile accident after the prom:

1. *Individual counseling and intervention.* Assessment of individual stress levels. Providing individuals a safe place to release stress energy. Helping adolescents feel comfortable in expressing how they feel. Providing death education for adolescents.

2. *Group grief work.* Providing an atmosphere for the seven adolescents as a group to deal with the deaths of their four classmates in particular and with the area of death and dying in general. Providing for group sessions

and projects that commemorate the deceased classmates. Group exploration of unfinished business through written or role-playing exercises. Provision for students to deal with the deaths outside the group within the school environment through peer support groups. Gray (1988) reported that bereaved teens in support groups found peers to be "most helpful," compared to other school-related workers, and that bereaved adolescents did not want to be singled out or treated in special ways (pp. 187–188).

In cases of sudden death, grief, and bereavement among adolescents, a great deal of shock, vulnerability, remorse, and other emotions will quickly emerge. Because most adolescents lack experience dealing with the death of their peers and because social influence is powerful and pervasive in a setting such as a high school, the use of adolescent group grief work is an ideal strategy for controlling distortions and rumors and for helping young people release grief energy and begin to resolve their feelings of loss.

The Cedar Grove High School counselor was attentive to the feelings of fear, shock, powerlessness, and emptiness that many students manifested. The counselor believed that a group would be an appropriate setting for the students to share their feelings of grief and vulnerability. The group grief work was also perceived to be an appropriate activity in which the school could nurture learning and provide appropriate modeling for handling real-life bereavement and commemoration. The counselor, meeting with the group in the group guidance room, served as the crisis worker. She met with several grief work groups during the days immediately following the deaths of the four students. Each group, though different in composition, shared a common theme of needing to deal with the deaths of their classmates. The counselor set the tone by introducing the topic and encouraging members to share their emotional responses to the loss. Later during the session, after the release of students' grief energy, the counselor began to use structured techniques to help them sharpen their memories and focus on reality.

CW: I really appreciate all of the expressions of your feelings you've given so freely. Before the session began today, I asked Peggy to go by the yearbook office and pick up a copy of this year's *Wildcat.* I also asked her to pick up some leftover photographs that the yearbook staff did not use. Peggy, would you like to share some of them with the group?

Peggy: I put filing cards in the pages of the annual that I thought we'd like to look at. Oh, and I've got some great shots of Lucille, Jerry, and Velma. I only found one of Phil, and that was in a group. But Phil's class picture is in there (pointing toward the yearbook), and all four of them look so real and so alive and so happy in the activities section.

The students in the group showed a great deal of interest and released a great amount of stress energy while examining the photographs of the deceased students. Later in the session, the group discussed death in general, the impact of death on the living, and their own deaths. The counselor was able to use another technique that is sometimes effective in group grief work: the epitaph exercise. Each group member was given four index cards and was instructed: "If you were given the responsibility for writing the epitaphs for Phil, Jerry, Lucille, and Velma, write down the exact words on the cards that would appear on their gravestones." The group shared their epitaphs and discussed them.

Eddie: I thought Cynthia's was really good when she wrote—about Jerry—"Here lies the Will Rogers of Cedar Grove," because he really did like everybody. [*Students nod in agreement.*]

Shirley: I almost cried when I wrote Velma's, and then I did when Sheila read Velma's. I just felt like I couldn't stand it. It's so true. I'm really going to miss that girl. [*Students nod in agreement. Long period of silence; thoughtful look on all faces.*]

CW: I think what we've done is to write down, in the briefest form, what we want to remember most about each of our beloved classmates.

Before the session ended, the counselor led the group in identifying the positive contributions that each of the deceased students had made and in verbalizing their good-byes to each of their departed classmates. The counselor was attempting to use the power and social influence of the group setting to enhance the emotional impact upon each member and to prepare each member to say good-bye, let go of the deceased, and begin to get ready to go on living.

Bereavement in Schools

The sudden death of a student, teacher, or principal may precipitate a bereavement crisis for an entire school or school community. As a proactive response, a preplanned interdisciplinary team approach to dealing with such crises has been widely used (Allan & Anderson, 1986; Hunt, 1987; Pelej, 1987; Sorensen, 1989; Stevenson, 1986; Zinner, 1987). A typical school crisis intervention team might include school counselors, school psychologists, school administrators, and other individuals possessing knowledge, skills, and experience with crisis intervention in schools. The team is convened at the onset of the crisis and addresses issues such as: (1) the nature of the school crisis, (2) the emotional needs of students, faculty, and staff, (3) identification of high-risk populations, (4) parental involvement and contact, and (5) immediate and long-term crisis intervention strategies (Sorensen, 1989, p. 426).

The crisis intervention team, responding to a sudden death affecting the school and community, would promptly take several initiatives to help students, faculty, and others. Examples of strategies the team might employ are (1) setting up mini-counseling centers, (2) convening small grief groups or support groups, (3) facilitating large group meetings, led by team members or consultants the team might bring in, (4) leading classroom discussions in targeted at-risk classes, (5) conducting faculty meetings for the purpose of dealing with feelings and coping strategies, (6) establishing a crisis information center for communicating with and offering support to the bereaved during the acute crisis phase, (7) covering classes for faculty who are especially vulnerable, (8) serving as curriculum consultants for helping faculty to develop classroom activities for responding to the specific crisis, (9) serving as individual grief counselors and support persons for students, faculty, and staff, (10) determining parental needs, guidance, and sharing, and ensuring that appropriate parental involvement is invited, and (11) serving as consultants for the building administrator in formulating press releases and dealing with the media (Sorensen, 1989).

Crisis intervention team members assess the particular needs of the bereaved school population and provide or acquire appropriate responses or services. Individually or in groups, team members may focus on the grief of a specific grade level, provide group discussion for particular subgroups, temporarily relieve bereaved teachers of classroom responsibilities, staff mini-counseling centers, or work with parents. The crisis intervention team provides the appropriate responses needed to nurture the healing process and foster a return to as near normalcy as possible.

Separation and Divorce

When Don Nakamura, age 32, an automobile salesman, came home and announced to Hattie, age 30, that he wanted a divorce, it shattered Hattie's world. The marriage had been going downhill for a long time, and during the preceding months Don had been staying out nights. Nevertheless, Hattie, a licensed practical nurse, wanted to patch things up and to have a child. But Don was adamant and Hattie finally reluctantly admitted that the marriage was over. She was still distraught, with feelings of grief, guilt, worthlessness, and failure. Hattie felt that her life was meaningless. She didn't want to face life alone; she was stuck in grief and felt that she was doomed to live the remainder of her life unfulfilled, without a husband or a child, because no decent man would ever want her. She felt like a complete failure and blamed herself for not succeeding in the marriage. Hattie found herself frozen in a state of grief, remorse, guilt, depression, and self-pity.

Intervention strategies provided and issues explored with Hattie during the days and weeks immediately following Don's announcement to her that he wanted a divorce were as follows:

1. *Individual counseling and intervention.* Assessment of Hattie's lethality level. Assessment of her coping skills and resources. Provision of a safe atmosphere for her to talk it out and cry. Assessment of available support persons. Consideration of her feelings of worthlessness, fear, failure, guilt, anger, depression, self-pity, and unfulfillment. Use of rational-emotive, reality therapy, and cognitive-behavioral modalities to help Hattie identify and successfully refute her negative and self-defeating beliefs and self-statements. Reprogramming her internal sentences and developing positive action steps that she can own, practice, and carry out independently of a helping person.

2. *Support group work.* Identification of divorce self-help groups for Hattie to use as supports. Assessment of her social needs on a time continuum from the present forward for several years. Use of the self-help group to assist her in making realistic plans for her personal and social adjustment to her new situation.

3. *Referral resources.* Assessment of Hattie's need for legal, vocational, and financial assistance. If necessary, identification of specific referral persons for her to contact immediately. (While interviewing her, careful assessment of statements reflecting her present autonomy and ability to attain her goals. For example, dependence on her husband's attorney, banker, or accountant may not serve her best interests. Many newly estranged wives find that they need a different attorney, banker, and accountant from the ones used by their spouses and that their vocational-development needs must be severed completely from those of the husband. Often this is a sudden and difficult switch. Therefore, the worker must be sensitive, supportive, realistic, and assertive because Hattie is so vulnerable during this phase of her separation).

The abrupt termination of relationships by separation is frequently accompanied by emotional responses found in other types of personal loss such as death. People who experience the loss of separation may exhibit shock, disbelief, denial, anger, withdrawal, guilt, and depression. Each person responds in unique ways. Some individuals will cry for several days. Some will verbally ventilate for days on end—to anyone who will listen. Some will go into a state of withdrawal, described by one person like this: "When he came in and told me he was leaving, packed his clothes, and left, I got in the bed and didn't move. I intended to stay there until I died."

The loss by separation may be the result of severance of a marriage, a love relationship, a gay or lesbian relationship, a business partnership, or any other close personal attachment. Helping people overcome the emotional and behavioral results of the loss of a relationship requires crisis intervention skills similar to those needed in other types of grief and bereavement.

In the case of Hattie, the client presented herself for crisis intervention several days after she had stayed in bed with the intention of crying and grieving herself to death. Hattie truly wanted to die after Don told her he was permanently leaving. At first her denial was so profound that she thought to herself, "This can never be. I will never be a divorcée. My parents must never know. My friends must never find out." Hattie did not talk to anyone about Don's leaving for several days. There was denial: "He really isn't leaving for good. He will be back. We will work things out." There was guilt: "What did I do to cause this? I must have been a terrible wife. I shouldn't have been so blind to his needs. If I just died in an accident, he could go on and marry the other woman and no one would ever have to know." There was anger: "I've a good mind to find her and pay her back for all the misery she's caused me."

Hattie experienced several stages of grief before she brought herself to the point of presenting her problem to the crisis worker.

CW: Well, Hattie, what brings you to see me today?

Hattie: My whole life is a wreck. It's really a mess. The main thing is that my marriage is breaking up. Well, I guess it has broken up. My husband's gone. Been gone over a week. I guess you could say that the marriage is down the tubes.

CW: You're feeling rather hopeless about the marriage. What has happened today, in relation to your marriage breakup, to impel you to come in right now?

Hattie: Well, I was tired of lying around feeling sorry for myself—thinking about killing myself or harming my husband's girlfriend. My intuition told me that neither one of those acts would solve anything, so I've come in here looking for better answers.

CW: Hattie, I'm really glad you decided to come today. What I want to find out first is whether you are in danger of suicide now. Are you still strongly contemplating suicide? Do you have a means at hand to do it? And how close are you to suicide now?

The crisis worker's first concern was Hattie's immediate safety. It appeared from her verbal and nonverbal cues that she was hopeful and stable enough to have some mobility. The fact that she came to present her problem was another positive factor. Then, when Hattie told the worker that she didn't have a definite plan or a definite means to kill herself, the worker proceeded with other steps in the crisis interview. At one point, Hattie appeared to be in a stage of "holding on," which Schneider (1984) described as having elements of anger, bargaining, and denial.

Hattie: I just can't believe this is happening to me. My whole world has caved in on me. This is simply horrible. I just can't stand it. I just don't know what I'm going to do without him.

CW: You're truly feeling terrible about the breakup of your marriage. But what I believe you're meaning is that this situation is causing you a great deal of hurt and causing you to make some major shifts in your life. But it seems to me you enormously complicate matters when you convince yourself, inside your head, that this is the most terrible catastrophe that could possibly happen to you. *Telling yourself* that you can't stand it and *believing* that it's horrible and that you're terrible seem to be an exaggeration that is getting in the way. That is different from telling yourself that it is very bad, and you hate it, but that you didn't cause it and that this isn't the end of the world—even though it may make your life very difficult for a while. You see where your catastrophizing, exaggerating, and awfulizing color your thinking and get in the way of your clearly and objectively assessing not only what has happened but also what your real options are, don't you?

Hattie: Well, yes. Since you put it that way, I guess I have come down harder on myself and on the problem than is necessary. I know it isn't really horrible, but I feel, at the time, that it's horrible and awful.

CW: Then your *believing* it's horrible and awful is the real culprit, isn't it? There is a difference between your beliefs and how things really are.

Hattie: You're right! It helps just to look at it differently, even though it doesn't solve my big mess.

CW: You're right. It doesn't solve it. But we can objectively examine it and together begin to figure out options you can choose if we know on the front end, even though you're grieving over your hurt, that we are not dealing with a world-shattering catastrophe.

The crisis worker was intervening by using elements of rational-emotive therapy (RET) described in Ellis and Grieger (1977). The worker was attempting to dispute the client's irrational beliefs about the separation and help her begin to direct her emotional energy toward the real issues. Hattie was an intelligent person who quickly responded to the rational ideas presented. But, as is typical in such cases dealing with the emotional state during loss, the worker knew that repetition, practice, support, and encouragement would need to be provided. A person in Hattie's state must have far more than just a one-shot session using RET to get her beyond her crisis and back to a state of equilibrium.

In addition to using RET as a crisis intervention strategy, the crisis worker also used a self-managed behavioral technique (Williams & Long, 1983) to help Hattie expend her grief energy over a period of several weeks. What Hattie did was to make a series of sound tapes—alone, at home—in a sequential and systematic manner. The purposes for making the tapes were (1) to serve as a mechanism for self-catharsis, (2) to present to the crisis worker her full story, (3) to clarify, in her own mind, the stages of grief she was going through, and (4) to document her progress on a set of cassette tapes that might be provided for other women to use in similar cases of loss. Hattie worked regularly and diligently on the self-taped sessions. The cassettes were quite useful to the crisis worker. But the main value of the behavioral plan was providing Hattie the purpose and the experience of doing it. She described in detail both her feelings and her actions throughout several stages: shock and disbelief, denial, anger, withdrawal, guilt, depression, searching, and resolution.

Hattie made eight cassette tapes. She reported that the most valuable and helpful aspect of the sound-taping activity was that of listening to her own tapes, which she found herself doing over and over. Hattie kept the cassettes with the stated intention of continuing to listen to them. But she later reported that after her crisis subsided, she didn't need to listen to them anymore.

Death of a Pet

The Thompsons, Hollis, age 36, Faye, age 33, and their adopted daughter, Dawn, age 4, were grieving over the death of Tinfoil, their aged terrier. Tinfoil had been like a member of the family. He had been a faithful companion to the Thompsons since they were newlyweds; he had been the affectionate and protective playmate of Dawn from the day the Thompsons got her through the adoption agency. Lately he had developed severe health problems, and the veterinarian had finally told the Thompsons that Tinfoil's medical condition made it necessary to terminate his life.

These were the intervention strategies provided and issues explored with the Thompson family during the days and weeks immediately following the death of their pet:

1. *Individual counseling and intervention.* Assessment of the levels of grief, guilt and stress in each—Hollis, Faye, and Dawn. Assessment of Dawn's understanding of the death of the pet. Provision of a period to grieve and release grief energy. Follow-up play therapy and ceremonial events as outlets for Dawn (Schoenberg, 1980, pp. 203–204).

2. *Group work.* Provision of an opportunity for the family to talk about Tinfoil's death in a realistic, factual, and honest manner. Use of the death of the pet to help Dawn to begin to develop her concept of death, free of misinformation. Provision of opportunities and activities for the family to commemorate the life of the pet and to reformulate the death of the pet within a context of growth.

Schoenberg (1980) has suggested that families use ceremonial events and play therapy to help deal with their grief following the death of a pet (pp. 203–204). Ceremonial events open up opportunities for discussion, sharing of feelings, and explanations to children. Play therapy provides opportunities for children to have healthy experiences and to take an active role in the family's grief work. Workers using play therapy techniques employ both objects of play and the process of play to enable children to think about, talk about, and develop positive attitudes about issues or events that might be too threatening or too complex for them to understand through abstract didactic instruction. Examples of play therapy objects that might be used are dolls, sandboxes, and a variety of toys. Some examples of the use of the process of play might be taking a trip, attending a funeral, and visiting the hospital. In the case of the Thompsons, both play therapy and ceremonial events were used.

Faye: We had a small funeral in the back yard. I helped Dawn invite a few of her close friends to the funeral, and our next-door neighbors mailed us a sympathy card. Hollis and Dawn dug Tinfoil's grave and we had a simple but beautiful graveside service. There were flowers and friends, and we paid tribute and said good-bye to him. It was a good thing for our family and for the friends who came. The funeral and our family discussions provided a good background later on for Dawn's play therapy. We even had another small ceremony when we put Tinfoil's collar on the bulletin board in Dawn's room. We're still grieving somewhat over his death, but it has been a learning experience for all of us, and I think Dawn will have a realistic and healthy view of death, loss, and grief as a result of these activities.

Such experiences as those described by Faye are undoubtedly "learning experiences" for adults as well as children. There are many other strategies that can be used to assist people who have lost a pet. For instance, where children are involved, puppets, artwork, sand play, photographs of the pet, and modeling clay are only a few of the play therapy techniques that might be used to stimulate discussion. Also, variations on ceremonial events can be developed to fit the needs of each specific situation involving loss of a pet. The strategies used in dealing with the loss of pets are aimed at the same goals as those used in any human loss: helping the grievers wind down their various stages of grief in healthy and growth-promoting ways.

Bereavement in the Elderly

Rosa and Robert Kizer, ages 82 and 85 respectively, had been living in a nursing home for four years. Robert had been there more than a year when Rosa had to join him. Robert had become immobile at the age of 73 following a stroke. Their three living children resided in other states and were busy with their own families, so Rosa placed Robert in the nursing home when he was 80 and she was no longer able to care for him because he required 24-hour nursing care. Robert's physical condition continued to deteriorate during his stay at the nursing home until he could not speak or move his body. He could turn his head a little and nod or shake his head for yes and no, and could swallow some liquid foods—but his eating had to be managed skillfully to avoid choking him. By this time Rosa was no longer housed in Robert's room because of the specialized care he required. Rosa was quite mobile physically, but her memory lapses kept her from assuming any role in caring for Robert. Rosa was in the dining room eating breakfast when one of the medical staff members came and requested that she come to Robert's room because they couldn't rouse him. When Rosa arrived at the room a staff physician met her and informed her that Robert had apparently died in his sleep.

Intervention strategies provided and issues explored with Rosa during the days and weeks immediately following the death of Robert were these:

1. *Individual counseling and intervention.* Assessment of Rosa's level of grief and coping ability. Provision of opportunities for Rosa to release her grief energy. Assessment of Rosa's physical and mental capacities to cope. Assessment of her children's ability to help. Examination of her economic, medical, legal needs. Use of therapeutic strategies such as person-centered therapy, reminiscence techniques, and validation therapy to help Rosa feel calm and secure, and to remember vividly that she is a worthwhile person and that she and Robert have had worthwhile lives.

2. *Group work.* Groups within the nursing home. Support groups.

3. *Referrals.* Medical. Religious. Organizations. Legal assistance. Rosa's church; her children; senior citizens' agencies.

Rosa Kizer continued to live in the nursing home following Robert's death. Her grief was alleviated by several factors: she was physically mobile, she had lots of friends in the nursing home and in the community, she was an outgoing person with an optimistic outlook on life, and she was visited regularly for several weeks by a crisis worker who used reminiscence and validation therapy techniques (American Association of Retired People, 1986). Even with the positive factors she had going for her, Rosa experienced periods of denial, isolation, loneliness, fear, anger, bargaining, and depression. The crisis worker's goal was to help Rosa through the various stages of grief, to achieve a satisfactory degree of reconciliation with and acceptance of Robert's death, and to begin to establish her postcrisis life as a worthwhile person.

Rosa: A lot of times I just mope around. Some of the time I get to feeling sorry for myself. Then, sometimes I forget and find myself walking down to Robert's room before I remember that he isn't there any more. My life seems so meaningless without him.

CW: [*Holding Rosa's hand and gently caressing the top of her hand and forearm.*] You're really missing him and you're also having trouble remembering. What would you like to recall most?

Rosa: Oh, I'd like to recall the times when all of us were at home and healthy. When the kids were home. But that seems so far away in the past.

CW: Rosa, I'd like to know what it means to you to vividly remember the good times in your life—like when your family was together.

The crisis worker was relaxed, talking in a soft and caring tone, and gently caressing Rosa. The worker had taken special care to arrive at Rosa's room at the exact appointment time (many older clients are very sensitive about people promising to come and see them, then arriving late). In facilitating Rosa's reminiscing, the worker was careful not to appear pressed for time or anxious to leave and go on to the next patient. (The "hurried and harried" behavior of caregivers gets on the nerves of many elderly clients and causes them to lose confidence in the caregiver.) The worker was careful to nurture Rosa's trust, which is absolutely necessary for helping people through validation therapy or reminiscence techniques.

Rosa: We lived out on the mountain then. Goodness gracious me, we had such a good time! All of us working hard then, but we played hard and enjoyed life too. [*Long pause. Rosa is smiling.*]

CW: Take just as long as you wish to think about life out on that mountain—just as vividly and clearly as you can get it in your mind. Just relax and take as long as you wish. Just take your memories back there and get hold of those good feelings you have about those good times.

Rosa: [*Long pause.*] Yes, yes! What a beautiful place and a beautiful time in life. We lived on the ridge overlooking a deep, green valley. Had such beautiful children. Grew about everything we ate. Yes, those were the times that warm one's heart. That was a glorious time. A sight for sore eyes! [*Long pause.*]

CW: It sounds wonderful! It sounds like it warms your heart right now, just remembering it clearly and telling me about it so clearly.

The crisis worker's objective was to get Rosa in touch with her vivid memories of real occurrences in her past, which she could recall, identify with, describe, and feel worthwhile about. The worker also wanted to feel and show genuine respect for and interest in Rosa's memories and descriptions. Such genuineness on the part of an interested listener is a good catalyst for sharing and validating one's own past. The worker assured Rosa that he appreciated the shared journey into her past and that he respected her for it and wanted to continue to do more on the next visit. Rosa was also encouraged, through cognitive-behavior techniques (Cormier & Cormier, 1985; Meichenbaum, 1985), to think about the past between visits and to be prepared to bring other important and memorable events into open expression. The worker reminded Rosa that she had the power, in her mind, to imagine and to go back and experience many healthy and happy times, and then to return in her mind to her room and feel a real sense of pride in her own private history of accomplishments.

Interviews were a small part of the overall individual work with Rosa. The support group, containing other elderly people who had recently experienced loss, was another important intervention strategy. The techniques for working with the elderly do not have to be highly formal, structured, or complicated. All intervention should be done by workers who live and model relationship skills (Cormier & Hackney, 1987; Egan, 1982) such as empathy, genuineness, acceptance, respect, warmth, and sincere caring in a relaxed and nonhurried way.

Loss Related to HIV Infection and AIDS Disease

Crisis workers are likely to encounter clients whose presenting problems include dealing with the phenomenon of HIV infection or disease. The six steps of crisis intervention and the triage assessment system presented in Chapters 2 and 3 are appropriate for use in assessing and helping HIV/AIDS clients. However, the worker must be prepared to consider additional dimensions such as stigma, personal rejection, prejudice, religious rejection, political apathy, cultural discrimination, legal oppression, fear of contagion, guilt, shame, and loss of self-esteem. According to Miller (1990, pp. 189–195), people living with acute HIV/AIDS-related problems may present serious psychological symptoms such as shock and denial, anxiety, depression, and other emotional traumas.

The HIV-infected person may experience any number of severe physical and emotional manifestations such as nausea, panic attacks, diarrhea, dizziness, skin rashes, lethargy, tremor, visual disturbances, sweating, depression, and sleeplessness. It is difficult to distinguish whether and to what extent these symptoms are related to the HIV infection itself or to its cognitive effects on clients (Miller, 1990, p. 190). However, HIV/AIDS clients, as opposed to many other crisis clients, have a good many reasons for developing anxieties. Their short-term and long-term medical prognosis may be grim. AIDS/HIV clients are particularly at risk of infection as well as being subject to the burden of stigma, marginalization, and social, occupational, domestic, and sexual hostility. They face potential abandonment, isolation, and physical pain. There are many more real problematic burdens in the lives of HIV-infected persons than the noninfected encounter. HIV-infected persons may feel it is impossible for them to alter their circumstances. It is difficult for them to maximize their future health and they have little control over assisting loved ones and family members to cope. Adequate medical/dental/welfare assistance may be very difficult to obtain. They may face negative social pressures and ostracism because they have been identified as homosexual/drug users/prostitutes/unfaithful. The HIV-infected person may also suffer from lack of privacy and confidentiality, feel the loss of dignity with increasing physical dependency, experience sexual unacceptability, and lose physical and financial independence. All of these factors mitigate against clients' coping mechanisms and may lead to what Miller (1990, p. 191) terms functional and social retreat and withdrawal as a direct response.

Kübler-Ross (1987), Miller (1990), Ostrow (1990), and others have documented a variety of difficult psychological as well as physical obstacles that people with HIV face. They may view their entire physical being as transformed and obsessively search for new bodily evidence of the disease progression; they may relentlessly pursue fads related to health and diet regimes; and they become preoccupied with illness, death, and avoidance of new infections. They may exhibit severe shock, denial, helplessness, self-blame, false hope of a cure, anger, frustration, guilt, and suicidal ideation. Denial of risk of HIV infection constitutes a pervasive and common problem in society (Bowers, 1991). Crisis workers faced with people living with HIV must be aware of these special factors and characteristics as they assess and engage in crisis intervention work.

Sources of help.   Crisis intervention with HIV-infected clients must start with sensitive and empathic listening. We recommend using the six-step method of relating to clients. Since clients may be experiencing an enormous array of situational, medical, and environmental problems, workers must be diligent in defining the total scope of problems, ensuring physical and psychological safety, and providing emotional supports. Crisis workers will usually find that there is very little they can do *for* clients. But in many communities, especially urban and suburban settings, there are a good many resources and alternatives to be used *with* them. Therein lies the necessity of knowing which resources and services are available at any given time and locale.

Crisis hot lines, sexual assault resource centers, library information services, and most centers that deal with crisis populations can usually provide referral information regarding specific services for HIV-infected clients. Some communities have specialized sources of help such as Aid to End AIDS Committees, gay/lesbian/bisexual support groups, AIDS/HIV hot lines, and AIDS hospices that offer direct information, assistance, and brokerage services for clients and their friends and families.

Crisis workers should have a ready list of referral resources that contains names of agencies or professionals, location, provisions for intake or obtaining services, and other pertinent information. Also, workers should be knowledgeable about HIV infection and disease issues, be able to accept diversity in people as well as their unique problems, and be empathic, nonjudgmental, and flexible in their approach to crisis work and clients.

Bereavement in HIV-infected clients.   Ansel's lover of six years died of AIDS 18 months ago. Last week Ansel lost his job as a bank teller and desperately needs a job. He suspects that the people at the bank found out that he, Ansel, tested HIV positive last May. Normally, Ansel is an intelligent, enthusiastic, energetic, outgoing, friendly, and positive individual. He is an exceptionally competent employee whom the bank was grooming for management work. Now he presents himself as unsure of himself, depressed, angry, nervous, and anxious.

Ansel: On top of everything else, I have never come out to my parents. I wouldn't mind telling my mom, but I would have real trouble revealing to my dad that I'm gay. I also worry that telling him that I've tested positive will be too much for his heart because he's had two bypasses already. I may have to find a cheaper place to live, too. I have too many things to deal with right now.

CW: Ansel, I'm really glad you came in here today. I can see that you are feeling really depressed today. Are you to the point of thinking about killing yourself?

The first thing the crisis worker does is to explore Ansel's lethality level. The crisis worker has the benefit of a brief intake statement and is prepared to explore the most pressing client concerns. But ensuring Ansel's safety takes first priority. Ansel's verbal and nonverbal responses and the worker's rapid assessment of his cognitive, affective, and behavioral functioning on the triage form (Affective—3, Cognitive—3, Behavioral—6, Total 12) give the worker the green light to proceed with further exploration of the problem with Ansel. Even so, the crisis worker is sensitive to any changes that might signal a sudden elevation of his cognitive, affective, or behavioral assessment scores.

CW: I'm happy to know that you're safe for now. Ansel, what do we most need to work on right now?

Ansel: I just don't see how I can handle everything, how I can make plans, so much is happening.

CW: You're overwhelmed with all the issues you are facing, and you're needing some help, understanding, and supports right now.

Ansel: It's been hard enough since my lover died. I still miss him terribly, and now I've lost my job—I have to tell my parents I'm gay—God! Gay and HIV positive, too!

CW: Ansel, I want you to know that I'm very sorry that you have lost your lover. You've suffered tremendous loss. The loss of your lover and now your job. I also sense your difficult struggle as you seek to tell your parents. I want to work with you and help you find some ways to deal with all these difficult and important things you are facing.

The crisis worker acknowledges the continued losses Ansel has faced as well as the problem of revealing to his parents his HIV status and the difficulty he will face in the future. Concomitantly, the crisis worker begins to think about what concrete actions Ansel will be imminently needing to take: employment counseling, support groups in order to help Ansel regain a sense of control over his life, and medical services. The research of Williams and Stafford (1991) indicates that a fundamental form of intervention with partners and adult family members is the use of peer groups to break down the prevalent feelings of isolation, enhance sharing of personal grief, and to promote healing (p. 425–426). Additional interventions found to be appropriate are providing adequate and accurate information to dispel anxiety about contagion issues, providing counseling in either group, family, or individual formats, and grief and bereavement work. Grief work was found to be "most effective in a group setting where, due to disparity of psychological adjustment levels, new members could gain hope for eventual healing of acute grief from grievers further along in the process" (p. 426).

Ansel was referred to an existing group at the Aid to AIDS Center that could provide the help he needed in an environment of warmth, acceptance, professional competence, and healing. The crisis worker followed up by contacting the center director to ensure that Ansel obtained the services he needed.

SOME REPRESENTATIVE REFERRAL SERVICES

We have indicated how important it is for crisis workers to become competent in using referral resources as an intervention strategy. We offer here a list of several representative resources. Most of the organizations and societies listed have branches in large cities. Local library information centers and crisis intervention agencies have information about how to reach these resources. The *Encyclopedia of Associations* (Burek, 1990) contains a comprehensive annotated national listing of major organizations.

American Association of Suicidology (AAS) (suicide)
2459 South Ash
Denver, CO 80222
Phone: (303) 692-0985
Telephone crisis hot lines and suicide prevention centers, located in major cities in the United States and staffed by volunteers trained in crisis intervention, are usually associated with AAS. AAS seeks to recognize and encourage suicidology (the study of suicide, suicide prevention, and related phenomena of self-destruction). It advances education, disseminates information through programs and publications, and cooperates with other organizations in suicidology.

Compassionate Friends (death of one's child)
P.O. Box 3696
Oak Brook, IL 60522-3696
Phone: (708) 990-0010
A nonprofit, nondenominational, informal self-help organization open to parents who have experienced the death of a child. Objectives are to promote and aid parents in the positive resolution of grief and to foster physical and emotional health of bereaved parents and siblings. More than 600 local chapters offer support and understanding by providing "telephone friends" who may be called, identifying sharing groups that meet monthly, and disseminating information concerning the grieving process. (Absorbed the organization Parents of Suicides in 1987.)

Concern for Dying (euthanasia)
250 West 57th Street
New York, NY 10107
Phone (212) 246-6962
or toll-free (800) 248-2122
Promotes public education to prevent the futile prolongation of the dying process and the assurance of patient autonomy with regard to treatment during terminal illness. Distributes "The Living Will" (document enabling individuals to express in writing their wishes regarding care during terminal illness). Sponsors a wide scope of interdisciplinary programs.

Hemlock Society (euthanasia)
P.O. Box 11830
Eugene, OR 97440
Phone: (503) 342-5748
FAX: (503) 345-2741
Supports the option of active voluntary euthanasia for the advanced terminally ill and the seriously incurably ill. Seeks to promote a climate of public opinion tolerant of the terminally ill individual's right to end his or her own life in a planned manner; and to improve existing laws on assisted suicide. Does not encourage suicide for any primary reason other than terminal illness; approves suicide prevention work; believes that the final decision to terminate one's own life should be one's own.

Hospice Association of America (care of terminally ill)
519 C Street, N.E.
Washington, DC 20002
Phone: (202) 546-4759
FAX: (202) 457-3540
Promotes concept of hospice, a philosophy of health care expressed through the provision of a variety of medical and nonmedical services to terminally ill patients and their families. Offers hospice referral services and consultations for medicare reimbursement problems.

Mothers Against Drunk Driving (MADD) (victims of drunk driving)
669 Airport Freeway, Suite 310
Hurst, TX 76053
Phone: (817) 268-6233
FAX: (817) 268-6827
Encourages citizen participation in working toward reform of drunk driving problems. Acts as voice of victims on behalf of communities, businesses, educational groups, and families. Supports highway patrol programs, state and federal reform of laws on drunk driving; provides public education programs. Maintains court monitoring programs; provides victim assistance; distributes information for victims, families, bereavement groups, judicial system. Operates Victim Outreach Program to help victims through the court process.

National AIDS Network (AIDS disease)
2033 M Street, N.W., Suite 800
Washington, DC 20036
Phone: (202) 293-2437
FAX: (202) 293-2587
More than 750 community-based groups providing AIDS education or direct services to individuals with AIDS. Serves as a resource center and networking agency for members and AIDS service organizations. Makes available financial aid to organizations that provide AIDS education or services; coordinates fund-raising activities.

National Sudden Infant Death Syndrome Foundation (NSIDSF)
   (sudden infant death syndrome)
10500 Little Patuxent Parkway, No. 420
Columbia, MD 21044
Phone: (301) 964-8000 or toll-free (800) 221-SIDS 24 hours a day
More than 70 local groups of concerned citizens, health professionals, and parents who have lost a child to sudden infant death syndrome (SIDS), a condition commonly known as crib death that accounts for about 6000 infant and child deaths in the United States annually. Assists bereaved parents who have lost a child to SIDS; works with families and professionals in caring for infants at risk due to cardiac and respiratory problems. Affiliated with the Sudden Infant Death Syndrome Alliance (SIDSA), same address, Columbia. MD.

Parents of Murdered Children (POMC) (murdered children)
100 E. Eighth Street, B-41
Cincinnati, OH 45202
Phone: (513) 721-5683
More than 65 regional and 40 state groups sponsor self-help organizations of parents whose children have been murdered. Fosters physical and emotional health; works to heighten societal awareness of problems faced by

those who survive a homicide victim. Provides information regarding the grieving process and the criminal justice system.

Society for the Right to Die (euthanasia)
250 W. 57th Street
New York, NY 10107
Phone: (212) 246-6973
FAX: (212) 586-6248
Engaged in educational, judicial, and legislative activities. Believes the rights of self-determination and privacy include the right to control decisions regarding one's own medical care. Opposes the use of medical procedures that prolong the dying process, causing unnecessary pain and suffering. Seeks to protect the rights of dying patients' providers—physicians, hospitals, and health-care personnel—from liability threats for complying with mandated desires of the terminally ill wishing to die.

SUMMARY

In this chapter we have outlined the major components of the dynamic stages of grief and death depicted in the models developed by both Kübler-Ross (1969) and Schneider (1984). We have also identified several types of loss, presented typical cases, and discussed strategies that crisis workers can use in counseling and intervention. A global perspective that can be drawn from the chapter is that crisis workers must be prepared to respect the privacy, individuality, and autonomy of the bereaved and to avoid the imposition of their own values upon the persons they seek to help.

Every human being will, at one time or another, suffer personal loss. During our lives most of us will encounter numerous people who are experiencing bereavement or grief as a result of some personal loss. What may be clearly perceived as a personal loss ranges from a devastating occurrence, such as the death of a spouse or a child, to what many people might view as an insignificant loss. In any event, it is an important loss if the individual perceives it as such.

Persons in helping roles are encouraged to make use of their personal assets, listening competencies, compassion, and skill at making referrals to assist the bereaved in coping, as best they can, with their own unique losses. Although the bereaved can never forget the loss and return to a state of complete precrisis equilibrium, they can be helped to reformulate their loss within a context of growth.

REFERENCES

Allan, J., & Anderson, E. (1986). Children and crisis: A classroom guidance approach. *Elementary School Guidance & Counseling, 21,* 143–149.

Alyson, S. (Ed.). (1990). *You can do something about AIDS* (2nd ed.). Boston: The Stop AIDS Project.

American Association of Retired People (AARP). (1986, September). Reminiscence: Thanks for the memory. *AARP News Bulletin,* p. 2.

Bahrick, A. S., & Sharkin, B. S. (1990). Pet loss: Implications for counselors. *Journal of Counseling and Development, 68,* 306–308.

Balk, D. E. (1990, August). *The many faces of bereavement on the college campus.* Paper presented at the annual meeting of the American Psychological Association, Boston, MA.

Becker, E. (1973). *The denial of death.* New York: Free Press.

Bertoia, J., & Allan, J. (1988). School management of the bereaved child. *Elementary School Guidance & Counseling, 23,* 30–38.

Blumenfeld, W. J., & Raymond, D. (1988). *Looking at gay and lesbian life* (Chapter 9, AIDS: Politics and precautions). Boston: Beacon Press.

Bordow, J. (1982). *The ultimate loss: Coping with the death of a child.* New York: Beaufort Books.

Bowers, D. (1991, September 16). Personnel communication.

Burek, D. M. (Ed.). (1990). *Encyclopedia of associations, 1991* (25th ed.) (Vol. I, Part 1, Part 2, and Part 3). Detroit: Gale Research.

Buscaglia, L. (1982). *The fall of Freddie the leaf: A story of life for all ages.* New York: Holt, Rinehart & Winston.

Campbell, C. A. (1990). Prostitution and AIDS. In D. G. Ostrow (Ed,), *Behavioral aspects of AIDS* (pp. 121–137). New York: Plenum Medical.

Christ, G. H., Moynihan, R. T., & Gallo-Silver, L. (1991). Human immunodeficiency virus and crisis intervention: A task-focused approach. In A. R. Roberts (Ed.), *Contemporary perspectives on crisis intervention and prevention* (pp. 70–82). Englewood Cliffs, NJ: Prentice-Hall.

Coleman, B. C. (1991, July 4). Experts say AIDS virus also represents a threat to the elderly. *Northwest Florida Daily News,* p. 12C.

Colgrove, M., Bloomfield, H. H., & McWilliams, P. (1976). *How to survive the loss of a love.* New York: Bantam Books.

Cormier, L. S., & Hackney, H. (1987). *The professional counselor: A process guide to helping.* Englewood Cliffs, NJ: Prentice-Hall.

Cormier, W. H., & Cormier, L. S. (1985). *Interviewing strategies for helpers: Fundamental skills and cognitive behavioral interventions* (2nd ed.). Pacific Grove, CA: Brooks/Cole.

Dagastino, A. (1991, September 17). Personal communication.

Des Jarlais, D. C., Friedman, S. R., & Woods, J. S. (1990). Intravenous drug use and AIDS. In D. G. Ostrow (Ed.), *Behavioral aspects of AIDS.* (pp. 139–155). New York: Plenum Medical.

Dickens, M. (1985). *Miracles of courage: How families meet the challenge of a child's critical illness.* New York: Dodd, Mead.

Downs, H., & Walters, B. (1986, May 15). *20/20 News Magazine* [Television program]. ABC Television Network.

Edelstein, L. (1984). *Maternal bereavement: Coping with the unexpected death of a child.* New York: Praeger.

Egan, G. (1982). *The skilled helper: Model, skills, and methods for effective helping* (2nd ed.). Pacific Grove, CA: Brooks/Cole.

Ellis, A., & Abrahms, E. (1978). *Brief psychotherapy in medical and health practice.* New York: Springer.

Ellis, A., & Grieger, R. (1977). *Handbook of rational-emotive therapy.* New York: Springer.

Freeman, L. (1978). *The sorrow and the fury: Overcoming hurt and loss from childhood to old age.* Englewood Cliffs, NJ: Prentice-Hall.

Galea, R. P., Lewis, B. F., & Baker, L. A. (1988). (Eds.). *AIDS and IV drug abusers: Current perspectives.* Owings Mills, MD: Rynd Communications, National Health Publishing.

Gibson, A. B., Roberts, P. C., & Buttery, T. J. (1982). *Death education: A concern for the living* (Fastback No. 173). Bloomington, IN: Phi Delta Kappa Educational Foundation.

Glasser, W. (1965). *Reality therapy.* New York: Harper & Row.

Gray, R. E. (1988). The role of school counselors with bereaved teenagers: With and without peer support groups. *The School Counselor, 35,* 185–192.

Gudas, L. (1990, August). *Children's reactions to bereavement: A developmental perspective.* Paper presented at the annual meeting of the American Psychological Association, Boston, MA.

Guerriero-Austrom, M. G., & Fleming, S. J. (1990, August). *Effects of sibling death on adolescents' physical and emotional well-being: A longitudinal study.* Paper presented at the annual meeting of the American Psychological Association, Boston, MA.

Gumaer, J. (1984). *Counseling and therapy for children.* New York: Free Press.

Hansen, J. C., & Frantz, T. T. (Eds.). (1984). *Death and grief in the family.* Rockville, MD: Aspen Systems Corporation.

Hughes, R. B. (1988). Grief counseling: Facilitating the healing process. *Journal of Counseling and Development, 67,* 77.

Hunt, C. (1987). Step by step: How your school can live through the tragedy of teen suicides. *American School Board Journal, 174,* 34–37.

James, R. K., & Myer, R. (1987). Puppets: The elementary school counselor's right or left arm. *Elementary School Guidance & Counseling, 21,* 292–299.

Johnson, S. M. (1977). *First person singular: Living the good life alone.* Philadelphia: Lippincott.

Koocher, G. (1975). Why isn't the gerbil moving? Discussing death in the classroom. *Children Today, 4,* 18–36.

Koop, C. E. (1990). Looking to the future. In S. Alyson (Ed.), *You can do something about AIDS* (2nd ed.) (pp. 28–30). Boston: The Stop AIDS Project.

Kübler-Ross, E. (1969). *On death and dying.* New York: Macmillan.

Kübler-Ross, E. (1975). *Death: The final stage of growth.* Englewood Cliffs, NJ: Prentice-Hall.

Kübler-Ross, E. (1981). *Living with death and dying.* New York: Macmillan.

Kübler-Ross, E. (1983). *On children and death.* New York: Macmillan.

Kübler-Ross, E. (1987). *AIDS: The ultimate challenge.* New York: Macmillan.

Kushner, H. S. (1983). *When bad things happen to good people.* New York: Avon.

Lane, K. E., & Dickey, T. (1988). New students and grief. *The School Counselor, 35,* 359–362.

Mantell, J. E., & Schinke, S. P. (1991). The crisis of AIDS for adolescents: The need for preventive interventions. In A. R. Roberts (Ed.), *Contemporary perspectives on crisis intervention and prevention* (pp. 185–217). Englewood Cliffs, NJ: Prentice-Hall.

Medvene, A. (1991). When a parent dies. Paper presented at Crisis Convening XV, Chicago.

Meichenbaum, D. (1985, May). Cognitive behavior modification: Perspectives, techniques, and applications. Two-day workshop, St. Louis, MO, presented by Evaluation Research Associates (Syracuse, NY).

Miller, D. (1990). Diagnosis and treatment of acute psychological problems related to HIV infection and disease. In D. G. Ostrow (Ed.), *Behavioral aspects of AIDS* (pp. 187–206). New York: Plenum Medical.

Minton, L. (1991, July 7). What a teenager with AIDS wants you to know. The most important thing: "A friend's support." *Parade: The Sunday Newspaper Magazine,* pp. 4–7.

Nieburg, H. A., & Fischer, A. (1982). *Pet loss: A thoughtful guide for adults and children.* New York: Harper & Row.

Osterweis, M., Solomon, F., & Green, M. (Eds.). (1984). *Bereavement: Reactions, consequences, and care.* Washington, D.C.: National Academy Press.

Ostrow, D. G. (Ed.). (1990). *Behavioral aspects of AIDS.* New York: Plenum Medical.

Pauley, J. (1986, June 3). *Divorce is changing America* ["White Paper" documentary]. National Broadcasting Company (NBC) News.

Pelej, J. (1987, April). Help your school survive a suicide. *Executive Educator,* pp. 26–31.

Rando, T. A. (1984). *Grief, dying, and death: Clinical interventions for caregivers.* Champaign, IL: Research Press.

Riordan, R. J., & Allen, L. (1989). Grief counseling: A funeral home–based model. *Journal of Counseling and Development, 67,* 424–425.

Savin-Williams, R. C., & Lenhart, R. E. (1990). AIDS prevention among gay and lesbian youth: Psychosocial stress and health care intervention guidelines. In D. G. Ostrow (Ed.), *Behavioral aspects of AIDS* (pp. 75–99). New York: Plenum Medical.

Schiff, H. S. (1977). *The bereaved parent.* New York: Crown Publishers.

Schneider, J. (1984). *Stress, loss, and grief: Understanding their origins and growth potential.* Baltimore: University Park Press.

Schoenberg, B. M. (Ed.). (1980). *Bereavement counseling: A multidiscipli-nary handbook.* Westport, CT: Greenwood Press.

Schonfeld, D. J. (1989). Crisis intervention for bereavement support: A model of intervention in the children's school. *Clinical Pediatrics, 28* 27–33.

Schwed, M. (1986, June 3). Hard numbers hit home in divorce documen-tary: A decade into epidemic, "bad news" is coming in. *The Commer-cial Appeal,* Memphis, p. C7.

Shucter, S. R. (1986). *Dimensions of grief: Adjusting to the death of a spouse.* San Francisco: Jossey-Bass.

Smith, W. J. (1985). *Dying in the human life cycle: Psychological, biomedi-cal, and social perspectives.* New York: Holt, Rinehart & Winston.

Sorensen, J. R. (1989). Responding to student or teacher death: Preplanning crisis intervention. *Journal of Counseling and Development, 67,* 426-427.

Staudacher, C. (1987). *Beyond grief: A guide for recovering from the death of a loved one.* Oakland, CA: New Harbinger.

Stephenson, J. S. (1985). *Death, grief, and mourning: Individual and social realities.* New York: Free Press.

Stevenson, R. (1986). How to handle death in the schools. *Tips for Princi-pals.* Reston, VA: National Association of Secondary School Principals.

Stone, H. W., (1972). *Suicide and grief.* Philadelphia: Fortress Press.

Tatelbaum, J. (1980). *The courage to grieve.* New York: Lippincott & Crowell.

Vinturella, L., & James, R. K. (1987). Sandplay: A therapeutic medium with children. *Elementary School Guidance and Counseling, 21,* 229–238.

Wass, H., & Corr, C. A. (1984). *Helping children cope with death: Guidelines and resources* (2nd ed.). New York: Harper & Row.

Wass, H., & Corr, C. A. (1985). *Childhood and death.* New York: Harper & Row.

Williams, R. J., & Stafford, W. B. (1991). Silent casualties: Partners, fami-lies, and spouses of persons with AIDS. *Journal of Counseling and De-velopment, 69,* 423–427.

Williams, R. L., & Long, J. D. (1983). *Toward a self-managed life style* (3rd ed.). Boston: Houghton Mifflin.

Worth, D. (1990). Women at high risk of HIV infection: Behavioral, pre-vention, and intervention aspects. In D. G. Ostrow (Ed.), *Behavioral aspects of AIDS* (pp. 101–119.) New York: Plenum Medical.

Zinner, E. (1987). Responding to suicide in schools: A case study in loss intervention and group survivorship. *Journal of Counseling and Devel-opment, 65,* 499–501.

CLASSROOM EXERCISES

I. Simulated Counseling with Prepared Cases

To gain experience and practice in dealing with various bereavement situa-tions, the class will work in small groups. Each group is assigned a different type of bereavement, selected from the following list:

Case of the Wynn family (death of a spouse)
Case of the Drake family (death of a child)
Case of the Nichols family (bereavement of a family following suicide)
Case of the Kirk family (bereavement in childhood)
Case of Cedar Grove High School (bereavement in adolescence)
Case of Hattie (separation and divorce)
Case of the Thompson family (death of a pet)
Case of Rosa (bereavement in the elderly)

Through role taking of bereaved clients in the various cases, students will spontaneously generate dialogue and crisis intervention techniques in each group.

Each group will select one or more clients from their assigned case. Group members will take the roles of the client(s), the crisis worker(s), and observer(s)/evaluator(s). A specified time limit will be given for the crisis intervention sessions, to be conducted simultaneously within each group. The crisis intervention session will begin as soon as the clients have had time to review the data of their case. While the crisis workers process the case with the clients, the observers/recorders will make a tape recording of the session, take notes, and be prepared to report on the effectiveness of the crisis intervention and to make suggestions for improvement.

Whenever the crisis intervention sessions have been completed, observers/reporters will make their reports to members of their particular groups. The exercise will be completed by providing time in each group for a summarizing discussion.

II. Simulated Counseling with Class-Developed Scenarios

Replicate the preceding exercise, except that each group has the task of generating a realistic bereavement situation for the role-taking exercise instead of using one of the eight cases described in the chapter. Group members can draw upon their own knowledge and experience for creating realistic scenarios. All groups should be cautioned to (1) refrain from using recognizable persons, places, or situations and (2) maintain confidentiality by refraining from mentioning the scenarios outside the classroom, even though only parts of real situations may have been simulated. The facilitator or instructor should monitor the group simulations to provide supportive counseling, after the activities have been completed, to any individual who identifies with the scenario so completely that a state of personal crisis is induced—a situation that is rare but possible.

At the conclusion of the exercise, individual role players will be instructed to verbally disassociate themselves from the roles they enacted during the simulation. The disassociation will be done within each small group.

CRISIS IN THE HUMAN SERVICES WORKPLACE

Part Three deals with helping the crisis worker (the counselor, the helper, the human services worker, the caregiver, and the agency leader) to cope with crises that might occur in the human services workplace.

The world in which we live and crisis workers function is becoming increasingly dangerous and violent for clients as well as human services professionals. Chapter 10, on violent behavior in institutions, provides information and techniques to help workers better understand and deal with both the volatile environment and the dilemmas of clients who strive to cope within that environment.

Hostage taking is another phenomenon of our modern milieu that has become increasingly prevalent. It is our fervent hope that readers will never be involved in a hostage-taking situation, but, far from one's control, it can happen to anyone at any time. Chapter 11, on hostage negotiation, contains concepts and strategies that could save the lives of both crisis workers and/or their clients, even though we hope that the reader's only such encounter will be restricted to these pages.

Our philosophy is that prevention of worker burnout should be a way of life for both individuals and agencies; that continuous learning or training is a preferred means of acquiring and maintaining helping attitudes, skills, and competencies; and that individual crisis workers can control their own personal and professional development, thereby enhancing their personal functioning as well as their value to society. Chapter 12, on human services workers in crisis, is written on the assumption that workers can avoid burnout by attending to their own physical, psychological, and emotional wellness. Individuals can not only prevent burnout but can also choose to positively and constructively nurture their own lifestyles, physical stamina, mental health, and personal vibrancy.

CHAPTER 10

Violent Behavior in Institutions

BACKGROUND

A variety of hazards now put human services professionals more at risk of being victims of violent behavior than they have been in the past. Probably the most noteworthy trend has been the increase in the number of substance-abuse clients. Given the variety of drugs available and the erratic behavior that accompanies them, the human services worker is confronted with a complex and sometimes dangerous job of assessment and treatment (Piercy, 1984).

Since the least restrictive environment movement and subsequent deinstitutionalization of patients in the 1970s, day care, halfway houses, and shelters have filled the gap left when the warehousing facilities of state mental institutions were emptied. Lack of facilities for transients, shortage of staff, and inability to monitor medication closely have created a fertile breeding ground for clients to regress to their previous pathological states (Reid, 1986).

Further, with increased societal and judicial awareness of the part that mental illness plays in crime, a number of individuals who would formerly have been incarcerated are now remanded to mental health facilities. Also, because of prison overcrowding, potentially violent people are released on early parole. Farmed out to halfway houses that are also understaffed, and assigned to parole officers who have tremendous caseloads, parolees do not always get the follow-up and supervision they need. Thus, human services workers are now being asked to deal with a wider variety of ex-felons than before (Appelbaum, 1984).

Finally, the increase in the number of elderly now institutionalized in nursing homes and hospitals has created a whole new population of potentially violent individuals. Casually dismissed as infirm and incapable of rendering harm to anyone, geriatric patients commit a disproportionate percentage of violent behavior against human services workers (Petrie, 1984, p. 107).

Institutional Culpability

By their very nature, most care providers are readily accessible to clientele and have minimal security checks. Therefore they are also easy prey to anyone who walks in off the street with intentions other than seeking services (Turner, 1984, pp. v–vi). Further, training for security and implementation of security devices cost time and money. Administrators trained solely in handling the financial, logistical, and personnel functions of institutions plus the responsibility of maintaining adequate patient care are unaware of what it takes to provide an adequately secure environment for their staff (Dyer, Murrell, & Wright, 1984).

Because of the negative publicity that accrues from violent incidents, institutions are loath to admit that they occur (Lanza, 1985). Such denials do not help the morale of workers; they lead the staff to feel powerless and frustrated (Lenehan & Turner, 1984, p. 253). Understaffing, overwork, poor physical environment, poorly educated nonprofessional staff, high staff turnover, absenteeism, on-the-job accidents, poor or incomplete communication between administration and staff, and lack of unifying treatment philosophy allow frustration to build within the staff and disrupt the treatment routine. As the staff transfer their frustration to the clients, the clients in turn become more threatened and start testing the limits of what will be tolerated. When staff attempt to impose behavioral limits under these erratic conditions, the outcome is often violent behavior by clients (Blair, 1991; Piercy, 1984, pp. 141–142).

Staff Culpability

Staff members are also culpable. There is a prevailing philosophy that because human services workers are caring, well-intentioned people, recipients of their services will act in reciprocal ways toward them (Turner, 1984, p. vii). The ostrichlike assumption that "it can't happen to me, and besides, there are so few violent incidents that I really don't need to be concerned" is fallacious (Dyer et al., 1984, p. 1). Madden, Lion, and Penna (1976) interviewed psychiatrists who had been assaulted and found that more than half of them could have predicted the assault if they had not been in denial and thought themselves immune from the threat.

From the client's viewpoint, becoming violent is invariably seen as a consequence of being provoked by the worker (Rada, 1981). Paradoxically, most staff have little idea what they or the institution do that is provocative. For many clients, treatment may be perceived as coercive, threatening, or frightening. When a client feels little control over treatment conducted by an authoritarian staff, the client's only option is to aggressively act out (Blair, 1991). Further, if the staff treatment philosophy is one where severe limit setting such as use of restraints, seclusion, medication, locked units, and assaults are "part of the territory," then a self-fulfilling prophecy is likely to develop that violent acting out is the norm and the only way to get attention. Conversely, failure of staff to set limits in a positive, firm, fair, and empathic manner where choices are clearly outlined is likely to result in limit testing that leads to violence. Particularly when client routine, status, or self-esteem is disrupted by dictatorially taking away food and drink, recreational time, cigarettes, furloughs, or other privileges without defining how those might be lost, giving any reason why they are lost, or explaining how they can be regained increases the potential for violence toward the limit setter (Blair, 1991).

Incidence

Mainly because of fear of bad publicity and inadequate reporting, statistics on violent behavior of clients toward workers in human services agencies are either poor or unavailable in most settings (Turner, 1984, p. v). The few studies conducted present a profile of violence that should serve as an eye opener for human services workers in general and crisis workers in particular. Lanza (1983) found that psychiatric nurses reported having been assaulted an average of seven times during an average of six years' service. Ruben, Wolkon, and Yamamoto (1980) found that 48% of psychiatric interns reported being assaulted during training. Schultz (1987) surveyed social workers and found the ratio of those who had violent clients as opposed to those who had not experienced violence was approximately 2 to 1.

Other studies have shown that 24% of human services workers experienced violent acts committed against them during their first year of service, and the rate escalated to 74% at some time during their tenure (Whitman, Armao, & Dent, 1976). Information garnered from congressional hearings on violence in federal hospitals during the years 1977 to 1980 showed increases of 16% in robbery, 33% in rape, 27% in assault, and 16% in physical arrests (House of Representatives Committee on Veterans Affairs, 1981). Even with these increases, Lion, Snyder, and Merrill (1981) believe that the incidence of assaults on patients and staff is underreported at a rate of about 5 to 1. Breakwell (1989) reports that health services workers are about 26 times more likely to be assaulted and seriously injured than the general public.

The point of citing these statistics is that the subject concerns you—not just somebody who works down the hall from you. For anyone who has ever seen a client wildly out of control and who has been injured or scared senseless in trying to contain that violence, one time is once too many (Lanza, 1985).

Legal Liability

Although health care providers may be the victims of assaults, they may also become legally liable for their actions, no matter how well intended those actions may be (Monahan, 1984). Such liability extends to the institutions and directors of those institutions, who may fall under a heading of "vicarious" civil and criminal liability (Dyer et al., 1984, p. 23). Numerous successful lawsuits have been brought against health care providers for failure to properly diagnose, treat, and control violent clients or protect third parties from assaultive behavior (Felthous, 1987).

Communication and consultation about potentially violent clients is extremely important. One of the better predictors of who will and will not be at risk to become violent is the pooled clinical judgment of human services workers who have come into contact with the client (Durivage, 1989; Werner, Rose, Murdach, & Yesavage, 1989). One of the primary reasons that cases have been decided in favor of the plaintiff involves the failure of one clinician to communicate with another clinician that a client has a history of violence and might present a future danger (Beck, 1988). From that standpoint, the institution and worker who wish to avoid a court appearance would do well to flag records of violent acts or ideation and relay that information to other members of the treatment team for feedback and possible action (Blair, 1991).

DYNAMICS OF VIOLENCE IN HUMAN SERVICES SETTINGS
Assessment

In 1974, the American Psychiatric Association did a study on the ability of the psychiatric profession to predict violence. Its conclusion was that such predictions were unreliable and lacked validity (American Psychiatric Association, 1974). This conclusion has been confirmed by other studies and reviews (Kirk, 1989; Monahan, 1988; Mulvey & Lidz, 1984; Valliant, Aser, Cooper, & Mammola, 1984). While Tanke and Yesavage (1985) have used the Brief Psychiatric Rating Scale to successfully differentiate high- and low-profile violence-prone clients from nonviolent controls, and Ostrow, Marohn, Offer, Crutiss, and Feczko (1980) have developed the Adolescent Antisocial Behavior Checklist to predict violent behavior in adolescents, even the highly esteemed MMPI has problems in reliably predicting violence (Sloore, 1988).

The current status of prediction and the "real world" of mental health care provision lead us to believe that the ability to predict who will and who will not become violent at what times and under what conditions has not been clearly established. Predictions are especially likely to be erroneous when crisis workers have little background information on clients and may not have time to make more than an "eyeball" assessment of the situation before they have to act. Currently, the controversy about the ability of both actuarial measurements and clinician assessment to predict violence continues (Webster, 1990). Yet, data do exist to present general profiles of clients who are more likely than others to become violent given the right constellation of conditions. Keeping the foregoing qualifiers—"general profiles" and "right conditions"—in mind, the following bases for profiling violence are "best bet" predictors.

Bases for Violence

There are biological, psychological, and social bases for violence. Biologically, low intelligence, hormonal imbalances, organic brain disorders, neurological and systemic changes of a psychiatric nature, disease, chemicals, or traumatic injury may lead to more violence-prone behavior (Hamstra, 1986; Heilbrun, 1990; Heilbrun & Heilbrun, 1989). Psychologically, specific situational problems, certain functional psychoses, and character disorders are predisposing to violence (Greenfield, McNeil, & Binder, 1989; Heilbrun, 1990; Heilbrun & Heilbrun, 1989; Klassen & O'Connor, 1988). Socially, modeling the behavioral norms of family, peers, and the milieu within which one lives can exacerbate violent tendencies (Tardiff, 1984a, p. 45; Wood & Khuri, 1984, p. 60). Finally, specific on-site physical environmental stressors such as heat, crowding, noise, conflict, and poor communication are triggers that can cause violence. When all these ingredients are mixed together, the results start to resemble the kinds of people and environments with which the crisis worker is likely to come in contact (Tardiff, 1984a, p. 45).

Age.   Males between the ages of 15 and 30 who come from the inner city and are members of a minority tend to be the most violent subgroup (Fareta, 1981; Kroll & Mackenzie, 1983). Next come elderly clients, who are disproportionately represented in the population that may be violent (Petrie, 1984, p. 107). Crisis workers tend to dismiss this group as being harmless. In a study of 200 cases of assault at the Cincinnati Veterans Administration Medical Center, Jones (1985) discovered that 58.5% of the assaults took place in the geriatric facility. This statistic is noteworthy because the institution also had a large psychotic and substance-abuse population.

Substance abuse.   Simonds and Kashani (1980) found high positive relationships between crimes committed against people and the use of amphetamines, phencyclidine (PCP), barbiturates, cocaine, and Valium®. Rada (1981) found that toxic reactions to illicit drugs such as PCP, LSD, barbiturates, amphetamines, and cocaine are common causes of violence in the emergency room. Therefore, for any human services worker, resources should include a *Physician's Desk Reference* (PDR) and the availability of a consulting physician for a fast diagnosis of the possible substance involved. Any initial assessment should be concerned not only with drug type but also with whether the drug is a prescription drug or of "street" manufacture so its potency may be determined (Piercy, 1984, p. 129).

Whereas barbiturates are commonly understood to depress the central nervous system, on occasion barbiturates may have an excitatory effect. Anyone coming off sedatives or depressants may be as disposed as or even more disposed to violent acting out than those who take stimulants. One of the most popular prescribed and abused drugs, Valium, is a classic example. Many people suffering from alcohol addiction will stop drinking and substitute large doses of Valium for alcohol. Effects of withdrawal from Valium may result in irritability and opposition to the health care setting and workers within that setting (Piercy, 1984, pp. 131–132).

The popularized versions of withdrawal from heroin as depicted by the media and press are close to reality. Particularly when addicts are suffering withdrawal, they are highly likely to perpetrate violence to secure the drug or the means to obtain it (Piercy, 1984, p. 135).

Amphetamines can cause feelings of power, euphoria, and extreme excitability. Other effects can include suspiciousness, wide fluctuations in mood, feelings of grandiosity, and extreme physical activity. Amphetamine abusers may overreact to mild and minor stimulations in their environment and at their worst become indistinguishable from paranoid or acute paranoid schizophrenics (Piercy, 1984, p. 132). Although downplayed in the media in comparison with users of other drugs, amphetamine abusers make up a large portion of the clientele that find their way into groups we run in the penal setting, and they have almost always been incarcerated because of violent crimes.

Alcohol has been associated with more than half of reported cases of violence in emergency rooms and one-fourth of reported cases in psychiatric institutions (Bach y Rita, Lion, & Climent, 1971). Alcohol releases the individual from fear of retribution and reduces cortical control to the point that inhibitions against morally and socially unacceptable conduct are lost (Piercy, 1984, p. 130). In the withdrawal stage, the individual may behave violently either because of being denied alcohol or, less commonly, because of hallucinosis, which causes the individual to fear imagined harm. The potential for violence is further increased when individuals who have a history of psychosis engage in alcohol or drug use (Klassen & O'Connor, 1988; Yesavage & Zarcone, 1983).

Predisposing history of violence.   A history of serious violence, including homicide, sexual attacks, assault, or threat of assault with a deadly weapon is one of the best predictors of future violence (Fareta, 1981; Monahan, 1981). Any background material that includes contact with the criminal justice system for aggravated felonies or a history of assaultive behavior while hospitalized should automatically put the human services worker on notice to be extremely cautious with the client (Klassen & O'Connor, 1988).

Psychological disturbance.   A variety of mental disorders fall within the category of psychological disturbance: the antisocial personality type, who has a history of violent behavior, emotional callousness, impulsivity, and manipulative behavior; the borderline personality, who floats in and out of reality, lacks adequate ego strength to control intense emotional drives, and repeatedly exhibits emotional outbursts; the paranoid, who is on guard against and constantly anticipating external threat and is willing and able to take action against that threat; the manic, who has elevated moods, hyperactivity, and excessive involvement in activities that may have painful consequences; the explosive personality, who has sudden escalating periods of anger; and the hallucinating schizophrenic, who is generally dysfunctional socially (Greenfield et al., 1989; Heilbrun, 1990;

Heilbrun & Heilbrun, 1989; Klassen & O'Connor, 1988; Wood & Khuri, 1984, p. 63).

Family history. A recent or past history of violence within the family is often carried into other environments. An early childhood characterized by an unstable and violent home is an excellent model for future violence (Wood & Khuri, 1984, pp. 65–66). A history of social isolation or lack of family and environmental support also may heighten potential for violence (Gomez, 1983; Heilbrun & Heilbrun, 1989). If a family member denies that the client has a history of violence, that testimonial should not be automatically accepted as the truth (Williams, Thornby, & Sandlin, 1989).

Time. Time in relation to the person's admission and tenure in the facility is critical. Admission on Friday or Saturday night during "party hours" significantly increases the potential for violence. The evening hours in geriatric and mental hospitals, with the onset of darkness, change of shift, and decrease in staff, often lead to client disorientation and states of confusion. The effects of this time period have become so notorious that they have been labeled the *sundown syndrome* (Piercy, 1984, p. 139). Mealtime, toileting, and bathing are also prime times for violent outbursts (Jones, 1985; Stokeman, 1982). Patients in both general and forensic psychiatric hospitals are more likely to be violent immediately after admission to the hospital (McNeil, Hatcher, Zeiner, Wolfe, & Myers, 1991; Star, 1984). For most patients committed involuntarily, the possibility of assault is significantly increased during the first 10 to 20 days after admission, and for paranoids it remains high during their first 45 days (Rofman, Askinazi, & Fant, 1980).

Presence of interactive participants. Violent behavior may be contingent on those who bring the person to the institution. Family members or friends who bring patients in for treatment often interact in a volatile manner with admitting staff, particularly if the staff are seen as abrasive and callous (Ruben, Wolkon, & Yamamoto, 1980) and treat either the patient or support persons in a curt or uncaring manner (Wood & Khuri, 1984, p. 58). Arguments that may be occurring between the client and support persons are easily transferred to staff. Further, when admonitions by distraught or intoxicated supporters to "fix" the client are not given immediate attention, they or the client may express grievances against the institution and staff by acting out. Any client who is accompanied to the institution by a police officer should be viewed as potentially violent (McNeil et al., 1991; Piercy, 1984, pp. 140–141).

Motoric cues. Close observation by the human services worker of physical cues will often give clues to emergent states predisposing to physical violence (Petrie, 1984, p. 115). Early warning signs include tense muscles; bulging, darting eye movements; staring or completely avoiding eye contact; closed, defensive body posture; twitching muscles, fingers, and eyelids;

body tremors; and disheveled appearance (Tardiff, 1989, p. 98; Wood & Khuri, 1984, p. 77). If the client is pacing back and forth, alternately approaching and then retreating from the worker, this may be a sign that the individual is gathering courage for an assault. The agitated client may have an expanded sense of personal space of up to eight feet in circumference, instead of three to four feet, and may be extremely sensitive to any intrusion into that space (Moran, 1984, pp. 244–246).

A number of verbal cues are precursors to violent action by the client. Heightened voice pitch, volume, and rapidity of speech may occur, particularly if the client has been using amphetamines. Confused speech content is reflective of confused thought. Finally, there is a high correlation between threats of violence and acting on those threats. The more specific the threat is as to the person, method, and time, the more seriously the threat should be taken (Tardiff, 1989, p. 99).

Multiple indicators.   The more the foregoing indicators are combined, the higher the potential for violence becomes (Klassen & O'Connor, 1988). Tardiff (1989) has indicated that if possible, the human services worker should attempt to assess all of these factors, and if they are present, the worker should clearly note the potential for violence on an intake form (p. 97). Tardiff further proposes that whether or not this information is available, one of the better verbal assessment techniques is to ask, "Have you ever lost your temper?" If the answer is "Yes!" the worker should proceed to ask how, when, and where this happened, and then perform an assessment much like that for suicide (p. 98). If any of the foregoing factors are apparent or are stated by the client, no matter how calm the client may appear to be, then a triage assessment of 10 on the interpersonal behavioral dimension should be made, the client's record should be flagged, and caution should be used in regard to the potential of the client to harm self or others.

INTERVENTION STRATEGIES

Because the institution itself plays such a large part in the who, what, why, how, and when of treatment, it may be viewed as an equal and contributing partner in resolving problems with clients who are disposed to becoming physically and verbally assaultive. No two institutions are alike with respect to a number of variables that affect what the institution can do about the problem of violence. The differences among a private, long-term mental health hospital for substance abusers, a state-supported halfway home for parolees, and a runaway shelter for teenagers supported by charity are great. Yet when confronted with clienteles that may be distraught, angry, fearful, and experiencing disequilibrium, they all have a common core of problems. Given the financial, legal, treatment, organizational, and philosophical limits that are idiosyncratic to each setting, the following intervention strategies should be viewed as a best "general" approach.

Security Analysis and Planning

One of the first steps in preventing violence is understanding what precautions the institution has taken to ensure safety of clients and staff. Although a health care facility should not strive for prisonlike security, certain precautions can be taken to ensure that workers are not put at extreme risk by their clientele. First and foremost, a security management analysis should be conducted by management with experts in the security field (Ishimoto, 1984, p. 211). The following questions are representative of what Ishimoto believes a security management analysis should entail in the areas of prevention, detection, response, and security education (pp. 211–216):

1. What are the institution's goals, functions, operations, organizational structure, and responsibilities?
2. Who is in charge of what security provisions?
3. What image considerations limit the amount of security?
4. What balance needs to be maintained between security of staff and provision of human services?
5. What is the geographical, environmental, and socioeconomic setting in which services are rendered?
6. What kinds of clientele make use of the facilities and what risk do they pose to others?
7. What kinds of provisions have already been made for staff, clients, visitors, and neighborhood security?
8. What kinds of training have staff received for emergencies?
9. What screening devices are available to monitor clientele, and are they reliable and valid?
10. What screening devices are used for personnel selection, and are they reliable and valid?
11. What physical security is available in the form of barriers, lighting, locks, and dispensing of keys?
12. What security personnel will be needed? Where and when?
13. Are there emergency contingency plans for a variety of problems, and do staff know what is expected of them under varying circumstances?
14. How do these outcome goals fit with Occupational Safety and Health Act requirements?

All staff should have input into these questions, and a comprehensive security plan should be worked out and disseminated. Such a plan should be comprehensive and simple, detailing who is responsible for what under which conditions. The plan should cover the entire domain of the institution, starting with the parking lot, moving through the front door to admissions, and proceeding through the building to encompass day-treatment facilities, staff offices, food services, pharmaceutical dispensaries, and client rooms (Ishimoto, 1984, pp. 209–223). Although initial costs in time and money for this service may be seen as burdensome by the administration, its net cost will be minimal if it avoids just one lawsuit by a client or staff member (Moran, 1984, p. 249). If such a survey is not taken, not only does the facility risk outbreaks of violence, but also the staff will perceive it as not being greatly concerned about what happens to them (Lewellyn, 1985).

Training

Planning is of little consequence if no training follows. Staff who have been trained in the methods, techniques, and procedures to follow have experienced increased confidence in their ability to deescalate violence and have significantly reduced assaultive behavior (Rice, Helzel, Varney, & Quinsey, 1985; Turnbull, Aitken, Black, & Patterson, 1990). Training should include both knowledge and skill building and should be ongoing, with immediate training for new members of the treatment team and continuing education for veterans (Dyer et al., 1984, pp. 12–15; Lewellyn, 1985; Turnbull et al., 1990). It should begin with the crisis intervention skills listed in Chapter 2 and additionally cover legal aspects, theories of aggression, reporting and recording of incidents, assessment of contextual and environmental variables, verbal defusing techniques, triggers of aggression, self-defense and restraint techniques, and follow-up staffing procedures (Blair, 1991; Rice et al., 1985; Turnbull et al., 1990). A critical component of training is not just talking about problems but gaining practice in solving them. There is no better way of doing this than in role-play situations, which can be videotaped for analysis and feedback by instructors and peers (Turnbull et al., 1990).

Adequate training should endow the crisis worker with the ability to make certain assumptions and take certain precautions when dealing with potentially violent clients (Turnbull et al., 1990; Zold & Schilt, 1984, pp. 98–99):

1. Assume the need to set limits and provide clear instructions with options that define what positive and negative consequences will occur.
2. Assume the client feels a number of debilitating emotions such as fear, depression, anxiety, helplessness, anger, rejection, and hopelessness and demonstrate concern by encouraging verbal ventilation through *how* and *when* questions, showing empathic concern by restatement and reflection of the client's feelings, and reinforcing appropriate behavior and communication of feelings.
3. Assume frustration of normal activity and boredom when the client is in residence and provide activities to keep the client fruitfully busy.
4. Assume a threat to the client's self-esteem, independence, and self-control and provide choices and opportunities to help in carrying out medical and psychological activities.
5. Assume tension and arousal and provide a calm and relaxing atmosphere, particularly in high-tension periods, by manipulating environmental variables and using a cooperative "we" approach.

6. Assume confusion and provide a careful explanation of all procedures to be employed, being particularly sure that all staff are operating from the same frame of reference.
7. Assume responsibility and provide for one primary staff member to act as chief caretaker and advocate of each client.
8. Assume disconnectedness and rootlessness if the client is to be institutionalized for any length of time and provide familiarity and psychologically calming anchors associated with pleasant memories.

While providing support through the foregoing proactive behaviors, the wise human services worker should observe a number of precautionary measures (Blair, 1991; Moran, 1984, p. 244; Piercy, 1984, p. 143; Turnbull et al., 1990; Wood & Khuri, 1984, p. 69):

1. Don't deny the possibility of violence when early signs of agitation are first noticed in the client.
2. Don't dismiss warnings from records, family and peers, authorities, or fellow workers that the client is violent.
3. Don't become isolated with potentially violent clients unless you have made sure that enough security precautions have been taken to prevent or limit a violent outburst.
4. Don't engage in certain behaviors that may be interpreted as aggressive, such as moving too close, staring directly into the client's eyes for extended periods of time, pointing fingers, or displaying facial expressions and body movements that would appear threatening.
5. Don't allow a number of the institution's workers to interact simultaneously with the client in confusing multiple dialogues.
6. Don't make promises that cannot be kept.
7. Don't allow feelings of fear, anger, or hostility to interfere with self-control and professional understanding of the client's circumstances.
8. Don't argue, give orders, or disagree when not absolutely necessary.
9. Don't be placating by giving in and agreeing to all the real and imagined ills the client is suffering at the hands of the institution.
10. Don't become condescending by using childish responses that are cynical, satirical, or otherwise designed to denigrate the client.
11. Don't let self-talk about your own importance be acted out in an officious and "know-it-all" manner.
12. Don't raise your voice, put a sharp edge on responses, or use threats to gain compliance.
13. Conversely, don't mumble, speak hesitantly, or use a tone of voice so low that the client has trouble understanding what you are saying.
14. Don't argue over small points, given strong opposition from the client.
15. Don't attempt to reason with any client who is under the influence of a mind-altering substance.
16. Don't attempt to gain compliance based on the assumption that the client is as reasonable about things as you are.

17. Don't keep the client waiting or leave a potentially violent client alone with freedom to move about.
18. Don't allow a crowd to congregate as spectators to an altercation.
19. Don't use *why* and *what* questions that put the client on the defensive.

These injunctions are not a recipe for avoiding violent confrontations, but they are general working procedures that will help the human services worker move adroitly with the client through the intervention stages.

Precautions Dealing with the Physical Setting

A few minimal safety precautions should be taken that deal with the physical settings of the institution in which staff members are most likely to become involved in potentially violent situations with clients. Two critical areas important to all crisis workers are the admissions area and the worker's office.

The reception or waiting-room area should offer a television set, reading material, and accessibility to snack areas. Availability of entertainment and food and drink gives clients and visitors an opportunity to become engaged in a pleasurable activity to offset the hostile feelings that may be engendered by the problems they are facing and defuse the stressful situation of admission (Wood & Khuri, 1984, pp. 79–80). One admonition is necessary with regard to food and drink. Clients who are extremely rebellious about entering the institution may attempt to choke themselves on foodstuffs or even swallow pull tabs from metal cans. The admissions staff should carefully monitor clients if they are allowed to eat or drink (McCown, 1986).

The admissions area should be clean and well kept, with furniture, carpet, and wall coverings well maintained. First impressions are lasting. If the client's first impression of a facility is that staff have little regard or respect for the facility, the client will have little reason to respect what goes on there either (Marohn, 1982). No sharp, movable objects, including furniture, should be available as potential weapons (McCown, 1986).

The area should be set up so that it is a choke point. Only one way into the rest of the facility should be available from the admissions area (Annis, McClaren, & Baker, 1984, p. 30). Depending on how much security is needed, the reception area may have electronically locked doors that separate it from the rest of the facility, sign-in sheets, identity check procedures, and metal detectors (Jones, 1984).

The admissions worker will make the first contact with the client and will engage the person during one of the most potentially violent moments the institution is likely to encounter. The admissions worker should be highly skilled in crisis intervention techniques and should have one primary job—*staying with and attending to the client being admitted!* Under no circumstances should a secretary, receptionist, or any other support person who is not professionally well versed in crisis intervention or who has other tasks to perform, such as typing letters or answering the telephone, be delegated to handle this important assignment. The admissions worker does not leave the client until all admitting procedures have been accomplished and the client is safely settled (McCown, 1986).

The admissions worker should never be left in a position of isolation from the rest of the staff (Turnbull et al., 1990). Security support equipment such as a body alarm (a button-activated device that when triggered will automatically send an alarm and position fix to security), an automatic dialer preset to in-house security and 911, convex mirrors to monitor the whole waiting area, panic buttons, closed circuit television monitoring equipment, button locks on elevators, and a metal detector at the entrance should be available (Doms, 1984, pp. 225–229; Jones, 1984; McCown, 1986; Wood & Khuri, 1984, pp. 79–80).

Personal work environments should also be safe. Desks should be set so that they allow for separation of client and worker, even though communicating across a desk is not the most desirable counseling setup. Space should be arranged to permit both the worker and the client clear access to the door. Any interview setting should provide an easy exit for the human services worker and should be so situated that the worker can leave the room without having to confront or cross within the personal space of the client. No potential weapons such as paperweights, letter openers, and sharpened pencils should be openly displayed or within easy reach of the client. The same personal warning devices and procedures recommended for the reception area should also be in place in workers' offices. This precaution is particularly critical because of the isolated nature of the therapy setting (Tardiff, 1984a, p. 50).

Although the institution and its precautions may cause human services workers some embarrassment and chagrin, workers should not disregard them. Our own work in penal institutions is a good example of what we are talking about. The corrections facility we work in mandates that a body alarm be worn at all times by the counselor, that a cocounselor be present in all groups, and that a guard be posted at all times within easy access of the group room. Occasionally group members may make snide remarks about these precautions. The worker may easily respond by stating, "I don't much like it either, but you guys know the rules," and injecting a little humor: "It's probably because they're afraid we might beat up on group members and want to protect you guys."

Stages of Intervention

Management of potentially violent situations should proceed in a sequential manner, based on a nine-stage model developed by Piercy (1984, pp. 147–148). The stages are as follows: (1) education, (2) avoidance of conflict, (3) appeasement, (4) deflection, (5) time out, (6) show of force, (7) seclusion, (8) restraints, and (9) sedation. For each of these stages, personal responsibility is paramount. Passing the buck is too easy and is likely to cause the very problems we are trying to avoid. Further, whether by circumstance or by design, the first person who comes in contact with the problem, usually the crisis worker, is the most likely to be the agitated client's focus of attention (Moran, 1984, pp. 233–234).

Stages 1 through 5 all rely heavily on talking instead of acting, in accordance with one of the primary goals of crisis intervention with violence-prone individuals: getting them to talk out rather than act out. This approach may seem obvious, but it is difficult to achieve. The agitated client clearly has a limited ability to talk and think through problems, as opposed to acting on them and giving little thought to the consequences (Tardiff, 1984a, p. 52).

As we move through the nine stages, we will follow Jason, a 15-year-old white male client, and Carol, a therapist who by most standards is an old pro. She has been at Seashore Village, an adolescent treatment facility, for four years. Jason is new to the business of institutions. He is not new to being angry, which he is right now as he sits with a deputy sheriff in the reception area waiting for Carol to come through the door. Jason's teenage years have been filled with petty larceny, truancy, alcohol and drug use, and parents who have gotten him out of one scrape after another. His latest escapade of stealing a car landed him in front of a juvenile court, and he was sent to Seashore as an alternative to the state juvenile correction system. His father, fed up with Jason's behavior and over the objections of his wife, has pushed for this placement. Jason feels betrayed and is extremely angry at his father for doing so.

Seashore itself is representative of a broad sample of institutions. It is neither the best nor the worst in terms of clients, staff, resources, and security measures. We are endeavoring to paint as representative a picture as possible, asking you to withhold judgments about the efficacy and appropriateness of these strategies in every institution. Our hope is that the procedures used in the case of Jason will cause you to think carefully about your own present or future role in an institution, compare the ideas proposed here with the requirements imposed upon you, analyze the procedures used, and make thoughtful comparisons between these techniques and the real world within which you operate.

Jason: [*Thinking to himself, hands sweating, slight tremors racing through his body.*]
Man, this place is scaring the hell out of me. How'd I ever get in this fix? What are they gonna do to me? I'll just bet a wrap-around suit with no arms in it. I'll be at the mercy of the rest of the crazies in here. I'll really go nuts if I stay here. I gotta get out of this place if it's the last thing I ever do.

Jason is extremely angry and anxious about what will happen to him, frustrated that he has lost control of his life and that what he has considered to be normal activity is going to be severely curtailed. He also feels extremely vulnerable, confused, bewildered, and alone. Jason's feelings are typical of those of a client who is being introduced to a long-term treatment facility for the first time (Blair, 1991; Zold & Schilt, 1984, p. 96).

As soon as Jason enters Seashore, admissions immediately calls the adolescent unit. At that time Carol comes quickly to the reception area and meets Jason. She immediately makes a fast visual assessment of Jason's verbal and nonverbal behavior as she enters the room and monitors Jason closely to see what his reaction to her initial query will be.

Carol: [*Thinking to herself.*] What's going on with this kid? Any signs he is agitated? Yes! He's pacing around, eyes darting to and fro, keeps cracking his knuckles, looking at the door and the cop. He'll run if he gets the chance! Muttering to himself. Who brought him in? Nobody else here but that cop over there. He keeps watching him. Must be an adjudication. If a cop brought him here, be careful until you know what's happening.

Carol picks up the file the deputy has brought, quickly looks it over, and finds the boy's name and rap sheet. A fast review tells her that Jason has been in a series of escalating scrapes with the law, that his parents are fed up with his behavior and feel he's out of control, and that he has been involved in fights when his explosive personality got out of control. Carol then stops briefly with the deputy and finds out what kind of a trip Jason had from the juvenile detention center.

Carol: [*Thinking to herself.*] OK! Check him out and see how stabilized he is and let him find out what's going to happen to him.

Stage 1: Education.   Clients need to be educated about what is happening to them and why and how it is happening. Reasoning and reassurance are given. One way of doing this is to assume the role of the client's advocate (Pisarick, 1981). Owning statements that indicate concern over the client's welfare are a good opening gambit. It must be assumed that in this new, strange, and alien environment the primary feeling of the client will be fear and anger (Rada, 1981). Open-ended questions and reflection of the client's feelings are crucial to conveying that the client's feelings count for something and are being taken into consideration (Turnbull et al., 1990).

Carol: Hi! My name's Carol, and you must be Jason. I'm the person who'll be working with you.

Jason: [*Gives a menacing look.*] Yeah! So what? [*Points to officer.*] The cop got me in here but I ain't gonna go any farther.

Carol: I understand how you feel. Most people who come here feel about the same way. Seems like everybody's against you, telling you what to do. I'd be angry too! I want you to know, though, that here at Seashore you're going to have some options about what happens.

Jason: Screw your options. I ain't stayin' here. [*Makes a menacing move toward Carol.*]

Carol: [*Senses move and moves back and a little to Jason's left, giving him some increased space.*] One of your immediate options is that I'd like you to come with me and meet some of the other kids here and have them tell you what's going on and see if what they have to say fits with what you're about. On the other hand, the court sent you here, and if you don't like the first option and want to fight it out, you could be carried back to the unit and we can wait until you've got yourself together. I understand you're angry, and I'd be angry too, but I'd like to know if you feel that fighting or running is gonna make it better for you and improve your situation rather than checking things out. So you've got a choice. I think you might be interested in meeting some of the other kids, but it'll have to be under peaceful conditions and you'll have to show me you can handle that starting right now.

In this initial meeting, the worker uses the technique of providing options (Turnbull et al., 1990). She is letting the client have some semblance of control of the situation but is also clearly outlining what the consequences of his choices are. As soon as possible she is going to model option therapy (McCown, 1986). Option therapy, in simple terms, says, "You always have a choice. You need to start deciding as soon as possible who's going to have control over those choices, you or us." Poor choices about appropriate behavior undoubtedly got Jason here in the first place. The worker immediately starts the educative process by proposing optional behaviors for Jason that will allow him opportunities to see clearly what his choices are and what the consequences of those choices will be (McCown, 1986).

Jason: Well . . . all right . . . lady, I'll give it a look-see, but I ain't promisin' nothin' after that.

Carol: I don't expect any more than that at the moment. What I want most for you is to see what's going on here and what some of the other kids think about what we do before you make any kind of promises. We don't lie and we don't make promises we can't keep, so let's go back and see the unit and meet some of the kids.

The worker has to make a quick judgment about how directive or nondirective to be. She is directive only to the extent of setting boundaries equivalent to how out of control the client is. Her other mission is to establish rapport and credibility with the client. She does this by accepting and acknowledging the client where he is and in turn stating the same from the institution's perspective. She offers no platitudes or false promises (Turnbull et al., 1990). Her technique of letting the client talk to other people on the unit is designed to let the client hear and see with his own ears and eyes what is going on without feeling he is getting a lot of propaganda. However, she will not provide a format for him to act out, and if in her judgment Jason is not controlled enough to make a tour with her, she will summon assistance and Jason will be escorted to an observation room (McCown, 1986).

Carol: [*Walking down the hall, with Jason two steps in front of her and a bit to the side.*] At each stop along our tour, I'll tell you what goes on. We have a lot of activities, so if you don't clearly understand what's happening or you want to know some more about it, just ask.

Jason's schedule is as follows:

7:00– 8:00	Stretch period, clean up room, lavatory, breakfast
8:00– 8:15	Community meeting, announcements
8:15–12:00	School
12:00–12:45	Lunch
12:45– 2:00	School
2:00– 3:00	Group problem solving
3:00– 4:00	Individual counseling
4:00– 5:00	Quiet time in room
5:00– 5:45	Dinner
5:45– 7:00	Special groups: assertiveness training, social skills, group counseling, family therapy, Alcoholics Anonymous, art therapy, and so on
7:00– 8:00	Group recreation in gym
8:00– 9:00	Free time, for recreation, phone calls, and such (privileges depend on level achieved)
9:00– 9:30	Shower, clean-up, bedtime (bedtime extended to 10:00 or 10:30 depending on level achieved)

Very little free time is available. For most individuals who enter a facility such as Seashore, a major problem has been too much free time and the inability to handle it well. Structuring the environment brings some badly needed discipline back into their lives. Particularly for adolescents, burning up energy in constructive ways is of paramount importance. Further, too much free time is a fertile breeding ground for acting out behavior (Vinick, 1986).

Seashore is also on a behavior management program that makes use of levels. Jason starts at entry level. Depending on how Jason operates in his environment, he will go up or down on the level system and will concomitantly receive more or fewer privileges. At an entry level, he will have few privileges—early bedtime, no passes—and will be under fairly close supervision. By conducting himself in a responsible manner, he may increase his level designation and gain access to a broader array of recreational activities, later bedtime, ground privileges, and weekend passes. The system is explained to Jason in a careful and clear manner, with emphasis on the fact that whether or not he moves to higher levels is his responsibility.

Educating a client about what is to happen medically and psychologically needs to be done slowly, methodically, and in nontechnical terms with numerous perceptual checks. Keeping explanations simple and helping the client to gain understanding ameliorates the situation, whereas complexity only increases the chance for violent behavior to occur (Moran, 1984, p. 234).

Jason: [*Somewhat belligerently.*] Like, what's this group meeting?

Carol: The group meets every day. We do two things there. First, putting this many kids together means that problems are going to arise. Within the limits of the institution we decide on a group basis how these problems will be handled. It's a one-person–one-vote program, and that includes the staff. The group decides how to tackle a community problem and then collectively makes a commitment to do something about it. Second, when problems between people arise, we all put our heads together and see how those problems can be solved. You don't necessarily have to accept an idea, but you must listen to what's being said.

Jason: I don't think I got anything to say to these nerds.

Carol: Maybe you don't. However, a lot of kids here do. You're not going to be here forever. Therefore, we look pretty hard at what's going on with you right now as you deal with other people here, how that behavior may or may not cause you problems, and what's down the road for you if you do decide to change some things in your life and what's likely if you don't. We don't ask you to love everybody here, but we do ask you to respect what they're trying to do, just as we ask them to respect you.

The human services worker's responses are from Glasser's reality therapy (1965, 1969) and focus on the issues of becoming involved, looking at alternatives, making value judgments, accepting no excuses, and assuming responsibility and consequences for one's actions. In this manner Carol goes over the entire schedule with Jason. While she explains the content of the program, she also makes sure to assess and reflect the emotional content of Jason's responses, again and again reinforcing the idea of options, responsibilities, and commitments.

Stage 2: Avoidance of conflict.   Avoidance of conflict and confrontation is attempted whenever possible. Matching threat for threat is likely to obtain for the human services worker exactly the opposite of control and containment of the situation (Dubin, 1981). If individuals can cool down on their own, with minimal monitoring, they should be given the option of doing so. Workers who delight in continuously pushing and escalating issues are not practicing good therapeutic intervention techniques and are clearly asking for trouble (Blair, 1991).

One week has elapsed since Jason's admission.

Jason: [*Standing in the hallway, shouting, shaking, and trembling, face flushed.*] If you think you or anybody else can make me stay in my room or in this place, you're crazier than I am. I just wanted a drink of water and Mr. Richardson started yelling at me that it was past quiet time. Just try stopping me and see what happens.

Carol: [*Quietly and calmly.*] Jason, if you'll calm down, I'll bring you a cup of water. Please go in your room. You can have your drink and we can talk about it.

If the client is fast approaching a point of no return, let ventilation of feelings occur. Although shouting, cursing, and yelling are not pleasant, they are better than hand-to-hand combat (McCown, 1986; Vinick, 1986). The worker should attempt to remove the agitated client from the vicinity of other residents who may aggravate the situation (Turnbull et al., 1990). This is best done by immediately asking the client to go to an area that is away from the other residents (McCown, 1986). If the client retains some semblance of control, the client's own room may be an appropriate place. If the client is fast losing control and cannot calm down, a better choice is a room that is devoid of stimuli. Such a place should be specifically prepared and reserved for this sort of occurrence. Once the client has relaxed to some degree, then the human services worker can establish the cause and degree of agitation by determining what occurred and then pointing out consequences (Vinick, 1986).

Carol: What are you angry about?

Jason: [*Still standing in the hallway, quite agitated.*] He was treating me just like my old man, just making me feel like a baby.

Carol: And what were you doing?

Jason: Hey, I was just going to get a drink of water. I still had two minutes until quiet time. He made me so mad I wanted to pick up a chair and bust him. I still feel like going after that jerk.

Carol: What will that accomplish?

Jason: It'll show him he can't push me around like my old man does.

Carol: If you do that, it'll just confirm that you need to be here. That you can't control yourself. Is that what you want?

Jason: Maybe I just don't care.

For those clients who do not respond to verbal attempts to defuse the situation, the next step for the human services worker is to give assurance that violent behavior by anybody, including both staff and clients, is unacceptable and then to indicate what the person's choices and consequences will become if the behavior persists (Wood & Khuri, 1984, pp. 67–68).

Carol: You can choose to pick up a chair, Jason, but that'll mean a number of things will happen. First, nobody is allowed to hit anybody else here, and that goes for both staff and kids. We won't permit anybody to do that because we don't want to see anybody hurt here. If it comes to that, we won't hurt you, but we will restrain you, something I'd not like to see happen. Second, if you choose to do that, no one else will get to hear your side of it and we won't have a chance to work your problem out with Mr. Richardson. Another choice would be to go back to your room and then ask for a drink. If you do that, I will get Mr. Richardson and we'll all sit down and work this through. Would you be willing to do that?

Clients should be confronted with their inappropriate behavior, but in a caring, supportive, and problem-solving way that is not tinged with sarcasm or challenge. If the situation is deteriorating so rapidly that the worker no longer feels that communication can be maintained, it may be fruitful to have someone else enter the scene who will be perceived as a neutral party by the client (Lakeside Hospital, 1988). This tactic is risky and involves a judgment call on the worker's part. Allowing clients to be rewarded for acting out by getting other people to come to the scene may reinforce inappropriate behavior and lead clients to believe that they and not the institution control the situation.

Jason: It ain't just Richardson, this whole place sucks. They won't let me do nothin'. And you don't understand either. Chaplain Gentry's the only guy who I can really talk to.

Carol: I understand that you're really disappointed and mad that you couldn't get a drink. I also know you're pretty angry at me and everybody else right now and about the last thing you want to do is go peacefully back to your room. I know that you and Chaplain Gentry are pretty close. Would you be willing to go to your room and wait quietly while I get him?

If the client does not choose this option then the worker will have to move the client to a safe place, which will be a time-out room. A show of force may be necessary to send a clear message: "If you can't handle yourself, we will."

Carol: Jason, I want you to go down to observation for 15 minutes and think this out. [*Speaking to technicians.*] Bob and Jerry, will you see that Jason gets to observation? In 15 minutes I'll be down to see if you're ready to talk this through.

Stage 3: Appeasement. Stages 3 and 4 are probably most appropriate in emergency situations in which the worker has little basis to judge the client's aggressiveness and violence and is unable to obtain immediate assistance. Appeasement is not applicable in a number of settings under ordinary circumstances, and if Jason had reached the point of being removed to involuntary time out, appeasement or deflection of feelings (Stage 4) would be highly inappropriate and run counter to good therapeutic practice.

However, in all situations we believe it is better to err on the side of humility than to project a "tough guy" image, regardless of the client's verbal barbs, threats, and exhortations. This recommendation does not mean that the human services worker should become a doormat to be walked all over by the client. It does mean that by operating in an empathic mode we should see just how frightening and alarming the situation is to the client. Alternately, any attempts by the workers to counter threat with threat in an emergency situation are likely to confirm the client's suspicions that bad things are going to happen.

Appeasement can be attempted if the client's demands are simple and reasonable, even if those demands are made in a bellicose manner. Early on it is better to grant demands and to defer worry about what "lessons" need to be taught until later (Piercy, 1984, p. 148). This approach may be difficult for some human services workers to accept because it is based on the idea that there is no winner or loser in a potentially violent confrontation between an agitated client and the institution (Moran, 1984, p. 234).

Jason: [*Enters the human services worker's office without an appointment, fists clenched, and starts shouting in an agitated, high-pitched voice.*] Listen, big shot!

I wanted to mail this letter to my girl, she doesn't know what's happened to me, and that jerk Richardson won't give me a stamp. I could bust all yer heads!

Carol: [*In a calm, collected voice.*] He's going by the rules, but I understand your concern. Please sit down at the table here and I'll see what can be done about getting a stamp.

The human services worker meets this demand because it is easily done and does not seriously conflict with institutional rules. She is also alone with an extremely agitated client who may or may not act out. There may be a discussion afterward with the other worker who gave the original order, but there needs to be a clear understanding among all workers that in emergencies, judgment calls may bend the rules a bit or countermand orders of others.

Stage 4: Deflection.   Deflection of angry feelings is attempted by shifting to other, less threatening topics. This may be done in a variety of ways. Asking the client to take a physically less threatening position focuses away from agitated motoric activity to problem solving (Wood & Khuri, 1984, p. 68).

Carol: [*Repeating her statement patiently, firmly, and respectfully.*] Jason, I understand how important it is for you to be able to write to your girlfriend. Please sit down. Then I'll get you a stamp and see if we can iron out this problem.

The human services worker literally and figuratively gets the client off his feet and in a less threatening operating mode (Epstein & Carter, 1988). The worker is also quietly but firmly setting limits by asking the client to sit. Since agitated individuals seldom listen closely to requests for compliance, Carol acknowledges Jason's feeling state and then uses the broken-record routine (Canter & Canter, 1982) of repeating her request. She is also employing another behavior management technique. By making a reward contingent upon a compliant behavior, Carol is using "Grandma's Law" (Becker, 1971). "Grandma's Law" basically states: "First you eat your spinach and then you get your ice cream."

By using problem-solving techniques, no matter how small the real or imagined injustice is, the human services worker conveys to the client an interest in the client as an individual and not just as another name in the institutional computer (Wood & Khuri, 1984, p. 71). Parceling out the problems into workable pieces, the worker removes them from the realm of the enormous and makes them solvable. A week later, in another confrontation over a variety of issues, the worker seeks to make the problem manageable.

Jason: I can't get nothin' done here. Everything's screwed up. School, home, people, the food, my freedom. It's a concentration camp.

Carol: OK. There seem to be at least three things that are really bugging you right now. Not being able to get a pass yet, the way your dad got angry in family therapy, and your problem with the math assignment yesterday. Together, I can see how it'd become overwhelming. Let's take them one at a time and see what can be done about each.

Until absolutely sure what the problem is, the human services worker should never make promises about what can or cannot be done when attempting to calm an agitated client (Wood & Khuri, 1984, p. 71).

Carol: I know that weekend pass is really important. You'd get to see your girlfriend, and you feel like you really deserve it. I'd like to see what could be done, but I can't give you a guarantee. A pass is based on good behavior and your level status. If you feel like you've gotten jerked around, griping about it won't help much. Very specifically, write down why you think you deserve the pass. I'll take it to the staffing this afternoon. Understand, though, I'll not use this as bait to get you to calm down.

Having the client write down problems also defuses angry feelings and acting out. In many instances, the client may just be testing limits. To write down clearly and logically what the problem is calls for time and effort, which very few clients will invest if the problem is not important (Epstein & Carter, 1988). Writing down the particulars of the problem is also cathartic for clients, allowing them to gain some emotional distance from it and view the situation in a more objective light (McCown, 1986).

When other more overt ploys are ineffective, the client may use manipulation and threat to obtain demands.

Jason: If you don't get that pass for me, you ain't much of a counselor and they'll be real sorry they didn't give it to me.

Carol: When you try and lay that guilt trip on me and make threats about what you'll do if you don't get your way, that's a pretty good indication that the staff's judgment was right and makes it even more difficult to act as your advocate. It's not so much any of the demands that you want, but more like pushing the limits to see how far you can get by manipulating and threatening me.

The response the human services worker makes is one from Adlerian psychotherapy called "avoiding the tar baby" (Dinkmeyer, Pew, & Dinkmeyer, 1979, p. 118). By responding directly to the client, the human services worker does not allow herself to be caught up in the manipulative trap the client lays for her. Although the response is confrontive, it is exceedingly effective with manipulative individuals because it deflects them from their game plan and causes them to consider the consequences of their actions (Wood & Khuri, 1984, p. 71).

When clients become agitated, despite the normal busy day and physical activity that help to burn up energy, deflection of anger through the use of physical activity can be helpful. Clients can take out their frustrations through activities that range from pounding on a heavy bag (Vinick, 1986) to tearing up telephone directories (McCown, 1986). At the same time, the human services worker can reinforce the client for acting in more appropriate ways. While teaching anger management skills may be more effective in the long run (LeCroy, 1988), appropriate and safe physical exertion to burn up angry feelings is an effective short-term solution.

Jason: [*Tearing up the Yellow Pages.*] Umphf! I . . . get so mad . . . I . . . Arggh! I . . . wish this phone book was that no-good SOB's face.

Carol: But in fact you haven't torn anybody's face off. You've made a good choice. Much better than when you were going around clobbering people. You don't have to pay any consequences at all for tearing up the phone book. You get it out of your system and get back in control.

Jason: [*Continues ventilating, until finally he runs out of energy and lets arms hang limply at side.*]

Carol: [*Continues to reinforce Jason for acting appropriately and within limits.*] Look at what you could have done. You could have swung a chair at Mr. Richardson, you could have punched me out, or trashed your room, all of which would have got you into hot water. The very kinds of things that got you here in the first place. But you didn't do that. What you did was perfectly acceptable and within the limits here.

Stage 5: Time out.   When clients cannot contend with the emotion of the moment, they are asked to go to a reduced-stimulus environment, to be alone and think things out. A clear assessment of how agitated the client is needs to be made at this point. In an initial meeting, the worker can estimate the client's remaining degree of control by the client's response to certain questions (Wood & Khuri, 1984, p. 68): How dangerous does the client feel in regard to self and others? Is the client able and willing to leave a high-stimulus situation for a few minutes to rest and think things over? If the client is not overly reactive, then the worker may ask the client to take a minimal time out in living quarters.

Jason: I don't want to sit, talk, or be reasonable. I want this scumbag place to do something!

Carol: Right now I can see there's no way this is going to get solved. You can go to your room and think things over. Go for 15 minutes. If you can come back and show me you're in control, that's it, no reduction in level, no write-ups, and it's forgotten.

If a threat is made directly to the human services worker, other staff, or clients, the policy should be mandatory time out with a clear and strong statement of reason (Vinick, 1986).

Carol: I've tried to work this through with you and you clearly don't want to hear it. When you continue to make threats, you're saying to me you're not willing to abide by the rules and are choosing to have rules enforced. I want you to go to the observation room for 30 minutes right now. At the end of that time I'll be around to see you. If you don't feel like talking you don't have to, but you can go back in the room for another 30 minutes. You can continue to do that until you're willing to talk to me about how you think you've been treated unfairly.

The human services worker states these conditions in a matter-of-fact manner and does not press the issue (Vinick, 1986). If the client is so agitated as to be beyond the grasp of reality and is unwilling to be compliant to the human services worker's request, then the worker needs help to contain the situation.

Stage 6: Show of force.   If the client is unable to proceed to time out or is otherwise noncompliant or acting out, then a show of force is needed (Piercy, 1984, p. 148). If the client is already agitated enough to warn the human services workers that help may be warranted, the interview should be carried out in an open hallway or large meeting room where the participants are in plain view of other staff members and the client can be restrained easily (Viner, 1982). The show of force indicates that any display of violence or threat of violence will not be tolerated and often helps disorganized clients to regain control of themselves (Wood & Khuri, 1984, p. 68). If this stage is reached, the potential for violence is high and the worker should not attempt to deal with the client alone. Either by paging help through an emergency code or by having assistance readily available, the worker needs to be able to summon enough help to demonstrate that compliance is now required (Lakeside Hospital, 1988).

The problem is that not all individuals give indications that they are about to become violent. Therefore, there are times when, through no fault of the worker, potentially violent situations occur when the worker is alone and not immediately able to call for assistance. The following procedures may keep the worker out of harm's way (Epstein & Carter, 1988; Lakeside Hospital, 1988; Moran, 1984, pp. 238–248; Turnbull et al., 1990).

1. *Stay calm and relaxed.* Tensing of muscles and agitated movement only fuel the situation and cause the client to expect that something bad (for the client) is about to happen. Knowing relaxation techniques such as simple deep breathing is extremely helpful because one is able to stay loose, anticipate client responses, and move quickly.

2. *Practice positive self-talk.* Even in the worst situations, running positive "billboards" through the mind's eye will help keep control of the situation.

3. *Do not stare at the client.* Whereas eye contact is fine in most counseling situations, it may be construed as a challenge in this situation. Focus on an imaginary spot on the client's upper chest about where the first button on a shirt would be, occasionally glancing at the eyes and other parts of the individual's body. Keeping focus on the centerline of the client's body will also let the human services worker avoid being faked out by extremity or eye movements.

4. *Stay arm's length away.* Make a judgment about how long the client's arms are and stay an arm's length and a bit more away. Estimating this distance on a continuous basis with other staff will keep the human services worker's distance perception well honed.

5. *Stay to weak side.* Know which of the client's hands is dominant and stay to the client's weak side. Chances are nine out of ten the client will be right-handed. In an aggressive stance, a person invariably places the foot of

the weak side forward, and wristwatches are usually worn on the weak arm. If the worker keeps to the weak side of the assailant, any blow aimed by the client is likely to have less power and be a glancing one.

6. *Keep arms at sides.* Folded arms are bad for two reasons. They imply hostility or authority and they put the worker at a distinct disadvantage because of the time it takes to unfold them and defend oneself.

7. *Assume a defensive posture.* Stand with feet slightly spread, face to face with the client but tending a bit to the client's weak side. Move the dominant leg slightly to the rear with the knee locked. Move the other leg slightly forward of the body and bent slightly at the knee. This position will allow the worker the best chance to stay upright, and staying upright is the best safeguard against being hurt.

8. *Avoid cornering.* Cornering occurs in three ways. When the client is placed in an angle formed by two walls or other objects, with the human services worker directly in front of the client, the only way out is through the worker. Exit cornering occurs when the individual cannot get out of a room without first crossing the personal space of the worker. Contact cornering occurs when the worker attempts to subdue a client by physical means. The client has two choices, ether to submit or to resist.

The premise in avoiding cornering is that even an agitated individual will seek to disengage if given the opportunity to do so without losing face. The human services worker should be careful to give the client space to exit the situation safely. A problem occurs in a private office where the worker does not have an easy escape exit. The easiest solution is to be so situated in an office that both the worker and the client can exit the room without having to cross the personal space of one another.

Although we would advise the worker to have a basic understanding of self-defense, under none but the most extreme circumstances do we believe that a worker should ever attempt bodily restraint of a client. The risk of physical injury is far too great and the client's trust in the worker will be destroyed.

9. *Avoid ordering.* When a client is threatening violence, attempting to order or command a client to do something is likely to aggravate the situation further. Staying with the basic empathic listening and responding skills used throughout this book is far more likely to lead to satisfactory results.

10. *Do perceptual checks.* Ask for help from the client. If current verbal responses are merely agitating the situation, check with the client as to what solutions or techniques might calm things down. If the client indicates for you to be quiet, that nothing you say or do will help, then be quiet.

11. *Admit mistakes.* If an error in judgment has been made, admit it and make an apology. If things have gone this far, do not be afraid to lose face.

12. *Do nothing.* If something will make matters worse, do nothing. If the client is determined to leave and help is not immediately available, let the client go. *Never* attempt to touch a client under these circumstances

without first indicating what you are about to do and getting the client's agreement to do so.

13. *Give validation.* In a sincere and empathic manner, acknowledge that the person has a good reason for feeling that way and let him or her leave.

All human services providers and especially crisis workers should undergo training in simple self-defense and take-down procedures (Blair, 1991; Turnbull et al., 1990). Neglecting to learn how to deal with a noncompliant teenager whom one of our coworkers thought could be manhandled cost the worker a broken rib. Following the incident, all human services personnel in the facility underwent training in physical self-defense and containment procedures. Numerous subsequent incidents were handled effectively without injury either to the clients or to the staff.

There are numerous facilities that provide such training for little or no charge. Local YMCAs or YWCAs and college continuing education courses may offer such instruction, or the local high school wrestling coach may even be prevailed upon. Instruction should be a priority of the institution, and *all* personnel should receive training.

Stage 7: Seclusion.   Seclusion may be generally differentiated from time out by its length, its setting, and its involuntary nature. Seclusion is a more severe type of limit setting for the client in a safe and secure environment where the client can reorganize thinking, feeling, and behavior (Holmes & Werner, 1966; Mattson & Sacks, 1978). There are three reasons for seclusion: (1) the client is agitated, hyperactive, verbally threatening, or damaging property; (2) the client is impulsive or intrusive and does not respond to limit setting; (3) the client is making suicidal gestures and is unable or unwilling to make a verbal contract about controlling behavior (Baradell, 1985).

In the confrontation with Jason, a response team has been called and is ready to take Jason to seclusion. Carol has slowly and carefully removed her jewelry to avoid cutting anyone in case she becomes involved.

Carol: I'd really like you to go on your own down to time out. It's up to you. You can go on your own right now or the technicians will take you to seclusion.

Even at this late hour, the worker is still attempting to allow Jason to exercise options and make choices (Baradell, 1985).

Jason: I ain't gonna go nowhere 'ceptin' outta here.

Carol backs away and the response team moves in. On a predetermined signal by the leader, they quickly take Jason down. One member holds his head, and the other four carry him to seclusion.

Once placed in seclusion, the client is oriented to what is going to occur, and a staff member is assigned to monitor the client. Checks are made at 15-, 30-, or 60-minute intervals, depending on the mental status of the client. Copies of nursing and general-care orders are given to both staff and the client. Seclusion has a low level of sensory input—no radio or television, no visitors—and emphasis is on biological needs. "Low level" does not mean that the client is sensorily deprived. It is important to prevent feelings of abandonment. The client is shown acceptance by the human services worker and reassured that seclusion is necessary and temporary and that the client can return to normal routine when behavior calms down (Baradell, 1985).

Carol: I'm sorry you chose to go to seclusion, Jason. You decided to exercise that option, but when you can agree to not make threats, control your behavior to the point you can talk this through, and make a written contract as to what you will do, you can come back out.

In an acute stage of agitation such as Jason has just experienced, it is no longer appropriate to explore conflicts or feelings (Ruesch, 1973). Carol's communication with the client is brief, direct, concrete, but kind. Given the sensory overload of the client, sleep is an excellent therapeutic modality, and the client should be allowed to use it (Baradell, 1985).

Seclusion or extended time out also has an effect upon other members of the community (Jones, 1976). Other residents will demonstrate a variety of feelings ranging from concern to fear. It is important that residents' questions be answered as fully as possible and plans made that incorporate their help in expediting the client's return to the community. Having a community meeting specifically for dealing with the concerns of the other residents is worthwhile. Many times the group can act as a therapeutic agent; encourage members to discuss how they can help the client by reinforcing or ignoring particular behaviors that caused the problem in the first place.

As the client is able to regain control, successive approximation is used to reintegrate the client back into the community. The goal of successive approximation is to break the total task into attainable small steps. A major fault of attempts to manage behavior is requiring total and immediate compliance to task. Verbal and written contracts ensure understanding of limits. The client discusses feelings about the experience with the human services worker and fully explores feelings of trepidation and stigma about returning to the community (Baradell, 1985). One negative footnote is appropriate here. A few clients may use seclusion as a way of achieving notoriety and a macho image (Gutheil, 1978). If such a hidden agenda is suspected, the human services worker should thoroughly discuss this problem with the other residents and obtain their help in being nonresponsive to the client's "tough" behavior.

Stage 8: Restraints.   If the client is acting out and will not go to seclusion, restraints will have to be used. Restraints are employed when it is evident that the client may be harmful to self or others (Tardiff, 1984a, p. 48). First, a response team that is trained to apply restraints to a client should be formed and be on call at all times (Wood & Khuri, 1984, p. 81). If the person is to be restrained, then adequate staff should be available and should consist of at least one person for each limb and another person who serves as leader, for a total of five members. Written guidelines and constant rehearsal of procedures with observation and critique should be made to keep the team's skills well honed (Tardiff, 1984b).

If at all possible, the crisis worker should not be involved in the episode, since involvement may erect barriers to future therapeutic endeavors. Once the decision to restrain the client has been made, then the team should move fast and no further attempts at communication should be made. In an emergency, if not enough staff are present to contain the client adequately, tossing a sheet over the client's head will provide enough distraction and be confining enough to enable staff to control the client (Vinick, 1986). At a predetermined signal, each staff member seizes and controls one extremity. With a backward motion the client is brought gently to the ground. The leader controls the client's head to prevent biting, and without choking, hitting, or verbal abuse the client is carried face down with four-point restraints to a room where five-point restraints may be applied and the client's condition monitored (Tardiff, 1984a, p. 47).

Restraints are most often employed in psychiatric facilities and are used in conjunction with a request from the nursing staff and backed by a doctor's order. Care needs to be taken in the use of restraints, and specific procedures as outlined in the American Nurses Association's (1974) *A Plan for the Implementation of the Standards of Nursing Practice* should be followed. When a client is placed in restraints, whether two-, four-, or five-point, close observation is absolutely necessary. Under no circumstances should clients be restrained without such guidelines and available professional medical staff.

Stage 9: Sedation.   If all else fails, then the client needs to be sedated. The problem now becomes clearly medical, and until the medical staff feels that medication is no longer necessary, there is little the human services worker can do.

With Jason, if sedation is needed, it does not mean the end of Jason's story. Stage 9 is essentially a complete time out for both Jason and the staff. For Jason, it will allow the sensory overload he is experiencing to diminish and return to normal limits. For the staff, it will give them time to reorganize their thoughts on how best to deal with this highly agitated adolescent. The overriding philosophy is that while plans may fail, people do not. This philosophy especially holds true for clients such as Jason who are resistant, aggressive, and noncompliant to treatment. When Jason comes out of sedation, the staff will start down the treatment road with him again and will have developed a new plan to deal with this angry young man.

THE VIOLENT GERIATRIC CLIENT

While medical science has been able to prolong the lives of Americans, the neuropsychiatric disorders concomitant with increased longevity remain beyond the reach of medical science at present. Alzheimer's disease is but one of many of the organic brain problems that the geriatric population currently faces. Accompanying the neuropsychiatric problems of the geriatric client are reduced judgment and increased impulsivity, which are precursors of violent behavior (Petrie, 1984, p. 107). The assumption that the elderly are passive recipients of care is misguided. Study after study indicates this clientele to be at risk with regard to violent behavior (Climent & Ervin, 1972; Johnson, Frankel, & Ferrence, 1975; Ochitill & Kreiger, 1982; Petrie, Lawson, & Hollender, 1982; Tardiff & Sweillam, 1980, 1982).

The case of Cliff demonstrates how the agitated and mildly disoriented elderly client can be stabilized without the use of medication. Reality orientation (Taulbee & Folsom, 1966), reminiscence (Butler, 1963), and remotivation (Garber, 1965) techniques are presented as workable options for the mildly disoriented elderly. The case of Grace shows how validation therapy (Feil, 1982) may be used with the severely disoriented elderly. The cases illustrate that the psychologically infirm elderly do not always have to spend this final stage of their lives in a chemically induced compliant state.

Mild Disorientation: The Case of Cliff

Cliff Hastings has lived a full and eventful life, but now, at the age of 74, he is a resident of a skilled nursing care facility. He was a strapping man who had worked all over the world on big construction projects until he was 72 years of age. He invented many engineering techniques in steamfitting and chilled water cooling systems. He was well respected by his men as a fair boss and had earned a worldwide reputation as a man whom one could call when there was an impossible job to be done. He lost his wife to cancer ten years ago, but submerged himself in his work and lived a highly productive life as a widower. He has had excellent relationships with his two children, Jan and Robert. Although they and their families are geographically distant from Cliff, they love their father very much and are very concerned about him.

At age 73, Cliff got up one morning, prepared to go to work, and fell flat on his face with a stroke. Although he recovered to the extent that he was able to shuffle around the house, lung complications set in. He was diagnosed as having emphysema and went on oxygen. Six months later, he was no longer able to take care of himself physically, was starting to have memory lapses, and was moved to Hursthaven Nursing Home by his children, who made the agonizing decision to place him there because of his physical and psychological infirmities.

At Hursthaven, he has become progressively more confused about people, places, and times, and when asked to do something has been either rebellious or passively resistant. A crisis was precipitated when he knocked an oxygen bottle over in the middle of the night because the "Arabs were after him" and broke the nose of a male attendant who tried to calm him down as he was attempting to struggle out of his bed. Cliff is about to meet a new type of human services worker. Her name is Marilyn and she is a gerontological counselor. She has just been retained by Hursthaven to deal with crisis situations like Cliff's.

Assessment.   Marilyn has thoroughly reviewed Cliff's chart and has discussed his case with the medical and primary care staff. Many of the primary care staff maintain that Cliff is noncompliant, badly disoriented, and dangerous, and they would like to keep him heavily sedated. Cliff's stroke, his unplanned aggressive outburst, his hostile and uncooperative behavior, his fear of the medical equipment, and his depression, plus the fact that his outburst was at night, all point toward vascular impairment (Petrie, 1984, pp. 110–111) and support the staff's contention that little but chemical restraints is left for Cliff. Marilyn decides to conduct her own assessment by interviewing Cliff. The worker has three purposes in mind: first, to determine the client's degree of disorientation and agitation; second, to use her therapeutic skills to reduce his disruptive behavior and help him return to a state of equilibrium with as little reliance on medication as possible; and third, to help Cliff use whatever resources he has to live this final stage of his life as fully as he is able.

Marilyn: Hello, I'm Marilyn. I don't believe I've met you. You seem pretty angry about something.

Cliff: [*Suspiciously.*] Who the hell are you?

Marilyn: I'm new here, part of the staff, and I'm getting around meeting all the residents. Sorry you're so angry. What can I do to help?

Cliff: I'm Cliff Hastings, and I'm mad as hell. Look at what those SOBs have done to me. I pay $3,000 a month for this place to strap me down. I'll kill the bastards if I get a chance. Can you get me out of here?

Marilyn: [*Speaking in a strong but soft and empathic voice, while pulling up a chair and sitting down directly in his line of sight.*] No! I can't right now. I guess I'd be mad too if I were strapped in like that. Do you know where you are?

Cliff: I'm in Hell and these people are all devils.

Marilyn: It may feel like that right now, but this is Hursthaven Nursing Home. Do you know that?

Cliff: Too damn well.

Marilyn: Do you know what day it is?

Cliff: Who cares? They're all the same in here.

The worker assesses Cliff's degree of contact with reality by determining how well oriented he is to person, place, and time. Although the client does not give specific, concrete responses, his retorts indicate that he is fairly well in touch with reality, given his present agitated state.

Marilyn: I'm sorry you're feeling so angry. Can I get you a drink of water?

Eliciting trust.   Offering food or drink to agitated clients tends to defuse the situation and make them more accepting of initiating overtures the worker may tender (Wood & Khuri, 1984, p. 67). The worker also sits down by Cliff and meets him at eye level. She places herself on his physical level and in his direct line of sight. Standing over a client who is confused tends to distort the caregiver's image in grotesque ways and may be very threatening (Wolanin & Phillips, 1981, p. 106).

Cliff: [*Takes a sip of water from cup Marilyn offers.*] Yeah, that's the least somebody around this place could do for the money I pay to be doped up and trussed up like a pig.

Marilyn: How do you feel?

Cliff: How the hell do you think I feel, young lady?

Marilyn: I guess I'd not only feel like a pig all trussed up, but mad as a wildcat in a gunnysack. How did this happen?

The crisis worker matches the vernacular of the client and interjects a bit of humor (Tomine, 1986). The worker is interested in knowing what happened, but her major concern is to continue posing open-ended questions to assess how much in touch with reality Cliff is and to let him know she is interested in and concerned about him. The worker manages to gain a working rapport with the client and explores last night's incident.

Marilyn: So what happened last night that got you in that fix?

Cliff: The Arab, he was after me. He was gonna strangle me, but nobody believes me. [*Points to attendant.*] That guy said it was one of the guys that work here at night. Said I busted his nose. Well, it was the Arabs. Sneaky devils.

Marilyn: Why do you think it was the Arabs?

Reality orientation.   The worker is taking a first step in attempting to relieve Cliff's confusion by using reality orientation (Taulbee & Folsom, 1966). Reality orientation focuses on anchoring clients to who they are, where they are, and why they are there. When a client's response or behavior is out of touch with reality, the worker asks the client a *why* question, in an approach contrary to that of most therapeutic interventions (Taulbee, 1978, p. 207). Marilyn does this because she is trying to find out the reason for the behavior. Once the worker knows that, then she can start to reorient the client.

Cliff: I spent a lot of time in Arabia, you know. Worked in construction. Put up a lot of refrigeration plants and steam systems. Hard to believe you'd need steam in that hothouse. Sometimes I wish I was back in Arabia. But that doesn't mean any damn camel choker can come in here in the middle of the night and kill me. I had plenty of close scrapes back there, and they didn't get me and they won't get me here.

Marilyn: [*Genuinely interested.*] Hey! That sounds pretty exciting. I've hardly been out of the Midwest. I'll bet you've seen some pretty hair-raising things and I can guess how you might think somebody was an Arab, being in a strange place like this.

Cliff rambles on for quite a while about his experiences there, with Marilyn listening and responding using person-centered techniques of attending, affirming, restating for clarification, reflecting feelings, and asking open-ended questions.

Pacing.   Cliff's response about working in Arabia gives the worker a clue about the image he saw attacking him in the night. However, she does not try to change his mind about what happened. The worker keeps pace with Cliff. She lets him tell his story without hurrying or trying to persuade him that he was mistaken last night. Patience is of maximum benefit in gaining the trust she will need if she is to accomplish anything with the client (Taulbee, 1978, p. 210). This approach is in direct contrast to that of most of the staff in the facility, who are pressed to get tasks accomplished in a specified time. Indeed, trying to gain compliance by coercing the client to meet institutional needs is likely to engender more agitated behavior.

Reminiscence therapy.   The worker's approach in urging Cliff to talk about his past is contradictory to most standard operating procedures and generally accepted counseling technique. Most therapeutic systems try very hard to keep clients in present time and view trips to the past as counterproductive to changing real-time problems. However, allowing geriatric clients to ruminate about past experiences can be therapeutically effective (Ebersole, 1978a, p. 145). Reminiscence therapy (Butler, 1963) is a nonthreatening experience that allows older clients to reflect on their lives and restore credibility to them (Miller, 1986). It also offers the opportunity for physical contact and validation for what the elderly have done with their lives (Baker, 1985). Memory dysfunction and personality disorganization is central to Cliff's current crisis and confusion. Reminiscence helps in personality reorganization and increases self-confidence because it draws on aspects of long-term memory that have been imprinted and can be recalled easily (Singer, Tracz, & Dworkin, 1991). Reminiscence can be therapeutic and healing for the client, while at a more basic level it is a simple, enjoyable sharing of anecdote that allows the worker to form a close affiliation with the client (Ebersole, 1978a, p. 145). Over the long term, using reminiscence can allow the following positive outcomes to occur (McMahon & Rhudick, 1964, pp. 292–298; Singer et al., 1991):

1. maintaining self-esteem in the face of declining physical capacities
2. coping with grief and depression resulting from personal losses
3. contributing significantly to a society of which the elderly client is still a member
4. retaining a sense of identity in an increasingly estranged environment
5. decreasing social and emotional isolation by involvement with others
6. decreasing depression and loneliness through social interaction
7. developing a renewed social network
8. renewing social skills.

Cliff: Yeah . . . [*Voice trails off.*] . . . I used to be hot stuff . . . but I'm not so hot now. Hell, half the time I don't even know who, what, or where I am.

Marilyn: [*Touches client's arm lightly with her hand.*] It sounds like that's pretty scary, having run things most of your life and now things are out of control.

Cliff: I hate to admit it, but that's right. All my life doing a job. Now I got to have help getting to the john! If that isn't something. How'd you like that? It embarrasses the hell out of me. They treat me like a 2 year old.

Marilyn: So being embarrassed and not being treated like a man is one of the worst parts of being here. I wonder what we might do to change that?

Anchoring. The worker uses a reflective statement of feeling to integrate the client's past with his present. By bringing up past incidents and hooking them to the present, the worker attempts to reinforce and help the client reassert his competence. She also uses touch to anchor Cliff psychologically to someone in the institution (Wolanin & Phillips, 1981, pp. 105–106). Prior to the assault, a kind but sterile atmosphere had existed for Cliff at Hursthaven. Like most human beings, he has not responded well to living in an emotional vacuum. Since the attack, the atmosphere between Cliff and the staff has become adversarial in nature. Marilyn needs to change Cliff's view of the staff as being against him and likewise the staff's view that Cliff is to be avoided. The worker will instruct primary care staff to start Cliff on a 24-hour orientation program once the present crisis is over. All staff members who come in contact with Cliff during the course of the day will introduce themselves, call Cliff by name, state the date, give a short preview of the next few hours' activities, and also explain any procedures, medical or otherwise, that they are carrying out. By consistently orienting the client, the staff takes a first step in treating confusion (Taulbee, 1978, p. 209).

The worker also picks up on Cliff's fear of losing control. Being wildly out of control is completely out of character for clients like Cliff, who are frightened at the prospect of losing their minds. Even more fears are generated when elderly clients sense someone is afraid of them or avoiding them because of fear of violence (Lion & Pasternak, 1973).

The crisis worker engages in a number of activities in this dialogue. The most important is that she has made a small but significant change in the interactional system that currently exists between Cliff and the staff by representing herself as an empathic, caring spokesperson for the institution and as an advocate for the client (Fisch, Weakland, & Segal, 1983). Second, she reflects his anger, fear, and loss of control. She acknowledges and validates his experiences. She is not just being platitudinous. She knows that the more he lacks current orientation, the more the staff will tend to avoid him. The more he is avoided the less contact he has with people, the more out of touch and disoriented he is likely to become (Petrie, 1984, pp. 114–115). The cycle can become deeper and deeper if uninterrupted and may cause even more disorientation and aggressive acts in the future (Miller, 1986).

Distinguishing between illusions and hallucinations. Marilyn understands that what agitated Cliff was probably not a hallucination, as the staff thinks, but more than likely an illusion. While piecing together the tale of the night before, she determines that one of the Sisters of Charity who works at the nursing home made rounds about the time Cliff became agitated. The sister's veil may have made her look like an Arab in the dim light. Thus, what Cliff saw was probably an illusion based in fact, not fiction. By proposing an explanation of the event, she allows Cliff to understand that he was not delusional but was misperceiving reality. The two problems are very different, and the difference is of great significance in calming the client. Although this may sound like a very pat conclusion, such happenings are all too common among mildly confused and disoriented clients. Many times, very definite, concrete stimuli create illusions that disrupt peace of mind for geriatric clients, leaving them to doubt their own perceptions. By being a bit of a detective, the worker may often be able to ascertain what is responsible for the illusion. It is extremely important for the worker to relate such a hypothesis to mildly confused clients like Cliff who are very much concerned about keeping in touch with reality (Wolanin & Phillips, 1981, p. 107).

Marilyn: [*Relates her hypothesis to the client.*] So I believe that you weren't really crazy last night, but actually saw Sister Lucy making rounds. If you think about it, it makes sense.

Cliff: I don't know. I still really believe there was an Arab in here.

Marilyn: From all you've told me about your experiences there, I can understand that. But I also know that when you're zonked out in a strange place with the medical equipment around and strangers passing to and fro, suddenly waking up and seeing things differently is not uncommon and doesn't mean you're nuts. I'll bet if you think about it, it has happened before. I know it has happened to me. There's a big difference between misunderstanding what you see and seeing something that isn't there. I'm not trying to change your mind, but maybe it's possible. I'd like you to think about it.

Sundown syndrome.   Because the event happened in the early evening, the sundown syndrome must be considered. Events that accompany the end of the day in an institution are strange and unsettling to residents who have been used to a regimen of activities based on their own time and the security of their own home. Unmet toilet needs, absence of a snack, different noises, decreased light, effects of sedatives, and presence of fewer personnel all add up to fear and strangeness without the support of another human being. These conditions can lead the client to act out (Wolanin & Phillips, 1981, p. 107). The worker will need to study the events surrounding the assault to determine if other factors in the institution caused Cliff to act out. Given the need to further assure Cliff about the reality of the situation, Marilyn relates the problems that occur with the approach of evening in the institution and makes some suggestions about how things might be changed to make this time less threatening.

Marilyn: So a lot of times when evening comes at Hursthaven things can get exciting for the reasons I mentioned. If you could make things here a bit more like home, what would they be?

Cliff: Well, I used to put my earphones on and listen to some country music and have a beer before I hit the hay. I don't know much else, just watch TV and stuff. No special furniture or anything. I lived in apartments most of my life.

Marilyn: I notice that there's not much of you in this room. It looks like a hospital room instead of Cliff's room. You mentioned a lot of items you collected over the years and picture albums of all your travels. Where are they?

Cliff: Oh, my kids just stored them away.

Marilyn: I'd like to see if we couldn't get some of those in here, dress the place up a bit so when people come by they'd know this was Cliff Hastings, world class engineer, who lives here.

Security blankets.   The worker is proposing that articles familiar to Cliff be brought into the room for two reasons. First, creating a familiar environment may go a long way toward creating a basis in reality for the fact that this is now Cliff's home and reconciling him to this stage in his life (Petrie, 1984, p. 116). Second, suddenly awakening in a medical environment with a variety of strange machines and tubes running in and out of one's body is extremely threatening because such foreign objects alter a person's body images and surroundings in a very negative way (Wolanin & Phillips, 1981, p. 106). Having familiar objects immediately visible can help the client reorient without becoming agitated in the process. Marilyn will check with administrative staff to see if Cliff's stereo equipment can be brought into his room. The worker will also check with medical staff to see if a bottle of beer in the evening will confound his medication. If possible, providing these amenities will further approximate the client's routine at home and provide orientation and security (Miller, 1986).

Remotivation.   Finally, the worker will attempt to involve Cliff in the activities of the institution. It is important to involve clients interpersonally and have them become physically and psychologically active in their environment. For people like Cliff who have been highly active throughout their lives, it is critical to fill idle time in meaningful ways to keep such clients from drifting into depression (Donahue, 1965). This does not mean forcing and cajoling clients into doing something contrary to what interests them. Playing bingo might be fun for many people, but forcing a person to engage in such an activity is inappropriate (Miller, 1986). After listening to Cliff, the worker makes a proposal designed to reinvolve him with the human race.

Marilyn: I don't know if this would be your cup of tea or not, but I'd like you to consider a proposition I have to make. Hursthaven has an alliance with St. Peter's Orphanage. None of those kids have anybody to care about them. I have a couple of boys in mind that I think you could do some good with. You've got some great stories that they'd love and probably some wisdom that could be helpful to those guys. They just mainly need a man to talk to, and I wonder if you'd be willing to help out.

The worker's agenda is twofold. She is truthful in what she tells Cliff. She also knows that the two boys will have a positive effect on Cliff in turn. Aged people seem particularly interested in sharing their experiences with the young (Ebersole, 1978b, p. 241). Cliff's candidness, wisdom, and trove of stories are likely to have a positive effect on two boys who are as anchorless as Cliff. He will have to get involved in the planning that the residents of Hursthaven carry out in coordinating activities with St. Peter's. Involvement with other members of the community, heretofore nil, will gently push him back into the mainstream, reinforce his dignity, and provide him with interaction that he will find meaningful and enjoyable. Engaging in this activity will give the client a stake in the community and will, Marilyn hopes, focus his psychic energy on something besides his own outcast state (Miller, 1986).

The worker is engaging in a variation of remotivation therapy at this point. Remotivation therapy is a group technique that is used to stimulate and revitalize individuals who are no longer interested in the present or the future (Dennis, 1978, p. 219). It is based on a combination of reminiscence and reality orientation. Remotivation attempts to persuade the client that he is accepted by others as an individual who has unique and important traits that make him distinguishable from everyone else (Garber, 1965). Remotivation therapy creates a bridge between the individual's self-perception and the perception of others. Reminiscing about one's experiences with the concrete world and identifying and asserting one's experiences through interactions with others often lead to strengthening the concept of reality. Being encouraged to describe oneself concretely as a person with roles and specific social functions and speaking accurately about past and present experiences gives a person strength (Dennis, 1978, p. 220).

While Marilyn's hypothesis is that Cliff will work better with young boys because he has been a mentor to numerous young engineers over his lifetime, many other elderly clients can profit from reminiscence groups that are composed of their peers (Singer et al., 1991). These groups enable the elderly to share their experiences with one another, come to terms with their past experiences, and use them for more meaningful living in the present. Such groups can do much to negate the loneliness, helplessness, and hopelessness that often pervade the elderly and that in turn lead to further physical and mental deterioration and result in crisis situations like Cliff's.

Severe Disorientation: The Case of Grace

Whereas Cliff is only mildly confused and fairly coherent as he ruminates about his past, many geriatric clients the worker will encounter have lost touch with reality. Verbalization of past events becomes commingled with fantasy. The standard regimen for working with geriatric clients has been to attempt to reality-orient them to the present. Such an approach becomes problematic for moderately confused clients and profoundly so for those who have almost entirely retreated from the reality of the present. Attempts to orient moderately-to-severely confused old, old clients to person, place, and time are generally futile. For many of these clients, nothing could be less worthwhile, for there is clearly not much in the present worth remembering (Miller, 1986).

Naomi Feil has seized upon this notion and has developed validation therapy (Feil, 1982). Her thesis is to acknowledge the feelings of the person no matter how irrational they may seem to be. By dignifying feelings the worker validates the person. To deny the feelings of the client is to deny past existence and thus deny the personhood of the individual.

Feil also believes that validating early memories enables clients to resolve the past and justify their role in old age. Positive outcomes from using the approach are restoration of self-worth, reduction of stress, justification of living, resolution of unfinished conflicts, and a better and more secure feeling for the client (Feil, 1982, p. 1). The worker continuously validates the client as a first step in restoring self-worth and affirming that at least one person is interested and concerned enough to listen to what the client's life has been. Anyone overhearing a dialogue between a worker and a client who has severely regressed into an irrational past would probably wonder at first whether the worker had also become senile. The worker must have some creative insight into the verbal meanderings and repetitive behaviors of the client in order for validation therapy to be effective (Miller, 1986). Listen to Marilyn as she attempts to convince an 83-year-old woman to go to dinner.

The woman, Grace, is standing in the hallway refusing to be moved. She is engaging in a rocking motion with her arms and softly humming to herself. Staff's efforts to get her to go to dinner have been fruitless and she is becoming increasingly agitated as a number of staff members are attempting to orient her and get her to comply with their requests. Marilyn enters this scene and asks the rest of the staff to leave them.

Grace: There, there! Don't you cry.

Marilyn: I see you're really concerned about your baby.

Grace: Yes, I've been up all night with Ellen. She must have colic, but I can't seem to get her to settle down. I need to get Dr. Heinz, he's our family doctor, a very good one, but I don't have anyone to hitch the team to go to town and get him.

Marilyn: It really worries you that Ellen doesn't seem to be getting any better. You must be awfully tired and hungry!

Grace: Even though Ellen's cranky, she's no bother, she's really a beautiful baby. It's just that her father isn't around much, he works on the railroad and I could use some help sometimes.

Marilyn: You must love her very much. Maybe we could go down to dinner together and you could tell me some more about her.

Grace: She's got to have quiet to get to sleep. It's too noisy there.

Marilyn: It's important to you that she gets to sleep. Perhaps we could have dinner served in your room. It'd be quiet there.

Grace: Well, I suppose, if you'd really like to.

In this short exchange the worker demonstrates two critical components of validation therapy. The client may well have lost the ability to comprehend and reason with any degree of complexity. By keeping communication short and simple, the worker avoids losing the client in a variety of ideas that may rapidly become overwhelming. The worker also responds directly and continuously to Grace's feelings, validating to her that the symbolic act she is engaging in is highly important (Miller, 1986).

Although the purpose of validation therapy is not to manipulate the client, the worker's approach is far better than forcibly taking the client to the dining room, where she will probably be so distraught over having to neglect her baby that she will not eat anyway. Whether Grace has ever had a baby named Ellen, or whether she is trying to resolve some shortcomings she has long felt in regard to mothering, is of little concern in the present moment. What is of concern is that the worker treat the situation as if it were real and of importance to the client and acknowledge the client's scattered thoughts and feelings in a congruent, empathic manner. Validation therapy is not intended to return the client to reality. However, for the human services worker who has to intervene in a crisis situation with the severely disoriented elderly, it does have the potential to calm them down, avoid situations conducive to acting out, and provide an effective therapeutic technique in an area where few have been found (Miller, 1986).

FOLLOW-UP WITH STAFF VICTIMS

Staff who are victims of violent attacks by clients may have emotional responses that include hypervigilance, startle responses, intrusive thoughts, and unresolved anger (Lenehan & Turner, 1984, p. 256), much like the victims of PTSD. Lanza (1984) found that nurses who had experienced such attacks had negative emotional, cognitive, and behavioral reactions up to a year afterward. It is extremely important to work through the aftermath of violent behavior suffered by staff, for two reasons: first, so that the victim does not become debilitated personally and professionally by the incident, and second, because other members of the staff will perceive that the institution takes such events very seriously and is concerned for their safety as well.

After an attack, staff members initially may ascribe blame to the victim to ease their own fear and trepidation about the possibility that it could happen to them. Under no circumstances should this be allowed to happen. Sympathy and support for the victim are vital. Pity, condescension, or subtle implications about provoking the assault should be avoided. Institutional support groups for victims of violence should be available (Stortch, 1991) and staff should be prepared to give immediate help with problem solving and decision making, such as determining injuries, providing medical transportation, staying with the victim, providing moral support, and helping with medical, legal, and police reports (Lenehan & Turner, 1984, pp. 255–256).

As soon as the victim is able, a psychological autopsy should be performed on the incident. A psychological autopsy examines in detail the situation that led to the violent episode. All staff members who are involved with the client attend the autopsy. It dissects what the staff and the client did behaviorally before, during, and after the incident. Further attention is given to the environmental setting to determine if it played a role in instigating the aggressive behavior. Hopefully, the autopsy will provide clues as to the *whys, hows,* and *whats* of the incident so it does not recur. The victim's opinions should be solicited and should be used as expert testimony. Staff gather to discuss what happened, work through feelings about the event, and generate options for preventing a recurrence (Lenehan & Turner, 1984, p. 259). By reviewing the traumatic experience, the victim is also able to deal with feelings of loss of security and control. As with any other type of violence, the victim needs to be able to review the assault for clues and causes as a way of resolving the traumatic experience (Lenehan & Turner, 1984, pp. 254–255). If the victim continues to have problems, then therapeutic help is called for and should be provided by the institution.

Murray and Snyder (1991) describe a consultation service of psychiatric nurses who track all of the assaults in a large metropolitan hospital. As soon as feasible, they sit down with the victim and attempt to obtain as complete a description as possible of what happened before, during, and after the assault. Questions are asked to enable the staff member to recall and verbalize additional aspects of the incident, including sensory experiences. A problem-solving approach is encouraged to support the natural tendency of the victim to want to learn from the incident and identify alternative approaches for the future.

SUMMARY

Violence in the human service's setting has increased exponentially in the past two decades. Increased abuse of drugs, closing down of the large state mental hospitals, increased adjudication of felons to mental health facilities, and increases in the geriatric population have been major contributors to this phenomenon. The problem pervades all parts of human services. Both service providers and their staffs have largely looked the other way, and when violence against staff has occurred it has been seen as going with the territory, or the victim has been blamed for being stupid and careless.

Since the range and type of institutions that provide extended care for clients with every conceivable type of problem is so broad, this chapter has endeavored to present interventional approaches that represent generically what all crisis workers need to know to stay out of harm's way and still provide effective service to their clientele. We examined two representative types of client: the male adolescent who is adjudicated as delinquent and the geriatric client who is suffering disorientation.

The techniques presented in this chapter range from option therapy to validation therapy. Designed to help clients, these techniques and others we have discussed are also intended to prevent the human services worker from being the object of an assault. Although neophytes to the human services business may dismiss the idea of being hurt by one of their clients, statistics indicate a strong likelihood that sometime during their career they will become victims of violence. The objective of this chapter has been to provide techniques that will minimize that chance.

REFERENCES

American Nurses Association. (1974). *A plan for the implementation of the standards of nursing practice.* Kansas City, MO: Author.

American Psychiatric Association. (1974). *Clinical aspects of the violent individual.* Washington, DC: American Psychiatric Association Press.

Annis, L. V., McClaren, H. A., & Baker, C. A. (1984). Who kills us? In J. T. Turner (Ed.), *Violence in the medical care setting: A survival guide* (pp. 19–31). Rockville, MD: Aspen Systems Corp.

Appelbaum, P. S. (1984). Hospitalization of the dangerous patient: Legal pressures and clinical responses. *Bulletin of the American Academy of Psychiatry and the Law, 12,* 323–329.

Bach y Rita, G., Lion, J. R., & Climent, C. E. (1971). Episodic dyscontrol: A study of 630 violent patients. *American Journal of Psychiatry, 128,* 1473–1478.

Baker, N. J. (1985). Reminiscing in group therapy for self-worth. *Journal of Gerontological Nursing, 11,* 21–24.

Baradell, J. G. (1985, February). Humanistic care of the patient in seclusion. *Journal of Psychosocial Nursing and Mental Health Services, 23,* 9–14.

Beck, J. C. (1988). The therapist's legal duty when the patient may be violent. *Psychiatric Clinics of North America, 11,* 665–679.

Becker, W. C. (1971). *Parents are teachers.* Champaign, IL: Research Press.

Blair, T. D. (1991, May). Assaultive behavior: Does provocation begin in the front office? *Journal of Psychosocial Nursing and Mental Health Services, 29,* 21–26.

Breakwell, G. M. (1989). *Facing physical violence,* London: Routledge.

Butler, R. (1963). The life review: An interpretation of reminiscence in the aged. *Psychiatry, 26,* 65–76.

Canter, L., & Canter, E. (1982). *Assertive discipline for parents.* Santa Monica, CA: Canter Associates.

Climent, C. E., & Ervin, F. R. (1972). Historical data in the evaluation of violent subjects. *Archives of General Psychiatry, 27,* 621–624.

Dennis, H. (1978). Remotivation therapy groups. In I. M. Burnside (Ed.), *Working with the elderly: Group processes and techniques* (pp. 219–235). North Scituate, MA: Duxbury Press.

Dinkmeyer, D. C., Pew, W. L., & Dinkmeyer, D. C., Jr. (1979). *Adlerian counseling and psychotherapy.* Monterey, CA: Brooks/Cole.

Doms, R. W. (1984). Personal distress devices for health care personnel. In J. T. Turner (Ed.), *Violence in the medical care setting: A survival guide* (pp. 225–229). Rockville, MD: Aspen Systems Corp.

Donahue, H. H. (1965). Expanding the program. *Hospital and Community Psychiatry, 17,* 117–118.

Dubin, W. R. (1981). Evaluating and managing the violent patient. *Annals of Emergency Medicine, 10,* 481–484.

Durivage, A. (1989). Assaultive behavior: Before it happens. *Canadian Journal of Psychiatry, 34,* 393–397.

Dyer, W. O., Murrell, D. S., & Wright, D. (1984). Training for hospital security: An alternative to training negligence suits. In J. T. Turner (Ed.), *Violence in the medical care setting: A survival guide* (pp. 1–18). Rockville, MD: Aspen Systems Corp.

Ebersole, P. P. (1978a). A theoretical approach to the use of reminiscence. In I. M. Burnside (Ed.), *Working with the elderly: Group processes and techniques* (pp. 139–154). North Scituate, MA: Duxbury Press.

Ebersole, P. P. (1978b). Establishing reminiscence groups. In I. M. Burnside (Ed.), *Working with the elderly: Group processes and techniques* (pp. 236–254). North Scituate, MA: Duxbury Press.

Epstein, M., & Carter, L. (1988). *Training manual for Headquarters staff.* Lawrence, KS: Headquarters, Inc.

Fareta, G. (1981). A profile of aggression from adolescence to adulthood: An 18-year follow-up of psychiatrically disturbed and violent adolescents. *American Journal of Orthopsychiatry, 51,* 439–453.

Feil, N. (1982). *Validation: The Feil method.* Cleveland, OH: Edward Feil Productions.

Felthous, A. R. (1987). Liability of treaters for injuries to others: Erosion of three immunities. *Bulletin of the American Academy of Psychiatry and Law, 15,* 115–125.

Fisch, R., Weakland, J. H., & Segal, L. (1983). *The tactics of change.* San Francisco: Jossey-Bass.

Garber, R. S. (1965). A psychiatrist's view of remotivation. *Mental Hospitals, 16,* 219–221.

Glasser, W. (1965). *Reality therapy.* New York: Harper & Row.

Glasser, W. (1969). *Schools without failure.* New York: Harper & Row.

Gomez, R. (1983). Demographic and nondemographic characteristics of psychiatric emergency patients. *Psychiatric Clinics of North America, 6,* 213–224.

Greenfield, T. K., McNeil, D. E., & Binder, R. L. (1989). Violent behavior and length of psychiatric hospitalization. *Hospital and Community Psychiatry, 40,* 809–814.

Gutheil, T. G. (1978). Observation on the theoretical basis for seclusion of the psychiatric inpatient. *American Journal of Psychiatry, 135,* 325–328.

Hamstra, B. (1986). Neurobiological substrates of violence: An overview for forensic clinicians. *Journal of Psychiatry and Law, 14,* 349–374.

Heilbrun, A. B. (1990). The measurement of criminal dangerousness as a personality construct: Further validation of a research index. *Journal of Personality Assessment, 54,* 141–148.

Heilbrun, A. B., & Heilbrun, M. R. (1989). Dangerousness and legal insanity. *Journal of Psychiatry and Law, 17,* 39–53.

Holmes, M. J., & Werner, J. A. (1966). *Psychiatric nursing in a therapeutic community.* New York: Macmillan.

House of Representatives Committee on Veterans Affairs. (1981, July 15). *Subcommittee on Hospital Health Care and Security Forces at VA Medical Center.* Washington, DC: U.S. Government Printing Office.

Ishimoto, W. (1984). Security management for health care administrators. In J. T. Turner (Ed.), *Violence in the medical care setting: A survival guide* (pp. 209–223). Rockville, MD: Aspen Systems Corp.

Johnson, F. G., Frankel, B. G., & Ferrence, R. G. (1975). Self-injury in London, Canada: A prospective study. *Canadian Journal of Public Health, 66,* 307–316.

Jones, J. (Speaker). (1984). *Counseling in correctional settings* (Cassette Recording No. 25–6611). Memphis: Memphis State University, Department of Counseling and Personnel Services.

Jones, M. (1976). *Maturation of the therapeutic community.* New York: Human Services Press.

Jones, M. K. (1985, June). Patient violence: Report of 200 incidents. *Journal of Psychosocial Nursing and Mental Health, 23,* 12–17.

Kirk, A. (1989). The prediction of violent behavior during short-term civil commitment. *Bulletin of the American Academy of Psychiatry and Law, 17,* 345–353.

Klassen, D., & O'Connor, W. A. (1988). A prospective study of predictors of violence in adult male mental health admissions. *Law and Human Behavior, 12,* 143–158.

Kroll, J., & Mackenzie, T. B. (1983). When psychiatrists are liable: Risk management and violent patients. *Hospital and Community Psychiatry, 34,* 29–37.

Lakeside Hospital. (1988). *Verbal techniques for de-escalating violent behavior.* Memphis, TN: Author.

Lanza, M. L. (1983). The reactions of nursing staff to physical assault by a patient. *Hospital and Community Psychiatry, 34,* 422–425.

Lanza, M. L. (1984). A follow-up study of nurses' reaction to physical assault. *Hospital and Community Psychiatry, 35,* 492–494.

Lanza, M. L. (1985, June). How nurses react to patient assault. *Journal of Psychosocial Nursing and Mental Health, 23,* 6–11.

LeCroy, C. W. (1988). Anger management or anger expression: Which is most effective? *Residential Treatment for Children and Youth, 5,* 29–39.

Lenehan, G. P., & Turner, J. T. (1984). Treatment of staff victims of violence. In J. T. Turner (Ed.), *Violence in the medical care setting: A survival guide* (pp. 251–260). Rockville, MD: Aspen Systems Corp.

Lewellyn, A. (Speaker). (1985). Counseling emotionally disturbed high school students: The Mattoon, Illinois, TLC program (Cassette Recording No. 12–6611). Memphis: Memphis State University, Department of Counseling and Personnel Services.

Lion, J. R., & Pasternak, S. A. (1973). Countertransference reactions to violent patients. *American Journal of Psychiatry, 130,* 207–210.

Lion, J. R., Snyder, W., & Merrill, G. L. (1981). Underreporting of assaults on staff in state hospitals. *Hospital and Community Psychiatry, 32,* 497–498.

Madden, D. J., Lion, J. R., & Penna, M. W. (1976). Assaults on psychiatrists by patients. *American Journal of Psychiatry, 133,* 422–425.

Marohn, R. C. (1982). Adolescent violence: Causes and treatment. *Journal of the American Academy of Child Psychiatry, 21,* 354–360.

Mattson, M. R., & Sacks, M. H. (1978). Seclusion: Uses and implications. *American Journal of Psychiatry, 135,* 1210–1212.

McCown, C. (Speaker). (1986). Counseling in an adolescent psychiatric treatment facility (Cassette Recording No. 7). Memphis: Memphis State University, Department of Counseling and Personnel Services.

McMahon, A., & Rhudick, P. (1964). Reminiscing: Adaptional significance in the aged. *Archives of General Psychiatry, 10,* 292–298.

McNeil, D. E., Hatcher, C., Zeiner, H., Wolfe, H. L., & Myers, R. S. (1991). Characteristics of persons referred by police to the psychiatric emergency room. *Hospital and Community Psychiatry, 42,* 425–427.

Miller, M. (Speaker). (1986). Counseling geriatric clients (Cassette Recording No. 14). Memphis: Memphis State University, Department of Counseling and Personnel Services.

Monahan, J. (1981). *The clinical prediction of violent behavior.* Rockville, MD: National Institute of Mental Health.

Monahan, J. (1984). The prediction of violent behavior: Toward a second generation of theory and policy. *American Journal of Psychiatry, 141,* 10–15.

Monahan, J. (1988). Risk assessment of violence among the mentally disordered: Generating useful knowledge. *International Journal of Law and Psychiatry, 11,* 249–257.

Moran, J. F. (1984). Teaching the management of violent behavior to nursing staff: A health care model. In J. T. Turner (Ed.), *Violence in the medical care setting: A survival guide* (pp. 231–250). Rockville, MD: Aspen Systems Corp.

Mulvey, E. P., & Lidz, C. W. (1984). Clinical considerations on the prediction of dangerous mental patients. *Clinical Psychology Review, 4,* 379–401.

Murray, G. M., & Snyder, J. C. (1991, July). When staff are assaulted: A nursing consultation support service. *Journal of Psychosocial Nursing and Mental Health Services, 29,* 24–29.

Ochitill, H. N., & Kreiger, M. (1982). Violent behavior among hospitalized medical and surgical patients. *Southern Medical Journal, 75,* 151–155.

Ostrow, E., Marohn, R. C., Offer, D., Curtiss, G., & Feczko, M. (1980). The Adolescent Antisocial Behavior Checklist. *Journal of Clinical Psychology, 36,* 594–601.

Petrie, W. M. (1984). Violence: The geriatric patient. In J. T. Turner (Ed.), *Violence in the medical care setting: A survival guide* (pp. 107–122). Rockville, MD: Aspen Systems Corp.

Petrie, W. M., Lawson, E. C., & Hollender, M. H. (1982). Violence in geriatric patients. *Journal of the American Medical Association, 248,* 443–444.

Piercy, D. (1984). Violence: The drug and alcohol patient. In J. T. Turner (Ed.), *Violence in the medical care setting: A survival guide* (pp. 123–152). Rockville, MD: Aspen Systems Corp.

Pisarick, G. (1981, September). The violent patient. *Nursing,* pp. 63–65.

Rada, R. T. (1981). The violent patient: Rapid assessment and management. *Psychosomatics, 22,* 101–109.

Reid, B. (Speaker). (1986). Counseling in half-way houses (Cassette Recording No. 9). Memphis: Memphis State University, Department of Counseling and Personnel Services.

Rice, M. E., Helzel, M. F., Varney, G. W., & Quinsey, V. L. (1985). Crisis prevention and intervention training for psychiatric hospital staff. *American Journal of Community Psychiatry, 13,* 289–304.

Rofman, E. S., Askinazi, C., & Fant, E. (1980). The prediction of dangerous behavior in emergency civil commitment. *American Journal of Psychiatry, 137,* 1061–1064.

Ruben, I., Wolkon, G., & Yamamoto, J. (1980). Physical attacks on psychiatric residents by patients. *Journal of Nervous and Mental Disease, 168,* 243–245.

Ruesch, J. (1973). *Therapeutic communication.* New York: Norton.

Schultz, L. C. (1987). The social worker as a victim of violence. *Social Casework, 68,* 240–244.

Simonds, J. F., & Kashani, J. (1980). Specific drug use and violence in delinquent boys. *American Journal of Drug and Alcohol Abuse, 7,* 305–322.

Singer, V. I., Tracz, S. M., & Dworkin, S. H. (1991). Reminiscence group therapy: A treatment modality for older adults. *Journal for Specialists in Group Work 16,* 167–171.

Sloore, H. (1988). Use of the MMPI in the prediction of dangerous behavior. *Acta Psychiatrica Belgica, 88,* 42–51.

Star, B. (1984). Patient violence/therapist safety. *Social Work, 29,* 225–230.

Stokeman, C. L. (1982). Questions and answers: Violence among hospitalized mental patients. *Hospital and Community Psychiatry, 33,* 986.

Stortch, D. D. (1991). Starting an in-hospital support group for victims of violence in the psychiatric hospital *Psychiatric Hospital, 22,* 5–9.

Tanke, E. D., & Yesavage, J. A. (1985). Characteristics of assaultive patients who do and do not provide visible cues of potential violence. *American Journal of Psychiatry, 142,* 1409–1413.

Tardiff, K. (1984a). Violence: The psychiatric patient. In J. T. Turner (Ed.). *Violence in the medical care setting: A survival guide* (pp. 33–55). Rockville, MD: Aspen Systems Corp.

Tardiff, K. (1984b). *The psychiatric uses of seclusion and restraint.* Washington, DC: American Psychiatric Association Press.

Tardiff, K. (1989). *Assessment and management of violent patients.* Washington, DC: American Psychiatric Press.

Tardiff, K., & Sweillam, A. (1980). Assault, suicide, and mental illness. *Archives of General Psychiatry, 37,* 164–169.

Tardiff, K., & Sweillam, A. (1982). The occurrence of assaultive behavior among chronic psychiatric inpatients. *American Journal of Psychiatry, 139,* 212–215.

Taulbee, L. R. (1978). Reality orientation: A therapeutic group activity for elderly persons. In I. M. Burnside (Ed.), *Working with the elderly: Group processes and techniques* (pp. 206–218). North Scituate, MA: Duxbury Press.

Taulbee, L. R., & Folsom, J. C. (1966). Reality orientation for geriatric patients. *Hospital and Community Psychiatry, 17,* 133–135.

Tomine, S. (1986). Private practice in gerontological counseling. *Journal of Counseling and Development, 68,* 406–409.

Turnbull, J., Aitken, I., Black, L., & Patterson, B. (1990, June). Turn it around: Short-term management for aggression and anger. *Journal of Psychosocial Nursing and Mental Health Services, 28,* 7–13.

Turner, J. (Ed.). (1984). *Violence in the medical care setting: A survival guide.* Rockville, MD: Aspen Systems Corp.

Valliant, P. M., Aser, M. E., Cooper, D., & Mammola, D. (1984). Profile of dangerous and non-dangerous offenders referred for pre-trial psychiatric assessment. *Psychological Reports, 54,* 411–418.

Viner, J. (1982). Toward more skillful handling of acutely psychotic patients. Part I: Evaluation. *Emergency Room Report, 3,* 125–130.

Vinick, B. (Speaker). (1986). Counseling in a state mental hospital (Cassette Recording No. 13). Memphis: Memphis State University, Department of Counseling and Personnel Services.

Webster, C. D. (1990). Prediction of dangerousness polemic. *Canadian Journal of Criminology, 32,* 191–196.

Werner, P. D., Rose, T. L., Murdach, A. D., Yesavage, J. A. (1989). Social workers' decision making about the violent client. *Social Work Research and Abstracts, 25,* 17–20.

Whitman, R. M., Armao, B. B., & Dent, O. B. (1976). Assault on the therapist. *American Journal of Psychiatry, 133,* 426–431.

Williams, W., Thornby, J., & Sandlin, P. D. (1989). Perceptions of prehospital dangerous behavior by psychiatric inpatients and their families. *Journal of Psychiatry and Law, 17,* 21–37.

Wolanin, M. O., & Phillips, L. R. (1981). *Confusion: Prevention and care.* St. Louis, MO: C. V. Mosby.

Wood, K. A., & Khuri, R. (1984). Violence: The emergency room patient. In J. T. Turner (Ed.), *Violence in the medical care setting: A survival guide* (pp. 57–84). Rockville, MD: Aspen Systems Corp.

Yesavage, J. A., & Zarcone, V. (1983). History of drug abuse and dangerous behavior in inpatient schizophrenics. *Journal of Clinical Psychiatry, 44,* 259–261.

Zold, A. C., & Schilt, S. C. (1984). Violence: The child and the adolescent patient. In J. T. Turner (Ed.), *Violence in the medical care setting: A survival guide* (pp. 85–106). Rockville, MD: Aspen Systems Corp.

CLASSROOM EXERCISES

I. Dealing with Verbal Abuse

The group is divided into dyads. One person in each pair assumes the role of the human services worker and the other person assumes the role of an agitated, verbally abusive client. The human services worker's job is to get the client under control. Since the dialogue will probably become rather loud, it is suggested that dyads be housed in separate offices or rooms if at all possible, or the exercise done outside of class.

The client will take a standing position and the human services worker will remain seated (all the better to intimidate the worker!). Another chair should be available for the client, but in the beginning the client must not sit down. The client may threaten, be noncompliant, yell, berate, gripe, say terrible things about the worker or the worker's parents, or otherwise try to cow and manipulate the worker into submission. However, when asked a question, the client must respond to the content being asked. Also, when a reflective statement is made by the worker, the client must respond by indicating the feeling state felt.

The worker may use any of the techniques discussed in this chapter or, for that matter, anything else that comes to mind. The mission for this exercise is to get the client to sit down. Continue the exercise for five to ten minutes with tape recorder on. At the end of the time switch roles. Whenever dyad partners have concluded their experiences of enactment of both worker and client roles, make sure that both persons verbally disassociate themselves from the roles to one another. At the end of both sessions, come back together as a group. Discuss the following questions:

1. How did you feel as the worker?
2. Were you able to stay relaxed and keep your wits about you?
3. How did you do that without becoming agitated yourself?
4. How did you attempt to gain compliance from the client?
5. What techniques worked and what didn't?

II. Staffing and Plotting a Strategy

Select some of the tapes made in the previous exercise. In groups of four or five, listen to the tapes and brainstorm what might be a more effective approach. Solicit the client for feedback on which seem to be the most effective ideas and why. See if the group agrees on which techniques for handling the client would be best. Is the group willing to commit as a team to employing the techniques? Process how the group feels about its decision after it has finished, particularly taking note of and discussing any ideas that may seem repugnant to some of the members.

III. Using Validation Therapy with a Disoriented Client

Working in dyads, one member assumes the role of a disoriented client who would like to talk about a past event that is of great importance. To make this event realistic, clients should think back to an important moment in their childhood and attempt to report that moment as if it were present time. While they are doing this, the human services workers should be doing their utmost to disregard this senseless patter and should be attempting to orient their clients to person, place, and time. The workers should also try to get their clients to complete some task. When approximately five minutes have elapsed, stop the dialogue and switch roles. At the end of another five minutes, again stop the dialogue and rejoin the group. Discuss these questions:

1. As the counselor, how did you feel in trying to orient the client?
2. How frustrated, if at all, did you become?
3. What did you try to do to get the client to be compliant?
4. How would you feel and what would you do if you had a busy schedule and had to gain compliance from the client?
5. As the client, what was your feeling about the worker's attempt to get you off your childhood memory and back to reality?
6. How did you respond when the worker kept trying to get you on task?

In the same dyads, the clients go back again to the early childhood memories. The workers will use validation therapy and pace with their clients as if the memories were real, alive, important, and very much here-and-now. Again the workers should attempt to have their clients comply with a task, but this purpose is secondary to responding empathically to the feelings and content of the memory. After the dialogue has continued for approximately five minutes, stop and switch roles. After another five minutes, again stop and rejoin the group. Discuss the following questions:

1. As the worker, how did you feel as you paced with the client?
2. How frustrated, if at all, did you become?
3. What did you do to stay at an empathic level with the client?

4. How compliant was the client to any requests you made?
5. As the client, how did you feel about the worker's attempts to listen and understand what you were saying?
6. How did you feel and what did you do when the worker attempted to gain compliance with the requested task?

CHAPTER 11

Hostage Crises

BACKGROUND

The following news brief appeared in the Memphis *Commercial Appeal* ("Insurance for Hostage Victims") on November 23, 1985:

> An insurance company has come up with a new policy. If you are worried about being taken hostage you can get an insurance policy for one million dollars that will pay off if you do not survive the incident. A one hundred thousand dollar reward will also be paid for information leading to the capture of the hostage takers—dead or alive.

The horrifying tragedies that take place a continent away from us, or in social institutions such as penitentiaries that are psychologically a continent away, make splashy headlines. Most of us assume that being taken hostage will happen to the other guy, certainly not us. Yet, if you had been a health care worker in a variety of settings from the Granite City, Illinois, Community Mental Health Center to St. Jude Children's Research Hospital in Memphis, Tennessee, you might have been exceedingly wise to take out such an insurance policy.

To bring the issue up close and personal, the human services worker is likely to meet individuals who have had their lives radically altered in what they may feel are very negative ways by human services agencies. The rise of the American health care system as a bureaucratic institution has led people to feel uncared for and ignored in times of emotional stress, particularly when they do not seem to have the ability to find coping mechanisms or resources on their own (Turner, 1984, p. 177). Just as hostage taking is a political act for terrorists too weak to cause revolution, it is, in the health care setting, a feeling act from people too weak to change what they believe to be grave injustices perpetrated on them by that system (Turner, 1984, p. 172).

This chapter will not make you a skilled negotiator in hostage situations. To become a negotiator takes a great deal of training. What this chapter will do is give you basic knowledge to help you survive a hostage situation or keep the situation at a reasonable level of stability until help arrives.

DYNAMICS OF HOSTAGE TAKING

For a positive outcome to occur, certain general dynamics of hostage takers need to be understood. First, hostage takers should be viewed as individuals who have reached an acute level of frustration. Second, the taking of hostages should be viewed as an attempt at problem solving. Third, hostage takers in most cases see hostages as mere pawns in a larger game and use them as bargaining chips throughout the negotiation process. Finally, the taking of hostages is an attention-seeking behavior to attract an audience, for without an audience the hostage taking is meaningless (Schlossberg, 1980, pp. 113–114).

Dynamically, there are two general classifications of behavior that may be observed in hostage takers: instrumental behavior and expressive behavior. Instrumental behavior has some recognizable goal that the perpetrator seeks to have fulfilled. Those engaging in expressive behavior seek to display their power. Of the two, the latter is the more difficult to understand, for such action appears to the casual observer to be senseless. There would seem to be no way that the perpetrators can gain anything except their own or others' destruction (Miron & Goldstein, 1978, p. 10). However, as an expressive gesture, such action is extremely powerful and indicates to the world at large that the perpetrators are able for a short while to take matters and destiny into their own hands. These dynamics combine variously to generate a number of types of hostage takers.

Types of Hostage Takers

If the negotiator can ferret out characteristics and identify the particular type of hostage taker being dealt with, then a valid triage assessment can be made and appropriate psychological and behavioral responses constructed. In general, with criminal types who are engaging in instrumental behavior, a rational, problem-solving approach that seeks a compromise in concrete terms is proposed. With psychotic or other emotionally disturbed types who are engaging in expressive behavior, emphasis is on affective techniques that use reflection of feelings and restatement of content. With terrorists who are "emotionally rational," a mix of the two basic techniques is probably best suited (Miron & Goldstein, 1978, pp. 96–97). We have omitted instrumental and instrumental/expressive hostage takers such as bank robbers and political terrorists from our discussion because of the unlikelihood of the worker's encountering these types. However, the true expressive types that the worker is likely to encounter are legion and are frequent recipients of service.

The mentally disturbed.   Mentally disturbed hostage takers suffer from various kinds of psychological maladies. A mentally disturbed person may or may not be in touch with reality. This individual will likely be a loner, acting in obedience to some intensely personal, often obscure impulse

(Cooper, 1981, p. 57), and may believe that taking hostages will carry out some sacred mission or prove that he or she can do something important (Fuselier, 1981a). In the case of the mentally disturbed, the most difficult task for the negotiator is predicting behavior. There are four major diagnostic categories of mentally disturbed hostage takers that the negotiator is likely to encounter.

The paranoid schizophrenic personality. Paranoid schizophrenics are out of touch with reality. They are easily recognized by their false system of beliefs and especially by their hallucinations or delusions. They often take hostages in order to carry out what they believe is a "master plan" or to obey "orders from some special person or deity" (Fuselier, 1981a). These psychotic individuals are frustrated; they want something and cannot get it. Paranoid schizophrenics are conflicted and have difficulty coping with even minimally stressful situations. Male paranoids typically have problems with gender identity and their religious beliefs. As a result, many of the situations where hostage taking occurs will involve these problem areas (Strentz, 1986). This combination of frustration and conflict produces a tremendous amount of anxiety. Excessive anxiety tends to make such individuals extremely sensitive and volatile, particularly when they are off their medication and their hallucinations are extremely active.

A variety of issues may underlie the paranoid schizophrenic's behavior. Lack of interpersonal trust, religious convictions, sexual dysfunction, persecutory beliefs about family or significant others, or extreme distrust of the negotiator, police, and authority in general make negotiating with this psychotic very difficult and dangerous (Strentz, 1986). Real time may be sped up or slowed down for the paranoid schizophrenic. Disassociation from reality is a hallmark of this type, and the negotiator will have to attempt to keep the dialogue at an even pace and keep the individual calm enough to stay in touch with the reality of the moment. Good negotiating strategy calls for reducing anxiety and at the same time attempting to create a problem-solving atmosphere (Maher, 1977, pp. 64–65). The best approach is to accept the paranoid schizophrenic's statements as true, although the negotiator should not agree with them. The negotiator should not try to convince the individual that he or she is wrong (Fuselier, 1981a). Empathic understanding of the beliefs of the paranoid and reflection of the disturbed individual's feelings are appropriate responses.

HT: The radio messages keep coming, even though I've told these people to shut their radios off. They're driving me crazy!

Neg: It must be really exasperating that they won't do what you tell you, particularly when all you want is peace and quiet.

The depressive personality. Hostage takers who are depressed seem to be in an incapacitated mental state. They are very confused people who identify themselves by their inability to make a firm decision. They may be characterized by slow, subdued speech, a negative outlook on life, and demands that are intermingled with references to death. Their hostages are frequently persons known to them. Depressed individuals are very unpredictable and are extremely dangerous. Often they are suicidal and may initiate a hostage taking in order to force the police to shoot them (Strentz, 1984, p. 185).

Persons suffering from depression have difficulty making decisions. In these cases, a problem-solving approach would most likely be futile. With the depressive, the negotiator must be firm and manipulative.

HT: I just don't know what to do, it's just a mess.

Neg: The mess will just get worse if you keep putting yourself deeper in this hole. Send the children out and we'll talk about you.

If the individual is suicidal, the negotiator needs to extract a commitment, no matter how tenuous, to keep the person from acting out a threat, and if possible change the subject to get the person's mind off the actions he or she is about to take. In the following dialogue, the negotiator attempts to shift the hostage taker's focus away from suicidal ideation and onto more effective communication. Negotiations in this case involve applying in a very paced way the intervention procedures described in the chapter on suicide.

HT: I wonder if you'd see that the picture albums get to the kids?

Neg: I'd be willing to help in any way I can, but I want you to agree to not do anything until we get all these other issues settled. By the way, would you mind speaking into the phone a little louder? My hearing isn't all that good and we must have a bad connection.

The inadequate personality. The inadequate personality usually displays a good deal of narcissistic, attention-seeking behavior. Many times this is an individual who has attempted a crime and has been caught in the process. Since the hostage-taking incident may be the high point of the person's life, the inadequate personality tends to stretch the situation for all it is worth. Identified by key phrases such as "I'll show them who's boss" and "Now they'll see what I can do," this hostage taker basks in the limelight of the situation. Such pronouncements are indicative of a low self-image. Therefore, the motivation for taking hostages may be to prove that the inadequate type can succeed at something. Yet, in the same instant, inadequate types may appear contrite and apologetic for their behavior. Initially, the inadequate personality type may state demands with considerable conviction and then turn around and provide the negotiator with several options (Strentz, 1984, p. 185). Negotiators need to be aware of and seize those options.

The primary strategy of the negotiator is to present problem-solving alternatives so that the hostage taker will not feel that he or she has "failed again." Playing up to this hostage taker's ego and helping the person to find a face-saving alternative is an excellent tactic. Inadequate personalities have a need to prove themselves to some "significant" others. The "I'll show them" statements are indicative of this need, and their true meaning ultimately may be the murder of the hostages if their egos are not handled with extreme care.

HT: I want a personal interview with the news director of Channel 3 right now. I've got some things I want to say. You do that and I'll let them go.

Neg: I understand how important it is to you to get on television. You let those people go now and I'll see that you get on the 10 o'clock news.

The antisocial personality. The antisocial personality repeatedly comes into conflict with society and is incapable of having significant loyalty to individuals, groups, or social values. Antisocial types tend to blame others and offer rationalizations for their behavior (American Psychiatric Association, 1987). The antisocial personality who takes hostages is generally engaged in an expressive act unless the individual is caught in the middle of a felony. The antisocial type is likely to dehumanize the hostages and should be considered extremely dangerous to them because the person will manifest little feeling for their well-being. Although antisocial personalities have not internalized moral values, they do understand their effect on others and are therefore potent adversaries. Although persons of this type lack emotional depth, they may display a wide range of skillful emotional overlays in place of true emotional responses (Lanceley, 1981, pp. 31–32).

The only concern of these hostage takers is for themselves. Therefore, the negotiator should be aware that this type has no compunction about doing anything to anybody. If at any point this hostage taker feels that hostages are a burden, they will be killed. The profound egocentricity of the antisocial type requires constant stimulation. A primary objective in the negotiation process is to keep the holder's attention and avoid having him or her turn attention to the hostages as a source of stimulus.

This person is not only streetwise but also policewise, so trickery is not a good idea. Also, the negotiator should avoid references to jail or hospitalization because antisocial types are likely to become highly agitated if they feel that they are going to lose their freedom or it is insinuated that they are crazy. Finally, the inflated ego of the antisocial type makes formation of Stockholm syndrome (where a close personal relationship may develop with a hostage) highly unlikely (Fuselier, 1981a).

HT: Don't give me that crap about "more time." You get that car in here or I start doing some fun things to this little 6-year-old, and her mommy gets to watch.

Neg: I know you're mad about the car, but you know I gotta go through procedures. I understand you could work the kid over, but I wonder if you've thought about the good that'll do you in the long run. It's your hide you're dealing with, too! So let's work on that side of it.

The estranged person.   Invariably the estranged hostage taker will know the hostage, who will probably be a spouse or lover. The estranged hostage taker is experiencing a breakdown in his or her interpersonal relationships. These breakdowns lead to domestic quarrels and, in turn, the escalating nature of the quarrels and the feared loss of the significant other lead the estranged person to commit the hostage taking. (Alcohol often provides the liquid courage necessary to carry out the hostage taking.) The estranged hostage taker seeks to coerce the maintenance of the relationship through forceful action. The most distinctive feature of this kind of hostage taking is its intensely personal nature and the unique purpose of the hostage taker in attempting continued domination over the significant other (Cooper, 1981, pp. 27–28).

As in any other domestic dispute, the negotiator should be extremely careful of this volatile situation and use empathic listening and responding skills to their fullest. With this type, the negotiator must contend with the highly personal nature of the hostage taking and the continued denial of reality. Intrinsic to intervention is the negotiator's ability to keep denial from turning into despair. The key to resolution is that the estranged hostage taker needs to be shown a graceful way out (Cooper, 1981, p. 28).

HT: It's not my fault. I've done everything she asked and then she still jilted me. If I can't have her, nobody will.

Neg: She really hurt you, then. I can start to see why you feel you had to do this. I'm wondering, though, if she can't see now just how strongly you feel. Perhaps you've made your point to her. You certainly have to me!

The institutionalized individual.   Institutionalized hostage takers are inmates who have a grievance, usually about conditions within the system in which they are confined. The only other reason for taking hostages is to obtain a passport to freedom. Hostage takings of this sort are usually deemed instrumental acts that are planned to produce concrete changes in the institution (Maher, 1977, p. 65). Only in a very few instances do inmates perpetrate a hostage situation as a desperate expressive act to obtain revenge. However, given the mix of violent individuals in most correctional settings, the situation, if not contained immediately, can become exceedingly dangerous for both hostages and other inmates.

HT: We want to see the warden and we want these 25 demands met and they ain't negotiable.

Neg: And I want to see and hear that the hostages are all right before we talk about any demands.

The wronged person.   The wronged hostage taker is dissatisfied or aggrieved by the system at large or a particular bureaucracy. Wronged individuals may be identified by the "crosses" they bear and the paranoia associated with their beliefs. These hostage takers feel so grossly discriminated against by the "establishment" that they seek to remake society to their own satisfaction (Cooper, 1981, p. 10).

Aggrieved or wronged individuals are high on the list of potential candidates with whom the human services worker may become involved—if not as a negotiator then as a hostage. Aggrieved individuals feel that no one in a position of responsibility will redress the terrible wrongs that have been done to them. After exhausting a variety of acceptable options within the system and still receiving no redress, these individuals may do something dramatic (Turner, 1984, p. 178).

Associated with this type of hostage taking is the high priority attached to publicity, for the hostage taker is usually motivated to make the public aware of the wrongs imposed by the particular authorities in question. Proper involvement of the media can enhance the opportunity for the release of the hostages, if the hostage taker perceives that a wrong will be made right by a public airing (Gladis, 1979).

HT: The doctors, nurses, the administrators, the psychologists, the social workers, they're all at fault. She wouldn't have died if they'd done their job. Everybody thinks this is such a hot-shot hospital. It's really Murder Incorporated, and people need to know the truth.

Neg: I realize what a terrible shock her death was, and how you trusted all those people. Yet you believe they let you down and should be exposed for the incompetent blunders they've made. Would you be willing to make a deal? If I can set it up so you can read that prepared statement you've got about the hospital, will you let those people out?

The religious fanatic.   Religious fanatics have the same inflexible and uncompromising attitude in their beliefs as political terrorists. But, unlike political terrorists, religious fanatics do not usually take hostages for offensive purposes. Rather, hostages are seen as sacrificial lambs that must be made to pay for the "sins" of the unrepentant. The taking of the American embassy in Iran in 1979 is a classic example of this situation. The hostage takers are unwilling to talk with those who are in a position to negotiate because they are not in the business of negotiation. What they are in the business of is atonement. Therefore, their demands are such that they are invariably impossible to meet—at least for a considerable time into the future.

Because religious zealots do not consider themselves accountable to anyone except their own deity, negotiations are very difficult and invariably call for outside help by someone whose nationality, religion, or some other attribute does not cast them in the "devil" category (Maher, 1977, p. viii). Hostages are subject to the religious and moral whimsy of such fanatics and may expect a long, arduous, and dangerous experience. Thus, the religious fanatic who is a hostage taker poses a particular problem to the negotiation process because such an individual must either die for the cause or relinquish it (Cooper, 1981, p. 45). As has been demonstrated over and over again in the Middle East, the former is more likely than the latter. In nearly every case of hostage taking by a religious fanatic, some sort of face-saving gesture will be required if the situation is to be resolved (Cooper, 1976, p. 104).

HT: This is God's will. If I allow you to pack me off to jail like a common thief, no one will believe in our holy cause.

Neg: What if we consider setting a low bond, maybe even self-recognizance? That way you wouldn't have to go to jail, and both your honor and your cause would be untarnished.

Stages of a Hostage Situation

Throughout the entire hostage episode, emotions of both parties move on a curve that oscillates between desperation and euphoria. As the episode is protracted, the cycle tends to dampen and retreat from both emotional extremes (Schreiber, 1978, p. 50). It is within this context that the following stages should be examined. There are four stages to a hostage situation: alarm, crisis, accommodation, and resolution (Strentz, 1984, pp. 189–194). The stages will be examined as they apply both to the hostage taker and to the hostage.

Alarm.   The alarm stage is the most traumatic and dangerous. Whatever the type of hostage takers, in this first stage their emotions are running exceedingly high, their reason may be diminished, and they may be extremely aggressive in their reaction to any perceived threat. To force their will upon the hostages, the general belief of the hostage takers is that hostages must be terrorized into submission. Therefore, hostage takers may be inclined to harass, abuse, or even kill anyone who seems to be interfering with their attempts to consolidate their position (Strentz, 1984, p. 190).

For the unprepared individual who suddenly becomes a hostage, the alarm stage is traumatic in every aspect. A previously tranquil situation now becomes a life-and-death one that pivots every minute. For the victim, defenseless and confused, the nightmarish experience takes on an unreal aspect. For many, denial of the reality of the situation sets in, particularly when those from whom they expect help seem to be doing nothing.

Effective coping at this early stage means immediately putting into place a strong will to survive and not succumbing to panic. Any sign of panic may cause the perpetrators to overreact to a highly charged situation and dramatically diminish the chances of survival (Strentz, 1984, p. 196). Hostages should disregard any notion of being a hero. Untrained, unarmed, and poorly conditioned civilians can best secure survival by maintaining low profiles (pp. 201–202) and staying calm and alert (Miron & Goldstein, 1978, p. 92).

Crisis.   The crisis stage marks the beginning of reason for the hostage takers. However, there is still a great deal of unpredictability and danger as they try to consolidate their position. Initial attempts at negotiation at this stage may be marked by outrageous demands and emotional diatribes by the hostage holders. Because of fear of assault by the authorities, hostage takers may move hostages to a more secure area or enlist their cooperation in making the area they are in more secure (Strentz, 1984, p. 191).

For the hostage, the crisis stage is the most critical because it sets the tone for the remainder of the situation. Hostage-captor interaction at this stage can either enhance or reduce hostages' chances of survival. Although denial by hostages may still be in place as a defense mechanism, the decision to face reality and engage in normal behavior generally provides some emotional relief and mental escape (Strentz, 1984, p. 203). If a hostage is in a position of responsibility, he or she cannot afford to lose emotional control. Dignified, nonthreatening behavior is the watchword. Hostages who are in positions of responsibility have to be very careful that they do not intimidate their captors. If their captors have inferiority feelings to begin with, they may see defiance as an attempt by the hostage to humiliate them. In particular, verbal humiliation is a precipitator of violence (p. 203).

At this stage, hostages may start to experience three problems: isolation, claustrophobia, and/or the loss of a sense of time. Individuals who are isolated will have to come to grips with the fact that the only human contacts they have may be extremely hostile toward them. Claustrophobia can take its toll even if the individual is not isolated and confined to a small cell. A problem that becomes very important is the loss of sense of time. By this stage, captors have usually removed personal items, including watches, from the hostages. Sense of time becomes very important to someone held captive who is hoping for rescue. Asking for such small favors as information about time or date puts hostages completely at the mercy of their captors. Hostage takers use such requests to good advantage in earning compliance from their captives (Strentz, 1984, p. 197). The message is, "We can do with you what we want. There is no hope other than what we give you!"

Accommodation.   The accommodation stage is the longest and most tranquil. For the hostage, the accommodation stage is marked by time dragging by. Boredom, punctuated only by moments of terror, is the hallmark of this stage. The crests and troughs of emotions that have occurred until this point are likely to induce fatigue in the hostage and hostage taker. If this stage becomes protracted, then there is a likelihood that what is known as the Stockholm syndrome, named after an aborted bank holdup in Sweden during which one of the hostages fell in love with her captor, will come into operation (Strentz, 1984, p. 198).

The Stockholm syndrome is possible if three conditions are met: extended period of time, not being isolated from one's captor, and positive contact between captor and captives (Fuselier, 1981b). The phenomenon comprises the three following elements (Strentz, 1984, p. 198):

1. Positive feelings are generated toward the hostage taker from the hostages.
2. Negative feelings are generated toward the authorities by the hostages.
3. Positive feelings are generated toward the hostages by their captors.

Evidence would seem to support the idea that this is not a well-gauged ploy on the part of the hostage to ensure survival. The phenomenon is probably an automatic, unconscious emotional response to the trauma of being taken hostage (Strentz, 1979, p. 2). It would seem that as people are thrown together, both captor and captive start to respond to one another on more personal terms. If this occurs, it becomes very hard to regard one another as faceless entities to be despised and used. Familiarity with each other provides a fertile ground for identification with the other's problems, hopes, fears, and outlook on life. If such positive identification by a hostage is reciprocated by the holder, the hostage's chances of survival go up considerably (Ochberg, 1977). During this stage it is not uncommon for hostages to feel that the authorities are the chief cause of the problem and that if they would only go home the siege would end (Strentz, 1984, p. 200).

The hostage can make use of this phenomenon. In as genuine a way as possible, the hostage should seek to build a positive relationship with his or her captors. The easiest way to do this is to be as real a person as possible by attempting to share the more personal aspects of one's life and attempt to elicit the same from the holders. If hostages make attempts to gain familiarity with the hostage takers, they would probably be wise to avoid political discussions with them, since such discussions accentuate differences between captor and captive (Miron & Goldstein, 1978, p. 92).

A captive who is a well-integrated individual may boost hostage morale by exploiting perceived weaknesses in the captors, although this is an extremely dangerous ploy if it backfires. The approach takes strength of character and is not generally recommended unless captives are isolated for a long period of time with only their own resources on which to fall back. In a protracted situation, hostages must take care of their physical needs. Eating and exercising are musts. Hostages should take whatever food is offered. Even if it is possible to do only flexibility exercises, they should be done on a regular basis (Strentz, 1984, p. 204).

Resolution.   In the resolution stage the hostage takers will have become fatigued as the long hours or days have taken their toll. The high expectations that they held early on will become dashed as they find that they have lost most of the bargaining chips. Whether there is a positive or negative resolution to the situation will depend on the ability of the negotiator to skillfully bring closure to the situation (Strentz, 1984, p. 193).

In particular, it is important to understand the difference between the behavior of a hostage taker who is planning to surrender and one who is planning to commit suicide (see the chapter on suicide for cues and rituals). Inadequate personality types are a high risk for the latter response. They may see surrender as just another in a long list of failures, whereas suicide may seem to be a positive solution. The problem with suicide is that the hostage taker may not have enough courage to accomplish the act on his or her own. To force the issue, the hostage taker may engage the police by failing to heed their instructions, firing at them, or firing at a hostage

(Strentz, 1984, pp. 193–194). If the hostage taker gives any cues at all during this final stage, the negotiator should be prepared to move immediately into a suicide prevention mode. Whatever the type, and however long and arduous the incident, the trained negotiator takes a purposeful and dignified approach to the surrender of the perpetrator.

If force has to be used, there will be a lot of confusion and noise. This is intentional on the part of the rescuers as a diversion. Hostages need to lie down if possible, or sit tight. Hostages should also keep their hands plainly visible by locking them behind their heads so that the rescuers clearly know who is a hostage and who is not. Hostages need to be calm and alert and follow orders of their rescuers explicitly (Strentz, 1984, pp. 205–206).

In the resolution stage, reaction of the hostages will be mixed, both toward the takers and toward their rescuers. Although relieved to be freed from the terror they have experienced, hostages may be hostile toward their rescuers and believe that the authorities were in the main responsible for having caused the trauma. Despite their recognition that their captors put them through a living hell and held the hostages' lives in their hands, hostages tend to feel that they in some way owe their holders for having given them their life back (Strentz, 1984, pp. 200–201).

Survivors of a hostage situation indicate that a variety of physical and psychological problems, ranging from paranoia about repeat occurrences and survival guilt to posttrauma anxiety attacks, may appear a long time after the incident. Survivors need to be aware that resolution of the situation may not necessarily mean the end of their problems associated with being taken hostage (Strentz, 1984, p. 201).

Characteristics of an Effective Negotiator

Since negotiation strategies are based on psychological principles, it would seem natural to employ psychologists, psychiatrists, or other mental health professionals as negotiators. Still, this is a controversial issue. There are a number of arguments against using mental health professionals as negotiators. First and foremost, hostage negotiations are a law enforcement operation and therefore should be dealt with in terms of immediate resolution of conflict rather than in terms of therapy. Second, the use of mental health professionals supplants the use of a negotiating-team approach, particularly if decisive physical action needs to be taken, and allows for a division of responsibility. Third, a mental health professional may not be nearly as wise in the use of street psychology as a person who has lived in and experienced the milieu of the hostage taker. Fourth, identification of the negotiator as a mental health professional may make hostage takers extremely agitated if they conclude that the authorities believe them to be mentally deranged (Maher, 1977, p. 9).

Yet a mental health professional, by virtue of training and personality characteristics, fits many of the criteria Miron and Goldstein (1978, pp. 93–94, 137–166) propose for selection of a negotiator. The resolution of this dilemma has been to make a psychologist a member of the negotiating team in a consultative capacity (Maher, 1977, p. 9). As a consultant, the psychologist serves as a resource person, adviser to the negotiator, intelligence gatherer, debriefer of victims and witnesses, and post hoc evaluator of the total response effort (Powitzky, 1979). Particularly as a consultant to the negotiator, the psychologist should

1. constantly assess the mental state of the hostage taker, as well as that of the negotiator
2. not become directly involved in the negotiations, thereby remaining as objective as possible
3. recommend techniques, approaches, or responses that will help resolve the situation (Fuselier, 1981b).

It should be understood that the only responsibility of the negotiator is to conduct all verbal interactions with the hostage taker to the successful conclusion of the situation (Fuselier, 1981b). To discharge such an awesome responsibility, the ideal negotiator will possess special characteristics. The following list is compiled from Miron and Goldstein (1978, pp. 93–94) and Maher (1977, pp. 17–18).

1. interpersonal sensitivity and empathic understanding
2. intellectual ability to deal with cognitive complexities
3. tolerance for ambiguity
4. positive self-concept
5. low authoritarianism
6. interviewing experience
7. past experience in stressful situations
8. verbal skills
9. flexibility, especially under pressure
10. firm but not overpowering manner
11. nonargumentativeness
12. nonsusceptibility to slurs about personhood
13. belief in the power of verbal persuasion
14. mature appearance
15. calm presence of mind
16. good physical condition
17. background in psychology, especially abnormal and social behavior
18. freedom from values associated with ethnic, racial, or religious background
19. street wisdom
20. familiarity with ideology of perpetrator if perpetrator is a terrorist
21. conciliation, compromise, and bargaining skills

What does not fit for a negotiator is the converse of the characteristics listed. Anyone who is high on authoritarianism, believes in physical force, power, and toughness, is rigid and inflexible, and works from a macho orientation has no business being a hostage negotiator (Miron & Goldstein, 1978, p. 94).

INTERVENTION STRATEGIES

Because hostage takings epitomize crisis conditions, the hostage negotiator is very much like an eclectic counselor who must have a variety of techniques to fit different and constantly changing situations. The only difference is that the negotiator is dealing with a victimizer rather than the victim, and the main object of the negotiator's attention is invariably holding a weapon.

Our six-step crisis intervention model provides the nucleus of the concepts and skills needed by negotiators to successfully intervene in hostage crises. Assessing the motives and emotional status of the hostage taker is an extremely important and delicate task because people's lives are generally at stake. Negotiators must be competent in listening and relationship skills because the hostage taker cannot be tested or evaluated in any normal way during the period of the emergency.

Triage assessment is especially difficult in these circumstances. Often, the negotiator has no way of knowing, other than what can be obtained verbally, what might be motivating the captor to take such extreme measures. Even then, the negotiator may have to make a determination based only on a verbal assessment taken over the telephone. A compounding problem is that the negotiator must determine a great deal of personal information beyond the current mental status of the perpetrator, including the expertise to carry out threats. At best, much of this information will be obtained from secondhand sources such as friends or relatives, who may provide a very biased picture of the captor. Worse, this entire scenario may take place with a great deal of noise, confusion, and a crowd and the media present. Understanding and assessing the degree of mobility/immobility that the hostage taker feels is of particular importance because the negotiator needs to decide how directive, collaborative, or nondirective to be. Examination of alternatives available is critical to the outcome of the negotiation. The negotiator will want to get the hostage taker to consider options other than killing the hostages.

The following intervention procedures would be universally recognized by hostage negotiation teams and can be considered to be constants in the negotiating process. Yet each hostage situation is an entity unto itself and cannot be reduced to any formula that works for all cases. Therefore, the successful negotiator, like other crisis interventionists, will be creative but will follow a standard procedure, take risks but proceed with caution, have empathy but believe in justice, and have patience but move decisively.

Containing the Scene

As in all other law enforcement operations, safety is the foremost consideration. In a hostage situation, inner and outer perimeters are secured around the hostage scene and a command post is established in the inner perimeter. This is the first step in the strategy of containment and negotiation. Containing and stabilizing the scene prevent the scope of the event from expanding (Schlossberg, 1980).

Gathering Information

The most important information the negotiator needs to know, as quickly as possible, is who the hostage taker is, to obtain a profile. Who are his or her close friends, relatives? Does he or she have children, a spouse, a girlfriend, a boyfriend? What kind of criminal record? How many arrests and for what? Is there a psychiatric record? Has the hostage taker ever been committed? Is he or she currently obtaining professional help? What is the professional's name, and is the professional available?

What kinds of specialized skills does the hostage taker have? What does the person know about weapons, explosives, electronics? Can the person fly, drive, operate special equipment? What kinds of special affiliations? Does the hostage taker belong to a religious order? a sect? a gang?

What are the individual's deviations? sexual preferences? Does the person use drugs, alcohol? What are his or her immediate problems—money? love life? parole problems? addiction? All of these pieces make up the puzzle of who the hostage taker is and perhaps will give the negotiator a clue to a positive solution (Miron & Goldstein, 1978, pp. 92–93).

The next piece of information to be determined is just who the hostages are. Are there really hostages? If so, how many, how old, and what sex are they? What is their current emotional state? Are they intelligent? Do they have potential for aggression? Does anybody need medical assistance or have special requirements? Are they related to their captor or complete strangers (Miron & Goldstein, 1978, p. 93)?

The last piece of initial information needed concerns the hostage site itself. What are safe observation positions? What are the safest approach and escape routes? Are there telephones or other means of communication present? What amount of space, number of rooms, obstacles, ventilation, and so on, compose the site? What is the access to food, water, toilet facilities?

Stabilizing the Situation

The initial tasks of the negotiator are to contain and stabilize the situation (Miron & Goldstein, 1978, p. 95). These initial minutes are the most critical for the hostages, and what the negotiating team does now will determine whether the situation is safely resolved (Turner, 1984, pp. 179–180). The negotiator's first goals are to calm the perpetrator and build rapport with him or her (Miron & Goldstein, 1978, p. 95). A low-key counseling approach that emphasizes reflective listening skills, letting the hostage taker know that the negotiator understands how strongly he or she feels, is an excellent opening strategy (Mirabella & Trudeau, 1981).

Neg: From what you're saying, you really feel angry at them. I understand how frustrated you are at the housing authority folks. It's as if they haven't heard a thing you've been saying.

It is important that the negotiator stay calm, especially during these opening gambits (Schreiber, 1978, p. 103). By tone of voice, choice of words, facial expression, and gestures, the negotiator models a calmness that will, one hopes, transfer itself to the hostage taker. Reassurance is part of the attempt to keep the situation tranquil (Miron & Goldstein, 1978, p. 97).

Neg: [*Sits down, takes off coat, lights a cigarette in view, but not in the same room or within reach of hostage taker.*] It doesn't seem like we're going any place for a while, so just take your time and tell me what it is you want. I'm sure we can reach a mutually agreeable solution.

The negotiator needs to allow the hostage taker the opportunity to ventilate feelings (Miron & Goldstein, 1978, p. 98). Ventilating provides a number of positive outcomes. The perpetrator's continued talking permits the negotiator to identify the person's mental state and personal problems and to assess the general atmosphere of the situation (Maher, 1977, p. 36). It is also very difficult for the hostage taker to remain emotionally charged and at the same time present lengthy discourses and answer questions about his or her problems to the negotiator (Miron & Goldstein, 1978, p. 98). One of the best ways to keep the perpetrator engaged is to ask open-ended questions.

Neg: I'm not sure I understand what you're really peeved about. How would you like them to set up the tenant grievance procedure with the housing authority? What would you see your role as being in that?

At the same time the negotiator must be careful not to intrude into the psychological space of the hostage taker (Maher, 1977, p. 36). Interpretive statements about the causal dynamics that motivate the hostage taker may generate hostility and increased agitation. To suggest that some personal inadequacy is at the root of the hostage taker's problem is unwise. The following type of statement is *not* suggested.

Neg: So it's really going way back to those inadequate feelings you had as a child. Your mother and father always put you down, so now you're really trying to show them how potent you are when in fact you really know that it isn't so.

Under no circumstances should the negotiator try to provoke the hostage taker. Arguing, demeaning remarks, outright rejection of demands, and sudden surprises have no place in the dialogue. Any signs of increased agitation or aggression in the hostage taker should be monitored carefully. Disjointed and speeded-up speech, flared nostrils, flushed cheeks, restlessness, pounding or shaking of fists, and so on, are all indicators that the negotiator needs to cool the situation down. One of the best ways to accomplish this is to distract the hostage taker by asking questions totally irrelevant to the situation or suggesting something contrary to what the perpetrator thinks the authorities might want (Miron & Goldstein, 1978, pp. 98–99).

Neg: You said you were interested in pro basketball and the Knicks in particular. Think they've got a chance against the Celtics tonight?

Neg: Well, if you think we're all infidel, godless swine, I guess that's your right. If you feel like you've got to let people know about your feelings, then maybe you ought to go on the radio. [*The negotiator and the media have previously worked out the conditions under which this would happen.*]

By trying to see the problem through the hostage taker's eyes, the negotiator tries to build rapport with the perpetrator. Using owning or "I" statements is one way the negotiator can establish a relationship with the hostage taker. Genuine and noncontrived self-disclosure about the negotiator's own life as it seems to apply to the conversation is a useful way of establishing the relationship and instigating reciprocal disclosure on the part of the hostage taker (Maher, 1977, p. 41).

Neg: I can sure understand that. I put in long hours, do good work, and still catch hell from the boss even though somebody else screwed up the job. It sure seems like the department isn't very damn grateful for all the effort I put out. Is that about the way you feel about your job?

Pacing the dialogue in a slow and purposeful manner is a key component in the negotiations and works in favor of the authorities. Although hostages may become depressed and question the handling of the situation as time drags by, delay is to their benefit. By not rushing, the negotiator allows the relationship to develop. Also, time wears down the resources of the hostage takers faster than it does those of the authorities. Lack of sleep, hunger, thirst, and unrelenting tension focus the hostage taker on the calm reasonableness of the negotiator and aid and abet the problem-solving process (Maher, 1977, p. 13; Miron & Goldstein, 1978, p. 99).

Neg: [*Eleven hours into negotiations.*] Man! I'm getting tired. Gonna get a cup of coffee and pump some caffeine in my body. How about taking a break off the heavy stuff and just talk some basketball for a while? Maybe if you want some coffee we could talk about that. [*The coffee will have some strings attached.*]

Finally, a good negotiator, like a good therapist, is excellent at restating the hostage taker's ideas back to him. This technique serves to clarify both to the hostage taker and to the negotiator what is really being said. It also builds rapport with the hostage taker because he or she is assured of being listened to very carefully. The hostage taker's words mean something and count for something with the negotiator (Miron & Goldstein, 1978, p. 102).

Neg: OK! Let me see if I understand you correctly. You want to read your manifesto over the radio, but you're worried that they'll ask you some questions you don't want to answer right now. You're also concerned that they'll try to keep your attention diverted so we can pull something on you. Is that about it?

Persuading the Hostage Taker to Give Up

The ultimate mission of the negotiator is to persuade the hostage taker to give up without harming anyone. There are a number of guidelines to which the negotiator should adhere in accomplishing this task. Persuasion should start with agreement with some of the perpetrator's ideas. Agreement in principle tends to soften the hostage taker's resistance to later negotiations (Miron & Goldstein, 1978, p. 103).

Neg: I agree with you. The scandalous conditions in public housing need to be aired, and you've done your research well.

The negotiator should start by negotiating smaller issues first, such as foodstuffs, medicine, cigarettes, and ways of communicating (Miron & Goldstein, 1978, p. 103). However, the negotiator should make it clear from the start that the hostage taker gets nothing without giving something in return (Maher, 1977, p. 13).

Neg: I'll see about getting the lights turned back on, but I want some indication that the people are all right.

The less attention paid to the hostages in the dialogue, the better. Continuous reference to hostages may exaggerate the hostage taker's sense of importance, turn his or her attention obsessively to them, and steer the dialogue away from resolution (Maher, 1977, p. 12).

Neg: Yes. I understand you'll start shooting one every 30 minutes if we don't comply with your demands, but what I'm not clear about is how you particularly want the transportation provided.

There is one exception to this rule, and that is an attempt by the negotiator to foster the Stockholm syndrome. Any action the negotiator can instigate to emphasize the human qualities of the hostages to the hostage taker should be considered. Most people have difficulty inflicting pain on another unless the victim remains dehumanized (Strentz, 1979, p. 10). Thus, flag words like "hostage" should never be used (Fuselier, 1981b). The negotiator should attempt to make the captives appear as human as possible.

Neg: I wonder if you could check on Mr. Smith and see how he's feeling. We understand from his wife that he has a heart problem. Also as a good-faith gesture we'd like you to let Mrs. Jones speak to her children. They don't have a father and they're pretty scared.

If at all possible, the negotiator should try to convince the hostage takers that their hostages are actually useless (Schreiber, 1978, p. 111). At points like this, closed questions are better than open-ended ones because they force yes or no answers and do not allow for a lot of philosophizing or emotional diatribe (Miron & Goldstein, 1978, p. 101).

Neg: How in the world are you going to make your escape with all those people, anyway? Seems to me like the old folks and kids are just going to slow you down. Besides that, you can't keep an eye on everybody at once when you're moving. Do you agree?

At some point in the negotiations there comes a time when the most powerful argument can be made to the most telling effect (Schreiber, 1978, p. 112). When that time comes, the negotiator must clearly and with conviction not only state what the facts are, but also give his or her conclusions (Miron & Goldstein, 1978, p. 103). There are some things that absolutely cannot be negotiated: firearms, exchange of hostages, and, most generally, drugs (Maher, 1977, p. 67). If drugs are part of the negotiation package, the effects should carefully be evaluated by a physician before they are ever made a bargaining tool (Maher, 1977, p. 39).

Neg: As a total package you've got to realize that it's unacceptable. The guns are not acceptable, for instance. However, there are some parts of the package I believe can be negotiated. Think about it! The rest of the package is a good one and we can make a deal on it.

Under most circumstances, friends, relatives, family, clergy, and other associates should not be brought to the scene. This is particularly true if the hostage taker asks for them, because he or she may want to kill them. If people such as these could help, the perpetrator would probably not be in this situation in the first place. If bringing such people to the scene becomes an absolute must, then the negotiator also needs to know clearly what their feelings are and needs to be close enough that he or she can hear what's going on (Maher, 1977, pp. 14–15, 67).

Neg: If we brought your wife down here, what could she do differently? You already said she never understands you. Why have her come?

The negotiator should argue both sides of any point. By presenting both sides, the negotiator is more likely to be taken seriously by the perpetrator. Further, the negotiator should argue against one or more unimportant aspects of the authorities' position as a way of showing how fair and open-minded the negotiator is (Miron & Goldstein, 1978, p. 104).

Neg: I can understand why you don't like having the area outside the building dark. I know it makes you nervous when you can't see what's going on. However, think about it from our side. The cops are just as nervous as you. What's to keep you from taking a shot at them if they're silhouetted? By the way, that letter you quoted to me that you want to read to the housing authority sounds pretty good and doesn't seem all that unreasonable to me. I can't see why the mayor is taking such a hard line in not letting you read it to the media.

A combination of delaying compliance, minimizing counterarguments, and promoting active listening with the perpetrator are excellent techniques when negotiations get down to the finish. In delaying compliance, the negotiator proposes that the perpetrator not make up his or her mind immediately, think it over, and see if he or she will not see it the negotiator's way at some future point. Immediately, the negotiator should follow up by offering weakened counterarguments to the proposition. Such counterarguments compromise and weaken the captor's own arguments. Finally, passive listening does little for the problem-solving process. Active listening should be used. The perpetrator should be asked to think about his or her position and what the consequences might be (Miron & Goldstein, 1978, pp. 103–104).

Neg: You've heard what the offer is. I know it's not everything you wanted. I know that reading that letter to the media is nonnegotiable, but what if I could get them to guarantee it right after you give up? The TV crews are all here and I don't think the city administration could get away with just hustling you off. I believe I could get authorization for you to do that. Why don't you roll it around for a while and see how it comes out? There's no rush.

Although it may seem irrational to do so, the negotiator should agree reluctantly with demands that may in reality benefit the authorities' position because these points may then be used to garner further concessions down the road (Miron & Goldstein, 1978, p. 106).

Neg: OK. If you really want a car instead of a bus, we'll see what we can do, but that's going to take some more time and I don't think my boss is gonna like it. [*The situation is beneficial to authorities because fewer hostages have the possibility of being moved.*]

The negotiator should refrain from making suggestions unless absolutely necessary. This tactic keeps the hostage taker in a decision-making process (Fuselier, 1981b). The perpetrator is then the one who has to make movement. Offering suggestions may also speed up time factors, which may not be advantageous to the negotiator (Miron & Goldstein, 1978, pp. 106–107).

Neg: You're the guy who's in control. You'll have to decide what to come back with. I'm just the go-between.

Two positions the negotiator must take that may seem in opposition to the goal are keeping the hostage taker's hopes alive and realizing that the hostage taker may have to be allowed to escape. The perpetrator must feel up until the time that all hostages are released that he or she has not undertaken the seizure in vain and that there is some hope of escape. One way of sustaining this assurance is by continuously reinforcing the hostage taker every time that he or she gives in on a point (Miron & Goldstein, 1978, pp. 105–107).

Neg: Personally, I really respect you for letting the old people and children go. I know that wasn't easy, but you did get agreement on your transfer conditions to the airport.

Neg: All right! We're agreed. The Barangan government has agreed to give you asylum and has provided the plane to take you to their country. As soon as you step inside the Baranga National Airliner, the last hostage at the foot of the ladder walks away. You clearly understand that if anything happens to that last hostage, that airliner, no matter who's on it, does not leave the airport. If anything bad happens, I have been instructed to tell you that we are not in the least concerned about what protests the Barangan government might have.

Negotiating in a Hostage Situation:
The Case of James

The scene is the diagnostic unit of a large penitentiary. Ricardo Cuervo, a psychologist, has just stepped out of his office. He almost runs into an officer escorting an inmate to some part of the unit. The inmate asks him in a rather abrasive manner, "Who are you?"

Ricardo responds civilly, "Do you need to see me?"

The response of the inmate is curt: "No! I ain't crazy!"

Ricardo reenters his office and thinks, "Something is wrong with that picture!" Stepping back out into the hall, Ricardo sees what was bothering him. First, the officer and inmate are standing still outside his door. There is no reason for the officer and the inmate to be together in the educational unit. Second, the inmate is a half step in back of the officer and pressing against his back.

The officer's face looks like he has seen a ghost, and he shouts, "Do what he says, he's got a shank!" (A shank is a prison-manufactured knife.) Ricardo does not know it yet, but he is about to become a hostage.

The inmate immediately says in a low, menacing voice, "Do what I say or he gets it right now!"

As Ricardo moves down the hall in front of the two, another psychologist happens along and becomes part of the procession. Before they are halfway down the hall, another corrections officer and a secretary are commandeered by the inmate. The inmate casts back and forth, looking for a sanctuary, and finally hustles his entourage into a small office of the secretary to the director of social services. The office is approximately 8′ by 12′ and has a doorway leading to the director's office. The office secretary, Sandra, is at once seized by the inmate, and the director, alarmed at what he sees taking place out of the corner of his vision, opens the adjoining office door. He is promptly taken captive by the inmate, who now threatens to kill the secretary if anyone does anything. Seven people are now the hostages of James Worthington, a convicted murderer of a clerk in a convenience store holdup.

Worthington, with a firm grip on Sandra and the shank pressed below her rib cage, is at the side of the outer door, with a peripheral view of the hallway. Two others, the original corrections officer and Delphinia, another secretary, are in front of Sandra's desk, situated three or four feet from the door to the hallway. The rest of the hostages, including Cuervo, are behind the desk, sandwiched between it and some file cabinets, away from the door to the director's office. This is the setting as the hostage situation, which is to last three hours, begins.

Ricardo: What do you want?

James: [*Very aggressive, labile, agitated, with eyes glazed and bulging and rigid posture.*] You shut the hell up. I know I'm gonna die today. This is it!

Sandra: [*Screaming.*] Don't hurt me! I'm afraid! Please put the knife away.

Officer: [*Arms waving in a random motoric way.*] Yeah, what do you want?

James: [*Becomes violently agitated and yanks the woman tighter to him and screams.*] Shut up, Goddammit! I'm goin' out today and I'll take every one of you with me. You think I give a shit about you?

(At this point a crowd and a lot of confusion invade the hallway. It is apparent that a riot alarm has been set off. A number of custodial officers attempt to get in the doorway.)

James: [*Shouting at the top of his lungs.*] Tell those bastards not to come in here or the woman dies, NOW!

Chorus from hostages: Stay out! He's got a knife! He means business! He'll kill her!

James: [*Screaming, with menacing gestures.*] I'll stick her, I mean it.

In these early moments of the alarm stage, the hostages, including Ricardo, make a big mistake by pushing the panic button. The screaming of the secretary and motoric movements of the officer are highly agitating to the hostage holder. The attempts by the psychologist to find out what the problem is are miscalculated. The hostage taker is engaging in expressive behavior and the instrumental response of the psychologist and the officer merely agitate James. Compounding James's agitation is the confusion in the hallway. The situation out there is far from contained. A custody captain comes to the door and tries to persuade James to throw out the knife.

James: I can't take it anymore—I've had enough of this bullshit!

Captain: [*In a commanding voice.*] Don't hurt the females.

James: If I'm gonna die, I might as well take as many of these mothers with me as I can.

Captain: [*In a more subdued voice.*] Tell me what the problem is, let's see if we can resolve it.

The captain's initial assessment is by the book. He responds in an instrumental way to the hostage taker by trying to find out what his goal is. Most incarcerated individuals are engaging in instrumental behavior when they take hostages and have clear-cut motives and demands. However, whatever has happened to James, it is plain that this is the wrong approach at this moment. Dr. Harold Deacon, director of psychology, is now on the scene outside the doorway. Although not trained as a hostage negotiator, Dr. Deacon offers his services to the captain.

Captain: Doc Deacon is out here and would like to talk to you.

James: I told you I ain't nuts. I don't wanta talk to no shrink.

Dr. Deacon makes a quick assessment of the hostage holder's behavior and responds in an empathic, expressive mode. The vehemence of James about his mental status tells Dr. Deacon that he is going to have to be very careful.

Dr. Deacon: Sounds as if you're pretty angry and nobody's listening to you.

James: That ain't the half of it, Doc.

The response by James gives Dr. Deacon two clues. First, he responds by acknowledging Dr. Deacon's reflective statement. The acknowledgment indicates that the hostage holder has a lot of angry feelings that need ventilating. Second, "the half of it" indicates that the holder does have some kind of agenda, but that there is more of an affective than cognitive basis to it at the moment. The dialogue continues for a few minutes as the holder angrily ventilates and Dr. Deacon responds in a deep empathic manner. Finally, Dr. Deacon takes a risk, one that probably would be seen as tactically unsound in most hostage situations.

Dr. Deacon: I'm really having trouble hearing from out here in the hallway. I wonder if I might step into the room?

James: No!

Dr. Deacon: I understand how you feel, but I really am having a hard time hearing you.

James: Well, OK! But I'm not coming out.

As Dr. Deacon enters the room, the original corrections officer taken by James, arms waving wildly, bolts out the door. James is unable to stop the officer because of his hold on Sandra. He immediately flies into a rage.

James: Come back here, you sonofabitch. You tricked me, Doc. Now I'm gonna cut her good.

This foolish, panic-stricken move by the officer is exceedingly dangerous. Although he makes good his escape, he immediately jeopardizes the other hostages. The hostage holder, fearing he may lose control of the rest of the hostages, will invariably feel he has to reassert his power over them in very aggressive ways. Dr. Deacon will have to respond quickly with a statement designed to restore some equilibrium to the situation.

Dr. Deacon: Hold it! That was stupid. But I'm here now. You've got me, the director of psychology. Frankly, I'm a helluva lot more valuable than he is. So relax. You've come out ahead in the deal.

James: [*Still highly agitated.*] OK! OK! I got you, it's cool. That jerk was driving me nuts anyways, wavin' his arms around like some freak.

In one respect, the officer's escape helps the situation. His uncontrolled behavior heightened the tension of the hostage taker. The officer's inability to get control of himself put the hostages in harm's way, given the high degree of emotional strain that James is experiencing. His departure allows

James to divert his attention from controlling the hostages to concentrating on what Dr. Deacon is saying.

Generally, going into the room would be unwise because it gives up another person to the situation. However, Dr. Deacon's assessment is that as James continues to ventilate, his voice has toned down and he is not swearing as much. Further, Dr. Deacon wants to be able to see clearly the nonverbal behavior of the hostage holder and measure it against verbal behavior presented. Dr. Deacon is having a hard time hearing, and although he uses the fact as a ploy to get into the room, it is something the hostage taker can accept as reasonable.

Dr. Deacon: [*About 30 minutes into the situation.*] Something's really hurting. I wonder if you could help me understand why you're so angry.

James: [*Slowly, but with increasing speed and vitriol, opens up.*] They wouldn't let me go to my grandfather's funeral. Gave me some jive talk that he wasn't on no relative list in my jacket. The social worker never even come back and give me an explanation after I asked him. No respect, man! None at all! Then last week, Furdy, down in metal shop, says I got me an attitude, says he's gonna lay me up for six months without pay. Sent my ass up to the PCC [Prison Classification Committee], which lays a lot of shuck on me—six months with no pay. Man! How they expect me not to have an attitude, the time hard enough without that? Those be unjust, unrighteous people, man! They don't listen to nothin'. I may be a con, but I deserve some respect, they really piss me off, man! Well, look at me and them now. I got seven hostages. Who's got the respect now? They damn sure gonna kill me when this is done so I might as well take as many with me as I can. Particularly that sucker over there. [*Points to the director of social services.*] He sat there this morning on the PCC and didn't say jack, didn't listen to a word I said. [*Turns menacingly to director of social services.*]

Dr. Deacon: [*Seeks to get James's focus of attention off the hostage and back to his feelings about the problem.*] It doesn't have to be that way. Nobody's going to hurt you. [*Rapidly but clearly restates the hostage taker's problems and feelings about the administration's response to them.*]

Deacon's restatement seeks to affirm and clarify for James that at least someone in the administration is now listening to him. He also seeks to affirm that James is still in good shape, that nothing irreparable has happened. It is extremely important that James understands he still has options at this point and that doing harm to the director will severely limit those options for him. The key feeling seems to be loss of respect. Dr. Deacon's assessment is that James is not overly angry with what happened as much as with how it happened. The information confirms for Dr. Deacon the negotiation approach he has taken with James and gives the psychologist information on areas he will need to pursue.

What Dr. Deacon hypothesizes from James's diatribe is that he feels both wronged and inadequate. Dr. Deacon needs to reinforce at any opportunity the respect James feels he has lost. He can also use this information to set up a problem-solving situation based on restoration of James's lost self-esteem to resolve the situation. Further, Dr. Deacon obtains two pieces of concrete information, the grandfather's death and the confinement to his cell with no work, pay, or privileges, that make James feel he has been unjustly dealt with by the authorities. The combined weight of these two problems, plus James's impulsivity, has pushed him over the edge. Somehow or another, Dr. Deacon needs to right the wrong done to James.

Dr. Deacon has another piece of information, which is alarming. The hostage taker has an axe to grind with one of the hostages, the director of social services. For the moment, all Dr. Deacon can do is hope to take attention and heat away from the director by refocusing attention to the problem. Dr. Deacon also understands from James's rapid mood swings and emotional outbursts that James is on the borderline of having a psychotic breakdown. Those swings need to be contained and stabilized.

By this time a professional negotiator has arrived in the hallway outside the office.

James: I don't want to talk to anybody here. [*To Cuervo.*] You, get me the governor on the phone. Or the commissioner of corrections.

Cuervo: I'd be glad to try, but I don't know the number.

James: [*Shouts out the door.*] Hey, I wanta talk to the governor or the commissioner. Somebody get 'em on the line.

Neg: [*Outside the room.*] They're not available. Tell me what you want and deal with me. Let's see what we can work out.

James: Screw you, I want the governor.

Although the negotiator is technically right in keeping the negotiations contained, his response creates a problem. Dr. Deacon has effectively taken over the negotiation role in the eyes of the hostage taker. For better or worse, Dr. Deacon is the controlling factor and the professional negotiator is now relegated to a backup role. Too many hands in the kitchen will spoil the soup. Dr. Deacon immediately picks up on this and regains control.

Dr. Deacon: James, it seems like what we have going can be solved between us. Whatever needs to be done, I'll see that it gets done.

James: You'll just say I'm crazy. Think I'm crazy?

Dr. Deacon: No, I don't think you're crazy. I believe you're under a lot of stress and feel like no one would listen to you to the point that you had to do something that would get some attention. I can't imagine anyone not being under a lot of stress given all that's happened to you and what's going on right now. I'd be willing to go up before a judge or the institutional administration and go to bat for you, but you have to give up your weapon and walk out if you want that from me.

Cuervo: Dr. Deacon's right. Anybody would feel the stress, I know I do.

James: You shut up! The doc's doin' the talkin'.

Even though Cuervo is also a psychologist, his reinforcement of Dr. Deacon does not help the situation. James sees Cuervo and the others as only one thing, bargaining tools. Cuervo and the other hostages would best be advised to be quiet and unobtrusive in the situation.

Meanwhile, Dr. Deacon has used James's question about being crazy as a wedge. He goes on to give James a plausible, rational reason that speaks directly to James's wounded pride. He is giving James a way out with some honor attached to it and in the bargain is saying that James has an ally. He is also saying that part of the bargain will be no violence. What's more, he is shifting attention away from the hostages to James's own well-being. Notice that no time limit is put on dropping the weapon, but Dr. Deacon states this as a logical prerequisite to the things that need to happen for James. It is now about one hour into the situation. Although James is still making some erratic emotional swings, he is much calmer than before.

In general, the crisis stage has passed and the accommodation stage has commenced. Dr. Deacon has seated himself on the edge of the desk, rolled up his shirt sleeves, loosened his tie, and put his hands in his pockets. At this point a subtle change occurs in James. He pulls a six-page letter from a back pocket and asks Dr. Deacon to look it over.

Dr. Deacon: I'm frankly amazed. This is a precise, articulate, well-written letter that clearly spells out specifics of your complaints. You've obviously thought this out carefully. It surely isn't the typical jailhouse crap I see. This is good information to support your case.

James: [*Flicker of a smile, head up.*] You really think so, Doc? Would you read it out loud to those guys out there?

Dr. Deacon has won a major victory here. The letter from James is well written, and Dr. Deacon can legitimately state that. By reinforcing James, he allows the hostage taker to regain some of his lost self-esteem. Dr. Deacon reads the letter, and it is decided that a copy of the letter should be made to give to the administration and the commission. James has calmed down quite a bit.

The one major expressive problem still centers on the director of social services, who continuously receives threatening and vicious statements from James. It seems that the director is the focal point for all of James's frustrations. Dr. Deacon decides that there must be a resolution to this problem before anything else can be accomplished.

James: Heeey, Mr. Dye-rec-tore! How you feel now, baby? You ain't so noncommitted now, are you, sucker? How'd you like to get your big fat ego punctured with this? [*Waves knife around.*]

Dr. Deacon: Well, my guess is that you're scaring the hell out of him, and if that's your intention you're doing a fine job.

James: Hey, Doc, I just want to make him feel like I did when he was sittin' up there this mornin' playin' God with me.

Dr. Deacon: What you're saying is, he made you lose your self-respect and you hurt because of that. Why don't you ask him how he feels now?

He interprets what James's feelings are and attributes the causality of those feelings directly to the hostage. What the hostage says will determine a lot about how the hostage taker reacts. However, Dr. Deacon knows the capabilities of the director of social services and believes that the bet is a good one.

Director of social services: James, I don't know what else to say but that I'm sorry you feel like I wasn't paying attention to you this morning. I sure wish you'd had the letter and read it, because that would have made a difference. I don't know if you believe I'm sincere or not, but I feel bad about it, particularly since some of these people might get hurt for something I did that could have been straightened out without all this.

Dr. Deacon: James, he said that pretty straight. How do you feel about that?

James: [*Visibly calmer.*] Yeah, man, well, we all make mistakes and yours was a big one.

Director of social services: Well, I'd say from what's happened, you're right.

James: How do I know I'll be safe if I let these people go?

It is now more than two hours into the situation. This is the first time that James has talked about letting people go and voiced a concern for his own well-being. It is a critical point in the situation that must not be missed. If Dr. Deacon can capitalize on it, the resolution stage is at hand.

Dr. Deacon: What's of most concern to you?

James: That I stay alive. I want to be transported to another institution. I don't want any of the guards to get up my backside here. I also want some guarantees that when I do go out of here, that I don't get worked over.

Dr. Deacon: I can't guarantee any of that, but let's pass it on to the captain. None of it sounds unreasonable. I can understand your concerns.

Dr. Deacon makes no promises, but he owns his feelings about James's position and further increases the bond between himself and the hostage taker. A good deal of negotiation now takes place about the possibility of a transfer, statements to the press, some new demands, how the transfer will take place, recriminations, how the hostages will be released, and a variety of other subjects. The exchanges proceed with Dr. Deacon serving as the conduit between James and the captain and professional negotiator.

Captain: We can do that. I got the OK from the commissioner. We could move you to Starkton.

James: How do I know I can trust you?

Captain: James, you and I have had dealings before, right, man? Did I ever run a game on you? Tell you I could do something and didn't? If I could do it, it got done. Isn't that right?

James: Doc, what do you think about that? Is he runnin' a game on me?

Dr. Deacon: I believe him, but how's that square with you? Is he right?

James: Yeah, man, I guess that's right. But what about all those other dudes?

Dr. Deacon: Look, I'll be willing to walk out of here with you and ride over to Starkton and see you get settled in over there. With me around there's no way that any of the officers would risk working you over.

James: OK. Let's work out the details.

When James checks the situation out with Dr. Deacon, it is a good indication that a bond of trust between the two has been established. Dr. Deacon serves as James's perceptual check throughout the negotiations but is careful to allow James to continue to feel that he is the person with ultimate responsibility. Final details are worked out between the captain, Dr. Deacon, and James. The women are let go first. The captain and negotiator come into the room and the other men are ushered out. James is given some paper and a pencil to write down some more statements he has to make to the media. To get the paper and pencil, he relinquishes the knife. Once his statement is finished, James is transported to another institution, with Dr. Deacon going along to be sure that he is safe.

In this hostage situation, although it took place in a penitentiary, James typifies the kind of emotionally overwrought person with whom human services workers are likely to come in contact in the course of their work. Even though Dr. Deacon had no formal training in hostage negotiation, he was able to use his considerable therapeutic and crisis intervention skills to resolve the situation. We are categorically in favor of using trained negotiators, but a professional negotiator may not always be available. The skills that human services workers like Dr. Deacon bring to the situation may be the best and most expert available. At such times, like it or not, the human services worker becomes a negotiator.

IF YOU ARE HELD HOSTAGE

Frank Bolz (1987), former chief hostage negotiator for the New York City Police Department, has outlined some basic ways to protect yourself if you are held hostage (pp.13–23; 66–71).

1. *Don't be a hero.* Accept the situation and be prepared to wait. This may be a challenge for human services workers who are used to being in control. For example, a counselor we knew at a college counseling center tried to take action on behalf of another counselor who was being threatened by a gun-carrying female client, and ended up being shot and killed. The client felt she had been wronged by the system and was in a highly agitated state. The counselor had never seen the woman before and had no idea of her potential for violence. Instead of keeping a low profile, attempting to minimally assess the woman's agitated state, practicing any of the calming techniques in this or the previous chapter, or merely waiting for police to arrive, the counselor attempted

to physically contain the woman. He attempted to make a heroic rescue and died trying. Attempting to overpower a captor is risky. The chances of your being able to react faster than a captor can bring a weapon to bear are practically nonexistent. Underestimating the physical ability of a captor who is excited and "pumped up" with adrenaline is exceedingly foolish, no matter how much stronger or more agile you may believe yourself to be.

2. *Follow instructions.* Particularly in the first minutes after being taken hostage, it is extremely important to follow instructions. Hostage takers are highly agitated in the initial moments of a hostage taking. Any resistance or hesitation in following directions is likely to indicate to the hostage takers that they must show they are in command of the situation. A clear way of demonstrating that they are now the ones in power is to physically hurt somebody.

3. *Don't speak unless spoken to.* As demonstrated by Ricardo Cuervo in this chapter, the highly honed verbal skills of a human services worker may be seen in a very negative way by a hostage taker. While the human services worker may make good use of verbal skills when the perpetrator initiates a dialogue, any attempts by the worker to take the lead in a conversation may result in the hostage taker feeling a loss of control.

4. *Don't make suggestions.* Attempting to problem-solve may well do the worker more harm than good. The hostage is in a subservient position. Any notion about being "helpful" is likely only to antagonize the captors. Only the authorities have the power to solve the problem. It is their job; they know what they are doing, so let them do it.

5. *Try to rest.* Although it may seem impossible at the time, conserving energy is important. No one can foretell how long the situation may go on. The roller coaster ride of emotions inherent in the situation is extremely energy draining. Being fully alert and acting in a logical and capable manner when the time is right requires having the psychic and physical energy to do so.

6. *Carefully weigh escape options.* Any attempt to escape should be weighed very, very carefully against the chances of being caught or provoking harm to other hostages. It does little good to come close to escaping. The odds must be highly in your favor and then weighed against how logical and planful you are at the moment and whether you have the physical capability and energy to escape.

7. *Request aid if needed.* Once the initial takeover is complete and the situation is clearly under the control of the hostage taker, it may be appropriate to ask for assistance, as in the case of medication. Do this directly and quietly to the hostage taker. Do not dwell on this issue, because constant queries may bring unwanted attention to you.

8. *Be observant.* If you are released and there are others still held hostage, you may be an invaluable source of information to the authorities. The number of perpetrators, their appearance, what their routine is, how

they are dressed, the affect and context of their conversation, the chain of command, where they are positioned, what other hostages are in the area, where they are located, and what kind of shape they are in are all important pieces of information that the authorities can use. Further, being observant enables you to keep mentally busy, avoid panic, and adapt to conditions that may change rapidly.

9. *Do not be argumentative.* Argumentativeness is likely to make you stand out and focus attention on you. As such, you may be perceived by your captors as a threat and treated accordingly. Philosophical, political, religious, or any other emotionally loaded topics should be met with simple agreement and validation of the captor's beliefs.

10. *Be patient.* It may appear that nothing is happening to relieve the situation. Remember that time is on the side of the authorities and you.

11. *Avoid standing out.* Besides avoiding verbally standing out, get rid of any identifying information that would make you seem like a threat, an important person, or an object of hatred. While we are extremely proud of our Memphis Police Department lapel pins that identify us as members of the Crisis Intervention Team, that silver shield with MPD on it would not be likely to be viewed as a positive attribute by a hostage taker.

12. *Treat captors with deference and respect.* One way of establishing the Stockholm syndrome is maintaining eye contact, not physically assuming an aggressive stance, speaking politely when spoken to, and gently establishing a personal relationship with the hostage taker. Remember that no matter how bizarre and ludicrous they may seem, the captors are operating out of an instrumental and/or expressive mode that makes absolute sense to them at the time. Responding in a respectful and empathic way to their expressive behavior can do much to temper volatility.

13. *Don't slight the seriousness of the situation by attempting to inject humor into it.* Making humorous remarks about the dilemma may cause the captors to perceive that they are not being taken seriously.

14. *Be careful of trickery.* Attempting to gain an advantage by resorting to tricks or subterfuge is extremely risky. If the captors find out you are attempting to deceive them, they may use you as a punitive example to other hostages.

15. *Do not embarrass your captors.* Many times hostage takers will not have the mental capabilities or the verbal abilities of the human services worker. By engaging in mental or verbal one-upmanship, you run the risk of embarrassing your captors and making them feel foolish. Undoubtedly, they will already have strong feelings about being taken advantage of by the establishment, which you may quickly be seen to represent if you make them feel inadequate.

16. *When rescue comes, follow directions of the rescuers precisely.* Rescuers may not know who captors and hostages are. Staying flat on the ground with hands and arms covering your head lets the rescuers know you are

not a threat to them. The worst possible scenario is for a rescuer to think you are not a hostage but a perpetrator and react by taking action against you. Many times during a hostage rescue, there will be a lot of noise and confusion, which is purposively designed by the rescuers. The urge to stand up and run should be tempered with the realization that by so doing you will put yourself in harm's way.

17. *Talk your feelings out after your release.* Immediately after your release, you most probably will be debriefed by the police, the FBI, or another law enforcement agency. This interview is important for two reasons. First, it provides the authorities with vital information to conduct future operations. Second, as Strentz (1991) reports, catharsis allows hostages to feel some relief that they are finally getting even with their captors. It is extremely important to experience catharsis. No matter how strongly you may feel that things are back in control or how much you may want to forget about the experience, the potential for posttraumatic stress disorder is much less when feelings about what happened are discussed as soon after the traumatic event as possible. Whether that dialogue is with a support system of relatives or friends or whether it is with a fellow professional, gaining psychological resolution and closure is critical.

SUMMARY

With wide-ranging access to the media as a format to air a variety of grievances, hostage taking has increased tremendously since 1970. A great deal of publicity surrounds terrorist hostage takings, but the human services worker is more likely to become involved with a variety of hostage-taker types who have little to do with worldwide political agendas.

Although hostage taking is certainly a crisis-oriented problem, it is unlike other crisis situations in that it is invariably a law enforcement operation and one that deals much more closely with the victimizer than with the victim. The art of crisis resolution in hostage taking is the art of negotiating and calls for experience, courage, physical stamina, guile, creativity, street smartness, and a variety of other attributes. Not every human services worker possesses qualities compatible with a negotiator's role.

Hostage takers come in a variety of types. Perpetrators of such events may be psychotic, be suffering from estrangement, feel they have been wronged, extol religious zealotry, believe fanatically in a political movement, or be dissatisfied with conditions in an institution, or they may have been caught in the middle of a crime. Understanding which type the hostage negotiator is dealing with is of critical importance because subsequent negotiating strategies will differ by type. In general, all hostage takers are engaged in either instrumental or expressive behavior or some combination of the two. Instrumental hostage takers are after a very clear, concrete goal. Expressive hostage takers are in pursuit of power.

A variety of negotiating techniques are available. These techniques range from the typical active listening and responding skills that most other crisis interventionists would commonly use to some very sophisticated and, perhaps, somewhat devious methods. One of the more famous techniques may be the attempt of the negotiator to try to generate the Stockholm syndrome in the hostage takers. The end point of all these techniques is to wear the hostage takers down enough that they will be willing to give up the hostages without further violence. In all hostage situations, time is most clearly on the side of the negotiators. Therefore, it is imperative that hostage negotiators proceed slowly and with patience.

For hostages, it is clear that keeping a low profile and staying psychologically and physically alert are the best initial moves in the early stages of this crisis situation. Panic and displays of emotional instability are to be avoided at all costs. If the situation becomes extended, hostages may attempt, in careful and congruent ways, to convey personal aspects of their lives to their captors. Becoming a person rather than a bargaining chip in the eyes of one's holders makes it very difficult for them to dehumanize the hostage to the point that he or she can be easily killed. Resolution for the hostage does not necessarily occur when the perpetrators are taken into custody and the hostages are freed. Poststress trauma may be associated with this crisis and call for extended psychological intervention.

REFERENCES

American Psychiatric Association. (1987). *Diagnostic and statistical manual of mental disorders* (3rd ed., rev.). Washington, DC: American Psychiatric Association.

Bolz, F. A. (1987). *How to be a hostage and live.* Secaucus, NJ: Lyle Stuart.

Cooper, A. (1976). Panelist's report. In R. D. Crelinsten, D. Laberge-Altmejd, & D. Szabo (Eds.), *Hostage-taking: Problems of prevention and control* (pp. 101–107). Montreal, Canada: Universite de Montreal.

Cooper, H. (1981). *The hostage-takers.* Boulder, CO: Paladin Press.

Fuselier, G. N. (1981a). A practical overview of hostage negotiations. *FBI Law Enforcement Bulletin, 50* (Pt. 1), 2–6.

Fuselier, G. N. (1981b). A practical overview of hostage negotiations. *FBI Law Enforcement Bulletin, 50* (Pt. 2), 10–15.

Gladis, S. D. (1979). The hostage terrorist situation and the media. *FBI Law Enforcement Bulletin, 48,* 10–15.

Insurance for hostage victims. (1985, November 23). *Commercial Appeal,* p. 2.

Lanceley, F. J. (1981). The antisocial personality as a hostage taker. *Journal of Police Science and Administration, 9,* 28–34.

Maher, G. F. (1977). *Hostage: A police approach to a contemporary crisis.* Springfield, IL: Charles C Thomas.

Mirabella, R. W., & Trudeau, J. (1981). Managing hostage negotiations: An analysis of twenty-nine incidents. *The Police Chief, 48,* 45–47.

Miron, M. S., & Goldstein, A. P. (1978). *Hostage.* Kalamazoo, MI: Behaviordelia.

Ochberg, F. M. (1977). The victims of terrorism: Psychiatric considerations. *Terrorism, 1,* 147–168.

Powitzky, R. J. (1979). The use and misuse of psychologists in a hostage situation. *The Police Chief, 46,* 30–33.

Schlossberg, G. (1980). Values and organization on hostage and crisis negotiation teams. *Annals of the New York Academy of Sciences, 347,* 113–116.

Schreiber, J. (1978). *The ultimate weapon: Terrorists and world order.* New York: Morrow.

Strentz, T. (1979, April). The Stockholm syndrome: Law enforcement policy and ego defenses of the hostage. *The Law Enforcement Bulletin,* pp. 1–11.

Strentz, T. (1984). Hostage survival guidelines. In J. Turner (Ed.), *Violence in the medical care setting: A survival guide* (pp. 183–208). Rockville, MD: Aspen Systems Corp.

Strentz, T. (1986). Negotiating with the hostage taker exhibiting paranoid schizophrenic symptoms. *Journal of Police Science and Administration, 14,* 12–16.

Strentz, T. (1991). Crisis intervention with victims of hostage situations. In A. R. Roberts (Ed.), *Contemporary perspectives on crisis intervention and prevention* (pp. 104–120). Englewood Cliffs, NJ: Prentice-Hall.

Turner, J. (1984). Hostage incidents in health care settings. In J. Turner (Ed.), *Violence in the medical care setting: A survival guide* (pp. 171–181). Rockville, MD: Aspen Systems Corp.

CLASSROOM EXERCISES
The Case of Mr. X

The setting is a human services agency. The only information available is that there is a man with a gun who has locked himself in a suite of offices on the second floor of the five-floor building. Eyewitnesses who have escaped from the scene describe the man as dressed in casual clothes, polite but very firm in giving directions and commands. One of the eyewitnesses thinks that she has seen him someplace before today, but she's not exactly certain where that was. There seem to be about six hostages in the second-floor area, but nobody knows just exactly how many clients and staff were there when the takeover occurred. Neither does anyone know for sure whether any hostages have been hurt, although they think not, even though several shots were fired and there was a lot of shouting in the initial minutes of the takeover. The police have contained the scene and have the telephone number of the second floor. An action news team from Channel 5 has just arrived, and a fairly large crowd is beginning to gather. As the principal negotiator, you have just arrived on the scene.

Simulated Negotiations with Mr. X

You will need two rooms for this activity and a telephone connection between the two. Audiotape and/or videotape recorders should be available in each room. Roles to be played are those of a hostage taker, four hostages, two negotiators, and a psychological consultant. The rest of the class, half in each of the two rooms, will be responsible for taking observational notes during the process. One way of handling observation is to assign certain members to monitor each of the actors in the role play.

Mr. X, the hostage taker, will have to decide which of the types, as outlined in this chapter, he will portray. He is not to tell anybody his type. Participants will have to decide on the basis of the hostage taker's actions as the drama unfolds, what his type is. The main objective of the hostage taker should be to get what he wants from the situation. What he wants, of course, depends on what his type is, and it is one of the missions of the negotiation team to find that out.

The hostages themselves should be portrayed as people in the crisis stage of the hostage situation. Things are starting to settle down, but there is still a lot of confusion. Hostages are advised to act on their own resources, using whatever skills and knowledge they have available. They must follow, to the best of their ability, the directives of the hostage taker. The one thing they cannot do is escape. The main objective of the hostages is to stay alive.

The negotiators are to act in coordination with one another, but only one negotiator is allowed to speak on the telephone at any time. The instructor may wish to rotate available class members in the role of negotiators. The negotiators are also on their own resources, but have the opportunity to consult with one another and the psychologist who is on the scene. The psychologist will not engage in any direct dialogue with the hostage taker, but will be available at all times to speak with the negotiators. The ultimate objective of the exercise is to get everyone, including the hostage taker, out safely.

Although it is impossible to draw out the exercise to the duration of a typical hostage situation, we recommend taking at least 45 minutes for the exercise. Upon completion of the exercise all role players will be called upon to verbally disassociate themselves from the parts they played. They will do this in front of the entire class. Questions to be discussed by the class following the disassociation activity are:

1. What type would you say the hostage taker was?
2. How did he demonstrate that?
3. How do you think the negotiators handled the situation?
4. What negotiating techniques did they use?
5. Can you specifically identify some of them?

6. At what points were the negotiators able to get the hostage taker to give in on some of his demands?
7. At what points did the negotiators have problems?
8. What were those problems?
9. What might the negotiators have done differently when they encountered problems?
10. How was the psychologist used?
11. Do you believe the psychologist was useful?
12. What else should the psychologist have done?
13. How did the hostages feel as they went through the experience?
14. How did they feel toward their captor?
15. How did they feel toward their rescuers?
16. How did they feel about their fellow hostages?
17. How did they feel about themselves after the siege was over?

An excellent additional assignment is to divide the class according to whether they were with the hostages or the negotiators. Discuss what their perceptions were and how they might have been different if they had exchanged rooms. The audio- or videotapes can be used to demonstrate what went on in each of the rooms and will add an objective perspective to what may become some very stimulating interchanges as various people defend their actions.

CHAPTER 12

Human Services Workers in Crisis: Burnout

BACKGROUND

Respond to the following questions with a yes or no.

1. Have you left parties early because the occasion offered you no opportunity to counsel?
2. Do you continue to counsel even though it interferes with your earning a living?
3. Do you sometimes have the "shakes" in the morning and find that this unpleasantness is relieved by counseling a little?
4. Do you repeat everything you hear? I mean do you repeat or paraphrase everything you hear?

These questions are part of Adams's (1989) humorous, satirical test of counseling addiction. Yet, the questions may not be too far off target when viewed in terms of another severe problem that strikes many professionals who are in the human services business—burnout! Burnout, though, is far from humorous. Burnout is not just some pop psychology term designed to elicit sympathetic responses from one's coworkers or spouse. It is a complex individual-societal phenomenon that affects the welfare of not only millions of human services workers but also tens of millions of those workers' clients (Farber, 1983, pp. vii, 1). Put in economic terms, billions of dollars are lost each year because of workers in all fields who can no longer function adequately in their jobs. Signs and symptoms of burnout include turnover, absenteeism, lowered productivity, and psychological problems (Riggar, 1985, p. xv). Yet, if burnout has been discussed in all occupations, why should it be endemic to the helping professions?

Helping Professionals: Prime Candidates

The bulk of writing and research that has been done on burnout has come from the helping professions. In the very nature of the job, intense involvement with people is a given, and generally these are people who are not at the highest levels of self-actualized behavior (Maslach, 1982b, pp. 32–33). Burnout tends to afflict people who enter their professions highly motivated and idealistic and who expect their work to give their life a sense of meaning (Pines & Aronson, 1988, p. 11). When many of the clients get worse instead of better despite all of the worker's skill and effort, burnout becomes a high probability for these idealistic people. Compounding the harsh realities of historically low success rates, the human services business is becoming tougher and tougher, as evidenced by the increasing amount of work done in intervening with severe psychological and physical traumatic events that range from sexual assault to murder (McRaith, 1991). This is the core of the helping professions, making them not just some of the most challenging but also some of the most stress-prone occupations. Thus, human services professionals must be able to tolerate a variety of complex problems that are generally couched in ambiguity, deal with conflict from both client and institution, and somehow meet a myriad of demands from the ecological framework in which they operate (Paine, 1982, p. 21). For the crisis worker, this is true many times over. Crisis center work settings are notorious for long and erratic hours, short pay, poorly functioning clients, immediate deadlines, a lack of control over when clients will arrive or phone, few second chances, repeat callers with chronic problems, hostile and emotionally "raw" clients, and interagency red tape. These are only a few of the stressors that assault crisis workers, making them prime candidates for burnout (Distler, 1990).

However, the question arises of whether burnout is really dynamically identifiable. Paine (1982, p. 11) and Maslach (1982b, p. 29) report critics who propose that burnout is "part of the job," so if a human services professional "can't stand the heat then he or she ought to get out of the kitchen," because there "always has been stress on this job and always will be."

Such cursory dismissal of burnout does not consider the major personal, social, and organizational costs that accrue when job stress turns into crisis (Paine, 1982, p. 11). Burnout is connected to loss of job productivity, impairment of inter- and intrapersonal relationships, and a variety of health problems. Burnout is not just part of the territory; it has major ramifications for both individuals and institutions (Maslach, 1982b, p. 39). It is a very real problem, with chronic occupational stress as a primary causal factor (Paine, 1982, p. 16; Tubesing & Tubesing, 1982, p. 156).

Definition

A historical definition of *burnout* places it as a child of the 1970s. The term comes from the psychiatric concept of patients who were burned out physically, emotionally, spiritually, interpersonally, and behaviorally to the point of exhaustion (Paine, 1982, p. 16). It was first coined as a workplace term by Herbert Freudenberger, who used it to describe young, idealistic volunteers who were working with him in alternative health care settings and who started to look and act worse than many of their clients (Freudenberger, 1974, 1975). Yet to define burnout adequately is not a simple task. To highlight this problem, Riggar's (1985) introduction to a comprehensive annotated bibliography on burnout lists 18 different definitions culled from the literature (pp. xvi–xvii).

A very broad definition depicts burnout as an internal psychological experience involving feelings, attitudes, motives, and expectations (Maslach, 1982b, p. 29). Being burned out means that the total psychic energy of the person has been consumed in trying to fuel the fires of existence. This energy crisis occurs because the psychic demand exceeds the supply (Tubesing & Tubesing, 1982, p. 156). It is experienced as a state of physical, mental, and emotional exhaustion caused by long-term involvement in emotionally demanding situations. It is accompanied by an array of symptoms including physical depletion, feelings of helplessness and hopelessness, disillusionment, negative self-concept, and negative attitudes toward work, people, and life itself. It represents a breaking point beyond which the ability to cope with the environment is severely hampered (Pines & Aronson, 1988, pp. 9–10).

DYNAMICS OF BURNOUT

Burnout is not generally perceived as a crisis event because its onset is slow and insidious. There is no one point or incident that is readily identifiable as the instigating trauma. Rather, it is a slow and steady erosion of the spirit and energy as a result of the daily struggles and chronic stress that are typical of everyday life and work (Pines & Aronson, 1988, p. 11). Because of the difficulty in identifying burnout, it becomes much easier to chalk it up as a character deficit. A crisis appears only when individuals are so defeated and exhausted by the environment that they take extraordinary means to find relief such as quitting a job or occupational field, developing a serious psychosomatic disease, becoming a substance abuser, or attempting suicide. What is even more problematic is that recovery from burnout is not always linear and tends toward chaos and crisis as the individual attempts to come to grips with core issues of vocation, personality, and relationships (Kesler, 1990). As a result, the precipitating crisis of job burnout may move toward a more global, existential crisis wherein individuals are in a state of crisis over living.

Occupationally, burnout occurs when past and present problems from one's job continuously pile up. The problems may come from a variety of sources: demanding and overbearing bosses, unending blizzards of paperwork, jack-of-all-trades-and-master-of-none job descriptions, tidal waves of clients, catastrophic dilemmas far beyond the expertise of the worker, iron-clad and unbending institutional rules and procedures, communication problems, and 16-hour work days. The problems may vary in degree and kind, but the result is a continuous and grinding interface between the person and the work environment (Pines & Aronson, 1988, pp. 43–44; Riggar, 1985, p. xvi). From the worker's standpoint, no short-term or long-term relief is forthcoming.

The nonspecific response of the body to any demand is stress. Humans need stress for optimal performance. However, there comes a point of maximal return for each person. That point is a function of genetic, biological, behavioral, and acquired physiological factors. Beyond that point, stress is harmful (Selye, 1974).

There are two types of stressors. Psychosocial stressors become stressors by virtue of the cognitive interpretation assigned to a stimulus (Ellis, 1973; Meichenbaum, 1977). Biogenic stressors possess some electrical or biochemical property that is capable of initiating a stress response. Coffee, amphetamines, exercise, and electrical shock produce stress regardless of one's cognitive interpretation of them. By far, though, the greater part of stress in a person's life is self-initiated and self-propagated (Everly, 1989, p. 7).

Environmental events may either "cause" the activation of the stress response or, more often, set the stage for it through cognitive-affective processing (Everly, 1989, p. 45). The actual stress response itself involves enervation of neurological, neuroendocrine, and endocrine systems either singularly or in tandem with one another, which in turn activates various physiological mechanisms directed toward numerous target organs (p. 47). In Selye's (1956) General Adaption Syndrome, overstimulation and excessive wear of target organs leads to stress-related dysfunction and disease. If the stressor is persistent and there is a chronic drain on adaptive energy, eventual exhaustion of the target organ will occur. The end result physiologically may be as dramatic as a heart attack or as common as a headache.

Burnout does not mean that a person is just stressed by a job. Stress occurs when there is a substantial imbalance (perceived or real) between environmental demands and the response capability of the individual. Stress can have both positive and negative effects. Burnout occurs when the stress becomes unmediated and the person has no support systems or other buffers to ease the unrelenting pressure (Farber, 1983, p. 14). The outcome is a person affected in every dimension of life by unlimited combinations of symptoms. Such a description very adequately meets the crisis conditions of being in a state of disequilibrium and paralysis.

Cornerstones of Burnout

Let us now look at three human services professionals who are experientially and professionally different, but by almost any definition are in the process of burning out.

Elaine. Elaine is a telephone counselor at the local rape crisis center. She has been a volunteer at the center for eight months and has been one of the best crisis workers ever employed there, smart, vivacious, cheery, and full of boundless zeal and energy. The director had thought it one of the best days' work she ever did when she persuaded Elaine to become a volunteer. Lately, Elaine has become exceedingly curt and short-tempered with her clients and fellow volunteers and has progressed to the point that all her coworkers give her a wide berth. They no longer invite her to go with them for lunch or even dally long in the coffee room when she enters. They are frankly fed up with her complaints about work, clients, and life in general. Elaine responds by blaming them for being uncommitted and redoubles her efforts to be the greatest crisis worker in the universe. Her professional relationships continue a downward spiral.

Mr. Templeton. Mr. Templeton has worked at Central Junior High School for two years. In that time he has instituted some sweeping changes in a guidance program that was, before he came, notorious for running attendance checks and not much more. Mr. Templeton's counseling approach changed all that. Formerly, the last place that students would have gone for help with personal problems would have been the counseling office. By getting out and explaining what his job was all about to students, faculty, parent groups, civic organizations, and anybody else who would listen, and indeed, making good on his promises, Mr. Templeton has turned the guidance office into something akin to a land office during the California gold rush. His principal, previously unimpressed with anything the counselor did with the exception of keeping track of the substitute teacher list, would now fight a circular saw to keep the likes of Mr. Templeton around. What the principal does not know is that Mr. Templeton has fantasies about sending the entire ninth grade to an Outward Bound camp in the Sahara Desert.

He has not had a new idea about how to improve the counseling program in six months and is wondering if maybe that stockbroker's job that he so capriciously turned down last year was not such a bad idea after all. As he considers all this, he wistfully looks at his wristwatch, then at the ninth grader sitting across from him, and wonders whether she is in his office because of grade problems or a problem at home. She has been talking for 30 minutes and he cannot remember two sentences she has said.

Josh. Josh is a social worker at an outpatient clinic for a community mental health center. He has worked there for five years. His patient load resembles something on the order of bus traffic to Mecca. He has just received a memorandum from the director further increasing his caseload by 20%, along with a rather curt directive to move on some of those old cases and get them off the clinic rolls. Josh is sitting in his friendly local tavern quietly getting drunk and wondering how he is going to put 20 people out on the street with no support. He is also mulling over what response he will make to his wife, who just this morning asked for a separation. Among the complaints she voiced, his job was prominent: the lousy pay for somebody with a master's degree, the long hours with no compensatory time, the emergencies in the middle of the night, and particularly forgetting he is the father of their two children and a husband to her. Josh stares across the bar and orders another drink. While waiting for his order, he swallows an antacid tablet for the dull, burning pain slowly working its way outward from the pit of his stomach.

What do these three human services professionals have in common? They are alike in that they are all empathic, sensitive, humane, idealistic, and people-oriented and have been highly committed and dedicated to their profession. However, like most other human services workers prone to burnout, they also tend to be overly anxious, obsessional, enthusiastic, and susceptible to identifying with their clients (Farber, 1983, p. 4). Role ambiguity, conflict, and overload, with too much or too little responsibility and too little authority characterize the dilemmas these workers face (Kesler, 1990; Olson & Dilley, 1988; Weiman, 1977). They may also contribute to role problems by expecting themselves to be "all things to all people," far beyond what the institution itself might expect (Distler, 1990). For each of them, one or more of the cornerstones of burnout have been laid (Farber, 1983, p. 6):

1. *Role ambiguity.* They lack clarity concerning rights, responsibilities, methods, goals, status, and accountability to themselves or their institutions.
2. *Role conflict.* Demands placed on them are incompatible, inappropriate, and inconsistent with values and ethics.
3. *Role overload.* The quantity and quality of demands placed on them have become too great.
4. *Inconsequentiality.* They have a feeling that no matter how hard they work, the outcome means little in terms of recognition, accomplishment, appreciation, or success.

They have, for a multiplicity of reasons, gotten cognitively, affectively, behaviorally, and physically into psychological hot water (Patrick, 1979; Watkins, 1983). They are ineffective for their clients, their organizations, their associates, their families, and, most of all, for themselves.

Generalizations from Research

The following points have been supported to varying degrees by research on burnout (Carroll & White, 1982; Grouse, 1984; Maslach, 1982a; Pines & Aronson, 1988):

1. All stressors can help lead to burnout.
2. Burnout is psychobiological.
3. Environmental factors other than work can be contributors.
4. A lack of effective interpersonal relationships exists.
5. Signs of burnout will occur, but recognition of them depends on the astuteness of the observer.
6. Symptoms sometimes appear quickly, but most usually occur over time.
7. Burnout is process- rather than event-oriented.
8. Burnout varies in severity from mild energy loss to death.
9. Burnout also varies in duration.
10. Burnout and resulting crisis can occur more than once.
11. Awareness varies from complete denial to full consciousness of the problem.

12. Burnout is infectious in that it puts additional stress on other workers.
13. Burnout is greatest for young workers and least for older workers.
14. Minorities tend to be less susceptible to burnout than whites.
15. Men and women are fairly similar with their experience of burnout.
16. Those who are single experience the most burnout while those with families experience the least.
17. Restorative and preventive measures have to be individually tailored because of the idiosyncratic nature of burnout.
18. No known personality trait or personality configuration in and of itself will cause burnout.
19. Burnout is not a disease and the medical model is not an appropriate analytical model.
20. Burnout should not be confused with malingering.
21. Burnout can lead to personal and professional growth as well as despair and trauma.

Myths That Engender Burnout

Candidates for burnout believe a number of myths about themselves and how they must operate in their environment (Everly, 1989; Friedman & Rosenman, 1974; Kesler, 1990; Pines & Aronson, 1988; Maslach, 1982a). They tend to distort the reality of the situation in typical Type A personality patterns (Friedman & Rosenman, 1974) such that they compose a variety of irrational statements about themselves and their work. These statements are modeled after Albert Ellis's (Patterson 1980, pp. 68–70) insane thoughts people say to themselves about their predicaments.

1. My job is my life, which means long hours, no leisure time, and difficulty delegating authority. Anxiety, defensiveness, anger, and frustration are the result when things do not go perfectly.

2. I must be totally competent, knowledgeable, and able to help everyone. Unrealistic expectations of performance, a need to prove myself, lack of confidence, and overriding guilt occur when I am not.

3. To accomplish my job and maintain my own sense of self-worth, I must be liked and approved of by everyone with whom I work. Thus, I cannot assert myself, set limits, say no, disagree with others, or give negative feedback. Therefore, I get manipulated by others in my work setting—including clients. Self-doubt, passive hostility, insecurity, and subsequent depression are the reward.

4. Other people are hardheaded and difficult to deal with, do not understand the real value of my work, and should be more supportive. Stereotyping and generalizing about specific problems and people occur and lack of creativity, wasted energy, and decreased motivation result. There is a defeatist attitude and a passive acceptance of the status quo.

5. Any negative feedback indicates there is something wrong with what I do. I cannot evaluate my work realistically and make constructive

changes. There is a great deal of anger with critics, which may manifest itself in either passive or aggressive hostility, depending on the person toward whom the anger is directed. Frustration and immobilization are the outcomes.

6. Because of past blunders and failures, things will not work the way they must. Old programs are not carried to fruition, nor are new ones created. Stagnation and decay in the work setting are the result.

7. Things have to work out the way I want. Extra hours, checking up on staff members' work, inability to compromise or delegate, overattention to detail, repetition of tasks, impatience with others, and an authoritarian style characterize behavior.

Symptoms of Burnout

Burnout is a multidimensional phenomenon, consisting of behavioral, physical, interpersonal, and attitudinal components. Behaviorally, it appears as a marked departure from the worker's former behavioral norm (Forney, Wallace-Schutzman, & Wiggers, 1982). Physically, burned-out workers feel worn out because of the extraordinary demands placed on their mental and physical resources, and they are drained below their former level of optimal and capable performance (Eastman, 1981; Everly, 1989; Hall, Gardner, Perl, Stickney, & Pfefferbaum, 1979; Pines & Aronson, 1988). Interpersonally, burnout pervades the worker's life, not only on the job site but also in other relationships and environments (Kesler, 1990; Watkins, 1983). Attitudinally, burnout represents a significant loss of commitment and moral purpose to one's work (Cherniss & Krantz, 1983; Pines & Aronson, 1988, p. 10).

The symptoms of burnout when collated appear as all the evils of Pandora's box let loose. We have gleaned them from a variety of sources and present them in Table 12-1 (page 546) for ready reference. Undoubtedly they are not all-encompassing. Certainly not all human services workers in crisis manifest all the symptoms listed. Yet, for the watchful observer, many will become noticeable, particularly if one looks back in time and ascertains if there have been any pronounced changes in the worker in regard to the presence or absence of symptoms.

Levels of Burnout

Burnout can be categorized as occurring at one of three levels: trait, state, and activity (Forney et al., 1982). At a trait level, it is all-pervasive, encompassing every facet of the worker's life. The worker is completely nonfunctional in regard to person, place, and time. The trait level of burnout is extremely serious and calls for immediate intervention in the worker's life.

At a state level, burnout may be periodic or situational. A classic example is what occurs during the period of full moon at a crisis line center. At such times it seems as if every crisis-prone person in town takes a signal from a lunar clock to go berserk. Although problematic, such crisis situations are relieved when the moon wanes, and the crisis line worker returns to some semblance of normalcy. However, over the long term, such state events contribute mightily to anticipatory anxiety, which, if not dealt with, can precipitate total burnout.

Finally, burnout may be activity based. Any activity that is performed over and over at an intense level, as in encounter group counseling of substance abusers or serving as a chaplain to the grief stricken in a trauma center, will invariably wear the armor off the most emotionally bulletproof crisis worker. A simple way of decreasing chances of burnout when the stressor is activity based is to change the routine. However, such change is not always easily accomplished or even recognized as needed.

Stages of Burnout

Another way of characterizing the road to burnout is by stages. Edelwich and Brodsky (1982, pp. 135–136) have delineated four stages through which the typical candidate for burnout goes.

Stage 1: Enthusiasm. The worker enters the job with high hopes and unrealistic expectations. As bright and shining as the worker's potential appears, if such idealism is not tempered by orientation and training programs that define what the worker can reasonably expect to accomplish, such a rose-colored view of human services work will inevitably lead to the stage of stagnation.

Stage 2: Stagnation. Stagnation occurs when the worker starts to feel that personal, financial, and career needs are not being met. Awareness may come from seeing individuals perceived as less able moving up the career ladder faster, pressures from home to meet increased financial obligations, and lack of personal intrinsic reinforcement for doing the job well. Astute management policy will head off stagnation by providing clear access up the career ladder, higher pay commensurate with increased job responsibilities, reduced overtime, and a variety of other incentives that clearly say to the worker, "You're doing a good job here, you're moving up in the organization, and we appreciate it." If intrinsic and extrinsic reinforcement does not occur, the worker will move into the next stage, frustration.

Stage 3: Frustration. Frustration clearly indicates that the worker is in trouble. The worker starts questioning the effectiveness, value, and impact of his or her efforts in the face of ever-mounting obstacles. Since the effects of burnout are highly contagious in the organizational setting, one person's frustration is likely to have a domino effect on others. Direct confrontation is necessary at this stage. One appropriate way of meeting frustration is to confront the problem head on by arranging workshops or support groups to increase awareness of the burnout syndrome and generate problem solving as a group. Workshops and support groups can make constructive use of discontent by bringing about changes within both the institution and the

TABLE 12-1 Symptoms of Burnout

Behavioral	Physical	Interpersonal	Attitudinal
Reduced quantity or efficiency of work	Chronic fatigue	Withdrawal from family	Depression
Use and abuse of alcohol and illicit drugs	Lower resistance	Compulsion to do all and be all at home	Feeling of emptiness
Increase in absenteeism	Maladies occurring at organ weak points	No mature interactions—keeping hidden agendas	Ranging from omnipotence to incompetence
Increase in risk taking	Colds and viral infections	Keeping everyone subservient	Cynicism
Increase in medication	Migraine	Feeling drawn to people less secure	Paranoia
Clock watching	Poor coordination	Reduction of significant others to status of clients	Compulsiveness and obsessiveness
Complaining	Ulcers	Breaking up of long-lasting relationships	Callousness
Changing or quitting the job	Insomnia, nightmares, excessive sleeping	Becoming therapeutically minded and overreacting to comments of friends	Guilt
Inability to cope with minor problems	Gastrointestinal disorders	No separation of professional and social life	Boredom
Lack of creativity	Facial tics		Helplessness
Loss of enjoyment	Muscular tension		Terrifying and paralyzing feelings and thoughts
Loss of control	Addiction to alcohol and/or drugs		Stereotyping
Tardiness	Increased use of tobacco and caffeine		Depersonalizing
Dread of work	Over- and undereating		Pessimism
	Hyperactivity		Air of righteousness
			Grandiosity

individual. Catching the problem at this stage may well lead back to a more tempered stage of enthusiasm. If the problem is not resolved, then the final stage, apathy, is reached.

Stage 4: Apathy. Apathy is burnout. It is a chronic indifference to the situation and defies most efforts at intervention. Apathy is truly a crisis stage: the individual is in a state of disequilibrium and immobility. Further compounding this stage are denial and little objective understanding of what is occurring. At this point psychotherapy is almost mandatory if reversal is to take place.

Worker-Client Relationships and Burnout

Maslach (1982b, pp. 36–37) has stated that the only human services workers who burn out are the ones who are on fire. Between a very real dedicatory ethic and at times an insatiable need to assist everyone with any type of problem, the idealistic human services worker sees his or her job as a call-

TABLE 12-1   (continued)

Behavioral	Physical	Interpersonal	Attitudinal
Vacillation between extremes of overinvolvement and detachment	Sudden weight gain or loss	Allowing clients to abuse privacy of home by calls or visits at any time	Sick humor, particularly aimed at clients
Mechanistic responding	Flare-ups in pre-existing medical conditions: high blood pressure, asthma, diabetes, etc.	No opportunity for or enjoyment in just being one's self	Distrust of management, supervisors, and peers
Accident proneness	Injury from high-risk behavior	Loneliness	Hypercritical attitude toward institution and coworkers
Suicide attempts	Missed menstrual cycle	Loss of authenticity	Hopelessness
Homocide attempts	Increased premenstrual tension	Loss of ability to relate even to clients	Entrapment in job and relations
	Injury from accident	Avoidance of close interpersonal contact	Free-floating feelings of inadequacy, inferiority, and incompetence
		Switch from open and accepting to closed and denying	Self-criticism
		Inability to cope with minor interpersonal problems	Perfectionism
		Isolation from or overbonding with staff	Rapid mood swings
		Increased expression of anger and mistrust	

ing. In an imperfect world, such an idealistic outlook can lead to overinvolvement and identification with the client—often to the detriment of the worker (Pines & Kafry, 1978).

As the human services worker becomes more deeply enmeshed in the helping relationship, it becomes harder and harder to say no to the demands of the client because of the worker's strong need to be accepted and liked. At this point, the worker has started to take on responsibility for the client. The worker's overinvolvement with the client may be manifested in a variety of ways. Extending the session beyond its usual time limit, taking and responding to phone calls at home at all hours of the night, experiencing hurt feelings over client failures, attempting dramatic cures on impossible cases, becoming panic stricken when well-laid plans go awry, refusing to withdraw from the case when it is clearly beyond the worker's purview, and losing one's sense of humor over the human dilemma are some of the many indicators that the worker is not paying attention to his or her own needs or, frankly, to the client's (Van Auken, 1979).

Under these circumstances, the helping relationship quickly comes to be seen by the worker as a chore, and the client may regress and act out as a way of announcing the client's awareness of the worker's apathetic attitude. As this psychological vortex continues, and the worker becomes even more overwrought and discouraged, termination of the therapeutic relationship by the client is the likely result (Watkins, 1983). Such negative reinforcement does little to mollify the worker's already bruised ego and leads further to a downward spiral into crisis. Faced with failure and mounting pressure to succeed, the worker is more and more likely to start taking on ownership of the client's problems.

At times, emotional aspects of the client may agitate feelings, thoughts, and behaviors that are deeply buried within the worker's own personality. When confronted with their own shortcomings, fears, faults, prejudices, and stereotypes as mirrored by the client, human services workers may begin behaving in inappropriate ways. Workers may act in ways designed to meet their own needs and not the clients'. The result is that clients are made to fit neatly into the workers' preconceived patterns for the way things ought to be (Freudenberger, 1977).

Particularly emotion-laden issues such as physical and sexual abuse of children, terminal illnesses, and chronic suicidal ideation are prime examples of content that may be exceedingly stressful to the worker because of strong feelings and experiences the worker may have about the problem (Daley, 1979). If the phenomenon of countertransference is not recognized and dealt with in positive ways, the human services worker ends up feeling guilty about having negative feelings toward the client and is not even sure why those feelings are occurring. Such feelings are antithetical to what the worker has been taught and put significant stresses on the worker.

The Culpability of Organizations

Much of the responsibility for burnout rests with the employing agency and its inability either to recognize or to do anything about organizational problems that lead to burnout (Everly, 1989, pp. 295–297; Pines & Aronson, 1988, pp. 97–111; Shinn & Mørch, 1983, p. 238). Savicki and Cooley (1987) compared degree of burnout with work environment and found that those workers who scored highest on burnout indexes felt that they had little impact on procedural and policy issues, lacked autonomy within the guidelines of the job structure, were unclear about agency objectives, had a high intensity of work assignments over extended periods of time, were highly restricted in how they could deal with clients, and felt generally unappreciated by their coworkers or supervisors. These findings should not be construed as representing "gripes" of the respondents. Numerous other studies (Barad, 1979; Maslach & Pines, 1977; Pines & Kafry, 1978; Pines &

Maslach, 1978) have substantiated findings that agencies that do not take pains to communicate clearly with and support their staff have high burn-out rates.

In contrast, those agencies that did allow input into the mission of the organization, were flexible in providing instrumental and emotional support to workers, and had support groups to help workers solve problems associated with the high stress of their jobs had workers with lower indexes of burnout (Everly, 1989, pp. 299–309; Pines & Aronson, 1988, pp. 107–111; Savicki & Cooley, 1987). These findings are also consistent with those of other studies (Barad, 1979; Pines & Kafry, 1978; Shinn & Mørch, 1983), which found equitable and supportive agency policies and practices to be one of the main determinants of whether there would be significant burnout of staff.

Private Practitioners and Burnout

The human services worker in private practice does not have to deal with the many institutional problems that assail agency workers. Yet the private practitioner has the potential for even greater problems with respect to the helping relationship. Although the aloneness that pervades a private practice is not the same as the isolation that agency workers sometimes impose on themselves when placed in high-stress situations, it can be more complete. Fenced off from other professionals by ethical and ecological boundaries, the private practitioner has few others with whom to discuss client problems. More important, there are few other individuals with whom they will discuss their own personal problems.

There are a variety of reasons for this state of affairs. First, so little is said about burnout that practitioners often attribute their experience to personal inadequacy (Maslach, 1982b, p. 37). In our society it is undesirable to admit our own limitations. A professional is expected to be in control (Pines & Aronson, 1988, p. 5). Second, Type A professionals typically see themselves as sociable, talented, responsive, performance-driven, and high achievers. Such individuals are not likely to feel secure enough to own or even recognize that there are too many things going on in their lives and that they are not being handled well. Third, given a Type A personality, practitioners tend to invest a great deal of time in the job as a means of finding a sense of fulfillment and identity. Competition and achievement serve as guiding values that correlate highly with the need to be seen as worthy and capable (Everly, 1989, p. 105; Freudenberger, 1982, p. 178; Maslach, 1982a, p. 66; Pines & Aronson, 1988, pp. 6–9).

Private practice is clearly a business. As such, it promotes the continuing fear that there will be no clients or that there will never be enough no matter how successfully the business is going (Mitchell, 1977, pp. 145–146). Every client termination raises questions: "Will there be someone to take her place?" "Will he pass the word along that I did him some good?" The private practitioner who is moving toward crisis invariably answers these questions negatively and redoubles his or her efforts to increase client loads and effect cures.

Starting and maintaining a private practice also call for maintaining a public presence. Whether such a presence involves making speeches to the Rotary Club on stress and the businessperson, consultation with the oncology staff on death and dying at the local hospital, or giving a workshop on discipline for Parents Without Partners, the continuous pressure of needing to be seen as active, abreast of current developments, and visible are part of the sales program that must constantly be maintained and upgraded.

Although the private practitioner is his or her own boss, being an independent businessperson also means being completely responsible for maintaining the practice. Long hours and difficult work periods are the rule rather than the exception. Because most clients work regular hours, private practitioners devote many evenings and weekends to their work. Usually there is no one to pick up caseloads, so vacations or even short respites are few and far between. The practitioner is caught in a double bind. First, lack of feeling in control is clearly associated with burnout (Freudenberger, 1977). Second, while continuously exerting and extending control, the private practitioner becomes extruded beyond all possible legitimate parameters of coping. The result is that the more the practitioner attempts to control the situation, the more out of control the situation is perceived and comes to be.

Self-Recognition of Burnout

Whatever the degree of burnout, human services workers and their organizations have a notorious blind spot. What they can detect in others and change by therapeutic intervention, they are generally unaware of in themselves. Further, they have extreme difficulty maintaining both the personal and professional objectivity to self-diagnose burnout or foster the discipline and devote the energy to integrate effective intervention strategies into their own lives (Spicuzza & Devoe, 1982). If they finally are confronted with the fact that something is terribly wrong in their professional lives, their initial maladaptive response is likely to be "What's wrong with me?" rather than "What can I do to change the situation?" If they are able to move to the second question, their typical operating mode is not to *change* the situation but rather to *increase* the amount of effort and subsequently *increase* the original problem (Pines & Aronson, 1988, pp. 5–9).

What is problematic about burnout is that its symptoms and causes are neither universal nor specific in nature (Forney et al., 1982). Recognizing burnout is not always easy. In a medical analogy, its presenting symptoms might look like anything from typhoid fever to a broken leg.

Nevertheless, whereas no formula can be applied to diagnose its onset or to treat it, the affliction does not have to be terminal (Forney et al., 1982). Indeed, given the variety of symptoms and dynamics presented, both preventive and curative measures can be taken. Before we delve into intervention, we want to be very clear that we agree with Watkins (1983) that no one, and we would go a step further and state that *absolutely* no one, who practices in the human services professions is immune to burnout. It is a dangerous malady that in its extremes can be vocationally or even physically lethal if not dealt with in assertive ways.

Further, it has been our experience that human services workers, like some of you who are reading this passage and are saying, "It'll never happen to me," are invariably the kinds of fellow professionals we end up treating—or, in the absence of treatment, become those who can no longer stand to ply the trade and quit, or, at the extreme, become substance abusers or suicidal. In these circumstances, the outcomes range from bad to worse. Bad for the profession and worse for you, the professional.

INTERVENTION STRATEGIES

The six-step model of crisis intervention described in Chapter 2 provides the essential guidelines for helping human services workers who find themselves frozen in the emotional state known as burnout. Emphasis in the application of the six-step method will usually focus on the directive end of the continuum. The crisis interventionist who helps a burned out human services worker will have to proceed in a very directive manner while confronting the client's irrational beliefs, proposing definite alternatives, and getting the client to commit to specific action steps that will get the person out of the state of immobility.

Assessment

Two types of instruments are important in determining burnout. The first type has to do with determining the degree of burnout in the individual. The most often used and commercially available, the Maslach Burnout Inventory (Maslach & Jackson, 1981a), measures three symptom patterns associated with burnout. The Emotional Exhaustion scale assesses feelings of being emotionally worn out by work. The Personal Accomplishment scale measures feelings of competence and achievement with work. The Depersonalization scale measures unfeeling and impersonal responses toward clients. The scales can also be combined to produce a total frequency and intensity score for burnout. Another self-administered burnout inventory by Pines and Aronson (1988, p. 220) measures physical, emotional, and mental exhaustion.

The second type of instrument measures the work setting. Typical of this type of assessment device is the Work Environment Scale (Moos, 1981), which measures ten different dimensions of an organizational component named *social climate*. Scales range across job commitment, support from coworkers and management, independence in decision making, efficient and planful approaches to tasks, performance pressure, role clarity, degree of control by management, variety and change in job, and physical comfort. Taken together, these two types of instruments provide a way of examining the degree of burnout in relation to environmental factors within the organization that may contribute to it (Savicki & Cooley, 1987). Combining these instruments with recognition of symptomology of burnout previously presented will yield a fairly comprehensive picture of how burned out the worker is and will dictate the degree of intervention necessary.

Counseling intervention for the human services worker suffering from burnout may best be considered in three distinct parts: intervention through training, intervention with the organization, and intervention with the individual. Triage assessment of the level of burnout is important in determining the type of intervention to be used. At a trait level, individual therapeutic intervention will clearly be warranted. At a state or activity level, training or organizational intervention may be sufficient. When the organization itself becomes a client, triage assessment would clearly include the administering of both burnout and work setting instruments to all members of the organization and following up that administration with individual interviews.

Intervention Through Training

Formal training in the human services field should include training designed to minimize burnout. Students should know the signs of burnout and be able to recognize them in themselves and others. Further, they should know how to operate effectively within the bureaucracy and be able to take care of themselves when placed under stress (Pines & Aronson, 1988, p. 194).

Whereas stress reduction techniques play an important role in reduction of burnout (Everly, 1989; Maslach, 1982a), stress reduction techniques alone are hardly enough. Such an approach attacks only the work load, and is not, in and of itself, preventive. It does not consider a variety of other equal and contributing problems. Unresolved personal issues, organizational problems, and conditions outside the work setting are key components in burnout (Everly, 1989; Maslach, 1982a; Pines & Aronson, 1988).

Early in a human services worker's training, and on an ongoing basis when in practice, emphasis needs to be placed on correcting worker attitudes that lead to overinvolvement. At least a part of training should focus on increasing therapeutic detachment and moderating idealism (Warnath & Shelton, 1976). Beginning human services practitioners need to have their rose-colored glasses gently removed so they can see that their good intentions are doing neither themselves nor their clients much good (Pines & Aronson, 1988, p. 194). Most particularly, students need to examine their limited insight into their own unresolved issues and conflicts and how those interact with those of their clients (Kell & Mueller, 1966; Watkins, 1983).

Intervention with the Organization

Much of the literature shows burnout to be situationally based (Kesler, 1990); thus, the organization can also be considered as client. When an organization is in danger of burnout, it is not just one individual but all those who work in the organization who should be involved in restructuring working conditions. Indeed, one of the major criticisms of burnout intervention has been the lack of change in the total system (Carroll & White, 1982, p. 56). What makes the major difference between obtaining peak performance from workers as opposed to having them burn out is whether the work environment is supportive or stressful (Pines & Aronson, 1988, p. 48). Particularly in human services work, failures are frequently observable and there is no clear way to define success (Daley, 1979). Further, any positive impact that the worker has on the environment receives little recognition (Freudenberger, 1977). Lack of positive reinforcement by the institution is not at all uncommon and fits neatly into an aversive management policy: "There is no such thing as burnout, only staff who don't work and have malicious motives toward the organization." Any executive director, department head, or CEO who believes the foregoing has a fool for counsel. As staff become increasingly burned out, they tend to fulfill management's negative predictions about them (Carroll & White, 1982, pp. 53–54). The direct and indirect cost to business and industry due to stress and subsequent burnout can be counted in the billions of dollars, in lost talent, and in poor delivery of services (Everly, 1989, pp. 296–297; Pines & Aronson, 1988, p. 10). While much is mentioned in the burnout literature about eradicating the negative aspects of the work environment, research indicates that a lack of positive features is significantly correlated with burnout independent of the presence of negative work features. Therefore, organizations should clearly attempt to identify and enhance the positive aspects of the work environment (Pines & Aronson, 1988, p. 48).

Human services organizations are notorious for having to live continuously on the edge of financial exigency. Lack of physical, human, and financial resources militates against comprehensive service provision and long-term planning. Organizations that face crises such as funding and human resource cutbacks often cope with problems by unwittingly adapting crisis characteristics and operating in a state of disequilibrium and immobility. Just letting the crisis "run its course" is no more appropriate for organizations than for individuals in crisis (Devine, 1984).

Therefore, from an ecological standpoint, the organization needs to move away from piecemeal interventions and apply techniques that have general inputs to the total organization rather than just inputs focused on individuals (Paine, 1982, p. 25). Ideally, interventions should be multifaceted and take into consideration both individual and environmental issues in a balanced and sensitive fashion (Carroll & White, 1982, p. 53).

When the total organization is burned out, Freudenberger (1975) suggests shutting it down for a period of time. At the least, shutting down gives staff a bit of breathing room. However, this approach is generally not enough if it involves only changing the office decor, having an office party, or having a one-shot in-service training program, because no lasting change takes place. Short of closing down, which is probably a pragmatic impossibility, the organization has a number of options.

As a start, the administration can take the time to articulate clearly the mission of the organization. Cherniss and Krantz (1983) found that organizations that have a clear ideology of purpose have reduced burnout in staff because they minimize ambiguity and doubt about what kind of action is to be taken. Time should be devoted both to establishing positive coworker and supervisory relationships and to reducing the rules, regulations, and paper blizzard that line staff face as they attempt to provide service to their clients (Savicki & Cooley, 1987). Improvement of job design, flexible hours, continuous supervision and training, intrinsic and extrinsic reinforcement, and emotional support are a few of many changes that will go a long way toward reducing burnout (Shinn & Mørch, 1983, p. 238).

Most attempts to deal with the organization by people who are burned out are typified by passively hostile actions that include physical, emotional, and mental withdrawal from problems the organization faces (Pines & Aronson, 1988, pp. 91–93). However, effective organizational change rarely is generated solely by the administration. To effect change in the organization, each individual must recognize there is an institutional problem and be responsible for doing something about it. Beginning to take responsibility for effecting change in a difficult situation is therapeutic in and of itself simply because it reduces the debilitating effects of the feeling of helplessness. Yet, workers who believe that everything about an organization is wrong and should be changed are the most likely to be burnouts. Some aspects of the bureaucracy cannot be changed short of destroying it. Thus, workers need to develop the ability to distinguish between those aspects of the organization that can be changed and those that cannot (Pines & Aronson, 1988, p. 29).

While it may seem that trying to deal with the many dimensions of a bureaucracy is equivalent to attempting to drain the ocean with a bucket, organizationally all dimensions of the work setting are interrelated. Participation in decision making (organizational dimension) is likely to have a positive effect on perceived autonomy (psychological dimension). Similarly, good relations between coworkers (social dimension) can reduce the negative impact of crowding (physical dimension) (Pines & Aronson, 1988, p. 48).

Social support systems. Social support systems are critical to avoiding burnout, whether they be at home or in the workplace (Distler, 1990; Kesler, 1990; Pines & Aronson, 1988). Support systems act as buffers for the individual and help maintain psychological and physical well-being over time (Pines, 1983, p. 157). However, in the human services business, chaotic work schedules militate heavily against strong social ties (Farber, 1983, pp. 16–17) and allow workers little time to enjoy positive interaction with one another because the focus is constantly on trying to solve client problems (Maslach, 1978). Although it is easy to give lip service to having adequate supports, when workers are experiencing stress, they cannot or do not make the effort to discriminate the various functions a support system can serve and are left with a vague feeling that they are not getting what they need but are not quite sure what that is (Pines, 1983, p. 172).

Social support systems have six basic functions: listening, technical support, technical challenge, emotional support, emotional challenge, and sharing social reality (Pines, 1983).

Listening. Periodically, all workers need someone to listen actively to them in an empathic manner without giving advice or making judgments (p. 158).

Technical support. When confronted with complex client problems, all workers need someone who can affirm confidence in their endeavors. Such a person must have the expertise to understand the complexities of the job and be able to give the worker honest feedback (p. 158).

Technical challenge. If workers are not intellectually challenged, they will stagnate. Intellectual contact with significant others stretches the worker in a positive way. Such challenges can come only from people who do not intend to humiliate or gain an advantage and who have professional expertise equivalent to that of the worker (p. 158).

Emotional support. Workers need someone to be on their side in difficult situations, even if the significant others do not necessarily agree totally with the workers. Professional expertise is not necessary for this function (pp. 158–159).

Emotional challenge. It is comforting for workers to believe that they have explored all avenues in attempting to resolve their problems. Support persons serve a valuable function when they question such assumptions and confront the worker's excuses. This function should be used sparingly, otherwise it may be construed as nagging (p. 159).

Sharing social reality. When workers become unsure of the reliability of their own perceptions about the reality of the situation, they need external validation. This function is especially important when workers feel that they are losing the ability to evaluate what is happening with their clients and with the organization (p. 159).

Although Maslach and Jackson (1981b) found that the support system of a spouse makes married workers less prone to burnout than their unmarried colleagues, it is impossible for one's spouse or close friend to fulfill all these tasks (Pines, 1983, p. 172). Clearly, the worker needs to have functioning support systems at the job site. How, then, might this occur if it does not happen spontaneously?

Support groups.   Within the organizational structure, time should be set aside for formal, structured support groups. Structurally, a support group resembles a problem-solving discussion group. The goal of such a group is to build a sense of competence and help workers feel that they can deal with the stresses they encounter in their work situation. A support group is a safe place for workers to disagree and challenge feelings of helplessness. The group serves as a cathartic agent for releasing pent-up emotions related to the job. Once catharsis occurs, members can realistically examine feelings associated with job stressors. By providing feedback, the support group validates for members that they are not alone in their feelings and reassures them that they are not abnormal in their response to the situation (Sculley, 1983, pp. 188–191).

The immediate goal for support groups is solving problems that lead to stress and burnout. Additionally, talking about stressful events and feelings of fallibility, anger, guilt, and depression, and making suggestions to improve group functioning through problem solving are priority issues for the group. The group should also fulfill the six basic functions suggested by Pines (1983).

To do this effectively, a support group not only needs the support of the administration but also must have a consultant/facilitator who is sensitive to the issues involved and can walk a tightwire between allowing the group to vent feelings and keeping the group in a problem-solving mode. The consultant/facilitator also needs to be in a position to provide the administration with information from the group that will allow for effective organizational change without becoming a "snitch" in the process (Sculley, 1983, pp. 193–194).

Workshops on burnout.   For a deeper level of intervention, we would propose institution of workshops that deal with burnout of the organization, with everybody in attendance, particularly administrative heads. The involvement of administration is critical at this juncture. If workers do not have confidence that organizational leadership is concerned, and if they believe that no lines of communication to their administrative supervisors are open, then little change is likely to result (Berkeley Planning Associates, 1977). Attendance of supervisors is crucial to ensure that everyone understands the sources of stress that occur in the work setting, because the factors that cause burnout in administrators are very different from those for direct service staff (Savicki & Cooley, 1987). We personally feel so strongly about the foregoing that we will not agree to do any workshops that propose organizational change unless all administrators agree to participate fully and for the duration of the workshop.

A comprehensive workshop should be designed to explore the individual symptoms of burnout, analyze personal, professional, and organizational sources of burnout, and culminate by forming personal contracts designed to counteract on-the-job disillusionment and stress (Baron & Cohen, 1982). Spicuzza and Devoe (1982) have proposed a mutual-aid group that would concentrate on cognitive strategies such as participant presentations, guest lectures, films, and reading assignments on causes of burnout, holistic health, alienation, isolation, organizational principles, and the art of effective management. Therefore, we suggest that Baron and Cohen's (1982) initiating procedures be followed and combined with the following three-stage paradigm proposed by Spicuzza and Devoe (1982).

Stage 1. All participants complete the Maslach Burnout Scale (Maslach & Jackson, 1981a) and then score themselves. To ascertain the degree of culpability of the organization in causing burnout, the Work Environment Scale (Moos, 1981) should also be administered. Participants are then asked to write down what personal contributions they have made to burnout in themselves and others in the organization. These comments are collected anonymously and put down on newsprint. The total group then processes these ideas with a view toward problem resolution. Processing of myths about how human services workers must be omniscient and omnipotent demonstrate clearly how such myths can exert stress on the individual. Finally, in this opening stage, organizational factors that are contributors need to be examined in the same way. Within the realities of what may be done, environmental factors that make for a positive or negative work setting need to be carefully examined.

There is inherent risk in such groups, and although most human services workers would extol risk taking as a necessary component of the healing process, for them to engage in such behavior is quite another story. Taking a risk may be especially intimidating in a group composed of members of the same organization. In such instances self-disclosure may be seen as individual weakness and failure at the job. Another problem is fear of recrimination for saying things that could reflect negatively on coworkers. To provide an atmosphere that is conducive to taking risks, we would propose that a group facilitator who is not a part of the organization be retained to lead the group.

Stage 2. At this point group members should feel safe enough to share some of their more deeply felt personal inadequacies in regard to their daily functioning. Relationships with clients, loss of empathy, guilt over therapeutic failures, absenteeism, drug and alcohol abuse, and family problems due to job stress are but a few of the many problems that may surface. Confidentiality and a no-recrimination clause are mandatory if the group is to make progress at this stage. It is extremely important that administrators understand and abide by these ground rules. As the group works its way through personal, professional, and organizational problems, members should gain increased understanding of themselves and their own situation within the organization. Members find they are not alone as others speak to the same kinds of problems.

Stage 3. The group members are asked to write down and discuss the positive aspects of their work setting. By doing this, they gain a positive outlook, and the workshop does not degenerate into a gripe session. The third stage is behaviorally oriented; that is, members are asked to concentrate on development of skills and behavioral plans to disrupt the burnout syndrome. Lots of social reinforcement should be provided by the leader and other group members for individuals as they plan new and more effective coping behaviors. Typically, relaxation and assertiveness training, realistic goal planning, more effective time management, systematic reinforcement schedules, restructured organizational policies, role clarity, clearer channels of communication, job changes, time sharing, and alternative compensation procedures for case overloads and long hours are some of the contractual agreements that may come out of the program. Whatever agreements are reached, whether for the organization or for the individual, they should be put down on paper in contractual, performance terms. Regular follow-up on the progress of both organizational and individual performance contracts is vital if the procedure is to have lasting effects.

Experience has taught us that such programs should be set up for approximately three half-day sessions and should be spread out over a period of three weeks. Adhering to this schedule gives participants time to digest material presented and also sustains interest for the return sessions. At the completion of the workshop, it may be suggested that support groups be formed to continue the work started.

The individual and the organization.   Vocationally, there are four major maladaptive responses to the onset of burnout. Workers may attempt horizontal job mobility (Pines & Aronson, 1988, p. 18). It is not uncommon for some human services workers we know to move to the same type of job on a different organization every one or two years. They continuously look for the "right" boss or organization when it is the job they are in that is causing their unhappiness. Others tire of the constant interaction with clients and decide to move vertically up the job ladder into administrative positions (p. 18). What they fail to realize is that their cynical and jaundiced view of the system will not be left behind but will be carried with them into a whole new set of stresses. It is an understatement to say that these people do not make very good bosses. There are also people who become what Pines and Aronson call "dead wood." These people have long ago decided that their best bet is to not "rock the boat" so they can make it to retirement. Nobody is ever sure of what their job really is. When asked to do something they will politely indicate they are too busy, or will agree with every idea put forth but venture none of their own, or will only contribute what is minimally necessary to escape notice or censure (p. 18). Finally, there are people who quit their job and the vocation, and in some instances this may be the wisest choice of all.

It should be apparent then that at the stage of frustration, choices may seem to be limited to job change or job stagnation, but the individual does have other options. First, clearly defining one's role within the organization is a high priority (Kesler, 1990). The worker should conduct a job analysis and determine which tasks are necessary, which are self-imposed, and which contribute to role overload (Pines & Aronson, 1988, p. 109). Through assertive negotiation with the administration, the worker needs to be able to define a reasonable work level and clearly apprise clients of the limits of service in regard to time as well as the amount and kind of service to be provided. While service to clients needs to be a high priority, other tasks should be clearly prioritized. If chores that do not have a high priority cannot be delegated, then serious consideration should be given to dropping them (Poliks, 1991).

Second, coping strategies are tied up in beliefs about the job (Bernstein, 1989). Regaining control of what is perceived to be an out-of-control situation is critical to avoiding burnout. Changing one's view of a setback from a catastrophe to a challenging problem to be solved is typical of those individuals who develop what Bernstein calls "stress hardiness" and is a critical cognitive component in avoiding burnout (Kesler, 1990). Keeping a log of daily stresses encountered, what, if any, behavioral and cognitive strategies were used, and how successful they were can provide an accurate behavioral record for monitoring and reinforcing successful coping behaviors (Pines & Aronson, 1988, p. 149).

Finally, if it is apparent that the organization is so entrenched and regressive that little change in policies and programs can be effected, it is probably time to look for greener occupational pastures. Since most people who are burned out quit their job before they are fired (Pines & Aronson, 1988, p. 39), it would behoove a worker who is in the frustration stage to consider what a near-future job change entails and start planning for it before reaching the apathy stage. Knowing company severance policies and state unemployment benefits, updating a resume, saving money, and commencing a job search are examples of prudent measures workers may take before they are so mentally, physically, and emotionally exhausted that there is little energy left for a major shift in one's life.

Intervention with the Individual

Direct action, in which the worker tries to master the environmental stressors, and palliative action, in which the worker attempts to reduce the disturbances when unable to manage the environment, are the two positive ways to cope with stress (Pines & Aronson, 1988, p. 144). Direct action is applied externally to the situational stressor in the environment, while palliative action is applied internally to one's cognitions and emotions about the stressor. Social support groups, workshops, assertiveness training, flex time, taking time off, salary increase, and role shifts are all examples of direct actions. Meditation, relaxation techniques, biofeedback, physical exercise with no ego involvement, adopting positive cognitions, engaging in leisure time pursuits, and adding more humor to one's life are all palliative "decompression activities" that allow the worker to put stressors aside (Pines & Aronson, 1988, p. 152; Poliks, 1991).

Whereas workers who are at the frustration stage may well be helped by being involved in self-initiated directive and palliative actions, those at the more serious stage of apathy will not (Edelwich & Brodsky, 1982, p. 137). In such cases, individual counseling is more appropriate (Baron & Cohen, 1982). Kesler (1990) has proposed using Arnold Lazarus's (1976) BASIC

ID (behavior, affect, sensation, imagery, cognition, interpersonal relationships, and drugs/biology) paradigm as a treatment approach to burnout. To this formulation Kesler adds an *S* for setting. Given the interactive effects of burnout across multiple facets of the individual, the BASIC IDS approach would seem valid in attacking burnout in a comprehensive way.

The following case illustrates many of the dynamics discussed in this chapter and portrays the crisis worker using combinations of direct and palliative actions in an abbreviated BASIC IDS approach. It should be clearly understood that neither symptoms nor intervention procedures are all-inclusive. For example, Tubesing and Tubesing (1982, p. 161) have listed 36 possible intervention strategies that cover physical, intellectual, social, emotional, spiritual, and environmental components of burnout, and those are not comprehensive by any means. Each worker is idiosyncratic and will not have the same constellation of presenting problems. Further, workers may be at varying degrees of immobility and disequilibrium according to where they are in the apathy stage. Therefore, no two persons will be alike in resolution of the crisis. The case presented is that of a professional with many years of experience and a doctorate, but neophytes should understand that Dr. Jane Lee is genotypical of any human services worker. Her case clearly points out that no worker is immune to burnout, no matter how much experience or expertise that worker may have.

Dr. Jane Lee is a striking, raven-haired 43-year-old woman with aquiline features, a low, melodious voice, aquamarine eyes that twinkle, and a smile that could serve as a toothpaste commercial. She is extremely witty and incisive of intellect, is widely read, and can talk as easily with truck drivers as she can with lawyers. At any social function people gravitate toward her. She seems to have been born with the natural empathy and easy familiarity that many people consciously work their whole life for, yet never quite obtain. Divorced for ten years, Jane has raised her only son and has been both mother and father to him while carrying on an exceedingly successful professional life.

Jane has a thriving practice in marriage and family therapy. She has a heavy client load and is clearing approximately $80,000 a year. She is seen by her peers as extremely capable, and her clients speak highly of her. Two of her areas of specialty are dealing with families who have suffered catastrophic illnesses and unraveling family dynamics of anorexics. Jane has been in private practice for eight years. Prior to entering private practice she worked in a community mental health facility. She was so skillful at therapy there that she rose to the directorship of the clinical program.

Jane graduated from a major university with a Ph.D. in counseling psychology and completed her internship in a VA hospital. She then successfully completed an American Association of Marriage and Family Therapists internship at a private clinic. She has written and published many articles on therapy for anorexics and the families of individuals suffering from catastrophic illnesses. She has also given many in-service programs and presentations at national human services conferences.

By any stretch of the imagination, Jane appears to be a highly competent, successful therapist and an exceptionally endowed woman overall. Her ability and demeanor have made her a role model that many women in her community aspire to emulate, not to mention some few men. As Jane sits down with the crisis worker, she is seriously considering driving her new Oldsmobile into a bridge abutment!

Jane: I came here today because of what you said to me the other night when we were having a drink. You pretty much have me pegged. I'm burned out even more than what you think, more than what I like to admit. Today I had a decision to make, whether to kill myself or come here. I came here but I'm not sure it's the right decision. If I killed myself it seems like it would just be over and done with. I've taken care of everything concerning Bobby, my son. He's practically through with college, and even though we're very close, I really think it'd be better for him if I were gone. He wouldn't have to put up with my lousy behavior, and believe me, it's lousy right now. There's enough insurance to get him finished up in school and he could sell the house. He's the only one that really matters besides my clients, and right now I'm not doing worth a damn with them. I'm probably hurting more than I help and I'm just not up to it anymore, so much pain and so damn little I can do about it. The only thing I can think about now when I go into a cancer ward is how bad the patients smell. Whoever said, "You don't have to smell them, all you gotta do is help them!" sure wasn't in this end of the business. I'm also starting to behave like those screwed-up anorexics I work with, too. It's starting to seem pretty reasonable to me that they aren't eating. Why the hell should they? Why the hell should I? Just sort of fade away and look thin while you're doing it. At least I'd make a great-looking corpse. Anyway, the main reason I came over today was to see if you'd be willing to take my clients. I've thought this over and you've got what it takes. I think you could help them, and if you agree, I'll start talking to them about coming over to your practice.

CW: What you just said scares the living hell out of me. There's a part of me that wants to run right out of here because what you're saying is really hitting home with the way I feel at times. There's another part of me that wants to tie you up in log chains until you come to your senses. Finally, there's another part of me that cares for you so much that I'm angry that you've let yourself get into this predicament. Most of all, though, I'm glad I made that reflection the other night and it finally sank in. I've seen you going downhill for quite a while now. My guess is that you didn't even know it was happening or just laid another piece of armor plate over yourself and said something like, "I've got to gut this through, I can't let down, I just need to work harder," or some of that other irrational garbage I hear you unload on yourself. First of all, I won't even consider what you said about the clients until we agree on one thing and that is you don't do any harm to yourself until we talk this through. So I want an agreement both as your therapist and as your friend that we shake on that before anything else happens. I won't take no for an answer. If that's not acceptable, we'll negotiate it. No matter what, we're now in this together.

The crisis worker is in a difficult position as the client's friend, fellow professional, and now as a therapist dealing with another human being in crisis. Because the crisis worker knows the client, she feels free to make some initial owning statements that let the client know exactly how she feels about the situation without becoming sympathetic in the bargain, which she could easily do because she has felt much the same way at prior times in her professional life (countertransference).

The crisis worker also makes an initial assessment of the lethality level of the client. Her reflective statement to the client a few evenings earlier was not made for idle conversation. The crisis worker has seen a slow but steady change coming over Jane in the last three months, and as she thinks about it, she sees that it was coming a good while before that. Jane has been keeping a stiff upper lip, but there have been indicators that all has not been well lately. She has been rather cynical about clients, as evidenced by her comment about how they smell. She has been suffering a variety of physical maladies that have ranged from unending colds to some severe gastrointestinal problems ominous enough to indicate that surgery might be needed in the near future.

As the crisis worker continues to assess the situation, she further realizes that Jane has truncated relationships with most of her acquaintances and has done this lately with the crisis worker on at least two occasions. Their relationship has been characterized by an easy rivalry, good comradeship, and just generally a lot of good times together without ever engaging in one-upmanship. Lately, though, the crisis worker has had the feeling that Jane has treated her more as a client than as a friend and has attributed some deeper psychological meaning to even the most innocent conversation. If Jane isn't doing that, she has been trying to direct the crisis worker in everything from approaches to clients to buying clothes. The crisis worker has had the uneasy feeling for quite a while that Jane was trying to remold her in ways to fit Jane's image of what she ought to be, and that is the exact opposite of how she would characterize their relationship over the years.

Finally, Jane's comments about getting things straightened out with her son and getting her professional affairs in order in regard to her clients lead the crisis worker to believe that Jane's lethality level is high and that she is serious about doing away with herself. The rather detached, mechanistic way that Jane has reported all this and her blank, hollow look are completely at odds with Jane's usual sparkle, which has been absent the past few months. Performing a quick synthesis of all this background data, what Jane is saying, and the depressed way she is looking and behaving, the crisis worker makes the assessment that Jane is not kidding about killing herself and that the threat must be taken seriously. The crisis worker immediately goes into a suicide prevention mode and institutes a verbal contract with Jane not to kill herself. Even though Jane is a practicing therapist, she is no different from any other client in this regard. Besides the threat of suicide, a triage assessment of Jane by a worker unfamiliar with burnout might cursorily dismiss her problem as typical "bitching" about one's work. While her outward demeanor is calm and collected, her affective responses are uncharacteristically angry and hostile for someone in the helping professions.

Her responses go farther than her job and indicate problems with social relationships, her personal integrity and identity, and her belief system in general. Behaviorally, anytime a human services worker seeks out another therapist, it is a sure bet the individual is in psychological hot water. As previously indicated, what human services workers can see in others they are not likely to see in themselves (Kesler, 1990). Even if Jane had not mentioned her suicidal ideation, an experienced crisis worker who had no previous knowledge of the client but understood the basic dynamics of burnout would give her a triage assessment score of 8 or 9 on the cognitive dimension. The crisis worker would then begin to do exploratory counseling across BASIC IDS components with the idea that her professional problems would be spreading out across other facets of her life (Lazarus, 1976).

Jane has done one thing right. She has gone to a significant other and is using that trusted other to self-disclose in a very intimate way some of her most troubled feelings (Maslach, 1976; Watkins, 1983). The crisis worker can juxtapose her own positive outlook as a stabilizing influence against the jaundiced world view that Jane currently has.

Jane: All right, I can agree to that. I know that's part of the procedure. Hell! I guess I knew you'd do that when I came in here. Maybe I'm only kidding myself about all this anyway, just a bit of the blues, feeling sorry for myself and all that crap.

CW: I'm glad you came here, for whatever reason, and I'm also glad you agree to our contract even though you know it's part of the program. I also don't believe that about having the blues, either. I think it's much more than that. I believe right now you're hurting quite a bit. I don't know why, though I've got some ideas that I'd like to explore with you. But first I'd like to hear what you think and feel is going on in your life right now.

While the crisis worker is acknowledging her regard for Jane, she is also doing quite a bit more. First, she has made a decision that she is going to take a pretty directive stance with Jane for the time being. The worker balances between making emotional challenges to the client and listening closely and accurately to Jane's problems. She also knows that Jane is extremely astute at the business they are engaged in, as evidenced by her comment about the contract. She is not going to let Jane play the game ahead of her. Her analysis is that Jane is out of control right now. This is a tough decision for the crisis worker to make and is a crucial point in the assessment process. The crisis worker needs not only to respect and support the wisdom of the client's choices but also to perform a realistic assessment of the client's strengths and weaknesses (Tubesing & Tubesing, 1982, p. 160). Above all, the crisis worker needs to stay closely in touch with the client's needs in the present moment (Van Auken, 1979). The crisis worker is therefore going to take control of the situation and will not sit back in a passive mode.

Jane: I don't know. I've dealt with all kinds of problems in my life and right now there's nothing I can really put my finger on. In comparison to what is going on now, I can tell you that going through the divorce with Jeff, taking off on my own to finish up the doctorate, and fighting my way up the ladder in the agency and then finally making a decision to go out on my own while raising Bobby make what's happening to me now seem like peanuts.

CW: Right! Those were really tough times, and you went through those like Superwoman. But that was then, and we're right here, right now, and from the looks of it you don't much feel like you're Superwoman, or Supermouse even, and what's happening in your life surely isn't peanuts or we wouldn't be having this talk right now. So what do you feel like right now?

The crisis worker acknowledges how tough the client has been, but will not let her get stuck in the past. The crisis worker wants to find out what is happening right now. What is more important about this now than it was a year ago? Further, the crisis worker will not let the client denigrate the problem. It is interesting that if Jane were the counselor here, she would probably ferret out what she has just done, retreating into the past, in a second. The difference is that Jane has really become a client, and although she may endeavor to be her own therapist or perhaps even be critical of the crisis worker's attempts to do therapy, she is as blind to the way she talks, thinks, and behaves as any other client. Jane's being a therapist gives her no edge in dealing with her own problems. In fact, her own expertise may militate heavily against her (Kesler, 1990).

Jane: All I can tell you is I'm washed out. Some little things, really. Like I get dates and appointments all mixed up. Last week topped that all off. I saw 44 clients last week. I think I got about a dozen appointments mixed up. I had people piling in on top of people, and my appointment book was really screwed up. It was a madhouse, and some of the people got agitated. A couple wound up cussing me out, and I probably deserved it. Nothing like that ever happened before.

CW: Never?

Jane: Well, to a far lesser extent. I've been strung out before, but I could always get it straightened out.

CW: How?

Jane: About every three months things would start to get out of hand. I'd just sit back and say, "Janie, old girl, you've got to get out of here for a while." I'd just hop in the car and take off for a weekend in Chicago. Check into a hotel, take in a show, and eat some really special meals, and use about half the hotel's hot water washing the clients off of me. Seems like that would clear the cobwebs out of my head.

CW: When was the last time you did that?

Jane: [*Wistfully.*] About nine months ago.

CW: Why so long?

Jane: Well, I bought that new office and went in and remodeled the whole thing. I contracted a lot of the stuff, but spent a lot of time on it myself. I cut the contractor a deal. If I could work on it too, he'd reduce the price.

CW: So being the omnipotent individual you are, you threw out at least one thing that keeps you on an even keel. In fact, rather than getting away from the office, you've been spending almost all your time there. Let's see, we've got a couple of characters running around inside of Jane—Dr. Jane, healer to the world, and Jane the carpenter. Wonder who else is inside there?

The crisis worker is looking for a link between the past and the present. If Jane had some coping mechanisms in the past, what were they? What's different about the way she has coped in the past and what she is doing now? What the crisis worker is doing here is very different from letting the client just wallow in the past. She is specifically looking for coping mechanisms in the past that can be linked to the present and what is happening in the present to keep those coping mechanisms from being put into place. She is also beginning to build a character repertoire with Jane in the hope that Jane can start to see all the various aspects of herself that are now motivating her to do some of the things she does (Butts, 1986). To set the stage for the client's regaining control of her life, the crisis worker proposes a positive character in Jane.

CW: I also heard a character that I'd call Janice. A person who knows when her stress bucket is full, and is practical and smart enough to get away from the crap that goes on at that office. Where have you stuck her?

Jane: Back up on the shelf with Janie?

CW: Who's Janie?

Jane: She's the gal who's a little crazy. Who can joke with her clients and get up in the middle of the night and go out and start seeding her lawn and sing Chuck Berry songs while she's doing it. [*Embarrassed.*] There's just no time for them right now. It's not just the new office, but I also needed another car, and since Bobby has changed schools there were a lot of added expenses in that. So I really needed to devote my time to building my caseload up to meet those financial obligations. If I can get through the next two years, I should have a lot of this behind me and can breathe easier.

CW: Well, I'm sure glad to hear you're planning on being around for the next two years, anyway. But that's not the question now, is it, because right now it sounds to me as if you're wrung out. You don't have any more energy to give, and you've set up on the wall a couple of people who are pretty important in recharging your batteries. Do you see how important they are and what it's cost you to do that?

The crisis worker is not yet making direct suggestions as to what Jane needs to do; however, she is hoping to raise Jane's consciousness to the fact that she has unconsciously changed her operating method. The crisis worker attempts to get her to recognize this by describing what these very positive characters have done for her and how there is a void in her life when they have been removed from it. By doing so, the crisis worker is attempting to marshal some very healthy defense mechanisms that have previously helped Jane cope well with the stressful life she leads.

Jane: I guess so, but I don't know how to get out of it.

CW: What will happen if you don't work on the office this next weekend?

Jane: The new plumbing isn't in. Clients wouldn't be able to use the bathroom. I'd also feel guilty for not working on it, the inconvenience and all.

CW: [*Laughing.*] Well, the first part of that problem is pretty easily handled. Call the porta-potty people. I can imagine a sign that says "The crap stops here" hanging from the door as clients walk in. [*Jane starts to smile and giggle for the first time since walking in the door.*] The other part of that is, who's the character laying a guilt trip on you? Tell me some more about her.

The crisis worker takes a little bit of a well-gauged risk here by injecting some humor into the situation. She does this because humor has been important in Jane's life, is helpful to her in coping, and turns her away from some of the cynicism she feels toward her clients and starts to allow her to laugh at herself a little. The ability to laugh at one's own foibles and some of the bizarre and ridiculously funny things that happen in our clients' lives cannot be overemphasized (Pines & Aronson, 1988, p. 154). Van Auken (1979) extols the judicious use of humor even in the most pathetic of situations. Getting a smile or a laugh from clients is a direct intrusion into the depressive thought processes and behaviors in which they are mired.

The crisis worker also starts to hammer a bit on Jane's guilt. Generally the crisis worker sees guilt as a pretty useless emotion, consumptive of energy that could be used in other, more positive ways. Guilt is invariably an emotion of the past, and whatever was done can never again be retrieved. It is one thing to learn from one's past mistakes and quite another to carry past, unfinished business into the present, particularly when one is feeling guilty about not measuring up.

Jane: That's Mother Superior. I get all kinds of lectures from her. [*Bitterly.*] She's just like Sister Angeline at St. Mary's, where I went to school. "Say your Hail Marys and Our Fathers, get your homework done. God doesn't like a shirker, watch how you dress, mind your manners, you're a young lady, ye reap what ye sow," ad nauseam. Jesus, I hated that!

CW: You hate it, but it sure sounds like you're living it. Small wonder you're feeling so lousy.

The crisis worker starts hooking up feelings with thoughts and actions. The response the crisis worker gets indicates that the burnout has spread out into the client's family life.

Jane: You know, I think that's maybe why Bobby and I are having problems right now. I really sound and act like a Mother Superior to him. Telling him what to do, always looking out for him. My Lord! He's 21 years old and I've started treating him like he was a 6 year old. I haven't ever done that before. He's about like some of those clients I have to lead around by the nose.

CW: Did you hear what you just said? "He's about like some of those clients I lead around." First of all, I didn't know that was the business you were in. Sounds like Jane the handywoman. Fix 'em up the way you do your office. Second, I wonder how many people outside the office you've decided to fix up and look out for. I have to tell you that's one of the kinds of feelings I've had around you lately. Sure a lot different from how things have been in our relationship.

With this information, the client gives the crisis worker a chance to plunge into some core issues that have definable behavioral outcomes. By stating how she deals with Bobby, Jane is manifesting another of the typical signs of burnout: trying to treat significant others in her life as if they were in the therapeutic situation. Jane has fallen into a burnout trap of trying to be omnipotent by controlling other people in her environment (Van Auken, 1979). Her relationship with Bobby is extremely important because one way of decreasing burnout is to have a satisfying family life, especially with one's children (Forney, Wallace-Schutzman, & Wiggers, 1982). Worse yet is that she has become autocratic in the therapeutic situation, so it is not surprising that a major component of her life that has been highly reinforcing to her is no longer so, and, in fact, has taken on some very negative connotations. The crisis worker lays that squarely on her. She is mixing up her characters and has replaced Dr. Jane with Jane the handywoman. This state of events is not so surprising since both characters are working in the same office. Jane needs a break in her day-to-day activities and needs to get away from the office to do it (Forney et al., 1982). Finally, the crisis worker relates and owns her own experience of having been treated the same way by Jane. She tries to make Jane aware that, like rings on a pond, the ripple effect from her burnout goes far beyond her immediate line of sight (Kesler, 1990).

CW: Indeed, I wonder about your relationships other than those with Bobby, myself, and your clients. Anyone else you're trying to control right now?

Jane: [*Frostily.*] If you mean men, absolutely no, or anybody else, for that matter. When I get home at night, I'm so bushed all I want to do is fall asleep, but then all those clients go tumbling around in my head, and I start thinking about car payments, mortgage payments, how to straighten things out with Bobby, and I wind up getting about two or three hours of sleep a night.

CW: So right now you're so exhausted that you'd just rather be alone.

Jane: That's right, but I feel like I ought to be out mingling with people. I'm so damned isolated anyway.

CW: OK! I can understand that, and I'd agree with you, but let's look at right now. Seems as if you really need some time to just curl up in the fetal position, turn the electric blanket up to nine, and get your batteries recharged. Could you do that? I mean seriously, just go home and go to bed, take the phone off the hook, put the answering service on until Monday, and not get up for the whole weekend.

Jane: I suppose.

CW: No supposes. If you don't want to do that, we'll look at something else. But right now you look like the *Grapes of Wrath* and just seem to really need to rest before you think about doing anything else. Are you willing to call the contractor up and tell him you won't be there Saturday and Sunday without feeling guilty about it?

Jane: I could use the rest. All right! I'll give it this weekend.

CW: Fine. But there's one more thing. If you really get to feeling blue, plug the phone in and call me at home. I also want a report next week, so what time do you want to come in?

Jane: Sounds like I'm a client.

CW: Sounds like you're right. [*Laughs.*]

The crisis worker is basically assisting Jane to make a simple commitment to do one thing—get some rest. A critical component in treating burnout is revitalization (Tubesing & Tubesing, 1982, p. 160). Jane is physically fatigued, and the first order of business is to get her physical batteries recharged. A number of other options are available at this juncture, but the crisis worker follows Tubesing and Strosahl's (1976) advice to let the client make the choice of what treatment is appropriate. Keying on the client's own words about needing sleep, the crisis worker follows up and gains commitment to a specific behavior that the client will engage in over the short term. This is not a dramatic first step, but considering the least dramatic steps first is probably the way to go (Van Auken, 1979). The most important objective of this initial encounter is finding some short-term intervention techniques that the client is able and willing to utilize (Freudenberger & Robbins, 1979).

A particular behavior the crisis worker touches on is the use of the telephone. Private practitioners are notorious for taking phone calls from clients at all hours of the night and on weekends. Van Auken (1979) urges human services workers not to let clients run or, for that matter, ruin their personal lives. The crisis worker makes sure that Jane follows this dictum. Finally, the worker provides emotional support, but once Jane is able to ventilate her feelings, the worker is going to move into a problem-solving mode. Getting Jane out of the office and into bed is a first step in alleviating her burnout.

Next week.

Jane: I'll have to admit I do feel better. Couldn't sleep at all Friday night, but I got ten hours in Saturday. I can't believe it! I woke up and I was all curled up in the fetal position. The clients looked somewhat better this week. I can't say it was wonderful, but at least I wasn't an ogre to them. I guess what bothers me most about that is that I've lost all my creativity.

CW: OK! Let's talk about that a bit. You haven't been paying very much attention to the right side of your brain, so what do you expect? What could you do creatively that isn't client involved that'd get the right side of your head going again?

Jane: I've got a couple of articles I've been putting off—how about that?

CW: Got anything to do with clients?

Jane: Yes.

CW: Is that going to help you out?

Jane: I don't guess so, the same old stuff, only I'm writing about it.

CW: What else, then?

Forney et al. (1982) propose that a variety of professional activities may be an excellent coping mechanism; nevertheless, the crisis worker confronts Jane about this suggested alternative. The crisis worker is fairly sure that the client's stress bucket is full to the brim professionally. Jane needs to become less, not more, involved in her professional life. Jane's response confirms the crisis worker's confrontation.

Jane: Well, there is something else. I bought this sailboat for Bobby and me. The Coast Guard Auxiliary is putting on a sailing class. It would sure surprise Bobby if the next time he came home I could handle that Y flyer.

CW: Is that something you want to do? Would like to do, not need to do it?

Jane: Yes!

CW: And not pile it on top of everything else. Really reserve some time for yourself to enjoy it.

Jane: You sure drive a hard bargain, but I can do it.

This is a wedge in the behavioral repertoire of the client that the crisis worker has been looking to find. Writer after writer in the burnout literature has promoted the use of leisure, particularly physical exercise, as a way of breaking up the dogmatic, work-brittle behavior of just going through the motions that often characterizes the burned-out human services worker (Dowd, 1981; Freudenberger & Robbins, 1979; Savicki & Cooley, 1982). By proposing for the client a combination of leisure, physical exercise, and quality time with her son, the crisis worker has neatly integrated a number of positive interventions. The crisis worker now takes on the main issue of the client's private practice.

CW: Fine. Let's talk about your practice for a while.

Jane: You know as well as I do about that. Sure, I've got a great caseload now. But who knows, it might dry up next week, and then where would I be? The bills don't wait.

CW: Has it ever dried up? Even in the last recession?

Jane: No, it hasn't, but I keep expecting the worst.

CW: You've been in private practice eight years now, right? Has it ever been such that you didn't have enough clients to keep the wolves away from your door?

Jane: No. I guess there's something else. I feel a little foolish saying this, but it's almost like if I don't live up to my reputation and take on those really tough cases, I start feeling like I'm not the queen of the mountain. I mean in the past, I've been real proud of that, but now I don't seem to feel anything but that there's an albatross around my neck.

CW: Sounds like Superwoman again. I frankly admire you for dealing with those terminals' families, and you're right! Not many could do that. But if there's no intrinsic payoff, why are you fooling yourself into thinking you can heal the whole world? See the trap you've put yourself into?

Jane: Well, no! I guess I don't.

CW: OK! I want to try something. Maybe you've used it on some of your clients before. It's a game of "Who Told You?" I want you to move over to my chair and ask that empty chair, which will represent Jane, some questions. I'm going to stand aside and process as we go along, but it'll mostly be up to you. I want you to use all your insight as a therapist and really bore in and go to work on Jane's fictional goals, those crazy things she tells herself that have no counterpart in reality. All right, let's start.

Jane as CW: [*Shifts chairs and gets a glitter in her eyes.*] OK, toots! Who told you you had to be Superwoman?

CW: Now shift back.

Jane: Nobody really, I've just got a lot of responsibilities.

Jane as CW: Responsibilities, my foot! You've been going up that success ladder so fast you've scorched the rungs. Always got to show them. Be number one. My God! You little twirp. You're 43 years old and you still think you're back on the VA ward. Got to show them you're better than any man. Volunteer for the worst cases. Scared to death you won't succeed. And when you did, you were scared you wouldn't succeed the second time. Who told you that?

Jane: Nobody! It was reality. I had to be better than the men there.

Jane as CW: That was 20 years ago, nerd! The only men you deal with now are your clients. And that's another thing, is that why you're so damned afraid of going out with any other man? And don't give me that stuff about getting burned again, you know why that divorce happened, and it sure doesn't have anything to do with having good social relationships now.

Jane: It's just that with the financial obligations for Bobby, I really don't have the time.

Jane as CW: [*Really angry and shouting.*] I won't have that! How long will you be responsible for him? He's 21 years old. Who supported you when you were 21? I'll tell you who. You did! You just use that as an excuse. Just like you use all those clients as an excuse. You don't fool me, you little martyr. Oh, sure! You get those strokes. [*Dripping sarcasm.*] Just like Annette here said, "I really admire you, Jane." You go around fooling everybody, but worst of all you fool yourself. Look at you. Sitting here the pathetic little wretch. You don't fool me. You're not little Miss Goody Two-Shoes. Behind all that depression is a really angry, bitter bitch who's always going around being everybody's servant. So just who told you you had to be that?

Jane: [*Breaks and sobs. The CW goes to Jane, gathers her into her arms, and hugs her for dear life. Five minutes elapse.*] Good Lord! I didn't realize that was all in there. I really got on a roll.

CW: Neither did I, but I figured if anybody could get it out, you could. What have you got out of that?

Jane: Besides spilling my guts, which I haven't done in 25 years, I see now how I got into this. I really set myself up.

CW: What do you want to do?

Jane: Well, I'm not going to kill myself literally or figuratively. I've got some living to do, and while I'm not going to quit the practice, there sure are going to be some limits put on it.

The "Who Told You?" technique is a combination of Adlerian, rational-emotive, and Gestalt therapy that is extremely powerful. Given a person with the kind of insight Jane has, it often has dramatic results in pointing out the way clients delude themselves. By using Jane as her own therapist, the crisis worker provides no one for the client to rationalize to, attack, manipulate, or otherwise attempt to fool but herself. For a person with Jane's abilities and insight, that seldom happens for very long. Underneath most depression lies anger. If that anger can be mobilized, then the client has taken a major step toward getting back into control of the situation. By putting Jane in a position to view her behavior from outside herself and also giving her a stimulus to attack her irrational ideas by the "Who Told You?" technique, the crisis worker provides an arena in which Jane can combat the apathy she is experiencing.

Such a dramatic shift to being mobile is uncommon among the general populace and in Jane's case is a condensed version of what may generally happen. The crisis worker often has to provide the stimulus statements that are the core of clients' irrational ideas because of clients' poor cognition of their own negative self-talk. However, in dealing with highly trained professionals, it is not uncommon for such rapid shifts to occur. Given the initial stimulus, they may pick up on the technique and provide their own dialogue with little or no help from the crisis worker. When emotional catharsis occurs, the crisis worker then takes a nondirective stance and serves as little more than a sounding board as their fellow professionals put reasonable parameters back into their lives. At that point, human services workers who are clients tend to be able to make good decisions quickly about the behavioral, emotional, and cognitive aspects of their lives. Indeed, if burnout syndrome is successfully overcome, it is not unreasonable to expect that human services workers will come back to their profession with hardier personalities, stronger commitments to self and profession, better self-temperance, a greater sense of meaningfulness, and increased vigor toward their environment (Kobasa, 1979). Further, new coping styles that include greater self-awareness, increased self-insight, and a more direct approach to problem solving are likely to result for those who successfully navigate these treacherous waters (Cooley & Keesey, 1981). Finally, it is our own observation that human services professionals who have successfully conquered burnout respond not only to their work but also to their daily living with calmer and wiser choices, behaviors, and work style.

In this vingette the crisis worker uses the BASIC IDS model to deal with multiple, overlapping issues in the client's life (Kesler, 1990). Jane's work load affects her relationship with her family and friends. Her role as mother affects her image of herself. Her image of herself affects her beliefs about her abilities as therapist and mother and finally affects her coping behaviors across the board. The crisis worker links all of these dimensions into a unified whole because each modality interacts with other modalities and should not be treated in isolation (Cormier & Cormier, 1985, p. 153). Jane's sailing expeditions not only will provide her with fun, relaxation, and togetherness with her son, but also are as necessary to her therapuetic functioning as her Ph.D. training. Achieving balance among the various parts of her life and compartmentalizing them to the extent that they do not start to run into or over one another allows Dr. Jane to be fully functioning in all of them and at the same time limits the stresses inherent in each (Pines & Aronson, 1988, p. 152).

SUMMARY

Burnout is not simply a sympathy-eliciting term to use when one has had a hard day at the office. It is a very real malady that strikes people and can have extremely severe consequences. It is prevalent in the human services professions because of the kinds of clients, environments, working conditions, and resultant stresses that are operational there. No one particular individual is more prone to experience burnout than another. However, by their very nature, most human services workers tend to be highly committed to their profession, and such commitment is a necessary precursor to burnout. Private practitioners may experience burnout even more severely than their counterparts in organizations because of their professional isolation. All human services workers, public or private, tend to be unable to identify the problem when it is their own. No one is immune to its effects.

Burnout moves through stages of enthusiasm, stagnation, frustration, and apathy. In its end stage, burnout is a crisis situation. The crisis takes many forms. It can be manifested behaviorally, physically, interpersonally, and attitudinally. It pervades the professional's life and can have effects on clients, coworkers, family, friends, and the organization itself.

Recognition of the beginning symptoms of burnout can alleviate its personal and organizational ramifications. Raising consciousness levels in regard to the dynamics of burnout in training programs and conducting on-the-job workshops are important ways of halting and ameliorating its effects. Support groups within the organization that provide instrumental and emotional resources to victims are important. In the past, burnout has been regarded as a malady that resides only within the individual. That view is archaic. Burnout should also be viewed in a systems perspective and as an organizational problem.

Intervention may occur on both an organizational and an individual level. At its end stage, burnout is a crisis situation that calls for immediate, direct, and reality-oriented therapeutic intervention. Given corrective remediation, victims of burnout can return to the job and again become productive.

REFERENCES

Adams, K. O. (1989). Have you been counseling too hard and too long? *The School Counselor, 36,* 165–166.

Barad, C. B. (1979). *Study of burnout syndrome among SSA field public contract employees.* Washington, DC: Social Security Administration, Office of Management, Budget, and Personnel, Office of Human Resources.

Baron, A., Jr., & Cohen, R. B. (1982). Helping telephone counselors cope with burnout: A consciousness-raising workshop. *Personnel and Guidance Journal, 60,* 508–510.

Berkeley Planning Associates. (1977). *Evaluation of child abuse and neglect demonstration projects, 1974–1977: Volume IX. Project management and worker burnout.* Washington, DC: U.S. Department of Commerce.

Bernstein, A. J. (1989). *Dinosaur brains.* New York: Wiley.

Butts, S. (Speaker). (1986). *Therapeutic techniques, marriage and family therapy* (Cassette Recording No. 6611-12). Memphis: Department of Counseling and Personnel Services, Memphis State University.

Carroll, J.F.X., & White, W. L. (1982). Theory building: Integrating individual and environmental factors within an ecological framework. In W. S. Paine (Ed.), *Job stress and burnout* (pp. 41–60). Beverly Hills, CA: Sage Publications.

Cherniss, C., & Krantz, D. L. (1983). The ideological community as an antidote to burnout in the human services. In B. A. Farber (Ed.), *Stress and burnout in the human service professions* (pp. 198–212). New York: Pergamon Press.

Cooley, E. J., & Keesey, J. C. (1981). Relationship between life change and illness in coping versus sensitive persons. *Psychological Reports, 48,* 711–714.

Cormier, W. H., & Cormier, L. S. (1985). *Interviewing strategies for helpers: Fundamental skills and cognitive behavioral interventions* (2nd ed.). Monterey, CA: Brooks/Cole.

Daley, M. R. (1979). Burnout—Smoldering problem in protective services. *Social Work, 58,* 375–379.

Devine, I. (1984). Organizational crisis and individual response: New trends for human service professionals [Special issue: Education and training in Canadian human services]. *Canadian Journal of Community Mental Health, 3,* 63–72.

Distler, B. J. (1990). *Reducing the potential for burnout.* Paper presented at Crisis Convening XIV, Chicago.

Dowd, E. T. (Ed.). (1981). Leisure counseling [Special issue]. *Counseling Psychologist, 9.*

Edelwich, J., & Brodsky, A. (1982). Training guidelines: Linking the workshop experience to needs on and off the job. In W. S. Paine (Ed.), *Job Stress and burnout* (pp. 133–154). Beverly Hills, CA: Sage Publications.

Ellis, A. (1973). *Humanistic psychology: The rational-emotive approach.* New York: Julian.

Everly, G. S. (1989). *A clinical guide to the treatment of the human stress response.* New York: Plenum Press.

Farber, B. A. (Ed.). (1983). *Stress and burnout in the human service professions.* New York: Pergamon Press.

Forney, D. S., Wallace-Schutzman, F., & Wiggers, T. T. (1982). Burnout among career development professionals: Preliminary findings and implications. *Personnel and Guidance Journal, 60,* 435–439.

Freudenberger, H. J. (1974). Staff burn-out. *Journal of Social Issues, 30,* 159–165.

Freudenberger, H. J. (1975). The staff burnout syndrome in alternative institutions. *Psychotherapy: Theory, research, and practice, 12,* 73–82.

Freudenberger, H. J. (1977). Burn-out: Occupational hazard of child care workers. *Child Care Quarterly, 6,* 90–99.

Freudenberger, H. J. (1982). Counseling and dynamics: Treating the end-stage person. In W. S. Paine (Ed.), *Job stress and burnout* (pp. 173–188). Beverly Hills, CA: Sage Publications.

Freudenberger, H. J., & Robbins, A. (1979). The hazards of being a psychoanalyst. *Psychoanalytic Review, 66,* 275–296.

Friedman, M., & Rosenman, R. (1974). *Type A behavior and your heart.* Greenwich, CT: Fawcett Publications.

Grouse, A. S. (1984). The effects of organizational stress on inpatient psychiatric medication patterns. *American Journal of Psychiatry, 141,* 878–881.

Hall, R. C. W., Gardner, E. R., Perl, M., Stickney, S. K., & Pfefferbaum, B. (1979). The professional burnout syndrome. *Psychiatric Opinion, 16,* 12–17.

Kell, B. L., & Mueller, W. J. (1966). *Impact and change: A study of counseling relationships.* New York: Appleton-Century-Crofts.

Kesler, K. D. (1990). Burnout: A multimodal approach to assessment and resolution. *Elementary School Guidance & Counseling, 24,* 303–311.

Kobasa, S. (1979). Stressful life events, personality, and health: An inquiry into hardiness. *Journal of Personality and Social Psychology, 37,* 1–11.

Lazarus, A. A. (1976). *Multimodal behavior therapy.* New York: Springer.

Maslach, C. (1976). Burned-out. *Human Behavior, 5,* 16–22.

Maslach, C. (1978). The client role in staff burn-out. *Journal of Social Issues, 34,* 111–124.

Maslach, C. (1982a). *Burnout—The cost of caring.* Englewood Cliffs, NJ: Prentice-Hall.

Maslach, C. (1982b). Understanding burnout: Definitional issues in analyzing a complex phenomenon. In W. S. Paine (Ed.), *Job stress and burnout* (pp. 29–40). Beverly Hills, CA: Sage Publications.

Maslach, C., & Jackson, S. E. (1981a). *The Maslach Burnout Inventory.* Palo Alto, CA: Consulting Psychologists Press.

Maslach, C., & Jackson, S. E. (1981b). The measurement of experienced burnout. *Journal of Occupational Behavior, 2,* 99–113.

Maslach, C., & Pines, A. (1977). The burn-out syndrome in the day care setting. *Child Care Quarterly, 6,* 100–113.

McRaith, C. F. (1991, April). *Coping with society's secret: Social support, job stress, and burnout among therapists treating victims of sexual abuse.* Paper presented at Crisis Convening XV, Chicago.

Meichenbaum, D. (1977). *Cognitive-behavior modification.* New York: Plenum Press.

Mitchell, M. D. (1977). Consultant burnout. In J. W. Pfeiffer & J. E. Jones (Eds.), *The 1977 annual handbook for group facilitators* (pp. 143–146). La Jolla, CA: University Associates.

Moos, R. H. (1981). *Work Environment Scale manual.* Palo Alto, CA: Consulting Psychologists Press.

Olson, M. J., & Dilley, J. S. (1988). A new look at stress and the school counselor. *The School Counselor, 35,* 194–198.

Paine, W. S. (1982). Overview of burnout stress syndromes and the 1980's. In W. S. Paine (Ed.), *Job stress and burnout* (pp. 11–25). Beverly Hills, CA: Sage Publications.

Patrick, P. K. S. (1979, November). Burnout: Job hazard for health workers. *Hospitals,* pp. 87–90.

Patterson, C. H. (1980). *Theories of counseling and psychotherapy* (3rd ed.). New York: Harper & Row.

Pines, A. M. (1983). On burnout and the buffering effects of social support. In B. A. Farber (Ed.), *Stress and burnout in the human service professions* (pp. 155–173). New York: Pergamon Press.

Pines, A., & Aronson, E. (1988). *Career burnout: Causes and cures.* New York: Free Press.

Pines, A. M., & Kafry, D. (1978). Occupational tedium in the social services. *Social Work, 23,* 499–507.

Pines, A. M., & Maslach, C. (1978). Characteristics of staff burnout in mental health settings. *Hospital and Community Psychiatry, 29,* 223–237.

Poliks, O. (1991, June). *Helping the helpers: Stress management and burnout prevention for schools.* Paper presented at the American School Counselor Association Conference, Des Moines, IA.

Riggar, T. F. (1985). *Stress burnout: An annotated bibliography.* Carbondale, IL: Southern Illinois University Press.

Savicki, V., & Cooley, E. J. (1982). Implications of burnout research and theory for counselor education. *Personnel and Guidance Journal, 60,* 415–419.

Savicki, V., & Cooley, E. J. (1987). The relationship of work environment and client contact to burnout in mental health professionals. *Journal of Counseling and Development, 65,* 249–252.

Sculley, R. (1983). The work-setting support group: A means of preventing burnout. In B. A. Farber (Ed.), *Stress and burnout in the human service professions* (pp. 198–212). New York: Pergamon Press.

Selye, H. (1956). *The stress of life.* New York: McGraw-Hill.

Selye, H. (1974). *Stress without distress.* Philadelphia: Lippincott.

Shinn, M., & Mørch, H. (1983). A tripartite model of coping with burnout. In B. A. Farber (Ed.), *Stress and burnout in the human service professions* (pp. 227–239). New York: Pergamon Press.

Spicuzza, F. J., & Devoe, M. W. (1982). Burnout in the helping professions: Mutual aid as self-help. *Personnel and Guidance Journal, 61,* 95–98.

Tubesing, D. A., & Strosahl, S. G. (1976). *Wholistic health centers: Survey research report.* Hinsdale, IL: Society for Wholistic Medicine.

Tubesing, N. L., & Tubesing, D. A. (1982). The treatment of choice: Selecting stress skills to suit the individual and the situation. In W. S. Paine (Ed.), *Job stress and burnout* (pp. 155–172). Beverly Hills, CA: Sage Publications.

Van Auken, S. (1979). Youth counselor burnout. *Personnel and Guidance Journal, 58,* 143–144.

Warnath, C. F., & Shelton, J. L. (1976). The ultimate disappointment: The burned-out counselor. *Personnel and Guidance Journal, 55,* 172–175.

Watkins, C. E. (1983). Burnout in counseling practice: Some potential professional and personal hazards of becoming a counselor. *Personnel and Guidance Journal, 61,* 304–308.

Weiman, C. (1977). A study of occupational stressors and the incidence of disease/risk. *Journal of Occupational Medicine, 19,* 119–122.

CLASSROOM EXERCISES
The Case of Steve

Steve is an elementary school guidance counselor. He has worked eight years in an urban school system. In that time he has built a guidance program from the ground up. Career awareness/exploration, developmental guidance, individual personal counseling, and parent-training groups are but a few of the activities he has instituted with little budget and no help. When there was no money for materials, Steve cajoled civic organizations. When students needed dental work and could afford none, Steve got it done free. He has counseled such problems as child abuse, suicide attempts, drug addiction, and home breakups and has done an excellent job. Teachers and parents have also sought him out for personal counseling; and he has done an excellent job with them too.

Steve is active in professional and civic organizations. When not working, Steve devotes a great portion of his time to his family: his wife, two daughters, and invalid mother. A keen sense of humor and a positive word for everybody typify Steve. His major recreational pursuits are working in his garden, carving duck decoys, and playing an occasional game of penny-ante gin rummy with some other teachers. Steve was just elected as outstanding educator of the year in the metropolitan area where he works. By any measure, Steve is doing an outstanding job, both professionally and personally.

Steve is just now at the American School Counselor Conference, which he has not missed in his tenure as a counselor. Actually, he is in a bar in the city in which the conference is being held. Steve is in the process of getting roaring drunk for the second day in a row. So far he has failed to put in an appearance at the conference, even to make a presentation he was scheduled to give. He cannot remember getting this inebriated since he got out of the service. To say that such behavior is highly unlike this conscientious young man is putting it rather mildly.

The only thing Steve is really sure of is that if he sees, hears, talks, or does anything that vaguely resembles counseling, he is afraid he will go stark raving mad. A not-so-subtle corollary to that neon sign that keeps flashing on and off in his head is that he no longer cares to be nice, friendly, brave, or obey any of the other Boy Scout laws to anyone for any reason. That includes his wife, with whom he had a fight before he left home. The fracas was over putting his mother into a nursing home. He immediately buries that horrid thought and broods over his shot of bourbon. At this particular moment, his good friend Mike, a buddy from Vietnam and graduate school days who is also a middle school counselor, walks into the bar, orders a beer, and sits down on a stool next to Steve. The following conversation takes place:

Mike: [*Cheerful but concerned.*] Hey, man! How you doin'? The chicks from Colorado told me you were in here getting hammered and said you told them to bug off. You must be getting choosy in your old age, those are some fine women. What's the deal?

Steve: If you want a drink, fine. If you wanta get inside my head, get the hell outta here and go back to the conference. I've had it with this stuff. I don't even know why I came, except this is a pretty nice bar. It's really quiet in here and people tend to their own business, catch my drift?

Mike: [*Smiling but dead serious.*] Uh huh! Well, watch my lips, screwball! This is the guy who sweated with you through the two worst pieces of your otherwise Prince Charming life. I am talkin' Nam and Stat II. I also remind you now that I am the godfather to your kids and haven't seen you this stewed up since we got back to Frisco from Nam. Besides which, I'm bigger than you and you can't throw me out. So what's eatin' on you, anyways? You're mad as hell about somethin'.

Steve: [*Angry but depressed.*] I don't know. I just know I don't want to be a counselor anymore. So much misery. I feel like the little Dutch boy with not enough fingers to stick in the dike. If I counsel one more person, I'll go nuts. Before I came here I put in my application at the post office to be a package sorter. At least I wouldn't have to listen or talk to packages, and the pay's better anyway.

I. Simulated Crisis Intervention Before the Group

A volunteer takes the role of Steve. The group leader takes the role of Mike and starts active listening in the "fishbowl" with Steve. After two minutes at most, without doing anything more than exploring the problem, the leader gets up and leaves the chair. The leader then invites any group member to come and sit in the leader's place and continue the dialogue in a crisis intervention mode. Any time a member becomes stymied, the member voluntarily gets up and leaves the chair. Another member is then invited to take the chair voluntarily. No questions are permitted by the rest of the group. Rather, any time a group member desires to offer input, that member gets up, taps the counselor on the shoulder, and sits down with Steve. This exercise should continue until Steve's situation is fully assessed and closure is reached regarding the crisis. At this point the leader can then process the counseling session. As openers, the following kinds of questions can be asked:

1. Did the crisis workers obtain an adequate assessment of the problem?
2. Referring to Table 12-1, what behavioral, physical, interpersonal, and attitudinal indicators lead you to believe that Steve is in crisis?
3. What problems do you foresee when a friend also gets cast in the role of crisis interventionist?
4. What special ethical considerations must the crisis worker bear in mind?
5. What makes the crisis of burnout different from other kinds of crises we have considered?

II. Simulated Intervention in Pairs

The group is divided into dyads: crisis worker and burned-out human services worker. Using the "Who told You?" technique, the human services worker starts a monologue about his or her gripes, complaints, frustrations, perceived shortcomings with clients, bureaucratic problems, and so on. (If participants do not currently hold a human services job, they can role-play Steve or one of the examples from the beginning of this chapter.) As the burned-out worker unfolds verbally, the crisis worker will use a combination of active listening skills and "Who Told You?"

Such an approach is designed to confront the irrational ideas and beliefs the burned-out worker has built up about his or her job. The crisis worker should be on the lookout for any of the 11 irrational ideas that Albert Ellis maintains are endemic to a neurotic society (Patterson, 1980, pp. 68–70):

1. It is essential that a person be loved or approved of by virtually everyone in the community.
2. A person must be perfectly competent and adequate and must achieve in order to be considered worthwhile.
3. Some people are bad, wicked, or villainous and therefore should be blamed or punished.
4. It is a terrible catastrophe when things are not as a person wants them to be.
5. Unhappiness is caused by outside circumstances, and a person has no control over it.
6. Dangerous or fearsome things are cause for great concern, and their possibility must be continually dwelt upon.
7. It is easier to avoid certain difficulties and self-responsibilities than to face them.
8. A person should be dependent on others and have someone stronger on whom to rely.
9. Past experiences and events are the determinants of present behavior; the influence of the past cannot be eradicated.

10. A person should be quite upset over other people's problems and disturbances.
11. There is always a right or perfect solution to every problem, and it must be found or the results will be catastrophic.

As the crisis worker detects irrational statements like these, he or she should confront the client with "Who Told you . . . ?" The idea is to confront the *shoulds, oughts,* and *musts* that propagandize clients into believing that they need to continue unproductive and debilitating ways of thinking and behaving. The exercise should be continued for 15 to 20 minutes and then the roles should be reversed. After the exercise is completed, all members rejoin the group and process the experience. Special emphasis should be given to comparing the irrational ideas brought out by each participant. The leader may want to list and tally each irrational idea so that all participants can start to experience the communality of ways in which they delude and fool themselves into making these irrational beliefs a dysfunctional part of their lives.

PART FOUR

NEW DIRECTIONS

The objectives of the final chapter of this book are (1) to highlight the evolution and importance of crisis intervention as a potent, innovative, and maturing subspecialty of psychotherapy, and (2) to empower crisis workers to progress toward more proactive, preventive, and creative initiatives than they have ordinarily taken in the past. We hope that the perspectives in "Off the Couch and into the Streets" will enhance the reader's vision of the future as well as personal and professional growth. Probably at no time in history has society had a greater need for competent, proactive crisis workers.

CHAPTER 13

Off the Couch
and into the Streets

Two recent and significant developments in the helping and human services professions define and give impetus to the emergent directions of the crisis intervention movement. First and foremost, crisis intervention has evolved into a major human services subspecialty (James & Gilliland, 1991). Second, it has become widely apparent that a reactive approach to crisis intervention is not enough; proactive and preventive models of systemwide crisis intervention need to be developed and implemented. The latter recognition, simply put, means that crisis work need not be only the purview of the mental health professional. These two developments, within the context of an increasingly complex society, provide the setting for this chapter.

THE EVOLUTION OF THE CRISIS
INTERVENTION SUBSPECIALTY

Crisis intervention has evolved from being a grassroots movement implemented by volunteers into a professional subspecialty with institutional support. Let us trace the process by which any particular type of crisis is first addressed by volunteers and later by professionals in institutions.

The need for crisis intervention services is at first unrecognized by the public and by existing institutions until such time as a critical mass of victims comes together to exert enough legal, political, or economic pressure to cause the particular crisis category, malady, or social problem to become formalized. Until that time, it remains nonformalized, nonprofessional, nonsubsidized. The problem is responded to or handled mainly through ad hoc nonformal means by former victims, current victims, friends, or significant others who are affected by the problem. Examples are Mothers Against Drunk Drivers (MADD) to try to reduce the number of young people killed by drunk drivers, the veterans groups organized to respond to the PTSD epidemic among military veterans following the Vietnam War, and the Aid to End AIDS Committee to prevent the spread of AIDS and enhance the quality of life of HIV-infected persons.

The Grassroots Movement

Initiators of crisis intervention services are generally concerned with one particular crisis category that personally affects them in some way. Typically, the crisis gets out of hand enough to cause noticeable problems before remedial responses are initiated. At first, the initiators are mavericks who are starting a victims' revolt. The revolt is against an entrenched status quo or power structure that shows little awareness of or responsiveness to the problem. The victims' revolt somehow manages to get an infant crisis agency started despite the benign neglect and reluctance of mainstream society. The infant agency is initially funded by private donations. The services are provided by ad hoc workers who are quite informally organized. The crisis agency gains access to public funding only after the agency has attained validation and some recognition by a substantial portion of the power structure. If, after a time, the infant crisis agency does not attain credibility sufficient to garner substantial private support or a modicum of public support, the agency begins to falter and eventually folds and ceases to operate.

Initially, community leaders may deny that the crisis exists or may recur. But, whenever the crisis persists, they finally come to realize that someone must become proactive—someone must exert the leadership, energy, time, resources, and resolve to confront the crisis problem. Thus, the formation of an agency is sanctioned or even encouraged. If the infant agency that is born from the necessity of containing the crisis succeeds and is publicly recognized as fulfilling a need, the quest to expand and mature begins.

The Importance of Volunteerism

Public validation. A stable cadre of volunteers can help an agency attain credibility, provide needed services to clients, and strengthen the financial condition by carrying out fund drives and locating financial assistance. Volunteerism is often the key to getting the infant crisis agency rolling. It is the grassroots influence that often captures the attention of the media, impels people to join as volunteers, and causes a greater number of clients and victims to seek the services of the agency. As the services increase and become publicized, political entities take note of the crisis problem and the services being rendered.

As mainstream institutions, such as governmental structures, become aware of the problem and as volunteer centers reach the saturation point where needs are obviously going unmet, some governmental or institutional funding is provided. Typically, as the numbers and needs of the clientele increase, the agency reaches the point where compassion and volunteerism alone cannot handle all of the complex personal, social, economic, psychological, and political problems that assail it.

Volunteers as front-line workers.   The use of trained volunteers as crisis workers has been a recognized component of many crisis centers and agencies for years (Clark & McKiernan, 1981; Roberts, 1991, p. 29; Slaikeu & Leff-Simon, 1990, p. 321). Probably the greatest number of front-line volunteers are used in staffing 24-hour suicide hot lines in major cities. Such hot lines require an enormous number of crisis workers because the crisis service never ceases—it must be provided seven days a week, 52 weeks a year. Roberts (1991, p. 29) reported that more than three-quarters of all crisis centers in the United States indicate that they rely on volunteer crisis workers and that such volunteers outnumber professional staff by more than six to one. Although volunteers cannot replace professionals, highly selective screening procedures and effective preservice and in-service training programs usually make the volunteer cadre in crisis centers the mainstay of services by hot lines in this country.

The Need for Trained Professional Consultants

As a crisis intervention center becomes oversaturated with numbers of clients and complex issues arise that are beyond the scope of the volunteers to handle, the need for professional assistance and/or formalized learning emerges. Also, the heavy demands of the client population impel the agency to create preservice and in-service training, using professional consultants to improve the knowledge and skills of the volunteers. Thus, training programs become systematically organized.

After the agency has established a formalized relationship with professionals to train the volunteers and act as volunteer backup consultants, the director can become more selective in screening, interviewing, and placing volunteers. Pairing newly acquired volunteers with experienced volunteers for apprenticeship periods tends to stabilize the volunteer work force. Thus, the agency begins to mature.

The Quest for Maturity and Power

It is essential that the agency in its developmental stages validate itself within the professional community. Some ways to do this are (1) ensuring that professionals in the human services/mental health field are represented on the agency's board of directors; (2) using professionals in the human services/mental health fields to facilitate both preservice and in-service training of volunteers; (3) legitimizing the mission and purpose of the agency, thereby helping the agency to garner support from charitable and governmental organizations; (4) providing a critical mass of people for the agency's own fund-raising efforts; and (5) gaining access to the political power structure.

As crisis agencies mature, they often gain proficiency in lobbying, public relations, political activity, the legislative process, gaining corporate backing, publishing newsletters, compiling lists for solicitation of funds, and getting leading power structure people involved. Fund raising becomes bigger and bigger business. If the agency is very successful, it may receive steady funding from a variety of sources—from local and state government, corporations, foundations, and charitable organizations such as the United Way.

Institutionalization. As crisis agencies become well known and as their clientele are drawn from a wider scope of the community (to the point that it goes beyond being handled by the grapevine/word of mouth/notepad system), it becomes apparent that if it is to continue to grow and serve its clients it must institutionalize itself. Thus, the seeds of the trappings of bureaucracy are born. To manage all the vital functions, it must centralize and formalize all aspects of the center operation. It takes on a formal board of directors, establishes rigorous auditing and record keeping functions, and requires more money, paid staff, and staff support.

As crisis agencies become crisis organizations they gain more power, prestige, and notoriety. They tend to attract the attention of the human services professions because they offer fertile fields for funded research, placement of practicum and internship students, and employment of graduates. Sometimes established and emerging agencies become involved in professional turf battles. Different agencies may serve the same client population and compete for volunteers and funding. Agencies may become defunct because of inadequate funding, inept leadership, lack of public interest, or overpowering competition from rival organizations. Crisis agencies sometimes attain eminent success, to the point that it becomes a vested interest of the human services professions to formalize the competencies of the personnel of such successful agencies through certification, licensure, and accreditation. The successful agencies may also tend to compete for resources and gain recognition through affiliating with national or regional agency networks and through linkages with national professional organizations and accrediting bodies.

Professionalization. Some agencies attain exemplary status through being recognized regionally or nationally as ranking among the top service providers in specific crisis categories. As a specialty evolves, it develops its own empirical base, professional research, and writings. For example, for crisis intervention, we have publications such as *Crisis Intervention;* the *Journal of Interpersonal Violence; Victimology; Violence and Victims; Response to the Victimization of Women and Children;* and the *Journal of Traumatic Stress.* A further manifestation of the professionalization of crisis intervention as a subspecialty is its textbooks. Such textbooks evolve in two ways.

1. Field-based experiential activities are written into narrative form and distributed through printed handouts to groups such as workshop and in-service training classes. The handouts are later edited and bound into either monographs or training manuals. Finally, the training manuals or

monographs are carefully revised and rewritten to form field-validated publications that appeal to people who want a straightforward, applied textbook.

2. Empirical research reports are collected, edited, and combined in theory and research-based texts. These books are valued by people who prefer materials based on proven scientific principles.

A particular book may follow either format or it may be a combination of the two. Crisis textbooks have tended to combine theory and practice in a unified whole as the need to train crisis workers has emerged. Formalized training in crisis intervention has necessitated the integration of theory and practice (Aguilera & Messick, 1982; Gilliland & James, 1988; Roberts, 1991; Slaikeu, 1990). As formal textbooks have become available, crisis agencies have tended to assimilate the text material into their training programs. Such assimilation has had the effect of further formalizing crisis intervention as a subspecialty among the psychological and human services professions.

Specialty areas may also attain a distinct level of recognition through building a base of national or regional affiliates, such as is evidenced through suicide hot lines, AA, spouse abuse centers, AIDS hot lines and assistance centers, and victim assistance programs. Local, state, regional, and national conferences are organized to provide for exchange of ideas and problem-solving strategies. (The annual Convening of Crisis Intervention Personnel sponsored by the University of Illinois at Chicago is an outstanding example of one of many such conferences.) The emergence of hundreds of crisis-oriented organizations in the 1970s and 1980s (Burek, 1992) attests to the dramatic transformation and national acceptance of crisis intervention as a pervasive subspecialty. Thus, the attainment and maintenance of maturity and professionalization have become the target goals of many crisis agencies or categories.

The Societal Impetus for Crisis Intervention

Why, from the 1970s to the present, has the crisis intervention movement experienced such extraordinary growth? Probably no one factor alone can explain why. The stresses, strains, and unprecedented changes that tear at the fabric of society itself may account for some of the reasons: lack of personal fulfillment, poverty, homelessness, the population explosion among the underclasses, increased experimentation with and use of drugs, alcoholism, the emergence of HIV infection and AIDS disease, the immediacy and power of the visual media to stir people's emotions and demand for action, the development and use of birth control pills by the middle and upper class, the feminist movement, the environmental movement, increased mobility of people, technological advances, rise in crime and terrorism are examples of possible catalysts. Perhaps the reasons that the demand arose for crisis agencies, journals, textbooks, courses, training, conferences, conventions, and such were that people everywhere felt a need to respond to the kinds of dilemmas individuals face every day—in their communities, families, work places, schools, and in the streets.

PROACTIVE AND PREVENTIVE MODELS OF CRISIS INTERVENTION

Crisis intervention organizations of all kinds tend to evolve pragmatically. They may spring from governmental research grants. They may develop from independently generated successful projects that gain local attention and later take on a national posture. The *Encyclopedia of Associations* (Burek, 1992), a comprehensive compilation and annotated description of organizations and agencies, offers some proof of the spectacular growth of crisis-oriented organizations during the 1970s and 1980s. Few crisis categories or situations have been omitted from some sort of widespread attention and organized response. Most of the organizations purport to deal with the specific targeted crisis category in not only reactive but also proactive and preventive modes.

Crisis Intervention in the Real World

Although crisis intervention theories and agencies applying those theories are barely two generations old, the spectacular growth and development since the 1950s has placed them virtually in the mainstream of mental health and human services (Blinder, 1991). No longer is crisis intervention considered the informal grassroots purview of paraprofessionals and volunteers. Rather, the theories, methodologies, and strategies of crisis intervention have come to be viewed as legitimate in both society and the mental health world (In Touch Hotline Counseling Center, 1991). People in general have become more positive in their acceptance of outreach strategies. There is less of a "blaming the victim" attitude. It has become accepted that dealing early on with a crisis is cost-effective (Roberts, 1991).

There are valid reasons for the widespread acceptance of crisis intervention as a therapeutic specialty. People in human services and political leadership positions have discovered that when they either ignore crisis situations or leave solutions entirely to the experts who have little political clout, lasting solutions elude them and the leaders themselves are blamed and held publicly responsible. Reactive responding has not worked very well. Leaders have discovered that endemic crisis problems will not easily go away; that reaction or no action may result in the problems' becoming pandemic or out of control. In a sense then, political expediency has dictated not only the widespread acceptance of effective crisis intervention strategies but also that crisis intervention become proactive and preventive.

The proactive and preventive concept has evolved all the way from the local to the national level. The Violence and Traumatic Stress Branch of the National Institute of Mental Health (NIMH, 1990) was created for the purpose of supporting research projects on the mental health sequelae resulting from exposure to traumatic life crises and catastrophic events. These experiences include interpersonal and mass violence, physical and sexual abuse, natural disaster, technological (human-made) hazards, accidents, forced relocation, and other individual and collective traumatic situations. The NIMH program supports research on the immediate and long-term psychopathological and stress reactions in victims, families, and service workers; on individual and environmental risk factors associated with the development of mental and physical disorder; and on informal support networks and programs designed to prevent and treat mental health problems.

The National Organization for Victim Assistance (NOVA) also evolved on a national level to respond to the needs of disaster victims in any community in the country (Young, 1991). NOVA's National Crisis Response Project (NCRP) is designed to address the emotional aftermath of communitywide disasters by sending out National Crisis Response Teams (NCRTs) to assist the affected communities or regions to quickly establish crisis response teams to respond to immediate needs as well as, to the extent possible, prevent crisis traumas from inflicting long-term emotional damage on disaster victims.

Both the NIMH and the NOVA models are examples of the use of governmental influence and resources to develop proactive and preventive strategies on a national to local scale. Basically, the NOVA model entails rapidly going out, taking action, and assisting communities to set up teams to contain and curtail disaster-caused trauma as effectively and efficiently as possible.

Cost and Managed Care Considerations

According to Blinder (1991), it was the business and industrial establishment, not the psychological community, that was responsible for the integration of crisis intervention into the framework of acceptable treatment modality and third-party insurance payment policy. Crisis intervention, short-term treatment, and brief therapy are often designated as treatments of choice in outpatient services, substance abuse rehabilitation, and inpatient psychiatric settings. Soaring costs of therapeutic and medical treatment have helped catapult crisis and short-term treatment to the forefront.

The concept of "managed care" (Blinder, 1991) has emerged to bring balance, efficiency, and maximization of benefit utilization to consumers of insured health care services. Crisis intervention is well suited to the managed care environment because of its rapid assessment, intervention and stabilization, facilitation of supports and resources, teaching of coping skills, formulation of prevention plans, and provision for enhanced insight and expedient return of clients to the community. Another important role of crisis intervention as a part of the managed care concept is the networking and referral function between case managers and others who are responsible for consumer health care. Such networking and use of crisis skills for enhanced communication and intervention often facilitate overcoming difficulties and red tape among family members, mental health facilities, hospitals, individual practitioners, Employee Assistance Programs (EAPs), and third-party insurance payers. The outlook for the continued growth and importance of crisis intervention skills and services is positive indeed, given the proven philosophy and methodology of crisis intervention and its immediacy, proximity, expectancy, visibility, and positive viability in the streets and neighborhoods where crises occur (In Touch Hotline Counseling Center, 1991; Roberts, 1991).

Collaborating/Networking

Successful crisis agency leaders understand the value of cooperation. Crisis intervention cannot be owned by any one organization, therapeutic modality, or discipline. In any city or community, what we call collaborating, networking, alliance building, systematizing, or the pooling of efforts works very well. Regardless of how efficiently local mental health agencies, police departments, local governments, health care systems, and other entities by themselves are run, collective efforts save time and money and make life easier for individual public servants. Effective collaborating/networking reaches not only different levels (local to national) but also different degrees of power, authority, and financial resources. Sometimes pressure politics, public relations, and public image building affect the course and extent of collaboration. For example, the plight of the Vietnam veterans suffering from PTSD was largely ignored until the problem spilled out of the streets and into the seats of power and authority—from personal crisis to politics. Whenever the PTSD problem began to impact members of Congress, the power of the federal government and the resources of the Veterans Administration were brought to bear not only to create a network of veterans centers throughout the country but also to slash the bureaucratic red tape to ensure that services to Vietnam veterans were taken to the streets where PTSD sufferers resided rather than requiring veterans to report to regular VA hospitals.

EMERGENT TRENDS IN CRISIS INTERVENTION

We have devoted several chapters in this book to specific crisis categories such as suicide, battering, sexual assault, hostage taking, and violent behavior in institutions. The crises that emerge from the streets call for crisis workers to respond not only reactively and with immediacy and presence, but also with proactivity and intentional planning for future directions. Thus, several types of programs of contemporary concern to crisis workers are

1. crisis stabilization programs
2. outreach programs
3. prevention programs

4. crisis response programs
5. programs to manage crisis situations in schools
6. programs to enable law enforcement officers' response to mentally ill and other persons in crisis.

Crisis Stabilization Programs

Crisis stabilization programs range from inpatient facilities such as the Crisis Stabilization Unit detailed in Chapter 3 that provided for short-term maximum safety and control to a variety of programs that exert less control over the safety needs of clients.

Crisis intervention managers in many communities have begun to organize systematic programs and initiatives to respond to crises and even to prevent crises from getting out of control. Crisis stabilization units, involving multidisciplinary talents from a broad community catchment area, are one vehicle that has been successful in providing alternatives to long-term hospitalization for people in crisis (Wilson, 1991). An alternative crisis stabilization program for some patients suffering from chronic emotional problems who formerly were hospitalized has been described by Leaman (1987). In that program, eligible patients spend an average of five days with a licensed foster care family in the family's home. Family members receive training and some cost reimbursement as foster care providers.

Halfway houses have also been used extensively as a short-term alternative to hospitalization for acutely disturbed chronic patients (Weisman, 1985). Such use of halfway houses combines crisis intervention techniques with techniques developed in halfway houses to enhance independent functioning and to counteract regressive, dependent behavior. Highly structured activities and expectations of appropriate behavior enable most patients to leave the halfway house within nine days and begin outpatient and day treatment programs.

Britton and Mattson-Melcher (1985) described a crisis stabilization program administered by a crisis intervention center in which chronically mentally ill persons are provided short-term housing, in lieu of hospitalization, with carefully selected families. The coordination of services, screening of home providers, assessment of needs, and use of referrals to the community are some of the components of the program.

Outreach Programs

Outreach programs have ranged from rapid response teams who deliver intervention at the geographical site of the crisis to workers who provide services at places wherever target populations are found.

Going to the scene of crises.   Several examples of the formation and use of rapid response outreach teams illustrate how going to the scene can be effective in ameliorating the devastating effects of crises. Brom and Kleber

(1989) described an outreach program aimed at preventing PTSD in victims of violence, such as bank robberies and hijackings. Proactive counseling and PTSD prevention strategies were developed through the organizations in which the victims worked. Essentially, the NIMH (1990) rapid response team concept was employed and served as a prime example of creatively taking crisis intervention service to the scene where it was needed, ensuring the safety of clients at the scene, and taking steps to prevent the trauma of the victims from generating future transcrises.

The July 19, 1989, crash of United Airlines Flight 232 in Iowa took more than 100 lives, and 185 survivors escaped. Shafer (1989a) described the anguish, shock, and wide range of human emotion that survivors, families, airline employees, and people in the community and the nation (via the visual media) felt. Short-term crisis counseling was quickly organized by the American Red Cross using rapid response teams of counselors, students, volunteers, and other caregivers. In this rather swift intervention process, whenever a victim was identified, airline personnel first contacted the rapid response teams to ensure that a counselor was with the family when officials delivered the tragic news. Crisis workers on the scene reported that their main goal was to get the survivors to express themselves and to give them permission to feel whatever emotions they were experiencing. For many, the greatest immediate need was to talk.

Modrak (1992) reported on the deployment of rapid response teams to the scenes of two separate tragedies. The first was the April 4, 1991, plane crash near Philadelphia. A plane carrying Pennsylvania Senator John Heinz collided with a helicopter, resulting in the crash of fiery sections of the plane and helicopter onto the Merion Elementary School grounds. The senator and others on both aircraft and two first-grade girls at the school were killed; three other children and two adults were wounded. A rapid response team composed of counselors, psychologists, and psychiatrists provided individual and group counseling, handed out referrals as appropriate, set up a crisis hot line, and formed a drop-in crisis center. The crisis services proved to be in constant demand as the team served the multiple victims generated by the plane collision and crash at the school.

Another tragedy reported by Modrak (1992) occurred on November 1, 1991, at the University of Iowa. The whole campus as well as the community was affected by an angry graduate student's shooting and killing five people and critically injuring another before fatally shooting himself. A crisis response team was organized by the University of Iowa Counseling Center. First priority was given to counseling eyewitnesses. Then, team members worked with individuals and groups identified as needing crisis intervention. University classes were canceled, a memorial service was televised for the student body and the community, needs assessments and appropriate referrals were made, open meetings of mourning were conducted during three consecutive mornings, and group sessions were held in every room of the student union in the afternoons.

The crisis response teams at both the University of Iowa and the Merion Elementary School found quick and effective means of responding to the needs of people at the scene of both crises. The two crisis teams recommended that communities establish networks for the formation of their own crisis teams to rapidly respond to sudden tragedies that can occur anyplace at any time (Modrak, 1992, p. 4).

Going to the crisis populations.   Pritchard, Brownstein, and Johnan (1989) described a creative youth-oriented outreach program that is a good example of taking crisis services to youth who would not likely come to a center or seek out services. Booths in shopping malls were set up to present vignettes to at-risk youth as a strategy to provide crisis information to youth in critical topics such as AIDS and teenage runaways.

University campuses are well suited to the process of taking crisis intervention services to the geographical locale of prospective clientele. White and Rubenstein (1984) assessed a unique program conducted by the Cornell University Psychological Services Center and local radio stations that broadcast hourly announcements targeted toward high-risk suicidal undergraduate students. Research on the effects of the program showed a significant increase in high-risk clients presenting for counseling services. Another example of college and university campus outreach, aimed at curbing campus violence, was sponsored by the American College Personnel Association (ACPA) (McGowan, 1992). That program targeted both the crisis problem and the population through setting up an outreach task force on campus violence to seek to improve institutional policy, organize and conduct workshops to educate administrators about ways to reduce violence on campuses, and develop a 102-page manual for dealing with violence in the university setting (pp. 9–10).

Intrater (1991) reported on outreach programs instituted to take services to three different youthful populations: (1) runaways, (2) "throwaways," and (3) pregnant teens and adolescent parents. From the Neon Street Center for Homeless Youth in Illinois, outreach services addressed a myriad of homeless youth needs such as obtaining food, housing, health care, education, and employment as well as alleviation of crises related to prostitution, sexual identity, substance abuse, HIV infection, teen pregnancy, and gang solicitation.

Prevention Programs

Roberts (1991) identified three types of contemporary prevention strategies used by professionals in the fields of public health, social work, and mental health (p. 146): primary, secondary, and tertiary prevention.

Primary prevention.   Primary prevention involves the intentional and proactive planning of strategies and activities to keep specific crises from developing in the first place. Examples of primary prevention are (1) parenting education programs to prevent child neglect/abuse; (2) HIV/

AIDS education programs to prevent the spread of the AIDS virus; (3) educational programs on college campuses to prevent date rape; and (4) educational programs for teenage males and females regarding the consequences of adolescent pregnancies.

Secondary prevention.   Secondary prevention strategies are designed to intervene in a particular crisis category early enough to contain and/or ameliorate the problem. Examples of secondary prevention are (1) providing counseling programs in Family Link/Runaway Houses to help families and teenage runners to control the behavior of running away; (2) establishing counseling services designed to stop battering behavior in households; (3) designing and implementing victim assistance programs to ensure that the rights of victims' (of crime or stark misfortune) are protected and honored.

Tertiary prevention.   Tertiary prevention entails the comprehensive use of crisis intervention strategies to contain and control the spread of the crisis. An example is the provision of a telephone hot line for suicidal people and mounting a public information program sufficiently strong so that virtually every suicidal person in the catchment area will call the hot line as an alternative to a suicide attempt.

Psychiatric emergency services.   The rise of psychiatric emergency services (PESs) over recent decades has begun to fill a definite void in the delivery of emergency crisis intervention. PESs are treatment facilities established for the express purpose of providing either emergency psychiatric outpatient or short-term psychiatric inpatient evaluation, emergency care, referral, and aftercare as alternatives to long-term hospitalization or makeshift psychiatric care in emergency rooms of general hospitals (Bassuk & Cote, 1983; Dubin & Fink, 1986). Not only have the numbers of PESs greatly increased and provided crisis intervention services in urban areas (McDermott & Gordon, 1984; Wellin, Slesinger, & Hollister, 1987), but also emergency services in rural areas have been enhanced as well (Bassuk & Cote, 1983; McDermott & Gordon, 1984). PESs have proven to serve the crisis intervention needs of the elderly (Dubin & Fink, 1986) and adolescents (Piersma & Van-Wingen, 1988) as well as the general population.

Many community mental health centers have established service components that amount to PESs. For example, we know of one mental health center that houses and operates an externally funded Victim Assistance Program. Another center has developed a comprehensive program of services for the homeless in an inner city. Still another center has set up a program for emergency vocational counseling for people in the community who suddenly lose their jobs due to plant closings. The growth and proliferation of PESs has followed the trend, started a couple of decades ago, to greatly reduce the inpatient population in mental health facilities. Although many users of PESs are probably former long-term inpatients, many other persons who need temporary psychiatric care receive quality emergency services that would otherwise be provided during hospitalization (Dubin & Fink, 1986).

Crisis Response Programs

Crisis response teams can be established as a direct reaction to an individual or community crisis or tragedy, or they can be intentionally planned and put into place before a crisis event occurs. Most such response teams are classified as secondary prevention strategies.

Local crises.   During the late summer and fall of 1990 a crisis response team was formed by community and college officials in Gainesville, Florida, to deal with the widespread fear precipitated by the unsolved murders of five young women students enrolled at the University of Florida and the Santa Fe Community College. According to Wakelee-Lynch (1990), the "university trauma team," composed of specialists from the university's counseling center, student affairs office, and student housing office, were brought together as a crisis response team to help the entire community cope with the fears, feelings of vulnerability, and panic that evolved pursuant to the crisis. In phase 1 of the crisis work the focus was on public safety and helping the primary survivors—for example, providing counseling and places of safety for families and friends of persons who were missing or had already been found murdered.

Phase 2 dealt with the recovery process. Nondirective counseling was provided for students who needed to focus on recognizing and verbalizing fears, feelings of anger, anxiety, irritability, and guilt. Follow-up research found that survivors' major need at that time was to be able to verbalize their feelings in a nonjudgmental climate. Using group and individual interventions, members of the crisis response team began to provide opportunities for students and friends to explore their feelings, deal with their grief, and activate other coping mechanisms and support systems needed to weather the crisis (Wakelee-Lynch, 1990, p. 3).

National crises.   A Gulf War–related crisis response program was reported by Coy (1991). That program, organized by school counselors, targeted students who were experiencing real fears and anxieties related to their parents, guardians, family members, neighbors, relatives, friends, or acquaintances being deployed to the Middle East region during Desert Shield and/ or Desert Storm. It was found that many children experienced war-related fears. School counselors and school psychologists formed the core of the crisis response movement. Many schools in both the United States and overseas (especially in military dependent schools) participated in the program. The response teams "provided formal and informal training for classroom teachers, organized support groups, provided individual and group counseling, and coordinated with community professionals to ensure a unified approach to children's needs" (p. 12).

National crisis response teams.   The rapid crisis response team movement received impetus and support on a national level with the establishment of the National Crisis Response Project by the National Organization for Victim Assistance (NOVA) in the late 1980s (Burek, 1992; Young, 1991). The National Crisis Response Project set up national crisis response teams (NCRTs) to assist communities following communitywide crises or disasters. The main objective of an NCRT in dealing with local community disaster is to form local crisis response teams that are in a position to deal with the community's grief reactions, stress effects, and posttraumatic stress disorder resultant from the disaster. According to Young (1991), the "project is based on the premise that disasters can cause individual and communitywide crisis reactions and that immediate intervention can provide communities with tools that are useful in mitigating long-term distress" (pp. 83–84).

NOVA, itself founded in 1975 (Burek, 1992, p. 1334), offers technical consultation, referral services, and public support to victim assistance training programs as well as providing direct services to victims, former victims, and others whose objective is to push for victims' rights. NOVA's NCRTs are dispatched in the event of communitywide disasters such as mass murders, plane crashes, and other traumatic crises. Whenever people in the affected communities are in crisis in the aftermath of the disaster, an NCRT reviews the types of stress reactions being experienced by the victims, works directly with the people needing intervention services, follows NOVA's guidelines in helping the people in need, and provides education for designated community leaders.

NCRTs are dispatched upon request of leaders in the affected community. "When a disaster occurs, NOVA is placed in contact with the community in one of two ways: either the community calls NOVA, or NOVA, on hearing of the tragedy, calls the community and offers assistance" (Young, 1991, p. 95). Three types of disaster service are available: (1) providing written material giving details of how to deal with the aftermath of disaster; (2) providing telephone consultation to leading caregivers in the area affected; and (3) sending in a trained team of volunteer crisis workers to assist the community.

Federal Emergency Management Agency (FEMA).   Sometimes more than one agency of the federal government coordinates the work of crisis response teams. Two instances of events during modern times that triggered such a coordinated effort were the San Francisco area earthquake and Hurricane Hugo in the southeastern United States, both of which occurred in 1989. The response teams were sent in by the National Institute of Mental Health (NIMH) and sponsored and funded by FEMA. In both disasters, FEMA and NIMH provided the widely affected areas with instruction, consultation, and expertise in developing local and regional support systems to cope with the enormous aftermath of these natural disasters (Shafer, 1989b). Teams of counselors, crisis workers, and other caregivers intervened with a wide range of populations and age groups (from children through senior citizens). Special emphasis was placed on enabling clients to cope with their psychological trauma with two important objectives in mind: to ensure their immediate safety and to help people of all ages in both regions to prepare themselves to face the future as free as possible from posttraumatic stress disorder.

Emergency telephone crisis services.   Probably the most obvious indicator of the public awareness and acceptance of the widespread availability of emergency crisis intervention has been the emergence of 911 telephone service. Of course the 911 service functions in addition to other established emergency components such as fire, police, sheriff, medical emergency, and ambulance listings that are in the front of most local telephone directories. The growth of crisis hot lines is another phenomenon in modern industrial societies that is indicative of people's increasing use of the telephone in calling for emergency help.

Whereas the 911 service as well as most of the other emergency listings in the front of most telephone directories function largely in the realm of physical emergencies, the crisis hot line is more often used as a first point of contact in psychological or emotional emergencies. Slaikeu (1990, pp. 105–141) refers to such emergency telephone help as "first-order intervention" or "psychological first aid." Indeed, the telephone is the most prevalent medium for the initial contact in most crisis service delivery. Even the vast outreach networks such as the services provided by NOVA, described in the previous section, depend heavily on the telephone as the basic mode of communication.

Many city and county libraries provide an information service, such as the LINC (Library Information Center) phone line, for public information and referral. LINC phone lines typically provide a wide range of telephone listings for all sorts of public needs, including all the emergency and crisis services in the local area.

Programs to Manage Crisis Situations in Schools

Crisis situations in schools have been on the rise since the 1950s (Palmo, Langlois, & Bender, 1988). The rapid societal changes that took place during the 1960s and 1970s were accompanied by more numerous and severe school crises than ever before (p. 97). Whereas in earlier times school leaders could deny the need for crisis intervention plans, such as establishing crisis response teams, the increased incidence of crisis and modern media reports of copycat suicides, hostage takers, murders, and other tragedies affecting school campuses made it necessary to the public safety for schools to become proactive in providing preventive, developmental plans. School counselors—initially trained and hired under the National Defense Education Act (NDEA) program in the late 1950s and 1960s to buttress the national science initiative through vocational and educational guidance and placement—in the 1970s, 1980s, and 1990s became key players in personal counseling and crisis prevention/intervention programs. Because of their training in mental health and related matters, counselors inherited the leadership roles in much of the crisis work in schools.

As societal changes such as proliferation of one-parent homes, broken homes, and blended families, an increase in the crime rate, and homelessness became prevalent in many communities, the role of schools shifted from *in loco parentis* (in place of the parent) to *school as parent.* In a sense, schools had to take over parental and societal roles that were abdicated by everyone else. Thus, crisis work with children—as they grappled with family, peers, drugs, teenage sex, AIDS, and just growing up—became only one of many social functions school leaders inherited by default.

Examples of situations that have occurred that have precipitated crises in schools include the following:

Alcoholic parents (Burk, 1972; Miller & Jang, 1977; Pattison & Kaufman, 1982)
Child and adolescent (students) suicide (Nelson & Slaikeu, 1990; Palmo et al., 1988; Weinberg, 1989)
Suicide ideation, threats, or attempts (Jobes & Berman, 1991; Kalafat, 1991; Palmo et al., 1988)
Child abuse (Kendrick, 1991)
Death of a parent (Gray, 1988)
Violence toward children (Daro, 1991)
Child terminal illness (leukemia) (Nelson & Slaikeu, 1990)
Death of a teacher (Sorensen, 1989)
Crisis of AIDS for adolescents (Mantell & Schinke, 1991)
Death of friends, as in a tragic accident claiming the lives of a group of students (Toubiana, Milgram, Strich, & Edelstein, 1988)
Teen pregnancy (Zabin & Streett, 1991)
Death of a sibling (Bertoia & Allan, 1988; Nelson & Slaikeu, 1990)
Family violence (Andrews, 1991)
Bereavement, loss, and grief (Bertoia & Allan, 1988; Hughes, 1988; Lane & Dickey, 1988; Riordan & Allen, 1989)
Economic crisis (Peeks, 1989)
War-related child crisis (Nelson & Slaikeu, 1990)

Responding to recurrent school crises. Warren and Gladych-Machniak (1990) described a crisis response team that created a community network for prevention/intervention regarding student suicide crises. A formalized suicide response team was formed in a Michigan community by bringing together professionals from the local community mental health center, the school administration, local human services agencies, and the school psychologist and staff. The focus was originally student suicide threats, but was later broadened to include tragic deaths. Although the crisis response team serves all schools in the district, it is not the goal or responsibility of the team to determine any school's needs, The convening of the response team to deal with recurrent crises is the prerogative of the school administration.

The Millard Public School District in Omaha, Nebraska, developed an exemplary and comprehensive game plan for crisis intervention in the schools (Millard Public Schools, 1991). The district formed a systemwide crisis response team of expert professionals for the purpose of providing leadership, support, and necessary information for schools experiencing a crisis such as that encountered in the aftermath of the sudden death of a student or staff member. That team, when called into action by the director of Pupil Personnel Services, can deal with any emergency that temporarily causes disruption in the school routine and is likely to cause emotional turmoil for staff and/or students. Besides a sudden death, the team can address other crises such as accidents causing severe injuries to staff or students, potentially life-threatening situations, natural disasters (such as tornados), child molestation (if widely known), child abduction, national/local emergencies, epidemic illness, or violence. Many school districts in this country have adopted standard suicide prevention models in particular and emergency trauma models in general because of widespread teenage and child suicides.

In cases of sudden death of a student or a teacher, or another tragedy affecting most of the school's population, crisis response teams can be called upon to intervene. Sorensen (1989) recommends that such school crisis response teams be preplanned, appointed, and oriented so that the assembly of the team does not occur during the crisis situation. A typical team responding to a student or teacher death might be composed of school counselors, school psychologists, school administrators, and mental health workers who have strong clinical skills, knowledge of how schools function, and experience with crisis work in school systems (p. 426).

Crisis intervention strategies that Sorensen (1989, p. 426) cites that the response team could use in dealing with shock over the sudden death of a student or teacher might include the following:

1. The school maintains its regular schedule, but crisis counseling stations are set up to accommodate student groups who need counseling, support, and/or guidance in order to cope.
2. The school's schedule might be altered if large groups of students need to meet with crisis response team members to talk, grieve, or receive comfort.
3. If needed, crisis response team members lead classroom discussions about student concerns.
4. A crisis counseling base clinic is set up to allow teachers to come for support as they attempt to handle their classes during the highly charged grief and emotional climate of the crisis.
5. Crisis response team members lead faculty meeting discussions focused on the concerns of faculty and students.

6. Crisis response team members cover classes for teachers who are too upset to do an effective job or who need time to recover from the shock of the tragedy.
7. Crisis response team members work alongside teachers developing classroom activities for dealing with the death or tragedy.
8. The crisis may bring to mind former crises, deaths, or other unfinished business in teachers or students. Crisis response team members counsel them about such revisited grief.
9. Parents of children who require special attention because of severe emotional trauma are contacted for information sharing and/or parental guidance.
10. Crisis response team members assist the school administration in developing and releasing statements to the media if necessary.

Kalafat (1991) and Nelson and Slaikeu (1990) recommend that educational leaders involve teachers and parents in meetings and discussions in a proactive manner to consider, make plans, and set up action steps to be taken before crises occur. Sooner or later every school will face some kind of emergency or crisis. The formulation, retention, and use of school crisis response teams during periods of calm and normalcy is a prevention/intervention type coping strategy that is widely recognized and recommended.

The uniqueness of the school setting.   School settings are unique and distinctive because of the tremendous burdens placed on them in recent years. Teachers, counselors, administrators, school social workers, and ancillary personnel bear an unprecedented responsibility as they attempt to provide a learning environment that is safe, proactive, and preventive for the full scope of society's children and youth amid the milieu of environmental problems that spill over into the schools. In addition to the issues of client safety and provision of competent crisis case management, the school setting has some unique legal implications that impact upon working with student crises such as suicidal threat (Palmo et al., 1988, p. 95). Parents rightfully expect the school to be responsible not only for providing the education but also for the care and safety of their children. Therefore, the possibility of charges of negligence is ever present and necessitates that the school err on the side of overcautiousness.

The school must take all threats of self-destruction seriously, immediately contact the parents or guardians, keep a current list of medical, psychological, and social referral resources for students and their families, maintain accurate records of actions and services provided, and carefully monitor the treatment and prognosis of the student.

It is essential that schools have in place specific procedures for dealing with emergencies. In every instance of a student crisis situation in school, someone should be designated to initiate the first step in the intervention. Procedures should be in place regarding who should contact the parent or guardian and who should make the primary decisions and take action steps needed to ensure the safety and well-being of the student or students.

Programs to Enable Law Enforcement Officers Response

It has been estimated that in recent years police officers typically have spent 80% to 90% of their working time on order maintenance activities, many involving crisis intervention (Luckett & Slaikeu, 1990, p. 228). Many of the calls officers respond to involve domestic disturbance or domestic violence, rated by police as having a higher degree of physical danger than any other calls they receive (Baumann, Schultz, Brown, Paredes et al., 1987). An increasing number of domestic disturbance calls involve police officers responding to a scene and having to confront a presumably mentally ill person or persons (Gillig, Dumaine, Stammer, Hillard, & Grubb, 1990, p. 663). Even though police departments do not relish having to divert much of their time away from providing for the public safety and enforcing the law, they have found themselves more and more in a modality of law enforcement/crisis intervention (Fein & Knaut, 1986; Gillig et al., 1990; Luckett & Slaikeu, 1990; Scales, 1991; Winter, 1991).

Police and the mentally ill/mentally disturbed.   Gillig et al. (1990) studied a sample of 309 police officers in Cincinnati and Hamilton County, Ohio, and found that during a one-month period, almost 60% of the officers had responded to at least one call where a presumably mentally ill person had to be confronted. Almost half of the officers had responded to more than one such call during the one-month period. According to Luckett and Slaikeu (1990), those figures are fairly standard throughout the country. The changing role of the police patrol officer to include all kinds of crisis calls means that the responding officer can never be sure of the situation he or she may encounter. This modern dilemma puts a heavy responsibility on the shoulders of law enforcement officers and, though many of them dislike spending their time on crises of a social service nature, they are accepting encounters with the mentally ill as an appropriate aspect of modern police work. They are also requesting more information, training, and collaboration with mental health and crisis intervention agencies (Gillig et al., 1990; Luckett & Slaikeu, 1990; Winter, 1991). The foregoing has highlighted a need to develop training models that include police crisis intervention (Luckett & Slaikeu, 1990, pp. 231–242).

Changing role of the police.   Front-line police work is rapidly being altered. Whereas a few years ago patrol officers concerned themselves mainly with *instrumental* crimes such as theft, robbery, and assault, today they additionally deal with a multitude of *expressive* kinds of crime, where individuals pose a serious threat to themselves or others because of their own anger, fear, vulnerability, depression, or other precipitant lack of emotional control. Police officers find themselves more and more faced with crimes of passion or confronted with mental or social problems that nobody else in society is willing or in a position to confront. Consequently, the new role of the police necessitates not only a higher degree of traditional professional police training but also a modicum of crisis intervention, mental health, counseling, and social work. That is indeed a tall order that many law enforcement personnel dislike yet realize is part of the territory of modern police work.

It was out of the milieu of police workers being confronted with an upsurge in the number of dispatch calls to the scene of *expressive* activity (by out-of-control individuals) that the Memphis Police Department developed and implemented two innovative and formidable programs that address the dangers to both police officers and the public: the Crisis Intervention Team (CIT) (James, 1990) and the Family Trouble Center (FTC) (Scales, 1991; Winter, 1991). The CIT program utilizes experienced police officers, trained in crisis intervention by experts in counseling and mental health, to intervene in on-the-spot crises to contain and control the situation before an act of violence occurs. The FTC program targets family violence situations by providing counseling and referral services to both battered persons and batterers who are identified in daily police reports.

The Crisis Intervention Team (CIT) program.   Because budget constraints, economic factors, and social problems have generated enormous numbers of homeless people, dumped onto the streets mental patients who formerly would have been hospitalized as inpatients, and increased drug use and abuse, there are now many more mentally disturbed persons who come into contact with the general public than ever before. Consequently, the Memphis city government, the mental health community, and the police department realized that incidents of police involvement with the mentally ill had resulted in the mentally ill themselves being vulnerable to serious harm and the increased possibility of police officers, untrained in dealing with the mentally ill, getting seriously injured or even killed. Why can't mental health workers take care of the enormous numbers of emotionally out-of-control people on the streets? Because it is a physical and fiscal impossibility to put enough mental health workers into the streets to monitor and serve the needs of these out-of-control people and to do so in accordance with the "least restrictive environment" movement in a democratic society. Spearheaded by the local affiliate of the Alliance for the Mentally Ill, the police department, the mental health community, the city government, and the counselor education and social work departments of two local universities formed a unique and creative alliance for the purpose of developing and implementing proactive and preventive methods of containing emotionally explosive situations in the streets that frequently led to violence. That encapsulates the founding of the CIT program.

Since the police were the first and often the only responsible officials on the scene of an out-of-control situation, calling in outside consultants proved unworkable. Therefore, the unique and cohesive alliance of several important community groups determined that highly trained and motivated police officers were the logical personnel to form a front-line assault on the crisis of dangerously expressive, out-of-control persons in the streets. The massive alliance effort resulted in the CIT program's becoming an example of how a successful program can work to accomplish the objectives of public safety and welfare, economic feasibility, and police accountability.

To comprehend what a difficult and delicate task it has been to bring to fruition a successful and workable CIT program, one must understand how the alliance network functions. The network consists of the Memphis city government and the Memphis Police Department (hereafter referred to as *the police*), the Alliance for the Mentally Ill, five of the six local community mental health centers, the emergency room components of public hospitals, academic educators from the Department of Counseling and Personnel Services at Memphis State University and from the School of Social Work at the University of Tennessee, the YWCA Abused Women's Services, the Sexual Assault Resource Center, and several private practice psychologists (hereafter referred to as *the mental health community*). The power, force, and success of the alliance derive from the process and fundamental working relationship that the police and mental health community have used to both form and maintain the CIT program. The alliance was formed because both the police and the mental health community realized that the problem of crisis in the streets was too severe for either to handle alone and that working together would make life much easier and safer for both as well as providing improved and safer service for clients and the community.

The alliance conducted a great many collaborative, systematic, and democratic meetings over a period of several months to hammer out a workable CIT blueprint. As a result of these meetings, key individuals from all segments of both police and community mental health developed effective working relationships with one another and learned a great deal about each other's problems, competencies, rules, and boundaries. Police were brought into mental health facilities for orientation into the world of mental health. Mental health personnel were brought into the police academy and accompanied police on patrols to learn about the problems, procedures, competencies, roles, and boundaries that law enforcement officers face in their everyday work. Then formal training was developed to ensure that not only the CIT officer selectees but also all supervisory-level police personnel understood the problems, objectives, and operational procedures of the CIT program.

The development and training phases provided some essential attitudinal and professional understanding between the police and the mental health community. As a result, CIT officers and their superiors know precisely what training and consultation resources the mental health community can provide. And the mental health professionals know what competencies and resources the police in general and the CIT officers in particular have to offer. Concomitantly, both sides develop mutual respect, understanding, trust, and cooperation. A CIT officer intervening with a distraught mental patient will likely listen empathically to the patient's feelings and concerns, be familiar with the mental health services available (will possibly know the patient's caseworker personally), and will, within the boundaries of professional ethics, communicate to the patient an understanding of the short-term needs of that person as well as a desire to provide for the immediate safety and referral requirements to contain and stabilize the patient's current crisis. The mental health center caseworker will also understand and have confidence in the CIT officer's ability to be a stabilizing and safety influence on the patient and will, if needed, likely call upon the CIT officer for emergency assistance with a particular client. The mental health caseworker may collaborate with the CIT officer in obtaining anecdotal information needed to enhance the patient's treatment plan and prevent the recurrence of that particular patient's crisis in the streets.

Based upon the trust and confidence built through the powerful and cohesive alliance described above, the police department opted to select experienced police patrol officers to receive training and then serve in the dual role of police officers and crisis intervention team specialists. Volunteers for the program had to have good records as officers, pass personality tests for maturity and mental stability, and be recommended, interviewed, screened, and selected to receive CIT training. The police department committed itself to putting trained CIT officers on duty in every precinct in the city, 24 hours every day. All upper-echelon supervisory officers received formal orientation about the role and function of CIT officers, so that whenever any call involving a suspected mentally disturbed person anywhere in the city is received, the CIT officer is the designated responsible law enforcement official at the scene—regardless of the rank—and all other officers at the scene serve as backups to the CIT officer who handles the case.

CIT training using mental health experts and providers.   An integral part of the CIT program is the special preservice training provided for the officers. The importance of effective training by competent, committed, motivated professionals cannot be overemphasized. We have found that the most effective trainers are flexible, innovative, enthusiastic, personable, and expert in their disciplines. We also insist that they ride with experienced CIT officers on a Friday or Saturday evening shift prior to the scheduled training of each new group of CIT officer selectees. The training is also greatly enhanced if the trainer can skillfully integrate the conceptual with the experiential. Realistic role play, use of video technology, playback, and discussion is essential. Most mental health workers cannot do that unless they are very conversant with the problems CIT officers face. Another fundamental element of the training is the use of the services of experienced CIT officers as training assistants. These assistants bring many valuable firsthand experiences into the learning environment that serve to heighten interest, enhance motivation, and provide realism.

The topics addressed by the CIT training and the professional personnel delivering the training on the first day are:

1. diagnostic and clinical issues related to the concept of danger in the mentally ill (by a clinical psychologist specializing in the handling of mentally ill persons acting out of control)
2. posttraumatic stress disorder (by two psychologists and one vet center counselor, all of whom specialize in PTSD)
3. treatment strategies and resources (by a senior clinical psychologist recently retired as executive director of a community mental health center)
4. patient rights and legal aspects of crisis intervention (by two attorneys).

The second day's training covers

1. crisis intervention (by a licensed clinical social worker who also directs a crisis stabilization unit)
2. suicide intervention (by a psychologist who specializes in suicidology and who also chairs the psychology division of a large medical university)
3. alcohol and drug behavior in the mentally ill (by a psychologist who specializes in alcohol and drug addiction)
4. psychotropic medications and side effects (by a psychiatrist who specializes in psychotropic medications).

On the third day, CIT candidates receive training in

1. verbal techniques of crisis intervention and practicum (by two university consultants who specialize in verbal techniques and role playing in crisis intervention training, assisted by two experienced CIT officers with whom the consultants have previously ridden on Friday and Saturday night patrols)
2. controlling aggressive behavior in the mentally ill (by a psychologist who has expertise in controlling verbally aggressive mentally ill people).

On the fourth day, participants receive training in

1. crisis intervention on-site in community mental health centers (one half-day training and orientation by mental health center personnel plus discussions with mental health workers and with mental patients themselves)
2. crisis intervention on-site in hospital settings (one half-day training and orientation by hospital personnel in large hospitals having mental patient facilities plus discussions with staff as well as with patients).

On the fifth day of training, participants are taught by Police Academy instructors. Components of that training include special equipment orientation (such as training in the use of the Taser gun, velcro leg straps, and a protective shield), techniques of mental patient scene control, and other police procedural requirements.

The training program employs cross-training by occasionally having all

CIT instructors ride in patrol cars with CIT officers during Friday and Saturday night shifts. The instructors are committed to serve as follow-up consultants for CIT officers.

By 1992 the Memphis Police Department had 95 trained CIT officers operating 24 hours each day in precincts in every part of the city, and a good many former CIT officers had been promoted to positions of leadership and responsibility in other key areas such as in the detective bureau. Active CIT officers respond to approximately 500 mental patient emergencies each month. When they are not involved in crisis intervention calls, the CIT officers perform regular patrol duties. The approach to utilization of these trained officers can be classified as the specialist-generalist model in that they serve in a dual role as CIT specialists and regular patrol officers. When a mental disturbance call is received, a CIT officer is immediately dispatched to the scene. The first year of operation (1988), CIT officers responded to 2478 mental disturbance calls, transported 1533 cases to mental health facilities, and used the Taser gun 14 times. Furthermore, officer injury-on-duty reports in handling mental disturbance calls decreased by 50% during the first eight months of the program in comparison to the same time period prior to the CIT program.

The Family Trouble Center (FTC) program.   An alliance process, quite similar to that described in the development of the CIT program, was used in the development and implementation of the FTC in Memphis. Two distinct populations were targeted for proactive and preventive intervention by the FTC. These were battered persons and batterers themselves. The FTC concept evolved out of the need of the police department and the mental health community to effectively reduce the level of battering and other forms of household violence and to reduce the number of repeat dispatches to the same addresses. For instance, computer printouts revealed that during a one-year period the police were dispatched up to 28 times to one particular household due to violence or threats of violence such as beatings. Both the police and the mental health community recognized the need for proactive and preventive strategies because of safety and efficiency considerations (Scales, 1991; Winter, 1991).

Several months of intensive collaborative planning by essentially the same police and mental health persons (alliance) who founded the CIT program laid the groundwork for the FTC. Three additional groups involved were the leadership of the Memphis Housing Authority, the Family Service of Memphis, and the judicial branches of both city and county governments. Also, the mayor's office provided a great deal of leadership and support for the formation of the FTC. The city government provided the physical facilities and the alliance sought and obtained two privately funded grants to enhance the initial start-up. The grants paid for a doctoral trainee's services as FTC director and for secretarial assistance.

In the evolution of the basic FTC operational blueprint, the collaborative alliance conducted needs assessments, planning sessions, and team-building sessions over a period of almost a year. During that blueprint-building period, a training program was developed and implemented for all the major players in the alliance; in other words, the planners first obtained training themselves. Then police patrol personnel as well as police supervisory and management personnel were trained in the FTC concept. Finally, volunteer crisis workers were trained. When the center opened, it was a full-blown proactive crisis intervention/prevention agency with several unique features:

1. a highly trained and competent director
2. a cadre of highly trained volunteers, mostly graduate students in counseling and social work
3. an attractive and functional physical facility in a strategic location
4. a thoroughly trained and competent police force whose front-line patrol personnel understood the FTC concept and whose police procedures included systematic reporting and referral of all household violence or threats of violence
5. a consistent and supportive judiciary that understood the FTC concept and was committed to ordering batterers to either serve jail time or receive treatment in the FTC's anger management clinic
6. a comprehensive counseling and referral clinic for battered persons
7. complete computerized printouts of all daily domestic disturbance dispatches (whereupon FTC counselors follow up on every instance of reported battering of any kind)
8. a comprehensive preservice and in-service training program for all volunteer counselors and anger management group facilitators
9. expert volunteer consultants, trainers, and anger management group leaders from the mental health community (counselor educators, social work educators, psychologists, psychiatrists, professional counselors, directors of other crisis agencies, university counseling center psychologists)
10. an effective network for collaboration and public and community relations
11. a child-care center to attend to children of battered parents who come to the FTC for counseling/referral services.

The FTC is a unique, creative, and comprehensive example of what a proactive and futuristic community crisis response center can be. Its development and implementation did not come easy. But the basic concepts of both the FTC and the CIT programs are not beyond the grasp of any community to organize and put into place. We include the following section to serve as a perspective, from our vantage point of heavy involvement in the development and implementation, on both the CIT and the FTC programs.

COMMUNITY DEVELOPMENT OF PROACTIVE-PREVENTIVE CRISIS INTERVENTION SERVICES

Probably every community has the resources, personnel, and expertise to develop and provide proactive-preventive crisis intervention services. The foregoing brief description of both the CIT and FTC programs provides an appropriate occasion for setting forth what we feel are some important considerations for communities or groups that are interested in initiating similar programs.

The Importance of Multidisciplinary Thinking

Crisis intervention programs should be planned and implemented by persons from different disciplines, perspectives, and cultural and training backgrounds. From the initial idea to the operational program, teamwork, cooperation, coordination, and collaboration are essential. There are many reasons to insist that crisis intervention programs of the future be based on multidisciplinary thinking. Such a process

1. enables cross-fertilization of ideas from many different conceptual and experiential points of view
2. includes patient advocate groups (such as the Alliance for the Mentally Ill in the Memphis programs) not only to serve as advocates but also to lobby, agitate, bring urgency for change to the forefront, and serve as a catalyst to bring different people/disciplines together
3. achieves collective power and clout
4. enables collaboration/cooperation among different people/disciplines that probably would not come together otherwise
5. minimizes turf battles/competition and vested interest (the volatile streets belong to no one professional group in particular, with the exception of the police)
6. ensures a multicultural mix in thinking about, planning, formulating, and implementing the program.

The Need for Innovative Alliances

The involvement of the Alliance for the Mentally Ill (AMI) of Memphis is an example of both appropriate use of the multidisciplinary approach and a pure form of proactive-preventive crisis intervention. The targeted crises were immediate, volatile, and located in every area of the city, and no segment of the community, except the police, had access to the crisis territory —the streets. Neither the police nor the mental health community alone had the means to cope with the crises. Such a milieu presented a prime opportunity to bring together all the components extant to solve the problem and to do so without the usual impediments of competition, jealousy, throat-cutting tactics, battles over turf, and other antagonistic factors. Also, an entity such as AMI was an ideal group to build cohesion and teamwork. Who could say no to that group when they were asking for reasonable and needed action to reduce the dangers to everyone? Who could possibly say no to strategies that would result in reduction of expressive crimes and even murder, stabilizing and containing out-of-control persons and violence that affects everyone? The truth is that when AMI obtained a firm commitment from a few key players in the police department and the mental health community, the remaining individuals and groups fell into line because it was clear that AMI was headed in the right direction. The result was the formation of an all-out community effort, relatively free of jealousies, blaming others, and credit or glory seeking. There was even pervasive excitement and relief that affirmative, nonpartisan, proactive steps were being taken to benefit the whole community and that the volatile streets would not be left to the police alone. The community alliance took the purest form of what crisis intervention can become—the bringing together of representatives of all mental health components to figure out ways to train and utilize police, paramedics, and others who are most likely to come into contact with distraught, out-of-control people.

A Blueprint for the Future

Clearly, the goal is not for police, paramedics, and other similar workers to become psychologists, psychiatrists, counselors, or social workers. Rather, the goal is to give those workers enough basic knowledge and skills to contain and stabilize out-of-control situations in the streets until enough equilibrium can be restored, specialized help or referral provided, or the person can be transported to a place of safety and assistance. Through built-in referral and consultation mechanisms, mental health personnel support, supplement, and function where the police leave off. Individual members of the police–mental health community alliance can do those jobs for which they are best suited and trained. The rich multidisciplinary and proactive-preventive approach we have described is radically different from traditional reactive crisis work. This approach is applicable to many community crisis situations. Perhaps it is a blueprint for the future of crisis intervention—for new directions. We view it as encouragement for people in communities to believe, "We've got people and situations like that. We can build teamwork and alliances like that. We have the expertise, resolve, motivation, and leadership to do that. We can form an effective and cohesive community action team." The important factor to take into account is that no one group or entity can or should do it alone.

The community alliance approach is quite a contrast to the national crisis response teams we have described elsewhere in this chapter. What we are talking about here is deriving the ideas, resources, and delivery of crisis intervention services from the community rather than depending on external expertise, even though expertise from without may at times be necessary and accepted. The community action concept also provides for the local community to assess its own needs, develop its own blueprint, formulate its own unique alliances, and utilize its own expert personnel to take proactive-preventive action steps in a systematic, measured, cost-effective, and autonomous fashion. We believe that any community, large or small, can create its own proactive-preventive crisis intervention teams using its own talents, leadership, and resources; and that such a procedure is cost-effective. We might note that almost all of the Memphis model components we have described were implemented at low or no cost. All of the mental health personnel contributed their time. The police department used its regularly budgeted resources to meet its CIT and FTC commitments without asking for any increase, even though it did obtain start-up funding for the FTC through a couple of privately financed grants. Otherwise, the total cost of both the CIT and FTC programs was formulated and met without any additional public funding.

SUMMARY

Although historically, crisis intervention has been largely limited to a reactive function of the human services professions, we have described two newly emergent directions that redefine that function. First, crisis intervention has evolved from being a grassroots movement that was driven mainly by volunteers, into a formidable professional subspecialty. Second, it has further advanced into the realm of proactive and preventive interventions while concomitantly responding to a continuously expanding number of different crisis categories. The impetus for these new directions, initiated by actions of people at the grassroots level, has spread from volunteers to professional human services specialists and to institutions.

Crisis intervention has taken on a proactive stance that includes outreach initiatives at both local and national levels. The philosophy of taking intervention services to the people in the streets or in the region has been widely accepted. The concept of networking and sharing ideas, strategies, and resources among diverse agencies has become common practice. Crisis interventionists have become more and more proactive and preventive in their training and their work. Public and private sources of support have come to recognize the wisdom and the economic benefits of prevention.

We have described representative and innovative strategies and specific examples of taking crisis intervention directly to the populations and locations where crises occur. Some of these were crisis stabilization programs, crisis response outreach teams, telephone interventions, crisis management in schools, a crisis intervention team approach to crises encountered by police officers, and a family trouble center for intervention with both victims of battering and batterers themselves. These programs are only a small sampling of the emerging world of crisis intervention that includes crisis workers in the modern complex arena of rapid response to human disasters and dilemmas as well as in the business of both ameliorating the effects of and preventing crises from occurring.

Last Words

If we have sounded enthusiastic and idealistic in our reporting on the proactive-preventive model of crisis intervention, it is because we are. We have been privileged to be totally immersed in every phase of the Memphis models—the CIT and the FTC programs. We have observed firsthand how effective highly trained police (CIT) officers can be under the most trying circumstances in the streets of Memphis. We have witnessed how effective our graduate student volunteers and practicum students can be in dealing with and counseling the most severely beaten clients and in learning and using group techniques to teach hostile and defensive batterers to control and manage their anger. We have ourselves participated in the hands-on crisis work. We have been involved in the conceptualizing, planning, training, and implementing of all phases of both the CIT and the FTC programs. These experiences have given us confidence that crisis intervention can and indeed should move off the couch and into the streets! We are quite sure that effective crisis intervention is more than reactive responding; that the new directions for crisis work clearly point toward systematic, collaborative, proactive, and preventive strategies involving highly skilled and motivated crisis workers from a wide variety of disciplines, competencies, and experiences.

REFERENCES

Aquilera, D. C., & Messick, J. M. (1982). *Crisis intervention: Theory and methodology* (4th ed.). St. Louis: C. V. Mosby.

Andrews, A. B. (1991). Crisis and recovery services for family violence survivors. In A. R. Roberts (Ed.), *Contemporary perspectives on crisis intervention and prevention* (pp. 121–145). Englewood Cliffs, NJ: Prentice-Hall.

Bassuk, E. L., & Cote, W. (1983). A network approach to rural psychiatric emergency training. *Hospital and Community Psychiatry, 34,* 233–238.

Baumann, D. J., Schultz, D. F., Brown, C., Paredes, R., et al. (1987). Citizen participation in police crisis intervention activities. *American Journal of Community Psychology, 15,* 459–471.

Bertoia, J., & Allan, J. (1988). School management of the bereaved child. *Elementary School Guidance and Counseling, 23,* 30–38.

Blinder, A. (1991, April). *Crisis intervention in the world of managed care—Legitimacy at last.* Paper presented at Crisis Convening XV, Chicago.

Britton, J. G., & Mattson-Melcher, D. M. (1985). The crisis home: Sheltering patients in emotional crisis. *Journal of Psychosocial Nursing and Mental Health Services, 23,* 18–23.

Brom, D., & Kleber, R. J. (1989). Prevention of post-traumatic stress disorders. *Journal of Traumatic Stress, 2,* 335–351.

Burek, D. M. (Ed.). (1992). *Encyclopedia of associations* (22nd ed.), Vol. 1, Part 2. Detroit: Gale Research.

Burk, E. D. (1972). Some contemporary issues in child development and the children of alcoholic parents. *Annals of New York Academy of Science, 197,* 189–197.

Clark, S. C., & McKiernan, W. (1981). Contacts with a Canadian "street level" drug and crisis centre, 1975–1978. *Bulletin on Narcotics, 33,* 23–31.

Coy, D. R. (1991, March). Gulf war impacts school counselors. *Guidepost,* pp. 12, 27.

Daro, D. (1991). Strategies and models in child abuse prevention. In A. R. Roberts (Ed.), *Contemporary perspectives on crisis intervention and prevention* (pp. 161–184). Englewood Cliffs, NJ: Prentice-Hall.

Dubin, W. R., & Fink, P. J. (1986). The psychiatric short procedure unit: A cost-saving innovation. *Hospital and Community Psychiatry, 37,* 227–229.

Fein, E., & Knaut, S. A. (1986). Crisis intervention and support: Working with the police. *Social Casework, 67,* 276–282.

Gillig, P. M., Dumaine, M., Stammer, J. W., Hillard, J. R., & Grubb, P. (1990). What do police officers really want from the mental health system? *Hospital and Community Psychiatry, 41,* 663–665.

Gilliland, B. E., & James, R. K. (1988). *Crisis intervention strategies.* Pacific Grove, CA: Brooks/Cole.

Gray, R. E. (1988). The role of school counselors with bereaved teenagers: With and without peer support groups. *The School Counselor, 35,* 185–192.

Hughes, R. B. (1988). Grief counseling: Facilitating the healing process. *Journal of Counseling and Development, 67,* 77.

In Touch Hotline Counseling Center (1991). *Proceedings of the Fifteenth Annual Convening of Crisis Intervention Personnel.* Chicago: University of Illinois at Chicago.

Intrater, L. C. (1991, April). *Working with homeless/throwaway youth in crisis.* Paper presented at Crisis Convening XV, Chicago.

James, R. K. (1990, April). *Training Memphis police officers for crisis intervention with the mentally disturbed.* Paper presented at Crisis Convening XIV, Chicago.

James, R. K., & Gilliland, B. E. (1991, April). *Future directions of crisis intervention.* Paper presented at Crisis Convening XV, Chicago.

Jobes, D. A., & Berman, A. L. (1991). Crisis intervention and brief treatment for suicidal youth. In A. R. Roberts (Ed.), *Contemporary perspectives on crisis intervention and prevention* (pp. 53–69). Englewood Cliffs, NJ: Prentice-Hall.

Kalafat, J. (1991). Suicide intervention in schools. In A. R. Roberts (Ed.), *Contemporary perspectives on crisis intervention and prevention* (pp. 218–239). Englewood Cliffs, NJ: Prentice-Hall.

Kendrick, J. M. (1991). Crisis intervention in child abuse: A family treatment approach. In A. R. Roberts (Ed.), *Contemporary perspectives on crisis intervention and prevention* (pp. 34–52). Englewood Cliffs, NJ: Prentice-Hall.

Lane, K. E., & Dickey, T. (1988). New students and grief. *The School Counselor, 35,* 359–362.

Leaman, K. (1987). A hospital alternative for patients in crisis. *Hospital and Community Psychiatry, 38,* 1221–1223.

Luckett, J. B., & Slaikeu, K. A. (1990). Crisis intervention by police. In K. A. Slaikeu (Ed.), *Crisis intervention: A handbook for practice and research* (2nd ed.) (pp. 227–242). Boston: Allyn & Bacon.

Mantell, J. E., & Schinke, S. P. (1991). The crisis of AIDS for adolescents: The need for preventive interventions. In A. R. Roberts (Ed.), *Contemporary perspectives on crisis intervention and prevention* (pp. 185–217). Englewood Cliffs, NJ: Prentice-Hall.

McDermott, P. M., & Gordon, C. I. (1984). The emergency psychiatric service system. *Crisis Intervention, 13,* 55–60.

McGowan, S. (1992, January). ACPA holds campus violence workshop. *Guidepost,* pp. 9–10.

Millard Public Schools. (1991). *Guidelines for the management of the aftermath of a suicide, sudden death, or other crisis.* Unpublished guidelines, Millard Public Schools, Don Stroh Administration Center, Omaha, Nebraska.

Miller, J. D., & Jang, M. (1977). Children of alcoholism: A 20-year longitudinal study. *Social Work Research, 13,* 23–29.

Modrak, R. (1992, January). Mass shootings and airplane crashes: Counselors respond to the changing face of community crisis. *Guidepost,* p. 4.

National Institute of Mental Health (NIMH). (1990, September). *Rapid assessment post-impact of disaster (RAPID)* (Program Announcement PA-91-04). Rockville, MD: Department of Health and Human Services, Public Health Service, Alcohol, Drug Abuse, and Mental Health Administration.

Nelson, E. R., & Slaikeu, K. A. (1990). Crisis intervention in the schools. In K. A. Slaikeu (Ed.), *Crisis intervention: A handbook for practice and research* (2nd ed.) (pp. 329–347). Boston: Allyn & Bacon.

Palmo, A. J., Langlois, D. E., & Bender, I. (1988). Development of a policy and procedures statement for crisis situations in the school. *The School Counselor, 36,* 94–102.

Pattison, E. M., & Kaufman, E. (Eds.). (1982). *Encyclopedic handbook of alcoholism.* New York: Gardner Press.

Peeks, B. (1989). Farm families in crisis: The school counselor's role. *The School Counselor, 36,* 384–388.

Piersma, H. L., & Van-Wingen, S. (1988). A hospital-based crisis service for adolescents: A program description. *Adolescence, 23,* 491–500.

Pritchard, L., Brownstein, J., & Johnan, M. (1989). The youth booth in the mall: Reaching youth in the 80's. *Prevention in Human Services, 6,* 87–92.

Riordan, R. J., & Allen, L. (1989). Grief counseling: A funeral home-based model. *Journal of Counseling and Development, 67,* 424–425.

Roberts, A. R. (Ed.). (1991). *Contemporary perspectives on crisis intervention and prevention.* Englewood Cliffs, NJ: Prentice-Hall.

Scales, P. K. (1991, April). *The Family Trouble Center: A domestic violence intervention project. Paper presented at Crisis Convening XV,* Chicago.

Shafer, C. (1989a, September). Counselors offer crisis intervention at Iowa crash site. *Guidepost,* pp. 1, 3, 6.

Shafer, C. (1989b, December). Recent disasters trigger NIMH response. *Guidepost,* pp. 1, 5.

Slaikeu, K. A. (Ed.). (1990). *Crisis intervention: A handbook for practice and research* (2nd ed.). Boston: Allyn & Bacon.

Slaikeu, K. A., & Leff-Simon, S. I. (1990). In K. A. Slaikeu (Ed.), *Crisis intervention: A handbook for practice and research* (2nd ed.) (pp. 319–328). Boston: Allyn & Bacon.

Sorensen, J. R. (1989). Responding to student or teacher death: Preparing crisis intervention. *Journal of Counseling and Development, 67,* 426–427.

Toubiana, Y. H., Milgram, N. A., Strich, Y., & Edelstein, A. (1988). Crisis intervention in a school community disaster: Principles and practices. *Journal of Community Psychology, 16,* 228–240.

Wakelee-Lynch, J. (1990, October). Florida crisis elicits aid from college officials and counselors. *Guideposts,* pp. 1, 3.

Warren, D. R., & Gladych-Machniak, K. (1990, April). *Network for a community response to a student suicide.* Paper presented at Crisis Convening XIV, Chicago.

Weinberg, R. B. (1989). Consultation and training with school-based crisis teams. *Professional Psychology Research and Practice, 20,* 305–308.

Weisman, G. K. (1985). Crisis-oriented residential treatment as an alternative to hospitalization. *Hospital and Community Psychiatry, 36,* 1302–1305.

Wellin, E., Slesinger, D. P., & Hollister, C. D. (1987). Psychiatric emergency services: Evolution, adaptation, and proliferation. *Social Science and Medicine, 24,* 475–482.

White, W. C., & Rubenstein, A. S. (1984). Crisis intervention on campus. *Crisis Intervention, 13,* 42–54.

Wilson, J. M. (1991, April). *Crisis stabilization: An alternative to hospitalization.* Paper presented at Crisis Convening XV, Chicago.

Winter, B. A. (1991, April). *The Family Trouble Center: A pilot program for domestic violence.* Paper presented at Crisis Convening XV, Chicago.

Young, M. A. (1991). Crisis intervention and the aftermath of disaster. In A. R. Roberts (Ed.), *Contemporary perspectives on crisis intervention* (pp. 83–103). Englewood Cliffs, NJ: Prentice-Hall.

Zabin, L. S., & Streett, R. (1991). The crisis of teen pregnancy and an empirically tested model for pregnancy prevention. In A. R. Roberts (Ed.), *Contemporary perspectives on crisis intervention and prevention* (pp. 240–255). Englewood Cliffs, NJ: Prentice-Hall.

Index

Abusive relationships, 186–187
Acceptance, 40
  in cases of PTSD, 189
  communicating, 46–47
  death and, 410
Acquired immune deficiency syndrome
    (AIDS), 417–418, 441–444
Adaptational theory, 18
Addiction, 332, 333–348 (*see also* Chemical
    dependency; Substance abuse)
Adolescent Alcohol Involvement Scale, 350
Adolescent Antisocial Behavior Checklist,
    458
Adolescents:
  bereavement in, 415, 431–433
  reactions to trauma by, 181
  suicide, 134, 138–140, 147–149
Adult Children of Alcoholics (ACOAs),
    343–347, 388–394
Affective domain scale, 79–80
Affective state, assessment of, 34
Age:
  bereavement and, 416–417, 439–441
  suicide and, 153
  violence and, 459
Alcohol abuse:
  aspects of, 325–327, 328–329
  background information on, 322
  in battered women, 277
  in batterers, 300–301, 309
  environmental cues for, 375–376
  in families, 339–343
  role in hostage taking, 508
  violence and, 460
  woman battering and, 271, 273
Alcoholism, 332, 334, 349
Alliance networks, functioning of, 603–604
"Alter-ego" exercises, 383–384
Alzheimer's disease, 483
Anchoring, in cases of geriatric violence,
    106, 487
Anger:
  in adult children of alcoholics, 345
  in battered women, 279–280, 282
  in battering men, 269
  in child sexual abuse victims, 245

Anger: (*continued*)
  cues, 305
  death and, 409
  deflection of, 475–477
  management groups, 297–311
  rape and, 230
  timeouts, 304
Antisocial personalities, 92, 507
Anxiety reactions, 108–109
Appeasement, 474–475
Applied crisis theory, 18–19, 24
Approach-avoidance behavior, 7
Assertiveness training, 245–246
Assessment, 33–38
  of adult children of alcoholics, 389–391
  of PTSD, 184, 185–187
  of batterers, 299–300
  of burnout, 551–552, 562
  in cases of geriatric violence, 484
  in cases of woman battering, 276–278
  of chemical dependency, 349–356
  of crisis severity, 33–35
  of current emotional status, 35–37
  of delayed rape trauma syndrome,
    246–247
  in hostage crises, 523–524
  of institutional violence, 458
  in long-term therapy versus crisis work,
    77–78
  neurological, 85–86
  for resources, 37
  in suicide, 37–38, 133–136
  summary of, 38
  triage system of, 79–85
Attitudes Toward Women checklist, 304

Bargaining, 409–410
BASIC ID approach, in treating burnout,
    559–560
Battered Woman Syndrome, 276
Battered-women's shelters, 289–296
Batterers:
  assessment of, 299–300
  intake interview for, 300–301
  treating, 297–311
  treatment goals for, 298–299

Battering, *see* Woman battering
Battering groups, 297–311
Beck, A. T., 21
Behavioral clues, to suicide, 135
Behavioral domain scale, 82–83
Behavioral learning model of addiction, 329
Being, client states of, 32–33
Bereavement, 22, 406–447
    conceptual approaches to, 409–412
    dynamics of, 407–418
    in HIV-infected clients, 443–444
    intervention strategies for, 418–444
    trauma and, 179
Bibliotherapy, 424–425
Birth defects, alcohol-related, 326–327
Borderline personality, 113–116
Brief Psychiatric Rating Scale, 458
Brunner/Mazel Psychological Stress Series, 212
Burnout, 453, 537–572
    classroom exercises related to, 576–579
    dynamics of, 539–551
    intervention strategies for, 551–572
    levels of, 544–545
    maladaptive responses to, 558–559
    myths that engender, 543–544
    organizational culpability for, 548–549
    private practitioners and, 549–550, 560–572
    research findings on, 542–543
    ripple effect of, 567
    self-recognition of, 550–551
    stages of, 545–546
    support for, 554–558
    worker-client relations and, 546–548
    workshops, 556–558

Caplan, G., 16
Case handling, 86–101, 116–120
Chemical dependency, 322–395 (*see also* Alcohol abuse; Substance abuse)
    aftercare for, 384–387
    assessment of, 349–356
    background information on, 322–333
    crisis points in, 358–362
    detoxification phase of, 362–363
    family treatment for, 376–384
    intervention strategies for, 348–388
    multivariate approach to, 347–348
    relapse to, 387–388
    terms related to, 332–333
    treatment, 363–367
Child abusers, treatment for, 243
Children:
    of alcoholic families, 339–341
    at battered-women's shelters, 295–296
    bereavement, 414–415, 428–431
    chemical dependency and, 382–383
    crisis intervention strategies for, 429–431
    death of, 413, 422–426
    PTSD in, 167, 181–185
    sexual abuse of, 186–187, 232–235

Children: (*continued*)
    suicidal, 136–138
    suicide intervention strategies for, 147–149
Child sexual abuse:
    case history in, 241–246
    classroom exercises related to, 260
    dynamics of, 235–238
    incidence of, 235–236
    phases of, 233–235
    prevention of, 246
Chronic crisis, 35, 101–102
Client functioning, determining, 79–85
Clients (*see also* Difficult clients)
    attending to immediate needs of, 56–57
    control and autonomy of, 31
    coping strengths of, 56
    emotional investment in, 418–419
    emotional strength of, 35–36
    focus on, 41
    immobile, 52
    manipulative, 112–116
    past history of, 14
    viewpoint of, 15
Client safety, 28–29, 53–54, 65–66, 89–90
Client threats, handling, 118–120
Closed questions, 39
Cocaine Addiction Self-Report, 350
Codependency, 336–339 (*see also* Dependency issues)
    characteristics of, 343–347
    defined, 332
    recovery process for, 393–394
Cognitive domain scale, 80–82
Cognitive model, 20–21, 24
Cognitive restructuring, 251–252
Cognitive state, assessment of, 34
Collaboration, in crisis intervention, 590
Collaborative counseling, 51, 66
Combat Exposure Scale, 185
Commitment:
    to abstain, extracting, 393
    in cases of burnout, 568
    for follow through, 58–59
    in hostage-taking situations, 506
    obtaining, 31–32, 66
    procedures, 104
    in telephone counseling, 90
Communication, 15, 40–47, 73, 270
Community alliance approach, 609
Community mental health centers, 101, 103–107
Compensation neurosis, 164
Confidentiality:
    in case handling, 116–120
    for HIV-infected persons, 442
    principles bearing on, 117–118
    suicide and, 150
Conflict avoidance, 472–474
Conflict Tactics Scale, 299, 304
Confrontation, 61–62, 197, 302, 370–373
Consistency, 45

Consultation, 62, 87, 118
Continuous Data Questionnaire (CDQ), 351
Control issues:
  in adult children of alcoholics, 345
  in battered women, 265, 270, 288
  for batterers, 269, 308
  in cases of burnout, 567
  following traumatic events, 183
  as an issue for rape survivors, 239
Coping, 29, 31, 55, 56, 66, 67, 346–347, 559, 565
Core listening skills, 28
Counseling (see also Individual counseling)
  at battered-women's shelters, 290–294, 295–296
  for batterers, 297–311
  collaborative, 51
  directive, 52–53
  nondirective, 50–51
  of suicidal clients, 136–147
  telephone, 86–101
Countertransference, 99, 419
Courtship violence, 296–297 (see also Woman battering)
Crime:
  alcohol-related, 327
  expressive, 601–602
  mental illness and, 455
Crisis (see also Trauma)
  attending incestuous relationships, 242–243
  characteristics of, 3, 4–5, 23
  factors in, 17
  going to the scene of, 591–593
  in the human services workplace, 453
  resulting from sexual abuse, 225
  in therapy sessions, 111
Crisis agencies, 585–588
Crisis case handling, 74–79
Crisis center work settings, 538
Crisis hotlines, 86–88, 90–101, 151, 226, 277–278
Crisis intervention:
  assessment in, 33–38
  listening in, 38–50
  models, 19–22
  multicultural perspectives in, 12–15
  programs, 608
  role play, 68
  services, 607–610
  skills, 27–73
  six-step model of, 27–32, 63–68
  strategies, 429–431
Crisis Intervention Team (CIT) program, 602–606
Crisis:
  programs, 591, 593–597
  severity, assessing, 33–35
  situations, 48
  textbooks, 586–587

Crisis: (continued)
  theory, 16–18, 24
  types, 101–103
  work, 74–78
Crisis workers:
  action strategies for, 53–59
  adult suicide and, 150–151
  effective, 7–12, 24
  guidelines for, 27–32
  personal grief among, 418–419
  self-assessment for, 53
  volunteers as, 585
Cross-cultural counseling, 13–15
Culture:
  bereavement and, 407–409
  role in chemical dependency, 323–324
  role in woman battering, 265–266
  sexual assault and, 230

Danger, crisis and, 4, 119
Death, 179, 407–409, 420–422 (see also Bereavement; Grief; Personal loss)
Defense mechanisms, addiction and, 333–336
Deflection, in violence intervention, 475–477
Delayed rape trauma syndrome, 246–253
Denial, 188
  addiction and, 334, 343
  chemical dependency and, 370
  death and, 409
  as the result of trauma, 181–182
  as a symptom of PTSD, 174–175
Dependency issues, 87 (see also Codependency)
  in adult children of alcoholics, 344
  in battering relationships, 268, 270, 271, 280, 291–292
Dependent personalities, 93
Depersonalization scale, 551
Depression, 80
  addiction and, 336
  in battered women, 276, 282, 293
  death and, 410
Desensitization, as a result of trauma, 180
Developmental crisis, 19, 102–103
Difficult clients, 59–62
Directive counseling, 52–53, 66, 563–564
Disclosure phase of child sexual abuse, 234
Disease model of addiction, 328–331
Disequilibrium, 32
Displacement, 183, 334, 338
Dissociative behavior, 112, 337
Divorce, 6, 415–416, 434–437
Domestic violence, 297 (see also Woman battering)
Drugs, 98, 323, 333 (see also Chemical dependency; Substance abuse)
Dual-diagnosis clients, 347–348
Dying with dignity, 131

Eclectic crisis intervention, 22–23, 24
Education:
    of adult children of alcoholics, 391–392
    for battered women, 289
    role in suicide prevention, 155, 157–158
    about sex offenders, 245–246
    in violence intervention, 469–472
    woman battering and, 271, 275
Egan, G., 45
Elderly people, 416–417, 439–441, 455 (see
    also Age; Old age)
Ellis, A., 21, 306
Emergency services, 594–595, 597
Emotional carryover, 8
Emotional Exhaustion scale, 551
Empathy, 40, 42–44
Enabling, 333, 336–339
Epitaph exercise, 433
Equilibrium/disequilibrium paradigm, 16
Equilibrium model, 20, 24, 32
Erikson, E., 22
Estrangement, as a result of trauma, 180
Ethics, confidentiality and, 117
Existential crises, 19
Expanded crisis theory, 17–18, 24
Expressive behavior, 504, 601–602

Facilitating movement, in battered women,
    280–284
Facilitative:
    assessment, 37
    listening, 47–50
    responding, 48
Family:
    dysfunction, 271
    history of violence in, 461
    intervention, in crisis creation, 361–362
    learned aggression in, 266
    responses to PTSD, 176–179, 202
    role in hostage crises, 520
    violence in, 272
Family Environment Scale, 304
Family therapy, 203–204, 376–384, 426,
    429
Feelings:
    assessment, in batterers, 307–308
    owning of, 39–40, 69–73
    writing to express, 201
Fetal alcohol syndrome, 326–327
Figley's Traumagram Questionnaire, 185
"First-order intervention," 597
Flashback episodes, 166
Flexibility, in crisis workers, 10
Flooding techniques, 184, 208, 244,
    251–252
Force, in violence intervention, 478–480
Formal counseling, 14

Gateway model of addiction, 328
General Adaptation Syndrome, 540
Genetic-predisposition model of addiction,
    328

Genuiness, 40, 44–46
Geriatric clients, violent, 482–492 (see also
    Age; Elderly people; Old age)
Gestalt techniques:
    for victims of PTSD, 209–210
    for resolving unfinished business, 223
Grief (see also Bereavement; Personal loss)
    in battered women, 292–293
    in child sexual abuse victims, 245
    crises, 16
    resolution, 252–253
Grieving process, 210
Group grief work, 431–432
Group therapy, 191–193, 427–428, 438
Growth, 4–5, 412
Guided imagery, 184
Guilt:
    in adult children of alcoholics, 345
    animated, 200
    in cases of burnout, 566
    trauma-induced, 179
Gulf War-related crisis response program,
    595

Habituation, defined, 333 (see also
    Chemical dependency; Substance
    abuse)
Hallucination, 98, 487–488
Histrionics, 92–93
Holding-on stage, in personal loss, 411, 436
Hostage crises, 453, 503–533
    background information concerning, 503
    case study illustrating, 522–529
    classroom exercises concerning, 534–536
    dynamics of, 504–514
    intervention strategies in, 515–529
    negotiators, 513–514
    self-protection during, 529–532
Hostage takers:
    persuasion of, 519–522
    types of, 504–510
Human immunodeficiency virus (HIV),
    417, 441–444
Human services:
    assistance programs, 86
    directories, 57
    workers, and burnout, 538
    workplace, 453, 458–462
Hypochondriasis, addiction and, 338–339
Hysterical neurosis, 164

"I" approach, 52
Illusions, in cases of geriatric violence,
    487–488
Immobility, 32, 52, 82–83
Impact of Events Scale, 185
Incest, 186–187, 233, 236, 237–238 (see
    also Child sexual abuse)
    exploration of, 248–249
    family crisis attending, 242–243
    reporting of, 228

Individual counseling:
  for bereavement, 421, 429, 431, 439
  for child sexual abuse victims, 244–245
  following a suicide, 426
  following separation or divorce, 434
  following the death of a pet, 438
Institutional crises, 151–152, 455–494
Intake interviews, 105, 186
Interactive participants, in violence, 461
Interpersonal theory, 18
Interventions, eclectic theory and, 22
Intrusive-repetitive phase of recovery, 188
Intrusive thoughts, as the result of trauma,
  182, 205–208
Irrational mental sets, disrupting, 373–374
"I" statements, 46

Kübler-Ross model, 409–410

Learned helplessness, 266–267, 280
Legalities, 117, 184, 457–458
Lethality level, 52
  assessment of, 105, 141
  in cases of burnout, 562
  characteristics of, 144
  in HIV-infected clients, 443
  in suicide, 134
  in telephone counseling, 89, 100–101
  Triage Assessment Form, 135–136
  in woman battering, 288, 300
Letting go, personal loss and, 411
Life-adjustment groups, 202
Lifestyle model of addiction, 329
Limitations, admitting, 549
Limit setting:
  with battered women, 282–283
  for borderline personalities, 113–114
  in telephone counseling, 94
Lindemann, E., 16
Listening:
  in crisis intervention, 38–50
  facilitative, 47–50
  in hostage crises, 525
  in woman-battering cases, 278
Long-term:
  case handling, 74–79
  crisis, 35
  disposition, determining, 106–107
  therapy, 74–78, 107–116
Loss, see Personal loss

MacAndrew Alcoholism Scale, 349
Maladaptive:
  behaviors, 18
  cognitions, 81
  defense mechanisms, 336–339
  responses, to burnout, 558–559
"Managed care" concept, 589
Manipulation:
  by clients, 112–116
  of hotline workers, 91–92
Maslach Burnout Inventory, 551, 557

Meichenbaum, D. H., 21
Mental disorders, violence and, 460–461
Mentally disturbed persons:
  as hostage takers, 504–507
  police and, 601
Michigan Alcohol Screening Test (MAST),
  304, 309, 350
Millon Clinical Multiaxial Inventory, 185
Minimizing, addiction and, 335
Minnesota Multiphasic Personality
  Inventory (MMPI), 185, 276, 349
Minuchin, S., 22
Mississippi Scale for Combat-Related
  Posttraumatic Stress Disorder, 185
Mortality patterns, 408
Motoric cues, to violence, 461–462
Multicultural perspectives, 12–15
Multiphasic treatment, of victims of PTSD,
  204

National crises, response programs for, 589,
  595, 596
Needs, immediate, 56–57 (see also Support)
Networking, 58, 288, 589–590
Neurological assessment, 85–86
Neurotransmitters, changes in, 85
Noncompliance, in borderline personalities,
  115
Nondefensiveness, 45
Nondirective counseling, 50–51, 66
Nonverbal behavior, confrontation and, 61
Nonverbal communication, 43–44
"Normal" behavior, 13
Numbing-type families, 178

Objective assessment, 33
Obsessive-compulsives, 93
Old age (see also Age; Elderly people)
  and suicide, 142–147, 153–154
Open-ended questions, 39, 50, 54–55, 67
  for difficult clients, 61
  exercise in using, 69
  in telephone counseling, 94
  in woman-battering cases, 281–282
Options, 55, 470
Outreach programs, 591–593
"Owning:"
  of clients' problems, 548
  defined, 37
  of feelings, 39–40, 69–73
  of options, 55

Pacing, 486, 518
Paranoids, 92
Paranoid schizophrenics, as hostage takers,
  505
Parent-survivor group work, 423–424,
  446–447
Passive aggression, addiction and, 338
Pedophiles, 235, 236
Peer-cluster model of addiction, 329
Personal Accomplishment scale, 551

Personal Experience Screening Questionnaire, 350
Personality patterns, in abusing men, 269–270
Personality tests, for detecting PTSD, 185
Personality traits, of alcoholics, 335–336
Personal loss, 410–417 (*see also* Bereavement; Grief)
Pets, death of, 416, 437–439
Physical cues, to violence, 461–462
Physical exercise:
  in combatting burnout, 569
  deflection of anger through, 476
Physical responses, to trauma, 183
Placater-type children, 340–341, 346
Planning, 31, 66
  of action steps, 55–56
  in telephone counseling, 90
Play therapy:
  for child sexual abuse victims, 244
  following the death of a pet, 438–439
  techniques of, 184–185
Police, 601–602
Pornography, rape and, 229
Positive-aggressives, 93
Positive and constructive thinking patterns, 29
Positive regard, communicating, 46–47
Posttraumatic stress disorder (PTSD), 5, 8, 17, 163–224
  affiliative responses and, 186
  background information on, 163–165
  in battered women, 276
  categories of families associated with, 177–179
  childhood sexual abuse and, 235, 237
  children and, 181–183
  conflicting diagnoses and, 167
  denial/numbing as a symptom of, 174–175
  diagnostic categorization of, 165–167
  dynamics of, 165–183
  education about, 249
  family responses to, 176–179
  family therapy and, 203–204
  helping other victims of, 210–211
  importance of acceptance in, 189
  incidence of, 169
  intervention, 183–190, 204–210
  intrusive-repetitive ideation as a symptom of, 175–176
  maladaptive patterns characteristic of, 179–181
  outreach programs for preventing, 592
  phases of recovery from, 187–188
  physiological responses to, 168–169
  preexisting psychopathology and, 167–168
  rape trauma as, 226
  residual impact of, 170
  symptoms of, 186
  therapeutic sequence for, 193–198

Posttraumatic stress disorder (PTSD) (*continued*)
  trauma type and, 170–171
  treatment risks in, 189–190
  veterans centers treatment of, 190–211
Power:
  in battering relationships, 265, 270, 280, 308
  among caregivers, 419
  in domestic violence, 299
  rape and, 229, 230
Precipitating events, 50
Precrisis functioning, 84–85
Prescriptive model of addiction, 328–329
Presenting crises, 101–103, 113
Prevention programs, *see* Crisis, programs
Primary prevention programs, 593–594
Priority setting, 68, 283
Privileged communication, 117
Problem-behavior proneness, 329
Problem definition, 13–14, 28, 54, 65, 89
Problem Drinker Scale, 350
Problem-solving strategies, 67
Professional distance, 99–100
Prohibition, effects of, 322
Projection:
  addiction and, 334
  of problems, 115
Psychiatric emergency services (PESs), 594–595
Psychic trauma, 163
Psychoanalytic model of addiction, 329
Psychoanalytic theory, 17
Psychodrama, in child therapy, 430
Psychodynamic approach to suicide, 130–131
Psychoeducation, about PTSD, 249
Psychological autopsy, 155, 162, 493
Psychological disturbances, violence and, 460–461
Psychological trauma, 17
Psychosocial:
  model of addiction, 329
  stressors, 540
  transition model, 21–22, 24
Psychotic breaks, 112
Psychotropic drugs, 85
Purdue PTSD scale, 185

Rape, 225, 226–232, 238–241
Rap groups, 191–193, 194–198
Rational-emotive therapy (RET), 21, 437
Rationalization, addiction and, 334
Reaction formation, addiction and, 335, 338
Reality orientation, 485–486
Reality therapy, 427, 472
Realness, 40
Recovery euphoria, 385–386
Reduced-stimulus environments, 477
Reenactment, of traumatic events, 182–183

Referral resources:
    for elderly bereaved persons, 439
    following separation or divorce, 435
    representative, 444–447
    using, 57–58
Reflective-transition phase of recovery, 188
Refocusing a crisis, 48
Regression, 109–110, 183, 204, 335
Relationship skills, 367–368
Relaxation exercises, 10, 52–53, 204, 305,
    478
Reminiscence therapy, 146, 440–441,
    486–487
Remotivation therapy, 489–490
Repression, addiction and, 335, 337
Rescue tendencies, avoiding, 419
Resource assessment, 37
Responding, as an aspect of listening,
    47–48
Restatement of ideas, 47–48, 68–69, 70,
    282, 518
Right-to-die issues, 149
Rogers, C. R., 40, 45
Role changes, chemical dependency and,
    386
Role overload, and burnout, 542
Role play, 10, 68, 432, 464
Roles, freedom from, 45

Safety, 28–29, 53, 65–66 (see also Client
    safety)
    of battered women, 277, 284–288, 301
    in hostage crises, 515–516
    from institutional violence, 466–467
    in telephone counseling, 89–90
    in the work environment, 467
Scale for Assessment of Suicide
    Potentiality, 134
Schneider model of response to
    bereavement, 410–412
Schools:
    bereavement in, 433–434
    crisis-intervention strategies for, 599–600
    crisis-management programs in, 597–601
Seclusion, in violence intervention,
    480–481
Security, institutional, 456, 463–464, 467
Sedation, in violence intervention, 482
Self-assessment, for crisis workers, 53
Self-defeating types, 93
Self-talk, 21, 478, 571
Separation, 415–416, 434–437
Sexual abuse, 6, 186–187, 193, 232–235
    (see also Child sexual abuse; Incest)
Sexual assault, 225–254. (see also Rape)
Silence, role of, 44
Situational clues, to suicide, 135
Situational crises, 19, 35
Situational supports, 29, 66
Six-step model of crisis intervention, 27–32,
    63–68
Sixteen Personality Factor, 185

Sociocultural models of addiction, 329
Sociological approach to suicide, 131
Spirituality, assessment of, 352
Spouses, death of, 412–413, 420–422
Spouse-survivor support groups, 421
Stabilization, in hostage crises, 516–518
Staff:
    culpability for violence, 456–457
    follow-up after violence involving,
        492–493
Stay-alive contracts, 150
Stockholm syndrome, 507, 511–512, 519
Stress:
    in battering relationships, 270–271
    burnout and, 540
    coping strategies for, 559
    management skills, 305
    reduction techniques, 552
    symptoms of, 168
Stress Event Test, 185
Substance abuse, 4–5, 7 (see also Chemical
    dependency)
    appraisal of, 105
    in battering, 271, 277, 300–301, 309
    defined, 332
    effect on mental health, 85–86
    inventories for, 350
    PTSD and, 186
    screening inventories, 304, 309, 349
    by Vietnam veterans, 174, 176
    violence and, 459–460
    workplace violence and, 455
Suicide, 100–101, 129–162, 593
    assessing potential, 37–38
    aspects of, 131–132
    in battered women, 277
    in batterers, 300
    bereavement following, 413–414,
        426–428
    burnout and, 562–563
    case histories in, 136–147
    classroom exercises, 161–162
    clues to, 134–135
    "democratic" nature of, 155
    dynamics of, 130–136
    education alternatives, 149
    hot lines, 585
    intervention strategies for, 147–154
    managing, 152–153
    myths about, 132–133
    post-intervention programs for, 156
    prevention of, 152, 154–156
    rates of, 129–130, 156
    risk factors in, 133–134
    threats of, 132
Sundown syndrome, 461, 488–489
Support:
    for battered women, 271, 278–280,
        291–292
    for burnout, 554–558
    after a child's death, 423–424
    for clients, 66

Support: (*continued*)
  after the death of a spouse, 421
  following separation or divorce, 435
  for HIV-infected persons, 442–443
  importance in PTSD, 176–179
  providing, 29, 53–54
  for rape survivors, 240–241
  in telephone counseling, 88–89
  for victims of child sexual abuse,
    241–246
Support groups:
  access to, 87
  interventionist's role in, 223–224
  for trauma victims, 198
Suppression:
  addiction and, 337
  and child sexual abuse, 234–235
Survival phase of child sexual abuse, 235
Survivor's guilt, 173, 179
Syndromatic clues, 134, 135
Systems theory, 17–18

Telephone counseling, 86–101
Termination anxiety, 110–111
Tertiary prevention programs, 594
Therapy:
  for battered women, 295
  for batterers, 297–311
  for children with PTSD, 184–185
  for child sexual abuse victims, 243–244
  for victims of delayed rape trauma
    syndrome, 247–253
Therapy sessions, crisis in, 111
Thought-stopping techniques, 208–209
Time factors, violence and, 461
Time outs, 477–478
Total listening worksheet, 72
Transcrisis, 35
  handling, 107–116
  points, 6–7, 107, 289, 348
  states, 5–7
Transgenerational violence, 306–307
Transposition of events, as a response to
    trauma, 183
Trauma (*see also* Crisis)
  behavioral and emotional changes
    attending, 177
  children's reactions to, 181–183
  denial/numbing response to, 174–175
  extinguishing, 249–250
  phases of recovery from, 187–188
  reexperiencing of, 205–207
  support groups and, 198
  types of, 170–171
Treatment, of chemical dependency, 324,
    347–348, 363–365, 366–367
Treatment recommendations, 106
Triage assessment, 33, 79–85
  of burnout, 552

Triage assessment (*continued*)
  in cases of bereavement, 420
  of chemical dependency, 350–351
  in hostage crises, 515
  Triage Assessment Form (TAF), 79,
    81–83, 120
Type A personalities, 543, 549

Unimodal expectations, 15

Validation therapy:
  in cases of geriatric violence, 491–492
  for elderly bereaved persons, 440
  using, 501–502
Verbal cues, to violence, 462
Victims, dynamics of, 306
Videotaping, as an assessment tool, 367
Vietnam veterans, 5, 165, 167–168,
    172–174, 176–179, 192–193
Violence:
  alcohol abuse and, 300–301
  confidentiality issues and, 116–117
  during courtship, 296–297
  cycle of, 305
  follow-up with staff victims of, 492–493
  in geriatric clients, 482–492
  in institutions, 453, 457
  legitimization of, 229
  predisposing history of, 460
  transgenerational, 306–307
  woman battering and, 272
Violent ideations, 100–101
Vocational counseling, 94–95

Walk-in crisis facilities, 101–107
"We" approach, 51
"Who Told You?" technique, 570–571
"Wishing and hoping" syndrome, 279
Woman battering, 261–313
  advice for, 311–312
  assessment in, 276–278
  background, 261–264
  centers versus shelters for, 289–296
  classroom exercises concerning, 319–321
  dynamics of, 265–275
  factors in, 271
  intervention strategies in, 275–289
  myths about, 272–274
Women:
  in battering relationships, 270
  responses to rape by, 230–231
  as wife-abuse workers, 275–276
Work Environment Scale, 551–552, 557
Work load, controlling, 558–559
Writing, 201, 476

"You" approach, 51

Zung and Beck Depression Scales, 185